PROLEGOMENA
TO
ANALYTICAL GEOMETRY

CAMBRIDGE UNIVERSITY PRESS

C. F. CLAY, Manager

LONDON : FETTER LANE, E.C. 4

LONDON : H. K. LEWIS AND CO., Ltd.,
136, Gower Street, W.C. 1

NEW YORK : THE MACMILLAN CO.

BOMBAY, CALCUTTA, MADRAS } MACMILLAN AND CO., Ltd.

TORONTO : THE MACMILLAN CO. OF CANADA, Ltd.

TOKYO : MARUZEN-KABUSHIKI-KAISHA

PROLEGOMENA
TO
ANALYTICAL GEOMETRY

IN ANISOTROPIC EUCLIDEAN SPACE OF THREE DIMENSIONS

BY

ERIC HAROLD NEVILLE

LATE FELLOW OF TRINITY COLLEGE CAMBRIDGE
PROFESSOR OF MATHEMATICS IN UNIVERSITY COLLEGE READING

CAMBRIDGE
AT THE UNIVERSITY PRESS
1922

PRINTED IN GREAT BRITAIN

MATRI

D.D.D.

AUCTOR

"Ye knowe eek, that in forme of speche is chaunge
With-inne a thousand yeer, and wordes tho
That hadden prys, now wonder nyce and straunge
Us thinketh hem; and yet they spake hem so,
And spedde as wel in love as men now do."

CHAUCER.

"In the vocabulary of the Sciences, words are fixed and dead, a botanical collection of colourless, scentless, dried weeds, a *hortus siccus* of proper names, each individual symbol poorly tethered to some single object or idea. No wind blows through that garden, and no sun shines on it, to discompose the melancholy workers at their task of tying Latin labels on to withered sticks."

RALEIGH.

"The method of 'postulating' what we want has many advantages; they are the same as the advantages of theft over honest toil. Let us leave them to others."

RUSSELL.

PREFACE

THE vitality of the mathematical form of speech is of a peculiar kind. Words grow, not by continuous and subtle variations in meanings already possessed, but by the acquisition of meanings entirely* new; meanings that are outgrown are neither dead nor discarded, but survive unchanged to be used when they are appropriate, and it often happens that an assertion can be interpreted to give a number of different theorems that are all true.

The first half of the present work is an account of the principles underlying the use of Cartesian axes and vector frames in ordinary space. The second half describes ideal complex Euclidean space of three dimensions, that is, three-dimensional 'space' where 'coordinates' are complex numbers and 'parallel lines' do meet, and develops a system of definitions in consequence of which the geometry of this space has the same vocabulary as elementary geometry, and enunciations and proofs of propositions in elementary geometry remain as far as possible significant and valid.

The arrangement of the material has been dictated by convenience for the structure as a whole, without regard to the logical relations between the initial assumptions. For this reason I have not called the volume a treatise on the foundations or on the principles of analytical geometry. Either description would have suggested a discussion of axioms, and the field to which this work belongs is not part of the region that extends for English readers from Russell's earliest work to Baker's latest; as far as I can judge yet, this work has no ground in common with the *Principles of Geometry*, and my debt to Russell, great as it is, is for the methods of the *Principles of Mathematics*, not for the philosophy of the *Foundations of Geometry*. The title 'Principles of Analytical Geometry' would have been no less misleading if the word had been associated with the formal logic of *Principia Mathematica*, or with the wide survey of general methods to which Darboux gave that very name.

The discussion falls into five parts. There is a preparatory book, that deals first with such fundamental matters as the avoidance of ambiguity in the measurement of angles and the meaning of the sign attached to the volume of a tetrahedron, and afterwards with the simplest kind of projection.

The second book is an introduction to vector analysis, and was written only after many efforts to utilise one or other of the current text-books. While ready to take for granted an acquaintance with the formal laws, I wished to protest both against the confusing notion that a vector *is* a piece of a line but

* Hence the bewilderment of the man in the street, who does not suspect, for example, that when an event is described as 'a point in a four-dimensional space where time is imaginary', five terms with which he is familiar are being used with technical meanings that he does not know.

is in some mysterious way indistinguishable from equal pieces of parallel lines, and against the assumption that lengths, curvatures, speeds, and the tensors of vectors generally, are intrinsically either signless or positive, a mischievous supposition which not only would encumber the geometry and mechanics of real space beyond endurance if it was not in practice ignored whenever it becomes inconvenient, but also is an insurmountable barrier to the extension of vector analysis from real to complex space. It seemed necessary to shew that the formal development of vector analysis is not complicated by the view* of the vector as duplex, and ultimately a compound of quotation and qualification gave place to a straightforward summary of the subject.

The beauty of the calculus of quaternions does not alter the fact that the geometer deals with the actual cosine of an angle and the actual square of a distance, not with the negatives of these numbers. I have therefore taken the line of Grassmann and Gibbs, and regarded as fundamental the negative of Hamilton's scalar product, and this I have ventured to call the projected product.

Some novelty will I think be found in the treatment of rotors. Much use has been made of the conception of the momental product of two rotors or of two sets of rotors, and the consideration of sets of rotors begins before couples have been mentioned. These are details of economy, not matters of principle, and everywhere I have refrained from lengthening the work by attack or defence.

The third book applies vector analysis to obtain formulae for use with Cartesian axes and with vector frames. The Cartesian frame is not assumed to be trirectangular, nor are the Hamiltonian unit vectors **i**, **j**, **k** mentioned. The claim that oblique frames are not more cumbersome than trirectangular in theoretical work is less extravagant than might be supposed. Vector frames are discussed partly because the discussion introduces in its simplest form a quantity of analysis that is fundamental in differential geometry, and partly because in complex space nul vectors are invaluable as vectors of reference but nul lines can not serve as axes of a Cartesian frame. Problems that involve the locating of lines by means of frames of reference explain the range of the second book by illustrating the utility for analytical geometry of the idea of the vector product and of the elements of the theory of rotors.

The following book is devoted to the construction of algebraic space. Mathematicians used complex space for many years without perceiving that the question of its existence or of its definition was one that needed to be considered. No flaw was recognised in the argument that because the points

* With regard to this view, I can not do better than repeat the words of the rôtisseur's son: "Au reste, je ne me flatte pas de tirer grand honneur de ces révélations. Les uns diront que j'ai tout inventé et que ce n'est pas la vraie doctrine; les autres que je n'ai dit que ce que tout le monde savait."

of intersection of a line and a circle are given by a quadratic equation, therefore a circle cuts every line in its plane in two points, which if they are not real are *ipso facto* imaginary. The success that waited on audacity blinded criticism. "The metaphysician, who should invent anything so preposterous as the circular points, would be hooted from the field. But the mathematician may steal the horse with impunity*."

By the time the mathematical conscience had become uneasy, dispute on the desirability of admitting complex numbers as coordinates was not possible, but on the justification to be offered different views have been held. The elegance of the theory by which von Staudt reduced every proposition which in analytical geometry would be described as involving a complex point to a proposition about real involutions, has led some writers to look for complex space *within* real space. The search is not to be encouraged: 'real' space with Euclidean properties is no less a creation of the mind than the complex space that is wanted. Accordingly, other mathematicians have constructed metrical geometry by means of quasi-geometrical axioms imposed on undefined 'points' and 'lines'. But the process is slow; the whittling of the set of axioms down to a logical minimum is a tedious exercise in which the student of analytical geometry may feel no interest and by which he should not be delayed.

There is a third method. "Il semble que, pour l'introduction et l'interprétation des imaginaires", wrote Darboux†, "il vaut mieux s'en tenir à la méthode analytique qui repose sur l'emploi des coordonnées rectilignes." In other words, *analytical geometry is to be developed from axioms expressed in the language of analytical geometry.* As far as I know, the details of such a development have not previously been worked out.

It is perhaps necessary to emphasise that complex space can not be constructed by the simple plan of attaching complex points to real axes. The assumption that we can take an ordinary Cartesian frame and 'let' coordinates relative to it have complex values is a mistake of the same kind as the illusion‡ that the natural numbers occur among the real numbers. A theory of algebraic space must account for the framework as well as for the points.

The fundamental axioms used in this book are axioms that involve vectors, and points are introduced only by their relation to vectors. The only reason for my adoption of this plan is that I have not found one that is simpler. To achieve *a* logical construction of complex space and *a* logical construction of ideal space is of the highest importance, but attempts to distinguish particular construc-

* Russell, *Foundations of Geometry*, p. 45, 1897.

† *Principes de Géométrie Analytique*, p. 3, 1917.

‡ See Russell, *Principles of Mathematics*, (1903), p. 150, and elsewhere. Without disputing that "the confusion of entities with others to which they have some important one-one relation...has produced the greatest havoc in the philosophy of mathematics", may we suggest that when we are aware of the confusion, it is no longer an error but a valuable economy? See pp. 243, 244 below.

tions as the best would be unprofitable* if not futile; so long as complex geometry and ideal geometry mean something, it does not much matter what the meanings are, nor is it even desirable for the geometer to be conscious continually of an interpretation of his words and symbols. It is however interesting to notice that in the axioms which Peano, deeply concerned with their interrelations, has formulated† for Euclidean space, vectors take the same precedence of points as here, and that Silberstein has shewn‡ that the question, irrelevant to us, whether this method introduces assumptions distinctive of Euclidean geometry at a stage that is premature from the standpoint of pure logic, must not be answered hastily.

The notions most difficult to extend to algebraic space are those in which direction is involved. In the substance of the chapter explaining the extension, I have not as far as I know been anticipated, and a comparison with the chapters of Darboux's *Principes de Géométrie Analytique* on the foundations of metrical geometry is interesting. Applied to anisotropic lines, the assertion§ that to determine a sense on a line is the same as to choose between the two values of a square root, is adequate for practical purposes, but a Frege-Russell definition of direction has the advantage of being applicable to nul lines.

An unusual degree of attention has been given to the isotropic plane, and the explicit appreciation of what are here called the two *aspects* of an isotropic plane is original.

This fourth book concludes with a proof that whatever are the values of the magnitudes fundamental in the frame from which space happens to have been constructed, a frame with assigned values for its fundamental magnitudes can be found: complex space is unique.

This work was begun as a preliminary chapter to an introduction to differential geometry. A collection of formulae for use with oblique axes was wanted. Such formulae are proved most readily by vector analysis, which for this purpose it would be barbarous to suppose established by means of rectangular axes, or by the equivalent means of **i**, **j**, and **k**. The first three books having been designed, the extension to the fourth book was inevitable.

But when it became clear that I was engaged not on the sections of a preliminary chapter but on a substantive treatise, the question of the scope of the work as a whole had to be faced. Callous though it might be to leave complex space without embracing infinity and the circular points, it seemed unnecessary to add another to the accounts of ideal space, and unprofitable to touch on this subject unless I was prepared to go as far as to include the expression of distances and angles by means of the absolute. The difficulty

* Compare De Morgan, on p. 94 of the little masterpiece *Trigonometry and Double Algebra*, 1849: "The student, if he should hereafter inquire into the assertions of different writers, who contend for what each of them considers as *the* explanation of $\sqrt{-1}$, will do well to substitute the indefinite article."

† See Russell's *Principles of Mathematics*, p. 432.

‡ *Projective Vector Algebra*, 1919.

§ *Principes*, pp. 138, 140, 180, 182.

vanished with the appearance in 1917 of Darboux's *Principes*; it is easy to leave off where a Darboux is beginning, and the questions with which this volume is concerned are precisely those whose answers Darboux assumes to be known.

The logical construction of ideal space from actual space, of which Darboux says nothing, was effected many years ago*, and the connection between the use of homogeneous coordinates and the recognition of points at infinity, on which Darboux touches in his introductory chapter, is familiar. The substitution of complex space for real space makes no difference to the arguments, but as exhibiting for Euclidean space the geometrical and the analytical theories in intimate relation, the account of ideal space in the first three chapters of book five is more than a mere transcript of existing material. Also the geometrical theory of quadriplanar coordinates given here has a generality that is uncommon.

The next chapter is somewhat outside the scheme of the volume. Its primary object is to explain, in preparation for the chapters that follow, how for algebraic curves and algebraic surfaces the ideas of tangents and tangent planes and of multiple points can be introduced without reference to limits; the subject has been developed considerably beyond the actual requirements. The restriction to algebraic loci is in many respects unnecessary, since the multiplicity of a number a as a root of an equation $f(z)=0$, where $f(z)$ is regular near a, is a definable integer without the assumption that $f(z)$ is a polynomial.

Chapter five of this book deals with circles, and chapter six with spheres. Stress is laid on the points at which the complex or ideal nature of the plane or of space becomes relevant, on the peculiarities of circles in an isotropic plane, and on the parabolic character of the section of a sphere by such a plane. The classification of coaxal systems of circles occupies two long sections, and illustrates well the variety of cases that can be covered by a single enunciation. To avoid misunderstanding, I may say here that I should be the last to discourage the student from asserting theorems as true 'in general' without delaying to examine exceptions and to frame conventional interpretations for their avoidance; it may be that these sections will play their most useful part as a warning. The book ends with a section on the rectilinear generators of the sphere.

The nature of limits in complex space and in ideal space is the subject of a brief appendix. A discussion of limits in the body of the work on a scale comparable with that on which other questions have been treated would have changed the balance entirely, but since the two extensions of space with which the volume is concerned introduce characteristic difficulties into the conception of a limit, some reference to these difficulties seemed desirable. The divorce of the notion of a limit from that of distance, which is essential if space is to

* See e.g. Russell, *Principles of Mathematics*, ch. xlvi, or Whitehead, *Axioms of Descriptive Geometry*, ch. iii (1907); both writers give references to the original sources.

be made complex, was effected by Jordan. But whereas Jordan *defines* a point P at infinity to be a limit of a set of points Γ if a homographic projection of P to an accessible point P' transforms Γ into a set of which P' is a limit, the definition proposed here is one directly in terms of tetrahedral coordinates, to which the distinction between accessible and inaccessible points is irrelevant; the two definitions are easily reconciled.

Nothing is said of cross ratios, nothing of the generality which is conferred on theorems that are nominally about circles and spheres by the arbitrariness of the coefficients in the fundamental expression for the square of a distance. These omissions place me in the happy position of being able to offer this volume as a preface to Darboux's, and I hope that they will also encourage the 'practical' reader to look here for the kind of account of complex space that he wants.

For the lack of uniformity in the scale and style of different parts of the volume I can only crave indulgence. The work grew spasmodically, sometimes forwards and sometimes backwards, during six years, and, as I have hinted, the reader whom at first I had in view was the beginner; hence some 'instructive' foot-notes and too free a use of italics. A preoccupation with differential geometry accounts for the wish to reserve suffixes for the indication of derivatives, and accounts therefore for a use of superior affixes that within the limits of the present volume is both unnecessary and unnatural. On the other hand, the extent of the cross-references made it impossible for me to make any considerable changes when the final scope of the volume had become apparent. A certain amount of formal repetition is inevitable, since one object of the work is to shew that formal repetition can be made possible; I have tried to exercise a reasonable moderation.

The background has long been common ground to mathematicians. The one individual debt is to Mr. Russell, whose influence will be recognised throughout; on its logical side, the work is an application of the Frege-Russell method of definition to problems that the pure mathematician, however ill-disposed to philosophy, can neither ignore nor delegate.

For fourfold assistance in passing the volume through the press I am very grateful to Mr. A. Robson of Marlborough College, who has read the proofs, criticised the arguments, verified the references, and compiled the indexes; this is a bald acknowledgment of laborious and invaluable help.

To praise the workmanship of the printers is superfluous; the reader has the result before him. But the author alone experiences the unfailing courtesy and forbearance of Mr. Peace and his staff, and I am glad to acknowledge my obligations; the casting of the semicircular brackets (see p. 123) is only one instance of the ready humouring of my whims.

TABLE OF CONTENTS

BOOK I

MEASUREMENT AND SIMPLE PROJECTION

BOOK II

VECTORS AND ROTORS

CHAPTER 1. VECTORS AND THEIR DECOMPOSITION

CHAPTER 2. PRODUCTS OF VECTORS

CHAPTER 3. ROTORS AND MOMENTS

CHAPTER 4. SETS OF ROTORS

BOOK III

CARTESIAN AXES AND VECTOR FRAMES

CHAPTER 1. TRIGONOMETRY OF PLANE AND SPHERICAL TRIANGLES

CHAPTER 2. THE CARTESIAN FRAMEWORK

CHAPTER 3. CARTESIAN AXES IN USE

CHAPTER 4. VECTOR FRAMES

CHAPTER 5. CHANGE OF AXES

BOOK IV

COMPLEX SPACE

BOOK V

IDEAL SPACE

BOOK V (*continued*)

CHAPTER 2. IDEAL SPACE IN ANALYSIS

CHAPTER 3. IDEAL VECTORS

CHAPTER 4. INTERSECTION AND ALTERSECTION OF LINES WITH PLANE CURVES AND WITH SURFACES

CHAPTER 5. CIRCLES IN IDEAL COMPLEX SPACE

BOOK V (*continued*)

CHAPTER 6. SPHERES IN IDEAL COMPLEX SPACE

APPENDIX

NOTE ON NUMERATION

It seemed necessary to present many of the logical chains in this volume in some detail, both to guide the beginner and to save time for the expert. To print as a theorem, with a paragraph to itself and the dignity of italics, every assertion of which subsequent use was to be made, would have been preposterous. The marginal numbers are designed to make reference easy with a minimum of adaptation of the text; the precise incidence of a number that does not refer to a formula or to a theorem set out formally is indicated by the mark °, which does not interrupt reading.

The system of numeration will be found, I hope, both simple and economical. The seventh section of the fourth chapter of the fifth book is called section 547. Within each section are subdivisions marked ·1, ·2, and so on, and definitions, equations, and assertions bear decimal numbers usually of two digits but occasionally of three; these decimal numbers are in order, but their second digits do not always run consecutively. When reference is made, the decimal part of the reference number is given in full, but the integral part is filled in, from the right, only as far as it differs from the number of the section in which the reference occurs. Thus the references in section 333 to ·14, 1·75, 23·4, and 234·25 are to a sentence in the text of the same section, a formula whose complete number is 331·75, a paragraph 323·4 in the preceding chapter, and a proposition in an earlier book. Ambiguity is impossible, but in the vast majority of references decimal entries only are required.

TABLE OF PARAGRAPHS RELATING TO THE ISOTROPIC PLANE

The following table enumerates the paragraphs in which details peculiar to isotropic vecplanes or isotropic planes are considered, but the sequence of paragraphs is not a self-contained account of the isotropic plane, for the sequence is not coherent nor are the paragraphs intelligible without reference to other parts of the volume. In many cases only part of a subsection is involved.

SUMMARY ACCOUNT OF SYMBOLS IN FREQUENT USE

Directions and their images are denoted by capital Greek letters, and Ω is used for the centre of the unit sphere; P′ stands for the direction reverse to P or the point diametrically opposite to P. Rays are denoted by small Greek letters, unprepared lines by small Latin letters.

Clarendon type is appropriated to undissected vectors; $\mathbf{r}'$ is the reverse of $\mathbf{r}$, and $\mathbf{0}$ is the zero vector. The vector in which the number r is associated with the direction P is denoted by r_{P}. A rotor is represented in the form $\mathbf{r}_k$ or in the form r_κ according to the light in which it is being regarded. A couple is expressed in terms of its component rotors as $(\mathbf{r}_k, \mathbf{r}_l')$, or in terms of its momental vector and the lines in which it is located as $\mathbf{R}_{kl}$.

The uses of script letters with vectors and rotors are explained as follows:

$\mathscr{A}\,\mathbf{rs}$, areal product	pp. 56, 217
$\mathscr{E}_\epsilon\mathbf{r}$, $\mathscr{E}\,\mathbf{r}$, vector derived by rotation ...	47, 217
$\mathscr{G}\,\mathbf{rs}$, projected product	54, 190
$\mathscr{M}\,\mathbf{r}_k\mathbf{s}_l$, $\mathscr{M}\,FG$, momental product ...	70, 76
$\mathscr{T}\,\mathbf{rst}$, spatial product	62, 196
$\mathscr{V}\,\mathbf{rs}$, vector product	57, 201

The angle of a plane Cartesian frame is denoted by ω; in space, α, β, γ are angles between axes of reference, A, B, Γ angles between planes of reference, and Υ is the sine of the frame. The polars of OXY, $OXYZ$ are denoted by OLM, $OLMN$.

For a plane vector frame $\mathbf{xy}$, the fundamental magnitudes are E, F, G, the areal magnitude is C; in three dimensions, the fundamental magnitudes are L, M, N, P, Q, R, the spatial magnitude is J. The polars of $\mathbf{xy}$, $\mathbf{xyz}$ are $\bar{\mathbf{x}}\bar{\mathbf{y}}$, $\bar{\mathbf{x}}\bar{\mathbf{y}}\bar{\mathbf{z}}$, and this derivative notation is extended to associated magnitudes. Amounts of the vectors of reference are denoted by U, V or U, V, W; for the use of amounts in an isotropic vecplane, see p. 221.

With reference to $OXYZ$, coordinates and components are x, y, z, projections are l, m, n; with reference to a vector frame attached to an origin O, the corresponding numbers are ξ, η, ζ and λ, μ, ν. The symbols by which umbral notation is most frequently applied are given by

$$c = (x, y, z), \quad p = (l, m, n), \quad \chi = (\xi, \eta, \zeta), \quad \upsilon = (\lambda, \mu, \nu),$$
$$\mathscr{G}\,\mathbf{rs} = \mathscr{C}\,c_{\mathbf{r}}c_{\mathbf{s}} = \mathscr{P}\,p_{\mathbf{r}}p_{\mathbf{s}} = S\chi_{\mathbf{r}}\chi_{\mathbf{s}} = \bar{S}\upsilon_{\mathbf{r}}\upsilon_{\mathbf{s}}.$$

The determinant whose typical element is a_{mn} is denoted by $[[a]]$.

When single letters are adequate, the distinction between actual and ideal is not reflected in the symbols used. But the ideal point which is determined from an actual origin O by the vector $\mathbf{r}$ and the number t is written as $(\mathbf{r}, t)$, and the ideal vector which the vector $\mathbf{r}$ and the number R combine to specify as $(\mathbf{r}, R)$.

The two focal points in an anisotropic plane are I and J; K is used for the one focal point in an isotropic plane, and also for an unspecified focal point either in an anisotropic plane or in space.

General rectilinear coordinates in a plane are α, β, γ, in space $\alpha, \beta, \gamma, \delta$; Cartesian coordinates rendered homogeneous become x, y, t or x, y, z, t, and the coordinates derived from an attached vector frame become ξ, η, τ or ξ, η, ζ, τ. By the use of ϵ for (α, β, γ) and $(\alpha, \beta, \gamma, \delta)$, it is possible to denote a homogeneous polynomial of degree n in rectilinear coordinates by $\Phi\epsilon^n$, and the corresponding multilinear function of n sets of coordinates by $\Phi\epsilon_1\epsilon_2 \ldots \epsilon_n$.

BOOK I

MEASUREMENT AND SIMPLE PROJECTION

CHAPTER I

DIRECTIONS AND ANGLES

110. Introduction. 111. The unit sphere and unit circles; spherical and circular images of directions. 112. Cyclic conventions. 113. Angles between coplanar directions. 114. Spatial conventions. 115. Angles between directions in space. 116. Prepared lines, prepared planes, and prepared space.

110. INTRODUCTION.

In the application of analysis to geometry the need first to be felt is of definiteness. There is a bewildering multitude of angles between one straight line and another, and there are numbers, such as the area of a triangle in a plane, that acquire in an algebraic treatment signs for which primitive definitions are unable to account. Our immediate object is to develop a language in which freedom and precision are not incompatible, and we have to begin by paying elaborate attention to elementary considerations relating to directions and measurements.

Generality is as desirable in analytical geometry as in pure algebra, but we can not follow the search for generality, leading in one direction to the employment of complex numbers and in another direction to the construction of a space with points at infinity, until we know what are the ideas and modes of expression that deserve generalisation.

111. THE UNIT SPHERE AND UNIT CIRCLES; SPHERICAL AND CIRCULAR IMAGES OF DIRECTIONS.

·1. The study of relations between directions, either in a plane or in three-
dimensional space, is much facilitated by a device familiar in optics and
astronomy and used in pure geometry by Gauss as long ago as 1827*. If Ω
is any point, the points at unit distance from Ω compose a sphere; each point
of this sphere is in a definite direction from Ω, and conversely in each direction
from Ω there is one and only one point of the sphere; by °*taking the point* P ·11
of the sphere to represent the direction ΩP we have a one-to-one correspondence
between the points of the sphere and directions in space, and °when it is ·12
difficult to visualise particular relations between directions in space it is often
easy to understand the corresponding relations between the associated points.

* In the great memoir, "Disquisitiones generales circa superficies curvas" (*Comment. Soc. Scient. Gottingensis recentiores*, vol. VI, and *Ges. Werke*, vol. IV; reprinted also in Liouville's edition of Monge's *Application de l'Analyse à la Géométrie*, and translated into German as Nr. 5 of Ostwald's *Klassiker der Exakten Wissenschaften* and into French for Gauthier-Villars' series of *Maîtres de la Pensée Scientifique*). The spherical representation of directions, which is often called the Gaussian representation, is explained in the first section of the paper.

A sphere of unit radius used for the representation of directions is called a
·14, ·15 °*unit sphere*, and the point corresponding to any direction is called the °*image*
or the spherical image of that direction. We use Ω always to denote the centre of the unit sphere we employ, and we use capital Greek letters to denote points of this sphere; also if P is any point of the sphere we denote by P′ the
·19 point diametrically opposite, so that °the direction of which P′ is the image is the reverse of the direction represented by P; often we speak of the direction whose image is P simply as the direction P.

·2. If p is any plane in space, there is one and only one plane through Ω parallel to p, and if this plane is q, every direction parallel to p is represented by a point common to q and the unit sphere:

·21 *All directions parallel to a single plane are represented spherically by points of one great circle;*

the two poles of the great circle represent the two directions at right angles to the plane.

·22 Directions which are parallel to one plane are described briefly as °*coplanar directions*, but we have to remember that *lines* in different planes may have
·23 *directions* that are coplanar; °any *two* directions *are* coplanar, since through any two points on a sphere a plane can be drawn to pass also through the centre of the sphere, but between three or more directions coplanarity is a significant relation.

·3. If all the directions with which we must deal are coplanar, and in particular if we are developing the theory of plane curves, a unit sphere gives
·34 place to a °*unit circle*. When our whole investigation is concerned with a single plane, naturally we use a unit circle lying in that plane, but in a study of three-dimensional space the unit circles corresponding to different planes have a common centre Ω and can not be assumed to lie in the planes which they represent. Parallel planes are represented by the same circle.

112. Cyclic conventions.

·1. If P, Σ are points of a unit circle, there are many lengths from one of these points to the other round the circle, and a length from P to Σ is also a length from Σ to P unless measurement in one direction round the circle is distinguished from measurement in the reverse direction. The first step therefore in the study of coplanar directions is to distinguish as positive and negative the two directions of measurement round a unit circle whose points represent the directions. We call an agreement to use the word positive of measurement in a particular direction round a circle and negative of measure-
·12 ment in the opposite direction a °*cyclic convention* for the circle. There are two cyclic conventions for any circle; in an investigation which uses only one unit circle we may adopt universally one of the conventions for that circle, and in every mathematical formula and theorem it is a matter of indifference which

convention is chosen, all that is essential being adherence to a choice once made. A cyclic convention actually adopted in a particular plane figure can be indicated, as on pp. 15 and 18 below, by the use of a barbed circle; if this indication is commonly omitted, that is because the counterclockwise convention is taken for granted.

A circle to which a definite cyclic convention is attached will be called a
°*prepared circle.* ·13

113. Angles between coplanar directions.

·1. Even after the adoption of a cyclic convention for a unit circle, there
is an infinity of angles, some positive and some negative, from any one direction ΩP whose image is in that circle to any other such direction ΩΣ, but
°any two of these angles differ by an integral multiple of 2π. We say that ·11
two angles are °*congruent* when they differ if at all by an integral multiple ·12
of 2π; °angles congruent in this sense have the same sine and the same ·13
cosine, and for many purposes two congruent angles are equivalent. It is not
legitimate to speak of *the* angle from ΩP to ΩΣ, but °with a cyclic convention ·14
for the great circle PΣ we may speak of *the* cosine and of *the* sine of the
angles from ΩP to ΩΣ, and we denote these functions by cos PΣ and sin PΣ;
we speak also of °*the* smallest positive angle from ΩP to ΩΣ, remarking that ·16
this angle is 0, not 2π, if P and Σ coincide*.

·2. °The angles from ΩΣ to ΩP are the negatives of the angles from ΩP ·21
to ΩΣ, and therefore

$$\cos \Sigma P = \cos P\Sigma, \quad \sin \Sigma P = -\sin P\Sigma: \qquad \cdot 22, \cdot 23$$

we can speak of *the* cosine of the angles *between* the two directions, but for
the sine the measurement must be explicitly *from* one of the directions *to* the
other. Unless P and Σ coincide or are diametrically opposite, the smallest
positive angle from ΩΣ to ΩP differs from the smallest positive angle from
ΩP to ΩΣ, and the smaller of these two angles is the smallest positive
angle °*between* the directions; in the case in which P and Σ represent opposite ·25
directions the smallest positive angle between the directions is π.

·3. When P is neither Σ nor Σ′, whether the smallest positive angle between
ΩP and ΩΣ is an angle from ΩP to ΩΣ or an angle from ΩΣ to ΩP depends
on the cyclic convention for the great circle PΣ. Conversely, °it is often con- ·32
venient to choose the cyclic convention by the condition that the smallest
positive angle *between* two particular directions ΩP, ΩΣ is an angle *from*
ΩP *to* ΩΣ, and it is to be noticed that this condition is ineffective only in
the cases in which the points P, Σ fail to determine a unique great circle on

* The peculiarity of the zero of directed numbers is not that it has *no* sign but that it has *both* signs. If we wish to exclude zero, we shall speak of numbers that are *strictly* positive or *strictly* negative as the case may be. Language in this matter is elastic; all that is incumbent on us is to be consistent, and the usage which we are here describing proves on the whole the most convenient for our purposes.

the unit sphere whose centre is Ω; this method of defining a particular direction of measurement round a unit circle is so common that instead of saying that the angle from ΩP to $\Omega\Sigma$ *which is numerically less than* π is to be positive we say briefly that *the angle* from ΩP to $\Omega\Sigma$ is to be positive.

·41 **·4.** We may add that °when the cyclic convention is known for a particular unit circle containing a point P, we can distinguish between the point in that circle which represents a direction *which makes* a given angle ϵ *with* ΩP and the point in the circle which represents a direction *with which* ΩP *makes* the angle ϵ; the distinction is especially valuable when ϵ is $\frac{1}{2}\pi$, each of the directions distinguished being then the reverse of the other.

·5. If P, Σ, T are points of a prepared unit circle and PΣ, ΣT, and PT are *definite* angles from P to Σ, from Σ to T, and from P to T, it does not usually
·51 happen that PT is the *sum* of PΣ and ΣT. But ° PT is always *congruent* with PΣ + ΣT so that

·52 $$\cos \mathrm{PT} = \cos(\mathrm{P}\Sigma + \Sigma\mathrm{T}), \quad \sin \mathrm{PT} = \sin(\mathrm{P}\Sigma + \Sigma\mathrm{T}).$$

If we regard PΣ, ΣT, and PT as *indefinite* symbols, each of which may denote any one of the angles of the congruence to which it belongs, then every value of PΣ + ΣT is a possible value of PT, and conversely, since every value of PT − ΣT is a value of PT + TΣ and therefore of PΣ, every value of PT is a possible value of PΣ + ΣT. With this interpretation of the symbols, we can invest the *equation*

·55 $$\mathrm{PT} = \mathrm{P}\Sigma + \Sigma\mathrm{T}$$

with the meaning that any value of either side is a value of the other side also.

An alternative method of introducing this equation is to regard such a symbol as ΛM as denoting not a single angle but the actual congruence of which the angles from Λ to M are the members; it must then be shewn that the class of angles obtained by adding a variable member of one congruence to a variable member of another is itself a congruence, and ·55 can be read as stating that the congruence formed in this way from PΣ and ΣT *is* the congruence PT. The difference between the two modes of treating the equation is not in the theorem that is asserted but in the meaning borne by the symbols. The second method is open to the objection that it would become necessary to allow symbols for congruences with differences other than 2π, since, for example, the halves of angles from Λ to M form a congruence with difference π; in consequence, the congruence-difference would have to be shewn explicitly, and this would rob the notation of its advantages.

To say that the equality ·55 does not *usually* hold if the symbols stand for definite angles is to understate the case; there is *no* rule which picks out a definite member of every congruence in such a way as to secure this equality. For example, if ΛM was defined to denote always the smallest positive angle from Λ to M, then if PΣ and ΣT were both greater than π it is $P\Sigma + \Sigma T - 2\pi$ that would be PT. Or if ΛM was restricted to denote an angle numerically not greater than π, then if PΣ and ΣT were both between $-\pi$ and $-\frac{1}{2}\pi$, the angle denoted by PT would be $P\Sigma + \Sigma T + 2\pi$. A refusal to contemplate limitations on the magnitude of angles might be defended adequately on the ground that restrictions are unnecessary, but we can in fact take the stronger position that *any* restriction must involve the denial of ·55 and must sooner or later prove tiresome, on that account if for no other reason.

114. Spatial conventions.

·1. Cyclic conventions for different great circles on a unit sphere are not sufficient to dispose satisfactorily of the difficulties connected with angles between directions in space. We can indeed frame a rule assigning the cyclic convention for every great circle on the sphere, but ° every such rule involves ·11
a kind of discontinuity fatal either to brevity or to accuracy.

·2. Consider for example only the great circles through a point Π and its opposite; let PΣP′Σ′ be the great circle of which Π, Π′ are the poles, let positive measurement round this great circle take the four points in the order named, and let positive measurement round the great circle through Π and P take these points and their opposites in the order Π, P, Π′, P′; the position of any point T in the semicircle PΣP′ may be defined by the length τ of the arc PT, and the cyclic convention in the great circle through Π and T being by hypothesis given by some definite rule, let us say that T is a positive point or a negative point according as positive measurement round the great circle takes T after Π and before Π′ or after Π′ and before Π; since by definition P is a positive point and P′ is negative, and since every point of the semicircle is either positive or negative, it follows that there are a positive point and a negative point indefinitely close together on the semicircle, and therefore that any formula involving the cyclic convention for a variable great circle through Π must present a discontinuity either as τ leaves 0 or as τ approaches π or as τ passes through at least one of the intermediate values.

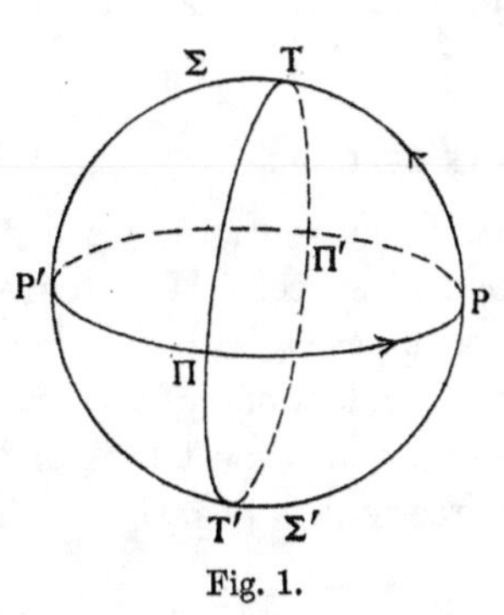

Fig. 1.

·3. The simple but fundamental fact enabling us to deal with angles between directions in space is that although standard directions are not to be imposed prematurely upon great circles, nevertheless ° *by a universal convention* ·31
each of the two directions round a great circle on any sphere may be associated with one of the two hemispheres separated by the circle. Travelling on the outside of a sphere round a great circle in one direction we have one hemisphere always on the right and the other always on the left, while if the direction in which we travel is reversed the hemispheres exchange characters; with respect to all the points in one of these hemispheres the circle is said to be described positively, while with respect to the points in the other hemisphere it is said

·35 to be described negatively. °*It is entirely immaterial whether the word positive is associated with the hemisphere on the right or with the hemisphere on the left, but in any one investigation the association must be the same in all the cases which occur.* A convention that associates in this connection the word positive with one of the words right and left and the word negative with the other we
·37 call for brevity a °*spatial convention.* There are two spatial conventions, and in our figures we shall adopt that which associates positive with left*, but the deduction of formulae and theorems from definitions is valid with either convention provided that no change of convention is permitted in the process.

·4. To appreciate the use of a spatial convention, let us revert to the example used already in this article. Since we are no longer attempting to assign only one direction of measurement round the circle ΠTΠ′, we can no longer describe the point T as *either* positive *or* negative, and if we make any use of the words we must say that every point is *both* positive *and* negative. If the spatial convention is such that Π is positive with respect to measurement from P to P′ through Σ, then if E is the point whose distance from P round the circle PΣP′Σ′ is $\tau+\frac{1}{2}\pi$, measurement from Π to Π′ through T is positive *with respect to* E, whatever the value of τ; if the spatial convention is reversed, and E is still defined as distant $\tau+\frac{1}{2}\pi$ from P, then for *every* position of T measurement from Π to Π′ through T is negative *with respect to* E; with neither convention can there be an abrupt change of sign if τ changes continuously.

115. Angles between directions in space.

·1. Having made a choice between the two spatial conventions, we can
·11 describe with precision the angles between directions in space. °If P, Σ are distinct points of the unit sphere not diametrically opposed, and T is any point of the sphere not on the great circle through P and Σ, one of the two directions of motion round the great circle is positive with respect to T and negative with respect to T′, and the other of these directions is negative with

* This convention is much the more natural in view of the universal convention that in a plane the standard rotation is counterclockwise; the most important works in which the contrary convention is adopted are Hamilton's, and his practice is not followed even by Tait and Joly, the chief of his disciples. The two conventions are usually distinguished as right-handed and left-handed, and here we have to record an anomaly: the convention that associates positive with left is often called right-handed. By de Candolle the botanist, to whom is attributed the first use of the words right-handed and left-handed in a geometrical sense, by Listing, the first to emphasise (*Göttinger Studien*, 1847; see pp. 817, 818, and figures on pp. 842, 850) the importance of a number of elementary distinctions, by Hamilton, who uses this convention in all his illustrations, and to the present day by writers on the circular polarisation of light, it is the association of positive with right that is called right-handed; nevertheless the majority of mathematical writers call the alternative convention right-handed, influenced either by the language of workshops or by a prejudice against using the word left-handed of the convention which they feel to be natural—the prejudice indeed which moved Hamilton to adopt the less natural usage *because* to him it appeared right-handed. It would be well if the use of the words right-handed and left-handed in geometry could be suspended for a generation, so that their reappearance with their original meanings might lead to no confusion.

respect to T and positive with respect to T′; if the first of these is the positive
direction for the great circle through P and Σ, the angles which ΩΣ makes
with ΩP are called the angles *from* the direction represented by P *to* the
direction represented by Σ *round* the direction represented by T, while the
angles which ΩΣ makes with ΩP if the positive direction of motion in the circle
is reversed are the angles from the direction of ΩP to the direction of ΩΣ
round the direction represented by T′. °If ϵ is one angle of the first class, the ·14
angles of the first class are the angles congruent with ϵ and the angles of the
second class are the angles congruent with $-\epsilon$; all the angles *between* two
directions ΩP, ΩΣ have the same cosine, and this is denoted simply by cos PΣ,
but the sine common to all the angles from ΩP to ΩΣ round a third direction
ΩT is the negative of the sine of the angles from ΩP to ΩΣ round the reverse
direction ΩT′. We have occasion often to notice that just as a choice of one
of two opposite directions as the direction round which to measure the angles
from ΩP to ΩΣ determines the sign of the sine of these angles, so on the
other hand °to choose this sign arbitrarily is to determine the one of any two ·18
opposite directions ΩT, ΩT′ round which the angles are measured, provided
only that the different directions ΩP, ΩΣ, ΩT are not coplanar. For the sake
of completeness we add that the angles from one direction to a coincident
direction are the even multiples, negative and zero as well as positive, of π,
and the angles from any direction to its reverse are the odd multiples,
negative and positive, of π; in these cases no reference is necessary to a third
direction.

116. Prepared lines, prepared planes, and prepared space.

·1. Every line in space has two directions, one the reverse of the other, and
°*a line associated specifically with one of its two directions we call a directed* ·12
*line, a prepared line, or a ray**, describing the ray as situated in the line
and calling the line the °*axis* of the ray; a line is the axis of two different rays, ·14
and each of these rays is said to be the °*reverse* of the other. The spherical ·16
image of the direction of a ray is called simply the spherical image of the ray,
and by an angle between two rays is meant an angle between their directions.
On a unit sphere a line has two images, the points representing its two directions; to overlook the existence of one of these images is to be inaccurate; to deal with both of them is to be prolix; to use instead of a sphere a surface on

* It is possible to define a ray as a line with one of its directions chosen as positive, thus allowing to each ray a positive and a negative direction; the effect is a complication of language, as far as I can see without compensation, for it is hardly simpler to speak of the negative direction of a ray than to speak of the reverse of the direction of a ray, while to speak of *the* direction rather than of the positive direction is a considerable advantage. The reader should know that the word ray is not consecrated wholly to the usage we adopt; Hamilton for example uses the word sometimes as equivalent to vector (*Lectures on Quaternions*, lect. 2, 1853) and sometimes as equivalent to half-line (*Elements of Quaternions*, p. 119, 1866; vol. I, p. 121 of Joly's edition).

which every line has a unique image* is to secure accuracy at an excessive price: the advantages of dealing rather with rays than with lines whenever direction and changes of direction have to be considered are exemplified abundantly in the course of our work, but they are only such as we should expect.

·2. In a plane as in a line there are two directions of measurement; in a line they are directions of linear measurement, but in a plane they are direc-
·21 tions of angular measurement or as we may say °*cyclic directions.*
·22 °*A plane associated with one of its cyclic directions is called a directed or prepared plane,* and if the cyclic direction is reversed the directed plane itself
·24, ·25 is said to be °*reversed.* °Rays in a prepared plane are represented on a unit sphere by points in a great circle; this great circle, which is said to represent
·26 the plane, is a °*prepared* circle. An angle from a ray λ to a ray μ measured in a prescribed cyclic direction will often be denoted by $\epsilon_{\lambda\mu}$.

·3. The use of a spatial convention in three-dimensional geometry is analogous to the use of a cyclic convention in plane geometry, and it is natural
·32 to say that the space with which a theorem deals is a °*directed* or *prepared space* if the statement of the theorem involves implicitly or explicitly a spatial convention. The one feature that appears to dwellers in a three-dimensional world to indicate an intrinsic difference between spatial conventions and cyclic conventions is that they themselves can perceive no process analogous to the continuous rotation by which a movable prepared great circle on a sphere can turn from coincidence with one directed circle to coincidence with the reverse circle or by which a movable prepared plane can turn from coincidence with one prepared plane to coincidence with the reverse plane.

·4. In figures, the direction of measurement in a ray is commonly indicated by an arrow-head; figure 2 shews a useful method of indicating the spatial conventions in figures drawn in perspective.

Fig. 2.

* Such a surface is easily defined: let γ be half of a great circle on a unit sphere, γ being defined to include one of its end points but not the other; then the surface consisting of the points of γ and of all points on one side of the great circle to which γ belongs is quite strictly a hemisphere, and in this surface every line has only one image. To use such a surface as this is obviously inconvenient, and is moreover not to deal with lines instead of rays but to take account of only one of the rays contained in each line.

CHAPTER I 2

MEASUREMENT IN PREPARED LINES AND PLANES

121. The partition of a ray by a point. 122. Steps; the lengths and directions of a step; congruent steps; addition of steps. 123. Distances from one line to another. 124. The partition of a prepared plane by a ray. 125. The sign of a triangle in a prepared plane. 126. Distance from a ray in a prepared plane; normals to a ray. 127. The area of a triangle; the universality of trigonometrical formulae.

121. THE PARTITION OF A RAY BY A POINT.

·1. Ordinary language recognises that it is natural to distinguish the points *on one side* from the points *on the other side* of a point in a line, of a line in a plane, and of a plane in space, but with unprepared lines, unprepared planes, and unprepared space, any association of the two sides with two antithetical words such as positive and negative or right and left is purely arbitrary*. In the case of a point in a line, it is obvious that if direction is given to the line a satisfactory convention, independent of any special point on the line, can be framed, and we shall see shortly that the use of prepared lines and planes and prepared space renders a definite treatment of the cases of a line in a plane and a plane in space equally within our power.

·2. If Q is any point of a ray ρ, the direction of another point R of ρ from Q is the direction of ρ or the reverse of this direction according as R is on one side or on the other side of Q; accordingly, °R is said to be on the positive side ·22
or on the negative side of Q in ρ according as R is in the direction of ρ or in the reverse direction from Q.

122. STEPS; THE LENGTHS AND DIRECTIONS OF A STEP; CONGRUENT STEPS; ADDITION OF STEPS.

·1. °The pair of points Q, R taken in this order is called† the *step* QR, or ·11
the step *from* Q *to* R; the same pair of points taken in the opposite order is

* It does not follow that the association is useless. For example, the use of areal coordinates x, y, z with the identity $x+y+z=1$ depends on the convention that each vertex of the triangle of reference is on the positive side of the corresponding side of the triangle, but no convention is implied as to the use of positive and negative with regard either to the sides of other lines in the plane or to directions along the sides of the fundamental triangle.

† In identifying the step with the ordered pair of points instead of regarding the step as some abstract entity *determined by* the pair of points, we are following the trend of modern logical mathematics and encouraging an attitude from which for example the use of complex numbers in geometry can be treated as something better than an ingenious analytical device. One advantage of the identification the reader can appreciate at once: as an abstracted entity a zero step presents formidable difficulties to the imagination, but an ordered pair of points does not become elusive if the two points coincide.

·12 the °*reverse* step RQ. If R coincides with Q, the step degenerates to QQ, the
·13 °*zero step* at Q; steps which are not zero steps are distinguished if necessary
·14, ·15 as °*proper* steps. A proper step lies in a definite line, called its °*axis*, and to
specify a proper step QR whose origin Q and axis are known to us, we must
describe also the distance between Q and R, and the side of Q on which R is
to be found; it follows that the steps which are simplest to describe are steps
in a *directed* line.

·21 **·2.** °A proper step QR in a ray ρ is called a *positive* step or a *negative* step
according as R is on the positive or the negative side of Q in ρ; if R is on the
positive side of Q in ρ, then Q is on the negative side of R in ρ and R is on
·22 the negative side of Q in the reverse of ρ; thus °the sign of a step in a ray is
changed by a reversal either of the order which distinguishes the step QR
from the step RQ or of the direction of the ray.

·31 **·3.** By the °*length* of a step QR in a ray ρ is meant the distance *from Q to
R in the direction of ρ*; this length is a real number, zero if the step is a zero
step and having the sign of the step if the step is proper; the magnitude of
the length is the signless number which is the distance *between Q and R*, and
this number is denoted by $|QR|$.

·41 **·4.** °A proper step QR in space has two directions, the two directions of its
axis, and two lengths, its lengths in these directions; the direction from Q to
R is called the positive direction of the step, and the direction from R to Q
the negative direction, and the corresponding lengths are the positive length
·43 and the negative length. °A zero step has the single length zero but has all
directions.

·5. Two steps which have a common direction and the same length in that
·51 direction are said to be °*congruent**; if P represents a common direction of
two congruent steps and r is their length in that direction, either r is different
from zero, both steps are proper, and the steps have in common the reverse
direction P′ and have the same length $-r$ in that direction, or r is zero and the
·52 steps are both zero steps. Whether zero or proper, °congruent steps have *all*
their directions common and have a common length in *each* of their directions;
·53 °all zero steps are congruent.

·61 **·6.** °A sum of two steps is defined as a single step only if the second of the
·62 components begins where the first ends; °the sum of two steps QR, RS is
·63 defined to be the step QS, and °if n steps can be arranged in a single chain
QR_1, R_1R_2, $R_2R_3 \ldots R_{n-1}S$ their sum can be expressed as a single step QS.
Since the sum of QR and RQ appears as QQ and the sum of RQ and QR as
·64 RR, °we are compelled to allow that the sum of a number of steps is not
independent of the order in which the steps are taken, even if the addition
·65 can be performed in more ways than one. °If two steps begin at the same point

* Or by some writers *equivalent*.

there is a unique step which can be added to one to produce the other, and this step is a difference between the two steps; more precisely, °$QS - QR = RS$. ·66
°If O is any point, any step QR can be expressed in the form $OR - OQ$, and ·67
therefore °all questions concerning steps may be replaced by questions con- ·68
cerning coinitial steps with an arbitrary origin.

123. Distances from one line to another.

·1. If a ray ν with direction represented by N cuts one curve or surface in a point F and in no other point and cuts another curve or surface in only one point G, the distance from the first curve or surface to the second along ν is the length of the step FG in the direction N. In general, we can not describe this distance except by specifying the actual ray in which it is measured, but there are two cases of exception which are important because examples of them occur in the most elementary geometry: °if all the steps from one curve ·13
or surface to another along different rays with the direction N are congruent, the common length of these steps is the distance from the first curve or surface to the second in the direction N, and °if there is one and only one ray which ·14
has the direction N and cuts each of two curves, it is the length of the step in this ray which is *the* distance from one curve to the other in the direction N. The first of these cases arises with two parallel planes and any direction which is not parallel to them, with a plane and a line parallel to the plane and any direction which is not parallel to the plane, and with two parallel lines and any direction which is parallel to a* plane containing the lines but is not a direction of the lines themselves; the second case, as we are about to shew, arises with two lines which are not parallel and any direction which is not coplanar with their directions.

·2. Two lines in a plane either meet or are parallel, and conversely if two lines meet or are parallel there is a plane containing them both; for two lines in space either to meet or to be parallel is the exception. If two lines meet, each is said†
to be a °*tractor* of the other; if several lines have a common tractor, the lines are ·21
said to be °*cotractorial*, or each of them is said to be cotractorial with the others. ·22
Two lines which neither meet nor are parallel are described as °*skew* to each other. ·23

·3. °If two lines l, m are parallel, every plane through one is parallel to the ·31
other, but if the lines are not parallel, the tractors of l which are parallel to m compose a plane L_m, the plane through l parallel to m, and the tractors of m which are parallel to l compose a parallel plane M_l, the plane through m parallel to l. If n is any line not parallel to the planes L_m, M_l, the planes L_n, M_n

* If the parallel lines are distinct, we may speak of *the* plane containing them; if they coincide, every direction is parallel to *a* plane containing them, but the statement is still true.

† The word is Cayley's (*Trans. Camb. Phil. Soc.*, vol. XI, p. 297, 1869; *Coll. Works*, vol. VII, p. 73); naturally the use of the word depends on the use of the word meet; in projective geometry a line is a tractor of a parallel line, but in metrical geometry, with which alone we are at present concerned, the only line which is both parallel to a line l and a tractor of l is l itself.

through l, m parallel to n neither coincide nor are parallel, and therefore they
·33 meet in a definite line: °*if there is no plane to which three lines are all parallel,
there is one and only one tractor of two of them which is parallel to the third,*
and in particular, taking the third at right angles to the planes which are
·34 parallel to the other two, °*two lines which are not parallel have a single normal
common tractor.* These theorems remain true if the lines whose tractors are
considered themselves intersect, but not if they are distinct and parallel; if
two distinct lines l, m cut in O, and if n is a line not parallel to the plane
containing l and m, the line through O parallel to n is the one line parallel to
n which cuts both l and m, and their one normal common tractor also passes
through O. Distinct parallel lines have no tractors which do not lie in the
plane containing them, but they have an infinity of normal common tractors.

·41 **·4.** °Measurement of distances between two lines by means of real numbers
becomes possible if we consider the lines in a definite order and give direction
to a tractor. If l, m are two lines which are not parallel and N is the image
of any direction not coplanar with the directions of the lines, there is one and
·42 only one line n of which N is a direction which cuts both l and m, and °*the
distance from l to m in the direction* N is the distance in that direction from
the point at which n is cut by l to the point at which n is cut by m; the normal
·43 distances from l to m are °the distances from l to m along their normal tractor.
If l and m are concurrent, their distance apart along every common tractor
which is not in their plane is zero, and in particular their normal distance
apart is zero, but their distance apart along a tractor coplanar with them
depends on the position of the tractor as well as on its directions. If however
the lines are parallel, their common tractors are coplanar with them, but the
distance from one to the other depends only on the direction in which it is
·45 measured, and in particular °the normal distances from one to the other remain
definite. In practice the distance in a given direction from one line to another
·49 can be calculated more readily than we might expect, for as we shall see* °it
is sometimes possible for us to find this distance without discovering a particular ray in which it is to be measured.

124. The partition of a prepared plane by a ray.

·1. To give direction to the line does not assist us to give names to the sides of a line in a plane unless† we give direction, that is, cyclic direction, to

* On p. 74 below; the method is applied later, on p. 162.

† An unwary reader may imagine for a moment that it is possible to perceive a right side and a left side of a ray in a plane, unassisted by a cyclic direction; the perception however implies a choice of a particular side of the plane in space from which to observe, and the substitution of positive and negative for right and left or for left and right requires a convention similar to the spatial convention. Given a spatial convention, the choice of one side of a plane as positive is in fact equivalent to the choice of a cyclic direction for the plane, but since the choice of a cyclic direction does not logically imply the use or the existence of a third dimension, to appeal to a third dimension at this stage is inartistic.

the plane, but it is easy to give a universal definition of the positive side of
a ray in a prepared plane. °If Q is any point of a ray ρ in a prepared plane, ·12
and R is a point of ρ on the positive side of Q, then if S is any point of the
plane not on ρ, the sign of the one angle from QR to QS which is numerically
between 0 and π depends on the cyclic direction for
the plane and on the side of the ray on which S is
situated, but is independent of the position of Q on
ρ and of the position of S on that side of ρ; °S is ·13
said to be on the positive side or on the negative side
of ρ according as this sign is positive or negative.
°If the cyclic direction of a prepared plane is reversed, ·14
the positive and negative sides of every ray in the
plane exchange characters, a fact to which we may direct attention by calling
the sides of a ray positive and negative *with respect to the cyclic direction
of the plane.*

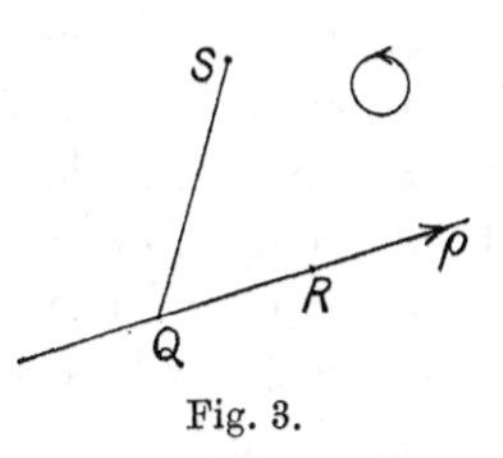

Fig. 3.

125. THE SIGN OF A TRIANGLE IN A PREPARED PLANE.

·1. Understanding the association of signs with the portions of a prepared
plane on the two sides of a ray, we can appreciate the characteristic known
as the *sign* of a triangle. If to the sides of a triangle QRS in a prepared plane
are given the directions from R to S, from S to Q, and from Q to R, then
°either every point within the triangle is on the positive side of each of the ·12
rays so formed or every point within the triangle is on the negative side of
each of these rays; °the triangle is said in the first case to be positive, in the ·13
second case to be negative. In other words, °if P is any point inside a triangle ·15
QRS, the angles numerically less than π from RS to RP, from SQ to SP, and
from QR to QP are either all positive for every position of P within the triangle or all negative for every position of P within the triangle, and the sign
of the triangle is the sign of these angles. °A reversal of the cyclic direction ·16
changes the sign of every triangle in the plane.

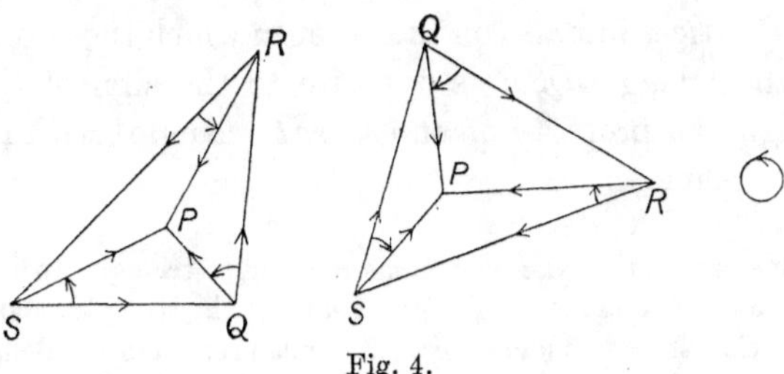

Fig. 4.

·2. In elementary geometry, two triangles ABC, FGH whose corresponding sides and angles are equal are themselves said to be equal, but if the triangles

are in one plane their equality may be accompanied by an intrinsic difference; although the angle numerically less than π from AB to AC is equal in amount to the angle numerically less than π from FG to FH, the directions of measurement of these two angles may differ. The triangles in a plane which are equal to a given triangle accordingly fall into two classes, and the division is often
·21 of importance; two coplanar triangles are said to be °*congruent* with each other *in the plane* containing them if the triangles are equal and the assumption of a cyclic direction by the plane confers on them the same sign, but if the triangles are equal and acquire different signs when their common plane is
·22 given cyclic direction, each triangle is said to be a °*reverse* of the other. For triangles in different *unprepared* planes the relation of equality is not analysed, but naturally two triangles in *prepared* planes are said to be congruent in those planes if they are equal and have the same sign, and a triangle in one prepared plane is said to be reverse of a triangle in another prepared plane if the triangles are equal and have different signs; a reversal of one only of the two planes interchanges congruence and reversion, but a simultaneous* reversal of both planes is without effect on congruence in the planes and on reversion. The difference which we are forced to recognise as possible between equal coplanar triangles we can perceive also as one of the possible differences between unequal triangles in a plane; even while dealing with an unprepared plane we can see that the difference is appropriately marked by a use of the words positive and negative, and when we have given a cyclic direction to the plane we remain in no doubt as to the manner in which the words are most suitably to be applied.

·31 **·3.** It is to be noticed that °the sign of a triangle depends not only on the position of its vertices but also on the order in which those vertices are taken†: the sign of the triangle QSR is opposite to the sign of the triangle QRS;
·32 explicitly, °sign is a property of an *ordered* triangle‡ with respect to a cyclic direction of its plane.

* It is for this reason that the definitions relating to triangles in a common unprepared plane are satisfactory; if one cyclic direction gave to the triangles a common sign and with the reverse direction their two signs were different, then from the definitions each triangle would be both congruent with and a reverse of the other; the definitions are adequate because this case can not occur.

† This is why we are apt to overlook for a time the importance of sign except with equal or similar triangles. Given two unrelated triangles we automatically denote their vertices in such a way as to give the triangles the same sign, but if equality or similarity determines the order of one set of vertices from the order of the other a fundamental difference of sign cannot escape our notice.

‡ As we regard the step QR as nothing but the ordered pair of points Q, R, so we may say that the ordered triangle QRS *is* the ordered triplet Q, R, S; the ordered triplet is naturally changed if its order is changed, but certain functions of the triplet are independent of the order, and certain functions are unaltered by some changes of the order though other changes affect them.

126. Distance from a ray in a prepared plane; normals to a ray.

·1. The distance of a point from a ray is a number to which in a prepared plane we can now attach a sign whenever the number is not zero, this sign being the sign attached to the side of the ray on which the point is situated; the distance *to* a ray *from* a point is the negative of the distance *of* the point *from* the ray. To put the matter otherwise, °in a plane containing a point R ·13
and a line t, there is one line e through R perpendicular to t, and this line cuts t in a definite point Q; if definite directions are given both to t, which becomes a ray τ, and to angular measurement in the plane, the direction of e, for the measurement of distances to and from τ, is defined as the direction which makes a positive right angle with the direction of τ, and the distances of R from τ and to τ from R are the distances from Q to R and from R to Q measured in this particular direction. Using the second form of definition we should not describe a vicious circle were we to define the positive side of a ray in a prepared plane as the side on which are the points whose distances from the ray are positive, but the distinction of sign is in reality more elementary than the ideas involved in perpendicularity, and there is no technical simplification to justify an inversion of the natural order.

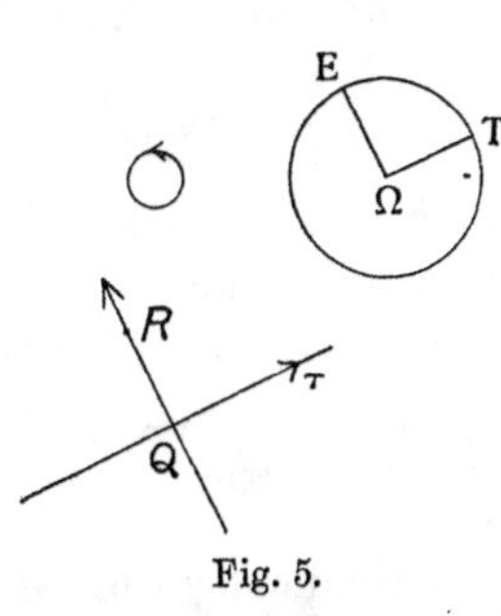

Fig. 5.

·2. The rays at right angles to a ray τ in a prepared plane may be classified into those whose direction is from the negative side of τ to the positive and those whose direction is from the positive side of τ to the negative; rays of the former class are called °*normals* to τ, and rays of the latter class are ·21
therefore normals to the reverse of τ or *reversed normals* to τ itself. In a prepared plane °we make a practice of using E_{P} or E_R for the image of the ·22
normals to rays whose direction is $\Omega\mathrm{P}$, and E alone in the case of normals to rays whose direction we are denoting consistently by $\Omega\mathrm{T}$.

·3. °The normal to the normal to a ray τ is not τ but the reverse of τ; in ·31
other words E_{E} is identical with T′ and never with T; to the unsymmetrical nature of the relation between rays and their normals in a prepared plane can be traced a want of symmetry in many regions of geometry.

127. The area of a triangle; the universality of trigonometrical formulae.

·1. The area of a triangle is not suffered to remain signless, an only survivor from the geometry of an unprepared plane, but °to this area is attached the ·11
sign of the triangle itself. To see the appropriateness of such a sign, we have only to consider a number of triangles with a common base ST and vertices

on a single line through a point Q on ST at right angles to the base; if the altitude QR of such a triangle is to receive a sign, by the specification of a direction of measurement along the line containing R, and if the area is to be equal to $\frac{1}{2}QR.ST$, the area also must acquire a sign; to give the area the sign of the triangle itself is the practice that enables us to make unreflecting use of familiar trigonometrical formulae.

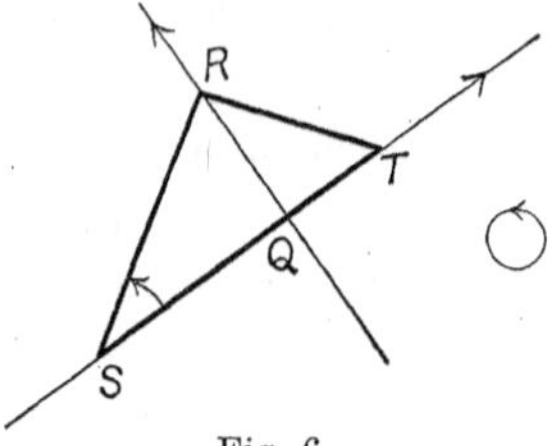

Fig. 6.

·2. To avoid detailed examination of different cases in subsequent work, it
·21 is worth our while to notice at once that °we can use the formulae of plane trigonometry without modification for steps of negative length, provided only that the directions *between* which we measure the angles from one step to another are the directions *in* which we measure the lengths of the steps.

·3. If ABC is a triangle, and D is the foot of the perpendicular from A on BC, the fundamental formulae

·31 $$BD = BA \cos CBA, \quad DA = BA \sin CBA, \quad \Delta = \tfrac{1}{2} BC \,.\, DA,$$

which contain implicitly all formulae relative to the triangle, do not depend in the least on the actual directions in which the steps are measured or on the signs of any of the steps involved, but require only that BD and BC should be measured in the same direction, that the direction in which DA is measured should make a positive right angle with this common direction, and that CBA should denote an angle *from* the direction in which BD and BC are measured
·35 *to* the direction in which BA is measured. °It is necessary to allow of the angles of a triangle either that at least one of them may be numerically greater that π or that their sum may be $-\pi$, but it is no drawback actually to make both of these admissions.

·4. For example, if the angle at B is obtuse and BC and BA are measured towards B, the numerically smallest angle denoted by CBA is the obtuse angle vertically opposite to

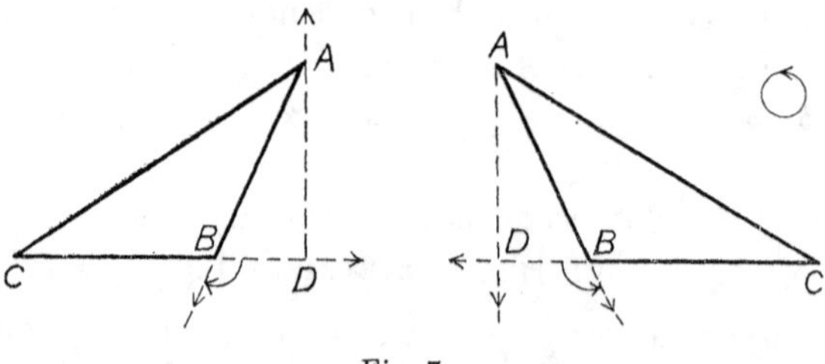

Fig. 7.

the internal angle at B, and therefore $\cos CBA$ is negative. Measured towards B, the length of BC is negative; hence the product $BC \cos CBA$ is positive, while since C and D

are on opposite sides of B the length of BD, measured in the same direction as the length of BC, also is positive. With the same triangle, the direction which makes a positive right angle with the direction of B from C is the direction from D to A or the direction from A to D according as the numerically smallest angle denoted by CBA is negative or positive; hence the sign of DA is opposite to the sign of $\sin CBA$, in agreement with the hypothesis that the length of BA is negative. Lastly, the triangle is positive or negative according as $\sin CBA$ is positive or negative, that is, according as DA is negative or positive, and therefore the sign of Δ is the sign of $BC \,.\, DA$. Of course the generality of the fundamental formulae ·31 does not require to be established by a direct consideration of all possible cases, but depends on the generality belonging to the circular functions themselves. On this subject see also 311 below.

CHAPTER I 3

MEASUREMENT IN SPACE

131. The partition of space by a prepared plane. 132. The sign of a tetrahedron. 133. The normals to a prepared plane; distance from a prepared plane. 134. The volume of a tetrahedron. 135. Angles between prepared planes.

131. THE PARTITION OF SPACE BY A PREPARED PLANE.

·1. A plane divides space as a line divides a plane, and just as by giving direction to the line and to the plane we can distinguish the positive from the
·12 negative side of the line, so °by giving direction to the plane and to space we can describe a point not in the plane as on the positive side or on the negative side. If Q is any point of a directed plane and R is any point not in the plane, the sign attached by a given spatial convention to angular measurement round QR in the cyclic direction of the plane depends on the side of the plane on which R is situated, and is otherwise independent of the positions
·14 of Q and R; ° the side of the plane on which R lies is called the positive or the negative side according as this sign is positive or negative.

·2. The bearing of the spatial convention on the naming of the sides of a directed plane is seen most clearly if we suppose a unit sphere described with its centre actually in the plane. The circle representing rays in the plane is then the circle in which the plane cuts the sphere, and the cyclic convention in this circle agrees with the cyclic direction of the plane. The spatial convention describes the points of the sphere on one side of the directed circle as positive, and the positive side of the prepared plane is the side on which these points are to be found.

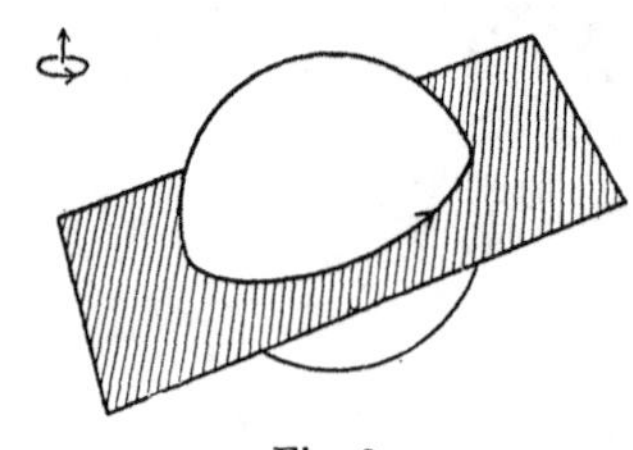

Fig. 8.

132. THE SIGN OF A TETRAHEDRON.

·11 **·1.** °In prepared space an ordered tetrahedron has a definite sign which is reversed if the spatial convention is changed and may be reversed if the order in which the vertices of the tetrahedron are taken is disturbed. If cyclic direction is given to the face QRS of the tetrahedron $QRST$ by the convention that in
·13 this face the triangle QRS is to be positive, °the ordered tetrahedron $QRST$ is said to be positive or to be negative according as T is on the positive or the negative side of the prepared plane QRS; if ρ, σ, τ are the rays in which the
·14 steps QR, QS, QT have positive lengths, °the sign of the tetrahedron is the

common sign of the angles numerically less than π from σ to τ round ρ, from τ
to ρ round σ, and from ρ to σ round τ. It is easy to shew that °the sign of ·15
the tetrahedron *RQST* is opposite to the sign of *QRST*, and thence that °a ·16
derangement of the order of its vertices leaves unaffected or reverses the sign
of an ordered tetrahedron according as the derangement is even or odd*.

·2. If two tetrahedra have corresponding edges equal in absolute length, then
any angle, length, area, or volume intrinsic to one of the tetrahedra is equal
numerically to the corresponding angle, length, area, or volume derived from
the other, and the two tetrahedra are said to be equal. In spite of equality,
two tetrahedra may exhibit the intrinsic difference which presents itself as
a difference in sign if the space containing the tetrahedra is prepared, and
two tetrahedra are said to be °*congruent* if they are equal and if they acquire ·23
the same sign when a spatial convention is adopted; if two tetrahedra are
equal but not congruent, each is said† to be a °*perverse* of the other. ·24

133. The normals to a prepared plane; distance from a prepared plane.

·1. If a line is perpendicular to a plane, both of the rays in the line are at
right angles to each of the corresponding prepared planes, but in prepared
space °each ray bears a special relation to each plane; a ray is said to be ·12
°*normal* to a prepared plane if it is at right angles to the plane and if its ·13
direction is from the negative side to the positive side of the plane; moreover,
°to say that a ray is normal to a plane is held to imply that the plane is pre- ·15
pared. If with one spatial convention a ray is normal to a plane, then with
the same convention the reverse of the ray is normal to the reverse of the
plane, and with the alternative convention the ray itself is normal to the
reversed plane.

·2. °The normals to a prepared plane are the rays represented by the ·21
positive pole of the corresponding prepared unit circle. Through any point *R*
of space passes one of these normals, this ray cuts the plane in a definite point
Q, and the distance of *R* from *Q* in the direction of the ray defines the
°distance of the point from the plane, while the negative of this distance is ·22
the °distance from the point to the plane. ·23

134. The volume of a tetrahedron.

·1. °The volume of an ordered tetrahedron *QRST* is given the sign of the ·11
tetrahedron, and is °one-third of the product of the area of the ordered triangle ·12

* Every derangement of a finite ordered class can be effected in many ways by a finite succession of simple interchanges: for example, to pass from *QRST* to *TRQS* we may interchange first *T* with *Q* and then *Q* with *S*, or proceeding on another plan we may pass through the orders *QRTS*, *RQTS*, *RTQS*; but for a particular derangement, either the number of interchanges must be even or the number of interchanges must be odd, and derangements are classified accordingly as even and odd derangements.

† Following Listing (*loc. cit.* p. 8 above, p. 830).

RST by the distance of *Q* from the plane of this triangle; either cyclic direction may be given to the plane containing the triangle, provided only that the same cyclic direction determines the signs both of the triangle and of the side of the plane on which *Q* is to be found, but a spatial convention has to be adopted before the sign of a tetrahedron is determinate.

·2. The area of a triangle ABC is one-half of the area of the parallelogram
of which AB, AC are adjacent sides, and is equal to $\frac{1}{2}AB\,.\,AC\,.\sin BAC$;
the volume of a tetrahedron $QRST$ is one-sixth of the volume of the parallelepiped of which QR, QS, QT are adjacent edges, and it is written in the
·23 form $\frac{1}{6}QR\,.\,QS\,.\,QT\,.\sin QRST$, where the last factor is called* the °*sine* of the
solid angle subtended at Q by the ordered triangle RST. Just as $\sin BAC$
·24 depends only on the directions of B and C from A, so °$\sin QRST$ depends only
on the directions of R, S, T from Q and not on the lengths of the edges QR,
QS, QT; indeed, if Β, Γ represent AB, AC on a unit circle we can write
$\sin \mathrm{B\Gamma}$ instead of $\sin BAC$, and if Ρ, Σ, Τ are spherical images of QR, QS, QT
we can write $\sin \Omega\mathrm{P}\Sigma\mathrm{T}$ instead of $\sin QRST$, and it is only because $\sin \mathrm{P}\Sigma\mathrm{T}$
might be used to denote the sine of an angle at Σ between the great circles
ΣΡ and ΣΤ that it is unwise to use this simpler symbol for the sine of the
solid angle.

If the lengths QR, QS, QT are all different from zero, the volume of the tetrahedron $QRST$ is zero if and only if the lines QR, QS, QT are all in one plane; hence

·26 *The sine* $\sin \Omega\mathrm{P}\Sigma\mathrm{T}$ *is zero if and only if the directions* Ρ, Σ, Τ *are coplanar.*

·3. The expressions given in ·1 and ·2 for its volume regard a proper or undegenerate tetrahedron as derived from a triangle by the introduction of a third
dimension: in the one case Q is taken as a point outside the plane of the triangle
RST, and in the other case QT is taken as a step not coplanar with the steps QR,
·32 QS. °Another derivation from a triangle regards the tetrahedron as generated
by a variable triangle of which the base is fixed and the vertex traces a line
of finite length, the plane of the triangle revolving round the fixed base; thus
·33 °a triangle XST whose vertex X moves from Q to R along the line joining
these points traces the tetrahedron $QRST$, and the same tetrahedron may be
generated similarly in five other ways. Viewing the construction in this light,
we concentrate our attention on two opposite edges of the figure instead of on
one vertex and a face or on three conterminous edges, and since the edges
·35 which we choose play different parts °there are two distinct modes of generation
corresponding to each pair of opposite edges. There is however a generation
of the tetrahedron by means of opposite edges in which the chosen edges play
similar parts, and this is among the most useful modes of developing the figure.

* This application of the word sine as well as the introduction of the function is due to von Staudt (*Crelle's J. f. d. M.*, vol. XXIV, p. 255, 1842). A line of argument different from that in the text is indicated in a foot-note on p. 103 below.

·4. Let l, m be the lines containing opposite edges QR, ST of a tetrahedron, let U be any point of l, and let V be any point of m; the tetrahedron being supposed not to degenerate into a plane figure, there passes through any point Z of UV a definite plane K to which both l and m are parallel, and if this plane cuts the four lines QS, RS, RT, QT in A, B, C, D, the lines AB, DC are
parallel to l and the lines AD, BC are parallel to m; °the figure $ABCD$ is a ·41
parallelogram whose sides depend in length on the position of Z but have the directions of l and m, and the tetrahedron may be regarded as generated by the motion of this variable parallelogram as Z moves from U to V, the sides parallel to l decreasing uniformly in numerical length from $|r|$, the length of QR, to zero, the sides parallel to m increasing uniformly in numerical length from zero to $|s|$, the length of ST, and the vertices describing straight lines.

·5. The volume of a tetrahedron is determinate if a pair of opposite edges is known, and the actual expression for the volume is both simple and valuable. With the notation of the last paragraph, let λ, μ be rays in l, m, let ν be a ray in the line through U and V, and let r, s, t be the lengths of QR, ST, UV in λ, μ, ν. Since the distance of any point X in λ from the plane through U and μ is a constant multiple of the distance of X from U, the volume of the tetrahedron $UXST$, as far as this volume depends on the position of X, also is a constant multiple of this distance, and
therefore °the volume of the tetrahedron ·51
$QRST$ is the product of r and a factor independent of the positions of Q and
R in λ. Hence °this volume is the pro- ·52
duct of rs and a factor independent alike of the positions of Q and R in λ and of the positions of S and T in μ. The value of the independent factor is readily obtained: if L, M are the points at unit distances from U, V along λ, μ, the factor is the volume of the tetrahedron $ULVM$, and if the line through M parallel to UV meets the line through U parallel to VM in P, this volume is that of the tetrahedron $ULVP$ and is $\frac{1}{6}t\sin\Omega\Lambda\mathrm{N}\mathrm{M}$, where Λ, M, N are the images of λ, μ, ν:

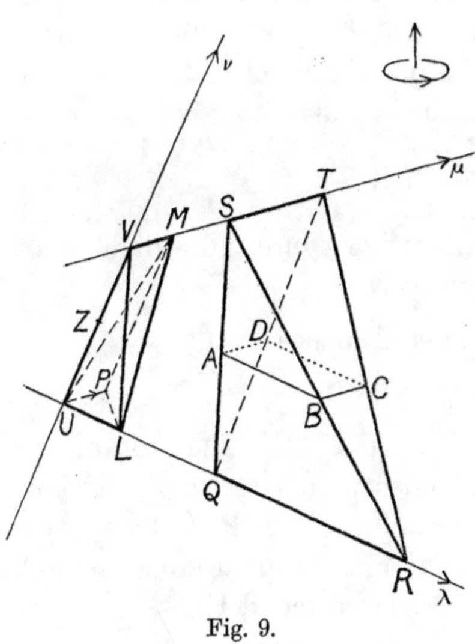

Fig. 9.

The volume of a tetrahedron of which opposite edges have lengths r, s in rays ·54
λ, μ *is* $-\frac{1}{6}rsd_{\lambda\mu\nu}\sin\Omega\Lambda\mathrm{MN}$, *where* $d_{\lambda\mu\nu}$ *is the distance from* λ *to* μ *along any ray* ν *which cuts them and* Λ, M, N *represent the directions of* λ, μ, ν.

If we wish to take ν at right angles to both λ and μ, we may appeal to the general formula or we may note that in this case the area of the triangle UST, with the cyclic direction that is positive with respect to λ, is $-\frac{1}{2}sd_{\lambda\mu}$ and the distance of L from the plane of this triangle is $\sin\epsilon_{\lambda\mu}$:

·55 *The volume of a tetrahedron of which opposite edges have lengths r, s in rays λ, μ is $-\frac{1}{6}rsd_{\lambda\mu}\sin\epsilon_{\lambda\mu}$, where $d_{\lambda\mu}$ is a normal distance from λ to μ and $\epsilon_{\lambda\mu}$ is an angle from λ to μ round the direction in which $d_{\lambda\mu}$ is measured,*

a result which is probably more used than the general theorem which includes
·56 it. It is to be remarked that °the last two theorems are true without any restrictions on the directions of the rays concerned, for if the rays λ, μ are parallel the factors $\sin \Omega\Lambda MN$ and $\sin\epsilon_{\lambda\mu}$ are zero, while if λ, μ are concurrent, then in the one theorem the factor $d_{\lambda\mu\nu}$ or the factor $\sin\Omega\Lambda MN$ is zero according as ν is not or is coplanar with λ and μ, and in the other theorem the factor $d_{\lambda\mu}$ is zero.

·6. The two theorems ·54, ·55 may of course be deduced from the generation of the volume by the area of a variable parallelogram. The area of the parallelogram described in ·4 is $(UZ\,.\,ZV/UV^2)\,rs\sin\epsilon_{\lambda\mu}$, and if $\frac{1}{2}z\,.\,UV$ is the distance of Z from the midpoint of UV this area is $\frac{1}{4}(1-z^2)\,rs\sin\epsilon_{\lambda\mu}$; moreover, the perpendicular distance of Z from the plane parallel to l and m and bisecting UV is $\frac{1}{2}z\,d_{\lambda\mu}$; hence the volume is numerically

·65 $$\tfrac{1}{8}rs\,d_{\lambda\mu}\sin\epsilon_{\lambda\mu}\int_{-1}^{+1}(1-z^2)\,dz,$$

which agrees with ·55, but the entry of the negative sign is more difficult to understand if the volume is calculated in this way.

·7. The equivalence of ·54 and ·55, and the equivalence of

$$\tfrac{1}{6}QR\,.\,QS\,.\,QT\sin QRST$$

and the product $\frac{1}{3}\times\frac{1}{2}QR\,.\,QT\sin RQT\times PS$, where P is the foot of the perpendicular from S on the plane QRT, establish what is perhaps the most useful of all formulae involving the sine of a solid angle: if Ρ, Σ, Τ are three points of a sphere whose centre is Ω, and Π is a pole of a great circle through Σ and Τ, then if the angles from Σ to Τ are measured round Π,

·72 $$\sin \Omega\mathrm{P}\Sigma\mathrm{T} = \cos \mathrm{P}\Pi \sin \Sigma\mathrm{T}.$$

135. Angles between prepared planes.

·11 **·1.** °An angle from one prepared plane to another may be defined as an angle from the direction normal to the first prepared plane to the direction normal to the second; the angles between two prepared planes have a common cosine, but if the planes are not parallel we can not give a definite sign to the sine of angles from one prepared plane to another except by reference to a
·13 direction which is not at right angles to their line of intersection. °The directions of the actual line of intersection are usually the most convenient directions

round which to measure the angles between prepared planes which are not parallel; round each of these directions the angles from one of the planes to the other compose a single congruence.

·2. Angles between prepared planes may be studied on a unit sphere. °If ·21
two such planes are parallel, the prepared great circles which represent them coincide in position and have the same direction or opposite directions according as the cyclic directions of the planes are identical or opposite. °If two ·22
prepared planes are not parallel, they are represented by two distinct circles, and their line of intersection is represented by the points of intersection of the circles; let these points be Λ, Λ′, and let the points at distances $\frac{1}{2}\pi$ from Λ along the two circles be P, Σ; the points P, Σ and the opposite points P′, Σ′, as well as the positive poles M, N of the two prepared circles, are situated on the great circle whose poles are Λ and Λ′, and whichever direction of measurement round this circle is adopted, the congruences of angles from P to Σ, from P′ to Σ′, and from M to N, are identical. At Λ, the prepared circles have definite directions, which are the directions of rays in the tangent plane to the sphere at Λ, and are in fact also the directions of

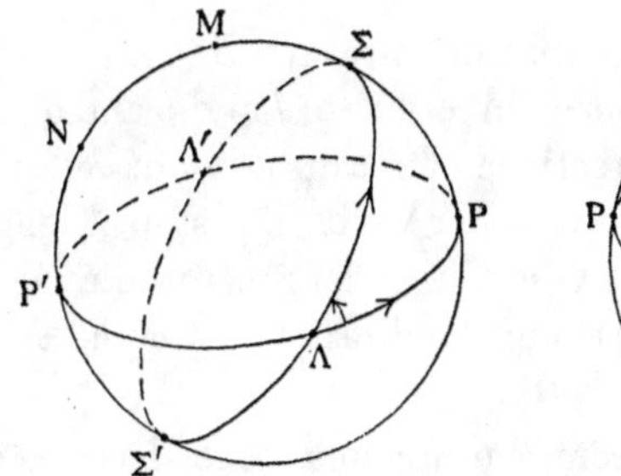

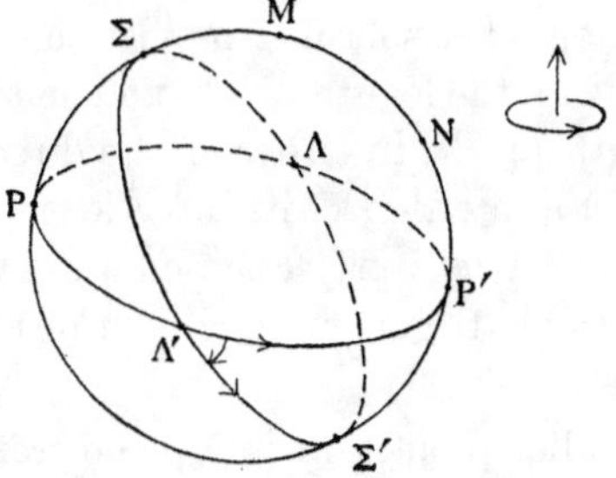

Fig. 10.

ΩP and ΩΣ; instead of measuring angles from the one prepared plane to the other round ΩΛ as angles from M to N, we may measure them as angles °from P to Σ, or as angles °at Λ from the direction of the quadrant ΛP to ·25, ·26
the direction of the quadrant ΛΣ, that is, from the first prepared circle to the second. °The directions of the two circles at Λ′ are represented not by P and ·27
Σ but by P′ and Σ′, but the angles from one plane to the other round the direction whose image is Λ′ can still be described as the angles at Λ′ from the first circle to the second; figure 10 is intended to shew the same sphere from different points of view, and to illustrate that °the angles at Λ′ are the ·29
negatives of the angles at Λ.

CHAPTER I 4

PARALLEL PROJECTION

141. Parallel projection in a plane; its effect on lengths. 142. The two kinds of parallel projection in space. 143. Parallel projection on a ray; its effect on lengths; distances between lines in space. 144. Parallel projection on a prepared plane; its effect on lengths, areas, and angles.

141. Parallel projection in a plane; its effect on lengths.

·1. If l and p are any two intersecting lines in a plane, and S is a point of
the plane, there is one line through S parallel to l, and this line meets p in
·11 a definite point P which is called the °*l-projection* of S on p; if l is at right
·12 angles to p, the l-projection is called the °*normal* projection, or briefly *the*
projection, of S on p, and if we wish to indicate that a projection is not assumed
to be normal we call it a projection by parallels or an oblique projection.

·2. A step ST has for its l-projection on p a definite step PQ. The lengths of
PQ depend on the lengths of ST and on the directions of l and p and of ST, and
·22 °the length of PQ in either of the directions of p can be compared with the
length of ST in either of its directions; in other words, if a step of length e in
a ray σ has for its l-projection on a ray ϖ a step of length f, the ratio of f to
e is expressible trigonometrically in terms of the directions of σ and ϖ and the
directions of l.

·3. Parallel projection in a plane from one ray on another has one characteristic which is not numerical. If the l-projection on ϖ of S in σ is P, then
the l-projections of the points on one side of S in σ are the points on one side
·32 of P in ϖ, so that °the positive side of S in σ projects as a whole either into the
·33 positive side of P or into the negative side of P in ϖ; moreover, °either the
two sides of all points in σ retain their signs after projection or the two sides
·34 of all points in σ exchange signs after projection, and we say that °*l-projection
from σ on ϖ or between σ and ϖ is negative or positive according as the signs*
·35 *of sides of points are affected or unaffected by the projection.* °The points
representing σ and ϖ on a unit circle lie on the same side or on opposite sides
of the diameter parallel to the axis of projection according as the projection
is positive or negative.

·4. Three methods suggest themselves for determining the ratio of the length of a projected step to the length of the original, and they lead to three different expressions. With the notation of the preceding paragraphs, if ι is a ray at right angles to l, and if the lines through S and T parallel to l, which contain the points P and Q, meet ι in G and H, the step GH is the normal

projection on ι of both ST and PQ; if then the directions of σ, ϖ, ι are represented by the points Σ, Π, I, the length of GH in ι can be expressed both as $e \cos \mathrm{I}\Sigma$ and as $f \cos \mathrm{I}\Pi$ and therefore °the value of f/e is $\cos \mathrm{I}\Sigma / \cos \mathrm{I}\Pi$; if the ·42
reverse of ι is used the expression obtained for f/e is $\cos \mathrm{I}'\Sigma / \cos \mathrm{I}'\Pi$, which has of course the same value as the expression found from I. Alternatively,

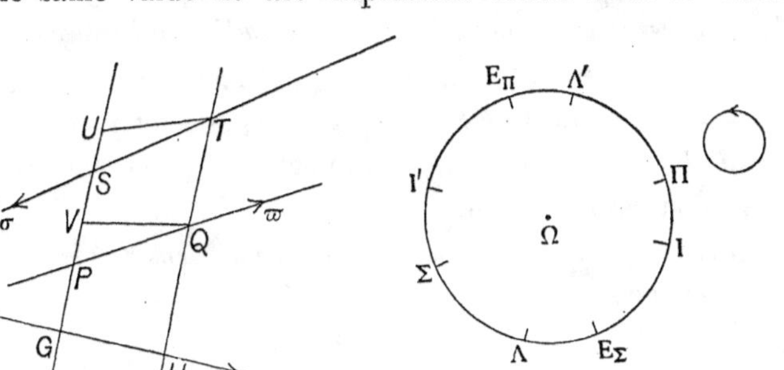

Fig. 11.

if Λ represents either direction along l, and PV, SU are steps in the direction of Λ with the same arbitrary length g in that direction, then since the areas of the triangles PQV, STU are equal in sign and amount, it follows that

$$\tfrac{1}{2} g f \sin \Pi\Lambda = \tfrac{1}{2} g e \sin \Sigma\Lambda,$$ ·43

and therefore that °f/e is equal to $\sin \Lambda\Sigma / \sin \Lambda\Pi$, on the assumption that angles ·44
from Λ to Σ and from Λ to Π are measured in the same direction. The relation between the two expressions found for f/e is obvious; the expression in terms of sines involves only directions immediately concerned in the projection, but is slightly ambiguous in form. In view of the three-dimensional problem to which we must proceed, we may mention a third method of expressing the result. If E_Σ, E_Π represent the directions normal to the rays σ, ϖ, cyclic direction having been given to the plane, then the distances of U from σ and V from ϖ are $g \cos \Lambda\mathrm{E}_\Sigma$ and $g \cos \Lambda\mathrm{E}_\Pi$, and the areas of the triangles STU, PQV are $\tfrac{1}{2} g e \cos \Lambda\mathrm{E}_\Sigma$, $\tfrac{1}{2} g f \cos \Lambda\mathrm{E}_\Pi$; thus °$f/e$ is expressed as $\cos \Lambda\mathrm{E}_\Sigma / \cos \Lambda\mathrm{E}_\Pi$, ·46
a ratio easily identified with $\cos \mathrm{I}\Sigma / \cos \mathrm{I}\Pi$.

·5. The reader will not fail to observe the advantage we have gained from our freedom* to use triangles of which the sides are real numbers and the angles may be negative or greater than π. Fettered to triangles with signless sides, we should have first to prove the formula

$$f \sin \Lambda\Pi = e \sin \Lambda\Sigma$$

or an equivalent for rays in the positive directions of the steps ST, PQ, and then to generalise the *result* by means of the identities

$$f \sin \Lambda\Pi = -f \sin \Lambda\Pi', \quad e \sin \Lambda\Sigma = -e \sin \Lambda\Sigma'.$$

Generalisation of results is a tedious distraction, whose avoidance justifies any attention devoted to first principles.

* In fig. 11, g is negative, U is on the negative side of σ, and V is on the positive side of ϖ; Λ is E'_I, and $\cos \Lambda\mathrm{E}_\Sigma$, $\cos \Lambda\mathrm{E}_\Pi$ are the negatives of $\cos \mathrm{I}\Sigma$, $\cos \mathrm{I}\Pi$.

·6. Altogether independent of the quantitative results of ·4 is the theorem that

·61 *If one step is the sum of a finite number of coplanar steps, any parallel projection, normal or oblique, of the sum on a line in the plane of the components is the sum of the corresponding projections of the individual components,*

an immediate deduction from definitions ·11 and 22·63, which might well be described as the fundamental theorem of plane trigonometry.

The success of the investigation in ·4 emphasises a theorem on which the very possibility of success depends:

·62 *In any parallel projection in a plane, congruent steps project on parallel lines into congruent steps.*

In other words,

·63 *In a parallel projection in a plane, if two steps that are congruent are projected on two rays that have the same direction, the projections have the same length.*

We must not attempt to *prove* ·62 or the corresponding theorem relating to projection in space. These theorems, in some form or other, are *assumed* in the geometrical definitions of the circular functions and in the spherical representation of directions, if not in the use of the word 'direction' itself, and to disentangle hypotheses from deductions would carry us back into that discussion of the logical foundations of elementary geometry which it is our intention to avoid; the assumptions that distinguish Euclidean geometry have been made, though not avowed, on almost every page of our first two chapters.

142. The two kinds of parallel projection in space.

·1. In space of three dimensions there are two kinds of oblique projection, projection on a line and projection on a plane. Through any point S of space there pass a single plane parallel to any given plane K and a single line parallel to any given line l; the plane cuts any line p which is not parallel to
·12 K in a definite point called the °*K-projection* of S on p, and the line cuts any
·13 plane N which is not parallel to l in a definite point called the °*l-projection* of S on N; if K is at right angles to p and l at right angles to N, the
·14 K-projection and the l-projection are called °*the* projections, or more fully the normal projections, of S on p and N, and a projection not assumed to be normal
·15 may be called °oblique or parallel.

·2. There is an obvious relation between projection on a plane and projection on any line in the plane:

·21 *If p is a line in a plane N, and if K is a plane not parallel to p and l a line parallel to K but not to N, then the K-projection on p of any point S is the m-projection on p of the l-projection of S on N, where m is parallel to the line of intersection of K and N.*

Particular cases of this theorem in which only one of the projections is normal need not delay us, but we remark that if K is at right angles to p, the lines at right angles to N are parallel to K, whence

If p is a line in a plane N, the projection on p of any point S is the projection on p of the projection of S on N. ·23

·3. A step in space projects on a line or on a plane into a step, and one characteristic of parallel projection is that

In parallel projection congruent steps project into congruent steps, ·31

a theorem that we shall be content to recognise, as in 1·6, from the success of calculations which would inevitably fail if the result were not true.

The numerical effects of projection on steps, on triangles, and on angles can be found without difficulty, but we have not to appeal to calculations for the theorem that

If one step is the sum of a finite number of other steps, any parallel projection of the sum, normal or oblique, on a line or on a plane, is the sum of the corresponding projections of the individual components. ·32

·4. It is interesting to compare the values of the analogous theorems 1·61, ·32. Since the whole of plane trigonometry may be made dependent on 1·61 without reference to ·32, the range of application of 1·61 is far wider than the range of application of ·32, in spite of the fact that the latter range includes the whole of spherical trigonometry. On the other hand, the fundamental theorems derivable from 1·61 can be proved and often have been proved without reference to the theory of projection, but the study of space offers such difficulties to perception and such variety in the different aspects of a single problem that to satisfactory progress in this study generality of treatment is essential and not merely desirable; whereas advance without 1·61 is sure but tiresome (the proof of the elementary expression of $\cos(A+B)$ as $\cos A \cos B - \sin A \sin B$, for example, requiring the consideration of a number of different cases), advance without ·32 is all but impossible.

143. Parallel projection on a ray; its effect on lengths; distances between lines in space.

·1. Projection from one ray on another in space, as in a plane, has a definite sign, and °this sign is positive or negative according as the images of the rays ·11
on a unit sphere lie on the same side or on opposite sides of the great circle representing the plane which guides the projection.

·2. If a step ST in a ray σ is projected on a ray ϖ by planes parallel to a plane K, the ratio of the length e of ST to the length f of its projection PQ can be expressed in three different forms in terms of the directions of σ and ϖ, whose images we suppose to be Σ, Π, and of the directions at right angles to the plane, which we represent by K and K′. If κ is a ray in the direction of K, the normal projections of ST and PQ on κ are identical, and $e \cos \mathrm{K}\Sigma$ and $f \cos \mathrm{K}\Pi$ are alternative expressions for a single length; hence °f is ·21
equal to $e \cos \mathrm{K}\Sigma / \cos \mathrm{K}\Pi$. If a* great circle through Σ and Π cuts the great circle representing K in the points Λ, Λ', then ST can be projected

* In general we might say *the* great circle, but the result is formally valid if Σ and Π coincide or are opposite to each other.

in a plane parallel to $\Omega\Lambda\Sigma$ by lines parallel to $\Lambda\Lambda'$ on a ray parallel to ϖ, and
·22 the projected step is congruent with PQ; hence °f is equal to $e \sin \Lambda\Sigma/\sin \Lambda\Pi$, on the assumption that $\Lambda\Sigma$ and $\Lambda\Pi$ are measured in the same direction round the great circle to which they belong. If on the great circle just used, I is a point distant by a quadrant from Λ,
·23 then °f is equal to $e \cdot \cos \mathrm{I}\Sigma/\cos \mathrm{I}\Pi$. A comparison of the third of the expressions for f with the first gives the equation

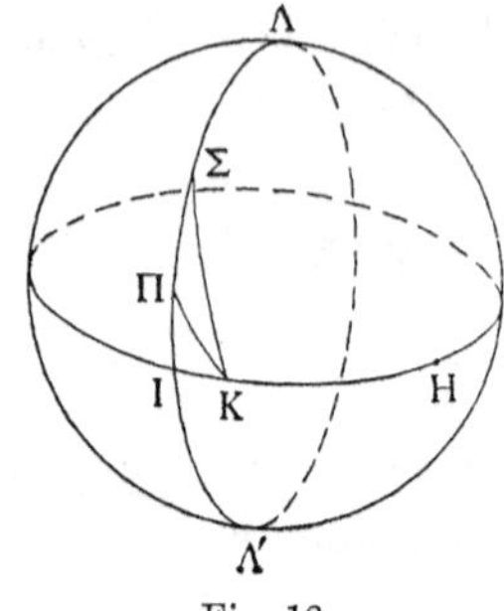

Fig. 12.

·24 $$\cos \mathrm{K}\Sigma/\cos \mathrm{K}\Pi = \cos \mathrm{I}\Sigma/\cos \mathrm{I}\Pi;$$

if we are acquainted with the rudiments of spherical trigonometry we recognise this equation as a consequence of the two formulae*

·25 $$\cos \mathrm{K}\Sigma = \cos \mathrm{KI} \cos \mathrm{I}\Sigma, \quad \cos \mathrm{K}\Pi = \cos \mathrm{KI} \cos \mathrm{I}\Pi,$$

·26 but °the simplest basis for spherical trigonometry is the theory of projection, and if ·24 is to be connected with ·25 it is best to replace ·24 by

·27 $$\cos \mathrm{K}\Sigma/\cos \mathrm{I}\Sigma = \cos \mathrm{K}\Pi/\cos \mathrm{I}\Pi,$$

an equation which shews that the ratio $\cos \mathrm{K}\Sigma/\cos \mathrm{I}\Sigma$ is actually independent of the position of Σ in $\mathrm{I}\Lambda$, and to *deduce*† that the value of $\cos \mathrm{K}\Sigma/\cos \mathrm{I}\Sigma$ for every such position of Σ is $\cos \mathrm{KI}$, its value when Σ is at I. Viewed apart from the theory of projection, ·24 shews that the value of $\cos \mathrm{K}\Sigma/\cos \mathrm{K}\Pi$ is $\cos \mathrm{I}\Sigma/\cos \mathrm{I}\Pi$ for *every* position of K in the great circle through I and K, and
·28 enables us to state a result including ·21 and ·23: °if H represents any direction in a plane at right angles both to K and to a plane to which σ and ϖ are parallel, other than a direction to which σ and ϖ are both at right angles, then f is equal to $e \cos \mathrm{H}\Sigma/\cos \mathrm{H}\Pi$.

·3. A valuable application of the idea of projection on a line is to the determination of the distance from one line to another in a given direction. Let K be a plane parallel to each of two lines l, m, let n be any line which is not parallel to K, let l, m meet their tractor parallel to n in F, G, and let P, Q be any two points on l, m; then the step FG is the K-projection of the step
·32 PQ on the tractor, and is therefore °congruent with the K-projection of the step PQ on n itself; hence we can find the lengths of the step FG in its two directions without determining the actual positions of F and G. In particular, if l, m are not parallel and n is any line at right angles to each of them, or if l, m are parallel and n is any line at right angles to them and parallel to a plane containing them, and if P is any point of l and Q any point of m, the

* See 313·14 on p. 102 below.

† We hasten to add in defence of the claim made in ·26 that this is not the natural method of deriving the elementary theorem used in ·25 from the theory of projection; as we shall see in 313·2, this theorem is an immediate corollary of 2·23.

distance from l to m in either direction of n is the distance in that direction
from the projection of P on n to the projection of Q on n, or in other words is
° the projection in that direction of the distance from P to Q. From the last ·33
result it follows that ° the distance between two lines along a normal tractor ·34
is numerically less than the distance between them along any other common
tractor, and the numerical value of this distance is therefore the ° *shortest* ·35
distance between the lines.

144. Parallel projection on a prepared plane; its effect on lengths, areas, and angles.

·**1**. More strikingly than the study of projection on a line the study of
projection on a plane is facilitated by the use of a unit sphere. Let N, N′
represent the directions at right angles to the plane N on which we are to
project, and Λ, Λ′ the directions of the axis of projection l; that the axis can
not be parallel to the plane implies that ° Λ, Λ′ are not in the great circle of ·12
which N, N′ are the poles.

·**2**. ° If a line s is parallel to l, all points of s have the same l-projection; ·21
° except in this case, the lines parallel to l through the points of s compose ·22
a plane whose intersection with the plane of projection is a line, the l-projection of s. On the unit sphere we can recognise the points representing the
directions of this projection; if Σ, Σ′ represent s, the great circle through Λ
and Σ is definite, because s is not parallel to l, and does not coincide with the
circle representing N, because, by ·12, Λ does not lie in this circle; ° the points ·23
Π, Π′ in which the great circle through Λ and Σ cuts the great circle representing N are the images of the directions of the l-projection of s on N.

·**3**. The axis of a ray σ projects on a plane N into a definite line p, and
each of the rays in p is a projection of σ by lines parallel to the axis of
projection; ° the l-projection of σ is positive on one of the two rays, negative ·32
on the other, and the rays may be distinguished accordingly as the positive
and the negative projection of σ on N. On the unit sphere, the point Σ
representing σ, the two points Λ, Λ′ representing the axis of projection, and
the two points Π, Π′ representing p, lie in one great circle, and Λ and Λ′ are
distinct from the others and divide the circle into two semicircles; of the
points Π, Π′, one lies in the same semicircle as Σ, and ° this one is the image ·34
of the positive l-projection of σ.

·**4**. The effect of parallel projection on the length of a step in a ray is to
be found by an application of the results of the last article, choice having been
made between the two projections of the ray. ° A ray σ and an l-projection ϖ ·41
of that ray on a plane N are contained in a single plane parallel to l, and
projection from σ to ϖ may be regarded as effected either by lines parallel to
l or by planes parallel to any plane containing l other than the plane parallel
to that in which σ and ϖ are to be found.

·5. For us the most important case of projection on a plane is parallel projection from one prepared plane to another, and this form of projection has the characteristic of sign. Let Σ, T represent two rays which are not parallel in a prepared plane M, and let Π, P represent the positive l-projections of these rays on a prepared plane N, the axis having Λ, Λ′ for its images; then the angles numerically less than π from Σ to T and from Π to P have
·52 necessarily the same sign if measured round Λ, and therefore °if measured in the cyclic directions of the two planes M, N these angles have the same sign or opposite signs according as the cyclic directions have the same sign or opposite signs with respect to Λ. The condition is independent of any particular pair
·53 of rays in M, and is unaltered by a substitution of Λ′ for Λ, and °*a parallel projection from one prepared plane on another is called positive or negative according as the cyclic directions of the two planes have the same sign or opposite signs with respect to a direction of the axis of projection.* An analytical
·54 criterion is readily enunciated: °*the sign of a projection from a prepared plane whose normals are represented by* M *on a prepared plane whose normals have the image* N *is the sign of* cos ΛM/cos ΛN, *where* Λ *represents either direction of the axis of projection.* In the case of normal projection, Λ can be taken
·55 coincident with N and °*the sign of a normal projection from one prepared plane on another is that of the cosine of the angles between the planes.*

·6. From the considerations adduced before the sign of a projection was defined it follows that

·61 *In parallel projection from one prepared plane on another, the two sides of a ray project into the two sides of the projection, and the sides retain or exchange signs according as the projection is positive or negative.*

A projection of an ordered triangle is an ordered triangle, and from the last result we deduce that

·62 *In parallel projection from one prepared plane on another, every ordered triangle preserves or reverses its sign according as the projection is positive or negative.*

·7. Perhaps the simplest general method for determining the effect of parallel projection on the area of a triangle in a prepared plane corresponds to the last method given in 1·4 for dealing with the corresponding question in two dimensions. If the l-projection of a triangle RST on a plane N is the triangle OPQ, and if RU, OV are congruent steps of length g in either of the directions of l, then the volumes of the tetrahedra $RSTU$, $OPQV$ have the same sign as well as the same amount; but if the direction in which RU, OV have the length g is represented by Λ and if normals to the directed planes containing the triangles have images M, N, then the distances of U and V from these planes are $g \cos \Lambda\mathrm{M}$ and $g \cos \Lambda\mathrm{N}$, and therefore the volumes of the tetrahedra are $\frac{1}{3}g \cos \Lambda\mathrm{M} \,.\, \Delta RST$ and $\frac{1}{3}g \cos \Lambda\mathrm{N} \,.\, \Delta OPQ$; hence

75 *If an ordered triangle of area* Δ *in a prepared plane whose normals are*

represented by M *is projected on a prepared plane whose normals are represented by* N, *by parallel lines of which one direction has the image* Λ, *the area of the projection is* Δ cos ΛM/cos ΛN; *if the projection is normal, the area is* Δ cos MN.

·8. Here we have taken the result for normal projection as a corollary of the more general theorem, but it is possible by an argument similar to the first argument used in 41 in the discussion of the projection of steps in a plane to derive the result for oblique projection from the special case. That the area of a normal projection of a triangle is numerically equal to Δ cos MN, in the notation we are using, is a familiar classical theorem, and leads directly to the numerical value of the area in any parallel projection, but an application of ·62 and of either ·54 or ·55 must be made if the simple and precise theorem ·75 is to be deduced.

·9. The effect of parallel projection on angles can be found immediately from the effects on lengths and areas. If steps QS, QT which have lengths s, t in the directions Σ, T project obliquely into steps OP, OR which have lengths p, r in the directions Π, P, and if M, N represent the normals to the planes QST, OPR, and Λ represents a direction of the axis of projection, then

$$\Delta OPR/\Delta QST = \cos \Lambda\mathrm{M}/\cos \Lambda\mathrm{N};$$

but

$$\Delta OPR = \tfrac{1}{2}pr \sin \Pi\mathrm{P}, \quad \Delta QST = \tfrac{1}{2}st \sin \Sigma\mathrm{T},$$

$$p/s = \sin \Lambda\Sigma/\sin \Lambda\Pi, \quad r/t = \sin \Lambda\mathrm{T}/\sin \Lambda\mathrm{P},$$

and therefore

$$\sin \Pi\mathrm{P}/\sin \Sigma\mathrm{T} = \cos \Lambda\mathrm{M} \sin \Lambda\Pi \sin \Lambda\mathrm{P}/\cos \Lambda\mathrm{N} \sin \Lambda\Sigma \sin \Lambda\mathrm{T}, \qquad \cdot 98$$

a trigonometrical formula in which the ambiguity is only apparent, since ΛΠ, ΛP belong to the same great circles as ΛΣ, ΛT and are to be measured in the same directions round those circles.

BOOK II

VECTORS AND ROTORS

CHAPTER II 1

VECTORS AND THEIR DECOMPOSITION

210. Introduction. 211. Proper vectors; the two directions and the two amounts of a proper vector; the zero vector; multiplication of a vector by a real number. 212. The representation of vectors by steps, and of sequences of vectors by chains of steps. 213. Addition of vectors; its associative and commutative character; subtraction and the minus sign. 214. Decomposition and projection of vectors in a prepared plane; rotation and erection. 215. Decomposition and projection of vectors in space. 216. Mean centres of sets of points, and of sets of loaded points.

210. Introduction.

In England, the word vector and its companions are usually held to belong to the vocabulary of applied mathematics, and their use in the proof of a proposition in geometry is regarded as eccentric if not unprofessional. If the adoption of this attitude here is mysterious, since Hamilton looked on his conceptions as geometrical and it was at Cambridge that kinematical methods and expressions were first made of service in the study of curves and surfaces, the attitude itself is mistaken. Nothing can be more in the spirit of analytical geometry than to associate numbers with directions, and it is this association that gives rise to the idea of a vector.

When we have described the particular association of numbers with directions to which the name of vector is given, the definition of a vector will be complete; whatever we may choose to add by way of comment, the concept of a vector is from that moment determinate. Moreover, we shall not have to explain what we mean by the equality of two vectors; the interpretation of such a collection of symbols as $\mathbf{r} = \mathbf{s}$, where $\mathbf{r}$ and $\mathbf{s}$ stand for vectors resulting, we may suppose, from distinct series of operations, is not in any sense arbitrary. But if into a theory of vectors we propose to introduce words and symbols which are *not* of universal application, we shall have to explain the meanings to be attached to *them*. It is open to us to adopt from arithmetic and analysis the *words* addition and subtraction and the corresponding signs, instead of inventing new terms and symbols, but what is to be meant by the sum of a number of vectors is purely a matter of definition; other special* uses of the word sum have logically nothing to do with the case.

* If $\mathbf{r}$ and $\mathbf{s}$ are any two vectors, there is of course a *class* of vectors which includes $\mathbf{r}$ and $\mathbf{s}$ and does not include any other vectors, but this class is not in any sense a sum of $\mathbf{r}$ and $\mathbf{s}$; it is the logical sum of *the class whose only member is* $\mathbf{r}$ and *the class whose only member is* $\mathbf{s}$.

This is not to deny that in preferring the word addition to a new word, we are influenced by the discovery that the operation to which it is to be attached has so much resemblance to algebraical addition that in manipulating symbols with their new meanings we are helped and not misled by our familiarity with them as originally used.

211. Proper vectors; the two directions and the two amounts of a proper vector; the zero vector; multiplication of a vector by a real number.

·11 **·1.** A °*proper vector*, as we shall use the phrase*, is a real number, positive
or negative, associated with a direction, together with the opposite number
associated with the reverse direction; if we denote the concept of the real
number r allied with the direction P by $r \downarrow \mathrm{P}$, the vector into which this
·13 concept enters is the °pair of concepts $(r \downarrow \mathrm{P}, -r \downarrow \mathrm{P}')$. The vector is not an
·14 *ordered* pair; that is to say, it is to be understood that °$(-r \downarrow \mathrm{P}', r \downarrow \mathrm{P})$ has
the same meaning as $(r \downarrow \mathrm{P}, -r \downarrow \mathrm{P}')$. The real numbers on which a vector
·15 partly depends are called the °*amounts* of the vector, and the vector in which
the amount r is associated with the direction P is called briefly the vector
·16 °r in P and is denoted by r_{P}; the vector r in P is identical with the vector
·18 $-r$ in P′, the vector r in P′ or $-r$ in P is called the °*reverse* of the vector r_{P}
·19 and is denoted by $-r_{\mathrm{P}}$, and two vectors are said to be °*equal and opposite* if
each is the reverse of the other.

·2. There is a temptation to regard the vector r_{P} as the simple concept $r \downarrow \mathrm{P}$ and to impose the equation

$$-r \downarrow \mathrm{P}' = r \downarrow \mathrm{P}$$

as a part of the definition of identity between vectors. Technically such a course introduces no errors, but logically it is indefensible; the concept $-r \downarrow \mathrm{P}'$ is not *the same* as the concept $r \downarrow \mathrm{P}$, and to introduce a notion of the *technical identity* of two concepts which are actually different brings us by questionable paths to a point which it is far better to take as the point of departure. In the present case, if we assert that there is a single vector which *is* both $r \downarrow \mathrm{P}$ and $-r \downarrow \mathrm{P}'$, we have still to admit that in some sense this vector has two directions and two amounts, and to make this admission is to allow that after all the vector is *not* the simple concept $r \downarrow \mathrm{P}$.

* The classical account of the word vector is on p. 15 of the *Lectures on Quaternions* (1853), but Hamilton was using the word many years earlier as one that would be familiar. For Hamilton a proper vector has only one direction and has a signless amount; towards the end of his work he deals (p. 665) with concepts obeying the laws of vectors and having complex amounts, and these he calls bivectors, but he introduces (p. 666) definite conventions, of which he recognises clearly (p. 669) the disadvantages, to avoid attributing two directions and two bitensors to each bivector. Actually mathematicians have not hesitated to use vectors with negative amounts, but that this practice logically involves giving to every proper vector two directions and two amounts is not commonly noticed, and there are many writers whose deductions are inconsistent with their definitions.

·3. °Of the two amounts of a proper vector one is positive and one negative, ·31
and it is possible to study systems of one-signed and signless vectors, defining
a positive vector as a positive number associated with a direction and a signless
vector as a signless number associated with a direction; °formulae relating to ·32
signless vectors are the same as formulae relating to positive vectors, and since
the signless vector $|q| \downarrow \mathrm{P}$ can be taken as corresponding to the vector
$(+|q| \downarrow \mathrm{P}, -|q| \downarrow \mathrm{P}')$, °any chain of reasoning involving the vectors which we ·33
shall use certainly can be conducted by means of signless vectors. The signless
vector is the simpler concept, having only one direction and one amount, but
technical convenience attaches to the vector with two amounts, and in mathematics it is *relations*, not *concepts*, that it is important to keep simple.

·4. °Of the two directions of a proper vector we call one the positive direc- ·41
tion and the other the negative direction, the positive direction being that in
which the amount is positive. There is a signless number $|q|$ such that the
two amounts of a vector **r** are $+|q|$ and $-|q|$; this signless* number is called
the °*tensor* of the vector and denoted by $|\mathbf{r}|$; if r is either amount of the vector, ·43
we incur no liability to error in denoting the tensor also by $|r|$.

·5. °As in other cases†, the implication of the word proper applied to a ·51
vector is that the amounts of the vector are not zero. The association of 0
with a direction P can of course be distinguished from the association of 0
with any other direction Σ, but it proves convenient‡ to identify the vector
0_Σ with the vector 0_P; the °*zero vector* has *all* directions, and the number ·53
associated with each direction of the zero vector is zero; the zero vector is
denoted simply by the symbol **0** without affix.

·6. It is natural to recognise in the vector of amount pr in the direction
P the °*product* of the vector of amount r in the same direction by the real ·61
number p, positive, zero or negative, and to denote the product of the vector **r**
and the real number p by $p\mathbf{r}$. The vector with tensor unity and positive
direction P is called the °*unit* vector in the direction P, and °any vector can ·62, ·63
be expressed as the product of the unit vector in either of its directions by its
amount in that direction; the unit vector in the direction P can of course be
denoted by 1_P. Unit vectors are known also as *radials* and as *orts*.

·7. A vector has no location in space, but it is often convenient to speak
of a vector as °*in* a line when it has the directions of the line, and °*in* a plane ·71, ·72
when it has directions possible for lines in the plane. °Coplanar vectors are ·73
vectors with coplanar directions. °The zero vector is in every line and in ·74
every plane.

* Here we are describing Hamilton's first use of the word tensor (*Lectures on Quaternions*, p. 57, 1853), abandoned with reluctance, if we may judge from a foot-note in his last work (*Elements of Quaternions*, p. 108, 1866; vol. I, p. 111 in Joly's edition). Nowadays the word tensor bears an entirely different meaning in mathematical literature.

† Compare 122·14 on p. 12 above. ‡ See 3·26 on p. 43 below.

212. The representation of vectors by steps, and of sequences of vectors by chains of steps.

·1. The relation between the lengths and the directions of a step in space is the same as the relation between the amounts and the directions of a
·12 vector; whether a step is proper or zero, °there is a single vector whose directions are the directions of the step and whose amount in each of these directions is the length of the step in that direction, and this vector is called the vector of the step; the vector of a zero step is the zero vector*.

·13 *Congruent steps are steps with the same vector,*

·14 and a step of which $\mathbf{r}$ is the vector is said to °*represent* $\mathbf{r}$. From any point O one and only one step OR can be drawn to represent a given vector $\mathbf{r}$, and the
·15 point R at which this step ends is itself said to represent $\mathbf{r}$ °*with reference to the origin* O.

The vector of a step AB is itself denoted by AB when there is no possibility of confusion; when a distinction must be made, the vector is usually denoted by $\overline{AB}$.

·2. A succession of vectors, $\mathbf{r}_1, \mathbf{r}_2, \mathbf{r}_3, \ldots$, finds its most graphic representation in a chain of steps. The origin of the first step is arbitrary, but each subsequent step begins where its predecessor ends, and the chain shews not only the vectors themselves, the kth step representing $\mathbf{r}_k$, but the order in which they are to be taken.

If $S_{01}S_{12}, S_{12}S_{23}, S_{23}S_{34}, \ldots$ and $T_{01}T_{12}, T_{12}T_{23}, T_{23}T_{34}, \ldots$ are two chains representing the same succession of vectors $\mathbf{r}_1, \mathbf{r}_2, \mathbf{r}_3, \ldots$, then because $S_{p-1,p}S_{p,p+1}$ and $T_{p-1,p}T_{p,p+1}$ are congruent, so also are $S_{p-1,p}T_{p-1,p}$ and $S_{p,p+1}T_{p,p+1}$. This being true for every value of p, the steps $S_{01}T_{01}, S_{12}T_{12}, S_{23}T_{23}, \ldots$ are all congruent:

·21 *If two chains of steps represent the same succession of vectors, the step from any point of one to the corresponding point of the other is congruent with the step from the origin of the former to the origin of the latter.*

It is to be observed that neither the representation nor the proposition requires the number of vectors to be finite; the succession may be unending, provided that the correspondence between the vectors and the natural numbers 1, 2, 3, ... is maintained throughout.

213. Addition of vectors; its associative and commutative character; subtraction and the minus sign.

·1. It is on the representation just described that the definition of the sum of a finite number of vectors is based. With the notation of the last paragraph, since $S_{n,n+1}T_{n,n+1}$ and $S_{01}T_{01}$ are congruent, so also are $S_{01}S_{n,n+1}$ and

* This is one reason why only one zero vector is recognised: the step OO itself is as definite as any other step.

$T_{01} T_{n,\,n+1}$; that is to say, °*in a chain representing a finite succession of vectors* ·11
$\mathbf{r}_1, \mathbf{r}_2, \ldots \mathbf{r}_n$, *the vector of the step from the beginning of the chain to the end does not depend on the origin of the chain at all*, but depends only on the actual succession of vectors. This is the vector which is called the sum of the vectors $\mathbf{r}_1, \mathbf{r}_2, \ldots \mathbf{r}_n$ and is denoted by $\mathbf{r}_1 + \mathbf{r}_2 + \ldots + \mathbf{r}_n$.

For the cases of two vectors and of three vectors there are alternative constructions for the sum that deserve mention.

Let OR represent a vector $\mathbf{r}$, and let OS and RN both represent a second vector $\mathbf{s}$; then by the definition, ON represents $\mathbf{r} + \mathbf{s}$, and because RN is congruent with OS, the figure $ORNS$ is a parallelogram :

If the coinitial steps OR, OS represent two vectors $\mathbf{r}$, $\mathbf{s}$, *the diagonal from O* ·13
of the parallelogram of which OR, OS are adjacent sides represents the sum $\mathbf{r} + \mathbf{s}$.

If in addition a third vector $\mathbf{t}$ is represented both by OT and by NK, then because OR, RN, NK represent $\mathbf{r}$, $\mathbf{s}$, $\mathbf{t}$ the sum $\mathbf{r} + \mathbf{s} + \mathbf{t}$ is the vector of OK, and because NK and OT are congruent, TK is congruent with ON and the plane through K parallel to ORS passes through T:

If the coinitial steps OR, OS, OT represent three vectors $\mathbf{r}$, $\mathbf{s}$, $\mathbf{t}$, *the diagonal* ·14
from O of the parallelepiped of which OR, OS, OT are adjacent edges represents the sum $\mathbf{r} + \mathbf{s} + \mathbf{t}$.

The constructions in ·13 and ·14 are inferior to the general construction for a sum, not only because the method is essentially* incapable of direct† extension to a larger number of vectors, but also in principle. They have however the merit of putting in evidence for the cases with which they deal a fundamental property: since the constructions are symmetrical,

The sum of two vectors or of three vectors is independent of the order in which ·15
the vectors are taken.

In fact, in the parallelogram of ·13, SN as well as OR represents $\mathbf{r}$, and therefore ON represents $\mathbf{s} + \mathbf{r}$, and it is equally easy to associate the six orders of the three vectors $\mathbf{r}$, $\mathbf{s}$, $\mathbf{t}$ with the six paths from O to K along edges of the parallelepiped of ·14.

·2. The operation of adding whole numbers in arithmetic involves, except in the simplest cases, assumptions of which we are apt to remain unconscious.

* Not that there is no direct interpretation of the sum of any number of vectors represented by coinitial steps. One that is extremely valuable is given as 6·31 on p. 51 below.

† Having found $\mathbf{r}_1 + \mathbf{r}_2$ by ·13, we could of course find $(\mathbf{r}_1 + \mathbf{r}_2) + \mathbf{r}_3$ by a second application of the same theorem, $\{(\mathbf{r}_1 + \mathbf{r}_2) + \mathbf{r}_3\} + \mathbf{r}_4$ by a third, and so on, and it is easy enough to prove—the result is a particular case of ·22 below—that $(\mathbf{r}_1 + \mathbf{r}_2 + \ldots + \mathbf{r}_{n-1}) + \mathbf{r}_n$ is $\mathbf{r}_1 + \mathbf{r}_2 + \ldots + \mathbf{r}_{n-1} + \mathbf{r}_n$ and that therefore the sum formed in this way by repeated use of ·13 would be the same as the sum defined by means of ·11. But this is not a direct geometrical construction like that of ·14, nor does the last foot-note refer to an inductive process of this kind.

An example, typical except that it does not introduce the complication of 'carrying', presents the steps of the process as follows:

$$\begin{aligned}123+514+341 &= (100+20+3)+(500+10+4)+(300+40+1)\\ &= 100+20+3+500+10+4+300+40+1\\ &= 100+500+300+20+10+40+3+4+1\\ &= (100+500+300)+(20+10+40)+(3+4+1)\\ &= 900+70+8\\ &= 978.\end{aligned}$$

Here the first step and the last shew the use of juxtaposition in arithmetic, and it is only in the step before the last that specific addition is performed. The intermediate steps depend on two general propositions: the second step and the fourth are valid because in an addition of this kind any group of *successive* numbers may be replaced by the sum of those numbers, a property expressed by saying that the addition of whole numbers is *associative*, and the third step can be taken because the value of the sum is independent of the order in which the numbers are added, an independence described by calling the addition *commutative*. The effect of the two properties is briefly that in adding any finite number of integers we may break up each of them into any number of others of which it is the sum and recombine the parts in any convenient manner. It is hardly necessary to say that merely to *call* a vector formed in a particular way from a number of others their sum is not to *confer* any of the properties associated with addition in arithmetic and algebra. The proof that addition of vectors is in fact both associative and commutative may be based on relations between addition of vectors and addition of real numbers, but the direct proof is too simple to be worth avoiding.

That

·22 *Addition of vectors is associative*

follows at once from the construction for the sum. If $R_{01}R_{12}, R_{12}R_{23}, \ldots R_{n-1,n}R_{n,n+1}$ is a chain of steps representing $\mathbf{r}_1, \mathbf{r}_2, \ldots \mathbf{r}_n$, then $R_{h-1,h}R_{h,h+1}, R_{h,h+1}R_{h+1,h+2}, \ldots R_{k-1,k}R_{k,k+1}$ is one chain that represents $\mathbf{r}_h, \mathbf{r}_{h+1}, \ldots \mathbf{r}_k$ and therefore $R_{h-1,h}R_{k,k+1}$ is one step that represents $\mathbf{r}_h+\mathbf{r}_{h+1}+\ldots+\mathbf{r}_k$. Hence the chain

$R_{01}R_{12}, R_{12}R_{23}, \ldots R_{h-2,h-1}R_{h-1,h}, R_{h-1,h}R_{k,k+1}, R_{k,k+1}R_{k+1,k+2}, \ldots R_{n-1,n}R_{n,n+1}$ represents the set of vectors

$$\mathbf{r}_1, \mathbf{r}_2, \ldots \mathbf{r}_{h-1}, (\mathbf{r}_h+\mathbf{r}_{h+1}+\ldots+\mathbf{r}_k), \mathbf{r}_{k+1}, \ldots \mathbf{r}_n,$$

and the vector of the step $R_{01}R_{n,n+1}$, which is the sum $\mathbf{r}_1+\mathbf{r}_2+\ldots+\mathbf{r}_n$, is also the sum $\mathbf{r}_1+\mathbf{r}_2+\ldots+\mathbf{r}_{h-1}+(\mathbf{r}_h+\mathbf{r}_{h+1}+\ldots+\mathbf{r}_k)+\mathbf{r}_{k+1}+\ldots+\mathbf{r}_n$.

It follows from ·22 that in forming the sum of any number of vectors we may replace any two *consecutive* members of the succession by their own sum, and
·23 so from ·15 that °the result would have been the same if these two vectors had come originally in the reverse order. Formally,

$$\begin{aligned}\mathbf{r}_1+\mathbf{r}_2+\ldots+\mathbf{r}_n &= \mathbf{r}_1+\ldots+\mathbf{r}_{h-1}+(\mathbf{r}_h+\mathbf{r}_{h+1})+\mathbf{r}_{h+2}+\ldots+\mathbf{r}_n \quad (\cdot 22)\\ &= \mathbf{r}_1+\ldots+\mathbf{r}_{h-1}+(\mathbf{r}_{h+1}+\mathbf{r}_h)+\mathbf{r}_{h+2}+\ldots+\mathbf{r}_n \quad (\cdot 15)\\ &= \mathbf{r}_1+\ldots+\mathbf{r}_{h-1}+\mathbf{r}_{h+1}+\mathbf{r}_h+\mathbf{r}_{h+2}+\ldots+\mathbf{r}_n \quad (\cdot 22).\end{aligned}$$

But if the number of objects in an ordered class is finite—and we have given no meaning to the sum of an infinite number of vectors*—any one

* Series of vectors are of the utmost importance, but their study naturally begins at a later stage.

arrangement can be transformed into any other by a finite number of interchanges of consecutive members*. Hence the sum of any finite number of vectors is wholly independent of the order in which the vectors are arranged:

Addition of vectors is commutative. ·24

Taken together, ·22 and ·24 imply that °in finding the sum of any finite ·25
number of vectors we may replace *any* group of these vectors by the sum of its members, for ·24 allows us to bring the vectors forming the group into succession, and ·22 is then applicable.

It is in order to secure uniqueness to the sum in all cases that we do not recognise different zero vectors: let $\mathbf{r}$, $\mathbf{s}$ be vectors which are not parallel, and let h, k be real numbers different from zero; $h\mathbf{r}-h\mathbf{r}$, $k\mathbf{s}-k\mathbf{s}$, $(h\mathbf{r}+k\mathbf{s})-(h\mathbf{r}+k\mathbf{s})$ are three zero vectors, and if the first is said to have only the directions of $\mathbf{r}$ and the second only the directions of $\mathbf{s}$, the third must be associated with the directions of $h\mathbf{r}+k\mathbf{s}$, and these depend on the ratio of h to k; if further $(h\mathbf{r}+k\mathbf{s})-(h\mathbf{r}+k\mathbf{s})$ is to be identical with $(h\mathbf{r}-h\mathbf{r})+(k\mathbf{s}-k\mathbf{s})$ we must conclude either that the vectors $h\mathbf{r}-h\mathbf{r}$, $k\mathbf{s}-k\mathbf{s}$ themselves depend on the values of h and k, or that the sum of two zero vectors is entirely indeterminate in direction even if the components have precise directions; briefly °we have to choose between having an infinity of ·26
zero vectors in a single pair of directions, having an infinity of directions for a single zero vector, and having an infinity of different sums to a single set of vectors, and it is the second convention which we adopt.

·3. Two elementary consequences of the definition of addition are often used, implicitly if not explicitly:

If a number of vectors have a common direction their sum has the same ·31
direction and its amount in that direction is the algebraic sum of the amounts of the individual vectors;

The sum of n vectors each with the amount r in the direction P *is the vector* ·32
of the amount nr in this direction.

If p is any real number and $\mathbf{r}$ is the vector r_P, it has been already agreed that $p\mathbf{r}$ denotes the vector $(pr)_P$; it follows from ·32 that the relation between multiplication by real numbers and addition is the same for vectors as for real numbers. Since we can interpret, in one and only one way, any expression of the form $p_1\mathbf{r}_1+p_2\mathbf{r}_2+\ldots+p_n\mathbf{r}_n$, we can use determinants in which the elements of one row or one column are vectors and the other elements are numbers. That such determinants are natural will be seen from examples in 334·4 and 337·5 below.

·4. Two obvious properties of the zero vector in addition, though explicit reference to them is seldom made, are important in connection with subtraction.

Addition of the zero vector produces no effect, ·41

since the zero vector is the vector of zero steps, and

If any vector is added to its reverse the sum is the zero vector, ·42

because a step OP followed by the reverse step PO gives the zero step OO.

* A process that must be effective is explained adequately by an example: the passage from 52413 to 12345 can be made by way of 52143, 51243, 15243, 12543, 12534, 12354.

·5. Subtraction is the operation which is cancelled by addition; the vector $\mathbf{r}-\mathbf{s}$ is to be defined by the equation

·51 $$(\mathbf{r}-\mathbf{s})+\mathbf{s}=\mathbf{r},$$

and it must be proved that there is one and only one vector which satisfies this condition. Let $\mathbf{s}'$ denote the reverse of $\mathbf{s}$. Then if there is a vector $\mathbf{t}$ such that

·52 $$\mathbf{t}+\mathbf{s}=\mathbf{r},$$

·53 this vector is such that $(\mathbf{t}+\mathbf{s})+\mathbf{s}'=\mathbf{r}+\mathbf{s}'.$

But identically
$$\begin{aligned}(\mathbf{t}+\mathbf{s})+\mathbf{s}' &= \mathbf{t}+\mathbf{s}+\mathbf{s}'\\ &= \mathbf{t}+(\mathbf{s}+\mathbf{s}')\\ &= \mathbf{t}+0\\ &= \mathbf{t},\end{aligned}$$

by ·22, ·41 and ·42; hence ·53 asserts that the only value *possible* for $\mathbf{t}$ is $\mathbf{r}+\mathbf{s}'$. On the other hand, since

$$(\mathbf{r}+\mathbf{s}')+\mathbf{s}=\mathbf{r}+\mathbf{s}'+\mathbf{s}=\mathbf{r}+(\mathbf{s}'+\mathbf{s})=\mathbf{r}+0=\mathbf{r},$$

·54 the value $\mathbf{r}+\mathbf{s}'$ of $\mathbf{t}$ does in fact satisfy ·52. Hence °subtraction of one vector from another is always possible, and

·55 $$\mathbf{r}-\mathbf{s}=\mathbf{r}+\mathbf{s}':$$

·56 *To subtract a vector* $\mathbf{s}$ *from a vector* $\mathbf{r}$ *is to add to* $\mathbf{r}$ *the vector reverse to* $\mathbf{s}$.

·61 **·6.** In ·56 we have one reason why °the vector reverse to $\mathbf{s}$ can be denoted by $-\mathbf{s}$; since the reverse of $-\mathbf{s}$ is $\mathbf{s}$,

·62 $$-(-\mathbf{s})=\mathbf{s},$$

·63 while ·55 can be written $\mathbf{r}-\mathbf{s}=\mathbf{r}+(-\mathbf{s}),$

·64 and $\mathbf{r}-\mathbf{s}'=\mathbf{r}+\mathbf{s}$

·65 is equivalent to $\mathbf{r}-(-\mathbf{s})=\mathbf{r}+\mathbf{s}.$

·66 Also by the definition adopted in 1·6, °if $\mathbf{r}$ is r_P the product of $\mathbf{r}$ by -1 is
·67 $(-r)_P$, and this again is the reverse of $\mathbf{r}$. Thus °the different uses of the minus sign with vectors are exactly parallel to the different uses of the same sign with real numbers, and our familiarity with the sign in algebra must be a help and not a hindrance in our operations with vectors.

214. Decomposition and projection of vectors in a prepared plane; rotation and erection.

·11 **·1.** °If two distinct lines m, n in a plane meet in a point O, if R is any point of the plane, and if P is a point of m and Q a point of n, then the figure $OPRQ$ is a parallelogram if and only if P is the n-projection of R on m and Q is the m-projection of R on n; from the definition of the sum of two vectors it follows that

·12 *If two lines in a plane are not parallel, any vector parallel to the plane can be expressed in one and only one way as the sum of vectors parallel to the two lines;*

if the vector is **r** and the lines are m and n, the component vectors are called
individually °the n-component of **r** in m or parallel to m and the m-component ·13
of **r** in n or parallel to n, and collectively they are called simply °the components ·14
of **r** in m and n. It is important to notice that ·12 is true of the zero vector as well as of proper vectors; applied to the zero vector, ·12 is equivalent to the following composite theorem:

The sum of two zero vectors is the zero vector; the sum of the zero vector and ·16
any proper vector is a proper vector, and the sum of two proper vectors can not be the zero vector if the vectors have different directions.

If two lines are at right angles they are not parallel, and therefore ·12 can be applied:

Any vector parallel to a plane can be expressed in one and only one way as the ·17
sum of a vector parallel to any line in the plane and a vector parallel to a perpendicular line in the same plane, and the component vectors are called the projection of the vector on or parallel to the line and the projection of the vector at right angles to the line.

·2. °The components and projections of which we have just been speaking ·21
are vectors; it is only if our attention is fixed on one of the directions of one of
these vectors that it is naturally concentrated also on a particular amount, but
one effect of using directed lines and planes is to give in some cases precisely
the definiteness we desire. If we form a component or projection of a vector
parallel to the axis of a ray, we can distinguish the amount of the component or
projection in the direction of the ray from the amount in the reverse direction,
and this °*amount* we call the component or projection of the vector in the ·22
direction of the ray; °a component or projection of a vector parallel to a *line* ·23
is a vector, but a component or projection of a vector in the direction of a *ray*
is a real number, which if it is not zero is positive or negative according as the
direction of the ray is the positive direction or the negative direction of the
component or projection parallel to the axis of the ray; instead of speaking of
a component or projection parallel to the axis of a ray we may speak of
a °vector-component or vector-projection parallel to the ray, and we may use ·24
the same compound words when dealing with undirected lines if we wish to
emphasise that the concepts described are not real numbers. In a prepared
plane, the projection of a vector **r** at right angles to a ray μ is °understood to ·25
be the projection of **r** on rays normal to μ, that is, on rays making with μ
a positive right angle; like the projection on μ itself, this projection is a definite
real number. The values of the components and projections described in the
present article can be obtained immediately by application of the results of
141; in particular, °the projections of a vector r_Λ on a ray μ and at right ·26

angles to μ are $r \cos \mathrm{M}\Lambda$ and $r \sin \mathrm{M}\Lambda$, where M is the spherical image of μ, and special cases of this result assert that

·27 *If the direction of a ray μ is one of the directions of a vector* **r**, *the projection of* **r** *on μ is the amount of* **r** *in that direction,*

and conversely that

·28 *If the projection of a vector* **r** *on a ray μ is an amount of* **r**, *the direction of μ is a direction of* **r**,

and that

·29 *The projection of a vector on a ray is zero if and only if the two are perpendicular.*

·3. If two vectors in a plane have projection zero on the same ray in that plane, the vectors have axes at right angles to that ray, and if further their projections at right angles to the ray are equal the vectors coincide; it follows that

·32 *If on every ray in a plane two vectors parallel to the plane have the same projection, the vectors are identical.*

It need hardly be remarked that the hypothesis of ·32 is much stronger than is necessary for the deduction of identity, but there are important applications in which the stringent condition is known to be satisfied. We can enunciate a general theorem of which a particular case gives the real ground of ·32; parallel lines which have one point in common coincide, and therefore

·33 *If m, n, q, r are four lines in a plane, subject to the conditions that q and r are not parallel, that m and q are not parallel, and that n and r are not parallel, then if two vectors have the same q-projection on m and the same r-projection on n, the vectors are identical.*

To take q coincident with n and r with m and to assert that a vector in a plane is completely determined by its components in any two distinct intersecting lines in the plane is only to affirm that the sum of two vectors is unique, but to suppose q at right angles to m and r at right angles to n enables us to state in language similar to that of ·32 that

·35 *If on each of two distinct intersecting rays in a plane two vectors parallel to the plane have the same projection, the vectors are identical,*

a result that can be expressed more simply and more usefully in the form that

·36 *A vector parallel to a plane is completely determined by its projections on any two rays in the plane provided that the rays are not parallel.*

·4. From 141·61 and the definition of the sum of a number of vectors follows the fundamental theorem

·41 *If a vector* **r** *is the sum of a finite number of coplanar vectors, and n is any line in the plane of the components, the n-components of* **r** *on any line or ray in this plane is the sum of the n-components on that line or ray of the vectors composing* **r**, with the special case

If a vector $\mathbf{r}$ *is the sum of a finite number of coplanar vectors, the projections of* $\mathbf{r}$ *on and at right angles to any line or ray in the plane of the components are the sums of the corresponding projections of the individual components of* $\mathbf{r}$*;* ·42

the n-components in the first of these theorems and the projections in the second are °vectors or real numbers according as the components and projections are on a line or on a ray. ·43

·5. If K is any direction in a directed plane and ϵ is a given angle, there is one and only one direction Λ such that ϵ is an angle from K to Λ in the plane, and the vector r_Λ, said to be obtained by rotating r_K through the angle ϵ, will be denoted by $\mathscr{E}_\epsilon r_K$; since the direction which makes an angle ϵ with K$'$ is Λ', the reverse of Λ, the vector $\mathscr{E}_\epsilon(-r)_{K'}$ is the vector $(-r)_{\Lambda'}$, which is identical with $\mathscr{E}_\epsilon r_K$; also if r_K is zero so also is r_Λ; thus if $\mathbf{r}$ is any vector °there is a definite vector $\mathscr{E}_\epsilon\mathbf{r}$ which is independent of the direction chosen, among the available directions, for the specification of $\mathbf{r}$. ·51

A case of especial value is that in which the angle ϵ is a positive right angle; °the vector $\mathscr{E}_{\frac{1}{2}\pi}\mathbf{r}$ we denote briefly by $\mathscr{E}\mathbf{r}$ and call the vector obtained by *erecting* $\mathbf{r}$. It is hardly necessary to add that for any two angles δ, ϵ ·52

$$\mathscr{E}_\delta\mathscr{E}_\epsilon\mathbf{r} = \mathscr{E}_\epsilon\mathscr{E}_\delta\mathbf{r} = \mathscr{E}_{\delta+\epsilon}\mathbf{r}, \qquad \cdot 53$$

and that

$$\mathscr{E}^2\mathbf{r} = \mathscr{E}_\pi\mathbf{r} = -\mathbf{r}, \qquad \cdot 54$$

$\mathscr{E}^2\mathbf{r}$ denoting $\mathscr{E}(\mathscr{E}\mathbf{r})$.

The effect of rotation on the sum of a number of vectors can be deduced from a series of elementary theorems. If Σ is any direction and T is the direction making with Σ the angle ϵ, and if r_Λ is the vector $\mathscr{E}_\epsilon r_K$, the projection of r_Λ in the direction T is $r\cos\Lambda\mathrm{T}$ and the projection of r_K in the direction Σ is $r\cos K\Sigma$; but by hypothesis ΣT is equal to KΛ, and therefore ΛT is equal to KΣ:

The projection of the vector $\mathscr{E}_\epsilon\mathbf{r}$ *in the direction making an angle* ϵ *with a direction* Σ *is equal to the projection of* $\mathbf{r}$ *in the direction* Σ*;* ·55

in particular

The projection of $\mathbf{r}$ *in any direction* T *is equal to the projection of* $\mathscr{E}\mathbf{r}$ *in the direction making a positive right angle with* T. ·56

Suppose now that the sum $\Sigma\mathbf{r}^{(m)}$ of a finite number of vectors $\mathbf{r}^{(1)}$, $\mathbf{r}^{(2)}$, ... is the vector r_K, that M is the direction making a positive right angle with K, and that Λ, N are the directions making a given angle ϵ with the directions K, M; by ·55, the projection of $\mathscr{E}_\epsilon\mathbf{r}^{(m)}$ on N is equal to the projection of $\mathbf{r}^{(m)}$ on M, and therefore by a double use of ·42 the projection of $\Sigma\,\mathscr{E}_\epsilon\mathbf{r}^{(m)}$ on N is equal to the projection of $\Sigma\mathbf{r}^{(m)}$ on M; by hypothesis the latter projection is zero, and therefore by ·29 the vector $\Sigma\mathscr{E}_\epsilon\mathbf{r}^{(m)}$ has directions at right angles to N; because KΛ, MN are equal, one angle from Λ to N is a positive right angle, and Λ is one direction of the vector $\Sigma\mathscr{E}_\epsilon\mathbf{r}^{(m)}$; lastly, the amount of $\Sigma\mathscr{E}_\epsilon\mathbf{r}^{(m)}$ in the direction Λ is by ·27 the projection of $\Sigma\mathscr{E}_\epsilon\mathbf{r}^{(m)}$ in that direction, and so by another double use of ·42 is the projection of $\Sigma\mathbf{r}^{(m)}$ in the direction K, which a second appeal to ·27 shews to be r:

·57 *If each of a finite number of vectors* $\mathbf{r}^{(1)}, \mathbf{r}^{(2)}, \ldots$ *is rotated through an angle* ϵ, *the sum of the vectors is rotated through the same angle;*

in symbols,
$$\sum_m \mathscr{E}_\epsilon\mathbf{r}^{(m)} = \mathscr{E}_\epsilon\sum_m \mathbf{r}^{(m)}.$$

In particular
$$\Sigma\mathscr{E}\mathbf{r}^{(m)} = \mathscr{E}\Sigma\mathbf{r}^{(m)}:$$

·58 *The sum of the vectors obtained by erecting any finite number of vectors in a directed plane is the vector obtained by erecting their sum.*

215. Decomposition and projection of vectors in space.

·1. In space of three dimensions the definitions and propositions of the last section have analogues of two distinct kinds, for we may extend them either by partial substitution of planes for lines or by an increase in the number of lines considered. The two forms of extension have interrelations, but their uses are independent.

One geometrical theorem that corresponds to 4·11
·11 is that °if a line l and a plane K meet in a point O, and R is any point of space, and if P is a point of l and Q a point of K, then the figure $OPRQ$ is a parallelogram if and only if P is the K-projection of R on l and Q is the l-projection of R on K; from this comes the theorem that

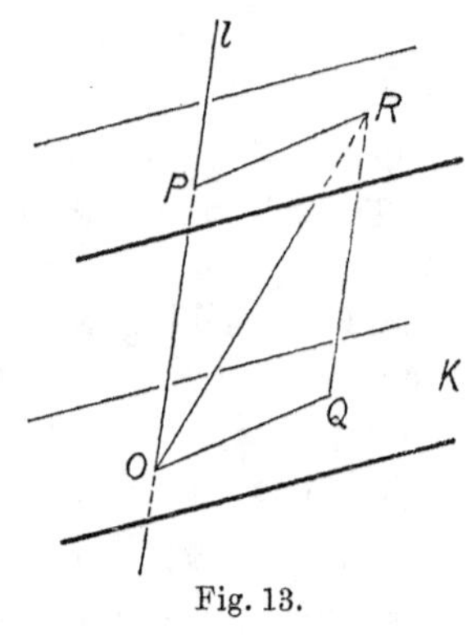

Fig. 13.

·12 *If a line and a plane are not parallel, any vector can be expressed in one and only one way as the sum of a vector parallel to the line and a vector parallel to the plane;*

if the vector is $\mathbf{r}$ and the line and plane are l and K, the component vectors
·13 are called the °*K-component* of $\mathbf{r}$ in l or parallel to l and the *l-component* of $\mathbf{r}$ in K or parallel to K. Taking the line and the plane at right angles we deduce two theorems, which justify useful definitions:

·14 *Any vector can be expressed in one and only one way as the sum of a vector parallel to any line and a vector at right angles to that line, and the components are called the projection of the vector on the line or parallel to the line and the projection of the vector at right angles to the line;*

15 *Any vector can be expressed in one and only one way as the sum of a vector parallel to any plane and a vector at right angles to that plane, and the components are called the projection of the vector in the plane or parallel to the plane and the projection of the vector at right angles to the plane.*

As in 4·2, we can distinguish between components and vector-components
and between projections and vector-projections, the °real numbers occurring ·16
with components and projections on a *ray* or at right angles to a *prepared*
plane; °a component parallel to a plane or at right angles to a line is essentially ·17
a vector-component. The values of components and projections of vectors on
rays are to be found from the formulae of **143** and **144**.

·2. If two lines are such that every line at right angles to one of them is at right angles also to the other, the two lines are parallel; arguing somewhat as in 4·3 we conclude that

If in every direction two vectors have the same projection, the vectors are identical; ·22

as with 4·32, the hypothesis of ·22 is stronger than the conclusion requires but is actually known to be satisfied in certain cases which present themselves. To reduce the hypothesis of ·22 to its weakest form we remark that two parallel planes which have a single common point coincide entirely, whence we conclude that

If three planes F, G, H have one and only one common point, and if l, m, n are any three lines such that l is not parallel to F, m to G, nor n to H, a vector is completely determined by its F-component in l, its G-component in m, and its H-component in n. ·23

The planes F, G, H must be distinct, but there is no reason why two of the lines l, m, n, or even all three of them, should not coincide.

If three directions are not coplanar, three planes to which these directions are at right angles have one and only one common point; hence

A vector in space of three dimensions is completely determined by its projections in any three directions that are not coplanar; ·24

in particular

A vector in space is completely determined by its projections on any three rays that are concurrent but not coplanar. ·25

·3. An alternative to ·11 as an extension of 4·11 to space is that °if l, m, n ·31
are three lines concurrent in a point O and not coplanar and R is any point
of space, and if F, G, H are points of l, m, n, then OR is a diagonal of a
parallelepiped of which OF, OG, OH are edges if and only if F, G, H are the
projections of R on l, m, n by planes parallel to the plane through m and n,
the plane through n and l, and the plane through l and m. From this it
follows that

Provided only that the directions of three lines l, m, n are not coplanar, any vector $\mathbf{r}$ in space can be expressed in one and only one way as the sum of three vectors parallel to the lines; the component of $\mathbf{r}$ parallel to l is the K-component of $\mathbf{r}$ parallel to l, where K is any plane parallel to both m and n, ·32 a result that can be obtained otherwise by a combination of ·12 with 4·12; an application of ·23 shews that if two vectors have the same set of components in three directions that are not coplanar the vectors are identical, but unlike ·23 and ·24 this is merely a particular case of the theorem that the sum of any finite number of vectors is a unique vector.

·4. From 142·32 and the definition of the sum of a number of vectors follows the fundamental theorem that

·41 *If a vector* **r** *is the sum of a finite number of other vectors, the K-component of* **r** *parallel to any line or in the direction of any ray is the sum of the K-components, parallel to that line or in the direction of that ray, of the vectors composing* **r**, *K being any plane not parallel to the line or ray,*

which we use repeatedly without explicit reference. Of ·41 the special case that

·42 *If a vector* **r** *is the sum of a finite number of other vectors, the projection of* **r** *parallel to any line or in the direction of any ray is the sum of the projections parallel to that line or in the direction of that ray of the vectors composing* **r**

·43 is invaluable; °if the projections or components are parallel to a line, they are vectors, but if they are in a given direction they are real numbers and the sum of the parts is an algebraic sum. The second part of ·32 enables us to deduce from 142·32 also that

·44 *If a vector* **r** *which is the sum of a finite number of other vectors* **s**, **t**, ... *is expressed as the sum of vectors with three assigned directions that are not coplanar, each of the three components of* **r** *is the sum of the corresponding components of the individual vectors* **s**, **t**, ...

It is possible to prove ·32 directly from 3·14 and to apply 142·32 to prove ·44 without making use of 3·22 or 3·24, modifying the enunciation of ·44 to require the order in which the components are taken to be the same as the order of the individual vectors **s**, **t**, ... Then 3·22 and 3·24 become corollaries of the theorems that in algebra the addition of real numbers is both associative and commutative, and the direct proofs in 3·2 are superfluous.

Complementary to ·41 and ·42 and following in the same way from 142·32 are the two results

·45 *If a vector* **r** *is the sum of a finite number of other vectors, and if K is any plane and l is any line not parallel to K, the l-component of* **r** *parallel to K is the sum of the l-components parallel to K of the vectors composing* **r**;

·46 *If a vector* **r** *is the sum of a finite number of other vectors, the projection of* **r** *parallel to any plane is the sum of the projections parallel to the same plane of the vectors composing* **r**;

in these theorems the components and projections are necessarily vectors.

216. MEAN CENTRES OF SETS OF POINTS, AND OF SETS OF LOADED POINTS.

·1. Let $R_1, R_2, \ldots R_n$ represent the vectors $\mathbf{r}_1, \mathbf{r}_2, \ldots \mathbf{r}_n$ with respect to the origin O, and let the vectors of the steps to these same points from another origin Q be $\mathbf{s}_1, \mathbf{s}_2, \ldots \mathbf{s}_n$. Then if $\mathbf{q}$ is the vector of OQ,

$$\mathbf{s}_1 = \mathbf{r}_1 - \mathbf{q}, \quad \mathbf{s}_2 = \mathbf{r}_2 - \mathbf{q}, \ldots \quad \mathbf{s}_n = \mathbf{r}_n - \mathbf{q},$$

and therefore by 3·56 and 3·25

$$\mathbf{s}_1 + \mathbf{s}_2 + \ldots + \mathbf{s}_n = (\mathbf{r}_1 + \mathbf{r}_2 + \ldots + \mathbf{r}_n) - n\mathbf{q}.$$ ·12

It follows that °$\mathbf{s}_1 + \mathbf{s}_2 + \ldots + \mathbf{s}_n$ is the zero vector if and only if Q is the point ·13
representing $(\mathbf{r}_1 + \mathbf{r}_2 + \ldots + \mathbf{r}_n)/n$ with respect to O:

Given any finite number of points $R_1, R_2, \ldots R_n$, there is one and only one point C ·14
such that the sum of the vectors of the steps $CR_1, CR_2, \ldots CR_n$ is the zero vector.

This point is called the °*mean centre* of the set of points $R_1, R_2, \ldots R_n$. ·15

It follows from 5·45 and 5·41 that

The mean centre of the projections, normal or oblique, of any set of points on ·16
a plane or a line is the projection of the mean centre of the set.

·2. Geometrical properties of the mean centre are easy to find. It follows from ·13 that

The mean centre of a set of points $R_1, R_2, \ldots R_n$ in a ray is the point whose ·21
distance from any point O of the ray is the arithmetic mean of the distances of $R_1, R_2, \ldots, R_n$ from O,

and from ·16 that

The sum of the distances of any number of points from any prepared plane ·22
through their mean centre is zero.

The only objection to using one or other of these properties for the definition of the point is that the existence of a point having the property requires some proof.

·3. From ·13 and ·12 we see that

If $R_1, R_2, \ldots R_n$ represent with respect to the origin O the vectors $\mathbf{r}_1, \mathbf{r}_2, \ldots \mathbf{r}_n$, ·31
then if C is the mean centre of $R_1, R_2, \ldots R_n$, the sum $\mathbf{r}_1 + \mathbf{r}_2 + \ldots + \mathbf{r}_n$ is n times the vector represented by C.

This is the generalisation of 3·13 and 3·14, but it depends on 3·24 and is not available, unless the whole mode of development of the subject is changed, to *prove* that the sum of the vectors is independent of their order.

·4. An immediate development of the idea of the mean centre is that of the
mean centre of a set of loaded points. A °*loaded point* is a point associated with ·41
a number, positive, zero, or negative; the idea of a loaded point is older and more primitive than that of a vector.

Suppose the points $R_1, R_2, \ldots R_n$ to be associated with the n numbers $m_1, m_2, \ldots m_n$. Then with the same notation as in ·1 we have

$$m_1\mathbf{s}_1 + m_2\mathbf{s}_2 + \ldots + m_n\mathbf{s}_n = (m_1\mathbf{r}_1 + m_2\mathbf{r}_2 + \ldots + m_n\mathbf{r}_n) - (m_1 + m_2 + \ldots + m_n)\mathbf{q}.$$ ·42

The conclusions to be drawn from ·42 depend on the value of the sum
·43 $m_1 + m_2 + \ldots + m_n$, which is called the °*total load* of the set.

·44 *If the total load of a set of loaded points is zero, the sum of the corresponding loaded vectors of steps to the points from an origin does not depend on the position of the origin.*

The case of a zero sum is exceptional. If $m_1 + m_2 + \ldots + m_n$ is not zero, there is a definite vector $(m_1 \mathbf{r}_1 + m_2 \mathbf{r}_2 + \ldots + m_n \mathbf{r}_n)/(m_1 + m_2 + \ldots + m_n)$, and therefore

·45 *If the total load of a set of loaded points $R_1, R_2, \ldots R_n$ is not zero, there is one and only one point C such that the sum of the corresponding loaded vectors of the steps $CR_1, CR_2, \ldots CR_n$ is the zero vector.*

This point C is called the mean centre of the set of loaded points, and the set
·47 is said to be °*concentrated* at the mean centre if the mean centre is associated with the total load of the set.

·**5**. From ·42 it follows that

·51 *If $m_1, m_2, \ldots m_n$ are any n numbers whose sum is not zero, and if $R_1, R_2, \ldots R_n$ are the points representing with respect to an origin O the vectors $\mathbf{r}_1, \mathbf{r}_2, \ldots \mathbf{r}_n$, then the sum $m_1\mathbf{r}_1 + m_2\mathbf{r}_2 + \ldots + m_n\mathbf{r}_n$ is the product by $m_1 + m_2 + \ldots + m_n$ of the vector represented by the mean centre of the loaded set obtained by associating $R_1, R_2, \ldots R_n$ with $m_1, m_2, \ldots m_n$.*

·52 In other words, ° the sum of the loaded vectors is the loaded vector of the concentrated set of points.

Applying 3·25 to ·52 we find that

·53 *In concentrating any finite set of loaded points, we may replace any group contained in the set by the loaded point obtained by the concentration of that group.*

It is ·53 that enables us to describe an inductive construction for the mean centre. If m_1 and m_2 are not both zero, $m_1\mathbf{r}_1 + m_2\mathbf{r}_2$ can not be zero unless $\mathbf{r}_1$ and $\mathbf{r}_2$ are parallel; hence the mean centre of two points R_1, R_2 with loads m_1, m_2 is collinear with R_1, R_2: it is therefore the point C_2 in $R_1 R_2$ such that
·54 $m_1 . CR_1 + m_2 . CR_2$ is zero, that is, °the point dividing $R_1 R_2$ in the ratio of m_2 to m_1. Having found C_2, we may find the mean centre of C_2 loaded with $m_1 + m_2$ and any third point R_3 loaded with a number m_3 different from $-(m_1 + m_2)$, and the process may be continued through any finite number of stages; the order in which the points are taken must satisfy the condition that none of the partial loads $m_1 + m_2$, $m_1 + m_2 + m_3, \ldots$ are zero, but if the total load is not zero this will not prevent the set from being exhausted.

We can adapt the process just described to finding the mean centre of a number of unloaded points by supposing the points given equal loads. The fact that the point so reached is independent of the order in which the points are taken is even in this case a geometrical theorem of some complexity.

CHAPTER II 2

PRODUCTS OF VECTORS

220. INTRODUCTION.

Multiplication, like addition, is a word whose use in relation to vectors is to be settled by definition. It was the triumph of Hamilton's genius to discover how the word could usefully be applied. Our purpose is not to follow in his footsteps, but to describe individually the functions that are of the greatest service in analytical geometry, shewing their interrelations but making no attempt to exhibit them as elements in a complete algebra. Our attitude is that there are certain numbers and vectors dependent on groups of vectors that are recognised to recur so persistently that it is worth while to attach special names and symbols to them*. These functions are all *distributive with respect to addition*, that is to say, if $\mathbf{r}$, any one of the variable vectors on which one of them depends, is expressed as the sum of a finite number of vectors $\mathbf{r}_1, \mathbf{r}_2, \ldots \mathbf{r}_n$, the value of the function for the argument $\mathbf{r}$ is the sum of its values for the arguments $\mathbf{r}_1, \mathbf{r}_2, \ldots \mathbf{r}_n$ severally. For this reason the functions are all called *products*, the distributive property being among the most important characteristics† of multiplication in algebra, where it finds expression in such identities as

$$a(p+q+\ldots)b = apb + aqb + \ldots.$$

Numerous relations between the functions to be described in this chapter will be found in chapter IV 1 below. The order of development of this subject, as of many others, is to a considerable extent arbitrary, and some different routes are followed and some are indicated in the latter of these two chapters.

* To illustrate by a particular case, to Hamilton the vector product $\mathcal{V}\,\mathbf{rs}$ is a vector associated with the product $\mathbf{rs}$ which is itself a definite quaternion, but to us (compare Burali-Forti, *Proc. Fifth Int. Congress of Math.*, vol. II, p. 488, 1912) $\mathcal{V}\,\mathbf{rs}$ is a vector dependent on the independent vectors $\mathbf{r}$, $\mathbf{s}$ and called a product only because

$$\mathcal{V}(\mathbf{r}_1+\mathbf{r}_2+\ldots)\mathbf{s} = \mathcal{V}\,\mathbf{r}_1\mathbf{s} + \mathcal{V}\,\mathbf{r}_2\mathbf{s} + \ldots, \quad \mathcal{V}\,\mathbf{r}(\mathbf{s}_1+\mathbf{s}_2+\ldots) = \mathcal{V}\,\mathbf{rs}_1 + \mathcal{V}\,\mathbf{rs}_2 + \ldots.$$

† Whitehead (*Universal Algebra*, p. 26, 1898) regards the distributive property as the one property necessary to justify the name of product.

221. The projected product of two vectors.

·1. If **r**, **s** are vectors of amounts r, s in the directions whose images are
·11 P, Σ,° the product $rs \cos \mathrm{P\Sigma}$ depends in value, though not in appearance, only on the vectors themselves, for if r', s' are the amounts of **r**, **s** in the reverse directions, then since r', s' are the negatives of r, s we have identically

$$r\,s \cos \mathrm{P\Sigma} = r'\,s \cos \mathrm{P'\Sigma} = r\,s' \cos \mathrm{P\Sigma'} = r'\,s' \cos \mathrm{P'\,\Sigma'}.$$

·12 °The product $rs \cos \mathrm{P\Sigma}$ is symmetrical with respect to the two vectors, but
·13 it can be described unsymmetrically, either as °the product of the amount of **s** in either of its directions by the projection of **r** in that direction, or similarly in terms of an amount of **r** and a projection of **s**, and we call the product the
·14 °*projected product** of the two vectors and denote it by $\mathscr{G}\,\mathbf{rs}$. Applying 15·42 to **r** and a ray in one of the directions of **s** and multiplying the projections by the amount of **s** in that direction, we deduce that

·15 *If of two vectors* **r**, **s** *the former is the sum of a finite number of components, the projected product of* **r** *and* **s** *is the algebraical sum of the projected products of* **s** *by the several components of* **r**,

with the extension that

·16 *If the vectors* **r**, **s** *are the sums of finite numbers h, k of components, the projected product of* **r** *and* **s** *is the algebraical sum of hk terms, each of which is the projected product of a component of* **r** *and a component of* **s**,

more symmetrical but less useful than the theorem from which it is derived: symbolically we have

$$\mathscr{G}(\sum_m \mathbf{r}^{(m)})\,\mathbf{s} = \sum_m \mathscr{G}\,\mathbf{r}^{(m)}\,\mathbf{s},$$

$$\mathscr{G}(\sum_m \mathbf{r}^{(m)})\,(\sum_n \mathbf{s}^{(n)}) = \sum_m \sum_n \mathscr{G}\,\mathbf{r}^{(m)}\,\mathbf{s}^{(n)},$$

where $\mathbf{r}^{(1)}, \mathbf{r}^{(2)}, \ldots$ are the components of the single vector $\Sigma\,\mathbf{r}^{(m)}$, and $\mathbf{s}^{(1)}, \mathbf{s}^{(2)}, \ldots$ the components of $\Sigma\,\mathbf{s}^{(n)}$. There are two modes of expressing these results briefly: we may say that

·17 *The projected product of two vectors is a linear function of each of them,*

·18 a magnitude $F(\mathbf{r})$ involving a vector **r** being called a °*linear function* of **r** if identically

$$F(\sum_m \mathbf{r}^{(m)}) = \sum_m F(\mathbf{r}^{(m)});$$

or we may assert that

·19 *The formation of the projected product is distributive for the decomposition of either of the vectors involved.*

* It is the negative of Hamilton's scalar product and is a special case of Grassmann's inner product; we do not propose to use quaternions, and the recurrence of negative signs in algebraical work is inconvenient. But I will not follow even Clifford and Gibbs in using Hamilton's name for a concept contradicting his, and I avoid the symbol $\mathscr{S}$ deliberately; $\mathscr{P}$ is required later, and $\mathscr{I}$ must be available for extracting the imaginary part of a complex expression, but $\mathscr{G}$, the initial of Gibbs and Grassmann, is not inappropriate.

·2. The projected product $\mathscr{S}\mathbf{rs}$ of two vectors **r**, **s**, being the product
$rs \cos \mathrm{P}\Sigma$, °vanishes if **r** or **s** is the zero vector or if the vectors are in perpen- ·21
dicular directions, and it is worth while to notice that owing to the convention
that the zero vector has all directions we can say that °*the projected product* ·22
of two vectors vanishes if and only if the vectors have directions at right angles;
the object of conventional language is to avoid the explicit mention of cases
apparently exceptional, and in this example the object is completely attained.

·3. From the form of the projected product follow the two results that °*the* ·31
projected product of two vectors is unaltered if an amount of one vector is interchanged with an amount of the other, of which the principal applications are applications of the particular consequence given in the following paragraph
as ·43, and that °*the projected product of two vectors is unaltered if one is* ·32
multiplied and the other divided by any real number, a trivial theorem on which the simplicity of the analysis connected with curvilinear coordinates in differential geometry is to a considerable extent dependent; in symbols ·31, ·32 take the forms

$$\mathscr{S} r_{\mathrm{P}} s_{\Sigma} = \mathscr{S} s_{\mathrm{P}} r_{\Sigma}, \tag*{·33}$$

$$\mathscr{S}\mathbf{rs} = \mathscr{S}(p\mathbf{r})(\mathbf{s}/p), \tag*{·34}$$

r, s denoting any real numbers and p denoting any real number other than zero; ·34 is a particular case of the simpler theorem that *if two vectors are multiplied by any two real numbers, the projected product of the vectors is multiplied by the algebraical product of the numbers*:

$$\mathscr{S}(p\mathbf{r})(q\mathbf{s}) = pq\,\mathscr{S}\mathbf{rs}. \tag*{·35}$$

The projected product of a vector **r** by itself is naturally denoted by $\mathscr{S}\mathbf{r}^2$
and may be called the °*projected square* of the vector; this is the square of ·36
each amount of the vector and is often useful in the calculation of amounts by means of ·16. The projected square of the vector of a step AB is the square of the lengths of AB and may be denoted usually by AB^2 without risk of confusion. More generally, it is almost always safe to use for the projected product of the vectors of two *collinear* steps AB, CD the elementary notation $AB\,.\,CD$.

·4. That °*the cosines of the angles between two directions is the projection in* ·41
either of the directions of a unit vector in the other is an observation so elementary that it is instructive to find it valuable, and a result of the same kind
is that °*the projection in any direction of any vector* **r** *is the projected product* ·42
of **r** *by a unit vector in the given direction*, from which follows the theorem of
symmetry that °*the projection in a direction* Σ *of a vector of amount* r *in a direc-* ·43
tion T *is equal to the projection in the direction* T *of a vector of the same amount in the direction* Σ, the most useful of the deductions from ·31. Even simpler than ·41 is the statement that

The cosine of the angles between two directions is the projected product of ·44
unit vectors in those directions,

from which in 313·1 below we derive the fundamental theorem of spherical trigonometry. One advantage of replacing directions by unit vectors is that decomposition becomes possible, and for this purpose ·44 allows more freedom than ·41.

222. The areal product of two vectors in a prepared plane.

·1. In a prepared plane, if r_{P}, s_{Σ} are any two vectors $\mathbf{r}$, $\mathbf{s}$ the product $rs \sin \mathrm{P}\Sigma$ no less that the product $rs \cos \mathrm{P}\Sigma$ is a number dependent only on
·11 the vectors $\mathbf{r}$, $\mathbf{s}$; we call this product the °*areal product* of $\mathbf{r}$ and $\mathbf{s}$, and denote it by $\mathscr{A}\,\mathbf{rs}$.

·12 *The areal product of two vectors in a prepared plane vanishes if and only if the vectors have parallel directions,*

the cases in which one vector is the zero vector being formally included. From 113·23,

·13 *The areal product* $\mathscr{A}\,\mathbf{sr}$ *is the negative of the areal product* $\mathscr{A}\,\mathbf{rs}$,

and for this reason it is sometimes desirable to lay stress on the order of the vectors by speaking of $\mathscr{A}\,\mathbf{rs}$ as a product of $\mathbf{r}$ *into* $\mathbf{s}$ or of $\mathbf{s}$ *by* $\mathbf{r}$.

If $\mathbf{r}$ is the vector r_{P} and Π is the direction which makes a positive right angle with P, the vector r_{Π} is the vector $\mathscr{E}\,\mathbf{r}$ obtained by erecting $\mathbf{r}$, and since $\sin \mathrm{P}\Sigma$ is $\cos \Sigma\Pi$, it follows that

$$\mathscr{A}\,\mathbf{rs} = \mathscr{G}\,\mathbf{s}\,(\mathscr{E}\,\mathbf{r}):$$

·14 *The areal product* $\mathscr{A}\,\mathbf{rs}$ *is the projected product of the vector* $\mathbf{s}$ *by the vector* $\mathscr{E}\,\mathbf{r}$ *obtained by erecting* $\mathbf{r}$.

This result with 14·58 enables us to apply 1·17 to deduce that

·15 *The areal product of two vectors in a prepared plane is a linear function of each of them:*

$$\mathscr{A}\,(\sum_m \mathbf{r}^{(m)})\,(\sum_n \mathbf{s}^{(n)}) = \sum_m\sum_n \mathscr{A}\,\mathbf{r}^{(m)}\,\mathbf{s}^{(n)}.$$

A slight change in ·14 gives a useful variation:

·16 $$\mathscr{A}\,\mathbf{s}\,(\mathscr{E}\,\mathbf{r}) = \mathscr{G}\,\mathbf{rs}.$$

·2. The concept of the areal product enables us to replace 14·12 by a theorem shewing the exact magnitudes of the components. If $\mathbf{k}$, a vector coplanar with $\mathbf{r}$ and $\mathbf{s}$, is identically $g\mathbf{r} + h\mathbf{s}$, then since $\mathscr{A}\,\mathbf{r}^2$ and $\mathscr{A}\,\mathbf{s}^2$ are zero,

$$\mathscr{A}\,\mathbf{ks} = g\,\mathscr{A}\,\mathbf{rs}, \quad \mathscr{A}\,\mathbf{rk} = h\,\mathscr{A}\,\mathbf{rs};$$

·21 *In a prepared plane, a vector* $\mathbf{k}$ *is decomposed into vectors parallel to given vectors* $\mathbf{r}$, $\mathbf{s}$ *that are not themselves parallel by the formula*

$$\mathbf{k}\,\mathscr{A}\,\mathbf{rs} = \mathbf{r}\,\mathscr{A}\,\mathbf{ks} + \mathbf{s}\,\mathscr{A}\,\mathbf{rk}.$$

Naturally if $\mathbf{r}$ and $\mathbf{s}$ are themselves parallel the decomposition fails, but the formula in ·21, though it loses interest, does not actually become false; $\mathscr{A}\,\mathbf{rs}$ vanishes, but if $\mathbf{r}$, $\mathbf{s}$ are r_{T}, s_{T},

$$\mathbf{r}\,\mathscr{A}\,\mathbf{ks} = rs\mathbf{1}_{\mathrm{T}}\,\mathscr{A}\,\mathbf{k}\mathbf{1}_{\mathrm{T}}, \quad \mathbf{s}\,\mathscr{A}\,\mathbf{rk} = rs\mathbf{1}_{\mathrm{T}}\,\mathscr{A}\,\mathbf{1}_{\mathrm{T}}\mathbf{k},$$

and so by ·13 the zero vector appears on the right of the equation as well as on the left: for *any* three vectors **k**, **r**, **s** in a prepared plane,

$$\mathbf{k}\,\mathscr{A}\,\mathbf{rs} = \mathbf{r}\,\mathscr{A}\,\mathbf{ks} + \mathbf{s}\,\mathscr{A}\,\mathbf{rk}. \quad ·22$$

Actually a simpler and more powerful method of dealing with the excepted case is to rely on the distributive property. If **r** and **s** are parallel but **r** is not the zero vector, then if **d** is any vector in the plane that is not parallel to **r**, the vector $\mathbf{s}-\mathbf{d}$ also is not parallel to **r**; that is to say, **s** can be expressed as $\mathbf{d}+\mathbf{e}$ where neither **d** nor **e** is parallel to **r**. Then

$$\begin{aligned}\mathbf{k}\,\mathscr{A}\,\mathbf{rs} &= \mathbf{k}\,\mathscr{A}\,\mathbf{r}(\mathbf{d}+\mathbf{e})\\ &= \mathbf{k}\,\mathscr{A}\,\mathbf{rd} + \mathbf{k}\,\mathscr{A}\,\mathbf{re}\\ &= \mathbf{r}\,\mathscr{A}\,\mathbf{kd} + \mathbf{d}\,\mathscr{A}\,\mathbf{rk} + \mathbf{r}\,\mathscr{A}\,\mathbf{ke} + \mathbf{e}\,\mathscr{A}\,\mathbf{rk}\\ &= \mathbf{r}(\mathscr{A}\,\mathbf{kd} + \mathscr{A}\,\mathbf{ke}) + (\mathbf{d}+\mathbf{e})\,\mathscr{A}\,\mathbf{rk}\\ &= \mathbf{r}\,\mathscr{A}\,\mathbf{ks} + \mathbf{s}\,\mathscr{A}\,\mathbf{rk}\end{aligned}$$

as in general.

Sometimes the vector to be decomposed is given not directly but as the vector obtained by erecting a given vector; the modification to meet this case is given at once by ·16 and ·13:

$$\mathscr{E}\,\mathbf{k}\,\mathscr{A}\,\mathbf{rs} = \mathbf{s}\,\mathscr{G}\,\mathbf{kr} - \mathbf{r}\,\mathscr{G}\,\mathbf{ks}. \quad ·23$$

If we suppose the vectors in ·23 all rotated through a right angle we have the alternative formula

$$\mathbf{k}\,\mathscr{A}\,\mathbf{rs} = \mathscr{E}\,\mathbf{r}\,\mathscr{G}\,\mathbf{ks} - \mathscr{E}\,\mathbf{s}\,\mathscr{G}\,\mathbf{kr}. \quad ·24$$

From ·24 and ·16 comes

$$\mathscr{A}\,\mathbf{ik}\,\mathscr{A}\,\mathbf{rs} = \mathscr{G}\,\mathbf{ir}\,\mathscr{G}\,\mathbf{ks} - \mathscr{G}\,\mathbf{is}\,\mathscr{G}\,\mathbf{kr}, \quad ·25$$

where **i** is any fourth vector in the plane.

·3. To be in a position to appreciate corresponding theorems in three dimensions, it is worth while to notice that

The area of the triangle QRS in a prepared plane is one half of the areal product of the vectors of the steps QR, QS. ·31

223. The vector product of two vectors.

·1. If r_{P}, s_{Σ} are two vectors **r**, **s** in space, $\sin \mathrm{P}\Sigma$ has meaning only if a direction T is assigned round which angles from P to Σ are to be measured, and the sign of $\sin \mathrm{P}\Sigma$ is changed if the direction round which measurement takes place is reversed. If Π is one direction at right angles to both P and Σ, we can avoid ambiguity by taking for $\sin \mathrm{P}\Sigma$ the sine of angles from P to Σ round Π and associating the resulting value of $rs \sin \mathrm{P}\Sigma$ definitely with the direction Π; then we must associate also with the reverse direction Π′ a number which is the negative of the number associated with Π, and therefore what we actually consider is not a *number* of the form $rs \sin \mathrm{P}\Sigma$ but the *vector*

$(rs \sin P\Sigma)_\Pi$, and this vector, which is called the *vector product* of **r** into **s** and denoted by $\mathcal{V}\mathbf{rs}$, depends only on **r** and **s** and on the spatial convention. Briefly

·11 *The vector product of* **r** *into* **s** *is the vector obtained by associating with each direction at right angles to both* **r** *and* **s** *the areal product of* **r** *and* **s** *in a prepared plane to which that direction is normal.*

A number of simple properties can be asserted at once.

·12 *The vector product* $\mathcal{V}\mathbf{sr}$ *is the reverse of the vector product* $\mathcal{V}\mathbf{rs}$;

·13 *The vector product* $\mathcal{V}\mathbf{rs}$ *is the zero vector if and only if the vectors* **r**, **s** *have parallel directions,*

a proposition that includes the statement that a vector product is the zero vector if either of the constituents is the zero vector. The symmetry of three-dimensional space is responsible for the theorem that

·14 *If* **r**, **s**, **t** *are three vectors mutually at right angles of which the first is a unit vector, and if* **t** *is the vector product of* **r** *and* **s**, *then* **s** *is the vector product of* **t** *and* **r**,

which is used explicitly in 336·3. An extension of ·14 can be expressed in the form

·15 *If* **s**, **t** *are two vectors at right angles, then*

$$\mathcal{V}\mathbf{t}(\mathcal{V}\mathbf{st}) = \mathbf{s}\,\mathcal{S}\mathbf{t}^2, \quad \mathcal{V}(\mathcal{V}\mathbf{st})\,\mathbf{s} = \mathbf{t}\,\mathcal{S}\mathbf{s}^2,$$

and we can remove the explicit condition from this enunciation by replacing the vector **t** by $\mathcal{V}\mathbf{rs}$, where **r** is arbitrary, for $\mathcal{V}\mathbf{rs}$ is necessarily at right angles to **s**:

·16 *For any two vectors* **r**, **s**,

$$\mathcal{V}(\mathcal{V}\mathbf{rs})\,\{\mathcal{V}\mathbf{s}(\mathcal{V}\mathbf{rs})\} = \mathbf{s}\,\mathcal{S}(\mathcal{V}\mathbf{rs})^2,$$

$$\mathcal{V}\{\mathcal{V}\mathbf{s}(\mathcal{V}\mathbf{rs})\}\,\mathbf{s} = \mathcal{S}\mathbf{s}^2\,\mathcal{V}\mathbf{rs}.$$

·2. If $\Omega\Pi$ is at right angles to ΩP and $\Omega\Sigma$ and if ΩT is the direction at right angles to $\Omega\Pi$ and ΩP such that there is a positive right angle from ΩP to ΩT round $\Omega\Pi$, then the vector product of r_P and t_T is $(rt)_\Pi$, and therefore $\mathcal{V}r_P s_\Sigma$ is the vector product of r_P and $(s \sin P\Sigma)_T$, that is, of r_P and $(s \cos \Sigma T)_T$, whence

·21 *The vector product of* **r** *into* **s** *is the vector product of* **r** *into the vector component of* **s** *at right angles to* **r**;

since also

·22 *If two vectors are multiplied by any two real numbers, the vector product of the vectors is multiplied by the algebraical product of the numbers,*

it follows that the vector product of r_P into **s** is the product by r of the vector product of 1_P into the component of **s** at right angles to P. But if P is at right angles to T and Π is at right angles to both of them, and if there is a positive right angle from P to T round Π, then there is a positive right angle from T to Π round P; hence

·23 *If the vector* **t** *is at right angles to the direction* P, *the vector product* $\mathcal{V}1_P\mathbf{t}$ *is the vector obtained by erecting* **t** *in a prepared plane to which* P *is normal.*

It follows from 14·58 that if $\mathbf{t}^{(1)}, \mathbf{t}^{(2)}, \dots \mathbf{t}^{(k)}$ are at right angles to P then

$$\mathcal{V}\, 1_{\mathrm{P}}\, (\Sigma \mathbf{t}^{(n)}) = \Sigma\, \mathcal{V}\, 1_{\mathrm{P}} \mathbf{t}^{(n)},$$

and therefore from ·22 that

If $\mathbf{t}^{(1)}, \mathbf{t}^{(2)}, \dots \mathbf{t}^{(k)}$ *are at right angles to* $\mathbf{r}$, *then* $\mathcal{V}\, \mathbf{r}\, (\Sigma \mathbf{t}^{(n)}) = \Sigma\, \mathcal{V}\, \mathbf{r}\mathbf{t}^{(n)}$. ·24

It follows from ·21 that if any k vectors $\mathbf{s}^{(1)}, \mathbf{s}^{(2)}, \dots \mathbf{s}^{(k)}$ have for their components at right angles to the vector $\mathbf{r}$ the k vectors $\mathbf{t}^{(1)}, \mathbf{t}^{(2)}, \dots \mathbf{t}^{(k)}$ and if their sum $\mathbf{s}$ has for its component at right angles to $\mathbf{r}$ the vector $\mathbf{t}$, then

$$\mathcal{V}\, \mathbf{rs} = \mathcal{V}\, \mathbf{rt},$$

$$\Sigma\, \mathcal{V}\, \mathbf{rs}^{(n)} = \Sigma\, \mathcal{V}\, \mathbf{rt}^{(n)};$$

but ·24 gives $$\Sigma\, \mathcal{V}\, \mathbf{rt}^{(n)} = \mathcal{V}\, \mathbf{r}\, (\Sigma \mathbf{t}^{(n)})$$

and 15·46 gives $$\mathbf{t} = \Sigma \mathbf{t}^{(n)},$$

and therefore for *any* set of vectors, and not merely for a set at right angles to $\mathbf{r}$,

$$\mathcal{V}\, \mathbf{r}\, (\Sigma \mathbf{s}^{(n)}) = \Sigma\, \mathcal{V}\, \mathbf{rs}^{(n)}, \qquad \cdot 25$$

and ·12 enables us to dispense with a separate proof of the corresponding equation

$$\mathcal{V}\, (\Sigma \mathbf{r}^{(m)})\, \mathbf{s} = \Sigma\, \mathcal{V}\, \mathbf{r}^{(m)} \mathbf{s}; \qquad \cdot 26$$

combining ·25 and ·26 we have

$$\mathcal{V}\, (\Sigma_m \mathbf{r}^{(m)})\, (\Sigma_n \mathbf{s}^{(n)}) = \Sigma_{mn}\Sigma\, \mathcal{V}\, \mathbf{r}^{(m)} \mathbf{s}^{(n)}:$$

If the vectors $\mathbf{r}, \mathbf{s}$ *are the sums of finite numbers* h, k *of components, the vector product of* $\mathbf{r}$ *and* $\mathbf{s}$ *is the sum of* hk *vectors each of which is the vector product of a component of* $\mathbf{r}$ *and a component of* $\mathbf{s}$, ·27

or briefly

The vector product of two vectors is a linear function of each of them. ·28

·3. Since the vector product $\mathcal{V}\, \mathbf{rs}$ is at right angles to $\mathbf{r}$ and $\mathbf{s}$, and the vector product $\mathcal{V}\, (\mathcal{V}\, \mathbf{rs})\, \mathbf{t}$ is at right angles to $\mathcal{V}\, \mathbf{rs}$, the vector product $\mathcal{V}\, (\mathcal{V}\, \mathbf{rs})\, \mathbf{t}$ is coplanar with $\mathbf{r}$ and $\mathbf{s}$ and is therefore expressible in the form $g\mathbf{r} + h\mathbf{s}$. An explicit formula is easily obtained. Consider first the case of a vector $\mathbf{k}$ which itself is coplanar with $\mathbf{r}$ and $\mathbf{s}$. Let Π be a direction of $\mathcal{V}\, \mathbf{rs}$; then if $\mathcal{A}\, \mathbf{rs}$ is the areal product of $\mathbf{r}$ and $\mathbf{s}$ in the plane to which Π is normal, $\mathcal{V}\, \mathbf{rs}$ is of amount $\mathcal{A}\, \mathbf{rs}$ in the direction Π and therefore $\mathcal{V}\, (\mathcal{V}\, \mathbf{rs})\, \mathbf{k}$ is the product by $\mathcal{A}\, \mathbf{rs}$ of the vector obtained by erecting $\mathbf{k}$ in this plane. That is to say, $\mathcal{V}\, (\mathcal{V}\, \mathbf{rs})\, \mathbf{k}$ is precisely the vector that is decomposed in 2·23, and

$$\mathcal{V}\, (\mathcal{V}\, \mathbf{rs})\, \mathbf{k} = \mathbf{s}\, \mathcal{S}\, \mathbf{kr} - \mathbf{r}\, \mathcal{S}\, \mathbf{ks}. \qquad \cdot 32$$

But any vector $\mathbf{t}$ can be expressed as the sum of a vector coplanar with $\mathbf{r}$ and $\mathbf{s}$ and a vector perpendicular to both $\mathbf{r}$ and $\mathbf{s}$, and if $\mathbf{k}$ is the first of these components it follows from 1·16 and 1·22 that

$$\mathcal{S}\, \mathbf{kr} = \mathcal{S}\, \mathbf{tr}, \quad \mathcal{S}\, \mathbf{ks} = \mathcal{S}\, \mathbf{ts}$$

and from ·21 that $$\mathcal{V}\, (\mathcal{V}\, \mathbf{rs})\, \mathbf{k} = \mathcal{V}\, (\mathcal{V}\, \mathbf{rs})\, \mathbf{t};$$

hence **t** can be substituted for **k** throughout ·32:

·33 *If* **r**, **s**, **t** *are any three vectors, then* $\mathscr{V}(\mathscr{V}\mathbf{rs})\mathbf{t} = \mathbf{s}\,\mathscr{S}\mathbf{rt} - \mathbf{r}\,\mathscr{S}\mathbf{st}$.

The identity in this theorem, of which ·15 is a trivial corollary, is invaluable.

224. The areal vector of a triangle.

·1. The process by which a pure number in the geometry of a prepared plane leads sometimes to a vector in the geometry of space deserves attention. The example we have had, in which occurs in the one case the areal product and in the other case the vector product of two vectors, is altogether typical, and it is easy to see the condition that renders the passage natural: by the spatial convention each direction normal to an unprepared plane in space is connected with one of the cyclical directions that can be given to the plane,
·11 and therefore °*if a magnitude is such as to depend for sign but not for absolute amount on the cyclical direction of a plane*, the association of the magnitude with a vector at right angles to the plane is inevitably suggested. Whether the introduction of the vector brings advantages is a question for discussion in each case, and the answer depends on the use that can be made of properties *characteristic* of vectors, that is to say, of the rules of vectorial addition and projection.

·2. It is 3·27 that justifies the introduction of the vector product; 125·16 suggests a vector derived from a prepared plane that requires justification of
·21 a different kind. By the °*areal vector* of a triangle QRS in space is meant the vector obtained by associating with each direction at right angles to the plane of the triangle the area of the triangle in the corresponding *prepared* plane; from **2**·31 and **3**·11,

·22 *The areal vector of the triangle QRS is one half of the vector product of the vectors of the steps QR, QS.*

Since we have given no meaning to the addition of triangles in different planes, the utility of areal vectors is not to be realised from propositions such as 3·27; but there is one operation, that of projection, which may be performed both on triangles and on vectors. We may deduce the effect of projection on an areal vector from 144·75, but a more satisfactory plan is to discover this effect directly, thereby reducing 144·75 to dependence on results in 143·2.

Suppose that the triangle QRS is projected by lines parallel to l on a plane K into the triangle ABC, and by the same lines on the plane through Q parallel to K into the triangle QFG; the triangles ABC, QFG have the same areal vector, and it is the second of these triangles that we consider. Let the lines through R, S parallel to l cut the plane through Q at right angles to l in X, Y, and to an assigned scale let QU, QV, QW represent the areal vectors of QRS, QFG, QXY. Since RX, SY are parallel to QW, the tetrahedra $QRSW$, $QXYW$ have the same volume; if however Γ, Λ are directions of QU, QW, and f, h are the lengths of QU, QW in those directions, the volume of $QRSW$ is equal to $\frac{1}{3}fh\cos\Gamma\Lambda$, because of the relation of QU to the triangle QRS, and because of the relation of QW to the triangle QXY the same

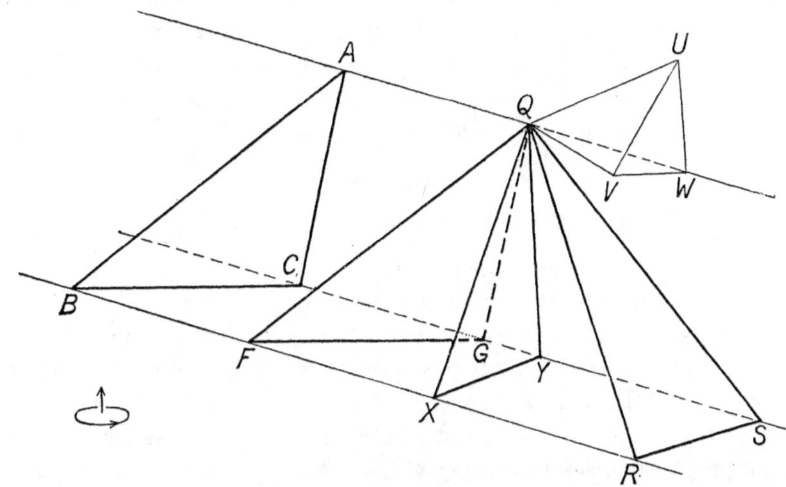

Fig. 14.

product $\frac{1}{3}fh\cos\Gamma\Lambda$ gives the volume of $QXYU$; it follows that the tetrahedra $QXYW$, $QXYU$ have the same volume, and therefore that the plane through U at right angles to l passes through W; similarly the plane through V at right angles to l passes through the same point, and therefore QV is a projection of QU by planes at right angles to l:

The areal vector of the projection of a triangle QRS on a plane K by lines ·23
parallel to l is the projection of the areal vector of QRS on a line at right angles to K by planes at right angles to l.

To prove the same result directly from properties of the vector product, let $\mathbf{r}$, $\mathbf{s}$ be the vectors of QR, QS, and let them be expressed as $\mathbf{b}+\mathbf{m}$, $\mathbf{c}+\mathbf{n}$, where $\mathbf{b}$, $\mathbf{c}$ are parallel to the plane K and $\mathbf{m}$, $\mathbf{n}$ are parallel to the line l. Then $\mathbf{b}$, $\mathbf{c}$ are the vectors of AB, AC, and the areal vectors of the triangles QRS, ABC are $\frac{1}{2}\mathcal{V}\,\mathbf{rs}$, $\frac{1}{2}\mathcal{V}\,\mathbf{bc}$; what we have to prove is that these vectors, of which the second is necessarily perpendicular to K, differ only by a vector perpendicular to l, and this follows from 3·27, for

$$\mathcal{V}\,\mathbf{rs} = \mathcal{V}\,(\mathbf{b}+\mathbf{m})\,(\mathbf{c}+\mathbf{n}) = \mathcal{V}\,\mathbf{bc} + \mathcal{V}\,\mathbf{mc} + \mathcal{V}\,\mathbf{bn} + \mathcal{V}\,\mathbf{mn}$$

and of the four vectors on the right, $\mathcal{V}\,\mathbf{mn}$ is the zero vector while $\mathcal{V}\,\mathbf{mc}$ is perpendicular to $\mathbf{m}$ and $\mathcal{V}\,\mathbf{bn}$ to $\mathbf{n}$.

·3. Although our work is to be confined strictly to the Euclidean plane and Euclidean space of three dimensions, we may permit ourselves the observation that the possibility of dealing in space with magnitudes that in a prepared plane depend on cyclical direction by means simply of vectors is a consequence, and analytically by far the most important consequence, of the three-dimensional character of space, which assures to a prepared plane a normal direction that is unique when the spatial convention is established. In space of more dimensions than three, directions at right angles to two directions are infinitely numerous, and there is no escape from the use of hypervectors, numbers associated with more directions than one.

225. THE SPATIAL PRODUCT OF THREE VECTORS.

·1. The most elementary problems involving three directions Ρ, Σ, Τ in space introduce the function $\sin \Omega \mathrm{P}\Sigma\mathrm{T}$, and so with three vectors **r**, **s**, **t** expressed as r_{P}, s_{Σ}, t_{T}, we have to consider the product $rst \sin \Omega \mathrm{P}\Sigma\mathrm{T}$; to reverse the direction in which **r** is measured is to change simultaneously the signs of r and $\sin \Omega \mathrm{P}\Sigma\mathrm{T}$, and therefore the product $rst \sin \Omega \mathrm{P}\Sigma\mathrm{T}$ depends on the vectors **r**, **s**, **t** themselves, not on the choice of directions for measuring
·11 them; we propose to call the product the °*spatial product** of **r**, **s**, **t** and to denote it by $\mathcal{T}\mathbf{rst}$. The spatial product $\mathcal{T}\mathbf{rst}$ depends for its sign on the order of the vectors involved and on the spatial convention, the sign but not the amount being changed by a simple interchange of two vectors:

·12 $$\mathcal{T}\mathbf{rst} = -\mathcal{T}\mathbf{rts} = -\mathcal{T}\mathbf{srt}.$$

Also from 134·26

·13 *The spatial product of three vectors vanishes if and only if the vectors have coplanar directions,*

the degenerate cases in which one of the vectors is zero or two are parallel being formally included, and

$$\mathcal{T}(f\mathbf{r})(g\mathbf{s})(h\mathbf{t}) = fgh\,\mathcal{T}\mathbf{rst}:$$

·14 *If three vectors are multiplied by any three real numbers, the spatial product of the vectors is multiplied by the algebraical product of the numbers.*

The simplest geometrical use of the spatial product is evident from the definition:

·15 *The volume of the tetrahedron QRST is one sixth of the spatial product of the vectors of the steps QR, QS, QT.*

* This, like the projected product, is the negative of Hamilton's scalar product; still avoiding $\mathcal{S}$, I have adopted $\mathcal{T}$ because the function is essentially *trilinear*. One reason why I am not convinced by Burali-Forti's arguments (*op. cit.* p. 53 above, pp. 487, 488) that any function that can reasonably be called a product should have an operational rather than a functional symbol, is that operational notation tends to put bilinear functions on a different footing from the majority of multilinear functions of higher orders.

·2. Perhaps the most important property of the spatial product comes from 134·72: if Π is a direction at right angles to Σ and T and sin ΣT is the sine of angles from Σ to T round Π, then

$$\sin \Omega P \Sigma T = \cos P\Pi \sin \Sigma T;$$

from this equation we have

$$rst \sin \Omega P \Sigma T = rst \sin \Sigma T \cos P\Pi = \mathscr{G} r_P (st \sin \Sigma T)_\Pi,$$

that is $$\mathscr{J}\mathbf{rst} = \mathscr{G}\mathbf{r}(\mathscr{V}\mathbf{st}):$$ ·21

The spatial product of any three vectors is the projected product of the first vector by the vector product of the second and third. ·22

An alternative proof of ·22 is virtually contained in 4·2; sometimes the formula

$$\mathscr{J}\mathbf{rst} = \mathscr{G}(\mathscr{V}\mathbf{rs})\mathbf{t}$$ ·23

is wanted instead of ·21. From ·22, ·12 or 3·28, and 1·17,

The spatial product of three vectors is a linear function of each of them, ·24

that is, $$\mathscr{J}(\sum_m \mathbf{r}^{(m)})(\sum_n \mathbf{s}^{(n)})(\sum_p \mathbf{t}^{(p)}) = \sum_m\sum_n\sum_p \mathscr{J}\mathbf{r}^{(m)}\mathbf{s}^{(n)}\mathbf{t}^{(p)}.$$

This implies $$\mathscr{J}(f\mathbf{r} + g\mathbf{s} + h\mathbf{t})\mathbf{st} = f\mathscr{J}\mathbf{rst},$$ ·25

for $g\mathbf{s} + h\mathbf{t}$, **s**, **t** are coplanar whatever the values of g and h, and so from ·13

$$\mathscr{J}(g\mathbf{s} + h\mathbf{t})\mathbf{st} = 0.$$

That the function $\mathscr{G}(\mathscr{V}\mathbf{rs})\mathbf{t}$ is more symmetrical in fact than in appearance can be deduced from 3·33 by substitution of $\mathscr{V}\mathbf{tr}$ for **t**. Since $\mathscr{V}\mathbf{tr}$ is perpendicular to **r**, the coefficient of **s**, which becomes $\mathscr{G}\mathbf{r}(\mathscr{V}\mathbf{tr})$, is then zero, and 3·33 yields

$$\mathscr{V}(\mathscr{V}\mathbf{tr})(\mathscr{V}\mathbf{rs}) = \mathbf{r}\,\mathscr{G}\mathbf{s}(\mathscr{V}\mathbf{tr}).$$ ·26

Interchange of **s** and **t** on the left merely reverses the vector, and therefore

$$\mathscr{G}\mathbf{t}(\mathscr{V}\mathbf{rs}) = \mathscr{G}\mathbf{s}(\mathscr{V}\mathbf{tr}).$$ ·27

Incidentally we have discovered a useful identity. Since $\mathscr{V}\mathbf{tr}$ and $\mathscr{V}\mathbf{rs}$ are both perpendicular to **r**, their vector product is a multiple of **r**, and ·26 shews the multiplier to be the spatial product itself:

$$\mathscr{V}(\mathscr{V}\mathbf{tr})(\mathscr{V}\mathbf{rs}) = \mathbf{r}\,\mathscr{J}\mathbf{rst}.$$ ·28

·3. The parts played by the areal product in a plane are shared in space between the vector product and the spatial product. In the extension of 2·21 it is spatial products that are concerned, for ·25 shews that if **k** is identical with $f\mathbf{r} + g\mathbf{s} + h\mathbf{t}$, then

$$f\mathscr{J}\mathbf{rst} = \mathscr{J}\mathbf{kst},\quad g\mathscr{J}\mathbf{rst} = \mathscr{J}\mathbf{rkt},\quad h\mathscr{J}\mathbf{rst} = \mathscr{J}\mathbf{rsk},$$

that is, that

For any four vectors **k**, **r**, **s**, **t**,

$$\mathbf{k}\,\mathscr{J}\mathbf{rst} = \mathbf{r}\,\mathscr{J}\mathbf{kst} + \mathbf{s}\,\mathscr{J}\mathbf{rkt} + \mathbf{t}\,\mathscr{J}\mathbf{rsk}.$$ ·32

This theorem supplies in its most compact form the quantitative element lacking in 15·32. If **r**, **s**, **t** are coplanar, the theorem does not become false, but while ceasing to give a decomposition of **k** it provides an identity that is anything but obvious:

·33 *If* **r**, **s**, **t** *are coplanar vectors and* **k** *is any vector whatever, then*

$$\mathbf{r}\,\mathscr{T}\mathbf{kst}+\mathbf{s}\,\mathscr{T}\mathbf{rkt}+\mathbf{t}\,\mathscr{T}\mathbf{rsk}=0.$$

There is a valuable companion to ·32, in the shape of a decomposition of an arbitrary vector **k** by means of vector products; this is the spatial equivalent of 2·24. Since **r** is perpendicular to both $\mathscr{V}\mathbf{tr}$ and $\mathscr{V}\mathbf{rs}$, the three vectors $\mathscr{V}\mathbf{st}$, $\mathscr{V}\mathbf{tr}$, $\mathscr{V}\mathbf{rs}$ cannot be coplanar if they are all proper vectors. Hence if **r**, **s**, **t** are three vectors that are not coplanar, any vector **k** must be expressible in the form $a\,\mathscr{V}\mathbf{st}+b\,\mathscr{V}\mathbf{tr}+c\,\mathscr{V}\mathbf{rs}$; the values of the coefficients a, b, c can be found at once, for by ·21

$$\mathscr{S}\mathbf{kr}=a\,\mathscr{T}\mathbf{rst},\quad \mathscr{S}\mathbf{ks}=b\,\mathscr{T}\mathbf{rst},\quad \mathscr{S}\mathbf{kt}=c\,\mathscr{T}\mathbf{rst}:$$

·34 *For any four vectors* **k**, **r**, **s**, **t**,

$$\mathbf{k}\,\mathscr{T}\mathbf{rst}=\mathscr{V}\mathbf{st}\,\mathscr{S}\mathbf{kr}+\mathscr{V}\mathbf{tr}\,\mathscr{S}\mathbf{ks}+\mathscr{V}\mathbf{rs}\,\mathscr{S}\mathbf{kt}.$$

This result, proved first under the restriction that **r**, **s**, **t** are not coplanar, can be extended to the excepted case by decomposition of one or more of the vectors **r**, **s**, **t**, and implies therefore that

·35 *If* **r**, **s**, **t** *are coplanar vectors and* **k** *is any vector whatever, then*

$$\mathscr{V}\mathbf{st}\,\mathscr{S}\mathbf{kr}+\mathscr{V}\mathbf{tr}\,\mathscr{S}\mathbf{ks}+\mathscr{V}\mathbf{rs}\,\mathscr{S}\mathbf{kt}=0.$$

It may be observed that ·32 and ·34 are equivalent, for on the one hand each of them implies that

·36 *For any five vectors* **l**, **m**, **r**, **s**, **t**,

$$\mathscr{S}\mathbf{lm}\,\mathscr{T}\mathbf{rst}=\mathscr{S}\mathbf{lr}\,\mathscr{T}\mathbf{mst}+\mathscr{S}\mathbf{ls}\,\mathscr{T}\mathbf{rmt}+\mathscr{S}\mathbf{lt}\,\mathscr{T}\mathbf{rsm},$$

and on the other hand each of them is deducible from ·36 in virtue of 15·22, or rather of the still narrower theorem that

·37 *If for every vector* **p** *the projected products* $\mathscr{S}\mathbf{pr}$, $\mathscr{S}\mathbf{ps}$ *are equal, then the vectors* **r**, **s** *are identical.*

·4. The spatial product plays a characteristic part in the deduction from 3·33 of an equally important identity. From 3·33, if **u** is any vector

·41 $$\mathscr{S}\mathbf{rt}\,\mathscr{S}\mathbf{su}-\mathscr{S}\mathbf{ru}\,\mathscr{S}\mathbf{st}=\mathscr{S}\{\mathscr{V}(\mathscr{V}\mathbf{rs})\,\mathbf{t}\}\,\mathbf{u};$$

the expression on the left only changes sign if **t** and **u** are interchanged, though on the right these vectors enter differently. We have however

·42 $$\mathscr{S}\{\mathscr{V}(\mathscr{V}\mathbf{rs})\,\mathbf{t}\}\,\mathbf{u}=\mathscr{T}(\mathscr{V}\mathbf{rs})\,\mathbf{tu}=\mathscr{S}(\mathscr{V}\mathbf{rs})\,(\mathscr{V}\mathbf{tu}),$$

by a double application of ·22, and the identity is now simple enough:

·43 *For any four vectors* **r**, **s**, **t**, **u**,

$$\mathscr{S}(\mathscr{V}\mathbf{rs})\,(\mathscr{V}\mathbf{tu})=\mathscr{S}\mathbf{rt}\,\mathscr{S}\mathbf{su}-\mathscr{S}\mathbf{ru}\,\mathscr{S}\mathbf{st}.$$

It is easy to return from ·43 to 3·33 by means of ·37, for ·42 and ·43 together imply ·41; the deduction, vicious in logic, is useful in practice, because ·43 unlike 3·33 imposes no tax on the memory in respect of signs.

CHAPTER II 3

ROTORS AND MOMENTS

231. Bound vectors.

·1. A vector involves a number associated with a direction; a vector °*localised* ·11
in a ray or a line involves a number associated not only with a direction but
also with a ray or a line which has that direction, and a vector °*anchored to* ·12
a point involves a number associated with a point as well as with a direction.
Localised and anchored vectors are called collectively °*bound* vectors, and in ·13
contrast with them simple vectors are said to be °*free*; to every bound vector ·14
corresponds a definite free vector. Any two free vectors have a single free
vector as their sum, but the sum of two bound vectors remains to be defined,
and the definition is to some extent arbitrary and to some extent dependent
on the nature of the bond; °it is not supposed that two bound vectors ·15
necessarily can be added to form a single vector, bound or free, but two
principles are adopted in the definition of addition if the word vector is used
even with a qualification: °*the sum of any number of bound vectors is in-* ·16
dependent of the order in which the vectors are taken, and °*if the sum of two* ·17
*bound vectors is a single vector, bound or free, the free vector corresponding to
the sum is the sum of the free vectors corresponding to the parts.* These principles
often require little supplementing by definitions to enable us to discover
criteria for the equality of the sums of two sets of bound vectors and standard
forms to which the sum of a set of bound vectors may be reduced.

232. Vectors anchored to a point.

·1. The extent to which the definition of a sum of two bound vectors is
arbitrary and the care that must be taken if inconsistencies are to be avoided
are well illustrated in the case of vectors anchored to a point; a vector **r** anchored
to a point O is often called a °*radius vector from* O, and we denote it by $\mathbf{r}_O$. ·11
It is natural to agree that °*if two vectors are anchored to the same point their* ·12
sum is a vector anchored to that point, and since the free vector corresponding
to the sum is given by a general principle, this agreement is sufficient completely to determine the sum in this case. As we have seen, every free vector
r can be represented relatively to a point O by a definite point R or a definite

step OR; the step, but not the point alone, involves in a definite manner both the vector $\mathbf{r}$ and the point O, and can serve quite precisely as a representative of the radius vector $\mathbf{r}_O$. It follows from our definitions and from 13·13 that if OR, OS represent in this way two vectors $\mathbf{r}_O$, $\mathbf{s}_O$ anchored to O, and if OT is the diagonal from O of the parallelogram of which OR and OS are sides, then the sum $\mathbf{r}_O + \mathbf{s}_O$ is the anchored vector $\mathbf{t}_O$ represented by OT, but it will be recalled that the *step* which must be added to OR to give OT as the sum is not OS but RT.

233. ROTORS; ADDITION OF CONCURRENT ROTORS.

·1. The study of vectors localised in lines is incomparably more important than the study of vectors associated with points; mathematics as a whole has suffered much from the appropriation of this subject by particular branches of applied mathematics when it should be regarded from the beginning as a fundamental part of pure mathematics, available for investigations that have no concern with statics and dynamics just as Cartesian coordinates may be used in work that has little relation to analytical geometry.

·21 **·2.** A vector localised in a line is called* a °*rotor*; a proper rotor has two amounts, one in each direction of its axis, but if the rotor is regarded as lying in a ray its amount in the direction of the ray can be distinguished from its amount in the opposite direction. Since the zero vector has every direction we are prepared to find that it can not be localised in any line; no purpose is
·22 served by associating the number zero with a single line, and the °*zero rotor* is the number zero associated with every line in a plane or in space according
·23 as our work has reference to two dimensions or to three. We °denote the rotor with vector $\mathbf{r}$ and axis k by $\mathbf{r}_k$, and the reverse rotor, which has the same axis and the reverse vector, by $\mathbf{r}_k'$; alternatively, if κ is a ray in the line k and the vector $\mathbf{r}$ has amount r in the direction of κ, we may denote the rotor $\mathbf{r}_k$ by r_κ. The rotor $\mathbf{r}_k$ may be represented by any step in k which has $\mathbf{r}$ for its vector.
·25 °The zero rotor may present itself in one of the forms $\mathbf{0}_k$, 0_κ, but when we wish to introduce it without reference to any particular axis we denote it by $\mathbf{0}_*$.

·3. The one principle of addition that supplements the general principles 1·16,
·31 1·17 implied in the use of the word vector is that °*concurrent rotors have for their sum a rotor through their point of concurrence.* This principle does not give us a direct definition of the sum even of two rotors if they do not intersect, but it enables us to give meaning to any assertion in which two sets of rotors are said to have or not to have the same sum. In the case of a set of concurrent rotors an actual sum is implicitly defined, for a rotor is known if its vector
·33 and one point of its axis are known, and therefore °*the sum of a set of rotors concurrent in a point O is the rotor through O whose vector is the sum of the vectors of the rotors belonging to the set.*

* The word is Clifford's (*Proc. Lond. Math. Soc.*, vol. IV, p. 381, 1873; *Math. Papers*, p. 182).

234. Moments of rotors in a prepared plane.

Among the most important concepts related to rotors is that of the moment of a rotor, which we define in this article for rotors in a prepared plane; the extension of the idea to space can be made, as in so many other cases, in two distinct ways.

·1. Let K represent one direction of the axis k of a rotor $\mathbf{r}_k$, let κ denote the ray obtained by the association of the direction K with k, and let r be the amount of $\mathbf{r}$ in the direction K. Then if Q is any point, and if a plane through Q and k is given cyclic direction, the product of r and the distance *of* Q *from* κ is called the °*moment of* $\mathbf{r}$ *about* Q in the prepared plane; to use K′ instead ·11
of K involves a change in the sign of r, but if the cyclic convention is untouched involves also a reversal of κ and therefore a change in the sign of the distance from the ray to the point: °if Q lies in k the moment is zero, and ·12
otherwise the moment depends only on Q, on $\mathbf{r}_k$, and on the cyclic convention for the plane through Q and k; °a reversal of the cyclic convention changes ·13
the sign of the moment.

·2. If $\mathbf{r}_k$ is the rotor r_κ and λ is the ray normal to κ through Q, and if the point of intersection of λ with κ is F, the distance q of Q from κ is the length of the step FQ in the ray λ, and it is the product rq that is the moment of r_κ about Q; moreover, if G is any point whatever of κ, the step FQ is the projection on λ of the step GQ:

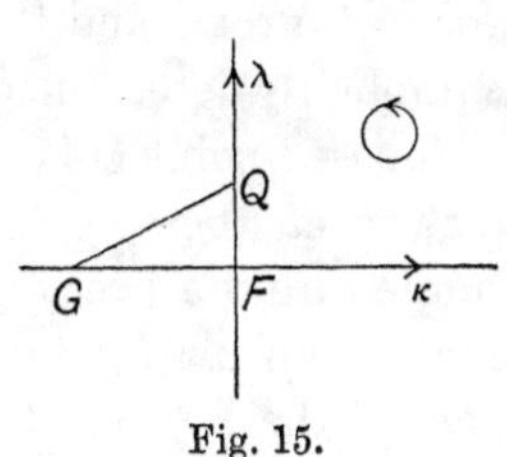

Fig. 15.

The moment of the rotor $\mathbf{r}_k$ *in a prepared plane about a point* Q *of the plane is the areal product of the vector* $\mathbf{r}$ *into the vector of any step from the axis* k *to the point* Q. ·21

If G is any point of k and O, Q are any two points of the plane, the vector of the step GQ is the sum of the vectors of the steps GO, OQ:

The moment of the rotor $\mathbf{r}_k$ *in a prepared plane about any point* Q *exceeds the moment of the same rotor about any other point* O *by the areal product of the vector* $\mathbf{r}$ *into the vector of the step* OQ; ·22

translating the areal product into a moment,

The moment of $\mathbf{r}_k$ *about* Q *exceeds the moment of* $\mathbf{r}_k$ *about* O *by the moment about* Q *of the rotor through* O *with the vector* $\mathbf{r}$. ·23

At first sight ·23 is a preposterous dressing up of the simplest of theorems on parallel lines and ·22 is designed solely to prevent the elementary nature of the theorem from being too apparent; we shall see however that ·23 is precisely the form that is required in the coordinate geometry of the plane and that both theorems have in three-dimensional work analogues that can not be enunciated more readily. Moreover we need not wait to find an application of ·21 in a valuable result that is by no means self-evident: if $\mathbf{q}$ is the vector of the step GQ and $\mathbf{r}_k$, $\mathbf{s}_l$, $\mathbf{t}_m$, ... are any rotors in the plane concurrent in G, the moments of these rotors about Q are the areal products $\mathscr{A}\mathbf{rq}$, $\mathscr{A}\mathbf{sq}$, $\mathscr{A}\mathbf{tq}$, ..., and by 22·15 the sum of these numbers is the areal product $\mathscr{A}(\mathbf{r}+\mathbf{s}+\mathbf{t}+...)\mathbf{q}$, which from ·21 is the moment about Q of the rotor through G with vector $\mathbf{r}+\mathbf{s}+\mathbf{t}+...$, that is, of the rotor that is defined in 3·33 as the sum of the concurrent rotors:

·24 *In a prepared plane, the moment of the sum of any finite number of concurrent rotors about any point is the sum of the moments of the individual rotors about that point;*

the proof has the merit of shewing the exact bearing of the concurrence—it is only because the axes k, l, m, ... have a common point G that the areal products $\mathscr{A}\mathbf{rq}$, $\mathscr{A}\mathbf{sq}$, $\mathscr{A}\mathbf{tq}$, ... involve a common vector $\mathbf{q}$.

In passing let us mention another simple and useful deduction from ·21. If $\mathbf{r}_k$ is the rotor of a step ST, and if $\mathbf{s}$, $\mathbf{t}$ are the vectors of the steps to S, T from a point Q, then from ·21 the moment of $\mathbf{r}_k$ about Q is $-\mathscr{A}\mathbf{rs}$; but $-\mathscr{A}\mathbf{rs} = \mathscr{A}\mathbf{s}(\mathbf{t}-\mathbf{s}) = \mathscr{A}\mathbf{st}$:

·25 *In a prepared plane, the moment of the rotor of a step ST about a point Q is the areal product of the vectors of the steps from Q to S and T.*

·31 **·3.** °The axis of a proper rotor is the aggregate of points about which the moment of the rotor is zero; it follows that if the vector $\mathbf{r}$ of a rotor and the moment R about a single point O are known, the axis k is implicitly determined, for by means of ·22 it can be discovered whether any proposed point Q is or is not on the axis. Actual construction is simple enough: the vector being given as r_{K}, a ray is drawn through O making a positive right angle with the direction K; the axis is the line at right angles to this ray through the point F which is such that the length FO, measured in the direction of the ray, is R/r. The construction fails if r is zero, but then the rotor is zero and the axis is essentially indeterminate; in every case,

·32 *A rotor in a prepared plane is determined completely by its vector together with its moment about any one point of the plane,*

while the construction proves that conversely

·33 *Given a point O, a vector r_{K}, and a number R, then provided that if r is zero so also is R, there is one and only one rotor having r_{K} for its vector and R for its moment about O.*

235. The momental vector of a rotor about a point.

·1. In space, rotors have moments of two kinds, intimately related and equally important. No convention gives sign to the distance of a point from a ray except in a prepared plane, and in space the moment of a rotor about a point is a vector, but in space rotors have moments about rays as well as about points, the moment of a rotor about a ray being a real number definite in sign as well as in amount.

·2. After 23·11 and 4·21 the definition of the moment of a rotor about a point is both easy and natural: in quite elementary terms, if a prepared plane is passed through the rotor r_κ and the point Q, the moment or °*momental* ·21
vector of r_κ about Q is the vector in which the direction normal to the plane is associated with the product by r of the distance *of* Q *from* κ in the plane, and it follows at once that

The momental vector of the rotor $\mathbf{r}_k$ *about the point* Q *is the vector product of* ·22
the vector $\mathbf{r}$ *into the vector of any step from the axis* k *to the point* Q,

whence from 23·25 as in 4·2 by the decomposition of the step we have

The momental vector of the rotor $\mathbf{r}_k$ *about the point* Q *is the sum of the* ·23
momental vector of the same rotor about any point O *and the vector product of the vector* $\mathbf{r}$ *into the vector of the step* OQ,

the proposition fundamental in the use of frames of reference for the specification of rotors, which may be expressed in the more homogeneous form that

The momental vector of $\mathbf{r}_k$ *about* Q *is the sum of the momental vector of* $\mathbf{r}_k$ ·24
about O *and the momental vector about* Q *of the rotor with vector* $\mathbf{r}$ *whose axis contains* O.

By the decomposition of $\mathbf{r}_k$ into any set of concurrent rotors we have from ·22,

The momental vector of the sum of any finite number of concurrent rotors ·25
about any point is the sum of the momental vectors of the individual rotors about that point.

Corresponding to 4·25 and proved in the same way is the theorem that

The momental vector of the rotor of a step ST *about a point* Q *is the vector* ·26
product of the vectors of the steps from Q *to* S *and* T.

·3. The argument leading to 4·32 can be repeated almost word for word on the basis of ·23. °The axis k of a proper rotor $\mathbf{r}_k$ is the aggregate of points ·31
about which the momental vector is zero, and if $\mathbf{r}$ and the momental vector about a single point O are known, ·23 can be used to discover whether any suggested point is or is not on the axis; if $\mathbf{r}$ is the zero vector, the rotor is the zero rotor:

A rotor in space is determined completely by its vector together with its ·32
momental vector about any one point.

The specification is redundant, since the vector and the momental vector are necessarily at right angles, but in spite of this defect it remains quite the most valuable form of specification in practice. The converse of ·32 must contain explicitly the hypothesis that the vectors are at right angles, but is in other respects similar to 4·33, and is established virtually by the same construction: if the momental vector about O is R_Λ and is not the zero vector, the prepared plane through O with Λ for its normal direction is a definite plane in which the rotor must lie, and in that plane the moment of the rotor about O is R, whence by application of 4·33 follows that

·33 *Given a point O and two vectors r_{K}, R_{Λ}, then provided that if r is zero so also is R and that otherwise the directions* K, Λ *are at right angles, there is one and only one rotor having r_{K} for its vector and R_{Λ} for its momental vector about O.*

236. The momental product of two rotors; the moment of a rotor about a ray; the mutual moment of two rays.

·1. Let $\mathbf{r}_k$, $\mathbf{s}_l$ be any two rotors, let P be a point of the axis k, let Q be a point of the axis l, and let $\mathbf{q}$ be the vector of the step PQ. By 5·22, the vector $\mathscr{V}\,\mathbf{rq}$ is the momental vector of $\mathbf{r}_k$ about Q and is independent of the position of P in k, and therefore the relation

·11
$$\mathscr{S}\,\mathbf{rqs} = \mathscr{G}(\mathscr{V}\,\mathbf{rq})\,\mathbf{s}$$

of 25·23 shews that the spatial product $\mathscr{S}\,\mathbf{rqs}$ also is independent of the position of P in k; it follows that the spatial product is independent also of the position of Q in l:

·12 *If $\mathbf{q}$ is the vector of the step PQ from a point in the axis of a rotor $\mathbf{r}_k$ to a point in the axis of a rotor $\mathbf{s}_l$, the spatial product $\mathscr{S}\,\mathbf{rqs}$ is a number independent both of the position of P in k and of the position of Q in l.*

·13 The number $\mathscr{S}\,\mathbf{rqs}$ we call the °*momental product* of $\mathbf{r}_k$ and $\mathbf{s}_l$ and denote by $\mathscr{M}\,\mathbf{r}_k\mathbf{s}_l$; to obtain the momental product $\mathscr{M}\,\mathbf{s}_l\mathbf{r}_k$ we have both to reverse the step of which $\mathbf{q}$ is the vector and to interchange $\mathbf{r}$ and $\mathbf{s}$ in the spatial product, and since each operation alone changes the sign of $\mathscr{S}\,\mathbf{rqs}$ the combined operation is without effect:

·14
$$\mathscr{M}\,\mathbf{s}_l\mathbf{r}_k = \mathscr{M}\,\mathbf{r}_k\mathbf{s}_l.$$

·2. We can discover at once a geometrical interpretation of the momental product; if P, Q are points in k, l, if PU is a step whose vector is $\mathbf{r}$ and QV is a step whose vector is $\mathbf{s}$, and if PX also is a step with vector $\mathbf{s}$, the spatial product $\mathscr{S}\,\mathbf{rqs}$ is six times the volume of the tetrahedron $PUQX$, and since the tetrahedra $UPQX$, $UPQV$ have the same sign as well as the same absolute volume, the volume of $PUQX$ is equal to the volume of $PUQV$:

·21 *The momental product $\mathscr{M}\,\mathbf{r}_k\mathbf{s}_l$ is six times the volume of any tetrahedron which has $\mathbf{r}_k$, $\mathbf{s}_l$ for the rotors of a pair of opposite edges.*

We can express the equation

·22
$$\mathscr{M}\,\mathbf{r}_k\mathbf{s}_l = \mathscr{G}(\mathscr{V}\,\mathbf{rq})\,\mathbf{s},$$

to which ·11 shews the definition of $\mathscr{M}\,\mathbf{r}_k\mathbf{s}_l$ to be equivalent, usefully in words, interpreting $\mathscr{V}\,\mathbf{rq}$ by means of 5·22:

·23 *If $\mathbf{R}$ is the momental vector of a rotor $\mathbf{r}_k$ about a point Q and $\mathbf{s}_l$ is any rotor through the same point, the momental product of the rotors $\mathbf{r}_k$, $\mathbf{s}_l$ is the projected product of the vectors $\mathbf{R}$, $\mathbf{s}$.*

From ·21 comes the condition of vanishing:

The momental product of two rotors is zero if and only if the rotors are coplanar, ·24

the rotors being actually coplanar if their axes intersect or are parallel, and formally coplanar if either of them is zero. As a particular case of 25·24,

$$\mathscr{I}(\sum_m \mathbf{r}^{(m)})\,\mathbf{q}\,(\sum_n \mathbf{s}^{(n)}) = \sum_m\sum_n \mathscr{I}\,\mathbf{r}^{(m)}\,\mathbf{q}\mathbf{s}^{(n)},$$

and this equation implies that

If each of two rotors $\mathbf{r}_k$, $\mathbf{s}_l$ is the sum of a finite number of concurrent rotors, the momental product of $\mathbf{r}_k$ by $\mathbf{s}_l$ is the sum of the individual momental products of components of $\mathbf{r}_k$ by components of $\mathbf{s}_l$; ·25

we run little risk of confusion in writing

$$\mathscr{M}(\sum_m \mathbf{r}_P^{(m)})(\sum_n \mathbf{s}_Q^{(n)}) = \sum_m\sum_n \mathscr{M}\,\mathbf{r}_P^{(m)}\,\mathbf{s}_Q^{(n)},$$

and we may express the result in the form that

The momental product of variable rotors through fixed points is a linear function of each of the rotors. ·26

·3. An obvious corollary of 25·14 is

$$\mathscr{M}(f\mathbf{r})_k(g\mathbf{s})_l = fg\,\mathscr{M}\,\mathbf{r}_k\mathbf{s}_l, \quad ·31$$

a formula of which the special cases

$$\mathscr{M}\,r_\kappa s_\lambda = s\,\mathscr{M}\,r_\kappa \mathbf{1}_\lambda, \quad ·32$$

$$\mathscr{M}\,r_\kappa s_\lambda = rs\,\mathscr{M}\,\mathbf{1}_\kappa \mathbf{1}_\lambda, \quad ·33$$

suggest the consideration of the functions $\mathscr{M}\,r_\kappa \mathbf{1}_\lambda$, $\mathscr{M}\,\mathbf{1}_\kappa\mathbf{1}_\lambda$, which bear to momental products the relations that projections and cosines bear to projected products.

·4. The momental product of r_κ and $\mathbf{1}_\lambda$ is called the °*moment* of the rotor r_κ about the ray λ. ·41

The moment of a rotor about a ray is zero if and only if there is a plane which contains them both; ·42

unless the rotor is zero, the ray and the rotor must be either parallel or concurrent. From ·25,

If a rotor $\mathbf{r}_k$ is the sum of any finite number of concurrent rotors, the moment of $\mathbf{r}_k$ about any ray is the sum of the moments of the components about that ray, ·43

and ·23 gives the useful theorem that

The moment of a rotor about any ray through a point Q is the projection on the ray of the momental vector of the rotor about Q, ·44

which combines with 5·24 to give a theorem of the same kind as the latter, namely,

The moment of a rotor $\mathbf{r}_k$ about any ray λ exceeds the moment of $\mathbf{r}_k$ about ·45

any ray ϖ parallel to λ by the moment about λ of a rotor with the vector $\mathbf{r}$ *through any point of ϖ,*

implying incidentally, since the point of ϖ is arbitrary, that

·46 *Two rotors with a common vector* have equal moments about any ray parallel to the plane containing their axes,*

a proposition of which a simple and important application is made in 43·5 below.

·5. If P is any point of the axis of a rotor $\mathbf{r}_k$, and λ is any ray, there passes through P one and only one prepared plane Λ to which λ is normal, and $\mathbf{r}_k$ can be resolved into a rotor $\mathbf{s}_m$ through P parallel to λ and a rotor $\mathbf{t}_n$ through P in Λ; by ·42 the moment about λ of the first of these components is zero, and therefore by ·43

·51 *The moment of a rotor about a ray is the moment about the same ray of the projection of the rotor on any plane which cuts it and is at right angles to the ray.*

Again, λ cuts Λ in a definite point Q, and in the prepared plane Λ the rotor $\mathbf{t}_n$ has a definite moment about Q; it follows from the definition of the momental vector that the momental vector of $\mathbf{t}_n$ about Q has for its amount in the direction of λ the moment of $\mathbf{t}_n$ about Q in Λ, and it follows from ·44 that this amount is the moment of $\mathbf{t}_n$ about λ in space:

·52 *If a rotor* $\mathbf{t}_n$ *is at right angles to a ray λ and the prepared plane through* $\mathbf{t}_n$ *to which λ is normal cuts λ is Q, the moment of* $\mathbf{t}_n$ *about λ in space is the moment of* $\mathbf{t}_n$ *about Q in the prepared plane.*

For giving a clear notion of the moment of a rotor about a ray, the construction we have just made repays examination. Since $\mathbf{r}$ is the sum of $\mathbf{s}$ and $\mathbf{t}$, these three vectors are coplanar, and assuming the rotor not to be parallel to the ray, the resolution of $\mathbf{r}_k$ takes place in the plane through k parallel to the ray, and this plane is unique. If $P^{(1)}$, $P^{(2)}$ are different points of k, the lines $m^{(1)}$, $m^{(2)}$ are parallel to each other and parallel to λ, and the lines $n^{(1)}$, $n^{(2)}$ are parallel to each other and at right angles to λ; the vectors $\mathbf{s}^{(1)}$, $\mathbf{t}^{(1)}$ associated with $m^{(1)}$, $n^{(1)}$ are the same as the vectors $\mathbf{s}^{(2)}$, $\mathbf{t}^{(2)}$ associated with $m^{(2)}$, $n^{(2)}$. The absolute distance of $Q^{(1)}$ from $n^{(1)}$ is the same as the absolute distance of $Q^{(2)}$ from $n^{(2)}$, this distance being simply the constant distance of λ from the plane through k parallel to λ; this is why the moment of $\mathbf{t}_n$ about

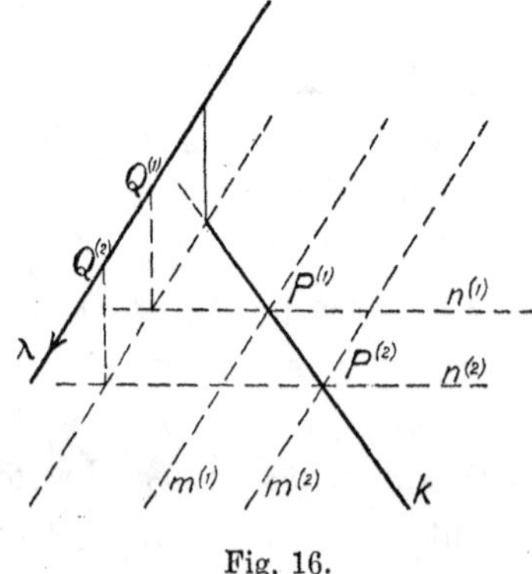

Fig. 16.

* And therefore with parallel axes.

λ is independent of the position of P. The absolute distance of $Q^{(1)}$ from $m^{(1)}$ is the absolute distance between $Q^{(1)}$ and $P^{(1)}$, and is as a rule different from the absolute distance of $Q^{(2)}$ from $m^{(2)}$; there is no difference between $\mathbf{s}^{(1)}$ and $\mathbf{s}^{(2)}$ to counteract this difference, but because the lines $m^{(1)}$, $m^{(2)}$ are parallel to λ the moments about λ of rotors in these lines vanish independently of the positions of the lines. The simplest expression for the moment of a rotor about a ray is evident from the construction: taking the rotor as r_κ, denoting the ray through P parallel to λ by μ, and one of the rays through P in n by ν, the amount of $\mathbf{t}$ in the direction of ν is $r \cos \epsilon_{\kappa\nu}$, and if Π is the direction making a positive right angle with N round M and d is the distance of Q *from* the plane through μ and ν in the direction of Π, the moment of $\mathbf{t}_n$ about λ, and therefore also the moment of r_κ about λ, is $rd \cos \epsilon_{\kappa\nu}$; the sign of d is covered by the choice of ν, which distinguishes Π from Π', and we can render the convention in the formula more obvious by substituting $\sin \epsilon_{\mu\kappa}$, or $\sin \epsilon_{\lambda\kappa}$, for $\cos \epsilon_{\kappa\nu}$, when the condition is that $\epsilon_{\lambda\kappa}$ is measured *round* the direction *in* which d is measured; the distance of Q from the plane is the shortest distance from κ to λ, and the most lucid form of the expression under consideration is $rd_{\kappa\lambda} \sin \epsilon_{\lambda\kappa}$, which could of course be deduced from ·21 and 134·55.

It is evident equally from the formula and from the construction that if h is a line parallel to k *in the plane through k parallel to* λ, the moment of $\mathbf{r}_h$ about λ is the same as the moment of $\mathbf{r}_k$ about λ; this is ·46 above.

It is possible to use ·51 and ·52, or the explicit expression $rd_{\kappa\lambda} \sin \epsilon_{\lambda\kappa}$, to *define* the moment of a rotor about a ray; the whole sequence of propositions relating to moments is changed, and in particular the proof of ·43 with a minimum of labour is an interesting exercise.

·6. The momental product $\mathscr{M} 1_\kappa 1_\lambda$ of unit rotors in rays κ, λ is called the °*moment* or the *mutual moment* of the two rays. ·61

The mutual moment of two rays is zero if and only if the rays are coplanar; ·62

The moment of a rotor r_κ about a ray λ is the product by r of the mutual moment of the rays κ, λ; ·63

The momental product of two rotors r_κ, s_λ is the product by rs of the mutual moment of the rays κ, λ. ·64

The mutual moment is a magnitude purely geometrical and intrinsic to the two rays, and a variety of expressions may be given for it. If P, Q are any points of κ, λ and if the step PQ has the length p in the direction Π, while K, Λ are the directions of κ, λ, it follows from ·64 that the mutual moment is $\mathscr{I} 1_{\mathrm{K}} p_\Pi 1_\Lambda$:

If p is the distance from the ray κ to the ray λ in the direction Π, the mutual moment of the rays is $-p \sin \Omega\Pi\mathrm{K}\Lambda$; ·65

in particular, if Π is at right angles to both κ and λ and $\epsilon_{\kappa\lambda}$ is an angle from

κ to λ round Π, the sine becomes $\sin \epsilon_{\kappa\lambda}$ and $-p$ can be written as $d_{\lambda\kappa}$, the corresponding shortest distance from λ to κ:

·66 *The mutual moment of the two rays κ, λ is the product $d_{\lambda\kappa} \sin \epsilon_{\kappa\lambda}$, where $d_{\lambda\kappa}$ is the shortest distance from λ to κ and $\epsilon_{\kappa\lambda}$ is an angle from κ to λ, the angle being measured round the direction in which the distance is measured.*

The last theorem gives the mutual moment in its simplest geometrical form; if we were guided by ·65 and ·66, we should naturally reverse the sign attached to this magnitude, but the theorem most important to secure is ·44, and an identification of $\mathscr{M}\,\mathbf{r}_k\mathbf{s}_l$ with $\mathscr{I}\,\mathbf{qrs}$, which obviously would be necessary to remove the negative sign from ·65, as clearly would introduce a negative sign into ·44; we may be reconciled on purely geometrical grounds to the signs in ·65 and ·66 by observing that if PU, QV are positive steps in the rays κ, λ, the sign of the ordered tetrahedron $PUQV$ is opposite to the sign of the product $d_{\kappa\lambda} \sin \epsilon_{\kappa\lambda}$.

When we know the mutual moment of two rays, we can use ·65 to calculate the distance from one to the other in a given direction without determining a cotractor along which this distance can be measured. More generally, if $\mathbf{p}$ is a given vector whose directions are not coplanar with those of two lines k, l,
·68 °there is only one step from k to l which has the directions of $\mathbf{p}$, and if the vector of this step is $j\mathbf{p}$, and proper rotors $\mathbf{r}_k$, $\mathbf{s}_l$ are located in the lines, then from the definition of the momental product, the multiplier j satisfies the equation

·69 $$j\,\mathscr{I}\,\mathbf{rps} = \mathscr{M}\,\mathbf{r}_k\mathbf{s}_l.$$

CHAPTER II 4

SETS OF ROTORS

241. Equivalence of two sets of rotors; the vector and the momental vectors of a set; the momental product of two sets. 242. Examples of equivalence. 243. Couples; the moments and the momental vector of a couple. 244. Equivalence of couples; addition of couples. 245. Reduction of sets of rotors; reduced sets. 246. Poinsot sets; motors; addition of motors; screws; intensity and pitch; momental products and virtual coefficients. 247. The reduced sets and the rotor-pairs with a given motor. 248. Uses of the word 'sum'.

241. Equivalence of two sets of rotors; the vector and the momental vectors of a set; the momental product of two sets.

·1. Since the rotors forming a given set can not as a rule be added together, it is necessary to consider how a set can be modified by such additions and decompositions as are possible.

If a set F of rotors is modified by the inclusion of the zero rotor or by the substitution for any concurrent rotors which it contains of the single rotor which is their sum, a set G is obtained which is a different set from F, but
F and G are said to be °*equivalent*; since F is obtained from G by the omis- ·11
sion of the zero rotor or by the substitution for a rotor contained in G of concurrent rotors of which that rotor is the sum, the definition implies that
°either of these operations applied to a set gives an equivalent set, save in ·12
the one case in which the original set comprises only the zero rotor; further,
°two sets of rotors that are equivalent to the same set are said to be equivalent ·13
to each other. For example, let $\mathbf{r}_k$, $\mathbf{s}_l$ be two rotors which do not intersect, let m be a line cutting both k and l, and let $\mathbf{t}_m$ be a rotor in m and $\mathbf{t}_m'$ be its reverse; the sum of $\mathbf{t}_m$ and $\mathbf{t}_m'$ is the zero rotor $\mathbf{0}_*$, while the sums $\mathbf{r}_k + \mathbf{t}_m$, $\mathbf{s}_l + \mathbf{t}_m'$ are definite rotors $\mathbf{u}_p$, $\mathbf{v}_q$; then the five sets of rotors $(\mathbf{r}_k, \mathbf{s}_l)$, $(\mathbf{r}_k, \mathbf{s}_l, \mathbf{0}_*)$, $(\mathbf{r}_k, \mathbf{s}_l, \mathbf{t}_m, \mathbf{t}_m')$, $(\mathbf{u}_p, \mathbf{s}_l, \mathbf{t}_m')$, $(\mathbf{u}_p, \mathbf{v}_q)$ are different but equivalent.

·2. The °*reverse F'* of a set F of rotors is the set whose members are the ·21
reverses of the members of F, and the °*compound* of a number of sets F, G, ·22
H, ... is the set composed of all the members of all the sets, a rotor which occurs in k of the components occurring k times in the compound. It is easy
to prove that °*the compound of any set of rotors and its reverse is equivalent* ·23
to the zero rotor, and that °*if two sets of rotors are equivalent so also are their* ·24
reverses, and from these theorems it follows that °*if two sets of rotors are* ·25
equivalent, the compound of either with the reverse of the other is equivalent to the zero rotor.

·3. There are certain magnitudes related to the rotors of a set which we can add, whether or not we can add the rotors themselves; we can add the
·31 vectors of the rotors, obtaining a single vector called the °*vector of the set*, we can add the momental vectors of the rotors about any point, obtaining the *momental vector* of the set about that point, and since the moment of a rotor about a ray and the momental product of two rotors are real numbers, we can add the moments of the rotors of a set about a ray, obtaining a single number
·32 called the °*moment of the set about the ray*, we can add the momental products
·33 of the rotors of a set with any single rotor, obtaining the °*momental product of the set and the rotor*, and we can add the momental products of the
·34 members of one set and the members of another set, obtaining the °*momental product of the two sets.* It follows from the definition of equivalence and from theorems 13·25, 35·25, 36·43, 36·25 that

·35 *Equivalent sets of rotors have the same vector, the same momental vector about any point, the same moment about any ray, and the same momental product with any other rotor or set of rotors,*

and that

·36 *The momental product of two sets of rotors is unaltered if for each is substituted any equivalent set;*

these theorems account for the importance of momental products, and because of this importance we denote the momental product of two sets F, G by
·37 $\mathscr{M}FG$ and the °*momental square* of a set F, that is, the momental product of F and any set equivalent to F, by $\mathscr{M}F^2$. The theorem that

·38 *The moment of any set of rotors about a ray is the projection on the ray of the momental vector of the set about any point of the ray*

is implied by 35·25 and 36·44, and is of considerable value; it is not implied by ·35 and 36·44 alone, for, as we shall see, a set of rotors is not in general equivalent to any single rotor. From 35·24 and 35·25,

·39 *If the vector of a set of rotors is* $\mathbf{r}$, *the momental vector of the set about a point Q is the sum of the momental vector of the set about any point O and the momental vector about Q of the rotor through O with vector* $\mathbf{r}$.

·4. By means of ·35 we can prove a result which is really of great importance although it is so naturally taken for granted that in practice reference is not made to it. It is certainly not self-evident that each of two distinct rotors can not be equivalent to some one complicated set of rotors. But if $\mathbf{r}_k$ and $\mathbf{s}_l$ are equivalent, then $\mathbf{r}$ is identical with $\mathbf{s}$, and if the momental vector of $\mathbf{r}_k$ about a point is zero then the momental vector of $\mathbf{s}_l$ about the same point also is zero; it follows that either $\mathbf{r}$ and $\mathbf{s}$ are zero or l passes through every point which lies in k, and since we regard two zero rotors as identical we can assert that

·43 *Rotors which are equivalent are identical.*

242. Examples of equivalence.

To realise the extent to which equivalent sets may differ in form although equivalence depends only on the composition and resolution of *concurrent* rotors, let us consider three examples.

·1. Let $\mathbf{r}_1, \mathbf{r}_2, \ldots \mathbf{r}_n$ be n *parallel* vectors, and let rotors be formed by locating these vectors in lines through points $P_1, P_2, \ldots P_n$; let $\mathbf{c}$ be any proper vector with the directions of the given vectors, and let

$$\mathbf{r}_1 = h_1\mathbf{c}, \quad \mathbf{r}_2 = h_2\mathbf{c}, \quad \ldots \quad \mathbf{r}_n = h_n\mathbf{c}.$$ ·11

Suppose first that the sum of the given vectors is not the zero vector; then $h_1 + h_2 + \ldots + h_n$ is not zero, and therefore if we associate the points $P_1, P_2, \ldots P_n$ with the numbers $h_1, h_2, \ldots h_n$ we have a loaded set with a definite mean centre C. Let O be the point such that the vector of OC is $\mathbf{c}$.

By the fundamental property of the mean centre, rotors with vectors $h_1 . CP_1, h_2 . CP_2, \ldots h_n . CP_n$ located in the lines $CP_1, CP_2, \ldots CP_n$ are together equivalent to the zero rotor; hence the given set of rotors through $P_1, P_2, \ldots P_n$ can be modified by the addition of these rotors. In the modified set, there are two rotors through the point P_k, namely, the rotors with vectors $\mathbf{r}_k$ and $h_k . CP_k$, that is, with vectors $h_k . OC$ and $h_k . CP_k$; these two rotors combine to form a single rotor through P_k with vector $h_k . OP_k$, and this rotor, because its vector is a multiple of the vector of OP_k, passes through O as well as through P_k. Thus the modified set is equivalent to a set concurrent in O, and this set is equivalent to a single rotor through O. The vector of the single rotor is of course $(\mathbf{r}_1 + \mathbf{r}_2 + \ldots + \mathbf{r}_n)$, as is in fact immediately evident from the construction in virtue of 16·51, which shews also why the axis of this rotor passes through C.

If any set of parallel rotors has a vector that is not the zero vector, the set is equivalent to a single proper rotor. ·13

The construction for the axis may be presented as a property of the mean centre:

If the total load of a set of loaded points is not zero, any set of parallel rotors through the points and proportional to the loads has the zero vector for its momental vector about the mean centre and zero for its moment about any ray through the mean centre. ·14

To deal with a set of parallel rotors in the excepted case in which the vector of the set is zero, let $\mathbf{s}_l$ be any proper rotor parallel to the set, and modify the set by including $\mathbf{s}_l$ and the opposite rotor $\mathbf{s}_l'$. The original set is equivalent to $\mathbf{s}_l$ together with the set formed by adding $\mathbf{s}_l'$ to the original set; this latter set has vector $\mathbf{s}'$, which is not the zero vector, and is therefore equivalent to *a single rotor with vector* $\mathbf{s}'$; if the axis of this rotor is l itself, the original set is equivalent to the zero rotor, but in general the axis is different from l.

·16 *If the vector of a set of parallel rotors is the zero vector, the set is equivalent either to the zero rotor or to a pair of rotors with vectors equal and opposite.*

In the first case the momental vector of the set about any point is the zero vector. In the second case the pair of rotors is not unique.

·2. The treatment of any set of rotors in a plane is simple: if any two of the rotors are not parallel they intersect and can be added, and the set is therefore equivalent either to a single rotor, which may be the zero rotor, or to a set of parallel rotors; applying to the last case the result of the last paragraph we find that

·27 *A set composed of any finite number of rotors in a plane is equivalent either to a single rotor, which may be the zero rotor, or to a pair of rotors with equal and opposite vectors.*

·3. One form of reduction of a set containing a finite number of rotors disposed in any manner in space is now evident. The number of rotors being finite, there are planes which have points in common with every axis, for if the axes are represented by points on a unit sphere, there are great circles passing through none of these points. If O is any point of a plane K, and p is any line not parallel to K, then as in **15·1** any rotor $\mathbf{r}_k$ through O can be resolved into a rotor through O parallel to p and a rotor through O in the
·31 plane K. Using the results of the last two paragraphs, we see that °a set containing any finite number of rotors is equivalent to a set containing not more than four rotors; since this method of finding a simple set equivalent to a given set is not actually convenient, it is not worth while to enumerate the different cases.

243. Couples; the moments and the momental vector of a couple.

·1. It is by no accident that in the first two of the examples we have just discussed the irreducible set takes the form of a pair of rotors with distinct axes and vectors equal and opposite, for the very feature that distinguishes rotors from vectors is that if two rotors $\mathbf{r}_k$, $\mathbf{r}_l$ have the same vector $\mathbf{r}$, then unless k and l coincide we do *not* write $\mathbf{r}_k = \mathbf{r}_l$ and therefore do *not* write $\mathbf{r}_k - \mathbf{r}_l = \mathbf{0}_*$: a pair of rotors with equal and opposite vectors is necessarily an irreducible element in the theory, and the manner in which elements of this kind combine with each other and with rotors has to be investigated.

·2. A pair of rotors $\mathbf{r}_k$, $\mathbf{r}_l'$ with equal and opposite vectors $\mathbf{r}$, $\mathbf{r}'$ and therefore
·21 with parallel axes is called a rotor-couple, or briefly a °*couple*; the plane through
·22 the axes k, l is definite unless the axes coincide, and is called the °*plane* of the
·23 couple. The couple $(\mathbf{r}_k', \mathbf{r}_l)$ is the °*reverse* of the couple $(\mathbf{r}_k, \mathbf{r}_l')$, and a couple

which is equivalent to the zero rotor is called a °*zero couple*; if the couple ·24
$(\mathbf{r}_k, \mathbf{r}_l')$ is zero, then $\mathbf{r}_k$ is equivalent to the reverse of $\mathbf{r}_l'$, that is, to $\mathbf{r}_l$: hence
from 1·43 °*a couple is zero only if its constituent rotors are zero or if the axes of* ·25
the constituents coincide, and from this it follows that

Two couples located in the same pair of distinct parallel lines are equivalent ·26
only if they are identical.

·3. A set of rotors and couples is a set of rotors with certain pairs taken
together, and °two such sets are *defined* to be equivalent if they are equivalent ·31
if no pairing is recognised: thus the set formed of two couples $(\mathbf{r}_h, \mathbf{r}_k')$, $(\mathbf{s}_l, \mathbf{s}_m')$
and a rotor $\mathbf{t}_n$ is equivalent to the set of five rotors $(\mathbf{r}_h, \mathbf{r}_k', \mathbf{s}_l, \mathbf{s}_m', \mathbf{t}_n)$ by
definition; if h intersects l and k intersects m, there are rotors $(\mathbf{r}+\mathbf{s})_p$ and
$(\mathbf{r}'+\mathbf{s}')_q$, and since if $\mathbf{r}+\mathbf{s}$ is $\mathbf{u}$ then $\mathbf{r}'+\mathbf{s}'$ is $\mathbf{u}'$ these rotors form a single
couple $(\mathbf{u}_p, \mathbf{u}_q')$, and in this case the original set of two couples and a rotor
is equivalent to a set with one couple and a rotor. °The vector of a couple, ·32
that is, the sum of the vectors of the constituent rotors, is the zero vector,
and therefore °the vector of a set of couples and rotors is the vector of the set ·33
of rotors alone, and °a set of rotors can not be equivalent to any set of couples ·34
unless the vector of the set of rotors is the zero vector.

·4. Neither in a plane nor in space does the moment of a couple require fresh definition, for in every case the moment is the sum of the moments of the constituent rotors, but moments of couples have important properties. In what follows we speak of moments rather than of momental vectors about a point in space, for the same language serves then to conduct parallel investigations.

The root of the theory of couples is in 35·24; let $(\mathbf{r}_k, \mathbf{r}_l')$ be any couple, let O be any point of l and let Q be any point of space; then by 35·24 the moment of $\mathbf{r}_k$ about Q is the sum of the moment of $\mathbf{r}_k$ about O and the moment of $\mathbf{r}_l$ about Q, and therefore the moment of the couple about Q is the moment of $\mathbf{r}_k$ about O; since the position of Q is independent of the position of O in l,

In space or in a plane, a couple has the same moment about every point, and ·41
this moment is the moment of either of the constituent rotors about any point in
the axis of the other;

the constant moment is naturally called simply *the* moment, and for a couple in space *the* momental vector also, of the couple. From ·41 and ·25 it follows that

A zero couple in a plane is a couple whose moment is zero, ·42

and that in space

A zero couple is a couple whose momental vector is the zero vector. ·43

The proposition

The moment of a couple about any ray is the projection on the ray of the ·44
momental vector of the couple,

which comes from 1·38, with its corollaries

·45 *The momental product of a couple and a rotor is the projected product of the vector of the rotor by the momental vector of the couple,*

·46 *The momental product of any two couples is zero,*

indicates the simplicity of the theory of couples.

·5. The fundamental result ·41 may of course be verified directly, not only in the elementary case of a couple in a prepared plane but also for a couple in space.

If a prepared plane through any point Q at right angles to the lines containing a couple $(\mathbf{r}_k, \mathbf{r}_l')$ meets k, l in K, L and r is the amount of $\mathbf{r}$ in the direction normal to the plane, the momental vectors of $\mathbf{r}_k$, $\mathbf{r}_l'$ about Q are vectors of amounts $r.QK$, $-r.QL$ in directions making positive right angles with the directions in which QK, QL are measured, and the sum of these vectors is the vector of amount $r.KL$ in the direction making a positive right angle with the direction in which KL is measured; the reference to Q disappears when the vectors are added, for the value of KL is independent not merely of the position of Q in the plane QKL but also of the position of Q in space.

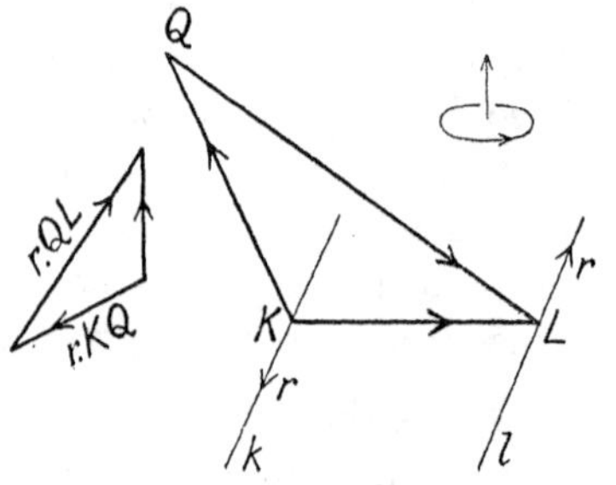

Fig. 17.

An interesting alternative method uses the idea of the moment about a ray as a momental product, replacing the ray by a unit rotor *that can be decomposed.* From 34·22 it follows that a couple has the same moment R about all rays with a common direction N at right angles to its plane, and therefore that the momental product of the couple and any rotor whose vector has the direction N and the amount t in that direction is tR; resolving a unit rotor in any ray λ through any point Q into a component of amount $\cos \mathrm{N}\Lambda$ in the ray through Q with the direction N and another component in a ray parallel to the plane of the couple, we deduce from 36·25 that the moment of the couple about λ is the sum of the momental products of the couple with these two components, and from 36·46 that the momental product of the couple and the second component is zero whatever the magnitude of this component; it follows that the moment of the couple about λ is $R \cos \mathrm{N}\Lambda$, and the importance of the vector R_{N} in connection with the couple is manifest.

61 **·6.** °If the momental vector $\mathbf{R}$ of a couple $(\mathbf{r}_k, \mathbf{r}_l')$ is known, then $\mathbf{r}$ can be found if k and l are known and l can be found if $\mathbf{r}_k$ is known; the couple
·62 may conveniently be °denoted by $\mathbf{R}_{kl}$; there is a certain redundance in this notation, for the directions of $\mathbf{R}$ are known if k and l are known, but there is redundance of the same kind if a single rotor is denoted by such a combination of symbols as $\mathbf{r}_k$. It should be added that a couple whose momental vector
·63 has P for one of its directions is often said to be °*about*, *round*, or *in* any line or ray which has the direction P, or even to be about, round, or in the direction P itself.

244. EQUIVALENCE OF COUPLES; ADDITION OF COUPLES.

·**1.** In the matter of equivalence there is a vital distinction between single couples and single rotors; as we have seen in 1·4, two different rotors can not be equivalent, but with couples the case is altered. From 1·35 it follows that

Equivalent couples have the same momental vector, ·11

and we proceed to establish the converse of this theorem.

·**2.** If $(\mathbf{r}_k, \mathbf{r}_l')$ and $(\mathbf{s}_m, \mathbf{s}_n')$ are two couples with the same proper momental vector $\mathbf{R}$, then k and l are parallel lines in one plane perpendicular to $\mathbf{R}$, and m and n are lines parallel to each other, but not necessarily to k and l, in a plane parallel to the plane containing k and l but not necessarily identical with this plane. In any case we can choose a pair of lines p, q coplanar with k, l and parallel to m, n, and we can find a vector $\mathbf{t}$ such that the couple $(\mathbf{t}_p, \mathbf{t}_q')$ has the momental vector $\mathbf{R}$.

The four vectors $\mathbf{r}_k, \mathbf{r}_l', \mathbf{t}_p', \mathbf{t}_q$ compose a coplanar set of which the vector, which is $\mathbf{r}+\mathbf{r}'+\mathbf{t}'+\mathbf{t}$, and the momental vector about any point, which is $\mathbf{R}+\mathbf{R}'$, are both zero. Hence from 2·27 and 3·43, this set is equivalent to the zero rotor, and therefore the couple $(\mathbf{r}_k, \mathbf{r}_l')$ is equivalent to the couple $(\mathbf{t}_p, \mathbf{t}_q')$.

The four vectors $\mathbf{s}_m, \mathbf{s}_n', \mathbf{t}_p', \mathbf{t}_q$ compose a parallel set of which the vector, which is $\mathbf{s}+\mathbf{s}'+\mathbf{t}'+\mathbf{t}$, and the momental vector about any point, which is $\mathbf{R}+\mathbf{R}'$, are both zero. Hence from 2·16 and 3·43, this set also is equivalent to the zero rotor, and therefore the couple $(\mathbf{s}_m, \mathbf{s}_n')$ is equivalent to the couple $(\mathbf{t}_p, \mathbf{t}_q')$.

Combining the two results, we find that $(\mathbf{r}_k, \mathbf{r}_l')$ and $(\mathbf{s}_m, \mathbf{s}_n')$ are equivalent. Adding that any two couples with momental vector zero are equivalent, we conclude that in any case

Couples with the same momental vector are equivalent. ·24

·**3.** The last theorem is the converse of ·11, and the two may be combined to give the simple theorem that

Equivalent couples are couples with the same momental vector. ·32

·**4.** If $(\mathbf{r}_k, \mathbf{r}_l')$ and $(\mathbf{s}_p, \mathbf{s}_q')$ are couples in the same plane or in parallel planes, a couple $(\mathbf{t}_p, \mathbf{t}_q')$ equivalent to $(\mathbf{r}_k, \mathbf{r}_l')$ can be located in p and q, on the assumption that these are distinct lines, and since the pair of couples $(\mathbf{s}_p, \mathbf{s}_q')$ and $(\mathbf{t}_p, \mathbf{t}_q')$ is equivalent to the single couple $(\mathbf{s}+\mathbf{t})_p, (\mathbf{s}+\mathbf{t})_q'$, °the pair of ·41
couples $(\mathbf{r}_k, \mathbf{r}_l')$ and $(\mathbf{s}_p, \mathbf{s}_q')$ also is equivalent to this couple; if p and q coincide, $(\mathbf{s}_p, \mathbf{s}_q')$ is equivalent to the zero rotor and °the pair of couples $(\mathbf{r}_k, \mathbf{r}_l')$ and ·42
$(\mathbf{s}_p, \mathbf{s}_q')$ is equivalent to the one couple $(\mathbf{r}_k, \mathbf{r}_l')$. Again, if $(\mathbf{r}_k, \mathbf{r}_l')$ and $(\mathbf{s}_p, \mathbf{s}_q')$ are couples in planes which intersect, and if A, B are any distinct points on the line of intersection, then through A, B can be drawn a pair of distinct parallel lines m, n in the plane of the first couple and a pair of distinct parallel lines s, t in the plane of the second couple; there is a couple $(\mathbf{u}_m, \mathbf{u}_n')$ equivalent to $(\mathbf{r}_k, \mathbf{r}_l')$, and there is a couple $(\mathbf{v}_s, \mathbf{v}_t')$ equivalent to $(\mathbf{s}_p, \mathbf{s}_q')$; $\mathbf{u}_m+\mathbf{v}_s$ is a

·43 rotor $\mathbf{t}_f$ through A, and $\mathbf{u}_n' + \mathbf{v}_t'$ is a rotor $\mathbf{t}_g'$ through B, and °the two rotors $\mathbf{t}_f$, $\mathbf{t}_g'$ compose a couple equivalent to the pair of couples $(\mathbf{r}_k, \mathbf{r}_l')$ and $(\mathbf{s}_p, \mathbf{s}_q')$.
·44 Hence °any pair of couples is equivalent to a single couple, and therefore

·45 *Any set formed of a finite number of couples is equivalent to a single couple,*

·46 which is called a °*sum* of the set. If the existence of an equivalent couple is known its form can be predicted, for by 1·35

·47 *The momental vector of a couple equivalent to a set of couples is the sum of the momental vectors of the individual couples.*

Direct proof of this important result is easy to construct in the case of two components, on the lines of the work proving the existence of a sum, and the result for any finite number of couples follows at once, but it must be said that the ingenuity which constructs such proofs is to a considerable extent wasted, for the proofs are apt to leave the reader wondering why the theorem happens to be true.

·**5.** The last theorem is of such a form as to imply its converse,

·51 *If one vector is the sum of a set of vectors, any couple of which this is the momental vector can be expressed as a sum of couples with the component vectors for momental vectors,*

which enables us to apply to the resolution of couples known results on the resolution of vectors. To take only the result immediately required, from 15·12 we see that

·52 *If a line k and a plane L are not parallel, any couple may be expressed as the sum of a couple in any plane at right angles to k and a couple in some plane at right angles to L,*

and taking for k a line at right angles to a plane K and for L a plane at right angles to a line l, we can write the same theorem in the form that

·53 *If a line l and a plane K are not parallel, any couple may be expressed as the sum of a couple in K and a couple in some plane through l.*

245. Reduction of sets of rotors; reduced sets.

·**1.** The only sets of rotors which as yet we have considered in detail are sets of concurrent rotors and sets of couples, but to pass from these special sets to sets of any kind requires only two simple results concerning the combination in a particular case of a rotor and a couple.

If $\mathbf{r}_l$ is a rotor and $(\mathbf{s}_m, \mathbf{s}_n')$ is a couple in a plane containing l, then if $\mathbf{s}$ is not the zero vector, $\mathbf{r}$ is different either from $\mathbf{s}'$ or from $\mathbf{s}$, and whether or not l is parallel to m and n the set $(\mathbf{r}_l, \mathbf{s}_m, \mathbf{s}_n')$ is equivalent either to a set of the form $((\mathbf{r}+\mathbf{s})_p, \mathbf{s}_n')$ or to a set of the form $((\mathbf{r}+\mathbf{s}')_q, \mathbf{s}_m)$; further, unless $\mathbf{r}$ is the zero vector no *couple* can have either of these forms, and the pair which is
·13 equivalent to $(\mathbf{r}_l, \mathbf{s}_m, \mathbf{s}_n')$ is equivalent to a single rotor $\mathbf{r}_k$: °*a couple and a*

proper rotor parallel to the plane of the couple are together equivalent to a single rotor with the vector of the given rotor. On the other hand, if $\mathbf{r}_k$ is any rotor and O is any point, and if l is the line through O parallel to k, the rotor $\mathbf{r}_k$ is equivalent to the set $(\mathbf{r}_k, \mathbf{r}_l, \mathbf{r}_l')$ which is equivalent to the rotor $\mathbf{r}_l$ and the couple $(\mathbf{r}_k, \mathbf{r}_l')$ together: ° *any rotor is equivalent to a rotor through an* ·16
arbitrary point together with a couple, the rotor anchored to the arbitrary point O having the vector of the given rotor $\mathbf{r}_k$, and the couple having for its momental vector the momental vector of $\mathbf{r}_k$ about O.

·2. We are now in a position to describe the simplest forms of sets of rotors equivalent to any given set F, which may be regarded either as a set of rotors and couples or as a set of rotors only. If O is any point of space, any rotor belonging to F is equivalent by ·16 to a rotor through O together with a couple, and therefore the set F is equivalent to a set of rotors concurrent in O together with a set of couples; the set of concurrent rotors is equivalent by 33·31 to a single rotor through O, and the set of couples is equivalent by 4·45 to a single couple, provided only that the numbers of rotors and couples are finite:

Any set F containing a finite number of rotors and couples is equivalent to a ·21
set composed of a single rotor through an arbitrary point O and a single couple; the rotor is the rotor through O whose vector is the vector of the set F, and for the couple may be taken any couple whose momental vector is the momental vector of the set F about the point O,

the last result coming simply from the fact that the momental vector about O of a rotor through O is necessarily the zero vector.

·3. A set composed of a rotor and a couple is called a °*reduced* set of rotors. ·31
If the set does not degenerate into a rotor alone or a couple alone, the axis of the rotor is called the *axis* of the set and the plane of the couple is called the *plane* of the set; the set is said to *pass through* any point of its axis or to be a reduced set *at* any such point. If a reduced set has a proper rotor but a zero couple, the set has a definite axis but no unique plane, while if the rotor is zero the set passes through every point of space. Should a reduced set formed of the rotor $\mathbf{s}_l$ and the couple $\mathbf{U}_{mn}$ be equivalent to a couple $\mathbf{V}_{pq}$, the vector $\mathbf{s}$ is zero and therefore $\mathbf{V}_{pq}$ is equivalent to $\mathbf{U}_{mn}$ itself. But for the set to be equivalent to a single rotor $\mathbf{r}_k$, it is sufficient that the pair of rotors $(\mathbf{r}_k, \mathbf{s}_l')$ be equivalent to the couple $\mathbf{U}_{mn}$; ° a reduced set is equivalent to a single rotor ·35
if and only if the rotor of the set is a proper rotor parallel to the plane of the couple. If two reduced sets are equivalent their rotors have the same vector, and it follows that

Equivalent reduced sets of rotors have parallel axes, and if two such sets have ·36
the same axis their rotors are identical and their couples are equivalent.

It is necessary for us to observe that the second part of this theorem has a species of converse; if equivalent reduced sets have rotors $\mathbf{r}_l$, $\mathbf{r}_p$ with distinct axes, and if the couples of the sets are $\mathbf{R}_{mn}$, $\mathbf{S}_{qr}$, then $\mathbf{S}_{qr}$ is the sum of the couples $(\mathbf{r}_l, \mathbf{r}_p')$, $\mathbf{R}_{mn}$; hence if $\mathbf{R}_{mn}$, $\mathbf{S}_{qr}$ have parallel planes, l and p are parallel to these planes and the sets are equivalent to a single rotor:

·37 *If equivalent reduced sets have distinct axes, the planes of their couples can not be parallel unless the sets are equivalent to a rotor alone;*

·38 moreover, °*if a reduced set is equivalent to a proper rotor, either the couple is zero or the plane of the couple is parallel to the axis of the rotor.*

·4. Let K be any plane which is not parallel to the axis l of a reduced set consisting of a rotor $\mathbf{r}_l$ and a couple $\mathbf{R}_{mn}$; by 4·53 a pair of couples $\mathbf{S}_{hk}$ and $\mathbf{T}_{st}$ can be found, together equivalent to $\mathbf{R}_{mn}$, with h and k parallel to l and the plane through s and t parallel to K, and by ·13, since $\mathbf{r}_l$ is parallel to the plane through h and k, there is a single rotor $\mathbf{r}_q$ equivalent to the set formed of the rotor $\mathbf{r}_l$ and the couple $\mathbf{S}_{hk}$; utilising ·21, ·36, and ·37 we have the theorem

·41 *If K is any plane not parallel to the vector of a set of rotors, there is one and only one line q parallel to this vector such that the equivalent reduced sets with q for axis have their couples in planes parallel to K.*

The construction by which this result has been proved fails if the vector $\mathbf{r}$ is zero, for there is then no single rotor equivalent to the compound of $\mathbf{r}_l$ and $\mathbf{S}_{hk}$ unless $\mathbf{S}_{hk}$ also is zero; in the same case ·37 can not be applied; but in the last enunciation the possibility of this failure is formally excluded, for if $\mathbf{r}$ is zero there are no planes not parallel to $\mathbf{r}$. If $\mathbf{r}$ is not zero, the construction does not fail if K is taken at right angles to $\mathbf{r}$, and if $\mathbf{r}$ is zero and K is parallel to a couple equivalent to the set, $\mathbf{r}$ may be regarded as located in any line at right angles to K; thus follows Poinsot's theorem*:

·43 *Whatever the nature of a set of rotors, there are equivalent reduced sets with axes at right angles to their planes, and unless the set is equivalent to a single couple the reduced sets of this form have a common axis.*

246. Poinsot sets; motors; addition of motors; screws; intensity and pitch; momental products and virtual coefficients.

·1. The last theorem shews that a rotor and a couple whose momental vector is parallel to the rotor form a set of a kind far more widely applicable

·11, ·12 than is at first apparent; such a set is called a ° *Poinsot set.* ° Equivalent Poinsot sets have the same rotor and their couples have the same momental vector; the vector and the rotor are parallel, and unless the rotor is zero the

·13 sets have a definite axis. Conversely, °all Poinsot sets with the same rotor

* Enunciated and proved by Poinsot (*J. de l'Éc. Poly.*, vol. VI (cah. 13), p. 184; read 1804, pub. 1806) for the concrete case of forces; so far were mathematicians at that time from appreciating the common element in dissimilar concepts that many years elapsed before the same theorem was proved for the case of angular velocities, and the fundamental identity of the theorems escaped the notice not only of Chasles, the first to enunciate the kinematical result, but of Poinsot himself, who discovered this result independently.

and the same momental vector are equivalent. Thus Poinsot's theorem pre-
pares us for the concept of a *motor*, the fundamental element in a calculus
more comprehensive and not less beautiful than the vector calculus: a motor
is* ° *a rotor associated with a parallel momental vector.* Completely decomposed, ·15
° a motor which is in no way degenerate depends on an axis l with its two ·18
directions Λ, Λ', a vector $\mathbf{r}$ with its two amounts $r, -r$ in the directions Λ, Λ',
which is located in the axis to form the rotor $\mathbf{r}_l$, and a momental vector $\mathbf{R}$
with two amounts $R, -R$ in the same directions, which is not located in l but
is limited by the condition that R/r is a linear magnitude.

·2. ° A motor is *not* a set of rotors. ° Every Poinsot set has a definite motor, ·21, ·22
and if F is any set of rotors, the Poinsot sets equivalent to F have a common
motor, which is called ° the motor of F: ·23

Every set of rotors has one definite motor, and equivalent sets are sets with ·24
the same motor.

The axis of the motor of a set of rotors is called the ° *Poinsot axis* or, for ·25
reasons that will be apparent in our next article, the ° *central axis* of the set, ·26
and the rotor and the momental vector of the motor are called the *principal rotor*
or *Poinsot rotor* and the *principal moment* or *Poinsot moment* of the set. ° The ·27
principal directions are definite even if the Poinsot rotor is zero, unless the
Poinsot moment also is zero. ° If m and n are any two distinct parallel lines ·28
whose plane is at right angles to the axis of a motor with momental vector $\mathbf{R}$, a
couple $\mathbf{R}_{mn}$ with this momental vector can be located in m and n and combined with the rotor of the motor to form a Poinsot set with the given motor;
thus not only has every set of rotors a definite motor but ° *every motor is the* ·29
motor of an infinity of sets of rotors.

·3. Theorems ·24 and ·29 provide the foundations for the theory of addition
of motors: if M is any finite set of motors, each member of M is the motor of
some set of rotors, and sets of rotors corresponding to the different members
of M can be compounded to form a single set of rotors; this set has a definite
motor, which depends only on the members of M, and is called the ° *sum* of ·31
M or of the members of M. The importance of motors depends partly on

* This use of motor is Clifford's (*Proc. L.M.S.*, vol. IV, p. 382, 1873; *Math. Papers*, p. 183). A combination of a force in a line and a couple round the same line is usually called a *dyname*, and this name is adopted by Ball for what Clifford calls a motor.

The word dyname is due to Plücker, whose language in introducing it (*Phil. Trans.*, vol. CLVI, p. 362, 1866) is far from clear; Routh's view (*Anal. Statics*, vol. I, p. 187, 1896) that to Plücker a dyname was any set formed of one force and one couple is defensible, though possibly the word was intended to denote any set of forces which is not equivalent to a single force, but it is at least certain that the idea was of some set of forces, and a motor is *not* a set of rotors, for the momental vector of a couple is not *identical* with the couple itself. The word having been coined, mathematicians may use it as they find best, and may even transfer it to the vocabulary of pure mathematics, leaving its place to be filled by the word *wrench* which Ball employs, but the origin of the word dyname can not be concealed, and although Clifford's word has a kinematical suggestion, this defect is a link with the word vector.

theorem ·24, but the analytical elegance of the motor calculus is due entirely
·32 to the fact that °*every* finite set of motors has a sum which is itself a motor*.

·4. The linear magnitude which is the quotient of the momental vector **R**
of a motor by the vector **r** of the rotor $\mathbf{r}_l$, or of the amount of **R** in either of
·41 its directions by the amount of **r** in the same direction, is called the °*pitch* of
the motor; if **r** is not zero the motor with rotor $\mathbf{r}_l$ and pitch p has momental
·42 vector $p\mathbf{r}$, but °although motors with the zero rotor and different momental
vectors are different motors it is impossible to distinguish between them on
the basis of pitch. The elements determining a motor may be introduced in
any order, and by considering the pitch in advance of the individual vectors
of which it is the ratio we find the relation between the motor calculus and
·43 the theory of screws. A °*screw* is a ray associated with a linear magnitude
which is the pitch of the screw. The motor with rotor $\mathbf{r}_l$, momental vector **R**,
and pitch p has the two screws obtained by associating the pitch p with the
two rays λ, λ' in the axis l; if one of these screws is given, the specification
of the motor may be completed by a statement of the amount of **r** in the
·44 direction of the screw, and this amount is called the °*intensity* of the motor
on the particular screw; if the screws with pitch p on the rays λ, λ' are denoted
by α, α' and if the amounts of **r** in the directions of λ, λ' are r, $-r$, the motor
·45 may be described as °the motor of intensity r on the screw α or as the motor
of intensity $-r$ on the screw α', or more briefly as the motor r on α or $-r$ on
·46 α'. It is to be noticed that °the two screws belonging to one motor differ in
·47 direction but not in pitch; °with the same numerical value $|p|$ for the pitch
and the same axis l for the ray there are four screws, that with pitch p in λ,
that with pitch p in λ', that with pitch $-p$ in λ, and that with pitch $-p$ in λ', and
·48 these are all distinct; it is the second that is the °*reverse* of the first, and a screw
·49 with pitch $-p$ is a °*perverse* of a screw with pitch p on the same axis.

·51 **·5.** Since the two vectors **r**, **R** of a motor are parallel, °their projected product
is the algebraic product rR of their amounts in a common direction; if there is
a proper finite pitch p, the projected product is expressible both as pr^2 and as
R^2/p; if the pitch is either zero or infinite, the projected product is zero. While in
many respects less important than the pitch, the product rR is far more easily
calculated in the common case in which the motor is given not directly but as
the motor of a specified set of rotors, and also therefore if the motor is given as
the sum of a number of motors. To understand this, we have only to consider
the form of the momental product of two reduced sets of rotors. From 3·45
·52 and 3·46, °the momental product of a reduced set with rotor $\mathbf{r}_l$ and couple $\mathbf{R}_{hk}$
and a reduced set with rotor $\mathbf{s}_m$ and couple $\mathbf{S}_{fg}$ is the sum

$$\mathscr{M}\,\mathbf{r}_l\mathbf{s}_m + \mathscr{G}\,\mathbf{r}\mathbf{S} + \mathscr{G}\,\mathbf{s}\mathbf{R};$$

if l is coplanar with m, and in particular if **r** coincides with **s**, the first term is

* In technical language, for the operation of addition motors and vectors yield *groups*
but rotors do not yield a group.

zero, and if further $\mathbf{R}$ coincides with $\mathbf{S}$ the second and third terms are equal: °*the momental product of any two reduced sets of which the rotors have the* ·53
same vector $\mathbf{r}$ *and the couples have the same momental vector* $\mathbf{R}$ *is twice the projected product of* $\mathbf{r}$ *and* $\mathbf{R}$; thus

The momental square of any reduced set is twice the projected product of the ·54
vector of its rotor by the momental vector of its couple.

If then we define the °*momental product of two motors* as the momental product ·55
of any two sets of rotors having those motors, we have the theorem that

The product of the amounts of the two vectors of a motor in either of the ·57
directions of the axis is half the momental square of the motor,

with the implication that

The momental square of a set of rotors is zero if the set is equivalent either ·58
to a single rotor or to a couple, but not otherwise.

·6. To give a trigonometrical expression for the momental product of two motors, we must suppose the rotors $\mathbf{r}_l$, $\mathbf{s}_m$ and the momental vectors $\mathbf{R}$, $\mathbf{S}$ given in the forms r_λ, s_μ and R_Λ, S_M in terms of rays λ, μ in the axes and amounts in the directions of these rays; then by ·52, 36·66, and 3·45 the momental product is

$$rsd_{\mu\lambda} \sin \epsilon_{\lambda\mu} + Rs \cos \epsilon_{\lambda\mu} + Sr \cos \epsilon_{\lambda\mu}; \qquad \cdot 61$$

if neither of the rotors $\mathbf{r}_l$, $\mathbf{s}_m$ is zero,

The momental product of two motors with intensities r, s *on screws* α, β *with* 62
finite pitches p_α, p_β *is*

$$rs\{(p_\alpha + p_\beta) \cos \epsilon_{\alpha\beta} - d_{\alpha\beta} \sin \epsilon_{\alpha\beta}\},$$

$-d_{\alpha\beta}$ being written for $d_{\beta\alpha}$. The linear magnitude which multiplies rs in this expression proves to be of great importance in the theory of screws, and its
half is called the °*virtual coefficient* of the two screws α, β and is denoted ·63
usually by $\varpi_{\alpha\beta}$; by 1·36 °the product $2rs\varpi_{\alpha\beta}$ for the motors of two sets of ·64
rotors can be evaluated directly from the sets themselves. The expression given in ·62 for the momental product of two motors is indeterminate if either of the motors has the zero rotor, but the momental product itself is in any
case definite and is given by the earlier expression ·61; °if both motors have ·65
the zero rotor, the momental product is zero whatever the momental vectors may be, but if one has a proper rotor r_λ and the other has the zero rotor and
momental vector S_M, °the momental product is $rS \cos \epsilon_{\lambda M}$, the projected ·66
product of the vectors r_Λ, S_M. It is to be added that °the virtual coefficient ·67
$\varpi_{\alpha\alpha}$ of two identical screws is simply the pitch p_α.

·7. The general question of the relation of the sum of a number of motors to the individual components we do not propose to consider, but we remark
that °it is only the position of the axis of which the determination remains to ·71
be effected. If the components have rotors with vectors $\mathbf{r}_1$, $\mathbf{r}_2$, ... on axes l_1, l_2, ... and have momental vectors $\mathbf{R}_1$, $\mathbf{R}_2$, ..., while the sum has rotor $\mathbf{r}_l$ and

·72 momental vector $\mathbf{R}$, then °the vector $\mathbf{r}$ is the sum of the vectors $\mathbf{r}_1, \mathbf{r}_2, \ldots$, and the vector $\mathbf{R}$, though it is not the sum of the vectors $\mathbf{R}_1, \mathbf{R}_2, \ldots$, is given in general if $\mathbf{r}$ is not zero by ·62 and 36·66, for if the components can all be regarded as motors with intensities $r_1, r_2, \ldots$ on screws $\alpha_1, \alpha_2, \ldots$ and if the virtual coefficient of the screws α_m, α_n is ϖ_{mn}, then r^2, being the projected square of $\mathbf{r}_1 + \mathbf{r}_2 + \ldots$, is given by

·74 $$r^2 = r_1^2 + r_2^2 + \ldots + 2r_1 r_2 \cos \epsilon_{12} + \ldots,$$

and for the product rR of the amounts of $\mathbf{r}$ and $\mathbf{R}$ in one of their common directions we have from ·57

·75 $$rR = \varpi_{11} r_1^2 + \varpi_{22} r_2^2 + \ldots + 2\varpi_{12} r_1 r_2 + \ldots.$$

We leave to the reader the discussion of the cases in which some of the components have the zero rotor and of those in which $\mathbf{r}$ itself is zero, and refer him to Ball's treatise for developments of the subject.

247. THE REDUCED SETS AND THE ROTOR-PAIRS WITH A GIVEN MOTOR.

·1. It is an easy matter to describe all the reduced sets equivalent to a given Poinsot set, and we have two reasons for giving a description in detail: Poinsot's theorem shews us that in fact we are considering the most general distribution of equivalent reduced sets, and we become acquainted with an arrangement of lines which is of importance in geometry.

·2. Let the rotor $\mathbf{r}_l$ and the couple $\mathbf{R}_{hk}$ form a Poinsot set with a given motor, let Λ denote one direction of l, let the amounts of the vectors $\mathbf{r}$, $\mathbf{R}$ in the direction Λ be r, R, and let the pitch R/r be p. Through a point Q of space draw a line f parallel to l, a line m at right angles to f to intersect l in a point O, and a line n at right angles to both f and m; let M represent a direction of m, let N represent the direction of n which makes with M round Λ a positive right angle, and let q be the distance from O to Q in the direction M. There are reduced sets through Q equivalent to the given Poinsot set F, and these sets have a common rotor $\mathbf{r}_f$ and a common momental vector $\mathbf{S}$; if $\mathbf{S}_{st}$ is the couple of one of these sets, the rotor $\mathbf{r}_f$ and the couple $\mathbf{S}_{st}$ are together equivalent to the rotor $\mathbf{r}_l$ and the couple $\mathbf{R}_{hk}$, and therefore the couple $\mathbf{S}_{st}$ is a sum of the couples $\mathbf{R}_{hk}$, $(\mathbf{r}_l, \mathbf{r}_f')$; hence by 4·47 $\mathbf{S}$ is the sum of the vector of amount R in the direction Λ and the vector of amount rq in the direction N. For all positions of Q in m the vector $\mathbf{S}$ is therefore at right angles to m, and a direction of $\mathbf{S}$ may be specified by the angles which the direction Λ makes with it round the direction M; if one of these angles is δ and the corresponding amount of $\mathbf{S}$ is S, then

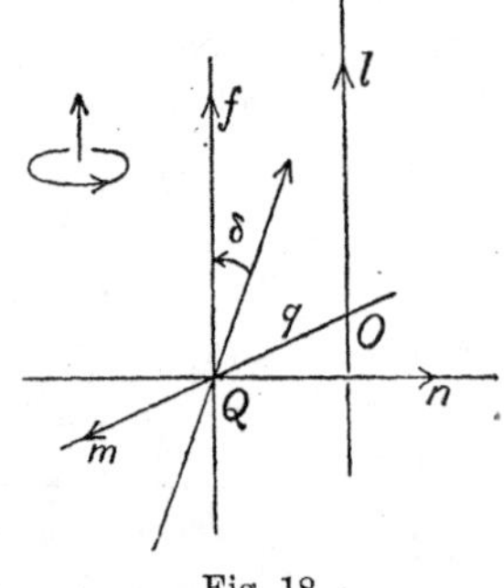

Fig. 18.

·21, ·22 $$S \cos \delta = R, \quad S \sin \delta = rq.$$

If neither R nor r is zero, and if δ varies continuously with q and is zero when
Q is at O, then °δ tends steadily towards $\frac{1}{2}\pi$ as q increases from zero through ·23
positive values, and tends steadily towards $-\frac{1}{2}\pi$ as q decreases from zero
through negative values; S has everywhere the sign of R and its numerical
value increases steadily and indefinitely with the numerical value of q; °at ·24
points equidistant from O and on opposite sides of O, the values of S are the
same and the values of δ are equal and opposite. If R but not r is zero, S is
not zero except when Q is at O, and therefore δ is $\frac{1}{2}\pi$ or $-\frac{1}{2}\pi$ except when
q is zero; the conventions that present the distribution in this case most
clearly as a limiting form of the general distribution °define δ either to be ·25
$\frac{1}{2}\pi$ when q is positive, 0 when q is zero, and $-\frac{1}{2}\pi$ when q is negative, or to
be $-\frac{1}{2}\pi$ when q is positive, 0 when q is zero, and $\frac{1}{2}\pi$ when q is negative;
then °S has everywhere except at O the same sign, and its numerical value ·26
increases steadily and indefinitely with the distance between O and Q, and it
is still true that at points equidistant from O and on opposite sides of O the
values of S are the same and the values of δ are equal and opposite. °If r but ·27
not R is zero, it is natural to regard δ as everywhere zero and S as equal to
R; °if R and r are both zero, S is everywhere zero and δ is entirely arbitrary; ·28
°in the last two cases, no simple conventions restore an analogy to the general ·29
distribution, and O is not distinguished intrinsically from other points of the line.

·3. We are now acquainted with the relations between equivalent reduced sets through different points on one line parallel to the axis of their common motor and through different points on one line intersecting this axis at right angles, or in brief through different points of a plane through the central axis; to complete our view we must consider different planes, and since equations ·21, ·22 involve no magnitude dependent on the position of the
plane we may say that ° the relation of a reduced set with any axis to the ·32
plane through that axis and the central axis is independent of the actual
position of this plane. If we imagine the line f of the last paragraph to rotate
round l, tracing a circular cylinder with radius q and axis l, then ° in every ·33
position of Q and f the line through Q with the directions of $\mathbf{S}$ touches this
cylinder, and the acute angle from a direction of this line to a direction of
f round an outward normal to the cylinder is everywhere the same, being the
acute angle whose tangent is rq/R, that is, °q/p, where p is the pitch of the ·35
motor; the name of central axis needs no further justification, and we note
that °the distribution about the central axis depends only on the pitch. ·36

·4. With the notation of ·2, we impose no restriction on the motor if we take one of the lines in which the couple $\mathbf{S}_{st}$ is located to intersect the axis of the rotor $\mathbf{r}_f$. But if s intersects f, the rotors in these lines are together equivalent to a single rotor, and therefore the rotor $\mathbf{r}_f$ and the couple $\mathbf{S}_{st}$ are together equivalent to a pair of rotors:

There is an infinity of rotor-pairs with any given motor. ·41

If the pair of rotors (s_κ, t_λ) is equivalent to a given set of rotors F, the set $F - s_\kappa$, obtained by compounding with F the reverse of s_κ, is equivalent to the single rotor t_λ, and therefore $\mathscr{M}(F - s_\kappa)^2$ is zero. On the other hand, by 6·58, if $\mathscr{M}(F - s_\kappa)^2$ is zero, then F is equivalent either to s_κ together with a single rotor or to s_κ together with a couple; the latter case is easily recognised, since it occurs if and only if the vector of s_κ is the vector of F.

Expressing the condition for $\mathscr{M}(F - s_\kappa)^2$ to be zero in the form

·42 $$\mathscr{M}F^2 - 2s\,\mathscr{M}F1_\kappa = 0,$$

we can distinguish several possibilities. If $\mathscr{M}F^2$ is zero, the condition requires s to be zero unless $\mathscr{M}F1_\kappa$, the moment of F about the ray κ, is zero, but is satisfied for every value of s in the exceptional case; this conclusion can be verified without difficulty by elementary arguments. If $\mathscr{M}F^2$ is not zero, ·42 is satisfied, for a given ray κ, by one definite value of s if the moment of F about κ is not zero, but can not be satisfied at all if this moment does vanish.

·51 **·5.** We* shall call a ray °*impotent* for a set of rotors if the moment of the
·52 set about the ray is zero. °If κ is impotent for a set F, so also is the reverse
·53 of κ, and the term may be applied to the line in which the rays lie. °A line or a ray that is impotent for F is impotent for every set equivalent to F, and therefore is said to be impotent for the motor of F.

It follows from 1·38 that

·54 *A line through a point Q is impotent for a given set of rotors if and only if it is perpendicular to the momental vector of the set about Q.*

If the momental vector is proper, the condition limits the line to a definite plane through Q; to discuss the relation of this plane to the central axis and the pitch would be to repeat the substance of ·2.

·6. Returning to ·42, we can now substitute for ·41 the more complete theorem that

·61 *If a line is neither impotent for a set of rotors nor in the principal directions of the set, there is one and only one rotor-pair that is equivalent to the set and has one of its constituents located in the line.*

·62 °The momental square of a rotor-pair is twice the momental product of the two constituents; hence

·63 *If two rotor-pairs are equivalent, the momental product of the constituents of one is equal to the momental product of the constituents of the other.*

·64 °A cotractor of two lines is impotent for any rotor-pair located in the lines. If the rotor $\mathbf{r}_l$ and the couple $\mathbf{R}_{mn}$ compose a Poinsot set equivalent to a rotor-pair $(\mathbf{s}_p, \mathbf{t}_q)$, then because $\mathbf{r}$ is $\mathbf{s} + \mathbf{t}$, a line perpendicular both to $\mathbf{s}$ and to $\mathbf{t}$ is perpendicular to $\mathbf{r}$ and therefore, if $\mathbf{r}$ is proper, to $\mathbf{R}$ also. Hence a normal

* We have to avoid the accepted term *nul*, because of its established position in the theory of complex space.

cotractor of p and q is impotent both for the couple $\mathbf{R}_{mn}$ alone and for the Poinsot set; it follows that the moment of $\mathbf{r}_l$ about the normal cotractor is zero:

If a rotor-pair is not equivalent to a couple, its central axis cuts at right angles ·66
any normal cotractor of the two lines in which the rotor-pair is situated.

248. Uses of the word 'sum'.

·1. Every set of vectors has a definite sum which is a vector, every set of motors has a definite sum which is a motor, but with the concepts of rotors and couples, which in a sense are intermediate between the concept of vectors and the concept of motors, addition presents features of difficulty.

·2. The case of couples is indeed peculiar; we can add, in a perfectly
natural sense, any number of couples, and the result is a couple, but ° there is ·21
no one couple which has the right to be called *the* sum; different processes of
addition in general lead to couples which though equivalent are distinct. If
we devote attention only to the momental vectors of couples, uniqueness of sum
reappears, but a °momental vector is not itself a rotor or a set of rotors, nor is it ·22
in any general sense a sum of a set of rotors, and momental vectors alone are
intrinsically incapable of serving the purposes for which couples are required.

·3. With rotors it is still more evident than with couples that there is difficulty in defining a sum, for in this case addition even is not generally possible. Were there only one Poinsot set equivalent to any set of rotors we might call that Poinsot set the sum, but in fact there is an infinity of such sets. We can find a pair of rotors equivalent to any set of rotors, but there is an infinity of such pairs and no one of them has an intrinsic claim to precedence.

·4. In short, we can not speak in an elementary sense of *the* sum of a number of couples or of a number of rotors; nevertheless, there are two different methods of effecting the economies which result from the use of the word sum.

·5. We can °*define the use of certain phrases into which the* WORD '*sum*' ·51
enters, and as long as our work contains the word only in the phrases defined,
the absence of a concept corresponding to the word can lead to no fallacies.

On this plan, we agree to *say* that two sets of rotors ° *have the same sum* or ·52
that one is *a sum* of the other as an alternative method of expressing that the
sets are equivalent, and to *say* that one set of rotors is ° *a sum* of a number ·53
of sets if the one set is equivalent to the compound of the others; in this
sense °a Poinsot set is a sum of any set to which it is equivalent. ·54

·6. But the method* of Frege and Russell can be used to define a definite concept as *the sum* of a set of couples or of rotors, and the definition can be

* Devised first by Frege (*Grundlagen der Arithmetik*, 1879) and independently by Russell (*Principles of Mathematics*, 1903) for dealing with the classical difficulties of number, and applied by these writers and others to the solution of a multitude of mathematical and philosophical problems.

made in a number of ways which are not equivalent. In the case of couples,
we can discover of any couple whether it is or is not equivalent to a sum of
a number of couples in the elementary sense, merely by examining whether
the momental vector of the proposed couple is or is not the sum of the
momental vectors of the individual couples; thus if C is any finite set of
couples, there is a definite class composed of all the couples that are equivalent
·62 to the set C, and °this *class* of couples may be defined as *the sum* of C or of
the members of C: that the class is itself infinite, in the sense of containing
an infinity of members, does not render the concept of the class less definite.
·63 From the definition it follows that °sets of couples with the same sum are
·64 equivalent sets; *a* sum of a number of couples may be defined to mean °a
couple belonging to *the* sum; with this definition we can not speak of a set
of two couples, for example, as a sum of a set of five couples, but in the case
of couples the word sum is naturally used to imply that reduction to the form
of a single couple has been effected.

·7. With rotors there is a difficulty of practice but none of principle; the
sum of a set F is to be a *class of sets equivalent to* F, and we have to decide
·71, ·72 whether this class is to consist of °*all* sets eqüivalent to F, or of °*all reduced*
·73 sets equivalent to F, or of °*all Poinsot* sets equivalent to F. In any case we
·74 have a *definite* concept, and in any case the statement that °equivalent sets
are sets with the same sum follows from the definition and is not itself a
definition; it is unnecessary for us to make an irrevocable choice, and indeed
we may distinguish the three classes as the complete sum, the reduced sum,
·75 and the Poinsot sum, but we notice that °if every compound of a number of
sets is to be a sum of the sets we must use the complete sum and sacrifice
any advantages that might follow from supposing a sum necessarily to have
a simple form.

·8. Whatever our language, notation must allow the equation

$$F + G = H,$$

where F, G, H refer to three sets of rotors, to assert that H is equivalent to a compound of F and G. Thus arises a problem similar to that presented in our first chapter (see p. 6) by the addition of angles. To effect a solution, we may suppose F, G, H to be indefinite symbols, denoting unspecified members of classes of equivalent sets, or we may regard them as symbols for the classes themselves. With either interpretation, the sign of equality has its universal meaning and is not misappropriated to serve as a sign of equivalence in the special sense which the latter word bears in the theory of rotors.

BOOK III

CARTESIAN AXES AND VECTOR FRAMES

CHAPTER III 1

TRIGONOMETRY OF PLANE AND SPHERICAL TRIANGLES

311. Plane triangles with directed sides. 312. Spherical triangles; the polar and the colunars of a spherical triangle. 313. Fundamental formulae and simple deductions. 314. The index of measurement and its uses.

311. Plane triangles with directed sides.

·1. An instructive exercise, and a valuable introduction to the work on
spherical triangles in the succeeding sections, which is essential to our progress,
is the formation of definitions for an ordered triangle whose sides are rays. We
take three rays α, β, γ in a plane; for the plane we assume a cyclic direction, and
°of the rays we assume only that no two of their axes are parallel. Then β and γ ·12
intersect in a point A, while γ and α intersect in a point B, and α and β in a
point C, and °either A, B, C are three distinct points, or they coalesce in a single ·13
point. The distances from B to C in the direction of α, from C to A in the direction
of β, and from A to B in the direction of γ, are called the °sides, or more fully ·14
the lengths of the sides, of the triangle, and are denoted by a, b, c; each of these
sides is a definite real number, but there is no reason to suppose any of them
positive, nor is there any relation between their signs. Angles at A from β
to γ are called °external angles of the triangle at A; the supplement of an ·17
external angle at A is an angle from γ to the reverse of β, and is called an
°internal angle at A; all internal angles at A are congruent, and one of these* ·18
angles is chosen arbitrarily to be described as °*the* first angle of the triangle ·19
and is denoted by A; the definitions of external and internal angles at B and
C are similar, and selection from among the internal angles provides B and C,
the second and third angles of the triangle; instead of making the selections
at A, B, C entirely independent, we may make one choice depend on the other
two in such a way as to retain the familiar value for the sum of the angles,
but with any combination of selections the sum is congruent with π, and there
is little to be gained by a limitation.

·2. It is to be noticed that °the values of the sides and angles of a triangle ·21
of rays depend on the order of the rays; if the triangle $\alpha\beta\gamma$ has sides a, b, c

* In order not to confuse, we describe a procedure in accord with elementary usage, but the reader will recognise that there is something to be said in favour of expressing formulae in terms of *external* angles A', B', C'. Theoretically this practice is natural, and of the two formulae

$$A'+B'+C'=2\pi, \quad A+B+C=\pi$$

the former leads to the more elegant identities, but the expression of a as $-b\cos C'-c\cos B'$ has nothing to recommend it, and for a right-angled triangle the use of external angles is quite indefensible.

and external angles A', B', C', the triangle $\alpha\gamma\beta$ has sides $-a$, $-c$, $-b$, and
·22 may be taken as having external angles $-A'$, $-C'$, $-B'$. °A triangle of rays is an ordered triangle in every definition, not merely in definitions involving
·23 implicitly the sign. °The sign of the triangle $\alpha\beta\gamma$ is taken to be the same as the sign of the triangle ABC, and not to depend on the directions of α, β, γ along the undirected lines BC, CA, AB.

·3. The perpendicular distances of A from α, of B from β, of C from γ, are the
·31 three °altitudes of the triangle, and we denote them by p, q, r. If a is positive, A is on the positive or the negative side of α according as the sign of the triangle is positive or negative, and the sign of p is the sign of the triangle;

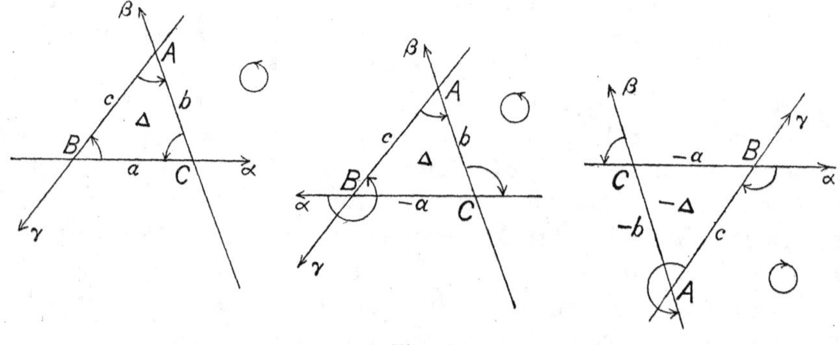

Fig. 19.

if a is negative, the direction from B to C is the reverse of the direction of α and the sign of p is opposite to the sign of the triangle; thus in any case
·34 °the sign of the product ap is the sign of the triangle, and $\frac{1}{2}ap$ is Δ, the area of the triangle:

·35 $$2\Delta = ap = bq = cr.$$

·4. If we denote the actual vectors of the steps BC, CA, AB by $\mathbf{a}$, $\mathbf{b}$, $\mathbf{c}$, the trigonometry of the triangle is contained in the relations

·41 $$\mathbf{a} + \mathbf{b} + \mathbf{c} = 0,$$

·42 $$\mathscr{G}\,\mathbf{bc} = -\,bc\cos A,$$

·43 $$\mathscr{A}\,\mathbf{bc} = bc\sin A.$$

Thus $$a^2 = \mathscr{G}\,\mathbf{a}^2 = -\,\mathscr{G}\,\mathbf{a}(\mathbf{b}+\mathbf{c}) = a(b\cos C + c\cos B)$$

·45 gives $$a = b\cos C + c\cos B,$$

and $$a^2 = \mathscr{G}\,\mathbf{a}^2 = \mathscr{G}(\mathbf{b}+\mathbf{c})^2 = \mathscr{G}\,\mathbf{b}^2 + \mathscr{G}\,\mathbf{c}^2 + 2\,\mathscr{G}\,\mathbf{bc}$$

·46 gives $$a^2 = b^2 + c^2 - 2bc\cos A,$$

while from ·41 $$\mathscr{A}\,\mathbf{a}(\mathbf{a}+\mathbf{b}+\mathbf{c}) = 0,$$

whence $$\mathscr{A}\,\mathbf{ca} = \mathscr{A}\,\mathbf{ab},$$

·49 giving $$c\sin B = b\sin C.$$

·5. Further, if s denotes $\frac{1}{2}(a+b+c)$, ·46 gives

$$bc(1+\cos A)=2s(s-a),\quad bc(1-\cos A)=2(s-b)(s-c),$$ ·51

whence on the one hand

$$\cos^2\tfrac{1}{2}A=s(s-a)/bc,\quad \sin^2\tfrac{1}{2}A=(s-b)(s-c)/bc,$$ ·52

and on the other hand

$$\Delta\cot\tfrac{1}{2}A=s(s-a),\quad \Delta\tan\tfrac{1}{2}A=(s-b)(s-c),$$ ·53

leading to $$\Delta^2=s(s-a)(s-b)(s-c),$$ ·54

$$\frac{\cos\frac{1}{2}B\cos\frac{1}{2}C}{s}=\frac{\sin\frac{1}{2}B\sin\frac{1}{2}C}{s-a}=\frac{\cos\frac{1}{2}(B-C)}{b+c}=\frac{\cos\frac{1}{2}(B+C)}{a},$$ ·55

$$\frac{\sin\frac{1}{2}B\cos\frac{1}{2}C}{s-c}=\frac{\sin\frac{1}{2}C\cos\frac{1}{2}B}{s-b}=\frac{\sin\frac{1}{2}(B-C)}{b-c}=\frac{\sin\frac{1}{2}(B+C)}{a}.$$ ·56

Since we have extracted no square roots, there can be no ambiguities in these formulae, but °it is not open to us to argue that the sines and cosines of the ·57
angles $\frac{1}{2}A$, $\frac{1}{2}B$, $\frac{1}{2}C$ are necessarily positive or to replace $\cos\frac{1}{2}(B+C)$ and $\sin\frac{1}{2}(B+C)$ by $\sin\frac{1}{2}A$ and $\cos\frac{1}{2}A$.

·6. If certain formulae of plane trigonometry threaten to evade us, we can recapture them by a simple device. The value of k given by

$$A+B+C=(2n+k)\pi,$$ ·61

where n is an integer and k is either $+1$ or -1, depends not only on the triangle itself, but on the measurements adopted for the angles; let k be
called the °*index of measurement*. Then since $\cos\frac{1}{2}(B+C)$, $\sin\frac{1}{2}(B+C)$ can ·62
be identified with $\sin\frac{1}{2}A$, $\cos\frac{1}{2}A$ if k is $+1$ and with $-\sin\frac{1}{2}A$, $-\cos\frac{1}{2}A$ if k is -1, we can write

$$\cos\tfrac{1}{2}(B+C)=k\sin\tfrac{1}{2}A,\quad \sin\tfrac{1}{2}(B+C)=k\cos\tfrac{1}{2}A,$$ ·63

and therefore

$$\frac{\cos\frac{1}{2}(B-C)}{b+c}=\frac{k\sin\frac{1}{2}A}{a},\quad \frac{\sin\frac{1}{2}(B-C)}{b-c}=\frac{k\cos\frac{1}{2}A}{a},$$ ·64

$$abc\cos\tfrac{1}{2}A\cos\tfrac{1}{2}B\cos\tfrac{1}{2}C=ks\Delta,\quad abc\cos\tfrac{1}{2}A\sin\tfrac{1}{2}B\sin\tfrac{1}{2}C=k(s-a)\Delta.$$ ·65

It is to be remembered that there is only *one* index; in formulae deduced by transposition from those given in full, k is unaltered.

312. Spherical triangles; the polar and the colunars of a spherical triangle.

·1. The spherical triangle* which is of use in analytical geometry is a triangle in which definite directions are given to the three great circles forming the sides. To specify a triangle of rays in a plane we may give the three

* With this section compare the early paragraphs in ch. 19 of Leathem's edition (1901) of Todhunter's *Spherical Trigonometry*; there *the* sides and *the* external angles are chosen to be positive and less than 2π, but it is equally useful in practice to suppose them positive or negative but numerically less than π, and we prefer not to commit ourselves to a particular system. The chapter on spherical trigonometry in Darboux's *Principes* (pp. 201–215),

vertices and the directions of the three sides, or we may state simply the three rays which form the sides; to describe a spherical triangle, we may state the three vertices and the directions of the three sides, but it is not sufficient to specify only the three prepared circles which form the sides without indicating which of the two points of intersection of each pair of sides is to be used as a vertex. For the sake of brevity we speak of *the* spherical triangle with assigned vertices, but it is to be understood that definite directions are given to the sides.

·2. There is one characteristic of a spherical triangle ABΓ which does not
depend on the directions of the sides. If the directions of the sides of the
triangle are determined by the convention that the least positive angles from
B to Γ, from Γ to A, and from A to B, in the directions of the sides, are all
·22 less than π, then* °either each vertex is on the positive side of the opposite
great circle or each vertex is on the negative side of the corresponding circle,
and the triangle itself is said to be positive in the one case, negative in the
other case; the sign of a particular spherical triangle is of course dependent
on the spatial convention, but whether two ordered spherical triangles have
the same sign or different signs depends on no arbitrary convention, and it is
·25 always a comparison of different triangles that is fundamental. °The sign of
the spherical triangle ABΓ on a sphere whose centre is O is the sign of the
tetrahedron OABΓ; two spherical triangles whose corresponding parts are
equal numerically are congruent if they have the same sign, but if their signs
differ each is a perverse of the other.

·3. If a, b, c are three prepared great circles forming the sides of a spherical
triangle ABΓ, the angles from B to Γ along a, from Γ to A along b, and from

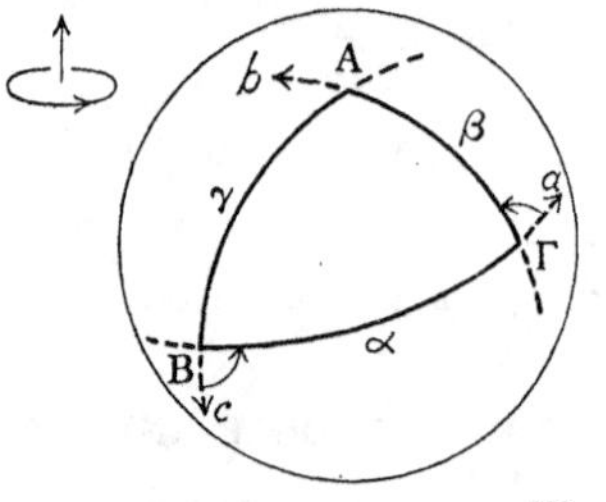

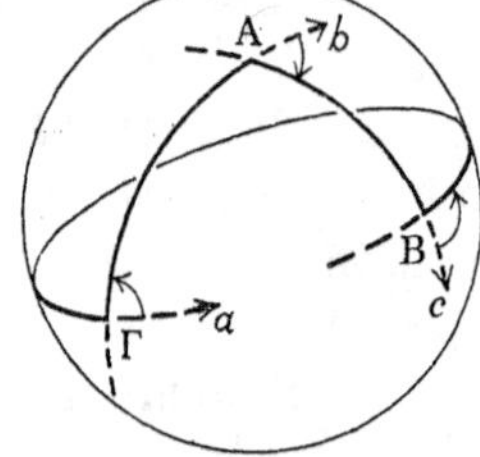

Fig. 20.

A to B along c, compose three congruences, and representative angles are
·31 chosen arbitrarily from these congruences to be called °*the* sides of the triangle
and to be denoted by BΓ, ΓA, AB, or by α, β, γ. Similarly the angles from b

develops the formulae without supposing the elements even to be real; it will be found that the treatment of complex space in Book V below does not depend on the formulae of this section or the next, but on the contrary enables us to interpret these sections retrospectively as valid on complex spheres. Darboux uses the external angles as a matter of course.

* The right-hand diagram in fig. 20, in which one of the least positive angles is between π and 2π, helps us to realise that the conclusion is dependent on the hypothesis.

to c round A, from c to a round B, and from a to b round Γ, compose three
congruences, and chosen members of these congruences are called °*the* external ·32
angles of the triangle and are denoted by Γ′AB, A′BΓ, B′ΓA or by A, B, Γ; by
subtracting the external angles from π we obtain the °internal angles. Any ·33
one of the sides or angles of a spherical triangle may have any value, positive
or negative, which is not an integral multiple of π, and between the circular
functions of the three sides and the three external angles there are many
relations, whose systematic study is the first concern of spherical trigonometry.
If O is the centre of the sphere on which the spherical triangle ABΓ is
situated, the function sin OABΓ of which we have already spoken is called
the °sine of the triangle itself; this function is independent of the directions ·34
of the sides of the triangle, and its sign is that of the triangle; every change
in the order of the vertices is without effect on the numerical value of the
sine, but while a cyclic* change leaves the sign also unaffected, a change that
is not cyclic reverses the sign:

$$\sin \mathrm{OAB\Gamma} = \sin \mathrm{OB\Gamma A} = \sin \mathrm{O\Gamma AB},$$ ·35

$$\sin \mathrm{OA\Gamma B} = -\sin \mathrm{OAB\Gamma}.$$

For brevity we shall °denote sin OABΓ by $\Upsilon_{\mathrm{AB\Gamma}}$, or when no ambiguity is ·36
possible by Υ simply.

·4. A definite spatial convention gives to the directed great circles a, b, c which
form the sides of the triangle ABΓ definite positive poles, and these we can
denote without risk of confusion by α, β, γ. Because β is a pole of b, Aβ is a
quadrant, and because γ is a pole of c, Aγ is a quadrant; hence °A is a pole ·42
of the great circle through β and γ, and similarly B, Γ are poles of the great
circles through γ and α and through α and β; to say that A, B, Γ are the
positive poles of the great circles $\beta\gamma$, $\gamma\alpha$, $\alpha\beta$, is to assign particular directions
to these great circles, and the circles with directions so determined we denote
by A, B, C. The triangle with α, β, γ for vertices and A, B, C for sides is
called the °*polar* of the triangle with A, B, Γ for vertices and a, b, c for sides, ·44
and a reader who is becoming impatient of our insistence on the possibility of
distinguishing between positives and negatives will welcome a definite justification of the drawing of such distinctions in the result that °*if one spherical* ·45
triangle is the polar of another the second is the polar of the first. °The sides ·46
of the polar triangle $\alpha\beta\gamma$ are congruent with the external angles of the original
triangle ABΓ, and conversely the external angles of $\alpha\beta\gamma$ are congruent with
the sides of ABΓ; in view of this result we actually °choose A, B, Γ for the ·47

* Fundamentally, the decisive feature is not whether the change is cyclic or acyclic but whether there is an even or an odd derangement of the four letters O, A, B, Γ (see 132·16 on p. 21 above, and the accompanying foot-note); the position of O being unalterable, the question is one of transpositions in the three letters A, B, Γ, and it is a peculiarity of interchanges with three symbols that cyclic changes are even and acyclic changes are odd; with any odd number of symbols all cyclic changes are even, but if the number is greater than three there are also acyclic changes which are even.

sides and α, β, γ for the external angles of the triangle $\alpha\beta\gamma$ when we wish to dwell on the relation between the two triangles; the statement that

·48 *If two spherical triangles are polars of each other, the sides of each are the external angles of the other,*

adds a definition to a theorem, and is typical of a number of enunciations of value in analytical geometry. The consideration of the sides and angles of the polar $\alpha\beta\gamma$ of a triangle ABΓ introduces to us no angles which we are not compelled to use in studying ABΓ itself, but the sine of the polar triangle, which is called the polar sine of ABΓ, is not expressible merely as a function of sin OABΓ, and has an independent importance*; it is to be remarked that
·49 the polar of a positive triangle may be either positive or negative. °The sine of the polar triangle will be denoted by $\upsilon_{AB\Gamma}$ or by υ alone.

·5. By the perimeter of the triangle ABΓ is meant the sum of the sides; this is usually denoted by 2σ. The sum of the angles is denoted by 2Σ and may be called the polar perimeter. The amount by which 2Σ falls short of 2π is the amount by which the sum of the *internal* angles exceeds π and is
·52 called for this reason the°*angular excess* of the triangle; if this angle is denoted† by E and the corresponding angle associated with the polar triangle by ϵ, we have

·55 $$2\sigma = \alpha + \beta + \gamma, \quad 2\Sigma = A + B + \Gamma,$$

·57 $$\epsilon = 2(\pi - \sigma), \qquad E = 2(\pi - \Sigma).$$

·6. The polar triangle is not the only triangle which can usefully be associated with a given triangle.

The circles b, c which meet in A meet also in the diametrically opposite point A', and the triangle with sides a, b, c and vertices A′, B, Γ is called the
·61 °*first colunar* of the triangle with sides a, b, c and vertices A, B, Γ. To leave unchanged the directions of a, b, c is to say that the vertices of the polar of A′BΓ are to be the same as the vertices of the polar of ABΓ, but since in reference to A′BΓ the circle through β and γ is to have A′ for its pole, the sides of the polar of A′BΓ are not the circles A, B, C but the circles A', B, C.
·63 Since the directions of measurement along a, b, c are unchanged, °the sides BΓ, ΓA′, A′B of the colunar are congruent with α, $\beta + \pi$, $\gamma - \pi$, while the

* The reader should be warned that writers on spherical trigonometry are in the habit of taking as fundamental the halves of the sines of a triangle and of its polar, which they call the norm of the sides and the norm of the angles of the triangle and denote by n and N. One elementary text-book quotes Salmon in support of calling the functions n and N sines; Salmon's phrase in the article quoted *is* ambiguous, but his practice is clear and consistent, and is that of von Staudt, which is followed in the text. The use of the norms is due to a comparison of 3·63 and 3·69 below with the classical formula 1·54 for the area of a plane triangle.

† Sometimes 2E is used, and often the excess is called the *spherical* excess. Name and notation are alike unhappy, for the differential geometry of *any* surface requires the angular excess of an arbitrary triangle, but not the half of the excess.

angles are congruent with $-A, B, \Gamma$; we define* *the* sides and *the* angles to have these values. °The perimeter of the colunar is then equal to the perimeter 2σ, and the polar perimeter has the value $2(\Sigma - A)$. °The sine of the colunar is $-\Upsilon$, and its polar sine is υ. ·64 ·65

Mere reversal of the side a of $AB\Gamma$ gives a triangle which bears to $AB\Gamma$ the relation which the polar of the first colunar of $AB\Gamma$ bears to the polar of $AB\Gamma$. This is a triangle whose polar is $\alpha'\beta\gamma$, and we may °take its sides to be $-\alpha, \beta, \gamma$ and its angles to be $A, B+\pi, \Gamma-\pi$; °its perimeter is then $2(\sigma-\alpha)$ and its polar perimeter 2Σ, while °its sine, independently of any convention, is Υ and its polar sine is $-\upsilon$. ·66 ·67 ·68

If the internal angles of a triangle on a sphere of unit radius are all positive and less than π, the triangle and its first colunar together compose a lune of angle A_i, where A_i is the internal angle, and therefore the sum of the areas of these two triangles is the fraction $A_i/2\pi$ of the area of the sphere, that is, is $2A_i$. But the triangle and its opposite together with the three colunars and their opposites compose the whole surface of the sphere. Hence $4(A_i + B_i + \Gamma_i)$ exceeds the area of the sphere by four times the area of the triangle:

On a sphere of unit radius, the area of a triangle each of whose internal angles is positive and less than two right angles is equal to the angular excess of the triangle. ·69

It is this theorem which gives interest to the angular excess, and to formulae by which it can be calculated logarithmically from the sides alone, without the evaluation of the individual angles.

·7. The effect of the existence of triangles related to any given triangle as we have described in ·4 and ·6 is that if

$$f(\alpha, \beta, \gamma, A, B, \Gamma) = 0$$

is a relation which holds between the sides and the external angles of any spherical triangle, the relation

$$f(A, B, \Gamma, \alpha, \beta, \gamma) = 0$$

is equally general, and so also are

$$f(\alpha, \beta+\pi, \gamma-\pi, -A, B, \Gamma) = 0,\ f(-\alpha, \beta, \gamma, A, B+\pi, \Gamma-\pi) = 0,$$
$$f(A, B+\pi, \Gamma-\pi, -\alpha, \beta, \gamma) = 0,\ f(-A, B, \Gamma, \alpha, \beta+\pi, \gamma-\pi) = 0,$$

and the eight relations derivable from these four by allowing β and γ to play the parts here assigned to α; it need hardly be said that the various changes do not necessarily yield distinct formulae.

·8. The fundamental relations between the sides and the angles of a triangle on a sphere can be thrown into many forms, differing in elegance and in utility, but the number of these results required for the purposes of analytical geometry

* It is seldom necessary to distinguish the colunar with sides $a, \beta+\pi, \gamma-\pi$ from the colunar with sides $a, \beta-\pi, \gamma+\pi$.

and for the manipulation of oblique axes is surprisingly small; usually we make direct application of the principles of projection and of the decomposition of vectors (notably of the theorems given in 215·3 and 221·1, applied by means of 221·41), and if we proceed to obtain a few trigonometrical results, it is rather to illustrate the application of these principles and to emphasise the generality of the formulae than from any insistent need of the formulae themselves.

313. Fundamental formulae and simple deductions.

·1. Let the directed circles b and c meet the circle A in the pairs of points Σ_1, Σ_1' and T_1, T_1', the points Σ_1, T_1 being distinguished from their opposites as the points of b, c among whose distances *from* A are *positive* quadrants; then in A the quadrants from Σ_1 to β and from T_1 to γ are positive, and therefore $\cos \Sigma_1 T_1$ is $\cos A$ and $\cos \Sigma_1' T_1$ is $-\cos A$; also, one of the angles from Σ_1' to Γ is $\frac{1}{2}\pi - \beta$, and one of the angles from B to T_1 is $\frac{1}{2}\pi - \gamma$. A unit vector in Γ is therefore the sum of $\cos\beta$ in A and $\sin\beta$ in Σ_1', and a unit vector in B the sum of $\cos\gamma$ in A and $\sin\gamma$ in T_1; symbolically,

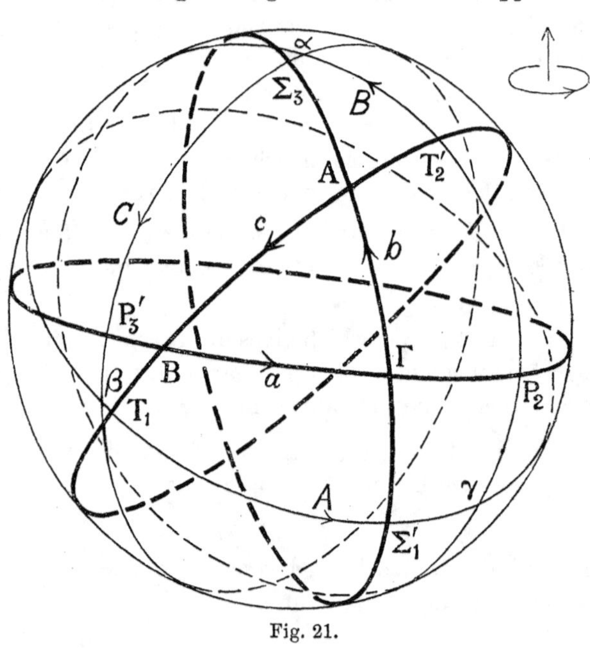

Fig. 21.

·11 $$1_\Gamma = (\cos\beta)_A + (\sin\beta)_{\Sigma_1'}, \quad 1_B = (\cos\gamma)_A + (\sin\gamma)_{T_1}.$$

By 221·44, $\cos \Gamma B$, which is $\cos\alpha$, can be regarded as $\mathscr{S} 1_\Gamma 1_B$, and by 221·16 we can calculate this projected product from ·11 as the sum of four parts; since

$$\cos AA = 1, \quad \cos AT_1 = 0, \quad \cos \Sigma_1' A = 0, \quad \cos \Sigma_1' T_1 = -\cos A,$$

the equality deduced is

·12 $$\cos\alpha = \cos\beta\cos\gamma - \sin\beta\sin\gamma\cos A,$$

the fundamental equation of spherical trigonometry, which implies not only the corresponding formulae for $\cos\beta$ and $\cos\gamma$ but also the complementary formulae obtained by its application to the polar triangle, namely,

·13 $$\cos A = \cos B\cos\Gamma - \sin B\sin\Gamma\cos\alpha$$

and its correlatives. For any triangle right-angled at A, ·12 gives

·14 $$\cos\alpha = \cos\beta\cos\gamma,$$

and for any triangle of which α is a quadrant, ·13 gives

$$\cos \mathrm{A} = \cos \mathrm{B} \cos \Gamma. \qquad \cdot 15$$

Of ·14 and ·15, the first is especially simple to use, since the cosines involved are independent of the directions of the sides of the triangle; moreover, it can be proved with less attention to detail than is necessary in the proof of the general formula ·12, for if the triangle is right-angled at A and Σ is *either* intersection of b with A and T *either* intersection of c with A, the projected product of $(\cos\gamma)_{\mathrm{A}} + m_{\Sigma}$ and $(\cos\beta)_{\mathrm{A}} + n_{\mathrm{T}}$ is $\cos\beta\cos\gamma$ whatever the values of m and n. In ·15, the cosines are independent of the directions of the sides of the polar triangle $\alpha\beta\gamma$, but depend on the directions of the sides of ABΓ.

·2. It is easy to frame proofs of ·12 and its consequences on the basis of projection and decomposition without the use of projected products. Since there are angles $\pi - \mathrm{A}$ from T_1 to Σ_1' and $\mathrm{A} - \frac{1}{2}\pi$ from Σ_1' to γ, the vector $\sin\beta$ in Σ_1' is the sum of $-\sin\gamma\cos\mathrm{A}$ in T_1 and $\sin\gamma\sin\mathrm{A}$ in γ, and the unit vector in Γ is the sum of these two vectors and $\cos\beta$ in A; since γ is at right angles to B, the projection $\cos a$ of 1_Γ on B is the sum of the two projections $\cos\beta\cos\gamma$, $-\sin\beta\cos\mathrm{A}\sin\gamma$. This proof of ·12 lacks the symmetry of the earlier proof, but is equally simple; in more complicated problems the use of projected products often imparts simplicity otherwise unobtainable, permitting as it does the decomposition of *two* vectors instead of the resolution of only one. In the case of a right-angled triangle, the simplest projective proof is perhaps an unsymmetrical proof: if the angles at A are right angles, the projection of 1_Γ on the plane OAB has the directions of A and A′ and its amount in the former of these directions is $\cos\beta$; the fundamental formula ·14 is therefore an immediate consequence of 142·23.

·3. The triangle $\mathrm{T}_2'\alpha\mathrm{A}$, where, in agreement with the notation of ·1, T_2' is the point of intersection of c and B separated from γ by a positive quadrant, is right-angled at T_2'; also one value of $\mathrm{T}_2'\mathrm{A}$ is $\frac{1}{2}\pi - \gamma$ and one value of $\mathrm{T}_2'\alpha$ is $\mathrm{B} - \frac{1}{2}\pi$; hence by ·14

$$\cos \mathrm{A}\alpha = \sin\gamma \sin \mathrm{B}, \qquad \cdot 33$$

and by applying this formula to the polar triangle we have

$$\cos \alpha\mathrm{A} = \sin\beta \sin\Gamma, \qquad \cdot 34$$

so that also*

$$\sin\beta\sin\Gamma = \sin\gamma\sin\mathrm{B}; \qquad \cdot 35$$

at once comes the set of formulae

$$\frac{\sin\alpha}{\sin\mathrm{A}} = \frac{\sin\beta}{\sin\mathrm{B}} = \frac{\sin\gamma}{\sin\Gamma}. \qquad \cdot 36$$

·4. The use of the functions Υ, υ enables us to introduce symmetry without loss of brevity: the result 134·72, proved in a manner which implied its

* From ·35 we have $\sin a \sin\beta\sin\Gamma = \sin\gamma\sin a\sin\mathrm{B}$, and therefore the three products $\sin\beta\sin\gamma\sin\mathrm{A}$, $\sin\gamma\sin a\sin\mathrm{B}$, $\sin a\sin\beta\sin\Gamma$ have a common value. The function sin OABΓ is often *defined* as the function with this value. Since then ·41, which is 134·72, follows at once from ·33, the relation of $\sin QRST$ to the volume of the tetrahedron $QRST$ is readily deduced.

generality, gives on application to a triangle and its polar the two sets of formulae

·41 $$\Upsilon = \cos A\alpha \sin \alpha = \cos B\beta \sin \beta = \cos \Gamma\gamma \sin \gamma,$$

·42 $$\upsilon = \cos A\alpha \sin A = \cos B\beta \sin B = \cos \Gamma\gamma \sin \Gamma;$$

whether in these we substitute expressions of the form contained in ·33 or expressions of the form contained in ·34 the result is the same, the two sets of formulae

·43 $$\Upsilon = \sin \beta \sin \gamma \sin A = \sin \gamma \sin \alpha \sin B = \sin \alpha \sin \beta \sin \Gamma,$$

·44 $$\upsilon = \sin B \sin \Gamma \sin \alpha = \sin \Gamma \sin A \sin \beta = \sin A \sin B \sin \gamma,$$

which give the sines of the triangles in the forms which are the most convenient although unsymmetrical. We can replace ·36 by

·45 $$\frac{\Upsilon}{\upsilon} = \frac{\sin \alpha}{\sin A} = \frac{\sin \beta}{\sin B} = \frac{\sin \gamma}{\sin \Gamma}.$$

The commonest symmetrical expression involving the sine of a triangle expresses the square of this function; we may obtain this formula without difficulty from ·43 and ·12, which give

$$\Upsilon^2 = \sin^2 \beta \sin^2 \gamma - (\cos \beta \cos \gamma - \cos \alpha)^2$$

and therefore

·46 $$\Upsilon^2 = 1 - \cos^2 \alpha - \cos^2 \beta - \cos^2 \gamma + 2 \cos \alpha \cos \beta \cos \gamma,$$

but the essence of the formula is that it can be exhibited in the form

·47 $$\Upsilon^2 = \begin{vmatrix} 1 & \cos \gamma & \cos \beta \\ \cos \gamma & 1 & \cos \alpha \\ \cos \beta & \cos \alpha & 1 \end{vmatrix},$$

and we shall presently find a point of view from which this determinantal form is understood and the crude passages from ·43 and ·12 to ·46 and ·47 are seen to lack even the virtue of necessity. Correlative to ·46 and ·47 are

·48 $$\upsilon^2 = 1 - \cos^2 A - \cos^2 B - \cos^2 \Gamma + 2 \cos A \cos B \cos \Gamma,$$

·49 $$\upsilon^2 = \begin{vmatrix} 1 & \cos \Gamma & \cos B \\ \cos \Gamma & 1 & \cos A \\ \cos B & \cos A & 1 \end{vmatrix}.$$

·5. Any deduction from the fundamental formulae already proved is valid if it does not involve extraction of a root.

For example, elimination of $\cos \beta$ and $\sin \beta$ between

$$\cos \alpha = \cos \beta \cos \gamma - \sin \beta \sin \gamma \cos A,$$

$$\cos \beta = \cos \gamma \cos \alpha - \sin \gamma \sin \alpha \cos B,$$

$$\sin \beta \sin A = \sin \alpha \sin B,$$

gives the relation

·51 $$\cos B \cos \gamma + \cot A \sin B + \cot \alpha \sin \gamma = 0,$$

as useful as it is inelegant; ·51 is typical of a group of six, and application of this group to the polar triangle reproduces the same group in a different order.

Again,

$$\Upsilon^2 = \sin\alpha\sin\beta\sin\Gamma\,.\,\sin\gamma\sin\alpha\sin B = \sin\alpha\sin\beta\sin\gamma\,.\,\sin\alpha\sin B\sin\Gamma,$$

that is, $$\Upsilon^2 = \upsilon\sin\alpha\sin\beta\sin\gamma, \qquad \cdot 52$$

and similarly or from the polar triangle,

$$\upsilon^2 = \Upsilon\sin A\sin B\sin\Gamma. \qquad \cdot 53$$

·6. From ·12 we have

$$\begin{cases}\sin\beta\sin\gamma\,(1+\cos A) = \cos(\beta-\gamma) - \cos\alpha = 2\sin(\sigma-\beta)\sin(\sigma-\gamma),\\ \sin\beta\sin\gamma\,(1-\cos A) = \cos\alpha - \cos(\beta+\gamma) = 2\sin\sigma\sin(\sigma-\alpha),\end{cases}$$

whence we can write both

$$\begin{cases}\cos^2\tfrac{1}{2}A = \sin(\sigma-\beta)\sin(\sigma-\gamma)/\sin\beta\sin\gamma,\\ \sin^2\tfrac{1}{2}A = \sin\sigma\sin(\sigma-\alpha)/\sin\beta\sin\gamma,\end{cases} \qquad \cdot 61$$

and

$$\Upsilon\cot\tfrac{1}{2}A = 2\sin(\sigma-\beta)\sin(\sigma-\gamma),\quad \Upsilon\tan\tfrac{1}{2}A = 2\sin\sigma\sin(\sigma-\alpha), \qquad \cdot 62$$

obtaining the valuable expression

$$\Upsilon^2 = 4\sin\sigma\sin(\sigma-\alpha)\sin(\sigma-\beta)\sin(\sigma-\gamma), \qquad \cdot 63$$

and the equalities

$$\begin{cases}\sin(\sigma-\alpha)\sin\tfrac{1}{2}B\sin\tfrac{1}{2}\Gamma = \sin\sigma\cos\tfrac{1}{2}B\cos\tfrac{1}{2}\Gamma,\\ \sin(\sigma-\gamma)\cos\tfrac{1}{2}\Gamma\sin\tfrac{1}{2}B = \sin(\sigma-\beta)\cos\tfrac{1}{2}B\sin\tfrac{1}{2}\Gamma,\end{cases} \qquad \cdot 64$$

which enable us to write

$$\frac{\cos\frac{1}{2}B\cos\frac{1}{2}\Gamma}{\sin(\sigma-\alpha)} = \frac{\sin\frac{1}{2}B\sin\frac{1}{2}\Gamma}{\sin\sigma} = \frac{\cos\frac{1}{2}(B-\Gamma)}{2\cos\frac{1}{2}\alpha\sin\frac{1}{2}(\beta+\gamma)} = \frac{\cos\frac{1}{2}(B+\Gamma)}{-2\sin\frac{1}{2}\alpha\cos\frac{1}{2}(\beta+\gamma)}, \qquad \cdot 65$$

$$\frac{\sin\frac{1}{2}B\cos\frac{1}{2}\Gamma}{\sin(\sigma-\beta)} = \frac{\sin\frac{1}{2}\Gamma\cos\frac{1}{2}B}{\sin(\sigma-\gamma)} = \frac{\sin\frac{1}{2}(B-\Gamma)}{-2\cos\frac{1}{2}\alpha\sin\frac{1}{2}(\beta-\gamma)} = \frac{\sin\frac{1}{2}(B+\Gamma)}{2\sin\frac{1}{2}\alpha\cos\frac{1}{2}(\beta-\gamma)}. \qquad \cdot 66$$

The correlatives of ·61, ·62, ·63 are

$$\begin{cases}\cos^2\tfrac{1}{2}\alpha = \sin(\Sigma-B)\sin(\Sigma-\Gamma)/\sin B\sin\Gamma,\\ \sin^2\tfrac{1}{2}\alpha = \sin\Sigma\sin(\Sigma-A)/\sin B\sin\Gamma,\end{cases} \qquad \cdot 67$$

$$\upsilon\cot\tfrac{1}{2}\alpha = 2\sin(\Sigma-B)\sin(\Sigma-\Gamma),\quad \upsilon\tan\tfrac{1}{2}\alpha = 2\sin\Sigma\sin(\Sigma-A), \qquad \cdot 68$$

$$\upsilon^2 = 4\sin\Sigma\sin(\Sigma-A)\sin(\Sigma-B)\sin(\Sigma-\Gamma). \qquad \cdot 69$$

Certain of these formulae are ambiguous in form though not in fact. For example, $\sin\sigma$ depends on the actual selections of α, β, γ, but a change of any one of these angles by 2π, which alters the sign of $\sin\sigma$, alters the sign also of every other denominator in ·65.

314. The index of measurement and its uses.

·1. From 3·61 it follows that

·11 $$\frac{\sin^2 \frac{1}{2}\mathrm{B} \sin^2 \frac{1}{2}\Gamma}{\sin^2 \sigma} = \frac{\cos^2 \frac{1}{2}\mathrm{A}}{\sin^2 \alpha},$$

·12 that is, that $$4\Upsilon^2 \sin^2 \tfrac{1}{2}\mathrm{A} \sin^2 \tfrac{1}{2}\mathrm{B} \sin^2 \tfrac{1}{2}\Gamma = \upsilon^2 \sin^2 \sigma,$$

and it is evident that 3·65 and 3·66 could be simplified to a considerable extent if the square roots could be extracted in ·11. Let us then write

·13 $$2\Upsilon \sin \tfrac{1}{2}\mathrm{A} \sin \tfrac{1}{2}\mathrm{B} \sin \tfrac{1}{2}\Gamma = k\upsilon \sin \sigma,$$

where k is necessarily either $+1$ or -1. The value of k is not intrinsic to the triangle, for to substitute $\mathrm{A} + 2\pi$ for A in ·13 without changing any of the
·14 other measurements would involve a change in k; we call k the °*index of measurement* of the triangle. It follows from 3·65 that, with the value of k defined by ·13,

·15 $$2\Upsilon \sin \tfrac{1}{2}\mathrm{A} \cos \tfrac{1}{2}\mathrm{B} \cos \tfrac{1}{2}\Gamma = k\upsilon \sin (\sigma - \alpha).$$

The value of the equal ratios in 3·65 is $k\upsilon/2\Upsilon \sin \frac{1}{2}\mathrm{A}$, that is, $k \cos \frac{1}{2}\mathrm{A}/\sin \alpha$, and the value of the equal ratios in 3·66 is $k\upsilon/2\Upsilon \cos \frac{1}{2}\mathrm{A}$, that is, $k \sin \frac{1}{2}\mathrm{A}/\sin \alpha$.

·2. We have now, using these values of the ratios, Delambre's formulae

·21 $$\begin{cases} \cos \tfrac{1}{2}\alpha \cos \tfrac{1}{2}(\mathrm{B}+\Gamma) = -k \cos \tfrac{1}{2}\mathrm{A} \cos \tfrac{1}{2}(\beta+\gamma), \\ \sin \tfrac{1}{2}\alpha \cos \tfrac{1}{2}(\mathrm{B}-\Gamma) = k \cos \tfrac{1}{2}\mathrm{A} \sin \tfrac{1}{2}(\beta+\gamma), \end{cases}$$

·22 $$\begin{cases} \cos \tfrac{1}{2}\alpha \sin \tfrac{1}{2}(\mathrm{B}+\Gamma) = k \sin \tfrac{1}{2}\mathrm{A} \cos \tfrac{1}{2}(\beta-\gamma), \\ \sin \tfrac{1}{2}\alpha \sin \tfrac{1}{2}(\mathrm{B}-\Gamma) = -k \sin \tfrac{1}{2}\mathrm{A} \sin \tfrac{1}{2}(\beta-\gamma); \end{cases}$$

the first or last member of this group, applied to the polar triangle, suffices to
·23 shew that ° the index of the polar triangle is the same as the index of the original triangle, and when this is known, the group reproduces itself. The identity of index can be expressed in many ways; for example, we have from ·13

·24 $$\sin \sigma \sin \Sigma = 4 \sin \tfrac{1}{2}\alpha \sin \tfrac{1}{2}\beta \sin \tfrac{1}{2}\gamma \sin \tfrac{1}{2}\mathrm{A} \sin \tfrac{1}{2}\mathrm{B} \sin \tfrac{1}{2}\Gamma.$$

·3. The problem of expressing Σ in terms of the sides only is equivalent to that of evaluating the angular excess or in elementary cases the area of the triangle, and is one on which some ingenuity has been expended.

Cagnoli's solution is given by combining

·31 $$2\upsilon \sin \tfrac{1}{2}\alpha \sin \tfrac{1}{2}\beta \sin \tfrac{1}{2}\gamma = k\Upsilon \sin \Sigma,$$

the correlative of ·13, with 3·52, when we have

·32 $$4k \cos \tfrac{1}{2}\alpha \cos \tfrac{1}{2}\beta \cos \tfrac{1}{2}\gamma \sin \Sigma = \Upsilon.$$

The numerical value of Υ is given in terms of the sides by 3·63, and we can write explicitly

·34 $$4 \cos^2 \tfrac{1}{2}\alpha \cos^2 \tfrac{1}{2}\beta \cos^2 \tfrac{1}{2}\gamma \sin^2 \Sigma = \sin \sigma \sin (\sigma - \alpha) \sin (\sigma - \beta) \sin (\sigma - \gamma).$$

·4. The modification of a formula due to Lhuilier is more difficult. From ·21 and ·22, treating Σ as $\frac{1}{2}A+\frac{1}{2}(B+\Gamma)$, we have

$$\cos\tfrac{1}{2}\alpha\,(1+k\cos\Sigma)$$
$$=\cos^2\tfrac{1}{2}A\,\{\cos\tfrac{1}{2}\alpha-\cos\tfrac{1}{2}(\beta+\gamma)\}+\sin^2\tfrac{1}{2}A\,\{\cos\tfrac{1}{2}\alpha-\cos\tfrac{1}{2}(\beta-\gamma)\},$$

$$\cos\tfrac{1}{2}\alpha\,(1-k\cos\Sigma)$$
$$=\cos^2\tfrac{1}{2}A\,\{\cos\tfrac{1}{2}\alpha+\cos\tfrac{1}{2}(\beta+\gamma)\}+\sin^2\tfrac{1}{2}A\,\{\cos\tfrac{1}{2}\alpha+\cos\tfrac{1}{2}(\beta-\gamma)\},$$

whence by use of 3·61

$$\cos\tfrac{1}{2}\alpha\sin\beta\sin\gamma\,(1+k\cos\Sigma) \qquad \cdot41$$
$$=8\sin\tfrac{1}{2}\sigma\sin\tfrac{1}{2}(\sigma-\alpha)\sin\tfrac{1}{2}(\sigma-\beta)\sin\tfrac{1}{2}(\sigma-\gamma)\{\cos\tfrac{1}{2}(\sigma-\beta)\cos\tfrac{1}{2}(\sigma-\gamma)-\cos\tfrac{1}{2}\sigma\cos\tfrac{1}{2}(\sigma-\alpha)\},$$

$$\cos\tfrac{1}{2}\alpha\sin\beta\sin\gamma\,(1-k\cos\Sigma) \qquad \cdot42$$
$$=8\cos\tfrac{1}{2}\sigma\cos\tfrac{1}{2}(\sigma-\alpha)\cos\tfrac{1}{2}(\sigma-\beta)\cos\tfrac{1}{2}(\sigma-\gamma)\{\sin\tfrac{1}{2}(\sigma-\beta)\sin\tfrac{1}{2}(\sigma-\gamma)+\sin\tfrac{1}{2}\sigma\sin\tfrac{1}{2}(\sigma-\alpha)\};$$

But identically*

$$\cos\tfrac{1}{2}(\sigma-\beta)\cos\tfrac{1}{2}(\sigma-\gamma)-\cos\tfrac{1}{2}\sigma\cos\tfrac{1}{2}(\sigma-\alpha)=\sin\tfrac{1}{2}\beta\sin\tfrac{1}{2}\gamma, \qquad \cdot43$$

$$\sin\tfrac{1}{2}(\sigma-\beta)\sin\tfrac{1}{2}(\sigma-\gamma)+\sin\tfrac{1}{2}\sigma\sin\tfrac{1}{2}(\sigma-\alpha)=\sin\tfrac{1}{2}\beta\sin\tfrac{1}{2}\gamma. \qquad \cdot44$$

Substituting in ·41, ·42 we have

$$\tfrac{1}{2}\cos\tfrac{1}{2}\alpha\cos\tfrac{1}{2}\beta\cos\tfrac{1}{2}\gamma\,(1+k\cos\Sigma) \qquad \cdot45$$
$$=\sin\tfrac{1}{2}\sigma\sin\tfrac{1}{2}(\sigma-\alpha)\sin\tfrac{1}{2}(\sigma-\beta)\sin\tfrac{1}{2}(\sigma-\gamma),$$

$$\tfrac{1}{2}\cos\tfrac{1}{2}\alpha\cos\tfrac{1}{2}\beta\cos\tfrac{1}{2}\gamma\,(1-k\cos\Sigma) \qquad \cdot46$$
$$=\cos\tfrac{1}{2}\sigma\cos\tfrac{1}{2}(\sigma-\alpha)\cos\tfrac{1}{2}(\sigma-\beta)\cos\tfrac{1}{2}(\sigma-\gamma),$$

and of these formulae, one gives $\cos^2\frac{1}{2}\Sigma$ and the other $\sin^2\frac{1}{2}\Sigma$, whether the index is positive or negative. To make a formal reduction we may write $k\cos\Sigma$ as $\cos\{\Sigma+\frac{1}{2}(1-k)\pi\}$, and division of one result by the other gives

$$\cot^2\{\tfrac{1}{2}\Sigma+\tfrac{1}{4}(1-k)\pi\}=\tan\tfrac{1}{2}\sigma\tan\tfrac{1}{2}(\sigma-\alpha)\tan\tfrac{1}{2}(\sigma-\beta)\tan\tfrac{1}{2}(\sigma-\gamma), \qquad \cdot47$$

or on the substitution of $\frac{1}{2}\pi-\frac{1}{4}E$ for $\frac{1}{2}\Sigma$,

$$\tan^2\{\tfrac{1}{4}E+\tfrac{1}{4}(1-k)\pi\}=\tan\tfrac{1}{2}\sigma\tan\tfrac{1}{2}(\sigma-\alpha)\tan\tfrac{1}{2}(\sigma-\beta)\tan\tfrac{1}{2}(\sigma-\gamma); \qquad \cdot48$$

this is the adaptation to the general triangle of Lhuilier's elegant formula for calculating the angular excess.

* Direct proof of these identities is superfluous. It follows from 3·61 that

$$\sin(\sigma-\beta)\sin(\sigma-\gamma)+\sin\sigma\sin(\sigma-a)=\sin\beta\sin\gamma,$$

and since a, β, γ are independent, this relation must be an *identity* deducible from the relation

$$2\sigma=a+\beta+\gamma.$$

Hence one consequence of the relation

$$\sigma=\tfrac{1}{2}a+\tfrac{1}{2}\beta+\tfrac{1}{2}\gamma$$

is the identity ·44, and one consequence of the relation

$$\sigma-\tfrac{1}{2}\pi=\tfrac{1}{2}(a-\pi)+\tfrac{1}{2}\beta+\tfrac{1}{2}\gamma$$

is the identity ·43.

·**5**. All the formulae of this article have of course their correlatives, and it will be found that changes also take place when they are applied to the colunars. If the first colunar is measured according to the conventions specified in 2·6, the only terms of ·13 to change are Υ and $\sin\frac{1}{2}\mathrm{A}$, which change sign, and therefore the index of the colunar is the same as that of the original triangle. As examples of the deductions that are possible may be mentioned

·51 $$\tfrac{1}{2}\cos\tfrac{1}{2}\alpha\sin\tfrac{1}{2}\beta\sin\tfrac{1}{2}\gamma\,\{1+k\cos(\Sigma-\mathrm{A})\} = \sin\tfrac{1}{2}\sigma\sin\tfrac{1}{2}(\sigma-\alpha)\cos\tfrac{1}{2}(\sigma-\beta)\cos\tfrac{1}{2}(\sigma-\gamma),$$

·52 $$\tfrac{1}{2}\cos\tfrac{1}{2}\alpha\sin\tfrac{1}{2}\beta\sin\tfrac{1}{2}\gamma\,\{1-k\cos(\Sigma-\mathrm{A})\} = \cos\tfrac{1}{2}\sigma\cos\tfrac{1}{2}(\sigma-\alpha)\sin\tfrac{1}{2}(\sigma-\beta)\sin\tfrac{1}{2}(\sigma-\gamma),$$

which come from ·45, ·46 without further investigation. Also from ·21, ·22 we have

$$-k\cos\tfrac{1}{2}\alpha\cos\Sigma = \cos^2\tfrac{1}{2}\mathrm{A}\cos\tfrac{1}{2}(\beta+\gamma)+\sin^2\tfrac{1}{2}\mathrm{A}\cos\tfrac{1}{2}(\beta-\gamma)$$
$$= \cos\tfrac{1}{2}\beta\cos\tfrac{1}{2}\gamma-\sin\tfrac{1}{2}\beta\sin\tfrac{1}{2}\gamma\cos\mathrm{A},$$

and therefore on substitution for cos A,

·53 $$-4k\cos\tfrac{1}{2}\alpha\cos\tfrac{1}{2}\beta\cos\tfrac{1}{2}\gamma\cos\Sigma = 1+\cos\alpha+\cos\beta+\cos\gamma;$$

application of this formula to the first colunar gives

·54 $$-4k\cos\tfrac{1}{2}\alpha\sin\tfrac{1}{2}\beta\sin\tfrac{1}{2}\gamma\cos(\Sigma-\mathrm{A}) = 1+\cos\alpha-\cos\beta-\cos\gamma.$$

CHAPTER III 2

THE CARTESIAN FRAMEWORK

321. Cartesian axes in a plane; countersymmetry; the polar of a plane frame. 322. Cartesian axes in space; the polar of a frame in space. 323. Components and projections. 324. Relations between components and projections. 325. Umbral notation.

321. Cartesian axes in a plane; countersymmetry; the polar of a plane frame.

·1. The Cartesian framework in a plane is composed only of two distinct directed lines, the axes, concurrent in a single point, the origin. The origin we denote by O, the axes are distinguished as the first axis or x-axis, denoted by $X'OX$ or by ξ, and the second axis or y-axis, denoted by $Y'OY$ or by η; the pair of axes forms the frame OXY. The points of an axis which lie on the positive side of the origin in that axis are said to compose the *positive half* of the axis, and the points which lie on the negative side to compose the *negative half*. Usually the symbols X, X', Y, Y' are not assigned to definite points in the axes; if X does denote a point, that point lies in the positive half of ξ,
and in any case °a point F is said to lie in OX if it is at O or on the positive ·18
side of O in ξ, even if X has been assigned to a definite point which in the literal sense is in OF; corresponding conventions attach to the uses of X', Y, Y'.

·2. We denote the images of ξ, η in a unit circle with centre Ω by Ξ, H. The two rays $\Xi'\Omega\Xi$, $\mathrm{H}'\Omega\mathrm{H}$, denoted also by ξ_Ω, η_Ω, determine a frame $\Omega\Xi\mathrm{H}$
parallel to OXY which is called the °*anchored frame* corresponding to OXY; ·22
if we have to deal with only one frame in a plane, often we can suppose Ω to coincide with O and avoid the mention of anchored frames, but if we have to compare frames with different origins the comparison of the directions of their axes is assisted by the use of parallel frames with a common independent origin. We notice that in the frame $\Omega\Xi\mathrm{H}$ the symbol Ξ is assigned to a definite point, the point of ξ_Ω whose distance from Ω in the direction of ξ_Ω is unity, but we say that a point F is *in* $\Omega\Xi$ even if literally F is in the prolongation of $\Omega\Xi$ beyond Ξ.

·3. The use of Cartesian axes in a plane does not imply the adoption of a cyclic convention for the plane: many of the results* of algebraical geometry are proved by means of coordinates but without reference to the measurement of angles. But in kinematical plane geometry cyclic direction is indispensable

* For example, results relating to the analysis of multiple singularities of curves and propositions in the theory of residuation.

and is assumed throughout. The fundamental characteristic which a cyclic
·31 convention confers on a frame is a sign: °a frame is said to be positive or
negative according as the positive half of the second axis is on the positive
side or on the negative side of the first axis, and a positive frame differs from
a negative frame even if the angles between the axes are the same in the two
frames. It is to be remarked that if the positive half of η is on the positive
·33 side of ξ then the positive half of ξ is °*necessarily on the negative side* of η;
fundamentally this is the asymmetrical* feature of plane geometry to which
allusion has been made already in 126·3.

·4. In a prepared plane, the angles from the x-axis to the y-axis of a frame
·41 compose a congruence, and of these angles we select one to be called °*the* angle
of the frame; this angle we denote by ω, adding if necessary some mark
·42 indicative of the frame to which it belongs. °The circular functions $\cos\omega$,
$\sin\omega$ are independent of all that is arbitrary in the choice of ω, and $\cos\omega$ is
·44 independent also of the cyclic direction of the plane, but °the sign of $\sin\omega$ is
the sign of the frame OXY itself and depends on this direction. If we have
only one frame to consider and the cyclic direction of the plane is not otherwise
determined, we may decide that the angle numerically less than π from ξ to
η is to be positive; if the cyclic direction and the two rays which are to serve
as axes are given, it may be possible for us to allot the parts of the two symbols
ξ, η in such a way that the frame is positive; but if both the cyclic direction
and the frame are given, the frame may be positive or negative, and if we have
to compare different frames we must be prepared to find them of different
·46 signs; °to assume either $\cos\omega$ or $\sin\omega$ to be essentially positive is to impose
·47 on our formulae a restriction at once unwarrantable and unnecessary. °The
angle ω is subject to only the one condition that it can not be an integral
·48 multiple of π. °The congruence to which the angle of the frame ΩΞH belongs
is the congruence to which ω belongs, and when we use ΩΞH as the anchored
·49 frame corresponding to OXY we °*define*† the angle of the anchored frame to
be identical with ω.

·51 **·5.** Two frames in a plane are said to be °*congruent* if on the giving of
direction to the plane the frames acquire congruent angles, and one frame in
·52 a plane is said to be a °*reverse* of another if the angle of one is congruent with
the negative of the angle of the other; the frames congruent with OXY and
·53 the reverses of OXY are the frames °*equal* to OXY in the plane of OXY.
A frame in one prepared plane may be congruent with, or a reverse of, a frame
in another prepared plane, but the relation of equality between two frames in
different planes can not be analysed if either plane is unprepared.

* The use of this word implies that symmetry is certainly absent; *unsymmetrical* is used if symmetry is not known to be impossible but is known to be accidental.

† Compare the comment on 12·48 above.

·6. Let x, y be two lines in a plane, concurrent in a point O, and let l, m be the lines through O at right angles to x, y; then the relation of the pair of lines x, y to the pair of lines l, m is the same as the relation of the pair of lines l, m to the pair of lines x, y. If however for lines we substitute rays, direct symmetry disappears and the restoration of some form of symmetry is an important matter; no angle from λ to ξ is congruent with any angle from ξ to λ unless ξ and λ are parallel, and if an angle from ξ to λ is a positive right angle the ray making a positive right angle with λ is the reverse of ξ.

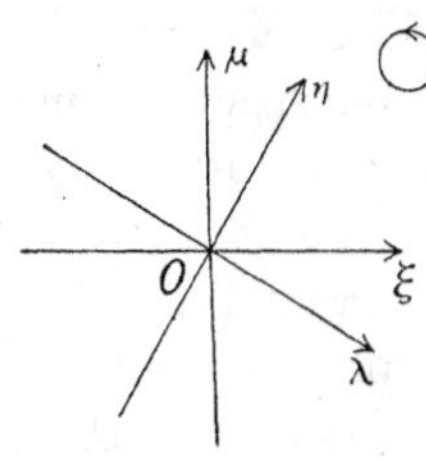

Fig. 22.

The species of symmetry which we can secure, which we
call °*countersymmetry*, is easily perceived from a figure, ·63
and is suggested by the consideration that if an angle from
ξ to η is a positive right angle the ray chosen for λ is to
coincide with ξ and the ray chosen for μ is to coincide
with η; °we take λ to be a reversed normal to η and μ to ·64
be a direct normal to ξ; then ξ is a reversed normal to μ
and η is a direct normal to λ, and therefore °the relation ·65
of ξ and η to λ and μ is the same as the relation of λ and μ
to ξ and η. °Countersymmetry results also if we take for λ a direct normal to ·66
η and for μ a reversed normal to ξ, and since in this case λ and μ coincide with
ξ and η if an angle from ξ to η is a negative right angle, we may refer to this
symmetry as °*negative* countersymmetry to distinguish it from the *positive* ·67
countersymmetry first described; if there is positive countersymmetry between
ξ, η and λ, μ, there is negative countersymmetry between ξ, η and λ', μ'.

·7. If two rays are not parallel, a ray at right angles to one of them is not
parallel to a ray at right angles to the other. Hence if two rays ξ, η are the
axes of a frame OXY in a directed plane, the reversed normal λ through O to
η and the direct normal μ through O to ξ are the axes of a frame OLM; this
frame is called the °*polar* frame, or the *direct* polar frame, of OXY, and its ·72
angle, which is congruent with $\pi-\omega$, is °defined to be $\pi-\omega$. The frame ·73
$OL'M'$ is called* the *retrograde* polar frame of OXY, and when used in that
capacity is defined also to have the angle $\pi-\omega$. °The frame OXY is itself ·74
the direct polar of OLM and the retrograde polar of $OL'M'$, while the direct
polar of $OL'M'$ and the retrograde polar of OLM are the same, the frame
$OX'Y'$, which is the *reflection* of OXY and is defined to have the angle ω.
We °denote the polar of a frame OXY consistently by OLM, and the corre- ·79
sponding anchored frame by $\Omega\Lambda\mathrm{M}$.

If the axes of a frame are rays selected from those intrinsic to a problem, they may be denoted already by symbols other than ξ, η, and a derivative notation for the polar frame may be wanted; we denote the polar of $\rho\sigma$ by $\overline{\rho}\overline{\sigma}$, of QRS by $Q\overline{R}\overline{S}$.

* To speak of the polar frames as the positive polar and the negative polar would be misleading, since the two frames have the same sign, which is that of the frame from which they are derived.

322. Cartesian axes in space; the polar of a frame in space.

·1. In space of three dimensions the axes of a frame are *three* rays, concurrent
·12 in the origin and not coplanar. We °denote the origin by O, the axes by $X'OX$, $Y'OY$, $Z'OZ$ or ξ, η, ζ, and the frame by $OXYZ$; as in a plane, an axis has a positive half and a negative half, and a point which is in ξ but not on the negative side of O in ξ is said to be *in* OX. Rays ξ_Ω, η_Ω, ζ_Ω parallel to
·15 ξ, η, ζ through a point Ω are the axes of a frame $\Omega\Xi\mathrm{HZ}$ which is the °*anchored frame* corresponding to $OXYZ$; the points Ξ, H, Z, the images of the axes ξ, η, ζ, are the vertices of a spherical triangle which is called the spherical
·16 triangle of the frame, or briefly the °*frame triangle*. In prepared space a frame
·17 has a definite sign, dependent on the spatial convention; °this sign is the sign of the frame triangle, and it is the common sign of the angles numerically less than π from η to ζ round ξ, from ζ to ξ round η, and from ξ to η round ζ. Often if only one frame has to be considered, we can determine the spatial convention by requiring this frame to be positive, or we can determine the direction of one axis in the undirected line containing it by requiring the frame to be positive, but sometimes we have to take the sign of a frame as we find it; to be really general, definitions and formulae must be applicable to frames of either sign.

·2. The planes OYZ, OZX, OXY are called the planes of the frame $OXYZ$; they are definite planes, for if two of the axes ξ, η, ζ lay in the same line the three axes would be coplanar; the plane OYZ is called the first reference plane, the yz-plane, or the x-plane, and the planes OZX, OXY have corresponding names. On the unit sphere the planes of the frame $OXYZ$ are represented by the three great circles in which are the sides of the frame triangle $\Xi\mathrm{HZ}$. It is not for all purposes necessary to adopt a spatial convention, and still less is it essential to give cyclic direction to the planes of a frame; moreover, to give cyclic direction to the planes of a particular frame is not to place ourselves in a position to give a satisfactory* cyclic direction to every plane. Nevertheless for the sake of brevity we give direction to the planes of a frame; we denote the prepared reference planes by Λ, M, N.

·3. The angles in Λ from η to ζ form one congruence, the angles in M from ζ to ξ form a second congruence, and the angles in N from ξ to η form
·31 a third congruence; °from each of these congruences one member is chosen, arbitrarily or in accordance with some principle that is itself arbitrary, and the three chosen angles, which we denote by α, β, γ, are called the biaxial
·32 angles of the frame $OXYZ$. Similarly three °biplanar angles A, B, Γ of the frame are obtained by selection from the congruences of angles from M to N
·33 round ξ, from N to Λ round η, and from Λ to M round ζ. °Of the angles α, β, γ, A, B, Γ none can be integral multiples of π, and of the angles $\pm\alpha\pm\beta\pm\gamma$, $\pm\mathrm{A}\pm\mathrm{B}\pm\Gamma$ none can be integral multiples of 2π, but the

* Compare 114·11 on p. 7 above.

biaxial angles and biplanar angles of a frame are not restricted in sign or required to lie within any specified limits, nor is the choice of one of these angles from the congruence to which it belongs dependent in any way on the selections made from the other congruences.

·4. In every congruence which does not consist of integral multiples of π there is one and only one angle numerically less than π, and our formulae are unchanged if we assume the biaxial angles and the biplanar angles of a frame to lie between $-\pi$ and π; also, to reverse Λ is to change the sign of a while leaving unaffected β and γ and the directions of ξ, η, ζ. Thus with given axes we may fix our ideas by supposing the biaxial angles and the biplanar angles to be numerically less than π and the biaxial angles to be positive; the cyclic directions of the planes of reference are then implicitly determined, and the biplanar angles are all positive or all negative according as the frame itself is positive or negative. No complications are caused by the adoption of the set of conventions just described, but in using a common phrase we have criticised the common practice: unnecessarily to *fix* an idea is almost always wrong, for an idea shews its strength in its mobility. In this connection see the end of 435·2 on p. 231 below.

·5. By giving direction to the plane OYZ we give direction also to the great circle through H and Z, and to a frame which has prepared planes as well as directed axes corresponds a spherical triangle of the kind considered in the last chapter. The sides of this triangle are congruent with the biaxial angles of $OXYZ$, and the external angles with the biplanar angles of $OXYZ$, and having chosen definite biaxial angles and biplanar angles for a frame, we
°define *the* sides and *the* external angles of the frame triangle to be identical ·51
with the chosen angles. The trigonometrical functions of the biaxial angles and biplanar angles of a frame are not independent, but the system of relations between these functions is a direct consequence of the relation of the angles to the frame triangle.

·6. The normals through O to the prepared planes Λ, M, N are called the normals of the frame $OXYZ$; they are three rays which we denote by λ, μ, ν, and they are the axes of a frame $OLMN$. Since μ is at right angles to ξ and ζ, and ν is at right angles to ξ and η, the plane through μ and ν is at right angles to ξ, and we denote this plane with the cyclic direction that renders ξ one of its normals by Ξ; similarly H, Z denote* the planes through O of which η, ζ are normals, and these are prepared planes of the frame $OLMN$. The frame $OLMN$ with λ, μ, ν for axes and Ξ, H, Z for planes is called the
°*polar* of the frame $OXYZ$ with ξ, η, ζ for axes and Λ, M, N for planes; the ·62
relation between the frames is °symmetrical and is described most simply by ·63
the statement that the normals of each frame are the axes of the other. As the points Ξ, H, Z are the images of the normals to the prepared planes denoted by the same letters, so we denote by Λ, M, N the images of the normals to the prepared planes Λ, M, N; the frame $\Omega\Lambda$MN is the anchored frame corresponding to $OLMN$, and is the polar of the anchored frame $\Omega\Xi$HZ.

* The use of Ξ, H, Z for prepared planes as well as for points of the unit sphere, and of Λ, M, N for points of the unit sphere as well as for prepared planes, involves no confusion.

The spherical triangle ΛMN is the frame triangle of *OLMN*, and it is the triangle described in 12·4 as the polar of ΞHZ. As with the polar of a
·66 spherical triangle so with the polar of a frame, we °define *the* biaxial angles of *OLMN* to be the biplanar angles of *OXYZ* and *the* biplanar angles of *OLMN* to be the biaxial angles of *OXYZ*; the signs of a three-dimensional frame and of its polar are not necessarily the same.

·7. Many functions of the six angles of a frame present themselves in work with oblique axes. The most important are indubitably the three cosines $\cos\alpha$, $\cos\beta$, $\cos\gamma$, which are independent not merely of the selections of α, β, γ from the congruences to which they belong but also of the cyclic directions of the planes of reference and of the spatial convention adopted. Next in value comes the sine of the frame triangle, which is called the sine of the frame;
·71 this function, which we °denote always by Υ, has the sign of the frame, and as we shall see in 4·4 its square is given in determinantal form by

·72
$$\Upsilon^2 = \begin{vmatrix} 1 & \cos\gamma & \cos\beta \\ \cos\gamma & 1 & \cos\alpha \\ \cos\beta & \cos\alpha & 1 \end{vmatrix},$$

and therefore in an expanded form by

·73
$$\Upsilon^2 = 1 - \cos^2\alpha - \cos^2\beta - \cos^2\gamma + 2\cos\alpha\cos\beta\cos\gamma,$$

but Υ itself can not be expressed rationally in terms of the biaxial angles
·74 alone, for °two frames may have the same biaxial angles but be of opposite signs. Complementary to the cosines of the biaxial angles are the cosines $\cos \mathrm{A}$, $\cos \mathrm{B}$, $\cos \Gamma$, which depend on the cyclic directions of the planes of the frame but not on the directions of the axes or on the spatial convention, but of more frequent occurrence in the sequel are $\cot \mathrm{A}$, $\cot \mathrm{B}$, $\cot \Gamma$, functions which depend on the directions both of axes and of planes. The sine of the polar frame, denoted by υ and determined from the equation

·75
$$\upsilon^2 = \begin{vmatrix} 1 & \cos\Gamma & \cos\mathrm{B} \\ \cos\Gamma & 1 & \cos\mathrm{A} \\ \cos\mathrm{B} & \cos\mathrm{A} & 1 \end{vmatrix}$$

by the condition that its sign is the sign of the polar frame, proves of less value than we should expect.

In terms of angles of both kinds we have as in 13·43, 13·44

·76
$$\Upsilon = \sin\beta\sin\gamma\sin\mathrm{A} = \sin\gamma\sin\alpha\sin\mathrm{B} = \sin\alpha\sin\beta\sin\Gamma,$$

·77
$$\upsilon = \sin\mathrm{B}\sin\Gamma\sin\alpha = \sin\Gamma\sin\mathrm{A}\sin\beta = \sin\mathrm{A}\sin\mathrm{B}\sin\gamma,$$

formulae which shew more clearly than ·72 and ·75 that for all undegenerate frames Υ and υ are different from zero, and that it is only when all the angles are congruent with right angles, positive or negative, that either Υ or υ is not numerically less than unity, while in the exceptional cases Υ and υ attain their numerical maximum together. The results corresponding to 13·41,

13·42 compose an important group of formulae, obtainable by direct application of 134·72, which we need usually in the form

$$\begin{cases}\cos \Lambda\Xi = \Upsilon \operatorname{cosec} \alpha = \upsilon \operatorname{cosec} \mathrm{A}, \\ \cos \mathrm{MH} = \Upsilon \operatorname{cosec} \beta = \upsilon \operatorname{cosec} \mathrm{B}, \\ \cos \mathrm{NZ} = \Upsilon \operatorname{cosec} \gamma = \upsilon \operatorname{cosec} \Gamma ;\end{cases}$$ ·78

the cosine of the angles between an axis of $OXYZ$ and an axis of $OLMN$ is zero unless the axes correspond, so that of the nine cosines of this form six are zero and the remaining three have their values given by ·78. If the sines of the biaxial angles of a frame are not positive, the sign of the frame is seen most readily from the set of formulae ·76; the set ·78 then gives the signs of $\cos \Lambda\Xi$, $\cos \mathrm{MH}$, $\cos \mathrm{NZ}$, and the cyclic directions of the planes follow at once.

The formulae

$$\Upsilon \sin \mathrm{A} \sin \mathrm{B} \sin \Gamma = \upsilon^2, \quad \upsilon \sin \alpha \sin \beta \sin \gamma = \Upsilon^2,$$ ·79

direct results of ·76 and ·77, are of interest as shewing that the sine of a frame can be expressed rationally in terms of the biplanar angles alone. Of the relations between the six angles of a frame we have repeated those which we are to find most useful, but every relation between the sides and the angles of a spherical triangle can be interpreted as a relation between the angles of a frame.

·8. If the six angles of one frame are congruent with the six angles of another, the frames are said to be °*congruent*, and if the six angles of one ·81
frame are congruent with the negatives of the six angles of another each frame is called a °*perverse* of the other. From the angles α, β, γ and the sine ·82
Υ, 13·12 gives cos A uniquely and 13·43 gives sin A uniquely; Υ^2 is given in terms of α, β, γ by 13·46, and the sign of Υ is without effect on cos A but determines the sign of sin A. The frames equal to $OXYZ$ are the frames whose biaxial angles have the same cosines as the biaxial angles of $OXYZ$, and a frame of this kind is congruent with $OXYZ$ or a perverse of $OXYZ$ according as its sign in prepared space is the same as or different from the sign of $OXYZ$.

·9. Compared with plane geometry the study of space of three dimensions has difficulties: to some mathematicians visualisation in space is almost impossible and spatial geometry is analysis of a particular kind; in problems of all kinds the presence of a third dimension involves a multiplication of possibilities. But in one respect at least geometry of three dimensions is the simpler: there is nothing in space analogous to countersymmetry in a plane, for in three dimensions to obtain a symmetrical relation between a frame and its polar we have only to take for each axis of the one the *corresponding* normal of the other; not until we become familiar with the extent to which countersymmetry affects the analysis relating to functions on a surface do we realise the simplicity to be expected when this feature is absent.

323. Components and projections.

·1. Success in dealing with oblique axes depends entirely on an abandonment of the classical attitude to an oblique frame; always it has been understood that with respect to such a frame a *direction* may be specified either by three ratios or by three cosines and that the elegance of a formula relating to directions depends on the judicious use of the double specification, but it has been taken for granted that a point must be indicated by its coordinates and a vector by its components. The failure to realise that there is a double specification for points and vectors as well as for directions is responsible for an avoidance of oblique frames which is both unwarrantable and mischievous.

·2. The coordinates of a point with respect to a frame are familiar lengths.
·21 In a plane, °the coordinates of R with respect to OXY are the distances from O, in the directions Ξ, H, of the η-projection of R on ξ and the ξ-projection
·22 of R on η, and they are denoted by x_R, y_R. In space, °the coordinates x_R, y_R, z_R of R with respect to $OXYZ$ are the distances from O, in the directions Ξ, H, Z, of the Λ-projection of R on ξ, the M-projection of R on η, and the N-projection of R on ζ, where Λ, M, N are as usual the planes of the frame. By the projections of R with respect to a frame, in space or in a plane, we
·23 mean °the distances of the normal projections of R on the axes from the origin, these distances being measured in the directions of the axes; we denote the projections in a plane by l_R, m_R and in space by l_R, m_R, n_R.

The components of a vector $\mathbf{r}$ with respect to a frame are the numbers already defined in 214 and 215 as the components of $\mathbf{r}$ with respect to the
·24 axes; °the components of $\mathbf{r}$ are the amounts, in the directions of the axes, of vectors parallel to the axes with $\mathbf{r}$ for sum, and we denote them in a plane
·25 by $x_\mathbf{r}, y_\mathbf{r}$ and in space by $x_\mathbf{r}, y_\mathbf{r}, z_\mathbf{r}$. °The projections of a vector with respect to a frame are its projections on the axes; the projection of a vector on an axis of a frame differs in no respect from the projection on any other ray. We denote the projections of $\mathbf{r}$ in a plane by $l_\mathbf{r}, m_\mathbf{r}$ and in space by $l_\mathbf{r}, m_\mathbf{r}, n_\mathbf{r}$.

The components and projections of a given vector with respect to two different frames are the same if the corresponding axes of the frames have
·26 the same directions, and in particular °the components and projections of a vector with respect to any frame are the same as the components and projections of the same vector with respect to the corresponding anchored frame. This result depends of course on the *freedom* of the vector; for example, the coordinates x_R, y_R, z_R of a point R with respect to the frame $OXYZ$ may be regarded as the components of a vector, and this vector like any other has the same components relative to $\Omega\Xi$HZ as relative to $OXYZ$, but in general the coordinates of R with respect to $\Omega\Xi$HZ are not x_R, y_R, z_R; there is no contradiction, for the coordinates of R relative to $\Omega\Xi$HZ are the components not of the vector of the step OR but of the vector of the step ΩR, and the two vectors differ by the vector of the step $O\Omega$.

·3. Each of the two sets of numbers used for specifying a vector has its characteristic property: in terms of the components, the vector can be described simply as °the sum of the three vector-components, x in OX, y in OY, ·31
z in OZ; on the other hand, each of the components is dependent on the directions of all the axes, but °each projection depends on the direction of the ·32
corresponding axis alone, being in fact the projected product of the vector by a unit vector in the axis.

·4. With respect to any frame, the ratios and cosines of the direction whose image is P may be identified with °the coordinates and projections of the point ·41
at unit distance from the origin in the direction in question, with °the co- ·42
ordinates and projections of the point P itself with respect to the corresponding anchored frame, and with °the components and projections of the unit vector ·43
1_P in the direction P; naturally we denote the first ratio by x_P and the first cosine by l_P, and we notice that °l_P is merely a brief alternative to cos ΞP. ·45

·5. The use of a unit circle or unit sphere in connection with points and vectors given by projections is obvious:

Referred to a frame OXY in a plane, the vector r_P in the plane and the point ·51
in the plane at distance r from O in the direction P *have projections* r cos ΞP, r cos HP;

Referred to a frame $OXYZ$ in space, the vector r_P and the point at distance r ·52
from O in the direction P *have projections* r cos ΞP, r cos HP, r cos ZP.

Equally important and hardly less evident are the relations of coordinates and components in the one case to the points Ξ, H, P and in the other case to the points Ξ, H, Z, P. In a plane, let F, G be the points in ξ, η such that OR is a diagonal of the parallelogram of which OF, OG are sides, and let X, Y be the points in ξ, η at unit distance from O; then

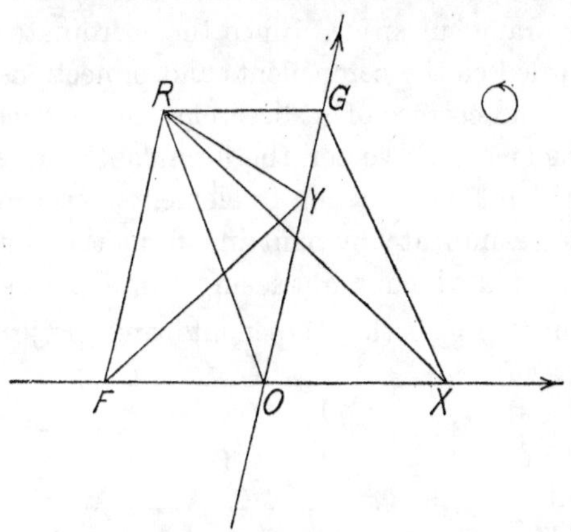

Fig. 23.

$$x_R = OF/OX = \Delta OFY/\Delta OXY;$$

thus $\begin{cases} x_R = \Delta ORY/\Delta OXY, \\ y_R = \Delta OXR/\Delta OXY, \end{cases}$ ·53

and since OX, OY, OR are of lengths 1, 1, r in the directions Ξ, H, P,

If X, Y are the points at unit distance from the origin along the axes of a ·54
frame OXY in a plane, the components of the vector r_P in the plane and the coordinates of the point R in the plane at distance r from O in the direction P *are the ratios of the areas of the triangles ORY, OXR to the area of the triangle OXY, and can be expressed trigonometrically as* r cosec ω sin PH, r cosec ω sin ΞP.

In space the argument is parallel; if X, Y, Z are the points at unit distance from O along the axes, and F is the L-projection of R on ξ, then x_R is the ratio of the volumes of the ordered tetrahedra $OFYZ$, $OXYZ$, and of these volumes the first is that of the tetrahedron $ORYZ$ and is $\frac{1}{6}r \sin \Omega\mathrm{PHZ}$, and the second is $\frac{1}{6} \sin \Omega\Xi\mathrm{HZ}$, that is, $\frac{1}{6}\Upsilon$:

·55 *If X, Y, Z are the points at unit distance from the origin along the axes of a frame $OXYZ$, the components of the vector r_P and the coordinates of the point R at distance r from O in the direction* P *are the ratios of the volumes of the tetrahedra $ORYZ$, $OXRZ$, $OXYR$ to the volume of the tetrahedron $OXYZ$, and are expressible trigonometrically as* $r\Upsilon^{-1} \sin \Omega\mathrm{PHZ}$, $r\Upsilon^{-1} \sin \Omega\Xi\mathrm{PZ}$, $r\Upsilon^{-1} \sin \Omega\Xi\mathrm{HP}$.

Comparing ·55 with ·54 we observe in ·54 the feature of countersymmetry; $\sin \Omega\Xi\mathrm{PZ}$, $\sin \Omega\Xi\mathrm{HP}$ may be written as $\sin \Omega\mathrm{PZ}\Xi$, $\sin \Omega\mathrm{P}\Xi\mathrm{H}$, and the three functions $\sin \Omega\mathrm{PHZ}$, $\sin \Omega\mathrm{PZ}\Xi$, $\sin \Omega\mathrm{P}\Xi\mathrm{H}$ depend symmetrically on the three points Ξ, H, Z, but $\sin \Xi\mathrm{P}$ is $-\sin \mathrm{P}\Xi$, and the dependence of the two functions $\sin \mathrm{PH}$, $\sin \mathrm{P}\Xi'$ on the two points Ξ, H is countersymmetrical.

324. Relations between components and projections.

·1. Of the two sets of elements relating a vector to an oblique frame, either alone suffices to determine the vector, and the vector determines the other; hence components can be expressed in terms of projections and projections in terms of components, and we proceed to obtain the actual formulae, first for a frame in a plane and then for a frame in space. Since the coordinates and projections of a point can be regarded as the components and projections of a radius vector, and since the ratios and cosines of a direction can be regarded as the components and projections of a unit vector, the formulae obtained in connection with a vector apply without modification to elements determining a point or a direction, a fact that we indicate by omitting from the symbols for components and projections the affix which might seem to limit their scope.

·2. The simplest formulae involving both components and projections express relations between elements of one kind relative to one frame and elements of the other kind relative to the polar frame. In themselves interesting, they are also useful in enabling us with a minimum of labour to duplicate many of our results.

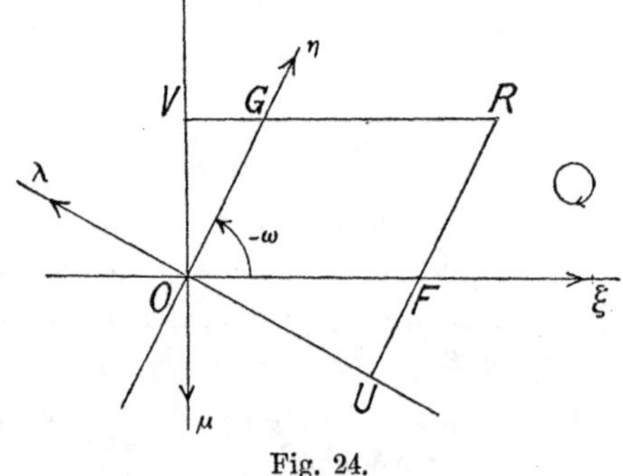

Fig. 24.

In a plane, the line through a point R which is perpendicular to the axis λ of the polar of a frame OXY is parallel to the axis η of OXY; hence (see figure 24, in which ω is supposed to be negative and the cyclic direction to be clockwise) the projection U of R on

λ is also the projection on λ of the η-projection F of R on ξ. The lengths of OF, OU, in the directions of ξ, λ, are $x, \bar{l}$, and one angle from λ to ξ is $\frac{1}{2}\pi - \omega$; hence $\bar{l}$ is equal to $x \sin \omega$. Similarly, since one angle from μ to η is $\omega - \frac{1}{2}\pi$ and the cosine of this angle also is $\sin \omega$, the projection $\bar{m}$ is equal to $y \sin \omega$. We may find l, m in terms of $\bar{x}, \bar{y}$ directly, by drawing lines through R parallel to λ, μ, but we may avoid the geometrical examination by recalling that OXY is the polar of OLM and noticing that the multipliers are as before $\cos \Xi\Lambda$, $\cos \mathrm{HM}$, and have still the value $\sin \omega$; from the theorem first proved, we deduce at once that l, m are equal to $\bar{x} \sin \omega, \bar{y} \sin \omega$:

In a plane, components x, y and projections l, m relative to a frame of angle ω are related to projections $\bar{l}, \bar{m}$ and components $\bar{x}, \bar{y}$ relative to the polar frame by the formulae ·22

$$\bar{l} = x \sin \omega, \quad \bar{m} = y \sin \omega,$$
$$l = \bar{x} \sin \omega, \quad m = \bar{y} \sin \omega.$$

In space, the same principle leads to similar results: the projection of R on the first axis of the polar of the frame $OXYZ$ is again the projection on that axis of the Λ-projection of R on the axis ξ; accordingly, °$\bar{l}$ is equal to $x \cos \Xi\Lambda$, ·23
and similarly l is equal to $\bar{x} \cos \Xi\Lambda$; from the values of the cosine given in 2·78 we see that $\bar{l}$ is equal to $x\Upsilon \operatorname{cosec} \alpha$, and that we can assert that l is equal to $\bar{x}\upsilon \operatorname{cosec} \mathrm{A}$ if we wish to lay stress on reciprocity, or that $\bar{x}$ is equal to $l\Upsilon^{-1} \sin \alpha$ if we wish to keep the polar frame in a subordinate position:

Components $\bar{x}, \bar{y}, \bar{z}$ and projections $\bar{l}, \bar{m}, \bar{n}$ relative to the polar of a frame $OXYZ$ are related to projections and components relative to $OXYZ$ itself by the formulae ·24

$$\bar{l} = x\Upsilon \operatorname{cosec} \alpha, \quad \bar{m} = y\Upsilon \operatorname{cosec} \beta, \quad \bar{n} = z\Upsilon \operatorname{cosec} \gamma,$$
$$\bar{x} = l\Upsilon^{-1} \sin \alpha, \quad \bar{y} = m\Upsilon^{-1} \sin \beta, \quad \bar{z} = n\Upsilon^{-1} \sin \gamma.$$

The results of the last two paragraphs may usefully be regarded in another light. In a plane, the distances of a point R from the rays ξ, η are the distances from O of the projections of R on the rays through O normal to ξ, η, that is to say, on the rays μ, λ':

In a plane, the point whose distances from the axes of a frame OXY are f, g is the point whose projections relative to the polar of OXY are $-g, f$, and the coordinates of this point with respect to the frame OXY itself are $-g \operatorname{cosec} \omega, f \operatorname{cosec} \omega$. ·25

Conversely, °*the normal distances of the point R from the axes ξ, η are* ·26
$y_R \sin \omega, -x_R \sin \omega$, a result of less value to us than is ·25. In ·25 and ·26 countersymmetry appears, and the corresponding propositions relative to space are simpler and if possible more obvious:

The point whose distances from the planes of a frame $OXYZ$ are f, g, h is the point having with respect to the polar frame the projections f, g, h and with respect to the frame $OXYZ$ the coordinates $f\Upsilon^{-1} \sin \alpha, g\Upsilon^{-1} \sin \beta, h\Upsilon^{-1} \sin \gamma$; ·27

The distances of the point R from the planes of the frame $OXYZ$ are ·28
$x_R \Upsilon \operatorname{cosec} \alpha$, $y_R \Upsilon \operatorname{cosec} \beta$, $z_R \Upsilon \operatorname{cosec} \gamma$.

·3. If x, y are the components relative to a plane frame OXY of a vector **r** in the plane of the frame, then **r** is the sum of the vectors x_{Ξ}, y_{H}, and so by 215·42 the projection of **r** on any ray is the sum of the projections of x_{Ξ}, y_{H} on that ray. But the projections of x_{Ξ}, y_{H} on ξ are x, $y\cos\omega$ and the projections of x_{Ξ}, y_{H} on η are $x\cos\omega$, y:

·31 *Relative to a frame of angle* ω, *projections* l, m *are given in terms of components* x, y *by the pair of formulae*

$$\left[\begin{array}{l} l = x + y\cos\omega, \\ m = x\cos\omega + y. \end{array}\right.$$

Applying this theorem to the polar frame, which has angle $\pi - \omega$, and substituting for $\bar{l}$, $\bar{m}$ and $\bar{x}$, $\bar{y}$ their values in terms of x, y and l, m, we deduce that

·32 *Relative to a frame of angle* ω, *components* x, y *are given in terms of projections* l, m *by the pair of formulae*

$$\left[\begin{array}{l} x\sin\omega = l\operatorname{cosec}\omega - m\cot\omega, \\ y\sin\omega = -l\cot\omega + m\operatorname{cosec}\omega. \end{array}\right.$$

We can of course deduce the formulae in ·32, in the form

$$x\sin^2\omega = l - m\cos\omega,$$
$$y\sin^2\omega = -l\cos\omega + m,$$

by a mere algebraical reversal of the formulae in ·31, but it is noteworthy that in some branches of geometry we meet more often with the pairs of coefficients $\operatorname{cosec}\omega$, $-\cot\omega$ and $-\cot\omega$, $\operatorname{cosec}\omega$ than with the pairs of coefficients 1, $-\cos\omega$ and $-\cos\omega$, 1.

The arguments by which ·31 and ·32 have been obtained are adequate to provide the corresponding theorems for a frame in space. The projections of x_{Ξ}, y_{H}, z_{Z} on ξ are x, $y\cos\gamma$, $z\cos\beta$, the projections of the same vector-components on the rays η, ζ can be expressed similarly, and corresponding to ·31 we have the result that

·33 *Relative to any frame in space, projections are given in terms of components by the set of formulae*

$$\left[\begin{array}{l} l = x + y\cos\gamma + z\cos\beta, \\ m = x\cos\gamma + y + z\cos\alpha, \\ n = x\cos\beta + y\cos\alpha + z. \end{array}\right.$$

Applying ·24, we find that x is given in terms of l, m, n by

$$x\Upsilon\operatorname{cosec}\alpha = l\Upsilon^{-1}\sin\alpha + m\Upsilon^{-1}\sin\beta\cos\Gamma + n\Upsilon^{-1}\sin\gamma\cos\text{B}:$$

·34 *Relative to any frame in space, components are given in terms of projections by the set of formulae*

$$\left[\begin{array}{l} x = l\Upsilon^{-2}\sin^2\alpha + m\Upsilon^{-1}\cot\Gamma + n\Upsilon^{-1}\cot\text{B}, \\ y = l\Upsilon^{-1}\cot\Gamma + m\Upsilon^{-2}\sin^2\beta + n\Upsilon^{-1}\cot\text{A}, \\ z = l\Upsilon^{-1}\cot\text{B} + m\Upsilon^{-1}\cot\text{A} + n\Upsilon^{-2}\sin^2\gamma. \end{array}\right.$$

The absence of negative signs from these formulae is one of the minor advantages secured by the use of *external* angles of the frame triangle.

·4. The direct passage from ·33 to ·34 is a superfluous exercise in algebra and trigonometry. What is interesting to remark is that the equivalence of the sets of formulae in these two theorems rests only on the values given in 134·72 for $\cos \Lambda\Xi$, $\cos \mathrm{MH}$, $\cos \mathrm{NZ}$, and is an adequate logical basis for spherical trigonometry, implying as it does that

Each of the determinants ·41

$$\begin{vmatrix} 1 & \cos\gamma & \cos\beta \\ \cos\gamma & 1 & \cos\alpha \\ \cos\beta & \cos\alpha & 1 \end{vmatrix}, \qquad \begin{vmatrix} \Upsilon^{-2}\sin^2\alpha & \Upsilon^{-1}\cot\Gamma & \Upsilon^{-1}\cot\mathrm{B} \\ \Upsilon^{-1}\cot\Gamma & \Upsilon^{-2}\sin^2\beta & \Upsilon^{-1}\cot\mathrm{A} \\ \Upsilon^{-1}\cot\mathrm{B} & \Upsilon^{-1}\cot\mathrm{A} & \Upsilon^{-2}\sin^2\gamma \end{vmatrix}$$

is the reciprocal of the other.

Since the divisor that converts the cofactor $1-\cos^2\alpha$ of the leading element of the first determinant into the leading element $\Upsilon^{-2}\sin^2\alpha$ of the second is Υ^2, this is the value of the first determinant; also the product of the determinants is unity:

The determinants in ·41 *have the values* Υ^2, Υ^{-2}. ·42

The first part of this theorem has been quoted already in 13·47 and 2·72.

Knowing the value of the first determinant, we have from the cofactor of $\cos a$,

$$\Upsilon \cot \mathrm{A} = \cos\beta\cos\gamma - \cos a, \qquad \cdot 43$$

a version of the fundamental formula 13·12. Further, ·41 implies three formulae typified by

$$\Upsilon^{-2}\sin^2 a + \Upsilon^{-1}\cot\Gamma\cos\gamma + \Upsilon^{-1}\cot\mathrm{B}\cos\beta = 1, \qquad \cdot 44$$

and six typified by

$$\Upsilon^{-1}\cot\mathrm{B}\cos\gamma + \Upsilon^{-1}\cot\mathrm{A} + \Upsilon^{-2}\sin^2\gamma\cos a = 0. \qquad \cdot 45$$

Multiplication by Υ^2 and substitution from the group to which ·43 belongs converts ·44 into

$$\Upsilon^2 = 1 - \cos^2 a - \cos^2\beta - \cos^2\gamma + 2\cos a\cos\beta\cos\gamma, \qquad \cdot 46$$

the expanded form of the determinantal expression, given previously as 13·46 and 2·73. The same operations reduce ·45 to an identity, but multiplication by $\Upsilon \sin \mathrm{B}$ alone gives

$$\cos\mathrm{B}\cos\gamma + \cot\mathrm{A}\sin\mathrm{B} + \Upsilon^{-1}\cos a\sin^2\gamma\sin\mathrm{B} = 0, \qquad \cdot 47$$

which is equivalent to 13·51.

·5. By the definitions of the magnitudes involved, the fundamental theorem 221·15 implies that, in the notation of 3·2,

The projected product of two vectors **r**, **s** *is expressible in the two forms* ·51

$$x_{\mathbf{r}} l_{\mathbf{s}} + y_{\mathbf{r}} m_{\mathbf{s}} + z_{\mathbf{r}} n_{\mathbf{s}}, \quad l_{\mathbf{r}} x_{\mathbf{s}} + m_{\mathbf{r}} y_{\mathbf{s}} + n_{\mathbf{r}} z_{\mathbf{s}},$$

whatever the reference frame,

a result that includes a large number of useful particular cases, of which the most elementary come from the less general theorem

The value of the projection of the vector **r** *in the direction represented by* Π *is expressible in the two forms* ·52

$$x_{\mathbf{r}} l_{\Pi} + y_{\mathbf{r}} m_{\Pi} + z_{\mathbf{r}} n_{\Pi}, \quad l_{\mathbf{r}} x_{\Pi} + m_{\mathbf{r}} y_{\Pi} + n_{\mathbf{r}} z_{\Pi},$$

which follows from the preceding if the projection is regarded as the projected product of **r** by a unit vector in $\Omega\Pi$. It is really on the first expression in ·51 that ·52 is based; that the projection can be written also as $l_\mathbf{r}x_\Pi + m_\mathbf{r}y_\Pi + n_\mathbf{r}z_\Pi$ is not an immediate deduction from 215·42, but instead of appealing to the notion of a projected product we may apply the elementary theorem to express the projection by means of the polar frame in the form $\bar{x}_\mathbf{r}\bar{l}_\Pi + \bar{y}_\mathbf{r}\bar{m}_\Pi + \bar{z}_\mathbf{r}\bar{n}_\Pi$; using ·24, we obtain at once the expression completing ·52.

By means of ·33 and ·34, we can give to ·51 a form in which only components are involved and another form in which projections appear alone:

·53 *The projected product of two vectors* **r**, **s** *is given in terms of their components by*

$$x_\mathbf{r}x_\mathbf{s} + y_\mathbf{r}y_\mathbf{s} + z_\mathbf{r}z_\mathbf{s} + (y_\mathbf{r}z_\mathbf{s} + z_\mathbf{r}y_\mathbf{s})\cos\alpha + (z_\mathbf{r}x_\mathbf{s} + x_\mathbf{r}z_\mathbf{s})\cos\beta + (x_\mathbf{r}y_\mathbf{s} + y_\mathbf{r}x_\mathbf{s})\cos\gamma$$

and in terms of their projections by

$$l_\mathbf{r}l_\mathbf{s}\Upsilon^{-2}\sin^2\alpha + m_\mathbf{r}m_\mathbf{s}\Upsilon^{-2}\sin^2\beta + n_\mathbf{r}n_\mathbf{s}\Upsilon^{-2}\sin^2\gamma$$
$$+ (m_\mathbf{r}n_\mathbf{s} + n_\mathbf{r}m_\mathbf{s})\Upsilon^{-1}\cot \mathrm{A} + (n_\mathbf{r}l_\mathbf{s} + l_\mathbf{r}n_\mathbf{s})\Upsilon^{-1}\cot \mathrm{B} + (l_\mathbf{r}m_\mathbf{s} + m_\mathbf{r}l_\mathbf{s})\Upsilon^{-1}\cot\Gamma.$$

If, instead of *substituting for* $l_\mathbf{s}$, $m_\mathbf{s}$, $n_\mathbf{s}$ in

·54 $$\mathscr{S}\mathbf{rs} = x_\mathbf{r}l_\mathbf{s} + y_\mathbf{r}m_\mathbf{s} + z_\mathbf{r}n_\mathbf{s}$$

from equations of the form ·33, we *eliminate* $x_\mathbf{r}$, $y_\mathbf{r}$, $z_\mathbf{r}$ *from* ·54 and equations of this form, we have

·55 $$\begin{vmatrix} 1 & \cos\gamma & \cos\beta & l_\mathbf{r} \\ \cos\gamma & 1 & \cos\alpha & m_\mathbf{r} \\ \cos\beta & \cos\alpha & 1 & n_\mathbf{r} \\ l_\mathbf{s} & m_\mathbf{s} & n_\mathbf{s} & \mathscr{S}\mathbf{rs} \end{vmatrix} = 0,$$

that is

·56 $$-\Upsilon^2\mathscr{S}\mathbf{rs} = \begin{vmatrix} 1 & \cos\gamma & \cos\beta & l_\mathbf{r} \\ \cos\gamma & 1 & \cos\alpha & m_\mathbf{r} \\ \cos\beta & \cos\alpha & 1 & n_\mathbf{r} \\ l_\mathbf{s} & m_\mathbf{s} & n_\mathbf{s} & 0 \end{vmatrix},$$

and a similar process gives the correlative formula

·57 $$-\Upsilon^{-2}\mathscr{S}\mathbf{rs} = \begin{vmatrix} \Upsilon^{-2}\sin^2\alpha & \Upsilon^{-1}\cot\Gamma & \Upsilon^{-1}\cot \mathrm{B} & x_\mathbf{r} \\ \Upsilon^{-1}\cot\Gamma & \Upsilon^{-2}\sin^2\beta & \Upsilon^{-1}\cot \mathrm{A} & y_\mathbf{r} \\ \Upsilon^{-1}\cot \mathrm{B} & \Upsilon^{-1}\cot \mathrm{A} & \Upsilon^{-2}\sin^2\gamma & z_\mathbf{r} \\ x_\mathbf{s} & y_\mathbf{s} & z_\mathbf{s} & 0 \end{vmatrix};$$

these results are of course equivalent to those contained in ·53.

Projected products, as will appear more clearly in Book IV, are the very stuff of which analytical geometry is made, and it is important that expressions for them should be as simple as possible to write. There is little need to be dissatisfied with ·51, but repeatedly to set down in full the expressions in ·53 would be intolerable, and we must consider what form of abbreviation is natural; we shall find that an improvement even in ·51 will suggest itself.

325. Umbral notation.

·1. The first expression given in 4·53 is linear and homogeneous in each of the sets of variables $x_{\mathbf{r}}, y_{\mathbf{r}}, z_{\mathbf{r}}$ and $x_{\mathbf{s}}, y_{\mathbf{s}}, z_{\mathbf{s}}$ and is symmetrical in the two sets; we abbreviate it first to*

$$\mathscr{C}\,(x_{\mathbf{r}}, y_{\mathbf{r}}, z_{\mathbf{r}})(x_{\mathbf{s}}, y_{\mathbf{s}}, z_{\mathbf{s}}),$$ ·11

calling $\mathscr{C}$ the component symbol of the frame. Similarly the second expression, a symmetrical bilinear homogeneous function of the two sets $l_{\mathbf{r}}, m_{\mathbf{r}}, n_{\mathbf{r}}$ and $l_{\mathbf{s}}, m_{\mathbf{s}}, n_{\mathbf{s}}$, we denote by

$$\mathscr{P}\,(l_{\mathbf{r}}, m_{\mathbf{r}}, n_{\mathbf{r}})(l_{\mathbf{s}}, m_{\mathbf{s}}, n_{\mathbf{s}}),$$ ·13

and we call $\mathscr{P}$ the projection symbol of the frame. If the two sets of variables in one of the expressions coincide, naturally we use an index, writing $\mathscr{C}\,(x, y, z)^2$ for $\mathscr{C}\,(x, y, z)(x, y, z)$ and $\mathscr{P}\,(l, m, n)^2$ for $\mathscr{P}\,(l, m, n)(l, m, n)$.

·2. Expressions of the two forms ·11, ·13 are so common that a further contraction which is often possible is very desirable. The three variables f, g, h which compose a set occurring in an expression of the form ·11 are not usually given as the components of a vector, though there is of course a vector with these three components. Often however there is a vector **r** such that f depends on $x_{\mathbf{r}}$, g on $y_{\mathbf{r}}$, and h on $z_{\mathbf{r}}$, and the dependence is the same in each case, or there are several vectors such that f depends in a particular fashion on their first components, and g and h depend in the same way on their second and third components; for example, if $x_{\mathbf{r}}, y_{\mathbf{r}}, z_{\mathbf{r}}$ are functions of a variable t, we have to deal with bilinear functions of the form

$$\mathscr{C}\,(dx_{\mathbf{r}}/dt, dy_{\mathbf{r}}/dt, dz_{\mathbf{r}}/dt)(x_{\mathbf{s}}, y_{\mathbf{s}}, z_{\mathbf{s}}),$$

and in connection with two vectors **r**, **s** the form of

$$\mathscr{C}\,(ax_{\mathbf{r}} + bx_{\mathbf{s}}, ay_{\mathbf{r}} + by_{\mathbf{s}}, az_{\mathbf{r}} + bz_{\mathbf{s}})^2$$

as a function of a and b deserves attention. Accordingly, ° *when f, g, h stand* ·21
for three groups of symbols derivable from a group involving† *an undefined symbol by the substitution for this undefined symbol of x, y, z in turn, the link (f, g, h) is replaced by the same group with the undefined symbol replaced by* c, this group being enclosed in semicircular brackets only if some enclosure is typographically necessary. Thus instead of $\mathscr{C}\,(dx_{\mathbf{r}}/dt, dy_{\mathbf{r}}/dt, dz_{\mathbf{r}}/dt)(x_{\mathbf{s}}, y_{\mathbf{s}}, z_{\mathbf{s}})$ we write $\mathscr{C}\,(dc_{\mathbf{r}}/dt)\,c_{\mathbf{s}}$, and instead of $\mathscr{C}\,(ax_{\mathbf{r}} + bx_{\mathbf{s}}, ay_{\mathbf{r}} + by_{\mathbf{s}}, az_{\mathbf{r}} + bz_{\mathbf{s}})^2$ we write $\mathscr{C}\,(ac_{\mathbf{r}} + bc_{\mathbf{s}})^2$. In these cases there is simultaneously a reduction in both

* The brackets which it is best to use in these contractions are not of precisely the ordinary form; we call them semicircular brackets.

† We have to avoid the word function, since we wish to include such cases as that of the first of the two examples just given. There is no reason to suppose that f does not involve y or z, or that *every* occurrence of x in f is replaced in the passage to g and h: for example, if $\phi(u, v, w)$ is a function of three variables, f, g, h may have the forms $\phi(x, x, z)$ $\phi(x, y, z)$, $\phi(x, z, z)$, and the link is replaced by $\phi(x, c, z)$. The matter is much easier to understand than to express in terms sufficiently general.

sets of variables, but the use of the notation in one link is quite independent of its use in another: thus whether or not further contraction is possible, $\mathscr{C}(x, y, z)(q, r, s)$ may be replaced by $\mathscr{C}c\,(q, r, s)$.

·3. We do not attempt to identify c with *one or other* of the components x, y, z; it is because c in isolation is meaningless that we can often omit semicircular brackets without danger of confusion. Adopting Sylvester's name*
·31 for a symbol meaningless in isolation, we call c the °*umbra* of the set of symbols x, y, z, and we denote the relation between c and the set by writing

·32 $$c = (x, y, z).$$

An umbra of the coordinates of a point with respect to orthogonal axes is used† by Lamé, but work with orthogonal axes can not reveal the extensive possibilities of an umbral notation.

For use with expressions containing the projection symbol $\mathscr{P}$ it is of the set of symbols l, m, n that an umbra is required, and we write

·33 $$p = (l, m, n).$$

·4. In elementary work it is with bilinear and quadratic expressions containing $\mathscr{C}$ and $\mathscr{P}$ that the use of umbral notation effects the most striking economy, but having introduced the notation we employ it as extensively as we can. The function $x_{\mathbf{r}} l_{\mathbf{s}} + y_{\mathbf{r}} m_{\mathbf{s}} + z_{\mathbf{r}} n_{\mathbf{s}}$ which appears in 4·51 and elsewhere may be regarded as a linear function of $l_{\mathbf{s}}, m_{\mathbf{s}}, n_{\mathbf{s}}$ with $x_{\mathbf{r}}, y_{\mathbf{r}}, z_{\mathbf{r}}$ for coefficients; in this aspect it is denoted by $(x_{\mathbf{r}}, y_{\mathbf{r}}, z_{\mathbf{r}})(l_{\mathbf{s}}, m_{\mathbf{s}}, n_{\mathbf{s}})$, and in the last form the links may be replaced by umbrae and the expression denoted by $c_{\mathbf{r}} p_{\mathbf{s}}$; when we regard the same function as linear in $x_{\mathbf{r}}, y_{\mathbf{r}}, z_{\mathbf{r}}$, with coefficients $l_{\mathbf{s}}, m_{\mathbf{s}}, n_{\mathbf{s}}$, we denote it more naturally by $(l_{\mathbf{s}}, m_{\mathbf{s}}, n_{\mathbf{s}})(x_{\mathbf{r}}, y_{\mathbf{r}}, z_{\mathbf{r}})$ or by $p_{\mathbf{s}} c_{\mathbf{r}}$; the function is the same in the two cases, and the distinction between $c_{\mathbf{r}} p_{\mathbf{s}}$ and $p_{\mathbf{s}} c_{\mathbf{r}}$, like the distinction between $\partial^2\phi/\partial x\partial y$ and $\partial^2\phi/\partial y\partial x$ when ϕ is a regular function, need not be remembered in the performance of analytical operations. To put the

* Introduced in 1851 in connection with determinants (*Phil. Mag.*, ser. 4, vol. I, p. 296; *Coll. Works*, vol. I, p. 242).

† First in his *Leçons sur les Fonctions Inverses des Transcendantes et les Surfaces Isothermes* (1857); the use is explained on p. 6. Accustomed to read that Lamé introduced the use of the symbol S to denote summation with respect to the three coordinates, and denoted $k(x) + k(y) + k(z)$, where $k(x)$ is any group of symbols involving x but not y or z, by $S\,k(x)$, I was amazed on making a belated first-hand acquaintance with his work to find that actually Lamé denotes this sum always by $S\,k(u)$. Considering that Lamé's method is not only more elegant but also more effective than that ascribed to him, since for example Lamé can distinguish the two functions

$$\frac{\partial^2\phi}{\partial x^2} + \frac{\partial^2\phi}{\partial y^2} + \frac{\partial^2\phi}{\partial z^2}, \quad \frac{\partial^2\phi}{\partial x^2} + \frac{\partial^2\phi}{\partial x\partial y} + \frac{\partial^2\phi}{\partial x\partial z}$$

as $S(\partial^2\phi/\partial u^2)$ and $S(\partial^2\phi/\partial x\,\partial u)$ but his professed followers have only the one contraction $S(\partial^2\phi/\partial x^2)$, it is difficult to understand the departure that has been made. Lamé regards his symbol u as denoting ambiguously one of the coordinates, a view which has disadvantages as well as advantages. In order to reserve u strictly for use as a curvilinear coordinate, I use c, suggested like $\mathscr{C}$ by the words component and coordinate.

present use of linked brackets more generally, we have only to write as a definition the formula $^{\circ}(f, g, h)(q, r, s) = fq + gr + hs$, and to say that any ·44
contraction in use for either of the links (f, g, h), (q, r, s) may be employed to effect further abbreviation*.

·5. An attempt must be made to answer one question: why cannot the notation $\mathscr{G}\mathbf{rs}$ for the projected product serve implicitly as a contraction for the bilinear functions that occur in 4·51 and 4·53?

One reply is that often the vectors are unknown until bilinearity in algebra calls attention to them.

Another reply, that to confuse the intrinsic function $\mathscr{G}\mathbf{rs}$ with its expression by means of a particular frame is to obscure the very nature if not to lose the advantages of coordinate geometry, can be explained by a simple example. If $\mathbf{r}^{(1)}, \mathbf{r}^{(2)}, \ldots \mathbf{r}^{(h)}$ and $\mathbf{s}^{(1)}, \mathbf{s}^{(2)}, \ldots \mathbf{s}^{(k)}$ are two sets of vectors, and if $x_{\mathbf{r}}{}^{(m)}, y_{\mathbf{r}}{}^{(m)}, z_{\mathbf{r}}{}^{(m)}$ are the components of $\mathbf{r}^{(m)}$ and $x_{\mathbf{s}}{}^{(n)}, y_{\mathbf{s}}{}^{(n)}, z_{\mathbf{s}}{}^{(n)}$ the components of $\mathbf{s}^{(n)}$, then in

$$\mathscr{C} \sum_m c_{\mathbf{r}}{}^{(m)} \sum_n c_{\mathbf{s}}{}^{(n)} = \sum_m \sum_n \mathscr{C} c_{\mathbf{r}}{}^{(m)} c_{\mathbf{s}}{}^{(n)} \qquad ·54$$

we have an identity in pure algebra which may logically be made the basis of the vectorial theorem

$$\mathscr{G} \Sigma \mathbf{r}^{(m)} \Sigma \mathbf{s}^{(n)} = \Sigma\Sigma \mathscr{G} \mathbf{r}^{(m)} \mathbf{s}^{(n)}, \qquad ·55$$

but the reasoning will be impossible to follow if the symbols in ·55 have to serve in a double capacity.

·6. We have described the use of umbral notation with reference to two particular bilinear functions already known to be wanted, but the method of contraction is applicable with any expression that is linear and homogeneous in each of several sets of variables. Since however there is a notation, such as

$$\Sigma\, a_{ij} u_i v_i, \quad i, j = 1, 2$$

to denote $\qquad a_{11} u_1 v_1 + a_{12} u_1 v_2 + a_{21} u_2 v_1 + a_{22} u_2 v_2,$

available for the general multilinear function, there is little to be said against restricting the umbral notation to the case of multilinear functions *symmetrical* in the different sets of variables involved, and since further the notation can be used much more freely with symmetrical than with unsymmetrical functions this restriction is in fact desirable.

If Tuv denotes a symmetrical homogeneous bilinear function of the two sets of variables (u_1, u_2, u_3), (v_1, v_2, v_3), we shall denote the coefficient of $u_i v_j$ in Tuv by T^{ij}; since Tuv is assumed to be symmetrical,

$$T^{32} = T^{23}, \quad T^{13} = T^{31}, \quad T^{21} = T^{12}. \qquad ·61$$

In Tuv, the coefficient of u_k is $T^{k1}v_1 + T^{k2}v_2 + T^{k3}v_3$, a linear function of (v_1, v_2, v_3), and the coefficient of v_k is $T^{1k}u_1 + T^{2k}u_2 + T^{3k}u_3$, which on account

* For example, if $k(x)$ is a group of symbols involving x, the expression $(1, 1, 1)\,k(c)$ denotes the sum $k(x) + k(y) + k(z)$, and by writing S for $(1, 1, 1)$ we could recover Lamé's notation, with c for u.

of the symmetry is the same linear function of (u_1, u_2, u_3) as $T^{k1}v_1 + T^{k2}v_2 + T^{k3}v_3$ is of (v_1, v_2, v_3). If then we write

·62 $$T^k = (T^{k1}, T^{k2}, T^{k3}) = (T^{1k}, T^{2k}, T^{3k}),$$

the coefficient of u_k in Tuv can be written as $T^k v$ and the coefficient of v_k in the same function as $T^k u$. Thus identically

·63 $$Tuv = (T^1u)\,v_1 + (T^2u)\,v_2 + (T^3u)\,v_3 = (T^1v)\,u_1 + (T^2v)\,u_2 + (T^3v)\,u_3,$$

and Tu may itself be regarded as an umbra of (T^1u, T^2u, T^3u). To write

·64 $$Tuv = (Tu)\,v = (Tv)\,u$$

is to express symbolically the precise form of the dependence of the function on the individual sets of variables.

It is here that the condition of symmetry is valuable. We can of course denote by Tuv an unsymmetrical function $\Sigma\Sigma T^{i,j}u_iv_j$, and shew the distinction between the linear functions $T^{k,1}w_1 + T^{k,2}w_2 + T^{k,3}w_3$ and $T^{1,k}w_1 + T^{2,k}w_2 + T^{3,k}w_3$ by writing $T^{k,}w$ for the one and $T^{,k}w$ for the other, but then to distinguish an umbra of $(T^{1,}w, T^{2,}w, T^{3,}w)$ from an umbra of $(T^{,1}w, T^{,2}w, T^{,3}w)$ with a view to giving significance to some such collection of symbols as ·64 requires a further complication that leaves the notation with few advantages over the elementary form with a symbol of summation.

The reader will observe that to propose contractions for the linear functions subsidiary to a given bilinear function is not to indulge in intelligent anticipation but simply to recall the manner in which the bilinear functions already found were actually constructed: 4·33 and 4·34 introduced three functions of x, y, z that we express as $\mathscr{C}^1c, \mathscr{C}^2c, \mathscr{C}^3c$ by writing

·65 $$\left[\begin{array}{lll} \mathscr{C}^{11} = 1, & \mathscr{C}^{12} = \cos\gamma, & \mathscr{C}^{13} = \cos\beta, \\ \mathscr{C}^{21} = \cos\gamma, & \mathscr{C}^{22} = 1, & \mathscr{C}^{23} = \cos\alpha, \\ \mathscr{C}^{31} = \cos\beta, & \mathscr{C}^{32} = \cos\alpha, & \mathscr{C}^{33} = 1, \end{array}\right.$$

and three functions of l, m, n, that we express as $\mathscr{P}^1p, \mathscr{P}^2p, \mathscr{P}^3p$ by writing

·66 $$\left[\begin{array}{lll} \mathscr{P}^{11} = \Upsilon^{-2}\sin^2\alpha, & \mathscr{P}^{12} = \Upsilon^{-1}\cot\Gamma, & \mathscr{P}^{13} = \Upsilon^{-1}\cot\mathrm{B}, \\ \mathscr{P}^{21} = \Upsilon^{-1}\cot\Gamma, & \mathscr{P}^{22} = \Upsilon^{-2}\sin^2\beta, & \mathscr{P}^{23} = \Upsilon^{-1}\cot\mathrm{A}, \\ \mathscr{P}^{31} = \Upsilon^{-1}\cot\mathrm{B}, & \mathscr{P}^{32} = \Upsilon^{-1}\cot\mathrm{A}, & \mathscr{P}^{33} = \Upsilon^{-2}\sin^2\gamma; \end{array}\right.$$

it was the substitution of these functions in 4·51, with arguments $x_{\mathbf{s}}, y_{\mathbf{s}}, z_{\mathbf{s}}$ and $l_{\mathbf{s}}, m_{\mathbf{s}}, n_{\mathbf{s}}$, that gave 4·53, and our abbreviations have been designed to give this important theorem the concise symbolical form

·67 $$\mathscr{G}\,\mathbf{rs} = \mathscr{C}\,c_{\mathbf{r}}c_{\mathbf{s}} = \mathscr{P}\,p_{\mathbf{r}}p_{\mathbf{s}}.$$

·7. Merely as shorthand the umbral notation which we have been explaining is invaluable*. But the symbolism is too algebraical in form to serve only as shorthand; inevitably such notation suggests a comparison between different groups of symbols which would be equivalent if the various symbols had a purely algebraical meaning, and if the laws of analysis are obeyed to

* See for example article 332 below.

any extent by the symbols the notation effects to that extent economy in thought as well as in material, while on the other hand if there is considerable departure from obedience to these laws then until the symbolism is very familiar the mental effort involved in its accurate use is a counterpoise to the mechanical effort avoided by its brevity.

We do not propose to elaborate the use of umbral notation into a formal calculus, and for the present we give only some simple formulae, verifiable immediately, from which the reader will gather that the notation is not readily misused. Using f and g for ordinary numbers, we have for any symmetrical bilinear function Tuv,

$$T(fu+gv)^2 = f^2Tu^2 + 2fg\,Tuv + g^2Tv^2, \qquad \cdot 71$$

$$\partial(Tuv)/\partial u_i = T^i v, \qquad \cdot 72$$

and if the variables u_1, u_2, u_3 and v_1, v_2, v_3 depend on a variable t while the coefficients of the bilinear function are constants,

$$d(Tuv)/dt = T(du/dt)v + Tu(dv/dt), \qquad \cdot 73$$

$$d(Tu^2)/dt = 2Tu(du/dt). \qquad \cdot 74$$

·8. It is for use with multilinear functions that we introduce umbral notation, but having umbral symbols at our command we use them also to abbreviate determinants. The determinants which occur most frequently in the early parts of analytical geometry are of the two forms

$$\begin{vmatrix} x_{\mathbf{r}} & x_{\mathbf{s}} & x_{\mathbf{t}} \\ y_{\mathbf{r}} & y_{\mathbf{s}} & y_{\mathbf{t}} \\ z_{\mathbf{r}} & z_{\mathbf{s}} & z_{\mathbf{t}} \end{vmatrix}, \quad \begin{vmatrix} l_{\mathbf{r}} & l_{\mathbf{s}} & l_{\mathbf{t}} \\ m_{\mathbf{r}} & m_{\mathbf{s}} & m_{\mathbf{t}} \\ n_{\mathbf{r}} & n_{\mathbf{s}} & n_{\mathbf{t}} \end{vmatrix},$$

r, **s**, **t** being known vectors, and we agree to write for these determinants

$$[c_{\mathbf{r}};\, c_{\mathbf{s}};\, c_{\mathbf{t}}], \quad [p_{\mathbf{r}};\, p_{\mathbf{s}};\, p_{\mathbf{t}}].$$

Should cases arise in which the constituents of one column or of one row of a determinant must be given explicitly while umbral notation is available for other columns or rows, we may proceed as in the parallel case of links, writing for example

$$[c_{\mathbf{r}};\, f, g, h;\, c_{\mathbf{t}}] = \begin{vmatrix} x_{\mathbf{r}} & f & x_{\mathbf{t}} \\ y_{\mathbf{r}} & g & y_{\mathbf{t}} \\ z_{\mathbf{r}} & h & z_{\mathbf{t}} \end{vmatrix}.$$

The limit of brevity is attained when a determinant can be contracted both vertically and horizontally. For example, if **q** is an umbral symbol for (**r**, **s**, **t**), it is possible to replace $[c_{\mathbf{r}};\, c_{\mathbf{s}};\, c_{\mathbf{t}}]$, $[p_{\mathbf{r}};\, p_{\mathbf{s}};\, p_{\mathbf{t}}]$ by $[[c_{\mathbf{q}}]]$, $[[p_{\mathbf{q}}]]$. With this notation, $[[\mathscr{C}]]$, $[[\mathscr{P}]]$ *denote*

$$\begin{vmatrix} 1 & \cos\gamma & \cos\beta \\ \cos\gamma & 1 & \cos\alpha \\ \cos\beta & \cos\alpha & 1 \end{vmatrix}, \quad \begin{vmatrix} \Upsilon^{-2}\sin^2\alpha & \Upsilon^{-1}\cot\Gamma & \Upsilon^{-1}\cot\mathrm{B} \\ \Upsilon^{-1}\cot\Gamma & \Upsilon^{-2}\sin^2\beta & \Upsilon^{-1}\cot\mathrm{A} \\ \Upsilon^{-1}\cos\mathrm{B} & \Upsilon^{-1}\cot\mathrm{A} & \Upsilon^{-2}\sin^2\gamma \end{vmatrix}.$$

Already in 4·5 we have had examples of determinants obtained by bordering. The determinants bordered in analytical geometry are almost all symmetrical in the first place, and such a determinant bordered by a vertical and a horizontal row with zero for their common element yields a symmetrical bilinear function of the bordering elements. We shall therefore use a notation explained sufficiently by saying that the determinant in 4·55 will be denoted by $[[[\mathscr{C}]]\, p_{\mathbf{r}}p_{\mathbf{s}};\ \mathscr{G}\mathbf{rs}]$, and the determinants in 4·56, 4·57 simply by $[[[\mathscr{C}]]\, p_{\mathbf{r}}p_{\mathbf{s}}]$, $[[[\mathscr{P}]]\, c_{\mathbf{r}}c_{\mathbf{s}}]$. Doubly bordered determinants are not unknown, and it would be natural to denote

$$\begin{vmatrix} 1 & \cos\gamma & \cos\beta & l_{\mathbf{r}} & l_{\mathbf{t}} \\ \cos\gamma & 1 & \cos\alpha & m_{\mathbf{r}} & m_{\mathbf{t}} \\ \cos\beta & \cos\alpha & 1 & n_{\mathbf{r}} & n_{\mathbf{t}} \\ l_{\mathbf{s}} & m_{\mathbf{s}} & n_{\mathbf{s}} & 0 & 0 \\ l_{\mathbf{u}} & m_{\mathbf{u}} & n_{\mathbf{u}} & 0 & 0 \end{vmatrix}$$

by $[[[\mathscr{C}]]\,(p_{\mathbf{r}};\ p_{\mathbf{t}})(p_{\mathbf{s}};\ p_{\mathbf{u}})]$, but a notation derived from the determinant is
·84 sometimes superfluous in view of the fact that °this determinant has the value

$$\mathscr{C}\,(m_{\mathbf{r}}n_{\mathbf{t}} - n_{\mathbf{r}}m_{\mathbf{t}},\, n_{\mathbf{r}}l_{\mathbf{t}} - l_{\mathbf{r}}n_{\mathbf{t}},\, l_{\mathbf{r}}m_{\mathbf{t}} - m_{\mathbf{r}}l_{\mathbf{t}})(m_{\mathbf{s}}n_{\mathbf{u}} - n_{\mathbf{s}}m_{\mathbf{u}},\, n_{\mathbf{s}}l_{\mathbf{u}} - l_{\mathbf{s}}n_{\mathbf{u}},\, l_{\mathbf{s}}m_{\mathbf{u}} - m_{\mathbf{s}}l_{\mathbf{u}}).$$

·9. Contractions will be used as freely in plane geometry as in three-dimensional work. It is true that the economy must be less marked, but it is far from negligible, and naturally it is easier to compare two-dimensional with three-dimensional formulae if all are expressed in the same style.

As far as possible, the *same* symbols are used as umbrae in plane geometry as in solid geometry, the context being trusted to prevent confusion. Thus we write

·92 $$c = (x,\ y),$$

·93 $$p = (l,\ m).$$

·94 Then the formulae $$\mathscr{G}\mathbf{rs} = c_{\mathbf{r}}p_{\mathbf{s}} = p_{\mathbf{r}}c_{\mathbf{s}}$$

are valid in the plane, the theorem being proved by the same argument as establishes the corresponding theorem in space, and we shall purposely use $\mathscr{C}$ and $\mathscr{P}$ for the component and projection symbols in a plane in order to reproduce literally the formulae

·95 $$\mathscr{G}\mathbf{rs} = \mathscr{C}\, c_{\mathbf{r}}c_{\mathbf{s}} = \mathscr{P}\, p_{\mathbf{r}}p_{\mathbf{s}};$$

it follows from 4·31 and 4·32 that the necessary definitions are

·96 $$\mathscr{C}\, c_{\mathbf{r}}c_{\mathbf{s}} \equiv x_{\mathbf{r}}x_{\mathbf{s}} + (x_{\mathbf{r}}y_{\mathbf{s}} + y_{\mathbf{r}}x_{\mathbf{s}})\cos\omega + y_{\mathbf{r}}y_{\mathbf{s}},$$

·97 $$\mathscr{P}\, p_{\mathbf{r}}p_{\mathbf{s}} \equiv l_{\mathbf{r}}l_{\mathbf{s}}\operatorname{cosec}^2\omega - (l_{\mathbf{r}}m_{\mathbf{s}} + m_{\mathbf{r}}l_{\mathbf{s}})\operatorname{cosec}\omega\cot\omega + m_{\mathbf{r}}m_{\mathbf{s}}\operatorname{cosec}^2\omega,$$

·98 implying $$\mathscr{C}^{11} = \mathscr{C}^{22} = 1, \quad \mathscr{C}^{12} = \mathscr{C}^{21} = \cos\omega,$$

·99 $$\mathscr{P}^{11} = \mathscr{P}^{22} = \operatorname{cosec}^2\omega, \quad \mathscr{P}^{12} = \mathscr{P}^{21} = -\operatorname{cosec}\omega\cot\omega.$$

CHAPTER III 3

CARTESIAN AXES IN USE

330. Introduction. 331. The evaluation of projected products in a plane; the specification of angles in a prepared plane; the evaluation of areal products. 332. The evaluation of projected products in space, of vector products, and of spatial products; Lagrange's identities. 333. The specification of rotors, of rays, and of lines, in a prepared plane. 334. The specification of prepared and unprepared planes in space. 335. The specification of rotors in space and of motors; the determination of pitch and of a central axis. 336. The specification of rays and lines in space. 337. Some problems in the analytical geometry of lines and rays.

330. INTRODUCTION.

The apparatus, geometrical and algebraical, required for the use of Cartesian axes, is now at our command. To see how it is handled, we can not do better than consider a number of fundamental questions of an elementary kind.

331. THE EVALUATION OF PROJECTED PRODUCTS IN A PLANE; THE SPECIFICATION OF ANGLES IN A PREPARED PLANE; THE EVALUATION OF AREAL PRODUCTS.

·1. In plane geometry, with

$$c = (x, y), \quad p = (l, m), \qquad \cdot 11$$

221·15 gives for any two vectors $\mathbf{r}$, $\mathbf{s}$

$$\mathscr{G}\mathbf{rs} = c_{\mathbf{r}}p_{\mathbf{s}} = p_{\mathbf{r}}c_{\mathbf{s}}, \qquad \cdot 12$$

and 24·31 and 24·32 shew how the expression can be expanded in terms of components alone or in terms of projections alone. Writing

$$\mathscr{C}\, c_{\mathbf{r}}c_{\mathbf{s}} \equiv x_{\mathbf{r}}x_{\mathbf{s}} + (x_{\mathbf{r}}y_{\mathbf{s}} + y_{\mathbf{r}}x_{\mathbf{s}})\cos\omega + y_{\mathbf{r}}y_{\mathbf{s}}, \qquad \cdot 13$$

$$\mathscr{P}\, p_{\mathbf{r}}p_{\mathbf{s}} \equiv l_{\mathbf{r}}l_{\mathbf{s}}\operatorname{cosec}^2\omega - (l_{\mathbf{r}}m_{\mathbf{s}} + m_{\mathbf{r}}l_{\mathbf{s}})\operatorname{cosec}\omega\cot\omega + m_{\mathbf{r}}m_{\mathbf{s}}\operatorname{cosec}^2\omega, \qquad \cdot 14$$

we can assert that

The value of the projected product of two vectors $\mathbf{r}$, $\mathbf{s}$ *in a plane is the value of the four equal expressions* ·15

$$\mathscr{C}\, c_{\mathbf{r}}c_{\mathbf{s}}, \quad c_{\mathbf{r}}p_{\mathbf{s}}, \quad p_{\mathbf{r}}c_{\mathbf{s}}, \quad \mathscr{P}\, p_{\mathbf{r}}p_{\mathbf{s}}.$$

The notation implies that

The projections of any vector are given in terms of the components by ·16

$$l = \mathscr{C}^1 c, \quad m = \mathscr{C}^2 c$$

and the components in terms of the projections by

$$x = \mathscr{P}^1 p, \quad y = \mathscr{P}^2 p,$$

and elimination between ·12 and ·16 gives the equations

·17 $$\left[[[\mathscr{C}]]\, p_{\mathbf{r}} p_{\mathbf{s}} ;\ \mathscr{G}\, \mathbf{rs} \right] = 0, \quad \left[[[\mathscr{P}]]\, c_{\mathbf{r}} c_{\mathbf{s}} ;\ \mathscr{G}\, \mathbf{rs} \right] = 0,$$

shewing that

·18 *The projected product of two vectors* $\mathbf{r}, \mathbf{s}$ *in a plane has the value of the equal expressions*

$$-\left[[[\mathscr{C}]]\, p_{\mathbf{r}} p_{\mathbf{s}} \right] / [[\mathscr{C}]], \quad -\left[[[\mathscr{P}]]\, c_{\mathbf{r}} c_{\mathbf{s}} \right] / [[\mathscr{P}]].$$

·19 °The determinants denoted here by $[[\mathscr{C}]]$, $[[\mathscr{P}]]$ have the values $\sin^2 \omega$, $\operatorname{cosec}^2 \omega$.

·2. Recalling the substance of 23·4 and 221·4, we can write down the following corollaries of ·15 and ·18:

·21 *The value of the projection of the vector* $\mathbf{r}$ *in the direction* Σ *is the value of the six equal expressions*

$$\mathscr{C}\, c_{\mathbf{r}} c_{\Sigma}, \quad c_{\mathbf{r}} p_{\Sigma}, \quad p_{\mathbf{r}} c_{\Sigma}, \quad \mathscr{P}\, p_{\mathbf{r}} p_{\Sigma}, \quad -\left[[[\mathscr{C}]]\, p_{\mathbf{r}} p_{\Sigma} \right] / [[\mathscr{C}]], \quad -\left[[[\mathscr{P}]]\, c_{\mathbf{r}} c_{\Sigma} \right] / [[\mathscr{P}]].$$

·22 *The cosine of the angles between two directions* P, Σ *is the value of the six equal expressions*

$$\mathscr{C}\, c_{\mathrm{P}} c_{\Sigma}, \quad c_{\mathrm{P}} p_{\Sigma}, \quad p_{\mathrm{P}} c_{\Sigma}, \quad \mathscr{P}\, p_{\mathrm{P}} p_{\Sigma}, \quad -\left[[[\mathscr{C}]]\, p_{\mathrm{P}} p_{\Sigma} \right] / [[\mathscr{C}]], \quad -\left[[[\mathscr{P}]]\, c_{\mathrm{P}} c_{\Sigma} \right] / [[\mathscr{P}]].$$

·23 *Two vectors* $\mathbf{r}$, $\mathbf{s}$ *have perpendicular directions if and only if the equal expressions*

$$\mathscr{C}\, c_{\mathbf{r}} c_{\mathbf{s}}, \quad c_{\mathbf{r}} p_{\mathbf{s}}, \quad p_{\mathbf{r}} c_{\mathbf{s}}, \quad \mathscr{P}\, p_{\mathbf{r}} p_{\mathbf{s}}$$

vanish, and if and only if the determinants $\left[[[\mathscr{C}]]\, p_{\mathbf{r}} p_{\mathbf{s}} \right]$, $\left[[[\mathscr{P}]]\, c_{\mathbf{r}} c_{\mathbf{s}} \right]$ *vanish.*

·24 *The square of the amounts of a vector is the common value of the equal expressions*

$$\mathscr{C} c^2, \quad cp, \quad \mathscr{P} p^2, \quad -\left[[[\mathscr{C}]]\, p^2 \right] / [[\mathscr{C}]], \quad -\left[[[\mathscr{P}]]\, c^2 \right] / [[\mathscr{P}]].$$

·25 *The square of the distances of the point Q from the origin of the reference frame is the common value of*

$$\mathscr{C} c_Q^2, \quad c_Q p_Q, \quad \mathscr{P} p_Q^2, \quad -\left[[[\mathscr{C}]]\, p_Q^2 \right] / [[\mathscr{C}]], \quad -\left[[[\mathscr{P}]]\, c_Q^2 \right] / [[\mathscr{P}]],$$

and the square of the lengths of the step RS is the common value of

$$\mathscr{C}(c_S - c_R)^2, \quad (c_S - c_R \between p_S - p_R), \quad \mathscr{P}(p_S - p_R)^2,$$
$$-\left[[[\mathscr{C}]] (p_S - p_R)^2 \right] / [[\mathscr{C}]], \quad -\left[[[\mathscr{P}]] (c_S - c_R)^2 \right] / [[\mathscr{P}]].$$

·26 *The ratios and the cosines of any direction* P *satisfy identically the equations*

$$\mathscr{C}\, c_{\mathrm{P}}^2 = c_{\mathrm{P}} p_{\mathrm{P}} = \mathscr{P}\, p_{\mathrm{P}}^2 = 1, \quad \left[[[\mathscr{C}]]\, p_{\mathrm{P}}^2 ;\ 1 \right] = 0, \quad \left[[[\mathscr{P}]]\, c_{\mathrm{P}}^2 ;\ 1 \right] = 0.$$

·3. In a prepared plane the use of actual angles for the specification of directions has obvious advantages. With respect to a frame OXY we may of course describe the direction whose image is T merely by stating an angle from Ξ to T, but to adopt this plan is to abandon hope of symmetry. Two courses suggest themselves, and of both use is made on occasion: we may use explicitly both an angle from Ξ to T and an angle from T to H, or we may use an angle to T from a bisector of the angles between Ξ and H.

In the first case, we °denote a chosen angle from Ξ to T by α, and a chosen angle from T to H by β; the sum of α and β is necessarily congruent with ω, and we choose α and β to satisfy the equality ·31

$$\alpha+\beta=\omega. \qquad \cdot 32$$

In the second case, we °denote by ξ an angle to T from the bisecting ray which makes an angle equal to $\frac{1}{2}\omega$ with the first axis; moreover, when passing from one method of description to the other we assume the equalities ·33

$$\alpha=\tfrac{1}{2}\omega+\xi, \quad \beta=\tfrac{1}{2}\omega-\xi, \qquad \cdot 34$$

which are of course consistent with ·32. The choice of the angles α, β, ξ is in no respect governed by the choice of ω, but when one of the three angles has been chosen the others are determinate; the expression of α and β in terms of ξ given by ·34 is unique, but we can express ξ in terms of α and β in a variety of ways, of which the most useful is

$$\xi=\tfrac{1}{2}(\alpha-\beta). \qquad \cdot 35$$

We speak of the direction ξ or of the direction $\{\alpha, \beta\}$; the direction which makes an angle ϵ with this direction is the direction $\xi+\epsilon$ or $\{\alpha+\epsilon, \beta-\epsilon\}$, and in particular the direction normal to ξ or $\{\alpha, \beta\}$ is $\xi+\frac{1}{2}\pi$ or $\{\alpha+\frac{1}{2}\pi, \beta-\frac{1}{2}\pi\}$.

With the familiar mixture of theorem and convention, the angles derived from the polar of OXY to correspond to α and β may be defined by

$$\bar{\alpha}=\tfrac{1}{2}\pi-\beta, \quad \bar{\beta}=\tfrac{1}{2}\pi-\alpha; \qquad \cdot 37$$

from ·32, the sum of these angles is $\pi-\omega$, which we have already agreed to regard as *the* angle of the polar frame, while the difference between the angles is $\alpha-\beta$ and therefore

$$\bar{\xi}=\xi; \qquad \cdot 38$$

the bisectors of the angles between the axes of any frame are the bisectors also of the angles between the axes of the polar frame, and ·38 shews that the conventions embodied in ·34 and 21·73 imply that ξ and $\bar{\xi}$ are measured from the same direction.

·4. Naturally the relations between the angles α, β and the ratios and cosines of the direction $\{\alpha, \beta\}$ are simple and useful. If we regard the angles as fundamental, we have

$$l=\cos\alpha, \quad m=\cos\beta, \qquad \cdot 41$$

$$x=\sin\beta/\sin\omega, \quad y=\sin\alpha/\sin\omega, \qquad \cdot 42$$

the last pair of formulae being a consequence of 23·54. If on the other hand we wish to replace trigonometrical symbols by algebraical we use the same pairs of formulae in the forms

$$\cos\alpha=l, \quad \cos\beta=m, \qquad \cdot 43$$

$$\sin\alpha=y\sin\omega, \quad \sin\beta=x\sin\omega. \qquad \cdot 44$$

The fact that each of the pairs x, y and l, m can be expressed in terms of the other is equivalent to the fact that, on account of ·32, each of the pairs $\cos\alpha, \cos\beta$ and $\sin\alpha, \sin\beta$ can be expressed rationally in terms of the other; actually, from

$$\beta = \omega - \alpha, \quad \alpha = \omega - \beta$$

we have

·45 $$\sin\omega\cos\alpha = \sin\beta + \cos\omega\sin\alpha, \quad \sin\omega\cos\beta = \sin\alpha + \cos\omega\sin\beta,$$

·46 $$\sin\omega\sin\alpha = \cos\beta - \cos\omega\cos\alpha, \quad \sin\omega\sin\beta = \cos\alpha - \cos\omega\cos\beta,$$

and of these formulae, which explain the introduction of symmetry by the use of the pair of angles α, β connected by ·32, the pair ·45 is equivalent to 24·31 and the pair ·46 to 24·32; it is obvious also that ·45 and ·46 imply that $\alpha+\beta$ is congruent with ω. An elementary illustration of the use of the angles α, β is to be remarked in the simplicity of the deduction from ·37, ·43, and ·44 of the relations between ratios and cosines relative to one frame and cosines and ratios relative to the polar frame. As a second illustration we obtain the ratios and cosines of the direction ΩE making a positive right angle with a given direction ΩT: we have

·47 $$\alpha_E = \alpha_T + \tfrac{1}{2}\pi, \quad \beta_E = \beta_T - \tfrac{1}{2}\pi,$$

·48 and therefore $$x_E = -m_T \operatorname{cosec}\omega, \quad y_E = l_T \operatorname{cosec}\omega,$$

·49 $$l_E = -y_T\sin\omega, \quad m_E = x_T\sin\omega;$$

it is easy to see that either of the equations

·491 $$l_T x_E + m_T y_E = 0, \quad x_T l_E + y_T m_E = 0$$

together with the relations between ratios and cosines of a single direction given in ·26 implies the relations

·492 $$\frac{x_E}{-m_T} = \frac{y_E}{l_T} = \frac{l_E}{-y_T\sin^2\omega} = \frac{m_E}{x_T\sin^2\omega} = \frac{1}{\sqrt{(\sin^2\omega)}},$$

but ·491, and therefore also ·492, is true not only of the elements defining the direction ΩE but also of the elements defining the reverse direction ΩE′, and we can not discover from ·491 alone which value of $\sqrt{(\sin^2\omega)}$ in ·492 is associated with E and which value with E′.

·5. Actual angles may be introduced in the study of vectors and steps as well as of directions. If $\mathbf{r}$ is the vector of amount r in the direction $\{\alpha, \beta\}$, then

·51 $$l_{\mathbf{r}} = r\cos\alpha, \quad m_{\mathbf{r}} = r\cos\beta,$$

·52 $$x_{\mathbf{r}} = r\sin\beta/\sin\omega, \quad y_{\mathbf{r}} = r\sin\alpha/\sin\omega,$$

and if the step ST has the length r in the direction $\{\alpha, \beta\}$, then

·53 $$l_T - l_S = r\cos\alpha, \quad m_T - m_S = r\cos\beta,$$

·54 $$x_T - x_S = r\sin\beta/\sin\omega, \quad y_T - y_S = r\sin\alpha/\sin\omega.$$

·61 **·6.** If r is a length of the step ST, °the direction in which ST has this length has ratios $(x_T - x_S)/r$, $(y_T - y_S)/r$ and cosines $(l_T - l_S)/r$, $(m_T - m_S)/r$,
·62 and therefore by ·48 and ·49 the °normal direction has cosines $-\{(y_T - y_S)/r\}\sin\omega$,

$\{(x_T - x_S)/r\}\sin\omega$ and ratios $-\{(m_T - m_S)/r\}\operatorname{cosec}\omega$, $\{(l_T - l_S)/r\}\operatorname{cosec}\omega$, and the projection in this direction of any vector $\mathbf{r}$ is expressible in either of the forms

$$r^{-1}\sin\omega\begin{vmatrix} x_T - x_S & x_{\mathbf{r}} \\ y_T - y_S & y_{\mathbf{r}} \end{vmatrix}, \qquad r^{-1}\operatorname{cosec}\omega\begin{vmatrix} l_T - l_S & l_{\mathbf{r}} \\ m_T - m_S & m_{\mathbf{r}} \end{vmatrix}, \qquad \cdot 63$$

or otherwise in either of the forms

$$r^{-1}\sin\omega\begin{vmatrix} 0 & x_{\mathbf{r}} & y_{\mathbf{r}} \\ 1 & x_S & y_S \\ 1 & x_T & y_T \end{vmatrix}, \qquad r^{-1}\operatorname{cosec}\omega\begin{vmatrix} 0 & l_{\mathbf{r}} & m_{\mathbf{r}} \\ 1 & l_S & m_S \\ 1 & l_T & m_T \end{vmatrix}. \qquad \cdot 64$$

Taking for $\mathbf{r}$ the vector of a step PR we have expressions for the projection of this step normally to the ray in which ST has the length r; in particular we can find the distance of R from this ray by placing P anywhere in the line through S and T. For example, by giving to $x_{\mathbf{r}}$, $y_{\mathbf{r}}$, $l_{\mathbf{r}}$, $m_{\mathbf{r}}$ the values $x_R - x_S$, $y_R - y_S$, $l_R - l_S$, $m_R - m_S$ we find for the perpendicular distance the expressions*

$$r^{-1}\sin\omega\begin{vmatrix} 1 & x_R & y_R \\ 1 & x_S & y_S \\ 1 & x_T & y_T \end{vmatrix}, \qquad r^{-1}\operatorname{cosec}\omega\begin{vmatrix} 1 & l_R & m_R \\ 1 & l_S & m_S \\ 1 & l_T & m_T \end{vmatrix}. \qquad \cdot 65$$

Multiplying these expressions by $\frac{1}{2}r$ we conclude that

The area of the triangle RST in a prepared plane is given in terms of the coordinates and in terms of the projections of the vertices with respect to a frame of angle ω by the expressions ·66

$$\tfrac{1}{2}\sin\omega\begin{vmatrix} 1 & x_R & y_R \\ 1 & x_S & y_S \\ 1 & x_T & y_T \end{vmatrix}, \qquad \tfrac{1}{2}\operatorname{cosec}\omega\begin{vmatrix} 1 & l_R & m_R \\ 1 & l_S & m_S \\ 1 & l_T & m_T \end{vmatrix}.$$

In the form

$$\begin{vmatrix} 1 & l_R & m_R \\ 1 & l_S & m_S \\ 1 & l_T & m_T \end{vmatrix} = \begin{vmatrix} 1 & 0 & 0 \\ 0 & 1 & \cos\omega \\ 0 & \cos\omega & 1 \end{vmatrix}\begin{vmatrix} 1 & x_R & y_R \\ 1 & x_S & y_S \\ 1 & x_T & y_T \end{vmatrix}$$

the relation between the two determinants in ·66 appears as an immediate consequence of 24·31, and the cyclic direction of the plane governs the sign of the area by determining the sign of the factor $\sin\omega$ or $\operatorname{cosec}\omega$.

Using umbral notation as suggested in 25·8, we can contract the expressions in ·63 to

$$r^{-1}\sin\omega\,[c_T - c_S;\ c_{\mathbf{r}}], \quad r^{-1}\operatorname{cosec}\omega\,[p_T - p_S;\ p_{\mathbf{r}}]. \qquad \cdot 67$$

* Algebraically it is evident that the same expressions will result if we substitute $x_R - (hx_S + kx_T)$ for $x_{\mathbf{r}}$, and so on, if h, k are any two numbers whose sum is unity. That is, with this condition $hx_S + kx_T$, $hy_S + ky_T$ are necessarily the coordinates of some point on the line ST, and 24·31 implies that $hl_S + kl_T$, $hm_S + km_T$ are the projections of the same point. This is to anticipate.

·68 To abbreviate those in ·65 and ·66 we may use °an umbra P for (R, S, T), when the expressions in question become

·69 $$\tfrac{1}{2}[1, 1, 1;\ x_P;\ y_P] \sin\omega, \quad \tfrac{1}{2}[1, 1, 1;\ l_P;\ m_P] \operatorname{cosec}\omega.$$

·7. Having worked in the last few paragraphs from first principles, we are able to appreciate that the use of wider notions enables us to recover the same results with much less labour. The vectors **r**, **s** can be expressed as $x_{\mathbf{r}}\mathbf{l}_{\Xi} + y_{\mathbf{r}}\mathbf{l}_{\mathrm{H}}$, $x_{\mathbf{s}}\mathbf{l}_{\Xi} + y_{\mathbf{s}}\mathbf{l}_{\mathrm{H}}$, and therefore from 222·15, that is, because the areal product is distributive,

·71 $$\mathscr{A}\,\mathbf{rs} = x_{\mathbf{r}}x_{\mathbf{s}}\,\mathscr{A}\,\mathbf{l}_{\Xi}^2 + x_{\mathbf{r}}y_{\mathbf{s}}\,\mathscr{A}\,\mathbf{l}_{\Xi}\mathbf{l}_{\mathrm{H}} + y_{\mathbf{r}}x_{\mathbf{s}}\,\mathscr{A}\,\mathbf{l}_{\mathrm{H}}\mathbf{l}_{\Xi} + y_{\mathbf{r}}y_{\mathbf{s}}\,\mathscr{A}\,\mathbf{l}_{\mathrm{H}}^2;$$

but from the definition of the areal product,

·72 $$\mathscr{A}\,\mathbf{l}_{\Xi}^2 = 0, \quad \mathscr{A}\,\mathbf{l}_{\Xi}\mathbf{l}_{\mathrm{H}} = \sin\omega, \quad \mathscr{A}\,\mathbf{l}_{\mathrm{H}}\mathbf{l}_{\Xi} = -\sin\omega, \quad \mathscr{A}\,\mathbf{l}_{\mathrm{H}}^2 = 0,$$

and therefore

·73 *The areal product of the vectors* **r**, **s** *is given in terms of the components of the vectors by the formula*

$$\mathscr{A}\,\mathbf{rs} = (x_{\mathbf{r}}y_{\mathbf{s}} - y_{\mathbf{r}}x_{\mathbf{s}}) \sin\omega,$$

and in terms of the projections by the formula

$$\mathscr{A}\,\mathbf{rs} = (l_{\mathbf{r}}m_{\mathbf{s}} - m_{\mathbf{r}}l_{\mathbf{s}}) \operatorname{cosec}\omega,$$

the second part of the theorem coming by an application of 24·22 and 21·73.

Umbral notation can be used in the formulae of ·73, giving

·74 $$\mathscr{A}\,\mathbf{rs} = [c_{\mathbf{r}};\ c_{\mathbf{s}}] \sin\omega = [p_{\mathbf{r}};\ p_{\mathbf{s}}] \operatorname{cosec}\omega.$$

A particular case of this gives the expressions in ·63, already in the abbreviated forms of ·67. From 222·31 and ·74 the area of the triangle RST is expressible in the forms

·75 $$\tfrac{1}{2}[c_S - c_R;\ c_T - c_R] \sin\omega, \quad \tfrac{1}{2}[p_S - p_R;\ p_T - p_R] \operatorname{cosec}\omega,$$

identifiable at once with those given in ·69.

332. The evaluation of projected products in space, of vector products, and of spatial products; Lagrange's identities.

After our experience of the application of 222·15 to the proof of the theorems of the last paragraph, we retain our full equipment for the first consideration of corresponding theorems in space.

·1. In the geometry of space we have agreed to write

·11 $$c = (x, y, z), \quad p = (l, m, n),$$

·12 $$\mathscr{C}\,c_{\mathbf{r}}c_{\mathbf{s}} = x_{\mathbf{r}}x_{\mathbf{s}} + y_{\mathbf{r}}y_{\mathbf{s}} + z_{\mathbf{r}}z_{\mathbf{s}} + (y_{\mathbf{r}}z_{\mathbf{s}} + z_{\mathbf{r}}y_{\mathbf{s}}) \cos\alpha + (z_{\mathbf{r}}x_{\mathbf{s}} + x_{\mathbf{r}}z_{\mathbf{s}}) \cos\beta + (x_{\mathbf{r}}y_{\mathbf{s}} + y_{\mathbf{r}}x_{\mathbf{s}}) \cos\gamma,$$

·13 $$\mathscr{P}\,p_{\mathbf{r}}p_{\mathbf{s}} = l_{\mathbf{r}}l_{\mathbf{s}}\Upsilon^{-2}\sin^2\alpha + m_{\mathbf{r}}m_{\mathbf{s}}\Upsilon^{-2}\sin^2\beta + n_{\mathbf{r}}n_{\mathbf{s}}\Upsilon^{-2}\sin^2\gamma + (m_{\mathbf{r}}n_{\mathbf{s}} + n_{\mathbf{r}}m_{\mathbf{s}})\Upsilon^{-1}\cot\mathrm{A} + (n_{\mathbf{r}}l_{\mathbf{s}} + l_{\mathbf{r}}n_{\mathbf{s}})\Upsilon^{-1}\cot\mathrm{B} + (l_{\mathbf{r}}m_{\mathbf{s}} + m_{\mathbf{r}}l_{\mathbf{s}})\Upsilon^{-1}\cot\Gamma,$$

for we have found in 24·33 and 24·34 that with this notation

The projections of any vector are given in terms of the components by ·14

$$l = \mathscr{C}^1 c, \quad m = \mathscr{C}^2 c, \quad n = \mathscr{C}^3 c,$$

and the components in terms of the projections by

$$x = \mathscr{P}^1 p, \quad y = \mathscr{P}^2 p, \quad z = \mathscr{P}^3 p,$$

and that consequently

The value of the projected product of two vectors **r**, **s** *is the value of the six equal expressions* ·15

$$\mathscr{C}\, c_{\mathbf{r}} c_{\mathbf{s}}, \quad c_{\mathbf{r}} p_{\mathbf{s}}, \quad p_{\mathbf{r}} c_{\mathbf{s}}, \quad \mathscr{P}\, p_{\mathbf{r}} p_{\mathbf{s}}, \quad -\big[[[\mathscr{C}]]\, p_{\mathbf{r}} p_{\mathbf{s}}\big]/[[\mathscr{C}]], \quad -\big[[[\mathscr{P}]]\, c_{\mathbf{r}} c_{\mathbf{s}}\big]/[[\mathscr{P}]],$$

where now, by 24·42, $[[\mathscr{C}]]$, $[[\mathscr{P}]]$ have the values Υ^2, Υ^{-2}.

·2. The corollaries of 1·15 and 1·18 enunciated in 1·2 can be repeated*, word for word and symbol for symbol; the interpretation of the symbols has changed, but the basis of the deductions is again in 23·4 and 221·4:

The value of the projection of the vector **r** *in the direction* Σ *is the value of the six equal expressions* ·21

$$\mathscr{C}\, c_{\mathbf{r}} c_{\Sigma}, \quad c_{\mathbf{r}} p_{\Sigma}, \quad p_{\mathbf{r}} c_{\Sigma}, \quad \mathscr{P}\, p_{\mathbf{r}} p_{\Sigma}, \quad -\big[[[\mathscr{C}]]\, p_{\mathbf{r}} p_{\Sigma}\big]/[[\mathscr{C}]], \quad -\big[[[\mathscr{P}]]\, c_{\mathbf{r}} c_{\Sigma}\big]/[[\mathscr{P}]].$$

The cosine of the angles between two directions P, Σ *is the value of the six equal expressions* ·22

$$\mathscr{C}\, c_{\mathrm{P}} c_{\Sigma}, \quad c_{\mathrm{P}} p_{\Sigma}, \quad p_{\mathrm{P}} c_{\Sigma}, \quad \mathscr{P}\, p_{\mathrm{P}} p_{\Sigma}, \quad -\big[[[\mathscr{C}]]\, p_{\mathrm{P}} p_{\Sigma}\big]/[[\mathscr{C}]], \quad -\big[[[\mathscr{P}]]\, c_{\mathrm{P}} c_{\Sigma}\big]/[[\mathscr{P}]].$$

Two vectors **r**, **s** *have perpendicular directions if and only if the equal expressions* ·23

$$\mathscr{C}\, c_{\mathbf{r}} c_{\mathbf{s}}, \quad c_{\mathbf{r}} p_{\mathbf{s}}, \quad p_{\mathbf{r}} c_{\mathbf{s}}, \quad \mathscr{P}\, p_{\mathbf{r}} p_{\mathbf{s}}$$

vanish, and if and only if the determinants $\big[[[\mathscr{C}]]\, p_{\mathbf{r}} p_{\mathbf{s}}\big]$, $\big[[[\mathscr{P}]]\, c_{\mathbf{r}} c_{\mathbf{s}}\big]$ *vanish.*

The square of the amounts of a vector is the common value of the equal expressions ·24

$$\mathscr{C}\, c^2, \quad cp, \quad \mathscr{P}\, p^2, \quad -\big[[[\mathscr{C}]]\, p^2\big]/[[\mathscr{C}]], \quad -\big[[[\mathscr{P}]]\, c^2\big]/[[\mathscr{P}]].$$

The square of the distances of the point Q from the origin of the reference frame is the common value of ·25

$$\mathscr{C}\, c_Q^2, \quad c_Q p_Q, \quad \mathscr{P}\, p_Q^2, \quad -\big[[[\mathscr{C}]]\, p_Q^2\big]/[[\mathscr{C}]], \quad -\big[[[\mathscr{P}]]\, c_Q^2\big]/[[\mathscr{P}]],$$

and the square of the lengths of the step RS is the common value of

$$\mathscr{C}\,(c_S - c_R)^2, \quad (c_S - c_R)(p_S - p_R), \quad \mathscr{P}\,(p_S - p_R)^2,$$
$$-\big[[[\mathscr{C}]]\,(p_S - p_R)^2\big]/[[\mathscr{C}]], \quad -\big[[[\mathscr{P}]]\,(c_S - c_R)^2\big]/[[\mathscr{P}]].$$

The ratios and the cosines of any direction P *satisfy identically the equations* ·26

$$\mathscr{C}\, c_{\mathrm{P}}^2 = c_{\mathrm{P}} p_{\mathrm{P}} = \mathscr{P}\, p_{\mathrm{P}}^2 = 1, \quad \big[[[\mathscr{C}]]\, p_{\mathrm{P}}^2;\ 1\big] = 0, \quad \big[[[\mathscr{P}]]\, c_{\mathrm{P}}^2;\ 1\big] = 0.$$

* Habitually to indulge in repetitions of this kind is to forgo the advantages implicit in the notation, but a few examples at this stage may be allowed.

·3. From the identities

·31 $$\mathbf{r} = x_{\mathbf{r}} 1_{\Xi} + y_{\mathbf{r}} 1_{\mathrm{H}} + z_{\mathbf{r}} 1_{\mathrm{Z}}, \quad \mathbf{s} = x_{\mathbf{s}} 1_{\Xi} + y_{\mathbf{s}} 1_{\mathrm{H}} + z_{\mathbf{s}} 1_{\mathrm{Z}},$$

which simply express the meaning of components, using 223·27 and the results of the forms

·32 $$\mathcal{V}\, 1_{\Xi}^2 = 0, \quad \mathcal{V}\, 1_{\mathrm{Z}} 1_{\mathrm{H}} = -\mathcal{V}\, 1_{\mathrm{H}} 1_{\mathrm{Z}},$$

we have

·33 $$\mathcal{V}\, \mathbf{rs} = (y_{\mathbf{r}} z_{\mathbf{s}} - z_{\mathbf{r}} y_{\mathbf{s}}) \mathcal{V}\, 1_{\mathrm{H}} 1_{\mathrm{Z}} + (z_{\mathbf{r}} x_{\mathbf{s}} - x_{\mathbf{r}} z_{\mathbf{s}}) \mathcal{V}\, 1_{\mathrm{Z}} 1_{\Xi} + (x_{\mathbf{r}} y_{\mathbf{s}} - y_{\mathbf{r}} x_{\mathbf{s}}) \mathcal{V}\, 1_{\Xi} 1_{\mathrm{H}};$$

since $\mathcal{V}\, 1_{\mathrm{H}} 1_{\mathrm{Z}}$, $\mathcal{V}\, 1_{\mathrm{Z}} 1_{\Xi}$, $\mathcal{V}\, 1_{\Xi} 1_{\mathrm{H}}$ are the vectors of amounts $\sin\alpha$, $\sin\beta$, $\sin\gamma$ in the directions normal to the planes of reference,

·34 *The vector product of* **r** *and* **s** *is the vector whose components in the polar of the frame OXYZ are* $(y_{\mathbf{r}} z_{\mathbf{s}} - z_{\mathbf{r}} y_{\mathbf{s}}) \sin\alpha$, $(z_{\mathbf{r}} x_{\mathbf{s}} - x_{\mathbf{r}} z_{\mathbf{s}}) \sin\beta$, $(x_{\mathbf{r}} y_{\mathbf{s}} - y_{\mathbf{r}} x_{\mathbf{s}}) \sin\gamma$,

and this, in virtue of 24·24, is equivalent to the assertion that the *projections* of the vector product $\mathcal{V}\,\mathbf{rs}$ in the frame $OXYZ$ itself are $\Upsilon(y_{\mathbf{r}} z_{\mathbf{s}} - z_{\mathbf{r}} y_{\mathbf{s}})$, $\Upsilon(z_{\mathbf{r}} x_{\mathbf{s}} - x_{\mathbf{r}} z_{\mathbf{s}})$, $\Upsilon(x_{\mathbf{r}} y_{\mathbf{s}} - y_{\mathbf{r}} x_{\mathbf{s}})$; the vectors **r** and **s** being the vectors whose components in the polar of $OXYZ$ are $l_{\mathbf{r}} \upsilon^{-1} \sin \mathrm{A}$, $m_{\mathbf{r}} \upsilon^{-1} \sin \mathrm{B}$, $n_{\mathbf{r}} \upsilon^{-1} \sin \Gamma$ and $l_{\mathbf{s}} \upsilon^{-1} \sin \mathrm{A}$, $m_{\mathbf{s}} \upsilon^{-1} \sin \mathrm{B}$, $n_{\mathbf{s}} \upsilon^{-1} \sin \Gamma$, ·34 gives the *components* of the vector product in $OXYZ$ directly as $\Upsilon^{-1}(m_{\mathbf{r}} n_{\mathbf{s}} - n_{\mathbf{r}} m_{\mathbf{s}})$, $\Upsilon^{-1}(n_{\mathbf{r}} l_{\mathbf{s}} - l_{\mathbf{r}} n_{\mathbf{s}})$, $\Upsilon^{-1}(l_{\mathbf{r}} m_{\mathbf{s}} - m_{\mathbf{r}} l_{\mathbf{s}})$, since by 22·79 the factor $\upsilon^{-2} \sin \mathrm{A} \sin \mathrm{B} \sin \Gamma$ which enters has the value Υ^{-1}:

·35 *If* **p** *is the vector product of* **r** *and* **s**, *then**

$$(x_{\mathbf{p}}, y_{\mathbf{p}}, z_{\mathbf{p}}) = \Upsilon^{-1} \left\| \begin{matrix} l_{\mathbf{r}} & m_{\mathbf{r}} & n_{\mathbf{r}} \\ l_{\mathbf{s}} & m_{\mathbf{s}} & n_{\mathbf{s}} \end{matrix} \right\|, \quad (l_{\mathbf{p}}, m_{\mathbf{p}}, n_{\mathbf{p}}) = \Upsilon \left\| \begin{matrix} x_{\mathbf{r}} & y_{\mathbf{r}} & z_{\mathbf{r}} \\ x_{\mathbf{s}} & y_{\mathbf{s}} & z_{\mathbf{s}} \end{matrix} \right\|.$$

·4. To evaluate the spatial product we make use of the identity

·41 $$\mathcal{J}\,\mathbf{rst} = \mathcal{S}(\mathcal{V}\,\mathbf{rs})\,\mathbf{t},$$

proved in 225·2, which gives

·42 $$\mathcal{J}\,\mathbf{rst} = c_{\mathbf{p}} p_{\mathbf{t}} = p_{\mathbf{p}} c_{\mathbf{t}},$$

where **p** denotes $\mathcal{V}\,\mathbf{rs}$; on substitution from ·35, we find that

·43 *The spatial product of the three vectors* **r**, **s**, **t** *is given by*

$$\mathcal{J}\,\mathbf{rst} = \Upsilon^{-1}[p_{\mathbf{r}}; p_{\mathbf{s}}; p_{\mathbf{t}}] = \Upsilon[c_{\mathbf{r}}; c_{\mathbf{s}}; c_{\mathbf{t}}].$$

Direct proofs of ·43 are easy to construct. It follows from† 225·24 that $\mathcal{J}\,\mathbf{rst}$ is a linear function of the set of components $x_{\mathbf{r}}, y_{\mathbf{r}}, z_{\mathbf{r}}$, a linear function of the set $x_{\mathbf{s}}, y_{\mathbf{s}}, z_{\mathbf{s}}$, and a linear function of the set $x_{\mathbf{t}}, y_{\mathbf{t}}, z_{\mathbf{t}}$, and from 225·12

* To write $(x_1, x_2, \ldots x_n) = M\,\|A\|$, where A is a rectangular array with n columns and $n-1$ rows, means that for $r = 1, 2, \ldots n$, $x_r = (-)^{r-1} M A_r$, where A_r is the determinant of the square array obtained by omitting from A the rth column. In other words, the notation means that for *arbitrary* values of n parameters $\lambda_1, \lambda_2, \ldots \lambda_n$,

$$\lambda_1 x_1 + \lambda_2 x_2 + \ldots + \lambda_n x_n = M\Delta,$$

where Δ is the determinant of the square array obtained by placing above A the row $\lambda_1, \lambda_2, \ldots \lambda_n$.

† In the text, 225·24 was deduced from 225·22, which is practically the relation from which ·43 has just been deduced, but it is easy to prove 225·24 without 225·22.

that this function suffers a reversal of sign but no other alteration if any two of the sets are interchanged; these conditions are sufficient* to imply that $\mathscr{T}\,\mathbf{rst}$ is a constant multiple of the determinant $[c_{\mathbf{r}};\ c_{\mathbf{s}};\ c_{\mathbf{t}}]$, and the multiplier is necessarily $\mathscr{T}\,1_{\Xi}1_{H}1_{Z}$, which is Υ. To avoid appealing to a general theorem on conditions implying a determinantal form, we can express $\mathscr{T}\,\mathbf{rst}$ as $\mathscr{T}(x_{\mathbf{r}}1_{\Xi}+y_{\mathbf{r}}1_{H}+z_{\mathbf{r}}1_{Z})(x_{\mathbf{s}}1_{\Xi}+y_{\mathbf{s}}1_{H}+z_{\mathbf{s}}1_{Z})(x_{\mathbf{t}}1_{\Xi}+y_{\mathbf{t}}1_{H}+z_{\mathbf{t}}1_{Z})$ and use 225·13 and 225·12, when it becomes evident that $\mathscr{T}\,\mathbf{rst}/\Upsilon$ is constructed from the components precisely by the rules which govern the expansion of the determinant $[c_{\mathbf{r}};\ c_{\mathbf{s}};\ c_{\mathbf{t}}]$. From one part of ·43 the whole theorem can be reconstructed, and ·35 follows without difficulty, for the first projection of $\mathscr{V}\,\mathbf{rs}$ is $\mathscr{S}\,1_{\Xi}(\mathscr{V}\mathbf{rs})$, that is, $\mathscr{T}\,1_{\Xi}\mathbf{rs}$.

·5. The simplest geometrical interpretations of ·35 and ·43 are evident:

If Π *is a direction at right angles to both the directions* P *and* Σ, *and if* ε *is an angle from* P *to* Σ *round* Π, *then* ·51

$$(x_{\Pi},\, y_{\Pi},\, z_{\Pi})\sin\epsilon=\Upsilon^{-1}\left\Vert\begin{matrix} l_{P} & m_{P} & n_{P}\\ l_{\Sigma} & m_{\Sigma} & n_{\Sigma}\end{matrix}\right\Vert,\quad (l_{\Pi},\, m_{\Pi},\, n_{\Pi})\sin\epsilon=\Upsilon\left\Vert\begin{matrix} x_{P} & y_{P} & z_{P}\\ x_{\Sigma} & y_{\Sigma} & z_{\Sigma}\end{matrix}\right\Vert.$$

If P, Σ, T *are any three directions in space,* ·52

$$\sin\Omega\mathrm{P}\Sigma\mathrm{T}=\Upsilon^{-1}[p_{P};\, p_{\Sigma};\, p_{T}]=\Upsilon\,[c_{P};\, c_{\Sigma};\, c_{T}].$$

The areal vector of the triangle QRS has the components ·53

$$\tfrac{1}{2}\Upsilon^{-1}[1,1,1;\ m_P;\ n_P],\quad \tfrac{1}{2}\Upsilon^{-1}[1,1,1;\ n_P;\ l_P],\quad \tfrac{1}{2}\Upsilon^{-1}[1,1,1;\ l_P;\ m_P]$$

and the projections

$$\tfrac{1}{2}\Upsilon\,[1,1,1;\ y_P;\ z_P],\quad \tfrac{1}{2}\Upsilon\,[1,1,1;\ z_P;\ x_P],\quad \tfrac{1}{2}\Upsilon\,[1,1,1;\ x_P;\ y_P],$$

where P is an umbra of (*Q, R, S*).

The volume of the tetrahedron QRST is given by the two expressions ·54

$$\tfrac{1}{6}\Upsilon\,[1,1,1,1;\ x_P;\ y_P;\ z_P],\quad \tfrac{1}{6}\Upsilon^{-1}[1,1,1,1;\ l_P;\ m_P;\ n_P],$$

where P is an umbra of (*Q, R, S, T*).

If any one of these theorems is known, the others can be deduced immediately.

The classical proof of ·53 may be presented as follows: if the triangle *QRS* is projected normally on the x-plane, then by 224·23 the areal vector of the projection is the projection of the areal vector of *QRS* on the normal to the plane; but by 142·23, the projection of Q on the x-plane is the point whose projections in that plane, referred to the frame OYZ, are m_Q, n_Q, and therefore by 1·66, which we may suppose established by elementary methods, the areal vector of the projection is of amount $\frac{1}{2}[1,1,1;\ m_P;\ n_P]\operatorname{cosec}\alpha$; this then is the projection of the areal vector of *QRS* on *OL*, and the first component of the areal vector in *OXYZ* follows from 24·24.

There is a far more elementary method, effective though inelegant, of proving a result equivalent to ·52. The fact that the equation of every plane has the form $fx+gy+hz=d$, which can be proved independently of any of the results of this article, implies algebraically that the equation of the plane through K parallel to the plane OUV is $[c-c_K;\ c_U;\ c_V]=0$,

* Compare Salmon, *Modern Higher Algebra*, foot-note to § 13 (p. 9 of 4th ed., 1885).

or in other words implies that if J is on this plane then $[c_J;\ c_U;\ c_V]=[c_K;\ c_U;\ c_V]$; if then* the plane through R parallel to OST meets OX in F, the plane through S parallel to OFT meets OY in G, and the plane through T parallel to OFG meets OZ in H,

$$[c_R;\ c_S;\ c_T]=[c_F;\ c_S;\ c_T]=[c_F;\ c_G;\ c_T]=[c_F;\ c_G;\ c_H];$$

but the construction makes the volumes of the tetrahedra $ORST$, $OFST$, $OFGT$, $OFGH$ equal, in sign as well as in amount, the volume of $OFGH$ is $\frac{1}{6}\Upsilon\, x_F y_G z_H$, and since in the determinant $[c_F;\ c_G;\ c_H]$ only the leading diagonal survives, the value of this determinant is the simple product $x_F y_G z_H$; hence the volume of $ORST$ is $\frac{1}{6}\Upsilon\,[c_R;\ c_S;\ c_T]$.

·6. It is interesting to observe that in the relation

$$\sin \Omega \mathrm{P\Sigma T} = \Upsilon^{-1}\,[p_{\mathrm{P}};\ p_{\Sigma};\ p_{\mathrm{T}}],$$

which forms part of ·52, every element can be described without reference to the fact that the directions $\Omega\Xi$, $\Omega\mathrm{H}$, $\Omega\mathrm{Z}$ have been supposed to be those of axes of coordinates, and that we can write

·62 $$\sin \Omega\Xi\mathrm{HZ} \sin \Omega\mathrm{P\Sigma T} = \begin{vmatrix} \cos \Xi\mathrm{P} & \cos \mathrm{HP} & \cos \mathrm{ZP} \\ \cos \Xi\Sigma & \cos \mathrm{H}\Sigma & \cos \mathrm{Z}\Sigma \\ \cos \Xi\mathrm{T} & \cos \mathrm{HT} & \cos \mathrm{ZT} \end{vmatrix},$$

an identity that includes 13·47 as a special case; since the proof of ·52 does not require P, Σ, T not to be coplanar, the symmetry of ·62 in the two sets of directions shews that the result is true unless *both* sets are coplanar, and it is easy to prove directly that in fact there are *no* exceptional cases.

Multiplying ·62 by the product $xyzrst$ of any six numbers, we have the identity

·63 $$\mathscr{I}\,\mathbf{xyz}\,\mathscr{I}\,\mathbf{rst} = \begin{vmatrix} \mathscr{G}\,\mathbf{xr} & \mathscr{G}\,\mathbf{yr} & \mathscr{G}\,\mathbf{zr} \\ \mathscr{G}\,\mathbf{xs} & \mathscr{G}\,\mathbf{ys} & \mathscr{G}\,\mathbf{zs} \\ \mathscr{G}\,\mathbf{xt} & \mathscr{G}\,\mathbf{yt} & \mathscr{G}\,\mathbf{zt} \end{vmatrix},$$

valid for any six vectors whatever.

·7. Since, like any other sets of direction ratios and cosines, those given in ·51 satisfy the identities of ·26, we have

·71 $$\sin^2 \epsilon = \Upsilon^{-2}\,\mathscr{C}\,(m_{\mathrm{P}} n_{\Sigma} - n_{\mathrm{P}} m_{\Sigma},\ n_{\mathrm{P}} l_{\Sigma} - l_{\mathrm{P}} n_{\Sigma},\ l_{\mathrm{P}} m_{\Sigma} - m_{\mathrm{P}} l_{\Sigma})^2,$$

·72 $$\sin^2 \epsilon = (m_{\mathrm{P}} n_{\Sigma} - n_{\mathrm{P}} m_{\Sigma})(y_{\mathrm{P}} z_{\Sigma} - z_{\mathrm{P}} y_{\Sigma}) + (n_{\mathrm{P}} l_{\Sigma} - l_{\mathrm{P}} n_{\Sigma})(z_{\mathrm{P}} x_{\Sigma} - x_{\mathrm{P}} z_{\Sigma}) + (l_{\mathrm{P}} m_{\Sigma} - m_{\mathrm{P}} l_{\Sigma})(x_{\mathrm{P}} y_{\Sigma} - y_{\mathrm{P}} x_{\Sigma}),$$

·73 $$\sin^2 \epsilon = \Upsilon^2\,\mathscr{P}\,(y_{\mathrm{P}} z_{\Sigma} - z_{\mathrm{P}} y_{\Sigma},\ z_{\mathrm{P}} x_{\Sigma} - x_{\mathrm{P}} z_{\Sigma},\ x_{\mathrm{P}} y_{\Sigma} - y_{\mathrm{P}} x_{\Sigma}^2),$$

·74 $$\sin^2 \epsilon = -\begin{vmatrix} 1 & \cos\gamma & \cos\beta & y_{\mathrm{P}} z_{\Sigma} - z_{\mathrm{P}} y_{\Sigma} \\ \cos\gamma & 1 & \cos\alpha & z_{\mathrm{P}} x_{\Sigma} - x_{\mathrm{P}} z_{\Sigma} \\ \cos\beta & \cos\alpha & 1 & x_{\mathrm{P}} y_{\Sigma} - y_{\mathrm{P}} x_{\Sigma} \\ y_{\mathrm{P}} z_{\Sigma} - z_{\mathrm{P}} y_{\Sigma} & z_{\mathrm{P}} x_{\Sigma} - x_{\mathrm{P}} z_{\Sigma} & x_{\mathrm{P}} y_{\Sigma} - y_{\mathrm{P}} x_{\Sigma} & 0 \end{vmatrix},$$

* In certain cases, the construction in this precise form will fail, unless the symbols R, S, T are permuted: the reader is left to fill in the outlines.

$$\sin^2\epsilon = -\begin{vmatrix} \Upsilon^{-2}\sin^2\alpha & \Upsilon^{-1}\cot\Gamma & \Upsilon^{-1}\cot\mathrm{B} & m_{\mathrm{P}}n_{\Sigma}-n_{\mathrm{P}}m_{\Sigma} \\ \Upsilon^{-1}\cot\Gamma & \Upsilon^{-2}\sin^2\beta & \Upsilon^{-1}\cot\mathrm{A} & n_{\mathrm{P}}l_{\Sigma}-l_{\mathrm{P}}n_{\Sigma} \\ \Upsilon^{-1}\cot\mathrm{B} & \Upsilon^{-1}\cot\mathrm{A} & \Upsilon^{-2}\sin^2\gamma & l_{\mathrm{P}}m_{\Sigma}-m_{\mathrm{P}}l_{\Sigma} \\ m_{\mathrm{P}}n_{\Sigma}-n_{\mathrm{P}}m_{\Sigma} & n_{\mathrm{P}}l_{\Sigma}-l_{\mathrm{P}}n_{\Sigma} & l_{\mathrm{P}}m_{\Sigma}-m_{\mathrm{P}}l_{\Sigma} & 0 \end{vmatrix}, \quad \cdot 75$$

and from 25·84 it appears that ·71, ·73 can be given the elegant form

$$\sin^2\epsilon = \Upsilon^{-2}\,[[[\mathscr{C}]]\,(p_{\mathrm{P}};\ p_{\Sigma})^2], \quad \cdot 76$$

$$\sin^2\epsilon = \Upsilon^{2}\,[[[\mathscr{P}]]\,(c_{\mathrm{P}};\ c_{\Sigma})^2], \quad \cdot 77$$

and that ·72 is equivalent to

$$\sin^2\epsilon = \begin{vmatrix} 1 & 0 & 0 & x_{\mathrm{P}} & x_{\Sigma} \\ 0 & 1 & 0 & y_{\mathrm{P}} & y_{\Sigma} \\ 0 & 0 & 1 & z_{\mathrm{P}} & z_{\Sigma} \\ l_{\mathrm{P}} & m_{\mathrm{P}} & n_{\mathrm{P}} & 0 & 0 \\ l_{\Sigma} & m_{\Sigma} & n_{\Sigma} & 0 & 0 \end{vmatrix} \quad \cdot 78$$

which can be transformed into ·76 or ·77 immediately.

·8. The formulae of the last paragraph are not independent of those giving $\cos\epsilon$, but the identities to which our attention is drawn by a comparison take a more general form if derived from ·35; the elementary identity

$$(rs\sin\epsilon)^2 = r^2s^2 - (rs\cos\epsilon)^2$$

gives for any two vectors

$$\mathscr{S}(\mathscr{V}\mathbf{rs})^2 = \mathscr{S}\mathbf{r}^2\,\mathscr{S}\mathbf{s}^2 - (\mathscr{S}\mathbf{rs})^2, \quad \cdot 81$$

and therefore

$$\mathscr{P}p_{\mathbf{r}}^2\,\mathscr{P}p_{\mathbf{s}}^2 - (\mathscr{P}p_{\mathbf{r}}p_{\mathbf{s}})^2 = \Upsilon^{-2}\,\mathscr{C}(m_{\mathbf{r}}n_{\mathbf{s}}-n_{\mathbf{r}}m_{\mathbf{s}},\ n_{\mathbf{r}}l_{\mathbf{s}}-l_{\mathbf{r}}n_{\mathbf{s}},\ l_{\mathbf{r}}m_{\mathbf{s}}-m_{\mathbf{r}}l_{\mathbf{s}})^2, \quad \cdot 82$$

$$\begin{vmatrix} l_{\mathbf{r}}x_{\mathbf{r}}+m_{\mathbf{r}}y_{\mathbf{r}}+n_{\mathbf{r}}z_{\mathbf{r}} & l_{\mathbf{r}}x_{\mathbf{s}}+m_{\mathbf{r}}y_{\mathbf{s}}+n_{\mathbf{r}}z_{\mathbf{s}} \\ l_{\mathbf{s}}x_{\mathbf{r}}+m_{\mathbf{s}}y_{\mathbf{r}}+n_{\mathbf{s}}z_{\mathbf{r}} & l_{\mathbf{s}}x_{\mathbf{s}}+m_{\mathbf{s}}y_{\mathbf{s}}+n_{\mathbf{s}}z_{\mathbf{s}} \end{vmatrix} \quad \cdot 83$$

$$= \begin{vmatrix} m_{\mathbf{r}} & n_{\mathbf{r}} \\ m_{\mathbf{s}} & n_{\mathbf{s}} \end{vmatrix}\begin{vmatrix} y_{\mathbf{r}} & z_{\mathbf{r}} \\ y_{\mathbf{s}} & z_{\mathbf{s}} \end{vmatrix} + \begin{vmatrix} n_{\mathbf{r}} & l_{\mathbf{r}} \\ n_{\mathbf{s}} & l_{\mathbf{s}} \end{vmatrix}\begin{vmatrix} z_{\mathbf{r}} & x_{\mathbf{r}} \\ z_{\mathbf{s}} & x_{\mathbf{s}} \end{vmatrix} + \begin{vmatrix} l_{\mathbf{r}} & m_{\mathbf{r}} \\ l_{\mathbf{s}} & m_{\mathbf{s}} \end{vmatrix}\begin{vmatrix} x_{\mathbf{r}} & y_{\mathbf{r}} \\ x_{\mathbf{s}} & y_{\mathbf{s}} \end{vmatrix},$$

$$\mathscr{C}c_{\mathbf{r}}^2\,\mathscr{C}c_{\mathbf{s}}^2 - (\mathscr{C}c_{\mathbf{r}}c_{\mathbf{s}})^2 = \Upsilon^2\,\mathscr{P}(y_{\mathbf{r}}z_{\mathbf{s}}-z_{\mathbf{r}}y_{\mathbf{s}},\ z_{\mathbf{r}}x_{\mathbf{s}}-x_{\mathbf{r}}z_{\mathbf{s}},\ x_{\mathbf{r}}y_{\mathbf{s}}-y_{\mathbf{r}}x_{\mathbf{s}})^2. \quad \cdot 84$$

The second of these identities is true independently of relations between l, m, n and x, y, z, and is a simple case of an identity invaluable in the applications of determinants to pure algebra; the first and third, which have often been used to establish* ·71 and ·73, are associated with the name of Lagrange.

Even ·82, ·83, ·84 may be generalised, for ·81 is only a particular case of 225·43:

$$\mathscr{S}(\mathscr{V}\mathbf{rs})(\mathscr{V}\mathbf{tu}) = \mathscr{S}\mathbf{rt}\,\mathscr{S}\mathbf{su} - \mathscr{S}\mathbf{ru}\,\mathscr{S}\mathbf{st}. \quad \cdot 85$$

* For trirectangular axes.

Algebraically the identity

·86
$$\begin{vmatrix} l_{\mathbf{r}}x_{\mathbf{t}}+m_{\mathbf{r}}y_{\mathbf{t}}+n_{\mathbf{r}}z_{\mathbf{t}} & l_{\mathbf{r}}x_{\mathbf{u}}+m_{\mathbf{r}}y_{\mathbf{u}}+n_{\mathbf{r}}z_{\mathbf{u}} \\ l_{\mathbf{s}}x_{\mathbf{t}}+m_{\mathbf{s}}y_{\mathbf{t}}+n_{\mathbf{s}}z_{\mathbf{t}} & l_{\mathbf{s}}x_{\mathbf{u}}+m_{\mathbf{s}}y_{\mathbf{u}}+n_{\mathbf{s}}z_{\mathbf{u}} \end{vmatrix} = \begin{vmatrix} m_{\mathbf{r}} & n_{\mathbf{r}} \\ m_{\mathbf{s}} & n_{\mathbf{s}} \end{vmatrix}\begin{vmatrix} y_{\mathbf{t}} & z_{\mathbf{t}} \\ y_{\mathbf{u}} & z_{\mathbf{u}} \end{vmatrix} + \begin{vmatrix} n_{\mathbf{r}} & l_{\mathbf{r}} \\ n_{\mathbf{s}} & l_{\mathbf{s}} \end{vmatrix}\begin{vmatrix} z_{\mathbf{t}} & x_{\mathbf{t}} \\ z_{\mathbf{u}} & x_{\mathbf{u}} \end{vmatrix} + \begin{vmatrix} l_{\mathbf{r}} & m_{\mathbf{r}} \\ l_{\mathbf{s}} & m_{\mathbf{s}} \end{vmatrix}\begin{vmatrix} x_{\mathbf{t}} & y_{\mathbf{t}} \\ x_{\mathbf{u}} & y_{\mathbf{u}} \end{vmatrix}$$

is verified even more easily than ·83.

By means of a determinant we can express $\mathscr{G}(\mathscr{V}\mathbf{rs})(\mathscr{V}\mathbf{tu})$ in terms of component symbols and the projections of $\mathscr{V}\mathbf{rs}$ and $\mathscr{V}\mathbf{tu}$, and therefore by means of component symbols and the *components* of **r**, **s**, **t**, **u**. Thus comes the identity

·87
$$\begin{vmatrix} \mathscr{C}c_{\mathbf{r}}c_{\mathbf{t}} & \mathscr{C}c_{\mathbf{r}}c_{\mathbf{u}} \\ \mathscr{C}c_{\mathbf{s}}c_{\mathbf{t}} & \mathscr{C}c_{\mathbf{s}}c_{\mathbf{u}} \end{vmatrix} = -\begin{vmatrix} \mathscr{C}^{11} & \mathscr{C}^{12} & \mathscr{C}^{13} & y_{\mathbf{r}}z_{\mathbf{s}}-z_{\mathbf{r}}y_{\mathbf{s}} \\ \mathscr{C}^{21} & \mathscr{C}^{22} & \mathscr{C}^{23} & z_{\mathbf{r}}x_{\mathbf{s}}-x_{\mathbf{r}}z_{\mathbf{s}} \\ \mathscr{C}^{31} & \mathscr{C}^{32} & \mathscr{C}^{33} & x_{\mathbf{r}}y_{\mathbf{s}}-y_{\mathbf{r}}x_{\mathbf{s}} \\ y_{\mathbf{t}}z_{\mathbf{u}}-z_{\mathbf{t}}y_{\mathbf{u}} & z_{\mathbf{t}}x_{\mathbf{u}}-x_{\mathbf{t}}z_{\mathbf{u}} & x_{\mathbf{t}}y_{\mathbf{u}}-y_{\mathbf{t}}x_{\mathbf{u}} & 0 \end{vmatrix}$$

which is independent of the meaning attached to the bilinear function $\mathscr{C}c_{\mathbf{p}}c_{\mathbf{q}}$ and can be verified at once if the determinant on the right is multiplied by

$$\begin{vmatrix} x_{\mathbf{r}} & y_{\mathbf{r}} & z_{\mathbf{r}} & 0 \\ x_{\mathbf{s}} & y_{\mathbf{s}} & z_{\mathbf{s}} & 0 \\ x_{\mathbf{m}} & y_{\mathbf{m}} & z_{\mathbf{m}} & 0 \\ 0 & 0 & 0 & 1 \end{vmatrix}$$

and the product by

$$\begin{vmatrix} x_{\mathbf{t}} & x_{\mathbf{u}} & x_{\mathbf{n}} & 0 \\ y_{\mathbf{t}} & y_{\mathbf{u}} & y_{\mathbf{n}} & 0 \\ z_{\mathbf{t}} & z_{\mathbf{u}} & z_{\mathbf{n}} & 0 \\ 0 & 0 & 0 & 1 \end{vmatrix},$$

where **m**, **n** are arbitrary. There is a similar identity with projections and projection symbols, but this is not algebraically a distinct result, for the algebraic proof of ·87 is not affected by the particular values of $\mathscr{C}^{11}$, $\mathscr{C}^{22}$, $\mathscr{C}^{33}$.

333. The specification of rotors, of rays, and of lines, in a prepared plane.

·1. We have seen in 234·32 that a rotor in a prepared plane is known completely if its vector and its moment about any one point of the plane are known, and if we are studying the plane by means of a Cartesian frame OXY it is natural to suppose that it is about the origin O that the moment is given. It is important to know the moment of a rotor $\mathbf{r}_k$ about any point Q of the plane in terms of the vector $\mathbf{r}$ and the moment R of $\mathbf{r}_k$ about O, and here again the results are ready for us: the vector of the step OQ is of course the vector with components x_Q, y_Q and projections l_Q, m_Q, and therefore by 234·22 and 1·73

If the vector of a rotor in a prepared plane is $\mathbf{r}$ *and the moment of the rotor about the origin of a frame OXY is R, the moment of the rotor about any point Q can be expressed in the two forms* ·12

$$(x_{\mathbf{r}}y_Q - y_{\mathbf{r}}x_Q)\sin\omega + R, \quad (l_{\mathbf{r}}m_Q - m_{\mathbf{r}}l_Q)\operatorname{cosec}\omega + R.$$

Two simple corollaries deserve mention. If $\mathbf{r}$ is a proper vector, the points about which the rotor has moment zero are the points whose coordinates and projections satisfy the equations

$$(y_{\mathbf{r}}x - x_{\mathbf{r}}y)\sin\omega = R, \quad (m_{\mathbf{r}}l - l_{\mathbf{r}}m)\operatorname{cosec}\omega = R; \qquad \cdot 13$$

these then are *equations of the axis of the rotor*, and incidentally we have verified that the rotor is determined completely by $\mathbf{r}$ and R, for if $\mathbf{r}$ is not zero the line in which the rotor is localised is determined uniquely by either of the equations ·13. And if a rotor is given by its vector $\mathbf{r}$ and by a point P through which it passes, °the moment of the rotor about the origin is ·14
expressible in the two forms $(y_{\mathbf{r}}x_P - x_{\mathbf{r}}y_P)\sin\omega$, $(m_{\mathbf{r}}l_P - l_{\mathbf{r}}m_P)\operatorname{cosec}\omega$; this is of course merely an analytical version of 234·21.

The vector of a step ST in a plane has components $x_T - x_S$, $y_T - y_S$ and projections $l_T - l_S$, $m_T - m_S$; it follows from ·14 that °the moment of the ·15
step, that is, the moment of the rotor of the step, about the origin, is expressible in the two forms

$$(x_S y_T - y_S x_T)\sin\omega, \quad (l_S m_T - m_S l_T)\operatorname{cosec}\omega.$$

It is even simpler to quote 234·25 than to use ·14, for ·15 then comes at once from 1·73, and the moment about an arbitrary point is deducible from 1·66 or 1·75.

·2. There are many ways of specifying a ray in a plane, and the last paragraph directs us to one of the most effective. We know (compare 23·4 above) that in describing a direction K by means of ratios we are virtually decomposing a unit vector $\mathbf{1}_{\mathrm{K}}$, and similarly the means adopted for describing a unit rotor 1_κ in a ray κ are valuable for identifying the ray κ itself. From this point of view, °a ray κ in a prepared plane is specified with reference to a Cartesian ·21
frame by three numbers, of which the first two are ratios or cosines defining the direction of the ray and are not independent, being subject to 1·26, and the third is the *moment* of the ray, that is, of a unit vector located in the ray, about the origin of the frame; we denote* the ratios by x_κ, y_κ, the cosines by l_κ, m_κ, and the moment by a_κ.

We may take a more elementary view of the moment as an element assisting us to identify a ray, for this moment is simply °the distance of the origin from ·23
the ray. If the ray κ has moment a_κ, the projection of O on κ is the point at distance a_κ from O in the direction making a *negative* right angle with the direction of κ, and is therefore by 1·48 and 1·49 the point of coordinates

* These symbols are of the kind we have used for rotors, but confusion is unlikely.

$a_\kappa m_\kappa \operatorname{cosec}\omega$, $-a_\kappa l_\kappa \operatorname{cosec}\omega$ and projections $a_\kappa y_\kappa \sin\omega$, $-a_\kappa x_\kappa \sin\omega$. Provided that a_κ is not zero, the axis of the ray is determined by the position of this point, but the direction of the ray in the line remains unknown, and the determination of this direction is precisely analogous to the determination from 1·26 of y_κ or m_κ when x_κ or l_κ is given, or, in the notation of 1·3, to the determination of one of the functions $\cos\alpha$, $\sin\alpha$ from the other. If a_κ is zero, the pairs of numbers $a_\kappa x_\kappa$, $a_\kappa y_\kappa$ and $a_\kappa l_\kappa$, $a_\kappa m_\kappa$ fail to indicate the direction of the ray. We meet with little encouragement if we attempt to specify a ray by means of two independent numbers. Returning in ·12 from moments to distances we see that

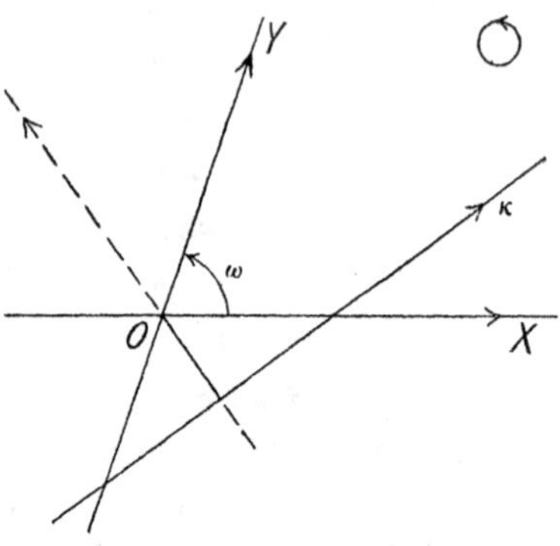

Fig. 25.

·25 *The distance of a point Q in a prepared plane from a ray κ is expressible in the forms*

$$(x_\kappa y_Q - y_\kappa x_Q)\sin\omega + a_\kappa, \quad (l_\kappa m_Q - m_\kappa l_Q)\operatorname{cosec}\omega + a_\kappa,$$

where a_κ is the distance of the origin from the ray,

·26 and we see also that if P is any point of the ray, °the distance a_κ is expressible as $(y_\kappa x_P - x_\kappa y_P)\sin\omega$ or $(m_\kappa l_P - l_\kappa m_P)\operatorname{cosec}\omega$.

There are two reasons for regarding a_κ first as a moment. On the one hand, we have then a definite reason for choosing the distance of O from κ rather than the distance from O to κ; algebraically, $(x_\kappa y_P - y_\kappa x_P)\sin\omega$ would serve as well as $(y_\kappa x_P - x_\kappa y_P)\sin\omega$, and by regarding the function primarily as a moment we avoid a tax on memory. On the other hand, a rotor has two directions and two distances from the origin, and to pass from the distance of a ray to the moment of a rotor would be to repeat much of 234. Moreover, as we are about to find, in the extension to the geometry of space the conceptions of distance and moment are both required, for while they are of equal utility they are applied to distinct problems.

·3. Equations for the axis of the ray κ are given from ·25:

·31 *The coordinates of a point on the axis of the ray κ satisfy the equation*

$$(y_\kappa x - x_\kappa y)\sin\omega = a_\kappa,$$

and the projections of a point on the same line satisfy the equation

$$(m_\kappa l - l_\kappa m)\operatorname{cosec}\omega = a_\kappa.$$

This result may be regarded in two ways as the interpretation of an equation satisfied by the *vector* from the origin to any point of the axis. If this vector is $\mathbf{r}$ and the vector of the ray is $\mathbf{k}$, the moment of the ray about the origin is given by 234·21 as $\mathscr{A}\mathbf{kr}'$:

·32 *The vector* $\mathbf{r}$ *from the origin to any point on the ray κ satisfies the equation*

$$\mathscr{A}\mathbf{kr} + a_\kappa = 0,$$

where $\mathbf{k}$ *is the vector of the ray and a_κ is the distance of the origin from the ray.*

he alternative point of view, natural if a ray in a plane is taken as analogous to a plane in space, is to suppose the ray κ specified by the unit vector $\mathbf{n}_\kappa$ *normal* to κ together with the distance a_κ; then if R is any point on the ray, he projection of RO in the normal direction is of length a_κ:

The vector $\mathbf{r}$ *from the origin to any point on the ray* κ *satisfies the equation* ·33

$$\mathscr{G}\,\mathbf{n}_\kappa\mathbf{r} + a_\kappa = 0,$$

where $\mathbf{n}_\kappa$ *is the unit vector normal to the ray and* a_κ *is the distance of the origin from the ray.*

·4. If what is to be specified is not a ray but an undirected line, the advantage of dealing with *unit* vectors disappears: a line may be identified by means of *any* proper vector located in it or by means of *any* proper vector to which it is perpendicular.

The first method repeats ·13:

The coordinates and projections of the points on a given line satisfy the equivalent linear equations $(y_{\mathbf{h}}x - x_{\mathbf{h}}y)\sin\omega = H$, $(m_{\mathbf{h}}l - l_{\mathbf{h}}m)\operatorname{cosec}\omega = H$, *where* $\mathbf{h}$ *is any vector with the directions of the line and* H *is the moment about the origin of the rotor obtained by locating* $\mathbf{h}$ *in the line.* ·41

The vector $\mathbf{h}$ is ineffective unless it is a proper vector, and we have to notice that the line determined by the vector $k\mathbf{h}$ and number kH is the same as the line determined by the vector $\mathbf{h}$ and number H: on this account the description of the line by means of $\mathbf{h}$ and H or by means of the three numbers $x_{\mathbf{h}}$, $y_{\mathbf{h}}$, H or the three numbers $l_{\mathbf{h}}$, $m_{\mathbf{h}}$, H is said to be °*homogeneous.* We can of ·42
course give ·41 a form purely vectorial:

The vector $\mathbf{r}$ *from the origin* O *to a variable point of a given line satisfies the equation* ·43

$$\mathscr{A}\,\mathbf{rh} = H,$$

where $\mathbf{h}$ *is any vector with the directions of the line and* H *is the moment about* O *of the rotor obtained by locating* $\mathbf{h}$ *in the line.*

For the alternative method, suppose $\mathbf{n}$ to be any vector perpendicular to the line, and $\mathbf{r}, \mathbf{s}$ to be the vectors from O to two points R, S of the line. Then $\mathbf{r}-\mathbf{s}$ is the vector of SR, and is therefore perpendicular to $\mathbf{n}$; that is

$$\mathscr{G}\,(\mathbf{r}-\mathbf{s})\,\mathbf{n} = 0,$$

and therefore $$\mathscr{G}\,\mathbf{rn} = \mathscr{G}\,\mathbf{sn}:$$

If $\mathbf{n}$ *is any vector perpendicular to a given line, the vector* $\mathbf{r}$ *from the origin to a variable point of the line satisfies an equation* ·46

$$\mathscr{G}\,\mathbf{rn} = N,$$

where N *depends on* $\mathbf{n}$ *but is independent of the position of the point on the line.*

In algebraical terms,

·47 *The coordinates and projections of the points on a given line satisfy the equivalent linear equations*

$$(l_{\mathbf{n}}x + m_{\mathbf{n}}y) = N, \quad (x_{\mathbf{n}}l + y_{\mathbf{n}}m) = N,$$

where **n** *is any vector perpendicular to the line and N depends only on the line and on the choice of* **n**.

·48 Here again we have a homogeneous specification of the line: °the line determined by $k\mathbf{n}$ and kN is the same as the line determined by **n** and N, but we can not say that the line is determined by $\mathbf{n}/N$, since N may be zero.

·5. The converse of ·46 is easily proved. Let the vector **r** from the origin to a variable point R satisfy the condition

·51 $$\mathscr{G}\,\mathbf{rn} = N,$$

where **n** is an arbitrary proper vector and N is a given number. Since **n** is a proper vector, it is possible first to find a particular vector **t** such that $\mathscr{G}\,\mathbf{tn}$ is not zero, and then by taking **s** as $(N/\mathscr{G}\,\mathbf{tn})\,\mathbf{t}$ to find a particular vector **s** such that

·52 $$\mathscr{G}\,\mathbf{sn} = N.$$

But from ·51 and ·52 follows

·53 $$\mathscr{G}\,(\mathbf{r}-\mathbf{s})\,\mathbf{n} = 0,$$

and this implies that if S is the point such that OS has the vector **s**, the point R satisfies ·51 if and only if the step SR is perpendicular to **n**.

·54 *If* **n** *is any proper vector in a plane and N is any number, the points in the plane whose vectors satisfy the condition*

$$\mathscr{G}\,\mathbf{rn} = N$$

compose a definite line.

·55 It follows that °every linear relation between the coordinates of a variable point expresses that there is some definite line on which the point is restricted to lie, for $ax + by$ can be regarded as the projected product of the vector of components (x, y) and the vector of projections (a, b), and the latter is not the
·56 zero vector unless a, b are both zero. Similarly °a linear relation between projections implies a linear restriction on the point.

The converse of ·43 may be deduced from ·54 and 222·14, or may be proved directly by arguments parallel to those just used; having found one point S whose vector **s** satisfies

$$\mathscr{A}\,\mathbf{sh} = H,$$

·58 we can replace $$\mathscr{A}\,\mathbf{rh} = H$$

by $$\mathscr{A}\,(\mathbf{r}-\mathbf{s})\,\mathbf{h} = 0,$$

which by 222·12 expresses that the point whose vector is **r** lies on the line
·59 through S with the directions of **h**: °every relation of the form of ·58 restricts the point which represents **r** with reference to a particular origin to a particular line.

334. The specification of prepared and unprepared planes in space.

·1. A prepared plane in space is identified with reference to a frame $OXYZ$ by the direction of its normals and the distance from it of the origin O; if the plane is S, we denote the ratios and the cosines of the normal direction by x_S, y_S, z_S and l_S, m_S, n_S, and the distance of O from S by a_S. If S_O is the plane through O parallel to S and with the same cyclic direction, the distance of any point Q from S is the sum of the distances of O from S and of Q from S_O; the first of these distances is a_S, and the second is the projection of the step OQ on any ray normal to S:

The distance from a prepared plane S to a point Q is expressible in the four ·12
forms

$$\mathscr{C} c_S c_Q + a_S, \quad p_S c_Q + a_S, \quad c_S p_Q + a_S, \quad \mathscr{P} p_S p_Q + a_S.$$

We deduce that if we are given the direction normal to a prepared plane S and one point P of the plane, we can obtain the distance a_S as the value of ·13
the four equal expressions

$$-\mathscr{C} c_S c_P, \quad -p_S c_P, \quad -c_S p_P, \quad -\mathscr{P} p_S p_P,$$

and this is otherwise evident, for the distance of O from the plane is the projection normal to the plane of any step to O from a point in the plane.

The normal projection of O on the plane S is the point at distance $-a_S$ from O in the direction normal to S; if a_S is not zero, the plane is determined save for its cyclic direction by the position of this point, but it is impossible to identify even an unprepared plane by means of this point if the plane contains the origin.

·2. It follows from ·12 that the points of the plane S are the points of which the coordinates satisfy the equation

$$p_S c + a_S = 0 \qquad \cdot 21$$

and the projections the equation

$$c_S p + a_S = 0. \qquad \cdot 22$$

As equations however ·21 and ·22 have little to recommend them: on the one hand the equations alone are insufficient to characterise the prepared plane, while on the other hand for the unprepared plane there is no advantage in dealing with a unit vector. If $\mathbf{n}$ is any vector perpendicular to a plane and $\mathbf{r}$, $\mathbf{s}$ are vectors from O to points of the plane, $\mathscr{G}(\mathbf{r}-\mathbf{s})\mathbf{n}$ is zero, and therefore $\mathscr{G}\mathbf{rn}$, where $\mathbf{r}$ may be regarded as variable, has a value independent of the position, in the plane, of the point to which $\mathbf{r}$ corresponds.

If $\mathbf{n}$ is any vector perpendicular to a given plane, the vector $\mathbf{r}$ from the ·23
origin to a variable point of the plane satisfies an equation

$$\mathscr{G}\mathbf{rn} = N,$$

where N depends on $\mathbf{n}$ *but is independent of the position of the point in the plane.*

·24 °The specification of the plane by means of a proper vector $\mathbf{n}$ and a number N is a *homogeneous* specification.

The converse of ·23, subject only to the restriction that $\mathbf{n}$ is not the zero vector, is also true. If $\mathbf{n}$ is not zero, we can find some vector $\mathbf{t}$ such that $\mathscr{S}\mathbf{tn}$ is not zero, and then writing $\mathbf{s}$ for $(N/\mathscr{S}\mathbf{tn})\,\mathbf{t}$ we have

$$\mathscr{S}\mathbf{sn} = N,$$

and therefore $$\mathscr{S}\mathbf{rn} = N$$

is equivalent to $$\mathscr{S}(\mathbf{r}-\mathbf{s})\,\mathbf{n} = 0,$$

which expresses that the step from the fixed point S which represents $\mathbf{s}$ to the variable point R which represents $\mathbf{r}$ is always perpendicular to $\mathbf{n}$.

·28 *If* $\mathbf{n}$ *is any proper vector and N is any number, the points representing with reference to an origin O a variable vector* $\mathbf{r}$ *that is subject only to the condition*

$$\mathscr{S}\mathbf{rn} = N$$

compose a definite plane.

·3. The algebraical equivalent of ·23 is that

·31 *The coordinates and projections of a variable point in a fixed plane satisfy the equivalent equations*

$$p_{\mathbf{n}}c = N, \quad c_{\mathbf{n}}p = N,$$

where $\mathbf{n}$ *is any vector perpendicular to the plane and N is a number independent of the position of the point in the plane.*

·32 Since any set of three numbers is the set of projections of some vector, °every linear relation between the coordinates of a variable point of space corresponds to a definite plane, and since any set of three numbers is the set of components

·33 of some vector, °so also does every linear relation between the projections of a variable point.

·4. It is to be emphasised that in the solution of problems ·23 can be used directly, and not merely after translation into ·31. As an example we may consider the determination of the point common to three planes given vectorially by equations

·41 $$\mathscr{S}\mathbf{ra} = A, \quad \mathscr{S}\mathbf{rb} = B, \quad \mathscr{S}\mathbf{rc} = C.$$

If the vectors $\mathbf{a}$, $\mathbf{b}$, $\mathbf{c}$ are not coplanar, the vector $\mathbf{r}$ which satisfies ·41 is expressible, like any other vector, both in the form $f\mathbf{a}+g\mathbf{b}+h\mathbf{c}$ and in the form $i\mathscr{V}\mathbf{bc}+j\mathscr{V}\mathbf{ca}+k\mathscr{V}\mathbf{ab}$, where f, g, h and i, j, k are numbers, and the values of these numbers are given by substitution in ·41. The simpler expressions are those for i, j, k, for 225·23 and 225·25 give at once three equations of which the first is

$$i\,\mathscr{T}\mathbf{abc} = A,$$

·43 and therefore $$\mathbf{r}\,\mathscr{T}\mathbf{abc} = A\,\mathscr{V}\mathbf{bc} + B\,\mathscr{V}\mathbf{ca} + C\,\mathscr{V}\mathbf{ab}.$$

The alternative substitution is not more difficult and yields

$$\mathbf{r}\begin{vmatrix} \mathcal{G}\mathbf{a}^2 & \mathcal{G}\mathbf{ab} & \mathcal{G}\mathbf{ac} \\ \mathcal{G}\mathbf{ba} & \mathcal{G}\mathbf{b}^2 & \mathcal{G}\mathbf{bc} \\ \mathcal{G}\mathbf{ca} & \mathcal{G}\mathbf{cb} & \mathcal{G}\mathbf{c}^2 \end{vmatrix} = \begin{vmatrix} \mathcal{G}\mathbf{a}^2 & \mathcal{G}\mathbf{ab} & \mathcal{G}\mathbf{ac} & \mathbf{a} \\ \mathcal{G}\mathbf{ba} & \mathcal{G}\mathbf{b}^2 & \mathcal{G}\mathbf{bc} & \mathbf{b} \\ \mathcal{G}\mathbf{ca} & \mathcal{G}\mathbf{cb} & \mathcal{G}\mathbf{c}^2 & \mathbf{c} \\ A & B & C & \mathbf{0} \end{vmatrix}, \qquad \cdot 44$$

which must of course be precisely equivalent to ·43. If actual coordinates or projections of the point of intersection are wanted, they are easily obtained from ·43 or ·44 by means of 2·15, 2·35, and 2·43, but if we prefer to obtain the coordinates, for example, by replacing ·41 by

$$p_{\mathbf{a}}c = A, \quad p_{\mathbf{b}}c = B, \quad p_{\mathbf{c}}c = C \qquad \cdot 45$$

we can actually recover 2·35 from ·43 and 2·43.

335. The specification of rotors in space and of motors; the determination of pitch and of a central axis.

·1. A rotor in space is specified with reference to a Cartesian frame by its vector and its momental vector about the origin of the frame. It is convenient sometimes to denote rotors by simple unaffected symbols, and if the rotor is ρ we denote its vector by **r** and its momental vector about the origin by **R**, but we use x_ρ for the first component of **r** and X_ρ for the first component of **R**, and so on, and write also in this connection

$$C = (X, Y, Z), \quad P = (L, M, N). \qquad \cdot 12$$

Since the vectors **r**, **R** are necessarily at right angles,

$$\mathcal{G}\,\mathbf{Rr} = 0, \qquad \cdot 13$$

a relation that may be expressed in any of the forms

$$\mathcal{C}\,C_\rho c_\rho = 0, \quad C_\rho p_\rho = 0, \quad P_\rho c_\rho = 0, \quad \mathcal{P}\,P_\rho p_\rho = 0. \qquad \cdot 14$$

Often °the components of **r** and **R** are called the *six components* of ρ and the ·15
projections of **r** and **R** the *six projections* of ρ, but it is a consequence of ·14 that usually it is advisable to associate the components of one of the vectors **r**, **R** with the projections of the other; the components and projections of **R** are called the °*momental* components and projections of ρ. That °any two vectors ·16, ·17
r, **R** subject to ·13 determine a rotor, provided only that if **r** is zero so also is **R**, follows from 235·33.

·2. The rotor ρ is equivalent to the compound of the rotor through O with vector **r**, which is denoted by ρ_O, and any couple with momental vector **R**; the rotor ρ_O can be resolved into rotors of amounts x_ρ, y_ρ, z_ρ in the rays ξ, η, ζ, and a couple with momental vector **R** can be regarded as the sum of couples about ξ, η, ζ with moments X_ρ, Y_ρ, Z_ρ about those rays. Thus the single rotor is expressed, with reference to any frame, as °a compound of three rotors in ·21
the axes of the frame and three couples round the axes of the frame, and the

six components of the rotor are the amounts of the component rotors and
·22 momental vectors. As for the six projections, while °l_ρ, m_ρ, n_ρ are the projec-
·23 tions of $\mathbf{r}$ on the axes ξ, η, ζ, it follows from 236·44 that °L_ρ, M_ρ, N_ρ are the
·24 moments of the rotor about the axes; °like the projection l_ρ, the moment L_ρ is independent of the directions of η and ζ as well as of the position of O in ξ.

·3. The fundamental problem of determining the moment of ρ about an arbitrary point Q is solved by the association of 235·23 with 2·35:

·31 *The momental vector of the rotor ρ about any point Q is the vector with components*

$$X_\rho + \Upsilon^{-1}(m_\rho n_Q - n_\rho m_Q), \quad Y_\rho + \Upsilon^{-1}(n_\rho l_Q - l_\rho n_Q), \quad Z_\rho + \Upsilon^{-1}(l_\rho m_Q - m_\rho l_Q)$$

and projections

$$L_\rho + \Upsilon(y_\rho z_Q - z_\rho y_Q), \quad M_\rho + \Upsilon(z_\rho x_Q - x_\rho z_Q), \quad N_\rho + \Upsilon(x_\rho y_Q - y_\rho x_Q).$$

We may use this result as we used the corresponding result 3·12. First we remark that

·32 *The coordinates and projections of points on the axis of the rotor ρ satisfy the sets of equations*

$$\Upsilon(yz_\rho - zy_\rho) = L_\rho, \quad \Upsilon(zx_\rho - xz_\rho) = M_\rho, \quad \Upsilon(xy_\rho - yx_\rho) = N_\rho,$$
$$\Upsilon^{-1}(mn_\rho - nm_\rho) = X_\rho, \quad \Upsilon^{-1}(nl_\rho - ln_\rho) = Y_\rho, \quad \Upsilon^{-1}(lm_\rho - ml_\rho) = Z_\rho;$$

the equations of the first set are equations of planes through the axis of the rotor parallel to the axes of the frame of reference, and the equations of the second set are equations of planes through the same line at right angles to the planes of reference. Unless the vector $\mathbf{r}$ is zero, at least two of the equations in each of the sets are significant* and represent planes that are not parallel; multiplying the equations of the first set by x_ρ, y_ρ, z_ρ and adding, and multiplying the equations of the second set by l_ρ, m_ρ, n_ρ and adding, we find that in each set, if $\mathbf{r}$ is not zero, the three equations are either incompatible or equivalent to only two equations, and that it is in virtue of the perpendicularity of $\mathbf{r}$ and $\mathbf{R}$, expressed in ·14, that the equations are compatible and represent a definite line. Next we note that

·33 *The rotor with vector $\mathbf{r}$ through a point P has the six components*

$$x_{\mathbf{r}}, y_{\mathbf{r}}, z_{\mathbf{r}}, \quad \Upsilon^{-1}(n_{\mathbf{r}} m_P - m_{\mathbf{r}} n_P), \quad \Upsilon^{-1}(l_{\mathbf{r}} n_P - n_{\mathbf{r}} l_P), \quad \Upsilon^{-1}(m_{\mathbf{r}} l_P - l_{\mathbf{r}} m_P)$$

and the six projections

$$l_{\mathbf{r}}, m_{\mathbf{r}}, n_{\mathbf{r}}, \quad \Upsilon(z_{\mathbf{r}} y_P - y_{\mathbf{r}} z_P), \quad \Upsilon(x_{\mathbf{r}} z_P - z_{\mathbf{r}} x_P), \quad \Upsilon(y_{\mathbf{r}} x_P - x_{\mathbf{r}} y_P).$$

The vector of the step ST has components $x_T - x_S$, $y_T - y_S$, $z_T - z_S$ and projections $l_T - l_S$, $m_T - m_S$, $n_T - n_S$; we may deduce the momental components and projections of the rotor of the step from ·33, but it is preferable to appeal

* An equation is significant if it is not merely an identity.

to 235·26 and 2·35, which give at once the components and projections required:

The rotor of the step ST has the six components ·35

$$x_T - x_S,\quad y_T - y_S,\quad z_T - z_S,$$
$$\Upsilon^{-1}(m_S n_T - n_S m_T),\quad \Upsilon^{-1}(n_S l_T - l_S n_T),\quad \Upsilon^{-1}(l_S m_T - m_S l_T),$$

and the six projections

$$l_T - l_S,\quad m_T - m_S,\quad n_T - n_S,$$
$$\Upsilon(y_S z_T - z_S y_T),\quad \Upsilon(z_S x_T - x_S z_T),\quad \Upsilon(x_S y_T - y_S x_T).$$

·4. A vectorial equation for the axis of the rotor ρ is given by 235·22:

The vector **r** *from the origin to any point of the axis of the rotor* ϖ *which has vector* **p** *and momental vector* **P** *satisfies the equation* ·41

$$\mathscr{V}\mathbf{rp} = \mathbf{P}.$$

This equation implies ·32, and is sufficient to determine the axis; indeed, from 2·35 and ·41 we can write down at once the equations of ·32, but as a rule we make direct use of ·41, either implicitly or explicitly; examples of the application of ·41 are to be found in section 7 of this chapter.

·5. It is easy to obtain analytical expressions for the momental product of two rotors σ, τ, by regarding each as compounded of a rotor through O and a couple, and arguing as in 246·5. The two rotors intersecting in O have momental product zero, and the momental product of any two couples is zero; hence from 243·45,

The momental product of two rotors σ, τ *is the sum of the projected product* $\mathscr{S}$**St** *and the projected product* $\mathscr{S}$**Ts**, *and may be calculated by means of a frame OXYZ with origin O by the addition of any one of the numbers* ·51

$$\mathscr{C}\, C_\sigma c_\tau,\quad P_\sigma c_\tau,\quad C_\sigma p_\tau,\quad \mathscr{P}\, P_\sigma p_\tau$$

to any one of the numbers

$$\mathscr{C}\, C_\tau c_\sigma,\quad P_\tau c_\sigma,\quad C_\tau p_\sigma,\quad \mathscr{P}\, P_\tau p_\sigma;$$

the two rotors are coplanar if the sum so found is zero.

·6. Every finitely numerous set of rotors has a vector and has with reference to any point a momental vector, and it follows from first principles that each component or projection of each of these vectors with regard to any frame is the sum of the corresponding components or projections of the individual members of the set. Symbolically, if ρ is a typical rotor of a set, the vector whose components and projections with respect to a frame $OXYZ$ are Σx_ρ, Σy_ρ, Σz_ρ and Σl_ρ, Σm_ρ, Σn_ρ is the vector of the set, and the vector whose components and projections with respect to the same frame are ΣX_ρ, ΣY_ρ, ΣZ_ρ and ΣL_ρ, ΣM_ρ, ΣN_ρ is the momental vector of the set about O. For a set F of rotors, we denote the sums Σx_ρ, Σl_ρ, ΣX_ρ, ΣL_ρ, and so on, by x_F, l_F, X_F, L_F, and so on, we write as for a single rotor

$$C = (X, Y, Z),\quad P = (L, M, N),$$

and we call X_F and L_F the first momental component and the first momental projection of the set relative to the frame $OXYZ$; sometimes we call the components $x_F, y_F, z_F, X_F, Y_F, Z_F$ collectively the six components of the set F, and the corresponding projections collectively the six projections. A set of rotors is not determined by its six components or by its six projections, but by 241·35

·63 *Equivalent sets of rotors are sets which have with reference to any frame the same six components and the same six projections,*

and we may call the components and projections the six components and the six projections of the *motor* of the set, when we find that

·64 *A motor is determined completely by its six components or its six projections with respect to any frame.*

·65 We have to observe that° for a motor or for a set of rotors there is no quantitative relation between the six components or between the six projections. The relation ·13 expressing that any momental vector of a single rotor is at right angles to the vector of the rotor has no counterpart in the case of sets of rotors, for given *any* two vectors $\mathbf{r}$, $\mathbf{R}$, we have only to take the rotor $\mathbf{r}_O$ through the point O and any couple of rotors with the momental vector $\mathbf{R}$, to have a set of three rotors of which the vector is $\mathbf{r}$ and the momental vector about O is $\mathbf{R}$; if as in 247·4 we suppose one of the rotors composing the couple to intersect $\mathbf{r}_O$, we may add this rotor to $\mathbf{r}_O$ and obtain a rotor-pair with the given vector and the given momental vector.

·7. The expressions given in ·31 for components and projections of the momental vector of a single rotor about any point are linear in the components and projections of the rotor, and therefore

·71 *The momental vector of any set F of rotors about any point Q has with reference to the frame $OXYZ$ the components*

$$X_F+\Upsilon^{-1}(m_F n_Q - n_F m_Q),\quad Y_F+\Upsilon^{-1}(n_F l_Q - l_F n_Q),\quad Z_F+\Upsilon^{-1}(l_F m_Q - m_F l_Q)$$

and the projections

$$L_F+\Upsilon(y_F z_Q - z_F y_Q),\quad M_F+\Upsilon(z_F x_Q - x_F z_Q),\quad N_F+\Upsilon(x_F y_Q - y_F x_Q).$$

If the vector of the set is zero, the momental vector is everywhere the same in directions and amounts, but if the vector is not zero, the set has a definite pitch q_F, which may be zero but is not infinite, and the central axis may be found from ·71 as the locus of points about which the momental vector is the vector with components $q_F x_F, q_F y_F, q_F z_F$ and projections $q_F l_F, q_F m_F, q_F n_F$. From this argument we find two sets of equations for the central axis, one set typified by

·72 $$X_F+\Upsilon^{-1}(m_F n - n_F m)=q_F x_F,$$

and the other set by

·73 $$L_F+\Upsilon(y_F z - z_F y)=q_F l_F;$$

the three equations of the first set would be incompatible without the equality

$$p_F C_F = q_F . p_F c_F, \qquad \cdot 74$$

and the three equations of the second set without the correlative equality

$$c_F P_F = q_F . c_F p_F; \qquad \cdot 75$$

·74 and ·75 give analytical expressions for the pitch q_F. A slightly different line of reasoning leads to the same result: if the vector of the set F is $\mathbf{f}$ and the central axis is k, the set formed of the rotor $\mathbf{f}_k$ together with any couple whose momental vector is $q_F\mathbf{f}$ is equivalent to the set F; hence the set obtained by subtracting from F a couple with momental vector $q_F\mathbf{f}$ is equivalent to a single rotor and the axis of this rotor is the central axis of F. But in order that

$$x_F, \quad y_F, \quad z_F, \quad X_F - q_F x_F, \quad Y_F - q_F y_F, \quad Z_F - q_F z_F$$

should be the six components and

$$l_F, \quad m_F, \quad n_F, \quad L_F - q_F l_F, \quad M_F - q_F m_F, \quad N_F - q_F n_F$$

the six projections of a *single* rotor, equations ·74 and ·75 must be satisfied, and the axis of the rotor is then given by equations such as ·72 or ·73. Vectorially, the axis and the pitch are given simultaneously by the one equation

$$\mathcal{V}\,\mathbf{r}\mathbf{r}_F = \mathbf{R}_F - q_F \mathbf{r}_F, \qquad \cdot 77$$

which *implies* $\quad q_F \mathcal{S}\,\mathbf{r}_F^2 = \mathcal{S}\,\mathbf{R}_F \mathbf{r}_F, \qquad \cdot 78$

since $\mathcal{S}\,(\mathcal{V}\,\mathbf{r}\mathbf{r}_F)\,\mathbf{r}_F$ is identically zero.

336. THE SPECIFICATION OF RAYS AND LINES IN SPACE.

·1. A ray is identified by means of the same numbers as a unit rotor in the ray, and the language and notation relating to the rotor are appropriated for the ray. If $\mathbf{k}$ is the unit vector in the direction of the ray κ, and $\mathbf{K}$ is the momental vector of the ray about the origin, then

$$\mathcal{S}\,\mathbf{k}^2 = 1, \quad \mathcal{S}\,\mathbf{K}\mathbf{k} = 0, \qquad \cdot 11$$

relations which may be translated in the usual fashion into equations involving components and projections; only four of the twelve elements defining a ray are algebraically independent, but a fifth is necessary if no ambiguous irrational is to appear. The three projections l_κ, m_κ, n_κ are the cosines of angles between the ray κ and the coordinate axes, and the three momental projections L_κ, M_κ, N_κ are the mutual moments of κ and these axes. From 5·51

The mutual moment $d_{\nu\mu} \sin \epsilon_{\mu\nu}$ of two rays μ, ν is the sum $\mathcal{S}\,\mathbf{M}\mathbf{n} + \mathcal{S}\,\mathbf{N}\mathbf{m}$, and the rays are coplanar, that is, either concurrent or parallel, if this sum is zero. ·12

From 5·41, the vector $\mathbf{r}$ of the step from the origin to a variable point of the ray satisfies the relation

$$\mathcal{V}\,\mathbf{r}\mathbf{k} = \mathbf{K}. \qquad \cdot 13$$

·2. The merit of the momental vector as a means of specifying a ray is that this vector involves no reference to a particular point of the ray or to a particular plane through the ray, but since rays often are defined by means of particular points or particular planes we gain confidence by discovering that in the commonest cases the momental vector can readily be ascertained.

Thus it is a corollary to 5·33 that

·21 *The ray with direction* Λ *through a point* S *has the six coordinates*

$$x_\Lambda,\quad y_\Lambda,\quad z_\Lambda,\quad \Upsilon^{-1}(n_\Lambda m_S - m_\Lambda n_S),\quad \Upsilon^{-1}(l_\Lambda n_S - n_\Lambda l_S),\quad \Upsilon^{-1}(m_\Lambda l_S - l_\Lambda m_S)$$

and the six projections

$$l_\Lambda,\quad m_\Lambda,\quad n_\Lambda,\quad \Upsilon(z_\Lambda y_S - y_\Lambda z_S),\quad \Upsilon(x_\Lambda z_S - z_\Lambda x_S),\quad \Upsilon(y_\Lambda x_S - x_\Lambda y_S).$$

If S, T are two distinct points and if r is a distance from S to T, the unit rotor in the ray through S and T with the direction in which r is measured is the rotor found by dividing the rotor of the step ST by r; hence from 5·35

·22 *If* r *is a distance from one point* S *to a distinct point* T, *the ray in which the distance is measured has the six coordinates*

$$(x_T - x_S)/r,\quad (y_T - y_S)/r,\quad (z_T - z_S)/r,$$
$$\Upsilon^{-1}(m_S n_T - n_S m_T)/r,\quad \Upsilon^{-1}(n_S l_T - l_S n_T)/r,\quad \Upsilon^{-1}(l_S m_T - m_S l_T)/r,$$

and the six projections

$$(l_T - l_S)/r,\quad (m_T - m_S)/r,\quad (n_T - n_S)/r,$$
$$\Upsilon(y_S z_T - z_S y_T)/r,\quad \Upsilon(z_S x_T - x_S z_T)/r,\quad \Upsilon(x_S y_T - y_S x_T)/r.$$

To the two values of r, namely the two square roots of r^2, correspond the two rays through S and T.

A third case of importance is that of a ray given by means of two planes which contain it, and for the sake of the comparison we treat this problem by three different methods. We take the planes to be prepared planes S, T, and we denote the rays through the origin normal to these planes by σ, τ. Any angle whose cosine is given by 2·22 is an angle between the planes, and if such an angle ϵ_{ST} is to be from S to T round the common ray κ, this ray is determinate and its direction is given by 2·51.

The plane through O normal to κ contains σ and τ and the momental vector $\mathbf{K}$ of κ about O; moreover, if this plane cuts κ in R, the momental vector is the vector obtained by rotating the vector of RO through a positive right angle. Hence the projections of $\mathbf{K}$ in directions making positive right angles with σ, τ are equal to the projections of RO on σ, τ themselves, that is, to the distances a_S, a_T of O from S, T. It follows from 24·25 that $\mathbf{K}$ is the sum of $-a_T \operatorname{cosec} \epsilon_{ST}$ in σ and $a_S \operatorname{cosec} \epsilon_{ST}$ in τ.

·24 *If* ϵ_{ST} *is an angle from a prepared plane* S *to a prepared plane* T, *the common ray round which this angle is measured has the six coordinates*

$$\left[\begin{array}{l}\Upsilon^{-1}(m_S n_T - n_S m_T)\operatorname{cosec}\epsilon_{ST},\\ \Upsilon^{-1}(n_S l_T - l_S n_T)\operatorname{cosec}\epsilon_{ST},\\ \Upsilon^{-1}(l_S m_T - m_S l_T)\operatorname{cosec}\epsilon_{ST},\end{array}\right.\qquad \left[\begin{array}{l}(a_S x_T - a_T x_S)\operatorname{cosec}\epsilon_{ST},\\ (a_S y_T - a_T y_S)\operatorname{cosec}\epsilon_{ST},\\ (a_S z_T - a_T z_S)\operatorname{cosec}\epsilon_{ST},\end{array}\right.$$

and the six projections

$$\begin{bmatrix} \Upsilon(y_S z_T - z_S y_T)\operatorname{cosec}\epsilon_{ST}, \\ \Upsilon(z_S x_T - x_S z_T)\operatorname{cosec}\epsilon_{ST}, \\ \Upsilon(x_S y_T - y_S x_T)\operatorname{cosec}\epsilon_{ST}, \end{bmatrix} \qquad \begin{bmatrix} (a_S l_T - a_T l_S)\operatorname{cosec}\epsilon_{ST}, \\ (a_S m_T - a_T m_S)\operatorname{cosec}\epsilon_{ST}, \\ (a_S n_T - a_T n_S)\operatorname{cosec}\epsilon_{ST}, \end{bmatrix}$$

where a_S, a_T are the distances of the origin from the two planes and the ratios and cosines are those of the normals to the planes.

Again we observe that there are two rays, distinguished by the sign of $\sin\epsilon_{ST}$, the function $\sin^2\epsilon_{ST}$ being given by 2·71 or 2·73.

It is not difficult to avoid the geometrical investigation that has preceded the enunciation of ·24. An equation to the plane through the line of intersection of two planes S, T and parallel to the first axis of the frame $OXYZ$ is to be found by eliminating x from the pair of equations

$$p_S c + a_S = 0, \quad p_T c + a_T = 0, \tag{·241}$$

and the simplest form of the eliminant is

$$(l_S m_T - l_T m_S)\,y + (l_S n_T - l_T n_S)\,z + (l_S a_T - l_T a_S) = 0\,; \tag{·242}$$

if the ray to be found is κ, 5·32 gives an equation for the same plane in the form

$$\Upsilon z_\kappa y - \Upsilon y_\kappa z - L_\kappa = 0, \tag{·243}$$

and since from 2·51, Υz_κ is equal to $(l_S m_T - m_S l_T)\operatorname{cosec}\epsilon_{ST}$ and $-\Upsilon y_\kappa$ is equal to $(l_S n_T - n_S l_T)\operatorname{cosec}\epsilon_{ST}$, it follows that L_κ is equal to $(a_S l_T - a_T l_S)\operatorname{cosec}\epsilon_{ST}$.

A third method treats the problem by vectors alone, and it is not to be denied that this is the best plan; if **s**, **t** are unit vectors normal to the planes, and **r** is the vector of the step from O to any point in the line of intersection,

$$\mathscr{S}\,\mathbf{rs} + a_S = 0, \quad \mathscr{S}\,\mathbf{rt} + a_T = 0\,; \tag{·244}$$

but if the ray of which we are in search has vector **k** and momental vector **K**, then

$$\mathbf{k} = \mathscr{V}\,\mathbf{st}\operatorname{cosec}\epsilon_{ST} \tag{·245}$$

by definition, and

$$\mathbf{K} = \mathscr{V}\,\mathbf{rk}, \tag{·246}$$

from ·13; substituting from ·245 in ·246 and using 223·33 we have

$$\mathbf{K} = (\mathbf{s}\,\mathscr{S}\,\mathbf{rt} - \mathbf{t}\,\mathscr{S}\,\mathbf{rs})\operatorname{cosec}\epsilon_{ST} = (a_S\mathbf{t} - a_T\mathbf{s})\operatorname{cosec}\epsilon_{ST}\,; \tag{·247}$$

·245 and ·247 together are equivalent to ·24.

·3. In using the momental vector in the specification of a ray we are not compelled to sacrifice such advantages as there are in knowing a particular point on the ray, for there is one point whose coordinates and projections have a form both simple and definite.

In ·13, **k** is a *unit* vector, and therefore if **r** can be taken perpendicular to **k**, 223·14 will become applicable and will shew that **r** is $\mathscr{V}\,\mathbf{kK}$; to take **r** perpendicular to **k** is to let **r** be the vector from O to the normal projection of O on κ:

·31 *The vector of the step from the origin O to its normal projection on a ray κ is the vector product* $\mathcal{V}\,\mathbf{kK}$, *and therefore this point has coordinates*

$$\Upsilon^{-1}(m_\kappa N_\kappa - n_\kappa M_\kappa),\quad \Upsilon^{-1}(n_\kappa L_\kappa - l_\kappa N_\kappa),\quad \Upsilon^{-1}(l_\kappa M_\kappa - m_\kappa L_\kappa)$$

and projections

$$\Upsilon(y_\kappa Z_\kappa - z_\kappa Y_\kappa),\quad \Upsilon(z_\kappa X_\kappa - x_\kappa Z_\kappa),\quad \Upsilon(x_\kappa Y_\kappa - y_\kappa X_\kappa).$$

·32 It follows that °the first coordinate and the first projection of any point on the ray are $sx_\kappa + \Upsilon^{-1}(m_\kappa N_\kappa - n_\kappa M_\kappa)$ and $sl_\kappa + \Upsilon(y_\kappa Z_\kappa - z_\kappa Y_\kappa)$, where s denotes the distance of the point in question from the projection of O on κ.

·4. A line is identified by means of *any* rotor of which it is the axis, that is, by means of any proper vector **h** which has its directions, together with the momental vector **H**, about the origin of coordinates, of the rotor obtained by locating **h** in the line; the two vectors are perpendicular, so that

·42 $$\mathcal{S}\,\mathbf{Hh} = 0,$$

but from 235·33 it follows that they are not subject to any other restriction except the negative one that **h** must not be the zero vector. The specification
·43 is variable, since **h** is not determinate, but it is also °*homogeneous*, for the pair of vectors k**h**, k**H**, for any proper value of k, fixes the same line as the pair of vectors **h**, **H**; this line will be called the line (**h**, **H**), or, if confusion is impossible, the line h.

Referred to a frame of reference, a line, like a ray, has six coordinates and six projections; but whereas the coordinates of a ray are six numbers individually significant and connected by two relations, the coordinates of a line will be proved to have only one relation between them, but significance
·44 attaches only to their ratios: °any expression which involves coordinates or projections of a line except through ratios alone is really concerned not with the line itself but with some particular rotor located in the line.

As an example, we can not attach, in relation to two lines (**m**, **M**), (**n**, **N**), any intrinsic value to the *expression* $\mathcal{S}\,\mathbf{Mn} + \mathcal{S}\,\mathbf{Nm}$, but the *equation*

$$\mathcal{S}\,\mathbf{Mn} + \mathcal{S}\,\mathbf{Nm} = 0$$

is unaltered if (h**m**, h**M**), (k**n**, k**N**) are substituted for (**m**, **M**), (**n**, **N**), and the equation, being the condition for the rotors obtained by locating **m**, **n** in the lines to have coplanar axes, describes a property of the lines:

·45 *The two lines* (**m**, **M**), (**n**, **N**) *are coplanar if and only if*

$$\mathcal{S}\,\mathbf{Mn} + \mathcal{S}\,\mathbf{Nm} = 0.$$

From 5·41 it follows that the vectorial equation of the line (**h**, **H**) is

·46 $$\mathcal{V}\,\mathbf{rh} = \mathbf{H}.$$

Combining this with 235·33 we can assert that

If $\mathbf{h}$, $\mathbf{H}$ *are any two vectors of which the first is not the zero vector, the points representing with reference to an origin O a variable vector* $\mathbf{r}$ *subject only to the condition* ·47

$$\mathscr{V}\mathbf{rh} = \mathbf{H}$$

compose a definite line.

To illustrate the direct application of the vectorial equation, let S be a point on the line $(\mathbf{m}, \mathbf{M})$ and T a point on the line $(\mathbf{n}, \mathbf{N})$. Then

$$\mathscr{G}\mathbf{Mn} = \mathscr{G}(\mathscr{V}\mathbf{r}_S\mathbf{m})\,\mathbf{n} = \mathscr{J}\mathbf{r}_S\mathbf{mn}, \qquad \cdot 48$$

$$\mathscr{G}\mathbf{Nm} = \mathscr{G}(\mathscr{V}\mathbf{r}_T\mathbf{n})\,\mathbf{m} = \mathscr{J}\mathbf{r}_T\mathbf{nm}, \qquad \cdot 49$$

and therefore $\qquad \mathscr{G}\mathbf{Mn} + \mathscr{G}\mathbf{Nm} = \mathscr{J}\mathbf{m}\,(\mathbf{r}_T - \mathbf{r}_S)\,\mathbf{n},$

from which ·45 follows at once.

·5. We can translate the three propositions 5·32, 5·33, 5·35 into assertions regarding a line; the first becomes

If a set of coordinates and projections of a line is ·51

$$x_h,\ y_h,\ z_h,\ X_h,\ Y_h,\ Z_h,\ l_h,\ m_h,\ n_h,\ L_h,\ M_h,\ N_h,$$

the planes through the line parallel to the axes of reference have equations

$$\Upsilon(yz_h - zy_h) = L_h, \quad \Upsilon(zx_h - xz_h) = M_h, \quad \Upsilon(xy_h - yx_h) = N_h,$$

and the planes through the line perpendicular to the planes of reference have equations

$$\Upsilon^{-1}(mn_h - nm_h) = X_h, \quad \Upsilon^{-1}(nl_h - ln_h) = Y_h, \quad \Upsilon^{-1}(lm_h - ml_h) = Z_h,$$

and the second becomes a corollary of this. A comparison of the third with ·22 suggests a similar modification of ·24, but if the intersection is to be treated as an unprepared line, there is no object in dealing with prepared planes; either by using ·24 or by adapting one of the proofs of that theorem, we find that

If $\mathbf{s}$, $\mathbf{t}$ *are vectors that are not parallel, the planes* ·54

$$\mathscr{G}\mathbf{rs} + S = 0, \quad \mathscr{G}\mathbf{rt} + T = 0$$

intersect in the line which has coordinates

$$\Upsilon^{-1}(m_\mathbf{s}n_\mathbf{t} - n_\mathbf{s}m_\mathbf{t}), \quad \Upsilon^{-1}(n_\mathbf{s}l_\mathbf{t} - l_\mathbf{s}n_\mathbf{t}), \quad \Upsilon^{-1}(l_\mathbf{s}m_\mathbf{t} - m_\mathbf{s}l_\mathbf{t}),$$
$$Sx_\mathbf{t} - Tx_\mathbf{s}, \quad Sy_\mathbf{t} - Ty_\mathbf{s}, \quad Sz_\mathbf{t} - Tz_\mathbf{s},$$

and projections

$$\Upsilon(y_\mathbf{s}z_\mathbf{t} - z_\mathbf{s}y_\mathbf{t}), \quad \Upsilon(z_\mathbf{s}x_\mathbf{t} - x_\mathbf{s}z_\mathbf{t}), \quad \Upsilon(x_\mathbf{s}y_\mathbf{t} - y_\mathbf{s}x_\mathbf{t}),$$
$$Sl_\mathbf{t} - Tl_\mathbf{s}, \quad Sm_\mathbf{t} - Tm_\mathbf{s}, \quad Sn_\mathbf{t} - Tn_\mathbf{s}.$$

If $(\mathbf{h}, \mathbf{H})$ defines a line and k is such that

$$k^2\mathscr{G}\mathbf{h}^2 = 1,$$

then $k\mathbf{h}$ is a unit vector and $(k\mathbf{h}, k\mathbf{H})$ defines a ray κ. It follows from ·31 that

·55 °the vector of the step from the origin to its normal projection on the line is $k^2 \mathscr{V}\,\mathbf{hH}$, that is, $\mathscr{V}\,\mathbf{hH}/\mathscr{S}\,\mathbf{h}^2$:

·56 *The normal projection of the origin O on the line h has for its first coordinate and its first projection*

$$\Upsilon^{-1}(m_h N_h - n_h M_h)/\mathscr{P} p_h^2, \quad \Upsilon(y_h Z_h - z_h Y_h)/\mathscr{C} c_h^2.$$

337. Some problems in the analytical geometry of lines and rays.

·**1.** We have often to deal with a plane through one ray parallel to another ray; the plane is definite provided that the two rays are not parallel, and the choice of a definite angle from one ray to the other corresponds to the choice of a definite cyclic direction for the plane. If the rays are σ, τ, and an angle from σ to τ is $\epsilon_{\sigma\tau}$, the ratios and cosines of the direction Π of the normal to the plane through σ parallel to τ are given by 2·51, and only the distance of the origin O from the plane remains to be determined; this distance a is the distance in the direction Π from σ to the ray τ_O through O parallel to τ, and therefore, by 236·66, $-a \sin \epsilon_{\sigma\tau}$ is the mutual moment of σ and τ_O, and by 236·44 this is the projection in the direction of τ of the momental vector of σ about O. By 221·42, this projection of the momental vector is the projected product $\mathscr{S}\,\mathbf{St}$, given in terms of components and projections by

$$\mathscr{S}\,\mathbf{St} = \mathscr{C}\, C_\sigma c_\tau = P_\sigma c_\tau = C_\sigma p_\tau = \mathscr{P} P_\sigma p_\tau,$$

and we see that

·11 *The distance of the origin from the plane through a ray σ parallel to a ray τ is* $-\mathscr{S}\,\mathbf{St}\operatorname{cosec}\epsilon_{\sigma\tau}$, *where $\epsilon_{\sigma\tau}$ is an angle from σ to τ measured round the direction in which the distance is measured.*

If $\epsilon_{\sigma\tau}$ continues to denote an angle *from σ to τ*, the distance of the origin from the plane through τ parallel to σ is $\mathscr{S}\,\mathbf{Ts}\operatorname{cosec}\epsilon_{\sigma\tau}$; the condition for the rays to intersect is

·12 $$(\mathscr{S}\,\mathbf{St} + \mathscr{S}\,\mathbf{Ts})\operatorname{cosec}\epsilon_{\sigma\tau} = 0.$$

This agrees with 6·12; the rays must be coplanar but not parallel.

Applied to 4·21 and 4·22, ·11 shews that the points on the plane through σ parallel to τ satisfy the equations

·13 $$p_\Pi c - \mathscr{S}\,\mathbf{St}\operatorname{cosec}\epsilon_{\sigma\tau} = 0, \quad c_\Pi p - \mathscr{S}\,\mathbf{St}\operatorname{cosec}\epsilon_{\sigma\tau} = 0;$$

if $\sin\epsilon_{\sigma\tau}$ is not zero, we may write these equations in the form

$$\Upsilon \begin{vmatrix} x & x_\sigma & x_\tau \\ y & y_\sigma & y_\tau \\ z & z_\sigma & z_\tau \end{vmatrix} = \Upsilon^{-1} \begin{vmatrix} l & l_\sigma & l_\tau \\ m & m_\sigma & m_\tau \\ n & n_\sigma & n_\tau \end{vmatrix} = \mathscr{S}\,\mathbf{St},$$

·14 that is, $$\Upsilon[c;\ c_\sigma;\ c_\tau] = \Upsilon^{-1}[p;\ p_\sigma;\ p_\tau] = \mathscr{S}\,\mathbf{St},$$

and it is in fact evident from 5·32 that the plane represented by ·14 passes through σ, and from the form of the equations that this plane is parallel to τ

as well as to σ. We can write down the equations ·14, or rather the equivalent vectorial equation, without any algebraic argument: if R is any point of the plane through σ parallel to τ, if τ_O is the ray through O parallel to τ and σ_R is the ray through R parallel to σ, then by 236·46 the mutual moment of σ_R and τ_O is the same as the mutual moment of σ and τ_O, which by 236·44 is $\mathscr{S}\,\mathbf{St}$, and by 236·13 this moment has the value $\mathscr{J}\,\mathbf{trs}$, where $\mathbf{r}$ is the vector of the step OR.

The equation of the plane through a ray σ parallel to a ray τ is ·15

$$\mathscr{J}\,\mathbf{rst} = \mathscr{S}\,\mathbf{St}.$$

Another proof of this equation is virtually contained in 6·46; if S is any point on σ, the point R is in the plane with which we are dealing if the vector of RS is coplanar with the vectors $\mathbf{s}$, $\mathbf{t}$, that is, if $\mathscr{J}\,\mathbf{rst}$ is equal to $\mathscr{J}\,\mathbf{r}_S\mathbf{st}$, and since $\mathscr{V}\mathbf{r}_S\mathbf{s}$ is $\mathbf{S}$, this last spatial product is $\mathscr{S}\,\mathbf{St}$.

But when we come to the *equation* of a plane, we are really dealing with an unprepared plane, and instead of rays we should be considering lines. The last argument by which ·15 has been proved is independent of the assumption that $\mathbf{s}$, $\mathbf{t}$ are *unit* vectors, and therefore

The equation of the plane through the line $(\mathbf{m}, \mathbf{M})$ *parallel to the line* $(\mathbf{n}, \mathbf{N})$ *is* ·16

$$\mathscr{J}\,\mathbf{rmn} = \mathscr{S}\,\mathbf{Mn},$$

it being assumed that the lines are not parallel.

·2. To find the point of intersection of a given line with a given plane is to find a vector $\mathbf{r}$ satisfying simultaneously

$$\mathscr{V}\,\mathbf{rs} = \mathbf{S}, \quad \mathscr{S}\,\mathbf{rt} = T, \tag{·21}$$

where T is a given number and $\mathbf{s}, \mathbf{S}, \mathbf{t}$ are given vectors such that $\mathbf{s}, \mathbf{t}$ are not zero and that

$$\mathscr{S}\,\mathbf{Ss} = 0; \tag{·22}$$

the algebraic problem is to solve the set of equations

$$\Upsilon(yz_s - zy_s) = L_s, \quad \Upsilon(zx_s - xz_s) = M_s, \quad \Upsilon(xy_s - yx_s) = N_s, \tag{·23}$$

$$l_{\mathbf{t}}x + m_{\mathbf{t}}y + n_{\mathbf{t}}z = T, \tag{·24}$$

where

$$L_s x_s + M_s y_s + N_s z_s = 0. \tag{·25}$$

If F is a particular point on the line, $\mathbf{r}_F + k\mathbf{s}$ is the typical vector of any point on the line, and this point is in the plane if

$$\mathscr{S}\,\mathbf{r}_F\mathbf{t} + k\,\mathscr{S}\,\mathbf{st} = T; \tag{·26}$$

with the value of k given by ·26,

$$\mathbf{r}\,\mathscr{S}\,\mathbf{st} = \mathbf{r}_F\,\mathscr{S}\,\mathbf{st} + (T - \mathscr{S}\,\mathbf{r}_F\mathbf{t})\,\mathbf{s} = T\mathbf{s} + \mathbf{r}_F\,\mathscr{S}\,\mathbf{st} - \mathbf{s}\,\mathscr{S}\,\mathbf{r}_F\mathbf{t} = T\mathbf{s} + \mathscr{V}(\mathscr{V}\,\mathbf{sr}_F)\,\mathbf{t},$$

by 223·33, and therefore since F is on the line,

$$\mathbf{r}\,\mathscr{S}\,\mathbf{st} = T\mathbf{s} + \mathscr{V}\,\mathbf{tS}, \tag{·27}$$

an equation which gives $\mathbf{r}$ explicitly unless $\mathbf{s}$ is perpendicular to $\mathbf{t}$, when the line is parallel to the plane and the problem is either insoluble or indeterminate.

The algebraic solution gives the same result almost more simply, since in this case the plausible assumption that a satisfactory solution is to be obtained by finding x from the last three of the four equations ·23, ·24 is not misleading; obviously these equations give

·29 $$p_{\mathbf{t}} c_s \,.\, x = T x_s + \Upsilon^{-1}(m_{\mathbf{t}} N_s - n_{\mathbf{t}} M_s).$$

·3. The conditions for the line

·31 $$\mathscr{V}\mathbf{rs} = \mathbf{S}$$

·32 to lie in the plane $$\mathscr{S}\mathbf{rt} = T$$

can be deduced from ·27 or ·29. One necessary condition is of course

·33 $$\mathscr{S}\mathbf{st} = 0,$$

and ·27 gives further conditions in the form

·34 $$T\mathbf{s} + \mathscr{V}\mathbf{tS} = \mathbf{0}.$$

It is to be noted however that ·22 and ·33 together imply that $\mathbf{s}$ and $\mathscr{V}\mathbf{tS}$ are parallel, so that only one additional relation is implied by ·34; this relation is naturally taken in the form

$$T\,\mathscr{S}\mathbf{s}^2 + \mathscr{S}\mathbf{s}\,(\mathscr{V}\mathbf{tS}) = 0,$$

·36 that is, $$T\,\mathscr{S}\mathbf{s}^2 = \mathscr{T}\mathbf{tsS}.$$

We can associate this condition with 6·55; if the line is parallel to the plane, the line is *in* the plane if a single point of the line is in the plane, and the equation that expresses that the normal projection of the origin on the line is in the plane is

$$\mathscr{S}\,(\mathscr{V}\mathbf{sS}/\mathscr{S}\mathbf{s}^2)\,\mathbf{t} = T,$$

which is equivalent to ·36.

·4. A particular case of the problem solved by ·27 is to determine the point in which a line $(\mathbf{p}, \mathbf{P})$ cuts the plane through a point Q containing two given vectors $\mathbf{s}$, $\mathbf{t}$. The equation of the plane is

·41 $$\mathscr{T}\mathbf{rst} = \mathscr{T}\mathbf{r}_Q\mathbf{st},$$

·42 that is, $$\mathscr{S}\mathbf{r}\,(\mathscr{V}\mathbf{st}) = \mathscr{T}\mathbf{r}_Q\mathbf{st},$$

and therefore the point is given by

$$\mathbf{r}\,\mathscr{T}\mathbf{pst} = \mathbf{p}\,\mathscr{T}\mathbf{r}_Q\mathbf{st} + \mathscr{V}(\mathscr{V}\mathbf{st})\,\mathbf{P},$$

which by 223·33 is equivalent to

·44 $$\mathbf{r}\,\mathscr{T}\mathbf{pst} = \mathbf{p}\,\mathscr{T}\mathbf{r}_Q\mathbf{st} - \mathbf{s}\,\mathscr{S}\mathbf{Pt} + \mathbf{t}\,\mathscr{S}\mathbf{Ps}.$$

A simple alternative to quoting ·27 is to assume the required value of $\mathbf{r}$ to be $f\mathbf{p} + g\mathbf{s} + h\mathbf{t}$; substitution in ·41 gives f, and g and h come from substitution in the equation of the line.

As a matter of pure algebra we have to take ·23, with p written for s, with the equation

$$[c\,;\; c_{\mathbf{s}}\,;\; c_{\mathbf{t}}] = [c_Q\,;\; c_{\mathbf{s}}\,;\; c_{\mathbf{t}}],$$

and we have at once

$$x_p[c_Q\,;\; c_{\mathbf{s}}\,;\; c_{\mathbf{t}}] = [x_p x,\; y_p x - \Upsilon^{-1}N_p,\; z_p x + \Upsilon^{-1}M_p\,;\; c_{\mathbf{s}}\,;\; c_{\mathbf{t}}],$$

which is easily seen to lead to ·44.

On the other hand it is not difficult to reach the results by reasoning more geometrical. Let σ_O, τ_O be rays through O such that the vectors **s**, **t** are vectors of amounts s, t in these rays, and let the line (**p**, **P**) meet the plane containing these rays in the point J; let this plane be given a cyclic direction, let ω be an angle from σ_O to τ_O, and let θ be an angle between the direction normal to the plane and one direction of the line. Then if **r** is expressed as $f\mathbf{p}+g\mathbf{s}+h\mathbf{t}$, the equation

$$f\mathscr{I}\,\mathbf{pst}=\mathscr{I}\,\mathbf{r}_Q\mathbf{st}$$

expresses that $\mathbf{r}-\mathbf{r}_Q$ is coplanar with **s** and **t**, and gs, ht are the coordinates of J in the plane. Hence by 24·26 the distances of J from the axes are $ht\sin\omega$, $-gs\sin\omega$, and the momental vectors of σ_O, τ_O about J are vectors with these amounts in the direction normal to the plane. So from 236·44 the momental products of *unit* vectors located in σ_O, τ_O by the rotor ϖ located in the given line are $hpt\sin\omega\cos\theta$, $-gps\sin\omega\cos\theta$, where p is the amount of **p** in the direction associated with the angle θ, and so finally the momental products of rotors with vectors **s**, **t** located through O by the rotor ϖ in the given line are

$$hpst\sin\omega\cos\theta,\quad -gpst\sin\omega\cos\theta,$$

that is to say, are $h\mathscr{I}\,\mathbf{pst}$, $-g\mathscr{I}\,\mathbf{pst}$, and since these same momental products are otherwise given by 236·23 as $\mathscr{G}\,\mathbf{Ps}$, $\mathscr{G}\,\mathbf{Pt}$, the values already found for g, h are recovered.

·**5**. An attempt to anticipate every question that can arise concerning intersections of lines and planes would be an absurdity, but there is one more set of problems of this kind that deserves explicit mention.

Let σ, τ be any two rays that are not parallel, and let $\epsilon_{\sigma\tau}$ be an angle between them; then there is one definite ray ϖ which cuts both σ and τ at right angles and has a direction round which $\epsilon_{\sigma\tau}$ is an angle from σ to τ; it is often necessary to know this ray and the points S, T in which it cuts σ, τ. The ratios and cosines of ϖ are given in 2·51.

This problem is included in a more general one which is in fact easier to discuss. If (**s**, **S**), (**t**, **T**) are two lines that are not parallel and **k** is any vector not coplanar with **s** and **t**, there is one and only one line parallel to **k** which cuts both (**s**, **S**) and (**t**, **T**), and the problem is to find the points S, T in which this line meets the given lines and the momental vector **K** of the rotor obtained by locating **k** in the line.

The simplest determination of **K** comes from 225·34. From 6·42 and 6·45,

$$\mathscr{G}\,\mathbf{Kk}=0,\quad \mathscr{G}\,\mathbf{Ks}+\mathscr{G}\,\mathbf{Sk}=0,\quad \mathscr{G}\,\mathbf{Kt}+\mathscr{G}\,\mathbf{Tk}=0. \qquad \cdot 51$$

Substituting in the identity of 225·34, taken in the form

$$\mathbf{K}\mathscr{I}\,\mathbf{kst}=\mathscr{G}\,\mathbf{Kk}\,\mathscr{V}\,\mathbf{st}+\mathscr{G}\,\mathbf{Ks}\,\mathscr{V}\,\mathbf{tk}+\mathscr{G}\,\mathbf{Kt}\,\mathscr{V}\,\mathbf{ks},$$

we have
$$\mathbf{K}\mathscr{I}\,\mathbf{kst}=\mathscr{G}\,\mathbf{Sk}\,\mathscr{V}\,\mathbf{kt}-\mathscr{G}\,\mathbf{Tk}\,\mathscr{V}\,\mathbf{ks}, \qquad \cdot 52$$

which is sufficient to determine **K**, since $\mathscr{G}\,\mathbf{Sk}$ and $\mathscr{G}\,\mathbf{Tk}$ are known and $\mathscr{I}\,\mathbf{kst}$ is not zero.

The positions of S and T can be found from ·15; identically from 225·32,

$$\mathbf{r}_S\mathscr{I}\,\mathbf{kst}=\mathbf{k}\mathscr{I}\,\mathbf{r}_S\mathbf{st}+\mathbf{s}\mathscr{I}\,\mathbf{kr}_S\mathbf{t}+\mathbf{t}\mathscr{I}\,\mathbf{ksr}_S,$$

$$\mathbf{r}_T\mathscr{I}\,\mathbf{kst}=\mathbf{k}\mathscr{I}\,\mathbf{r}_T\mathbf{st}+\mathbf{s}\mathscr{I}\,\mathbf{kr}_T\mathbf{t}+\mathbf{t}\mathscr{I}\,\mathbf{ksr}_T,$$

but from ·15, $\mathscr{I}\mathbf{r}_S\mathbf{st} = \mathscr{G}\,\mathbf{St}, \quad \mathscr{I}\mathbf{r}_T\mathbf{ts} = \mathscr{G}\,\mathbf{Ts},$

$$\mathscr{I}\mathbf{r}_T\mathbf{sk} = \mathscr{I}\mathbf{r}_S\mathbf{sk} = \mathscr{G}\,\mathbf{Sk}, \quad \mathscr{I}\mathbf{r}_S\mathbf{tk} = \mathscr{I}\mathbf{r}_T\mathbf{tk} = \mathscr{G}\,\mathbf{Tk},$$

·545 and therefore $\mathbf{r}_S\,\mathscr{I}\,\mathbf{kst} = \mathbf{k}\,\mathscr{G}\,\mathbf{St} + \mathbf{s}\,\mathscr{G}\,\mathbf{Tk} - \mathbf{t}\,\mathscr{G}\,\mathbf{Sk},$

·546 $\mathbf{r}_T\,\mathscr{I}\,\mathbf{kst} = -\mathbf{k}\,\mathscr{G}\,\mathbf{Ts} + \mathbf{s}\,\mathscr{G}\,\mathbf{Tk} - \mathbf{t}\,\mathscr{G}\,\mathbf{Sk}.$

From ·545 and ·546,

$$\mathscr{V}\mathbf{r}_S\mathbf{r}_T(\mathscr{I}\,\mathbf{kst})^2 = -(\mathscr{G}\,\mathbf{St} + \mathscr{G}\,\mathbf{Ts})(\mathscr{G}\,\mathbf{Sk}\,\mathscr{V}\mathbf{kt} - \mathscr{G}\,\mathbf{Tk}\,\mathscr{V}\mathbf{ks})$$

and therefore these formulae imply not only

$$(\mathbf{r}_T - \mathbf{r}_S)\,\mathscr{I}\,\mathbf{kst} = -\mathbf{k}\,(\mathscr{G}\,\mathbf{St} + \mathscr{G}\,\mathbf{Ts}),$$

but also $\mathscr{V}\mathbf{r}_S\mathbf{s}_T\,\mathscr{I}\,\mathbf{kst} = -\mathbf{K}\,(\mathscr{G}\,\mathbf{St} + \mathscr{G}\,\mathbf{Ts}),$

from ·52, in agreement with 235·26, for if S and T do not coincide, $(\mathbf{r}_T - \mathbf{r}_S, \mathscr{V}\mathbf{r}_S\mathbf{r}_T)$ is the same line as $(\mathbf{k}, \mathbf{K})$. But whether or not S and T coincide,

$$\mathbf{K} = -\mathscr{V}\mathbf{kr}_S = -\mathscr{V}\mathbf{kr}_T,$$

by the very definition of $\mathbf{K}$, and this enables us to reproduce ·52 from ·545 and ·546.

We may find $\mathbf{K}$ not in terms of vector products, but in the form $f\mathbf{k} + g\mathbf{s} + h\mathbf{t}$, for substituting this expression in ·51 we have

$$f\,\mathscr{G}\,\mathbf{k}^2 + g\,\mathscr{G}\,\mathbf{ks} + h\,\mathscr{G}\,\mathbf{kt} = 0,$$

$$f\,\mathscr{G}\,\mathbf{ks} + g\,\mathscr{G}\,\mathbf{s}^2 + h\,\mathscr{G}\,\mathbf{st} = -\,\mathscr{G}\,\mathbf{Sk},$$

$$f\,\mathscr{G}\,\mathbf{kt} + g\,\mathscr{G}\,\mathbf{st} + h\,\mathscr{G}\,\mathbf{t}^2 = -\,\mathscr{G}\,\mathbf{Tk},$$

and therefore

·55 $$\mathbf{K}\begin{vmatrix} \mathscr{G}\,\mathbf{k}^2 & \mathscr{G}\,\mathbf{ks} & \mathscr{G}\,\mathbf{kt} \\ \mathscr{G}\,\mathbf{ks} & \mathscr{G}\,\mathbf{s}^2 & \mathscr{G}\,\mathbf{st} \\ \mathscr{G}\,\mathbf{kt} & \mathscr{G}\,\mathbf{st} & \mathscr{G}\,\mathbf{t}^2 \end{vmatrix} = \begin{vmatrix} 0 & \mathbf{k} & \mathbf{s} & \mathbf{t} \\ 0 & \mathscr{G}\,\mathbf{k}^2 & \mathscr{G}\,\mathbf{ks} & \mathscr{G}\,\mathbf{kt} \\ \mathscr{G}\,\mathbf{Sk} & \mathscr{G}\,\mathbf{ks} & \mathscr{G}\,\mathbf{s}^2 & \mathscr{G}\,\mathbf{st} \\ \mathscr{G}\,\mathbf{Tk} & \mathscr{G}\,\mathbf{kt} & \mathscr{G}\,\mathbf{st} & \mathscr{G}\,\mathbf{t}^2 \end{vmatrix}.$$

If the cotractor of $(\mathbf{s}, \mathbf{S})$ and $(\mathbf{t}, \mathbf{T})$ is to be perpendicular to them both, we may take

·56 $$\mathbf{k} = \mathscr{V}\,\mathbf{st}.$$

Then $\mathscr{G}\,\mathbf{Sk} = \mathscr{I}\,\mathbf{Sst}, \quad \mathscr{G}\,\mathbf{Tk} = \mathscr{I}\,\mathbf{Tst},$

$$\mathscr{I}\,\mathbf{kst} = \mathscr{G}\,(\mathscr{V}\,\mathbf{st})^2 = \mathscr{G}\,\mathbf{s}^2\,\mathscr{G}\,\mathbf{t}^2 - (\mathscr{G}\,\mathbf{st})^2,$$

·571 and therefore $\mathbf{r}_S\,\mathscr{G}\,(\mathscr{V}\,\mathbf{st})^2 = \mathbf{s}\,\mathscr{I}\,\mathbf{Tst} - \mathbf{t}\,\mathscr{I}\,\mathbf{Sst} + \mathscr{V}\,\mathbf{st}\,\mathscr{G}\,\mathbf{St},$

·572 $\mathbf{r}_T\,\mathscr{G}\,(\mathscr{V}\,\mathbf{st})^2 = \mathbf{s}\,\mathscr{I}\,\mathbf{Tst} - \mathbf{t}\,\mathscr{I}\,\mathbf{Sst} - \mathscr{V}\,\mathbf{st}\,\mathscr{G}\,\mathbf{Ts},$

·573 $$\mathbf{K}\,\mathscr{G}\,(\mathscr{V}\,\mathbf{st})^2 = \begin{vmatrix} 0 & \mathbf{s} & \mathbf{t} \\ \mathscr{I}\,\mathbf{Sst} & \mathscr{G}\,\mathbf{s}^2 & \mathscr{G}\,\mathbf{st} \\ \mathscr{I}\,\mathbf{Tst} & \mathscr{G}\,\mathbf{st} & \mathscr{G}\,\mathbf{t}^2 \end{vmatrix};$$

to substitute in ·52 from ·56 and then to apply 223·33 is to reach ·573 by a more difficult route.

The effect of dealing with rays instead of lines is that certain of the vectors become unit vectors. This has no bearing on the general investigation, but if

ϖ is to be a *ray* perpendicular to σ and τ and if $\epsilon_{\sigma\tau}$ is to be an angle from σ to τ round ϖ, the vector denoted in ·56 by $\mathbf{k}$ becomes $\mathbf{p}\sin\epsilon_{\sigma\tau}$ and the momental vector $\mathbf{P}$ of the *ray* is $\mathbf{K}\operatorname{cosec}\epsilon_{\sigma\tau}$. Instead of ·571, ·572, ·573 we have

$$\mathbf{r}_S\sin^2\epsilon_{\sigma\tau} = \mathbf{s}\,\mathcal{J}\,\mathbf{Tst} - \mathbf{t}\,\mathcal{J}\,\mathbf{Sst} + \mathbf{p}\sin\epsilon_{\sigma\tau}\,\mathcal{G}\,\mathbf{St}, \qquad \cdot581$$

$$\mathbf{r}_T\sin^2\epsilon_{\sigma\tau} = \mathbf{s}\,\mathcal{J}\,\mathbf{Tst} - \mathbf{t}\,\mathcal{J}\,\mathbf{Sst} - \mathbf{p}\sin\epsilon_{\sigma\tau}\,\mathcal{G}\,\mathbf{Ts}, \qquad \cdot582$$

$$\mathbf{P}\sin^3\epsilon_{\sigma\tau} = \begin{vmatrix} 0 & \mathbf{s} & \mathbf{t} \\ \mathcal{J}\,\mathbf{Sst} & 1 & \cos\epsilon_{\sigma\tau} \\ \mathcal{J}\,\mathbf{Tst} & \cos\epsilon_{\sigma\tau} & 1 \end{vmatrix}. \qquad \cdot583$$

Translated into elements referring to a Cartesian frame, ·545, ·546 give for any coordinate or projection w,

$$w_S\,\mathcal{J}\,\mathbf{kst} = \quad w_{\mathbf{k}}\,\mathcal{G}\,\mathbf{St} + w_{\mathbf{s}}\,\mathcal{G}\,\mathbf{Tk} - w_{\mathbf{t}}\,\mathcal{G}\,\mathbf{Sk}, \qquad \cdot591$$

$$w_T\,\mathcal{J}\,\mathbf{kst} = -\,w_{\mathbf{k}}\,\mathcal{G}\,\mathbf{Ts} + w_{\mathbf{s}}\,\mathcal{G}\,\mathbf{Tk} - w_{\mathbf{t}}\,\mathcal{G}\,\mathbf{Sk}; \qquad \cdot592$$

we can make a similar version of ·55, but in general simpler expressions come from ·52, which gives

$$X_\kappa[p_\kappa;\, p_{\mathbf{s}};\, p_{\mathbf{t}}] = -\begin{vmatrix} 0 & m_\kappa & n_\kappa \\ \mathcal{G}\,\mathbf{Sk} & m_{\mathbf{s}} & n_{\mathbf{s}} \\ \mathcal{G}\,\mathbf{Tk} & m_{\mathbf{t}} & n_{\mathbf{t}} \end{vmatrix},\; L_\kappa[c_\kappa;\, c_{\mathbf{s}};\, c_{\mathbf{t}}] = -\begin{vmatrix} 0 & y_\kappa & z_\kappa \\ \mathcal{G}\,\mathbf{Sk} & y_{\mathbf{s}} & z_{\mathbf{s}} \\ \mathcal{G}\,\mathbf{Tk} & y_{\mathbf{t}} & z_{\mathbf{t}} \end{vmatrix}, \qquad \cdot593$$

formulae deducible immediately, the first from the set of linear equations

$$p_\kappa C_\kappa = 0,\; p_{\mathbf{s}}C_\kappa = -\,\mathcal{G}\,\mathbf{Sk},\; p_{\mathbf{t}}C_\kappa = -\,\mathcal{G}\,\mathbf{Tk},$$

the second from the equivalent set

$$c_\kappa P_\kappa = 0,\; c_{\mathbf{s}}P_\kappa = -\,\mathcal{G}\,\mathbf{Sk},\; c_{\mathbf{t}}P_\kappa = -\,\mathcal{G}\,\mathbf{Tk}.$$

Perhaps the simplest process for discovering ·591 algebraically is to suppose F, G to be particular points of the lines s, t and $f\mathbf{s}$, $j\mathbf{k}$, $g\mathbf{t}$ to be the vectors of the steps FS, ST, TG; then f, j, g are determined by the set of equations

$$\begin{cases} x_F + fx_{\mathbf{s}} + jx_{\mathbf{k}} + gx_{\mathbf{t}} = x_G, \\ y_F + fy_{\mathbf{s}} + jy_{\mathbf{k}} + gy_{\mathbf{t}} = y_G, \\ z_F + fz_{\mathbf{s}} + jz_{\mathbf{k}} + gz_{\mathbf{t}} = z_G. \end{cases} \qquad \cdot594$$

If between these equations and

$$x_F + fx_{\mathbf{s}} = x_S$$

we eliminate f, j, g, we have x_S given by the equation

$$\begin{vmatrix} x_S - x_F & x_{\mathbf{s}} & 0 & 0 \\ x_G - x_F & x_{\mathbf{s}} & x_{\mathbf{t}} & x_{\mathbf{k}} \\ y_G - y_F & y_{\mathbf{s}} & y_{\mathbf{t}} & y_{\mathbf{k}} \\ z_G - z_F & z_{\mathbf{s}} & z_{\mathbf{t}} & z_{\mathbf{k}} \end{vmatrix} = 0,$$

that is, by

$$x_S[c_{\mathbf{s}};\ c_{\mathbf{t}};\ c_{\mathbf{k}}]=x_{\mathbf{s}}[c_G;\ c_{\mathbf{t}};\ c_{\mathbf{k}}]+\begin{vmatrix} x_F & 1 & 0 & 0 \\ x_{\mathbf{s}}x_F & x_{\mathbf{s}} & x_{\mathbf{t}} & x_{\mathbf{k}} \\ x_{\mathbf{s}}y_F & y_{\mathbf{s}} & y_{\mathbf{t}} & y_{\mathbf{k}} \\ x_{\mathbf{s}}z_F & z_{\mathbf{s}} & z_{\mathbf{t}} & z_{\mathbf{k}} \end{vmatrix}$$

$$=x_{\mathbf{s}}[c_G;\ c_{\mathbf{t}};\ c_{\mathbf{k}}]-\begin{vmatrix} 0 & x_{\mathbf{t}} & x_{\mathbf{k}} \\ x_{\mathbf{s}}y_F-y_{\mathbf{s}}x_F & y_{\mathbf{t}} & y_{\mathbf{k}} \\ x_{\mathbf{s}}z_F-z_{\mathbf{s}}x_F & z_{\mathbf{t}} & z_{\mathbf{k}} \end{vmatrix}$$

$$=\Upsilon^{-1}x_sP_tc_{\mathbf{k}}-\Upsilon^{-1}[0,\ -N_s,\ M_s;\ c_t;\ c_{\mathbf{k}}]$$

$$=\Upsilon^{-1}x_sP_tc_{\mathbf{k}}-\Upsilon^{-1}\{x_t(M_sy_{\mathbf{k}}+N_sz_{\mathbf{k}})-x_{\mathbf{k}}(M_sy_t+N_sz_t)\},$$

that is, by $$\Upsilon x_S[c_{\mathbf{k}};\ c_s;\ c_t]=x_{\mathbf{k}}P_sc_t+x_sP_tc_{\mathbf{k}}-x_tP_sc_{\mathbf{k}},$$

and this is one of the formulae covered by ·591; the process fails to make clear why all the formulae to be found should have the same form.

Since $j\mathbf{k}$ is the vector of a step from the line s to the line t, the spatial product $\mathscr{I}\mathbf{s}\,(j\mathbf{k})\,\mathbf{t}$ is by definition the momental product of the rotors by which the lines are being identified; hence from 5·51,

$$j\mathscr{I}\mathbf{skt}=\mathscr{G}\,\mathbf{St}+\mathscr{G}\,\mathbf{Ts}.$$

By this equation, which may be verified from ·545 and ·546 or from ·594, we can determine the coefficient j without finding the positions of the points S, T.

CHAPTER III 4

VECTOR FRAMES

340. Introduction. 341. Coefficients and polar coefficients; the polar of a vector frame. 342. The evaluation of projected products; the fundamental magnitudes and the polar magnitudes of a vector frame; relations between coefficients and polar coefficients. 343. The evaluation of vector products and of spatial products. 344. Vector frames in a plane. 345. Attached frames and their use. 346. Attached frames and Cartesian frames; loaded Cartesian frames.

340. Introduction.

In many investigations, vectors may profitably be described not by reference to a Cartesian frame but by their relations to a given set of vectors, or as we may say by reference to a vector frame.

Examples are to be found in 36·2 and 37·5: in 36·247 and 37·573 a desired vector was regarded as found when it was expressed in the form $b\mathbf{s} + c\mathbf{t}$ with known values of b and c, the vectors $\mathbf{s}$ and $\mathbf{t}$ being given, and in 37·545 and 37·55, with three known vectors $\mathbf{k}$, $\mathbf{s}$, $\mathbf{t}$ the problem was taken to be the expression of unknown vectors in the form $a\mathbf{k} + b\mathbf{s} + c\mathbf{t}$.

These cases are isolated, if characteristic, and do not indicate a need for a systematic treatment, but since the construction of algebraic space, real or complex, depends on familiarity with vector frames, some consideration of vector frames is part of our task. The notation adopted is in part traditional in differential geometry and in part designed for use in that subject.

341. Coefficients and polar coefficients; the polar of a vector frame.

·1. Three vectors $\mathbf{x}$, $\mathbf{y}$, $\mathbf{z}$ in space are adequate to be the constituents of a vector frame if *every* vector in space can be expressed in the form $f\mathbf{x} + g\mathbf{y} + h\mathbf{z}$, where f, g, h are numbers; the condition both necessary and sufficient for this
is that °the vectors $\mathbf{x}$, $\mathbf{y}$, $\mathbf{z}$ are not coplanar; an equivalent form is that the ·12
spatial product $\mathscr{S}\,\mathbf{xyz}$ is not zero. Assuming this condition fulfilled, we must take the vectors of reference in a definite order, but we have no selections to make analogous to those which determine the angles of a Cartesian frame; a spatial convention is however assumed, and this gives to the spatial product $\mathscr{S}\,\mathbf{xyz}$ a definite value which we denote by J and call the °*spatial* ·13
magnitude of the frame. °*The spatial magnitude of a vector frame is necessarily* ·14
different from zero.

·2. If $\mathbf{r}$ is any vector, we denote by $\xi_{\mathbf{r}}$, $\eta_{\mathbf{r}}$, $\zeta_{\mathbf{r}}$ the three numbers such that

$$\mathbf{r} = \xi_{\mathbf{r}}\mathbf{x} + \eta_{\mathbf{r}}\mathbf{y} + \zeta_{\mathbf{r}}\mathbf{z},$$ ·21

and we call these numbers the °*coefficients* of $\mathbf{r}$ in the vector frame $\mathbf{xyz}$. We ·22 can exhibit the coefficients individually as ratios of spatial products, for we have seen in 225·32 that

$$\mathbf{r}\,\mathcal{J}\mathbf{xyz} = \mathbf{x}\,\mathcal{J}\mathbf{ryz} + \mathbf{y}\,\mathcal{J}\mathbf{xrz} + \mathbf{z}\,\mathcal{J}\mathbf{xyr},$$

and this, in our present notation, is equivalent to

·23 $$\xi_{\mathbf{r}} : \eta_{\mathbf{r}} : \zeta_{\mathbf{r}} : 1 = \mathcal{J}\mathbf{ryz} : \mathcal{J}\mathbf{xrz} : \mathcal{J}\mathbf{xyr} : J.$$

The numbers which correspond to the projections in a Cartesian frame are projected products, and we write

·24 $$\lambda_{\mathbf{r}} = \mathcal{G}\mathbf{xr}, \quad \mu_{\mathbf{r}} = \mathcal{G}\mathbf{yr}, \quad \nu_{\mathbf{r}} = \mathcal{G}\mathbf{zr}.$$

·25 It will appear in ·4 that these numbers are appropriately called the °*polar coefficients* of **r**.

For contracted notation we write

·26 $$\mathbf{f} = (\mathbf{x}, \mathbf{y}, \mathbf{z}),$$

·27 $$\chi = (\xi, \eta, \zeta), \quad \upsilon = (\lambda, \mu, \nu).$$

·29 Thus ·21 is written $\mathbf{r} = \chi_{\mathbf{r}}\mathbf{f}.$

·3. The frame to be taken as polar of the vector frame **xyz** is of course a frame $\bar{\mathbf{x}}\bar{\mathbf{y}}\bar{\mathbf{z}}$ in which each constituent is perpendicular to two of the three vectors composing the original frame:

·31 $$\mathcal{G}\mathbf{y}\bar{\mathbf{x}} = \mathcal{G}\mathbf{z}\bar{\mathbf{x}} = \mathcal{G}\mathbf{z}\bar{\mathbf{y}} = \mathcal{G}\mathbf{x}\bar{\mathbf{y}} = \mathcal{G}\mathbf{x}\bar{\mathbf{z}} = \mathcal{G}\mathbf{y}\bar{\mathbf{z}} = 0.$$

These conditions are not sufficient to determine the polar frame, and we utilise the freedom that remains, to secure a simplicity unapproachable with Cartesian axes.

From ·31, if **r** can be expressed both as $\xi\mathbf{x} + \eta\mathbf{y} + \zeta\mathbf{z}$ and as $\bar{\xi}\bar{\mathbf{x}} + \bar{\eta}\bar{\mathbf{y}} + \bar{\zeta}\bar{\mathbf{z}}$, then identically

·32 $$\mathcal{G}\mathbf{xr} = \bar{\xi}\,\mathcal{G}\mathbf{x}\bar{\mathbf{x}}, \quad \mathcal{G}\mathbf{yr} = \bar{\eta}\,\mathcal{G}\mathbf{y}\bar{\mathbf{y}}, \quad \mathcal{G}\mathbf{zr} = \bar{\zeta}\,\mathcal{G}\mathbf{z}\bar{\mathbf{z}},$$

·33 $$\mathcal{G}\bar{\mathbf{x}}\mathbf{r} = \xi\,\mathcal{G}\bar{\mathbf{x}}\mathbf{x}, \quad \mathcal{G}\bar{\mathbf{y}}\mathbf{r} = \eta\,\mathcal{G}\bar{\mathbf{y}}\mathbf{y}, \quad \mathcal{G}\bar{\mathbf{z}}\mathbf{r} = \zeta\,\mathcal{G}\bar{\mathbf{z}}\mathbf{z},$$

and it is evident that the maximum of simplicity will be attained if we are able to take

·34 $$\mathcal{G}\mathbf{x}\bar{\mathbf{x}} = \mathcal{G}\mathbf{y}\bar{\mathbf{y}} = \mathcal{G}\mathbf{z}\bar{\mathbf{z}} = 1.$$

Now if **p** is any proper vector perpendicular to both **y** and **z**, a vector $\bar{\mathbf{x}}$ satisfies the last two of the conditions

·35 $$\mathcal{G}\mathbf{x}\bar{\mathbf{x}} = 1, \quad \mathcal{G}\mathbf{y}\bar{\mathbf{x}} = 0, \quad \mathcal{G}\mathbf{z}\bar{\mathbf{x}} = 0$$

if and only if it is a multiple $a\mathbf{p}$ of **p**. The first condition then becomes

·36 $$a\,\mathcal{G}\mathbf{xp} = 1;$$

since **x** is not coplanar with **y** and **z**, $\mathcal{G}\mathbf{xp}$ is not zero, and ·36 is satisfied by a unique value of a, which is not zero. Thus there is one and only one vector
·37 $\bar{\mathbf{x}}$ that satisfies ·35, and this is a proper vector: °*a vector frame in space has a unique polar.* Moreover, from the form of ·31 and ·34,

·38 *The relation between a vector frame and its polar is a symmetrical relation.*

·**4**. With the simplification which $\bar{\mathbf{x}}, \bar{\mathbf{y}}, \bar{\mathbf{z}}$ have been chosen to effect, ·32, ·33 become

$$\mathcal{G}\,\mathbf{xr} = \bar{\xi}, \quad \mathcal{G}\,\mathbf{yr} = \bar{\eta}, \quad \mathcal{G}\,\mathbf{zr} = \bar{\zeta}, \qquad \cdot 41$$

$$\mathcal{G}\,\bar{\mathbf{x}}\mathbf{r} = \xi, \quad \mathcal{G}\,\bar{\mathbf{y}}\mathbf{r} = \eta, \quad \mathcal{G}\,\bar{\mathbf{z}}\mathbf{r} = \zeta, \qquad \cdot 42$$

and may be summarised in the assertion that

The polar coefficients of a vector in a vector frame are the coefficients of the same vector in the polar frame. ·43

Explicitly, if $\lambda_{\mathbf{r}}, \mu_{\mathbf{r}}, \nu_{\mathbf{r}}$ are defined as in ·24, then

$$\mathbf{r} = \lambda_{\mathbf{r}}\bar{\mathbf{x}} + \mu_{\mathbf{r}}\bar{\mathbf{y}} + \nu_{\mathbf{r}}\bar{\mathbf{z}}, \qquad \cdot 44$$

or in contracted notation, $$\mathbf{r} = \upsilon_{\mathbf{r}}\bar{\mathbf{f}}. \qquad \cdot 45$$

From ·43 comes a theorem that we might have derived directly from 215·24:

A vector in space is completely determined by its projected products with any three vectors that are not coplanar. ·46

·**5**. Since $\bar{\mathbf{x}}$ is perpendicular to both **y** and **z**, it is a multiple of their vector product. It follows therefore from the identity of $\mathcal{G}\,\mathbf{x}\,(\mathcal{V}\,\mathbf{yz})$ with $\mathcal{J}\,\mathbf{xyz}$ that $\mathcal{V}\,\mathbf{yz}$ is $J\bar{\mathbf{x}}$. The same conclusion follows a comparison of ·44 with 225·34, which can be written

$$J\mathbf{r} = \lambda_{\mathbf{r}}\,\mathcal{V}\,\mathbf{yz} + \mu_{\mathbf{r}}\,\mathcal{V}\,\mathbf{zx} + \nu_{\mathbf{r}}\,\mathcal{V}\,\mathbf{xy}:$$

The polar of the frame **xyz** *is formed of the vectors* ·51

$$J^{-1}\mathcal{V}\,\mathbf{yz}, \quad J^{-1}\mathcal{V}\,\mathbf{zx}, \quad J^{-1}\mathcal{V}\,\mathbf{xy}.$$

Here the reciprocal nature of the relation between the frames is concealed.

From ·51 and 225·28

$$\mathcal{V}\,\bar{\mathbf{y}}\bar{\mathbf{z}} = J^{-2}\mathbf{x}\,\mathcal{J}\,\mathbf{xyz} = J^{-1}\mathbf{x}; \qquad \cdot 52$$

but if $\bar{J}$ is the spatial magnitude of the polar frame,

$$\mathcal{V}\,\bar{\mathbf{y}}\bar{\mathbf{z}} = \bar{J}\mathbf{x}, \qquad \cdot 53$$

since ·51 applies to the polar frame; hence

$$J\bar{J} = 1: \qquad \cdot 54$$

The spatial magnitude of the polar of a frame is the reciprocal of the spatial magnitude of the frame. ·55

A direct proof of ·54 is furnished by 32·63, on substitution from ·31 and ·34.

342. The evaluation of projected products; the fundamental magnitudes and the polar magnitudes of a vector frame; relations between coefficients and polar coefficients.

·**1**. If the first of two vectors **r**, **s** is given by its coefficients and the second by its polar coefficients, the projected product is determinable from first principles; we have

$$\mathcal{G}\,\mathbf{rs} = \mathcal{G}\,(\xi_{\mathbf{r}}\mathbf{x} + \eta_{\mathbf{r}}\mathbf{y} + \zeta_{\mathbf{r}}\mathbf{z})\,\mathbf{s} = \xi_{\mathbf{r}}\,\mathcal{G}\,\mathbf{xs} + \eta_{\mathbf{r}}\,\mathcal{G}\,\mathbf{ys} + \zeta_{\mathbf{r}}\,\mathcal{G}\,\mathbf{zs}, \qquad \cdot 11$$

that is, $$\mathcal{G}\,\mathbf{rs} = \chi_{\mathbf{r}}\upsilon_{\mathbf{s}}, \qquad \cdot 12$$

and similarly $$\mathcal{G}\,\mathbf{rs} = \upsilon_{\mathbf{r}}\chi_{\mathbf{s}}. \qquad \cdot 13$$

In these formulae the vectors **x**, **y**, **z** are not involved, except in so far as the coefficients and polar coefficients depend on them, but it is otherwise if the vectors **r**, **s** are given both by coefficients or both by polar coefficients.

·**2**. It follows from the distributive and commutative properties that the projected product $\mathcal{G}(\xi_{\mathbf{r}}\mathbf{x}+\eta_{\mathbf{r}}\mathbf{y}+\zeta_{\mathbf{r}}\mathbf{z})(\xi_{\mathbf{s}}\mathbf{x}+\eta_{\mathbf{s}}\mathbf{y}+\zeta_{\mathbf{s}}\mathbf{z})$ of any two vectors **r**, **s** is given by

·21 $$\mathcal{G}\,\mathbf{rs} = L\xi_{\mathbf{r}}\xi_{\mathbf{s}} + M\eta_{\mathbf{r}}\eta_{\mathbf{s}} + N\zeta_{\mathbf{r}}\zeta_{\mathbf{s}} + P(\eta_{\mathbf{r}}\zeta_{\mathbf{s}}+\zeta_{\mathbf{r}}\eta_{\mathbf{s}}) + Q(\zeta_{\mathbf{r}}\xi_{\mathbf{s}}+\xi_{\mathbf{r}}\zeta_{\mathbf{s}}) + R(\xi_{\mathbf{r}}\eta_{\mathbf{s}}+\eta_{\mathbf{r}}\xi_{\mathbf{s}}),$$

where

·22 $$L=\mathcal{G}\mathbf{x}^2,\quad M=\mathcal{G}\mathbf{y}^2,\quad N=\mathcal{G}\mathbf{z}^2,\quad P=\mathcal{G}\mathbf{yz},\quad Q=\mathcal{G}\mathbf{zx},\quad R=\mathcal{G}\mathbf{xy}.$$

The coefficients L, M, N, P, Q, R are called the *fundamental magnitudes* of the frame; in order to write ·21 briefly in the form

·23 $$\mathcal{G}\,\mathbf{rs} = S\chi_{\mathbf{r}}\chi_{\mathbf{s}},$$

24 we put $$L=S^{11},\quad P=S^{23}=S^{32}$$

and so on, and we observe that from 32·63

·25 $$J^2 = \begin{vmatrix} L & R & Q \\ R & M & P \\ Q & P & N \end{vmatrix},$$

a formula that we can abbreviate to

·26 $$J^2 = [[S]].$$

The projected product $\mathcal{G}\mathbf{xr}$, which is the polar coefficient $\lambda_{\mathbf{r}}$, is the coefficient of $\xi_{\mathbf{s}}$ in ·21; explicitly this coefficient is the linear function

$$L\xi_{\mathbf{r}} + R\eta_{\mathbf{r}} + Q\zeta_{\mathbf{r}},$$

denoted by $S^1\chi_{\mathbf{r}}$;

·28 *The polar coefficients of any vector are given in terms of the coefficients themselves by the formulae*

$$\lambda = S^1\chi,\quad \mu = S^2\chi,\quad \nu = S^3\chi.$$

·**3**. In terms of their polar coefficients the vectors **r**, **s** take the forms $\lambda_{\mathbf{r}}\bar{\mathbf{x}}+\mu_{\mathbf{r}}\bar{\mathbf{y}}+\nu_{\mathbf{r}}\bar{\mathbf{z}}$, $\lambda_{\mathbf{s}}\bar{\mathbf{x}}+\mu_{\mathbf{s}}\bar{\mathbf{y}}+\nu_{\mathbf{s}}\bar{\mathbf{z}}$, and therefore

·31 $$\mathcal{G}\,\mathbf{rs} = \bar{L}\lambda_{\mathbf{r}}\lambda_{\mathbf{s}} + \bar{M}\mu_{\mathbf{r}}\mu_{\mathbf{s}} + \bar{N}\nu_{\mathbf{r}}\nu_{\mathbf{s}} + \bar{P}(\mu_{\mathbf{r}}\nu_{\mathbf{s}}+\nu_{\mathbf{r}}\mu_{\mathbf{s}}) + \bar{Q}(\nu_{\mathbf{r}}\lambda_{\mathbf{s}}+\lambda_{\mathbf{r}}\nu_{\mathbf{s}}) + \bar{R}(\lambda_{\mathbf{r}}\mu_{\mathbf{s}}+\mu_{\mathbf{r}}\lambda_{\mathbf{s}}),$$

where $\bar{L}, \bar{M}, \bar{N}, \bar{P}, \bar{Q}, \bar{R}$ are constants called the *polar magnitudes* of the frame **xyz** and given by

·32 $$\bar{L}=\mathcal{G}\bar{\mathbf{x}}^2,\quad \bar{P}=\mathcal{G}\bar{\mathbf{y}}\bar{\mathbf{z}},$$

and so on. To abbreviate ·31 we write

·33 $$\bar{L}=\bar{S}^{11},\quad \bar{P}=\bar{S}^{23}=\bar{S}^{32},$$

and so on, so that with υ for (λ, μ, ν), ·31 becomes

·34 $$\mathcal{G}\,\mathbf{rs} = \bar{S}\upsilon_{\mathbf{r}}\upsilon_{\mathbf{s}}.$$

The coefficients of $\lambda_{\mathbf{s}}, \mu_{\mathbf{s}}, \nu_{\mathbf{s}}$ in ·31 are $\bar{S}^1 v_{\mathbf{r}}, \bar{S}^2 v_{\mathbf{r}}, \bar{S}^3 v_{\mathbf{r}}$, and these are the polar coefficients of $\mathbf{r}$ in the frame $\bar{\mathbf{x}}\bar{\mathbf{y}}\bar{\mathbf{z}}$, and therefore are the coefficients $\xi_{\mathbf{r}}, \eta_{\mathbf{r}}, \zeta_{\mathbf{r}}$:

The coefficients of any vector are given in terms of the polar coefficients by the formulae ·35

$$\xi = \bar{S}^1 v, \quad \eta = \bar{S}^2 v, \quad \zeta = \bar{S}^3 v.$$

·**4**. Since either of the frames **xyz**, $\bar{\mathbf{x}}\bar{\mathbf{y}}\bar{\mathbf{z}}$ is deducible from the other, the fundamental magnitudes of the frames are related. Either set of magnitudes can indeed be determined from the other; the explicit results are all derivable from the relation

$$\mathscr{G}(\mathscr{V}\mathbf{rs})(\mathscr{V}\mathbf{tu}) = \mathscr{G}\mathbf{rt}\,\mathscr{G}\mathbf{su} - \mathscr{G}\mathbf{ru}\,\mathscr{G}\mathbf{st} \qquad \cdot 41$$

which we have seen in 225·43 to hold between any four vectors, for this equality combines with 1·51 to give at once the typical equations

$$J^2\bar{L} = MN - P^2, \quad J^2\bar{P} = QR - LP, \qquad \cdot 42$$

$$\bar{J}^2 L = \bar{M}\bar{N} - \bar{P}^2, \quad \bar{J}^2 P = \bar{Q}\bar{R} - \bar{L}\bar{P}. \qquad \cdot 43$$

But results such as these are seldom used, the relation between the sets of magnitudes being applied as a rule in another form. If we substitute for λ, μ, ν from ·28 in ·35 we have

$$\left[\begin{array}{l} \xi = \bar{S}^1 S^1 \xi + \bar{S}^1 S^2 \eta + \bar{S}^1 S^3 \zeta, \\ \eta = \bar{S}^2 S^1 \xi + \bar{S}^2 S^2 \eta + \bar{S}^2 S^3 \zeta, \\ \zeta = \bar{S}^3 S^1 \xi + \bar{S}^3 S^2 \eta + \bar{S}^3 S^3 \zeta, \end{array}\right. \qquad \cdot 44$$

where, in agreement with 25·62 and 25·44, $\bar{S}^i S^j$ denotes $\bar{S}^{i1} S^{1j} + \bar{S}^{i2} S^{2j} + \bar{S}^{i3} S^{3j}$, and since the formulae in ·44 are true for any vector whatever, they are identities; hence

The value of the sum $\bar{S}^i S^j$ is unity or zero according as i and j coincide or differ. ·46

On the assumption that J^2 is not zero, the relation asserted by ·46 between the two sets of magnitudes is algebraically equivalent to the relation deduced from ·41, for on the one hand ·46 can be verified from ·42 or ·43, and on the other hand ·46 by giving the values of the three expressions $\bar{S}^i S^1$, $\bar{S}^i S^2$, $\bar{S}^i S^3$ provides three linear equations of which one is not homogeneous for the determination of $\bar{S}^{i1}$, $\bar{S}^{i2}$, $\bar{S}^{i3}$ as functions of L, M, N, P, Q, R.

The substance of the last paragraph can be regarded in the light of pure algebra. The sets of coefficients ξ, η, ζ and λ, μ, ν are two sets of variables, related linearly to each other; one set of formulae of transformation is given in ·28, and the set given in ·35 is the reciprocal set. If we lay no stress on this aspect, it is not only because we are concerned primarily with geometry, but also because the work as it presents itself to us involves a restriction of symmetry and a restriction in the number of variables: to pursue an algebraical investigation in which these restrictions are irrelevant without abandoning them would be only less undesirable than to enter here on a discussion of the elements of the general theory of linear substitutions.

343. THE EVALUATION OF VECTOR PRODUCTS AND OF SPATIAL PRODUCTS.

·1. We have seen that the vector products $\mathscr{V}\,\mathbf{yz}$, $\mathscr{V}\,\mathbf{zx}$, $\mathscr{V}\,\mathbf{xy}$ are $J\bar{\mathbf{x}}$, $J\bar{\mathbf{y}}$, $J\bar{\mathbf{z}}$, and that the vector products $\mathscr{V}\,\bar{\mathbf{y}}\bar{\mathbf{z}}$, $\mathscr{V}\,\bar{\mathbf{z}}\bar{\mathbf{x}}$, $\mathscr{V}\,\bar{\mathbf{x}}\bar{\mathbf{y}}$ are $J^{-1}\mathbf{x}$, $J^{-1}\mathbf{y}$, $J^{-1}\mathbf{z}$; we deduce the equations

·11 $$\mathscr{V}(\xi_{\mathbf{r}}\mathbf{x}+\eta_{\mathbf{r}}\mathbf{y}+\zeta_{\mathbf{r}}\mathbf{z})(\xi_{\mathbf{s}}\mathbf{x}+\eta_{\mathbf{s}}\mathbf{y}+\zeta_{\mathbf{s}}\mathbf{z}) = J(\eta_{\mathbf{r}}\zeta_{\mathbf{s}}-\zeta_{\mathbf{r}}\eta_{\mathbf{s}})\bar{\mathbf{x}}+J(\zeta_{\mathbf{r}}\xi_{\mathbf{s}}-\xi_{\mathbf{r}}\zeta_{\mathbf{s}})\bar{\mathbf{y}}+J(\xi_{\mathbf{r}}\eta_{\mathbf{s}}-\eta_{\mathbf{r}}\xi_{\mathbf{s}})\bar{\mathbf{z}},$$

·12 $$\mathscr{V}(\lambda_{\mathbf{r}}\bar{\mathbf{x}}+\mu_{\mathbf{r}}\bar{\mathbf{y}}+\nu_{\mathbf{r}}\bar{\mathbf{z}})(\lambda_{\mathbf{s}}\bar{\mathbf{x}}+\mu_{\mathbf{s}}\bar{\mathbf{y}}+\nu_{\mathbf{s}}\bar{\mathbf{z}}) = J^{-1}(\mu_{\mathbf{r}}\nu_{\mathbf{s}}-\nu_{\mathbf{r}}\mu_{\mathbf{s}})\mathbf{x}+J^{-1}(\nu_{\mathbf{r}}\lambda_{\mathbf{s}}-\lambda_{\mathbf{r}}\nu_{\mathbf{s}})\mathbf{y}+J^{-1}(\lambda_{\mathbf{r}}\mu_{\mathbf{s}}-\mu_{\mathbf{r}}\lambda_{\mathbf{s}})\mathbf{z}:$$

·13 *In the vector frame* $\mathbf{xyz}$, *the vector product of the vectors* $\mathbf{r}$, $\mathbf{s}$ *has the coefficients*

$$J^{-1}(\mu_{\mathbf{r}}\nu_{\mathbf{s}}-\nu_{\mathbf{r}}\mu_{\mathbf{s}}),\quad J^{-1}(\nu_{\mathbf{r}}\lambda_{\mathbf{s}}-\lambda_{\mathbf{r}}\nu_{\mathbf{s}}),\quad J^{-1}(\lambda_{\mathbf{r}}\mu_{\mathbf{s}}-\mu_{\mathbf{r}}\lambda_{\mathbf{s}}),$$

and the polar coefficients

$$J(\eta_{\mathbf{r}}\zeta_{\mathbf{s}}-\zeta_{\mathbf{r}}\eta_{\mathbf{s}}),\quad J(\zeta_{\mathbf{r}}\xi_{\mathbf{s}}-\xi_{\mathbf{r}}\zeta_{\mathbf{s}}),\quad J(\xi_{\mathbf{r}}\eta_{\mathbf{s}}-\eta_{\mathbf{r}}\xi_{\mathbf{s}}).$$

·2. We can infer the theorem that

·21 *For any three vectors* $\mathbf{q}$, $\mathbf{r}$, $\mathbf{s}$ *the spatial product is given with reference to a vector frame by*

$$\mathscr{S}\,\mathbf{qrs} = J[\chi_{\mathbf{q}};\ \chi_{\mathbf{r}};\ \chi_{\mathbf{s}}] = J^{-1}[\upsilon_{\mathbf{q}};\ \upsilon_{\mathbf{r}};\ \upsilon_{\mathbf{s}}],$$

from ·13 and 225·21, but it is more interesting to remark that

·22 $$J\,\mathscr{S}\,\mathbf{qrs} = [\upsilon_{\mathbf{q}};\ \upsilon_{\mathbf{r}};\ \upsilon_{\mathbf{s}}]$$

is a version of 32·63, and that if we regard the coefficients of $\mathbf{q}$, $\mathbf{r}$, $\mathbf{s}$ as projected products in the polar frame, then

·23 $$\bar{J}\,\mathscr{S}\,\mathbf{qrs} = [\chi_{\mathbf{q}};\ \chi_{\mathbf{r}};\ \chi_{\mathbf{s}}]$$

is another version of the same theorem. The distributive property of the spatial product also leads to

·24 $$\mathscr{S}\,\mathbf{qrs} = J[\chi_{\mathbf{q}};\ \chi_{\mathbf{r}};\ \chi_{\mathbf{s}}]$$

if the coefficients of the vectors are taken to have their primary meaning.

·3. Algebraical identities can be derived from ·13 as from 32·35 in 32·8. But in geometry it is usually easier to appeal directly to the vectorial relations which such identities represent than to use the identities themselves.

344. VECTOR FRAMES IN A PLANE.

·1. The theory of a vector frame in a plane agrees in its main lines with the theory of a frame of the same kind in space, but at one point there is a divergent track due to the countersymmetry of the prepared plane.

A plane vector frame is formed of two vectors $\mathbf{x}$, $\mathbf{y}$ which are not parallel, taken in a definite order; the areal product $\mathscr{A}\,\mathbf{xy}$, which is not zero, we denote

·12 by C and call the °*areal magnitude* of the frame.

The vector $\mathbf{r}$ can be expressed as $\xi_{\mathbf{r}}\mathbf{x} + \eta_{\mathbf{r}}\mathbf{y}$, and $\xi_{\mathbf{r}}$, $\eta_{\mathbf{r}}$ are called the *coefficients* of $\mathbf{r}$, while $\mathscr{G}\mathbf{xr}$, $\mathscr{G}\mathbf{yr}$ are called the *polar coefficients* and denoted by $\lambda_{\mathbf{r}}$, $\mu_{\mathbf{r}}$.

·**2.** The polar frame $\bar{\mathbf{x}}\bar{\mathbf{y}}$ is defined by the equations

$$\mathscr{G}\,\mathbf{y}\bar{\mathbf{x}} = \mathscr{G}\,\mathbf{x}\bar{\mathbf{y}} = 0, \qquad \cdot 21$$

$$\mathscr{G}\,\mathbf{x}\bar{\mathbf{x}} = \mathscr{G}\,\mathbf{y}\bar{\mathbf{y}} = 1, \qquad \cdot 22$$

exactly as in three-dimensional work, and again these equations lead to

$$\mathscr{G}\,\bar{\mathbf{x}}\mathbf{r} = \xi_{\mathbf{r}}, \quad \mathscr{G}\,\bar{\mathbf{y}}\mathbf{r} = \eta_{\mathbf{r}}, \qquad \cdot 23$$

and being symmetrical in the two sets of vectors imply also

$$\mathbf{r} = \bar{\mathbf{x}}\,\mathscr{G}\,\mathbf{xr} + \bar{\mathbf{y}}\,\mathscr{G}\,\mathbf{yr}: \qquad \cdot 24$$

The polar coefficients of a vector in one frame are the coefficients in the polar frame. ·25

The vectors $\bar{\mathbf{x}}$, $\bar{\mathbf{y}}$, having the pairs of directions at right angles to $\mathbf{y}$, $\mathbf{x}$, are multiples of the vectors $\mathscr{E}\,\mathbf{y}$, $\mathscr{E}\,\mathbf{x}$ obtained by erecting $\mathbf{y}$, $\mathbf{x}$, and it follows from the identities

$$\mathscr{G}\,(\mathscr{E}\,\mathbf{y})\,\mathbf{x} = -\mathscr{A}\,\mathbf{xy}, \quad \mathscr{G}\,(\mathscr{E}\,\mathbf{x})\,\mathbf{y} = \mathscr{A}\,\mathbf{xy},$$

cases of 222·14, that $\mathscr{E}\,\mathbf{y} = -C\bar{\mathbf{x}}, \quad \mathscr{E}\,\mathbf{x} = C\bar{\mathbf{y}}:$ ·26

The frame polar to $\mathbf{xy}$ *is formed by* $-C^{-1}\,\mathscr{E}\,\mathbf{y}$ *and* $C^{-1}\,\mathscr{E}\,\mathbf{x}$. ·27

The relation between the areal constants of a frame and its polar is given most directly by 222·25, for

$$\mathscr{A}\,\mathbf{xy}\,\mathscr{A}\,\bar{\mathbf{x}}\bar{\mathbf{y}} = \mathscr{G}\,\mathbf{x}\bar{\mathbf{x}}\,\mathscr{G}\,\mathbf{y}\bar{\mathbf{y}} - \mathscr{G}\,\mathbf{x}\bar{\mathbf{y}}\,\mathscr{G}\,\mathbf{y}\bar{\mathbf{x}}$$

reduces on account of ·21 and ·22 to

$$C\bar{C} = 1: \qquad \cdot 28$$

The areal magnitude of the polar of a frame is the reciprocal of the areal magnitude of the frame. ·29

The same result comes if ·26 is applied to the polar frame, for then

$$\mathscr{E}\,\bar{\mathbf{y}} = -\bar{C}\mathbf{x}$$

and therefore $\mathscr{E}^2\,\mathbf{x} = -C\bar{C}\mathbf{x},$

a relation that must be reconciled with the universal relation

$$\mathscr{E}^2\,\mathbf{r} = -\mathbf{r}.$$

·**3.** Since $\mathbf{r} = \xi_{\mathbf{r}}\mathbf{x} + \eta_{\mathbf{r}}\mathbf{y},$

the erected vector $\mathscr{E}\,\mathbf{r}$ is given by

$$\mathscr{E}\,\mathbf{r} = \xi_{\mathbf{r}}\,\mathscr{E}\,\mathbf{x} + \eta_{\mathbf{r}}\,\mathscr{E}\,\mathbf{y}, \qquad \cdot 32$$

and therefore by $\mathscr{E}\,\mathbf{r} = C\,(\xi_{\mathbf{r}}\bar{\mathbf{y}} - \eta_{\mathbf{r}}\bar{\mathbf{x}});$ ·33

hence $\mathscr{G}\,(\mathscr{E}\,\mathbf{r})\,\mathbf{s} = C\,(\xi_{\mathbf{r}}\,\mathscr{G}\,\bar{\mathbf{y}}\mathbf{s} - \eta_{\mathbf{r}}\,\mathscr{G}\,\bar{\mathbf{x}}\mathbf{s}),$

that is, $\mathscr{A}\,\mathbf{rs} = C\,(\xi_{\mathbf{r}}\eta_{\mathbf{s}} - \eta_{\mathbf{r}}\xi_{\mathbf{s}}).$ ·35

This formula, expressed in terms of the polar frame, becomes

·36 $$\mathscr{A}\,\mathbf{rs} = C^{-1}(\lambda_{\mathbf{r}}\mu_{\mathbf{s}} - \mu_{\mathbf{r}}\lambda_{\mathbf{s}}),$$

which multiplied by C is simply a version of 222·25:

·37 *The areal product of the vectors* $\mathbf{r}$, $\mathbf{s}$ *is given by*

$$\mathscr{A}\,\mathbf{rs} = C(\xi_{\mathbf{r}}\eta_{\mathbf{s}} - \eta_{\mathbf{r}}\xi_{\mathbf{s}}) = C^{-1}(\lambda_{\mathbf{r}}\mu_{\mathbf{s}} - \mu_{\mathbf{r}}\lambda_{\mathbf{s}}).$$

·4. For work in a plane we write

·41 $$E = \mathscr{G}\mathbf{x}^2, \quad F = \mathscr{G}\mathbf{xy}, \quad G = \mathscr{G}\mathbf{y}^2,$$

·42 $$\bar{E} = \mathscr{G}\bar{\mathbf{x}}^2, \quad \bar{F} = \mathscr{G}\bar{\mathbf{x}}\bar{\mathbf{y}}, \quad \bar{G} = \mathscr{G}\bar{\mathbf{y}}^2,$$

and we see that because the projected product is distributive

·43 $$\mathscr{G}\,\mathbf{rs} = E\xi_{\mathbf{r}}\xi_{\mathbf{s}} + F(\xi_{\mathbf{r}}\eta_{\mathbf{s}} + \eta_{\mathbf{r}}\xi_{\mathbf{s}}) + G\eta_{\mathbf{r}}\eta_{\mathbf{s}},$$

·44 $$\mathscr{G}\,\mathbf{rs} = \bar{E}\lambda_{\mathbf{r}}\lambda_{\mathbf{s}} + \bar{F}(\lambda_{\mathbf{r}}\mu_{\mathbf{s}} + \mu_{\mathbf{r}}\lambda_{\mathbf{s}}) + \bar{G}\mu_{\mathbf{r}}\mu_{\mathbf{s}}.$$

To express these formulae briefly, we write

·45 $$E = S^{11}, \quad F = S^{12} = S^{21}, \quad G = S^{22},$$

·46 $$\bar{E} = \bar{S}^{11}, \quad \bar{F} = \bar{S}^{12} = \bar{S}^{21}, \quad \bar{G} = \bar{S}^{22},$$

·47 $$\chi = (\xi, \eta), \quad \upsilon = (\lambda, \mu)$$

·48 so that $$\mathscr{G}\,\mathbf{rs} = S\chi_{\mathbf{r}}\chi_{\mathbf{s}} = \bar{S}\upsilon_{\mathbf{r}}\upsilon_{\mathbf{s}},$$

·49 to which we may add $$\mathscr{G}\,\mathbf{rs} = \chi_{\mathbf{r}}\upsilon_{\mathbf{s}} = \upsilon_{\mathbf{r}}\chi_{\mathbf{s}}.$$

·5. The relations between ξ, η and λ, μ for any vector take symbolically the same form as the corresponding relations in space: on the one hand

·51 $$\lambda = S^1\chi, \quad \mu = S^2\chi,$$

·52 and on the other hand $$\xi = \bar{S}^1\upsilon, \quad \eta = \bar{S}^2\upsilon.$$

·53 Explicitly, $$\lambda = E\xi + F\eta, \quad \mu = F\xi + G\eta,$$

·54 $$\xi = \bar{E}\lambda + \bar{F}\mu, \quad \eta = \bar{F}\lambda + \bar{G}\mu.$$

·6. The relations between the polar magnitudes $\bar{E}, \bar{F}, \bar{G}$ and the fundamental magnitudes E, F, G may be found explicitly by applications of the identity

·61 $$\mathscr{G}(\mathscr{E}\mathbf{r})(\mathscr{E}\mathbf{s}) = \mathscr{G}\,\mathbf{rs},$$

·62 which gives $$C^2\bar{E} = G, \quad C^2\bar{F} = -F, \quad C^2\bar{G} = E,$$

·63 $$\bar{C}^2E = \bar{G}, \quad \bar{C}^2F = -\bar{F}, \quad \bar{C}^2G = \bar{E}.$$

But, again as in the case of frames in space, the valuable identities are not these, but simpler relations which come from the identities

·64 $$\xi = \bar{S}^1S^1\xi + \bar{S}^1S^2\eta, \quad \eta = \bar{S}^2S^1\xi + \bar{S}^2S^2\eta,$$

where now $\bar{S}^iS^j$ denotes $\bar{S}^{i1}S^{1j} + \bar{S}^{i2}S^{2j}$; from ·64 we have a theorem expressed by the enunciation of 2·46, with the present interpretation of the symbols, but it is not a laborious matter* to write out all the identities implied: they are

$$\bar{E}E+\bar{F}F=1,\quad \bar{E}F+\bar{F}G=0,\quad \bar{F}E+\bar{G}F=0,\quad \bar{F}F+\bar{G}G=1. \qquad \cdot 67$$

It is not C itself but C^2 which enters into ·62, and C^2 is given in terms of E, F, G by the identity

$$(\mathscr{A}\,\mathbf{xy})^2=\mathscr{G}\,\mathbf{x}^2\,\mathscr{G}\,\mathbf{y}^2-(\mathscr{G}\,\mathbf{xy})^2,$$

which is a particular case of 222·25 and implies

$$C^2=EG-F^2; \qquad \cdot 68$$

the correlative formula $\bar{C}^2=\bar{E}\bar{G}-\bar{F}^2$ ·69

does not need independent proof.

345. Attached frames and their use.

·1. The processes described in the last chapter for the location of points and planes, rays and rotors, by means of a Cartesian frame $OXYZ$, are essentially definitions of vectors which relate the entities in question to the one point O; the vectors having been defined, the subsequent use of the frame $OXYZ$ in their specification is merely one way of discussing their interrelations. It follows that to use a vector frame **xyz** for similar work we have only to associate with the frame a definite origin of reference O. Then, for example, a prepared plane is located by the direction normal to the plane together with the length in that direction of the normal step to O from the plane; the direction can be treated as a unit vector, and the length as the amount of a given vector in a given direction.

The frame **xyz** *attached* to an origin O we denote by O**xyz**. There is no reason why the coefficients and polar coefficients of the vector of a step OR should not be called the coordinates and projections of R in the vector frame.

Attached frames may be used in a plane as well as in space; there are no special features that call for comment.

·2. The vectorial equations of planes and lines involve only the origin of reference and are the same whether a vector frame or a Cartesian frame is being used, but in the algebraic equations which replace these vectorial equations the variables naturally are numbers appropriate to the frame in use. With a Cartesian frame the variables associated with a variable point R are coordinates or projections of R; with an attached vector frame O**xyz** they are coefficients or polar coefficients of the vector of OR.

* In the branch of differential geometry which is the developed subject to which this article is most nearly allied, it has not been usual to introduce symbols for the magnitudes $\bar{E}, \bar{F}, \bar{G}$; I am convinced that the presentation of the subject has suffered not a little from the omission.

In the matter of algebra the change is slight. If the vectors **x**, **y**, **z** are vectors of amounts U, V, W in the directions of the axes of a Cartesian frame $OXYZ$, then

·21 $$\mathbf{r} = \xi_{\mathbf{r}}\mathbf{x} + \eta_{\mathbf{r}}\mathbf{y} + \zeta_{\mathbf{r}}\mathbf{z} = U\xi_{\mathbf{r}}\mathbf{1}_{\Xi} + V\eta_{\mathbf{r}}\mathbf{1}_{\mathrm{H}} + W\zeta_{\mathbf{r}}\mathbf{1}_{\mathrm{Z}},$$

·22 and therefore $$x_{\mathbf{r}} = U\xi_{\mathbf{r}}, \quad y_{\mathbf{r}} = V\eta_{\mathbf{r}}, \quad z_{\mathbf{r}} = W\zeta_{\mathbf{r}},$$

while on the other hand

·23 $$\mathscr{G}\,\mathbf{xr} = U\mathscr{G}\,\mathbf{r1}_{\Xi}, \quad \mathscr{G}\,\mathbf{yr} = V\mathscr{G}\,\mathbf{r1}_{\mathrm{H}}, \quad \mathscr{G}\,\mathbf{zr} = W\mathscr{G}\,\mathbf{r1}_{\mathrm{Z}},$$

·24 and therefore $$\lambda_{\mathbf{r}} = Ul_{\mathbf{r}}, \quad \mu_{\mathbf{r}} = Vm_{\mathbf{r}}, \quad \nu_{\mathbf{r}} = Wn_{\mathbf{r}}.$$

·3. The modifications of 34·31 and 36·51 are obvious, and can be made either by means of ·22 and ·24 or from the vectorial equations.

In place of the equations in 34·31 appear

·31 $$\upsilon_{\mathbf{n}}\chi = N, \quad \chi_{\mathbf{n}}\upsilon = N,$$

and conversely every linear relation between the coordinates of a point in a vector frame corresponds to a definite plane, and so does every linear relation between the projections.

In a vector frame a line (**k**, **K**) has six coordinates, ξ_k, η_k, ζ_k, Ξ_k, H_k, Z_k, the coefficients of **k** and **K**, and six projections λ_k, μ_k, ν_k, Λ_k, M_k, N_k, the polar coefficients of the same vectors; the specification is homogeneous, and the coordinates and projections are connected by the identity

·33 $$\mathrm{X}\upsilon = \Upsilon\chi = 0,$$

·34 where $$\mathrm{X} = (\Xi, \mathrm{H}, \mathrm{Z}), \quad \Upsilon = (\Lambda, \mathrm{M}, \mathrm{N}).$$

Equations of the line, that is, of particular planes through the line, are given with reference to the vector frame simply by translation of their vectorial forms; thus, since every vector **r** from O to a point on the line satisfies

$$\mathscr{V}\,\mathbf{rk} = \mathbf{K},$$

it follows from 3·13 that every point on the line satisfies

·36 $$J(\eta\zeta_k - \zeta\eta_k) = \Lambda_k,$$

which is the equation of a plane parallel to **x**, and also

·37 $$J^{-1}(\mu\nu_k - \nu\mu_k) = \Xi_k,$$

which is the equation of a plane parallel to $\bar{\mathbf{x}}$.

346. Attached frames and Cartesian frames; loaded Cartesian frames.

·1. The Cartesian frame $OXYZ$ can be compared with the vector frame $O\mathbf{1}_{\Xi}\mathbf{1}_{\mathrm{H}}\mathbf{1}_{\mathrm{Z}}$, the components x, y, z and the projections l, m, n of a vector in the Cartesian frame being the coefficients ξ, η, ζ and the polar coefficients λ, μ, ν of the same vector in the vector frame. In this way many results in the previous two chapters can be deduced as particular cases of the corresponding theorems in the present chapter. But the deduction fails *if there is explicit mention of the polar frame*, for the polar of the vector frame $\mathbf{1}_\Xi \mathbf{1}_\mathrm{H} \mathbf{1}_\mathrm{Z}$ is formed of the vectors $(\sec \Xi\Lambda)_\Lambda$, $(\sec \mathrm{HM})_\mathrm{M}$, $(\sec \mathrm{ZN})_\mathrm{N}$, and in general these are not unit vectors, and the vector frame which they compose does not correspond to the frame $OLMN$ which is the polar of $OXYZ$; in fact the polar coefficients λ, μ, ν of a vector $\mathbf{r}$ in $\mathbf{1}_\Xi \mathbf{1}_\mathrm{H} \mathbf{1}_\mathrm{Z}$ are the projections l, m, n of $\mathbf{r}$ in $OXYZ$, and these are not the components of $\mathbf{r}$ in $OLMN$. In defining the polar of a vector frame we have taken advantage of the possibility of choosing the magnitudes of the polar vectors to secure a simplicity more complete than is attainable with the Cartesian frame, where only the directions of the polar are at our command.

·2. Instead of deducing Cartesian formulae from vectorial, we can describe what is effectively a vector frame attached to a point O by means of a Cartesian frame in such a manner that the vectors themselves are thrown into the background. Suppose U, V, W to be three numbers, subject to the condition that no one of them is zero but unrestricted in sign, let X, Y, Z be the points at unit distance from O on the axes of a Cartesian frame $OXYZ$, and let F, G, H be the points on the same axes at distances U, V, W from O. The Cartesian coordinates x, y, z of a point R are the ratios of the volumes $ORYZ$, $OXRZ$, $OXYR$ to the volume $OXYZ$, but the position of R is described equally well by the ratios of the volumes $ORGH$, $OFRH$, $OFGR$ to
the volume $OFGH$; the latter ratios we call the °*adapted coordinates* of R in ·21
the frame obtained by °*loading* $OXYZ$ with the set of numbers U, V, W, and ·22
we denote these adapted coordinates by ξ, η, ζ. From the equalities such as

$$ORGH/OFGH = ORYZ/OFYZ = (ORYZ/OXYZ)/(OF/OX) \qquad \cdot 23$$

we have the relations between the adapted and the Cartesian coordinates:

$$\xi = x/U, \quad \eta = y/V, \quad \zeta = z/W. \qquad \cdot 24$$

·3. The ratios of a direction and the components of a vector are adapted to a loaded frame in the same way as the coordinates of a point. The set of formulae giving projections l, m, n in terms of adapted components ξ, η, ζ is found by the substitution of $U\xi, V\eta, W\zeta$ for x, y, z in 24·33 and is

$$\left[\begin{aligned} l &= U\xi + V\eta\cos\gamma + W\zeta\cos\beta, \\ m &= U\xi\cos\gamma + V\eta + W\zeta\cos\alpha, \\ n &= U\xi\cos\beta + V\eta\cos\alpha + W\zeta; \end{aligned}\right.$$

this set lacks the symmetry of the set from which it has been derived, the coefficient $W\cos\alpha$ of ζ in m differing from the coefficient $V\cos\alpha$ of η in n, but symmetry is at once restored if we take the equations in the form

$$\left[\begin{aligned} Ul &= \xi U^2 + \eta UV\cos\gamma + \zeta WU\cos\beta, \\ Vm &= \xi UV\cos\gamma + \eta V^2 + \zeta VW\cos\alpha, \\ Wn &= \xi WU\cos\beta + \eta VW\cos\alpha + \zeta W^2. \end{aligned}\right. \qquad \cdot 31$$

·32 We write therefore $\lambda = Ul, \quad \mu = Vm, \quad \nu = Wn,$

·33 $L = U^2, \quad M = V^2, \quad N = W^2, \quad P = VW \cos\alpha, \quad Q = WU \cos\beta, \quad R = UV \cos\gamma$

·34 and we have λ, μ, ν, the °*adapted projections* of a point or vector, or the *adapted cosines* of a direction, given in terms of adapted coordinates, components, or ratios, by the symmetrical set of formulae

·35 $$\lambda = L\xi + R\eta + Q\zeta, \quad \mu = R\xi + M\eta + P\zeta, \quad \nu = Q\xi + P\eta + N\zeta,$$

which leads necessarily to a *symmetrical* set

·36 $$\xi = \bar{L}\lambda + \bar{R}\mu + \bar{Q}\nu, \quad \eta = \bar{R}\lambda + \bar{M}\mu + \bar{P}\nu, \quad \zeta = \bar{Q}\lambda + \bar{P}\mu + \bar{N}\nu$$

expressing ξ, η, ζ as functions of λ, μ, ν. That the use of Ul, Vm, Wn is the natural complement to the use of x/U, y/V, z/W is seen otherwise if we aim at presenting the cosine of angles between two directions Π, K in a form $\lambda_\Pi \xi_K + \mu_\Pi \eta_K + \nu_\Pi \zeta_K$ analogous to the elementary form $l_\Pi x_K + m_\Pi y_K + n_\Pi z_K$. Expressions for the coefficients in ·35 in terms of U, V, W and frame angles are found by a comparison of ·36 with 24·34; writing $U\xi$ for x, λ/U for l, and so on, and putting also

·37 $$J = \Upsilon UVW,$$

we have from 24·34 three formulae of the type

·38 $$\xi = \lambda J^{-2} V^2 W^2 \sin^2\alpha + \mu J^{-1} W \cot \Gamma + \nu J^{-1} V \cot \mathrm{B},$$

·39 and therefore $\bar{L} = J^{-2} V^2 W^2 \sin^2\alpha, \quad \bar{P} = J^{-1} U \cot \mathrm{A}.$

·4. The polar of the loaded frame with which we are dealing is of course to be a frame obtained by loading the polar of the Cartesian frame $OXYZ$ but the numbers $\bar{U}$, $\bar{V}$, $\bar{W}$ to be associated with this polar are at our disposal to be selected in the manner which, while retaining the symmetry of the relation between a frame and its polar, leads to the simplest relations between adapted components in one frame and adapted projections in the other. Whatever numbers are chosen, we have from 24·23

·41 $$\bar{\lambda} = \xi U \bar{U} \cos \Xi\Lambda, \quad \bar{\mu} = \eta V \bar{V} \cos \mathrm{HM}, \quad \bar{\nu} = \zeta W \bar{W} \cos \mathrm{ZN},$$

·42 $$\lambda = \bar{\xi} U \bar{U} \cos \Xi\Lambda, \quad \mu = \bar{\eta} V \bar{V} \cos \mathrm{HM}, \quad \nu = \bar{\zeta} W \bar{W} \cos \mathrm{ZN};$$

if then we define the polar amounts to satisfy

·43 $$U\bar{U} \cos \Xi\Lambda = V\bar{V} \cos \mathrm{HM} = W\bar{W} \cos \mathrm{ZN} = 1,$$

a definition that is always valid since none of the cosines can vanish, we secure all the symmetry and simplicity we can wish. Explicitly,

·44 $$\bar{U} = (\Upsilon^{-1} \sin\alpha)/U, \quad \bar{V} = (\Upsilon^{-1} \sin\beta)/V, \quad \bar{W} = (\Upsilon^{-1} \sin\gamma)/W,$$

and with these polar amounts

·45 *The adapted components of any vector in a loaded frame are the adapted projections of the same vector in the polar frame.*

It follows from ·45 and ·33 that the coefficients in ·36 are given by

·46 $$\bar{L} = \bar{U}^2, \quad \bar{P} = \bar{V}\bar{W} \cos \mathrm{A},$$

and so on, and it is an easy matter to return from ·44 and ·46 to ·39.

·5. The vector frame attached to an origin marks the limit of our work. Let us consider for a moment the extensions which are most evident.

A vector attached to a point gives place readily to a rotor located in a definite line through the point, and if in the same way a vector frame attached to O can be regarded as a frame composed of three rotors concurrent in O, there is an immediate extension to a frame composed of three rotors that are not assumed to be concurrent. It is true that in general a rotor ρ can be specified completely by its *relations* to three given rotors: the vector $\mathbf{r}$ of the rotor can be expressed in terms of the vectors of the given rotors, and the axis is determinate if the momental product of ρ and each of the rotors of reference is known. But it is not possible to express an arbitrary rotor as a *sum* of multiples of three standard rotors, however these rotors are chosen; indeed, if we are to construct a rotor frame *to deal with rotors by decomposing them* we must have not fewer* than six rotors of reference. If we can decompose any rotor we can decompose any† motor, since we can then resolve the constituents of any *set* of rotors, and if the unit of our work is the motor we shall construct our frame of motors rather than of rotors. The ultimate frame for analysis in which motors play the leading part is composed then of six motors, unrestricted except by the condition that they are independent, and between the attached vector frame and the general motor frame the only frame deserving of detailed study is a frame bearing to the motor frame the same relation as that of the Cartesian frame to the attached vector frame; this‡ is the frame formed of six *screws* of arbitrary axis and pitch, and its use is developed exhaustively in Ball's classical work.

The conception of a loaded Cartesian frame is a timorous one, from which the formulae fundamental in the theory of a vector frame are reached by steps that are tentative. Nevertheless, the weaker§ idea is not without value.

* The theorem is virtually Möbius's. If the rotors of reference, specified with the help of an origin O, are $(\mathbf{p}_1, \mathbf{P}_1)$, $(\mathbf{p}_2, \mathbf{P}_2)$, ..., the problem of decomposing the rotor $(\mathbf{r}, \mathbf{R})$ is equivalent to that of finding a *single* set of numbers a_1, a_2, ... such that

$$\mathbf{r}=a_1\mathbf{p}_1+a_2\mathbf{p}_2+\ldots,\quad \mathbf{R}=a_1\mathbf{P}_1+a_2\mathbf{P}_2+\ldots.$$

There are six scalar equations, and the problem may be expected to be insoluble unless there are six variables, implying six rotors of reference. In the problem of utilising an attached vector frame, the equations are of the form

$$\mathbf{r}=a_1\mathbf{p}_1+a_2\mathbf{p}_2+\ldots,\quad \mathbf{R}=A_1\mathbf{p}_1+A_2\mathbf{p}_2+\ldots,$$

and the six variables imply only three vectors of reference. This simple enumeration renders the result intelligible, but of course does not afford a proof.

† This is why five rotors can not form a frame adequate for the decomposition even of pure rotors, although a rotor requires only five magnitudes to characterise it; a motor involves six independent numbers.

‡ Compare 246·4 on p. 86 above.

§ Weaker because in complex space there are attached vector frames that have no loaded Cartesian counterparts.

The loaded frame can be introduced with effect into analytical work from which the explicit mention of vectors is excluded: here is a concession to prejudice, for vectors and rotors are not less native to the realms of geometry than are circles and planes. A stronger case for the consideration of this frame rests on its relative finality; it is difficult to see how in three dimensions the idea of a Cartesian frame is to be modified further, unless there is some sense in which the origin as well as the axes can be loaded. But it is impossible to conjecture the value of motor frames in geometry, and if we are to pause at the attached vector frame, it is satisfactory to recognise that there is one aspect in which this frame does not admit of generalisation.

CHAPTER III 5

CHANGE OF AXES

350. Introduction. 351. Ratio schemes and cosine schemes. 352. Effects of a change of axes on the components and projections of a vector. 353. Relations between the schemes of a transformation. 354. Change of axes in a plane. 355. Change of vector frames. 356. Change of origin; effects of a change on the vectors used to specify points and rotors.

350. INTRODUCTION.

The method adopted in 36·2 and 37·4 for finding elements to specify a required ray or point with reference to a frame $OXYZ$, is virtually the discovery of corresponding elements with reference to another frame, followed by a passage from this frame to $OXYZ$; in 36·2 the subsidiary frame was the Cartesian frame formed by the rays through O parallel to κ, σ, τ, in 37·4 it was the attached vector frame that we should now denote by $O\mathbf{pst}$.

Again and again this feature presents itself in analytical geometry: there is no effort to describe all the points which have to be considered in a single investigation by means of a single frame, but at every stage reference is made to the frame which appears best adapted for immediate use. The process in the paragraphs quoted is entirely characteristic, and as it was possible for us to use it without having explicit 'formulae of transformation' at hand, so as a rule no reference should be made to general formulae, but reliance should be placed in individual cases on the methods, obvious in themselves, by which such formulae are obtainable. If after this assertion we proceed to obtain general formulae, the reason is that this course seems the simplest along which to indicate the methods themselves.

351. RATIO SCHEMES AND COSINE SCHEMES.

·1. Let $OXYZ$, $O^0X^0Y^0Z^0$ be any two Cartesian frames, and let us distinguish all symbols relating to the second frame by the affix indicated; thus we are to denote by Υ the sine of the first frame, by $\mathscr{C}^0$ the component symbol of the second frame, by ξ the ray OX, and by $y_{\mathbf{r}}$, $m^0{}_{\mathbf{r}}$ the second component of a vector $\mathbf{r}$ with reference to the first frame and the second projection of the same vector with reference to the second frame, while n_{η^0}, $n^0{}_{\eta^0}$ denote the cosines of the angles between the y-axis of the second frame and the z-axes of the two frames,—the second of these cosines is expressible otherwise as $\cos\alpha^0$, but the first depends on the relations between the two frames.

·**2.** If a frame is used for the identification of vectors only, the position of the origin is irrelevant. It is therefore worth while to consider in detail the manner of describing the relations between the directions of the axes, before discussing questions that involve the origin.

The directions of ξ^0, η^0, ζ^0 with respect to $OXYZ$ may be given either by ratios or by cosines, the complete specification being expressed in a scheme or matrix of one of the forms

·23, ·24

$$\begin{array}{c|ccc} & x & y & z \\ \hline X^0 & x_{\xi^0} & y_{\xi^0} & z_{\xi^0} \\ Y^0 & x_{\eta^0} & y_{\eta^0} & z_{\eta^0} \\ Z^0 & x_{\zeta^0} & y_{\zeta^0} & z_{\zeta^0} \end{array} \qquad \begin{array}{c|ccc} & l & m & n \\ \hline X^0 & l_{\xi^0} & m_{\xi^0} & n_{\xi^0} \\ Y^0 & l_{\eta^0} & m_{\eta^0} & n_{\eta^0} \\ Z^0 & l_{\zeta^0} & m_{\zeta^0} & n_{\zeta^0} \end{array}$$

while a similar scheme of one of the forms

·25, ·26

$$\begin{array}{c|ccc} & x^0 & y^0 & z^0 \\ \hline X & x^0{}_\xi & y^0{}_\xi & z^0{}_\xi \\ Y & x^0{}_\eta & y^0{}_\eta & z^0{}_\eta \\ Z & x^0{}_\zeta & y^0{}_\zeta & z^0{}_\zeta \end{array} \qquad \begin{array}{c|ccc} & l^0 & m^0 & n^0 \\ \hline X & l^0{}_\xi & m^0{}_\xi & n^0{}_\xi \\ Y & l^0{}_\eta & m^0{}_\eta & n^0{}_\eta \\ Z & l^0{}_\zeta & m^0{}_\zeta & n^0{}_\zeta \end{array}$$

expresses the directions of axes of $OXYZ$ with reference to $O^0X^0Y^0Z^0$. In general no two of these schemes are identical, but there are intimate relations between the four of them.

352. Effects of a change of axes on the components and projections of a vector.

·**1.** The most important question, and perhaps also the simplest to answer, concerns the relation between the components and projections of a vector $\mathbf{r}$ relative to $OXYZ$ and the components and projections of the same vector relative to $O^0X^0Y^0Z^0$. To abbreviate the formulae that occur we write

·11 $$\chi = (\xi, \eta, \zeta).$$

·**2.** By the definition of components, $\mathbf{r}$ is the sum of the vector $x_\mathbf{r}$ in ξ, the vector $y_\mathbf{r}$ in η, and the vector $z_\mathbf{r}$ in ζ, and to obtain $x^0{}_\mathbf{r}$, $y^0{}_\mathbf{r}$, $z^0{}_\mathbf{r}$ we have only to decompose the same vector into vectors in ξ^0, η^0, ζ^0; supposing the elements of the ratio scheme 1·25 known, we can express a unit vector in ξ as the sum of $x^0{}_\xi$, $y^0{}_\xi$, $z^0{}_\xi$ in ξ^0, η^0, ζ^0, and we can dissect in the same way unit vectors in η, ζ; there follows then the set of formulae

·21 $$\begin{cases} x^0{}_\mathbf{r} = x_\mathbf{r} x^0{}_\xi + y_\mathbf{r} x^0{}_\eta + z_\mathbf{r} x^0{}_\zeta, \\ y^0{}_\mathbf{r} = x_\mathbf{r} y^0{}_\xi + y_\mathbf{r} y^0{}_\eta + z_\mathbf{r} y^0{}_\zeta, \\ z^0{}_\mathbf{r} = x_\mathbf{r} z^0{}_\xi + y_\mathbf{r} z^0{}_\eta + z_\mathbf{r} z^0{}_\zeta, \end{cases}$$

·22 that is, $$x^0{}_\mathbf{r} = c_\mathbf{r} x^0{}_\chi, \quad y^0{}_\mathbf{r} = c_\mathbf{r} y^0{}_\chi, \quad z^0{}_\mathbf{r} = c_\mathbf{r} z^0{}_\chi.$$

The constitution of the formulae is perhaps clearer in umbral notation than when the expressions are written in full.

If it is the ratio scheme 1·23 that is supposed known, we have in the same way $$x_{\mathbf{r}} = c^0{}_{\mathbf{r}} x_{\chi^0}, \quad y_{\mathbf{r}} = c^0{}_{\mathbf{r}} y_{\chi^0}, \quad z_{\mathbf{r}} = c^0{}_{\mathbf{r}} z_{\chi^0},$$ ·23

and because this set of equations giving $x_{\mathbf{r}}, y_{\mathbf{r}}, z_{\mathbf{r}}$ in terms of $x^0{}_{\mathbf{r}}, y^0{}_{\mathbf{r}}, z^0{}_{\mathbf{r}}$ is equivalent to the set ·22 which gives $x^0{}_{\mathbf{r}}, y^0{}_{\mathbf{r}}, z^0{}_{\mathbf{r}}$ explicitly in terms of $x_{\mathbf{r}}, y_{\mathbf{r}}, z_{\mathbf{r}}$, the set of coefficients occurring in one of the sets of equations is said to be the *reciprocal* of the set of coefficients occurring in the other set of equations, and the scheme composed of one set of ratios is called the ° *reciprocal* ·25
of the scheme composed of the other set.

If knowing the elements of the scheme 1·23 we wish to determine $x^0{}_{\mathbf{r}}, y^0{}_{\mathbf{r}}, z^0{}_{\mathbf{r}}$ in terms of $x_{\mathbf{r}}, y_{\mathbf{r}}, z_{\mathbf{r}}$, we may reverse the set of equations ·23 algebraically, obtaining*

$$x^0{}_{\mathbf{r}} : y^0{}_{\mathbf{r}} : z^0{}_{\mathbf{r}} : 1 = [c_{\mathbf{r}}\,;c_{\eta^0}\,;c_{\zeta^0}] : [c_{\xi^0}\,;c_{\mathbf{r}}\,;c_{\zeta^0}] : [c_{\xi^0}\,;c_{\eta^0}\,;c_{\mathbf{r}}] : [c_{\xi^0}\,;c_{\eta^0}\,;c_{\zeta^0}].$$ ·26

The significance of ·26 is apparent from 23·55 and 32·43: $\frac{1}{6}\Upsilon\,[c_{\mathbf{r}}\,;c_{\eta^0}\,;c_{\zeta^0}]$ and $\frac{1}{6}\Upsilon\,[c_{\xi^0}\,;c_{\eta^0}\,;c_{\zeta^0}]$ are the actual volumes, calculated by means of the frame $OXYZ$, of two tetrahedra whose volumes have the ratio of $x^0{}_{\mathbf{r}}$ to unity.

·3. The last consideration shews immediately that if it is the cosine scheme 1·24 that is given, then

$$x^0{}_{\mathbf{r}} : y^0{}_{\mathbf{r}} : z^0{}_{\mathbf{r}} : 1 = [p_{\mathbf{r}}\,;p_{\eta^0}\,;p_{\zeta^0}] : [p_{\xi^0}\,;p_{\mathbf{r}}\,;p_{\zeta^0}] : [p_{\xi^0}\,;p_{\eta^0}\,;p_{\mathbf{r}}] : [p_{\xi^0}\,;p_{\eta^0}\,;p_{\zeta^0}],$$ ·31

for by 32·43 the volumes of the same two tetrahedra are expressible also as $\frac{1}{6}\Upsilon^{-1}[p_{\mathbf{r}}\,;p_{\eta^0}\,;p_{\zeta^0}]$ and $\frac{1}{6}\Upsilon^{-1}[p_{\xi^0}\,;p_{\eta^0}\,;p_{\zeta^0}]$.

* Not all text-books give the simplest method of effecting such a reversal. To find $y^0{}_{\mathbf{r}}$, for example, it is sufficient to regard the equations as three equations, linear and not homogeneous, in the *two* variables $x^0{}_{\mathbf{r}}, y^0{}_{\mathbf{r}}$; the condition of coexistence is the determinantal equation

$$[c_{\xi^0};\ y^0{}_{\mathbf{r}} c_{\eta^0} - c_{\mathbf{r}};\ c_{\zeta^0}] = 0,$$

in which no confusion of signs is possible. Similarly to find from the set of equations ·23 the value in terms of $x_{\mathbf{r}}, y_{\mathbf{r}}, z_{\mathbf{r}}$ of a given linear function $fx^0{}_{\mathbf{r}} + gy^0{}_{\mathbf{r}} + hz^0{}_{\mathbf{r}} - k$, we merely add to the given set the equation

$$p + k = fx^0{}_{\mathbf{r}} + gy^0{}_{\mathbf{r}} + hz^0{}_{\mathbf{r}},$$

where it is the value of p that we have to find; eliminating from the four equations the three variables $x^0{}_{\mathbf{r}}, y^0{}_{\mathbf{r}}, z^0{}_{\mathbf{r}}$ we have the equation

$$\begin{vmatrix} p+k & f & g & h \\ x_{\mathbf{r}} & x_{\xi^0} & x_{\eta^0} & x_{\zeta^0} \\ y_{\mathbf{r}} & y_{\xi^0} & y_{\eta^0} & y_{\zeta^0} \\ z_{\mathbf{r}} & z_{\xi^0} & z_{\eta^0} & z_{\zeta^0} \end{vmatrix} = 0,$$

which gives p without risk of error in the form

$$-\begin{vmatrix} k & f & g & h \\ x_{\mathbf{r}} & x_{\xi^0} & x_{\eta^0} & x_{\zeta^0} \\ y_{\mathbf{r}} & y_{\xi^0} & y_{\eta^0} & y_{\zeta^0} \\ z_{\mathbf{r}} & z_{\xi^0} & z_{\eta^0} & z_{\zeta^0} \end{vmatrix} \Bigg/ \begin{vmatrix} x_{\xi^0} & x_{\eta^0} & x_{\zeta^0} \\ y_{\xi^0} & y_{\eta^0} & y_{\zeta^0} \\ z_{\xi^0} & z_{\eta^0} & z_{\zeta^0} \end{vmatrix}.$$

Just as ·26 comes from the reversal of ·23, so ·31 is equivalent to

·32 $$l_{\mathbf{r}} = c^0{}_{\mathbf{r}} l_{\chi^0}, \quad m_{\mathbf{r}} = c^0{}_{\mathbf{r}} m_{\chi^0}, \quad n_{\mathbf{r}} = c^0{}_{\mathbf{r}} n_{\chi^0},$$

and these formulae can in fact be deduced by an argument parallel to that giving ·21: $\mathbf{r}$ being decomposed into $\xi^0{}_{\mathbf{r}}$, $\eta^0{}_{\mathbf{r}}$, $\zeta^0{}_{\mathbf{r}}$ along the axes of $O^0X^0Y^0Z^0$, the projections of $\mathbf{r}$ and its parts on OY for example are

$$m_{\mathbf{r}}, \quad x^0{}_{\mathbf{r}} m_{\xi^0}, \quad y^0{}_{\mathbf{r}} m_{\eta^0}, \quad z^0{}_{\mathbf{r}} m_{\zeta^0}.$$

Regarding $l_{\mathbf{r}}$, $m_{\mathbf{r}}$, $n_{\mathbf{r}}$ as projections of $\mathbf{r}$, we may calculate them from the frame $O^0X^0Y^0Z^0$ by any of the formulae in 32·21; thus we have

·33 $$l_{\mathbf{r}} = \mathscr{C}^0 c^0{}_{\mathbf{r}} c^0{}_{\xi} = c^0{}_{\mathbf{r}} p^0{}_{\xi} = p^0{}_{\mathbf{r}} c^0{}_{\xi} = \mathscr{P}^0 p^0{}_{\mathbf{r}} p^0{}_{\xi}.$$

To pass from components in one frame to components in another when it is a cosine scheme that is given, it is best to use projections, implicitly if not explicitly, as stepping stones. Thus we may use 32·14 to replace ·32 by

·34 $$\mathscr{C}^1 c_{\mathbf{r}} = c^0{}_{\mathbf{r}} l_{\chi^0}, \quad \mathscr{C}^2 c_{\mathbf{r}} = c^0{}_{\mathbf{r}} m_{\chi^0}, \quad \mathscr{C}^3 c_{\mathbf{r}} = c^0{}_{\mathbf{r}} n_{\chi^0},$$

or we may take from ·31

·35 $$x^0{}_{\mathbf{r}} = [\mathscr{C} c_{\mathbf{r}} ; p_{\eta^0} ; p_{\zeta^0}]/[p_{\xi^0} ; p_{\eta^0} ; p_{\zeta^0}],$$

and so on, where $\mathscr{C}$ serves as an umbra for $(\mathscr{C}^1, \mathscr{C}^2, \mathscr{C}^3)$, that is to say, where

$$\mathscr{C} c_{\mathbf{r}} = (\mathscr{C}^1 c_{\mathbf{r}}, \mathscr{C}^2 c_{\mathbf{r}}, \mathscr{C}^3 c_{\mathbf{r}}).$$

353. Relations between the schemes of a transformation.

·1. Since no restriction has been placed on the vector $\mathbf{r}$ whose relations to the two frames have been considered, the formula

$$l_{\mathbf{r}} = c^0{}_{\mathbf{r}} p^0{}_{\xi}$$

which is part of 2·33 can be nothing but

$$l_{\mathbf{r}} = c^0{}_{\mathbf{r}} l_{\chi^0}$$

which appears in 2·32, and therefore

$$l^0{}_{\xi} = l_{\xi^0}, \quad m^0{}_{\xi} = l_{\eta^0}, \quad n^0{}_{\xi} = l_{\zeta^0}.$$

These relations between the two cosine schemes are perfectly straightforward, concealed only by our notation; by definition, the elements of the first column of 1·24 are the cosines of angles between OX and the three axes of the second frame, and the elements of the first row of 1·26 are these same cosines:

·13 *The two cosine schemes connecting two Cartesian frames are composed of the same elements, but the rows of each scheme are the columns of the other.*

·2. The relation between the two ratio schemes is not as elementary as that between the two cosine schemes. Generally speaking, the two ratio schemes have no elements in common.

The whole theory is implicit in the assertion that the two sets of equations 2·22, 2·23, regarded as connecting the two sets of variables $(x_{\mathbf{r}}, y_{\mathbf{r}}, z_{\mathbf{r}})$, $(x^0{}_{\mathbf{r}}, y^0{}_{\mathbf{r}}, z^0{}_{\mathbf{r}})$, are algebraically equivalent. This consideration alone, for example, shews that the elements of one ratio scheme can be deduced from those of the other without any knowledge of the angles of either frame. Explicit results are ready to hand, for we need only compare 2·22 with 2·26 to find the typical formulae

$$x^0_\xi : y^0_\xi : z^0_\xi : 1 = (y_{\eta^0} z_{\zeta^0} - z_{\eta^0} y_{\zeta^0}) : (y_{\zeta^0} z_{\xi^0} - z_{\zeta^0} y_{\xi^0}) : (y_{\xi^0} z_{\eta^0} - z_{\xi^0} y_{\eta^0}) : [c_{\xi^0} ; c_{\eta^0} ; c_{\zeta^0}]. \qquad \cdot 22$$

But the simplest and for many purposes the most useful relations between elements of the two schemes are not relations expressing elements of one scheme in terms of elements of the other, but are relations involving three elements from each scheme; if in the equations of the set 2·22 we substitute for $x_{\mathbf{r}}$, $y_{\mathbf{r}}$, $z_{\mathbf{r}}$ their values given in 2·23 we have

$$\begin{aligned} x^0_{\mathbf{r}} = x^0_{\mathbf{r}} (x_{\xi^0} x^0_\xi + y_{\xi^0} x^0_\eta + z_{\xi^0} x^0_\zeta) \\ + y^0_{\mathbf{r}} (x_{\eta^0} x^0_\xi + y_{\eta^0} x^0_\eta + z_{\eta^0} x^0_\zeta) \\ + z^0_{\mathbf{r}} (x_{\zeta^0} x^0_\xi + y_{\zeta^0} x^0_\eta + z_{\zeta^0} x^0_\zeta), \end{aligned} \qquad \cdot 23$$

and similar expressions for $y^0_{\mathbf{r}}$, $z^0_{\mathbf{r}}$, and since $x^0_{\mathbf{r}}$, $y^0_{\mathbf{r}}$, $z^0_{\mathbf{r}}$ are independent, these are only the *identities*

$$x^0_{\mathbf{r}} = x^0_{\mathbf{r}}, \quad y^0_{\mathbf{r}} = y^0_{\mathbf{r}}, \quad z^0_{\mathbf{r}} = z^0_{\mathbf{r}};$$

in the same way substitution from 2·22 in 2·23 gives expressions equivalent to the identities

$$x_{\mathbf{r}} = x_{\mathbf{r}}, \quad y_{\mathbf{r}} = y_{\mathbf{r}}, \quad z_{\mathbf{r}} = z_{\mathbf{r}};$$

eighteen distinct relations between the elements of the ratio schemes can be deduced, but they are all comprised in the statement that

If each element of any one row of one of the mutually reciprocal ratio schemes relating the directions of the axes of two frames is multiplied by the corresponding element of any column of the other of the two schemes, and the three products are added, the result is unity if the row and the column correspond but is otherwise zero. ·24

We can express the results of ·24 in umbral notation, the typical set of formulae apparent from ·23 being

$$c_{\xi^0} x^0_\chi = 1, \quad c_{\eta^0} x^0_\chi = 0, \quad c_{\zeta^0} x^0_\chi = 0. \qquad \cdot 25$$

The identities implied in ·24 involve *all* the relations between the elements of the two ratio schemes which are independent of the angles of the frames; for example, the three identities

$$c_{\xi^0} x^0_\chi = 1, \quad c_{\xi^0} y^0_\chi = 0, \quad c_{\xi^0} z^0_\chi = 0 \qquad \cdot 26$$

can be solved as simultaneous equations for expressing x_{ξ^0}, y_{ξ^0}, z_{ξ^0} in terms of the elements of the first ratio scheme, and the three identities ·25 as simultaneous equations for expressing x^0_ξ, x^0_η, x^0_ζ in terms of elements of the second ratio scheme; each element of one scheme may in fact be found in this way from two distinct sets of equations, but the two solutions give expressions which are identical and not merely equivalent.

·3. That ·26 has the same form as 2·22 is of course no coincidence; from one point of view, ·26 merely makes for one special vector the assertion that 2·22 makes for every vector. It must not be forgotten that the elements of ratio schemes and cosine schemes are actual ratios and cosines of directions. For this reason, for example, 32·26, 32·22 can be applied to give

$$\mathscr{C}\, c_{\xi^0}{}^2 = p_{\xi^0} c_{\xi^0} = \mathscr{P}\, p_{\xi^0}{}^2 = 1,$$

$$\mathscr{C}\, c_{\eta^0} c_{\zeta^0} = p_{\eta^0} c_{\zeta^0} = c_{\eta^0} p_{\zeta^0} = \mathscr{P}\, p_{\eta^0} p_{\zeta^0} = \cos \alpha^0,$$

and for this reason also 32·52 implies that the determinant of each cosine scheme is the product of the sines of the two frames, and that the determinant of the scheme describing the direction ratios of $O^0X^0Y^0Z^0$ with reference to $OXYZ$ is Υ^0/Υ.

354. Change of axes in a plane.

·1. Of change of axes in two dimensions in cases which have parallels in the three-dimensional problems already considered we say nothing, but the description of directions by means of actual angles, as in 31·3, presents the question in a simple manner peculiar to plane geometry, for with the obvious notation we have for any vector **r**

·11 $$\alpha_{\mathbf{r}} = \alpha^0{}_{\mathbf{r}} + \alpha_{\xi^0}, \quad \beta_{\mathbf{r}} = \beta^0{}_{\mathbf{r}} + \beta_{\eta^0}.$$

While the whole theory is implicit in ·11, these formulae are not specially adapted to serve us here. They deserve mention rather for the light which they throw on the theory of *moving* axes in a plane, which is beyond the scope of this volume.

355. Change of vector frames.

The problem of changing from one vector frame to another need engage our attention only for a short space, for we did in effect transform the same problem for Cartesian frames into a special case of the present one.

·1. The relation between two frames **xyz**, $\mathbf{x}^0\mathbf{y}^0\mathbf{z}^0$ is supposed defined either by one of the schemes

·11, ·12

	$\mathbf{x}$	$\mathbf{y}$	$\mathbf{z}$
$\mathbf{x}^0$	$\xi_{\mathbf{x}^0}$	$\eta_{\mathbf{x}^0}$	$\zeta_{\mathbf{x}^0}$
$\mathbf{y}^0$	$\xi_{\mathbf{y}^0}$	$\eta_{\mathbf{y}^0}$	$\zeta_{\mathbf{y}^0}$
$\mathbf{z}^0$	$\xi_{\mathbf{z}^0}$	$\eta_{\mathbf{z}^0}$	$\zeta_{\mathbf{z}^0}$

	$\mathbf{x}^0$	$\mathbf{y}^0$	$\mathbf{z}^0$
$\mathbf{x}$	$\xi^0{}_{\mathbf{x}}$	$\eta^0{}_{\mathbf{x}}$	$\zeta^0{}_{\mathbf{x}}$
$\mathbf{y}$	$\xi^0{}_{\mathbf{y}}$	$\eta^0{}_{\mathbf{y}}$	$\zeta^0{}_{\mathbf{y}}$
$\mathbf{z}$	$\xi^0{}_{\mathbf{z}}$	$\eta^0{}_{\mathbf{z}}$	$\zeta^0{}_{\mathbf{z}}$

which state the coefficients of the elements of one frame in the other frame, or by one of the schemes

·13, ·14

	$\mathbf{x}$	$\mathbf{y}$	$\mathbf{z}$
$\mathbf{x}^0$	$\lambda_{\mathbf{x}^0}$	$\mu_{\mathbf{x}^0}$	$\nu_{\mathbf{x}^0}$
$\mathbf{y}^0$	$\lambda_{\mathbf{y}^0}$	$\mu_{\mathbf{y}^0}$	$\nu_{\mathbf{y}^0}$
$\mathbf{z}^0$	$\lambda_{\mathbf{z}^0}$	$\mu_{\mathbf{z}^0}$	$\nu_{\mathbf{z}^0}$

	$\mathbf{x}^0$	$\mathbf{y}^0$	$\mathbf{z}^0$
$\mathbf{x}$	$\lambda^0{}_{\mathbf{x}}$	$\mu^0{}_{\mathbf{x}}$	$\nu^0{}_{\mathbf{x}}$
$\mathbf{y}$	$\lambda^0{}_{\mathbf{y}}$	$\mu^0{}_{\mathbf{y}}$	$\nu^0{}_{\mathbf{y}}$
$\mathbf{z}$	$\lambda^0{}_{\mathbf{z}}$	$\mu^0{}_{\mathbf{z}}$	$\nu^0{}_{\mathbf{z}}$

which give polar coefficients, and we find it convenient to denote the first two of these schemes by $\mathrm{X}(\mathbf{f}^0/\mathbf{f})$, $\mathrm{X}(\mathbf{f}/\mathbf{f}^0)$, and the last two by $\Upsilon(\mathbf{f}^0/\mathbf{f})$, $\Upsilon(\mathbf{f}/\mathbf{f}^0)$, where X, Υ are suggested by χ, υ.

Since each element of a polar scheme is the projected product of the vectors which determine its position in the scheme, $\nu^0{}_{\mathbf{y}}$ for example denoting $\mathscr{G}\,\mathbf{yz}^0$, the two polar schemes $\Upsilon(\mathbf{f}^0/\mathbf{f})$, $\Upsilon(\mathbf{f}/\mathbf{f}^0)$ are formed of the same nine elements, the rows of one scheme being the columns of the other; we describe the relation between the schemes by saying that each is obtained by transposing the other, and we write

$$\Upsilon(\mathbf{f}^0/\mathbf{f}) = \mathscr{H}\{\Upsilon(\mathbf{f}/\mathbf{f}^0)\}, \quad \Upsilon(\mathbf{f}/\mathbf{f}^0) = \mathscr{H}\{\Upsilon(\mathbf{f}^0/\mathbf{f})\}. \qquad \cdot 17$$

The relation between the schemes $\mathrm{X}(\mathbf{f}^0/\mathbf{f})$, $\mathrm{X}(\mathbf{f}/\mathbf{f}^0)$ is the same as the relation between the schemes of ratios in the earlier work: the equations defining $\mathbf{x}^0$, $\mathbf{y}^0$, $\mathbf{z}^0$ in terms of $\mathbf{x}$, $\mathbf{y}$, $\mathbf{z}$ are algebraically equivalent to the equations defining $\mathbf{x}$, $\mathbf{y}$, $\mathbf{z}$ in terms of $\mathbf{x}^0$, $\mathbf{y}^0$, $\mathbf{z}^0$, and we say that each of the schemes $\mathrm{X}(\mathbf{f}^0/\mathbf{f})$, $\mathrm{X}(\mathbf{f}/\mathbf{f}^0)$ is the reciprocal of the other, writing

$$\mathrm{X}(\mathbf{f}^0/\mathbf{f}) = \mathscr{J}\{\mathrm{X}(\mathbf{f}/\mathbf{f}^0)\}, \quad \mathrm{X}(\mathbf{f}/\mathbf{f}^0) = \mathscr{J}\{\mathrm{X}(\mathbf{f}^0/\mathbf{f})\}. \qquad \cdot 19$$

·2. Given the relation between $\mathbf{xyz}$ and $\mathbf{x}^0\mathbf{y}^0\mathbf{z}^0$, the relation between either of the frames $\mathbf{xyz}$, $\bar{\mathbf{x}}\bar{\mathbf{y}}\bar{\mathbf{z}}$ and either of the frames $\mathbf{x}^0\mathbf{y}^0\mathbf{z}^0$, $\bar{\mathbf{x}}^0\bar{\mathbf{y}}^0\bar{\mathbf{z}}^0$ is implicitly determined, and the object of the notation of the last paragraph is to enable us to express this relation briefly in the three cases. The fundamental relation by means of which we pass from a frame to its polar is

$$\mathrm{X}(\mathbf{f}^0/\bar{\mathbf{f}}) = \Upsilon(\mathbf{f}^0/\mathbf{f}), \qquad \cdot 21$$

which is merely a version of 41·43, adapted to frames; since the relation of $\mathbf{xyz}$ to $\bar{\mathbf{x}}\bar{\mathbf{y}}\bar{\mathbf{z}}$ is symmetrical, ·21 implies

$$\Upsilon(\mathbf{f}^0/\bar{\mathbf{f}}) = \mathrm{X}(\mathbf{f}^0/\mathbf{f}). \qquad \cdot 22$$

Combining ·22 and ·21 with ·19 and ·17, we have

$$\Upsilon(\bar{\mathbf{f}}^0/\bar{\mathbf{f}}) = \mathrm{X}(\bar{\mathbf{f}}^0/\mathbf{f}) = \mathscr{J}\{\Upsilon(\mathbf{f}/\mathbf{f}^0)\} = \mathscr{J}\mathscr{H}\{\Upsilon(\mathbf{f}^0/\mathbf{f})\}, \qquad \cdot 23$$

$$\mathrm{X}(\bar{\mathbf{f}}^0/\bar{\mathbf{f}}) = \Upsilon(\bar{\mathbf{f}}^0/\mathbf{f}) = \mathscr{H}\{\mathrm{X}(\mathbf{f}/\mathbf{f}^0)\} = \mathscr{H}\mathscr{J}\{\mathrm{X}(\mathbf{f}^0/\mathbf{f})\}. \qquad \cdot 24$$

It will be observed that in double changes of the special kinds that occur here the order of transformation does not matter: it makes no difference whether we interchange rows and columns before or after constructing the reciprocal scheme; symbolically,

$$\mathscr{J}\mathscr{H} = \mathscr{H}\mathscr{J}. \qquad \cdot 25$$

·3. To evaluate the magnitudes connected with a frame $\mathbf{x}^0\mathbf{y}^0\mathbf{z}^0$ by means of a frame $\mathbf{xyz}$ to which $\mathbf{x}^0\mathbf{y}^0\mathbf{z}^0$ is related we have only to bear in mind intrinsic interpretations of these magnitudes. Because J^0 is the spatial product $\mathscr{T}\,\mathbf{x}^0\mathbf{y}^0\mathbf{z}^0$, we have from 43·21

$$J^0 = J\,[\chi_{\mathbf{x}^0}\,;\,\chi_{\mathbf{y}^0}\,;\,\chi_{\mathbf{z}^0}] = J^{-1}\,[\upsilon_{\mathbf{x}^0}\,;\,\upsilon_{\mathbf{y}^0}\,;\,\upsilon_{\mathbf{z}^0}], \qquad \cdot 31$$

and because L^0, P^0 are the projected products $\mathscr{G}(\mathbf{x}^0)^2$, $\mathscr{G}\,\mathbf{y}^0\mathbf{z}^0$, we have from 42·23

·32 $$L^0 = S\chi_{\mathbf{x}^0}{}^2, \quad P^0 = S\chi_{\mathbf{y}^0}\chi_{\mathbf{z}^0},$$

·33 and from 42·34 $$L^0 = \bar{S}\upsilon_{\mathbf{x}^0}{}^2, \quad P^0 = \bar{S}\upsilon_{\mathbf{y}^0}\upsilon_{\mathbf{z}^0}.$$

To write down the polar magnitudes of $\mathbf{x}^0\mathbf{y}^0\mathbf{z}^0$ we appeal to ·24, for the relation
$$\mathrm{X}(\bar{\mathbf{f}}^0/\bar{\mathbf{f}}) = \mathscr{H}\{\mathrm{X}(\mathbf{f}/\mathbf{f}^0)\}$$
is equivalent to the set of relations

·34 $$\bar{\mathbf{x}}^0 = \xi^0_{\mathbf{x}}\bar{\mathbf{x}} + \xi^0_{\mathbf{y}}\bar{\mathbf{y}} + \xi^0_{\mathbf{z}}\bar{\mathbf{z}}, \quad \bar{\mathbf{y}}^0 = \eta^0_{\mathbf{x}}\bar{\mathbf{x}} + \eta^0_{\mathbf{y}}\bar{\mathbf{y}} + \eta^0_{\mathbf{z}}\bar{\mathbf{z}}, \quad \bar{\mathbf{z}}^0 = \zeta^0_{\mathbf{x}}\bar{\mathbf{x}} + \zeta^0_{\mathbf{y}}\bar{\mathbf{y}} + \zeta^0_{\mathbf{z}}\bar{\mathbf{z}},$$

·35 and implies $$\bar{L}^0 = \bar{S}(\xi^0_{\mathbf{f}})^2, \quad \bar{P}^0 = \bar{S}\eta^0_{\mathbf{f}}\zeta^0_{\mathbf{f}},$$

·36 and so on, and also $$\bar{J}^0 = \bar{J}[\xi^0_{\mathbf{f}}; \eta^0_{\mathbf{f}}; \zeta^0_{\mathbf{f}}],$$

which being identical with

·37 $$\bar{J}^0 = \bar{J}[\chi^0_{\mathbf{x}}; \chi^0_{\mathbf{y}}; \chi^0_{\mathbf{z}}]$$

is equivalent to $$J = J^0[\chi^0_{\mathbf{x}}; \chi^0_{\mathbf{y}}; \chi^0_{\mathbf{z}}],$$

and restates a part of ·31, reversing the rôles of the two frames. The resemblance between ·35 and ·32 is deceptive; it is somewhat of an accident that we can denote with so little trouble functions connected with the *rows* of the scheme $\mathscr{H}\{\mathrm{X}(\mathbf{f}/\mathbf{f}^0)\}$, and for the rows of the scheme $\mathscr{J}\{\Upsilon(\mathbf{f}/\mathbf{f}^0)\}$, which would occur in formulae analogous to ·33, we have no notation ready.

·4. The formulae connecting the coefficients of any vector $\mathbf{r}$ in $\mathbf{xyz}$ with the coefficients of the same vector in $\mathbf{x}^0\mathbf{y}^0\mathbf{z}^0$ depend simply on the identity

·41 $$\chi^0_{\mathbf{r}}\mathbf{f}^0 = \chi_{\mathbf{r}}\mathbf{f},$$

or on the interpretation of the coefficients as ratios of spatial products. Since polar coefficients are coefficients in a polar frame, a single set of formulae combines with the transformations of ·2 to give the results in every case required, but we can deal directly with polar coefficients by treating them as projected products. To read $\xi^0_{\mathbf{r}}$, $\eta^0_{\mathbf{r}}$, $\zeta^0_{\mathbf{r}}$ from ·41 as coefficients of $\mathbf{x}^0$, $\mathbf{y}^0$, $\mathbf{z}^0$, we must be able to express each of the vectors $\mathbf{x}$, $\mathbf{y}$, $\mathbf{z}$ in terms of the vectors $\mathbf{x}^0$, $\mathbf{y}^0$, $\mathbf{z}^0$, that is to say, we must know the scheme $\mathrm{X}(\mathbf{f}/\mathbf{f}^0)$; we have then

·42 $$\mathbf{x} = \chi^0_{\mathbf{x}}\mathbf{f}^0, \quad \mathbf{y} = \chi^0_{\mathbf{y}}\mathbf{f}^0, \quad \mathbf{z} = \chi^0_{\mathbf{z}}\mathbf{f}^0,$$

and so from ·41 $$\chi^0_{\mathbf{r}}\mathbf{f}^0 = \xi_{\mathbf{r}}\chi^0_{\mathbf{x}}\mathbf{f}^0 + \eta_{\mathbf{r}}\chi^0_{\mathbf{y}}\mathbf{f}^0 + \zeta_{\mathbf{r}}\chi^0_{\mathbf{z}}\mathbf{f}^0$$
$$= \chi_{\mathbf{r}}\xi^0_{\mathbf{f}}\mathbf{x}^0 + \chi_{\mathbf{r}}\eta^0_{\mathbf{f}}\mathbf{y}^0 + \chi_{\mathbf{r}}\zeta^0_{\mathbf{f}}\mathbf{z}^0:$$

·43 *The coefficients of any vector in the frame* $\mathbf{x}^0\mathbf{y}^0\mathbf{z}^0$ *are given in terms of the coefficients of the same vector in the frame* $\mathbf{xyz}$ *by the formulae*
$$\xi^0_{\mathbf{r}} = \chi_{\mathbf{r}}\xi^0_{\mathbf{f}}, \quad \eta^0_{\mathbf{r}} = \chi_{\mathbf{r}}\eta^0_{\mathbf{f}}, \quad \zeta^0_{\mathbf{r}} = \chi_{\mathbf{r}}\zeta^0_{\mathbf{f}},$$
where the coefficients in each expression are the elements of the corresponding column of the scheme $\mathrm{X}(\mathbf{f}/\mathbf{f}^0)$.

·44 In $$\lambda^0_{\mathbf{r}} = \upsilon_{\mathbf{r}}\chi_{\mathbf{x}^0}, \quad \mu^0_{\mathbf{r}} = \upsilon_{\mathbf{r}}\chi_{\mathbf{y}^0}, \quad \nu^0_{\mathbf{r}} = \upsilon_{\mathbf{r}}\chi_{\mathbf{z}^0}$$

we have merely versions of 42·13, but we can exhibit ·44 as a deduction from ·43 by observing that if $\lambda^0_{\mathbf{r}}$, $\mu^0_{\mathbf{r}}$, $\nu^0_{\mathbf{r}}$ are to be expressed in terms of $\lambda_{\mathbf{r}}$, $\mu_{\mathbf{r}}$, $\nu_{\mathbf{r}}$, the coefficients come from the columns of X $(\bar{\mathbf{f}}/\bar{\mathbf{f}}^0)$, and therefore by ·24 from the rows of X $(\mathbf{f}^0/\mathbf{f})$. Reference to 42·12 or to the identity

$$X(\mathbf{f}/\bar{\mathbf{f}}^0) = \mathscr{H}\Upsilon(\mathbf{f}^0/\mathbf{f})$$

gives us $$\lambda^0_{\mathbf{r}} = \chi_{\mathbf{r}}\upsilon_{\mathbf{x}^0}, \quad \mu^0_{\mathbf{r}} = \chi_{\mathbf{r}}\upsilon_{\mathbf{y}^0}, \quad \nu^0_{\mathbf{r}} = \chi_{\mathbf{r}}\upsilon_{\mathbf{z}^0}, \qquad \cdot 45$$

which can be written also as

$$\lambda^0_{\mathbf{r}} = \chi_{\mathbf{r}}\lambda^0_{\mathbf{f}}, \quad \mu^0_{\mathbf{r}} = \chi_{\mathbf{r}}\mu^0_{\mathbf{f}}, \quad \nu^0_{\mathbf{r}} = \chi_{\mathbf{r}}\nu^0_{\mathbf{f}}. \qquad \cdot 46$$

There remains the expression of $\xi^0_{\mathbf{r}}, \eta^0_{\mathbf{r}}, \zeta^0_{\mathbf{r}}$ in terms of $\lambda_{\mathbf{r}}, \mu_{\mathbf{r}}, \nu_{\mathbf{r}}$, involving the elements of the scheme X $(\bar{\mathbf{f}}/\mathbf{f}^0)$, which is $\mathscr{J}\{\Upsilon(\mathbf{f}^0/\mathbf{f})\}$; we have

$$\xi^0_{\mathbf{r}} = [\upsilon_{\mathbf{r}}; \mu^0_{\mathbf{f}}; \nu^0_{\mathbf{f}}]/[\lambda^0_{\mathbf{f}}; \mu^0_{\mathbf{f}}; \nu^0_{\mathbf{f}}], \qquad \cdot 47$$

or in another form $$\xi^0_{\mathbf{r}} = [\upsilon_{\mathbf{r}}; \upsilon_{\mathbf{y}^0}; \upsilon_{\mathbf{z}^0}]/[\upsilon_{\mathbf{x}^0}; \upsilon_{\mathbf{y}^0}; \upsilon_{\mathbf{z}^0}], \qquad \cdot 48$$

and so on, a formula that can be deduced either from the nature of the scheme $\mathscr{J}\{\Upsilon(\mathbf{f}^0/\mathbf{f})\}$, or by an algebraical reversal of ·46 or ·45 followed by an interchange of the two frames **xyz**, $\mathbf{x}^0\mathbf{y}^0\mathbf{z}^0$, or from 43·21, which asserts that $[\upsilon_{\mathbf{r}}; \upsilon_{\mathbf{y}^0}; \upsilon_{\mathbf{z}^0}]$ has the value $J\mathscr{T}\,\mathbf{r}\mathbf{y}^0\mathbf{z}^0$; reference to 43·21 gives in the same way

$$\xi^0_{\mathbf{r}} = [\chi_{\mathbf{r}}; \chi_{\mathbf{y}^0}; \chi_{\mathbf{z}^0}]/[\chi_{\mathbf{x}^0}; \chi_{\mathbf{y}^0}; \chi_{\mathbf{z}^0}], \qquad \cdot 49$$

for direct use if X $(\mathbf{f}^0/\mathbf{f})$ is known.

356. Change of origin; effects of a change on the vectors used to specify points and rotors.

·1. To describe the relation of one Cartesian frame to another or of one attached vector frame to another requires, in addition to a scheme relating the unattached frames in the one case or the directions of the axes in the other case, only a specification of the vector of the step from one origin to the other; this vector may be given by its components or its projections in either of the Cartesian frames, or by its coefficients or its polar coefficients in either of the vector frames. As far as the frames are used only for the analysis of vectors, no change is produced by the attachment.

·2. To see the effect of a change of axes on the specification of directions, points, and other concepts with which we have to deal, we have only to consider the intrinsic nature of the numbers used in the specification.

The ratios and cosines of a direction are the components and projections of a vector which in itself is independent of the frame of reference, and the formulae of sections 2 and 5 of this chapter apply to this as to any other vector.

The coordinates and projections of a point are the components and projections of a vector, but this vector depends on the origin of the frame. Formulae already given in this chapter connect the description of the vector of the step O^0R by means of the frame $O^0X^0Y^0Z^0$ or $O^0\mathbf{x}^0\mathbf{y}^0\mathbf{z}^0$ with the description of *this same vector* by means of the frame $OXYZ$ or $O\mathbf{xyz}$. But in the frames $OXYZ$ and $O\mathbf{xyz}$ it is the vector of the step OR, not the vector of the step O^0R, that is fundamental, and if we wish to pass from coordinates or projections of R relative to one frame to coordinates or projections relative to the other frame we must remember that the vector of OR is the sum of the vector of O^0R and the vector of OO^0.

A plane is described by means of a direction and a distance; the relations between the elements describing the direction with reference to one frame and the elements describing the same direction by means of another frame are such as we have been considering; the relation between the distances of O and O^0 from the plane is given in terms of the position of O^0 relative to $OXYZ$ or of O relative to $O^0X^0Y^0Z^0$ by an application of 34·12.

The vector of a rotor is intrinsic to the rotor, and calls for no discussion; the momental components and momental projections of a rotor with respect to a frame are derived from the momental vector of the rotor about the origin of the frame; the formulae that connect the components and projections of the momental vector of a rotor about a point Q with respect to one frame with the components and projections of the momental vector about *the same point* Q with respect to another frame are in no particular affected by the nature of the vector, but the application of these formulae to the momental components and projections of the rotor with respect to the frame $O^0X^0Y^0Z^0$ or $O^0\mathbf{x}^0\mathbf{y}^0\mathbf{z}^0$ gives the components and projections with respect to $OXYZ$ or $O\mathbf{xyz}$ of the momental vector of the rotor about the point O^0; the momental components and projections of the rotor with respect to $OXYZ$ and $O\mathbf{xyz}$ depend on the momental vector about O, and an application of some proposition of the type of 35·31 is necessary if they are to be derived from the momental vector about O^0. There is a method of deriving momental components and projections differing slightly from the method just indicated; momental *projections* with respect to any Cartesian frame are moments of a rotor about the axes of the frame, and momental projections with respect to any attached vector frame are actual momental products; playing this part, momental projections relative to one frame can be calculated directly by means of 35·51 from specifications relative to another frame, and the passage from momental projections to momental components can then be made if necessary by means of the usual formulae connecting components in a frame with projections in the same frame.

What has been said of a single rotor applies, *mutatis mutandis*, to a set of rotors and to a ray. The vector of a set of rotors is independent of the origin, as is the unit vector by which the direction of a ray is subjected to analysis. But the vector to which the momental components and projections belong is the momental vector about the origin, and suffers an intrinsic change, given by 241·39 or 235·24, if the origin moves from O^0 to O.

BOOK IV

COMPLEX SPACE

CHAPTER IV 1

ALGEBRAIC VECSPACE

410. Introduction. 411. The fundamental properties of a three-dimensional algebraic vector field; triplets and inner products. 412. Projected products and fundamental magnitudes; spatial products and spatial directions; prepared vecspace; the polar of a frame. 413. Veclines and vecplanes; perpendicularity. 414. Vector products. 415. Nul vectors; isotropic veclines and vecplanes.

410. Introduction.

The formulae of Chapter III 4 and article 355 suggest the means of constructing an algebraic space whose properties depend only on those of real numbers. One outcome of this construction is to *prove* that the properties of geometrical space which are reproduced in algebraic space are mutually consistent—in other words, that in the assumptions of Euclidean geometry there is no latent contradiction. Were this its whole effect, the formation of the algebraic space corresponding to the space of geometry would be the concern only of those philosophers who investigate the logical foundations of mathematics. But there are developments of another kind. A construction with real numbers is always a challenge to perform a corresponding construction with complex numbers, and there is in fact no stage in the construction of algebraic space at which a hypothesis as to the nature of the numbers used is necessary: it is no harder* to build an *algebraic* space that is complex than to build one that is real. Complex algebraic space as a whole does not in any sense correspond to the space with which we have been dealing hitherto, but just as the algebra of complex numbers is more uniform than the algebra of real numbers and gives invaluable help in the study of theorems relating to real numbers alone, so the space in which coordinates are complex is the space in which analysis can work most freely, and attracts mathematicians both for this reason and because many of its features imply properties of real algebraic

* And of course no easier: to 'let' the coordinates be complex instead of real, while the axes are still vaguely supposed to be Cartesian, is an absurdity the acceptance of which should have disposed long ago of the claim that mathematics is a training in accuracy of thought, and yet writers as scrupulous as possible to face all *analytical* difficulties seem to admit complex points in this very way.

Hamilton's bivector, regarded as a pair of vectors (just as a complex number is a pair of real numbers), has no logical flaw, and there is a corresponding complex space of which the element is a pair of ordinary points, but the direct contemplation of the bivector and the point-pair seems to me to be a hindrance rather than a help in the technical task of framing definitions and constructions by which the language of ordinary geometry acquires useful significance in complex space.

space which can be transferred to the space of ordinary geometry. The services of complex vectors and complex frames in the study of Euclidean space alone render some account of complex space a natural part of our work. Difficulties arise because, whereas in dealing with ordinary space we have accepted position and direction as undefined and avoided the explicit recognition that absolute position and absolute direction are indeterminable if not meaningless, in constructing algebraic space we are unable to shirk issues by appealing to preconceptions that it is not our business to criticise.

411. The fundamental properties of a three-dimensional algebraic vector field; triplets and inner products.

·1. The propositions of geometry depend not at all on any hypothesis as to the nature of points and vectors themselves, but on the relations which are assumed to hold between vectors and vectors and between vectors and points.

The relations which are suggested by Euclidean geometry and reproduced in algebraic space of three dimensions are as follows:

·11 °Any three vectors subject only to the condition expressed by saying that they are not coplanar or that their spatial product is not zero can form a vector frame;

·12 °If $\mathbf{x}, \mathbf{y}, \mathbf{z}$ form a frame, an arbitrary vector $\mathbf{r}$ can be expressed symbolically in one and only one way in the form $\xi_\mathbf{r}\mathbf{x}+\eta_\mathbf{r}\mathbf{y}+\zeta_\mathbf{r}\mathbf{z}$, written briefly as $\chi_\mathbf{r}\mathbf{f}$, where

$$\chi=(\xi, \eta, \zeta), \quad \mathbf{f}=(\mathbf{x}, \mathbf{y}, \mathbf{z}),$$

and $\xi_\mathbf{r}, \eta_\mathbf{r}, \zeta_\mathbf{r}$ are numbers; no two vectors have the same set of coefficients in a given frame;

·13 °There is a vector $(\chi_\mathbf{r}+\chi_\mathbf{s})\mathbf{f}$, that is, $(\xi_\mathbf{r}+\xi_\mathbf{s})\mathbf{x}+(\eta_\mathbf{r}+\eta_\mathbf{s})\mathbf{y}+(\zeta_\mathbf{r}+\zeta_\mathbf{s})\mathbf{z}$, and this vector depends only on the vectors $\mathbf{r}, \mathbf{s}$, of which it is called the sum, not on the vectors $\mathbf{x}, \mathbf{y}, \mathbf{z}$;

·14 °Associated with any two vectors $\mathbf{r}, \mathbf{s}$ there is a number $\mathscr{S}\mathbf{rs}$, their projected product, which is independent of the vectors of reference $\mathbf{x}, \mathbf{y}, \mathbf{z}$, and the function $\mathscr{S}\mathbf{rs}$ is linear and homogeneous in each of the sets of coefficients $(\xi_\mathbf{r}, \eta_\mathbf{r}, \zeta_\mathbf{r})$, $(\xi_\mathbf{s}, \eta_\mathbf{s}, \zeta_\mathbf{s})$ and is a symmetric function of the two vectors;

·15 °The difference of position between any two points P, Q is determined by, and may in fact be identified with, a definite vector, the vector of the step PQ; if this vector and the position of one of the points are known, the position of the other point is fixed;

·16 °If R, S, T are any three points, the sum of the vectors of the steps RS, ST is the vector of the step RT.

In the geometry of ordinary space, two other conditions are fulfilled:

·17 °Projected products, and the coefficients of vectors in vector frames, are real numbers;

·18 °The projected square $\mathscr{S}\mathbf{r}^2$ is essentially positive unless the three coefficients $\xi_\mathbf{r}, \eta_\mathbf{r}, \zeta_\mathbf{r}$ are simultaneously zero.

To say that if the former of these additional restrictions is removed there
is no object in retaining any restriction similar to the latter, is to understate
the case; it is in no slight degree for the sake of analytical processes requiring
freedom from the latter that it is worth while to break away from the former.
We proceed therefore to investigate consequences of the first six assumptions,
without any suggestion as to what points and vectors are supposed to be: to
us a field of vectors or a °*vecspace** is to mean primarily a class for whose ·19
members the first four assumptions are true,—with some interpretation of the
plus signs in the identity $\mathbf{r} = \xi_{\mathbf{r}}\mathbf{x} + \eta_{\mathbf{r}}\mathbf{y} + \zeta_{\mathbf{r}}\mathbf{z}$ that allows the symbols to be
manipulated exactly as in algebra,—and a space is to be a class with whose
members some field of vectors is associated in the manner prescribed by the
fifth and sixth conditions. For convenience we use always definite words that
are applicable, strictly speaking, only in the study of a *given* vector field and
a *given* space, but in this we are merely adopting a custom which is common,
though sometimes concealed, in every branch of geometry as well as in other
parts of mathematics.

Geometry is the study of relations between points, but since we propose to derive the properties of space from the relation of points to vectors, we find it convenient to discuss relations between vectors and the problems of measurement in a vecspace before giving any attention to points.

·2. Something must be said of the numbers† that are to serve as coefficients or as projected products. In the conditions already made, it is implicitly assumed that these numbers compose a single group such that the sum and the product of any two of them belong to this group. Doubtless some progress could be made without further assumptions, but to work rapidly we not only subtract and divide but extract square roots and introduce angles by defining numbers to serve as sines and cosines. In fact the only number-groups that we really contemplate are the group formed of all the real numbers and the group formed of all the complex numbers. The real group provides a real algebraic vecspace and real algebraic space, while the complex group gives a complex vector field and complex space. Our object is to suggest definitions and constructions which, while they enable the language of ordinary geometry to be transferred to the geometry of real algebraic space, are significant when the space is complex.

·3. By assuming the possibility of subtraction, we assume implicitly that
there is a °*zero vector*, definable as a vector which can be added to any vector ·31
without producing any effect; °if $\mathbf{0}$ denotes a zero vector, $\mathbf{r} + \mathbf{0}$ is identical ·32

* The need for this word and the cognate *vecplane* and *vecline*, all of which are used in my *Fourth Dimension* (1921), seems imperative if vectors are discussed before points.

† These are supposed to be of one of the kinds with which elementary algebra is familiar: we are not concerned to tabulate such properties as that subtraction is possible and multiplication commutative.

with $\mathbf{r}$. Thus $(\xi_\mathbf{r}+\xi_0)\,\mathbf{x}+(\eta_\mathbf{r}+\eta_0)\,\mathbf{y}+(\zeta_\mathbf{r}+\zeta_0)\,\mathbf{z}$ as well as $\xi_\mathbf{r}\mathbf{x}+\eta_\mathbf{r}\mathbf{y}+\zeta_\mathbf{r}\mathbf{z}$ is an expression for $\mathbf{r}$, and therefore

·33 $$\xi_\mathbf{r}+\xi_0=\xi_\mathbf{r},\quad \eta_\mathbf{r}+\eta_0=\eta_\mathbf{r},\quad \zeta_\mathbf{r}+\zeta_0=\zeta_\mathbf{r}.$$

·34 Hence in any field °there is only one zero vector, and that is a vector whose
·35 coefficients in every frame are all zero*. °If the coefficients in any one frame are zero, the vector satisfies ·33 and therefore ·32, and is therefore the zero vector.

·**4.** One doubt may be dispelled at once: to shew that we are not about to waste time by studying self-contradictory concepts, we can give an example in which the properties ascribed to vectors and points are certainly to be found.

Let an ordered set of three numbers be called a *triplet*, and let the number $fp+gq+hr$ be called the *inner product* of the triplets (f, g, h), (p, q, r). Also let $\kappa(l, m, n)$, where κ is any number of the same kind as the elements of the triplets, mean the triplet $(\kappa l, \kappa m, \kappa n)$, and let $(f, g, h)+(p, q, r)$ mean $(f+p, g+q, h+r)$. Then the arbitrary triplet (x, y, z) is expressible in terms of three *given* triplets (f, g, h), (l, m, n), (p, q, r) in the form

$$\xi(f, g, h)+\eta(l, m, n)+\zeta(p, q, r)$$

if and only if ξ, η, ζ can be found simultaneously to satisfy the three equations

$$\xi f+\eta l+\zeta p=x,\quad \xi g+\eta m+\zeta q=y,\quad \xi h+\eta n+\zeta r=z:$$

any three triplets whose determinant does not vanish can serve as a frame.

If the two triplets (x, y, z), (a, b, c) are expressed in the forms

$$\xi(f, g, h)+\eta(l, m, n)+\zeta(p, q, r),\quad \alpha(f, g, h)+\beta(l, m, n)+\gamma(p, q, r),$$

their inner product $xa+yb+zc$ is

$$(\xi f+\eta l+\zeta p)(\alpha f+\beta l+\gamma p)$$
$$+(\xi g+\eta m+\zeta q)(\alpha g+\beta m+\gamma q)$$
$$+(\xi h+\eta n+\zeta r)(\alpha h+\beta n+\gamma r).$$

As a *function* of $\xi, \eta, \zeta, \alpha, \beta, \gamma$ this expression has coefficients depending on the three triplets (f, g, h), (l, m, n), (p, q, r), but the *value* of the expression for a *given* pair of triplets (x, y, z), (a, b, c) does not depend on the triplets of reference, the simple explanation being that a change in the triplets of reference affects the values of $\xi, \eta, \zeta, \alpha, \beta, \gamma$ no less than the values of the six numbers

$$f^2+g^2+h^2,\quad l^2+m^2+n^2,\quad p^2+q^2+r^2,$$
$$lp+mq+nr,\quad pf+qg+rh,\quad fl+gm+hn,$$

which are the coefficients of

$$\xi\alpha,\qquad \eta\beta,\qquad \zeta\gamma,$$
$$\eta\gamma+\zeta\beta,\qquad \zeta\alpha+\xi\gamma,\qquad \xi\beta+\eta\alpha,$$

* The *meaning* of zero in this assertion varies with the kind of numbers in use, though the same *symbol* is employed in every case.

in the expression for the inner product; and it is to be observed that as a function of the sets of variables (ξ, η, ζ), (α, β, γ), the inner product $xa + yb + zc$ is homogeneous, bilinear, and symmetrical.

Thus triplets with their inner products possess relations exactly of the kind postulated of vectors with their projected products. Further, the triplet (x, y, z) is obtainable from the triplet (a, b, c) by the addition of the triplet

$$(x - a, y - b, z - c),$$

and for any third triplet (l, m, n),

$$(l - a, m - b, n - c) + (x - l, y - m, z - n) = (x - a, y - b, z - c).$$

Hence if triplets can serve as vectors, they can serve equally well as points. And all that is necessary if a complex vector-field and complex space are required is to use complex numbers as the elements of the triplets.

Here it must be said that there are arguments against the obvious and easy course of *defining* vectors and points as triplets and reducing analytical geometry to a branch of the calculus of extension. Comparison with ordinary geometry is sufficient to arouse discontent with this method: a proposal to *identify* a point with its set of coordinates in some particular frame could emanate only from a logician in difficulties or a teacher in a hurry, and the logician at any rate would have no reason to choose a trirectangular frame. But discontent is no argument; the course taken by a puzzled logician *might* be logically necessary, and it is for us to shew that in this case the plan apparently simple is really both unnecessary and undesirable.

To suppose it necessary to define vectors otherwise than by their mutual relations is to mistake the nature of mathematics. The normal form of a mathematical theorem is an assertion that if certain *relations* hold then other *relations* also hold. What the concepts are between which the relations hold is always* a matter of indifference; to find that in a particular instance the relations do hold is important if the instance is so interesting in itself that it is desirable to know what general theories are applicable in its study, and may be of service if no other proof is available that the relations are mutually compatible, but to present the consequences of a set of relations as a theory of one particular set of concepts between which the relations hold is a double error, apt on the one hand to obscure the effects of the relations by modifications due only to the nature of the subject-matter, and on the other hand to cause ambiguities of language if not of thought if later the same relations are recognised between concepts of a different kind.

It is precisely when regarded as a deduction from relations of a prescribed form without any assumption as to what a vector is, that the theory of vectors has its purest and most adaptable form.

* Compare Russell (*Mysticism and Logic*, p. 75, 1917; reprinted from *International Monthly*, 1901): "Mathematics may be defined as the subject in which we never know what we are talking about, nor whether what we are saying is true."

Even if attention is concentrated on the relations, at first sight the inner product seems only a special case of a projected product and it can not be taken for granted that all relations between triplets imply relations of exactly the same form between vectors of every kind. If it is in fact true that in every class that we are prepared to call a field of vectors there must be a frame such that the projected product of any two vectors is the inner product of their sets of coefficients in this frame, not only is this a matter that requires proof, but the proof must be based on a study of the general relation, and until the proof is forthcoming it remains an open question whether the assumption that the projected product has the form of an inner product is not an implicit limitation on the vecspace to be studied.

To produce a last argument, we can say that a treatment that defines vectors as triplets can hardly avoid defining points in the same way. But if no distinction can be drawn between vectors and points, it becomes almost impossible to reproduce the language of elementary geometry, and premature simplicity exacts as usual a heavy toll: for example, it is necessary to say that any *three* triplets are *punctually* coplanar, but that the triplets (f, g, h), (l, m, n), (p, q, r) are *vectorially* coplanar only if

$$\begin{vmatrix} f & g & h \\ l & m & n \\ p & q & r \end{vmatrix} = 0,$$

and that the *four* triplets (f, g, h), (l, m, n), (p, q, r), (x, y, z) are *punctually* coplanar if

$$\begin{vmatrix} f, & g, & h, & 1 \\ l, & m, & n, & 1 \\ p, & q, & r, & 1 \\ x, & y, & z, & 1 \end{vmatrix} = 0.$$

412. Projected products and fundamental magnitudes; spatial products and spatial directions; prepared vecspace; the polar of a frame.

·1. From the assumption as to its character, the projected product $\mathscr{G}\,\mathbf{rs}$ is necessarily given by a formula that can be written

·11 $$\mathscr{G}\,\mathbf{rs} = L\xi_{\mathbf{r}}\xi_{\mathbf{s}} + M\eta_{\mathbf{r}}\eta_{\mathbf{s}} + N\zeta_{\mathbf{r}}\zeta_{\mathbf{s}} + P(\eta_{\mathbf{r}}\zeta_{\mathbf{s}} + \zeta_{\mathbf{r}}\eta_{\mathbf{s}}) + Q(\zeta_{\mathbf{r}}\xi_{\mathbf{s}} + \xi_{\mathbf{r}}\zeta_{\mathbf{s}}) + R(\xi_{\mathbf{r}}\eta_{\mathbf{s}} + \eta_{\mathbf{r}}\xi_{\mathbf{s}}),$$

·12 or briefly $$\mathscr{G}\,\mathbf{rs} = S\chi_{\mathbf{r}}\chi_{\mathbf{s}},$$

where the six coefficients L, M, N, P, Q, R are independent of $\mathbf{r}$ and $\mathbf{s}$ and have therefore the values of the six particular projected products $\mathscr{G}\,\mathbf{x}^2$, $\mathscr{G}\,\mathbf{y}^2$, $\mathscr{G}\,\mathbf{z}^2$, $\mathscr{G}\,\mathbf{yz}$, $\mathscr{G}\,\mathbf{zx}$, $\mathscr{G}\,\mathbf{xy}$. It is convenient to have symbols for the three projected products $\mathscr{G}\,\mathbf{xr}$, $\mathscr{G}\,\mathbf{yr}$, $\mathscr{G}\,\mathbf{zr}$, which are given in terms of the *fundamental magnitudes* L, M, N, P, Q, R and of $\xi_{\mathbf{r}}, \eta_{\mathbf{r}}, \zeta_{\mathbf{r}}$ by ·11, and we write

$$\lambda_{\mathbf{r}} = \mathscr{G}\,\mathbf{xr} = S^1\chi_{\mathbf{r}}, \quad \mu_{\mathbf{r}} = \mathscr{G}\,\mathbf{yr} = S^2\chi_{\mathbf{r}}, \quad \nu_{\mathbf{r}} = \mathscr{G}\,\mathbf{zr} = S^3\chi_{\mathbf{r}}, \qquad \cdot 14$$

$$\upsilon = (\lambda, \mu, \nu). \qquad \cdot 15$$

Then identically
$$\mathscr{G}\,\mathbf{rs} = \upsilon_{\mathbf{r}}\chi_{\mathbf{s}} = \chi_{\mathbf{r}}\upsilon_{\mathbf{s}}, \qquad \cdot 16$$
and in particular
$$\mathscr{G}\,\mathbf{r}^2 = \upsilon_{\mathbf{r}}\chi_{\mathbf{r}}. \qquad \cdot 17$$

It is to be observed that no additional hypothesis is required to secure the important identity

$$\mathscr{G}\,\mathbf{r}\,(\mathbf{s}+\mathbf{t}) = \mathscr{G}\,\mathbf{rs} + \mathscr{G}\,\mathbf{rt}. \qquad \cdot 18$$

·2. For ordinary space, spatial direction is accepted from experience, and spatial products are defined without reference to projected products or to the decomposition of vectors. We have now to shew that we can introduce spatial directions and spatial products into the theory of algebraic space without additional indefinables, in such a way as to reproduce the algebraic relations that hold between spatial products and projected products in ordinary space. The corresponding questions for vector products and areal products are considered in due course.

If $\mathbf{x}, \mathbf{y}, \mathbf{z}$ are themselves given in terms of three vectors $\mathbf{x}^0, \mathbf{y}^0, \mathbf{z}^0$ by expressions

$$\mathbf{x} = \chi^0_{\mathbf{x}}\mathbf{f}^0, \quad \mathbf{y} = \chi^0_{\mathbf{y}}\mathbf{f}^0, \quad \mathbf{z} = \chi^0_{\mathbf{z}}\mathbf{f}^0, \qquad \cdot 21$$

then
$$\mathbf{r} = \xi_{\mathbf{r}}\mathbf{x} + \eta_{\mathbf{r}}\mathbf{y} + \zeta_{\mathbf{r}}\mathbf{z} = \chi_{\mathbf{r}}\xi^0_{\mathbf{f}}\mathbf{x}^0 + \chi_{\mathbf{r}}\eta^0_{\mathbf{f}}\mathbf{y}^0 + \chi_{\mathbf{r}}\zeta^0_{\mathbf{f}}\mathbf{z}^0;$$
hence $\mathbf{x}^0, \mathbf{y}^0, \mathbf{z}^0$ form a frame, and the coefficients of $\mathbf{r}$ in this frame are given by

$$\xi^0_{\mathbf{r}} = \chi_{\mathbf{r}}\xi^0_{\mathbf{f}}, \quad \eta^0_{\mathbf{r}} = \chi_{\mathbf{r}}\eta^0_{\mathbf{f}}, \quad \zeta^0_{\mathbf{r}} = \chi_{\mathbf{r}}\zeta^0_{\mathbf{f}}. \qquad \cdot 22$$

Since the vectors $\mathbf{x}, \mathbf{y}, \mathbf{z}$ as well as the vectors $\mathbf{x}^0, \mathbf{y}^0, \mathbf{z}^0$ compose a frame, an arbitrary set of values of $\xi^0_{\mathbf{r}}, \eta^0_{\mathbf{r}}, \zeta^0_{\mathbf{r}}$ must lead to a corresponding set of values of $\xi_{\mathbf{r}}, \eta_{\mathbf{r}}, \zeta_{\mathbf{r}}$ which is unique, and therefore the determinant of the set of equations ·22, regarded as equations to determine $\xi_{\mathbf{r}}, \eta_{\mathbf{r}}, \zeta_{\mathbf{r}}$ in terms of $\xi^0_{\mathbf{r}}, \eta^0_{\mathbf{r}}, \zeta^0_{\mathbf{r}}$, must not be zero; this determinant is expressible as $[[\chi^0_{\mathbf{f}}]]$.

From ·22 and the rule for forming the product of two determinants, it follows that if $\mathbf{r}, \mathbf{s}, \mathbf{t}$ are any three vectors and $\mathbf{p}$ denotes $(\mathbf{r}, \mathbf{s}, \mathbf{t})$, then

$$[[\chi^0_{\mathbf{p}}]] = [[\chi_{\mathbf{p}}]]\,[[\chi^0_{\mathbf{f}}]]; \qquad \cdot 23$$

thus $[[\chi^0_{\mathbf{f}}]]$ is the ratio of a function independent of $\mathbf{x}, \mathbf{y}, \mathbf{z}$ to a function independent of $\mathbf{x}^0, \mathbf{y}^0, \mathbf{z}^0$, or since it depends on nothing but these six vectors, is the ratio of a number depending only on the frame $\mathbf{x}^0\mathbf{y}^0\mathbf{z}^0$ to a number ·24
depending only on the frame $\mathbf{xyz}$.

The last conclusion is easily confirmed. If $[[S]]$ denotes the value of the determinant

$$\begin{vmatrix} L & R & Q \\ R & M & P \\ Q & P & N \end{vmatrix},$$

which may otherwise be denoted by $[[\mathscr{G}\,\mathbf{ff}]]$, ·14 gives

·25 $$[[\upsilon^0_{\mathbf{f}}]] = [[S^0]]\,[[\chi^0_{\mathbf{f}}]]$$

and ·16 gives $$[[S]] = [[\upsilon^0_{\mathbf{f}}]]\,[[\chi^0_{\mathbf{f}}]];$$

hence $$[[S]] = [[S^0]]\,[[\chi^0_{\mathbf{f}}]]^2,$$

·28 °and $[[\chi^0_{\mathbf{f}}]]$ is the ratio of a square root of $[[S]]$ to a square root of $[[S^0]]$.

·3. Let us describe a set of three vectors $(\mathbf{r}, \mathbf{s}, \mathbf{t})$ associated with a particu square root p of $[[\mathscr{G}\,\mathbf{pp}]]$ as a *directed triplet** of spatial product p, and let say that the directed triplet in which $(\mathbf{r}', \mathbf{s}', \mathbf{t}')$ is associated with p' spatially codirectional with the directed triplet in which $(\mathbf{r}'', \mathbf{s}'', \mathbf{t}'')$ is associa with p'' if when the vectors are referred to a frame **xyz**

·31 $$p'\,[[\chi_{\mathbf{p}''}]] = p''\,[[\chi_{\mathbf{p}'}]].$$

From ·23 it follows that if two directed triplets are spatially codirectio with a third triplet whose spatial product is not zero they are spatially directional with each other. Hence directed triplets fall naturally into t classes such that any two members of the same class are spatially codirection If $(\mathbf{r}, \mathbf{s}, \mathbf{t})$ associated with p is a member of one class, $(\mathbf{r}, \mathbf{s}, \mathbf{t})$ associated w $-p$ is a member of the other class; any directed triplet of spatial prod

·32 zero belongs to both classes. The two classes are called the two °*spatial dir tions*, and if $(\mathbf{r}, \mathbf{s}, \mathbf{t})$ associated with p is a member of one of these classes

·33 is called the °spatial product of **rst** *in this direction.* There is no difference character between the two spatial directions—in fact if $(\mathbf{r}, \mathbf{s}, \mathbf{t})$ associa with p is in one direction, $(\mathbf{s}, \mathbf{r}, \mathbf{t})$ associated with p is in the other direction but it is always to be assumed, in the absence of specific assertion to contrary, that spatial products are measured in the same direction. In ot

·34 words, the space which is studied is a °*prepared space*, in which it is a defin square root of $[[\mathscr{G}\,\mathbf{pp}]]$ that is associated with $(\mathbf{r}, \mathbf{s}, \mathbf{t})$; this square root

·35 be called simply °*the* spatial product of **rst**, and is denoted by $\mathscr{J}\,\mathbf{rst}$. Th for any two sets of vectors $(\mathbf{r}', \mathbf{s}', \mathbf{t}')$, $(\mathbf{r}'', \mathbf{s}'', \mathbf{t}'')$ referred to any frame,

·36 $$\mathscr{J}\,\mathbf{r}'\mathbf{s}'\mathbf{t}'\,.\,[[\chi_{\mathbf{p}''}]] = \mathscr{J}\,\mathbf{r}''\mathbf{s}''\mathbf{t}''\,.\,[[\chi_{\mathbf{p}'}]].$$

We denote the spatial product of the three vectors forming the frame **x** by J, and since the determinant $[[\chi_{\mathbf{f}}]]$, in which every element of the princi diagonal is 1 and every other element is 0, has the value 1, we have a particular case of ·36, for any three vectors referred to this frame,

·37 $$\mathscr{J}\,\mathbf{rst} = J\,[[\chi_{\mathbf{p}}]],$$

·38 whence $$\mathscr{J}\,(\mathbf{q}+\mathbf{r})\,\mathbf{st} = \mathscr{J}\,\mathbf{qst} + \mathscr{J}\,\mathbf{rst},$$

·39 $$\mathscr{J}\,\mathbf{srt} = \mathscr{J}\,\mathbf{rts} = -\,\mathscr{J}\,\mathbf{rst}.$$

·4. There is one case in which the discussion just completed seems sup fluous. It is not inconsistent with the assumptions 1·11—1·14 to suppose t *every* determinant of the form $[[\mathscr{G}\,\mathbf{pp}]]$ is zero. But the algebraic space wh

* This use of the word triplet is of course entirely distinct from the use in 1·4 above

results from this supposition* has so little resemblance to Euclidean space that it is outside our province to pursue the investigation. We add therefore an explicit assumption to those already made:

For at least one set of three vectors **r**, **s**, **t** *the determinant* ·42

$$\begin{vmatrix} \mathscr{G}\mathbf{r}^2 & \mathscr{G}\mathbf{rs} & \mathscr{G}\mathbf{rt} \\ \mathscr{G}\mathbf{sr} & \mathscr{G}\mathbf{s}^2 & \mathscr{G}\mathbf{st} \\ \mathscr{G}\mathbf{tr} & \mathscr{G}\mathbf{ts} & \mathscr{G}\mathbf{t}^2 \end{vmatrix}$$

does not vanish.

And it follows from ·37 that

The necessary and sufficient condition for three vectors to form a frame is that their spatial product is not zero. ·43

With the introduction of spatial products, ·25 may be changed to

$$[[\nu^0{}_\mathbf{f}]] = J^0 J, \qquad \cdot 44$$

or with **r**, **s**, **t** substituted for $\mathbf{x}^0$, $\mathbf{y}^0$, $\mathbf{z}^0$, to

$$[[\mathscr{G}\mathbf{pf}]] = \mathscr{J}\mathbf{rst}\,\mathscr{J}\mathbf{xyz}, \qquad \cdot 45$$

which is more obviously general and requires no restrictions whatever to be placed on the six vectors, for if either side of ·45 is zero so also is the other. Another form of ·45 is a formula for a spatial product in terms of polar coefficients, namely,

$$\mathscr{J}\mathbf{rst} = J^{-1}[[\nu_\mathbf{p}]]. \qquad \cdot 46$$

The identity $$[[\mathscr{G}\mathbf{pp}]] = (\mathscr{J}\mathbf{rst})^2, \qquad \cdot 47$$

a special case of ·45 that we need for reference, only reiterates part of the definition of $\mathscr{J}\mathbf{rst}$.

·5. The actual coefficients of a vector **r** in a frame **xyz** can be found at once from the consideration that

The spatial product of three vectors is zero if two of the three coincide, ·51

for this proposition, with ·38, implies

$$\mathscr{J}(\xi_\mathbf{r}\mathbf{x} + \eta_\mathbf{r}\mathbf{y} + \zeta_\mathbf{r}\mathbf{z})\,\mathbf{yz} = \xi_\mathbf{r}\mathscr{J}\mathbf{xyz},$$
$$\mathscr{J}\mathbf{x}(\xi_\mathbf{r}\mathbf{x} + \eta_\mathbf{r}\mathbf{y} + \zeta_\mathbf{r}\mathbf{z})\,\mathbf{z} = \eta_\mathbf{r}\mathscr{J}\mathbf{xyz},$$
$$\mathscr{J}\mathbf{xy}(\xi_\mathbf{r}\mathbf{x} + \eta_\mathbf{r}\mathbf{y} + \zeta_\mathbf{r}\mathbf{z}) = \zeta_\mathbf{r}\mathscr{J}\mathbf{xyz},$$

that is, $$J\xi_\mathbf{r} = \mathscr{J}\mathbf{ryz}, \quad J\eta_\mathbf{r} = \mathscr{J}\mathbf{xrz}, \quad J\zeta_\mathbf{r} = \mathscr{J}\mathbf{xyr}, \qquad \cdot 53$$

or in one formula, $$\mathbf{r}\,\mathscr{J}\mathbf{xyz} = \mathbf{x}\,\mathscr{J}\mathbf{ryz} + \mathbf{y}\,\mathscr{J}\mathbf{xrz} + \mathbf{z}\,\mathscr{J}\mathbf{xyr}. \qquad \cdot 54$$

·6. The assumption that the determinant $[[S]]$ of the frame **xyz** does not vanish has a bearing on ·14, since this is the condition for $\xi_\mathbf{r}$, $\eta_\mathbf{r}$, $\zeta_\mathbf{r}$ to be determinable from this set of equations if $\lambda_\mathbf{r}$, $\mu_\mathbf{r}$, $\nu_\mathbf{r}$ are given:

* But so far is the supposition in question from being logically absurd, that complex space of four dimensions *necessarily* has three-dimensional 'sections' with this very peculiarity, just as in the complex space with which we are dealing there are planes, called isotropic planes, in which geometry takes a form that is anything but commonplace. A space in which ·42 is not true is said to be *isotropic*.

·61 *If the spatial product of three vectors is not zero, any fourth vector is determinate if its projected products with these three are known.*

On the assumption that every set of numbers is a possible set of coefficients in the frame **xyz**, it follows also that every set of numbers is a possible set of projected products in this frame. In particular, the sets of equations*

·62
$$\left[\begin{matrix} \mathscr{G}\,\mathbf{x}\bar{\mathbf{x}} = 1, & \mathscr{G}\,\mathbf{y}\bar{\mathbf{x}} = 0, & \mathscr{G}\,\mathbf{z}\bar{\mathbf{x}} = 0, \\ \mathscr{G}\,\mathbf{x}\bar{\mathbf{y}} = 0, & \mathscr{G}\,\mathbf{y}\bar{\mathbf{y}} = 1, & \mathscr{G}\,\mathbf{z}\bar{\mathbf{y}} = 0, \\ \mathscr{G}\,\mathbf{x}\bar{\mathbf{z}} = 0, & \mathscr{G}\,\mathbf{y}\bar{\mathbf{z}} = 0, & \mathscr{G}\,\mathbf{z}\bar{\mathbf{z}} = 1, \end{matrix}\right.$$

determine three definite vectors $\bar{\mathbf{x}}$, $\bar{\mathbf{y}}$, $\bar{\mathbf{z}}$. From these equations

·63
$$\mathscr{G}\mathbf{x}\,(\lambda\bar{\mathbf{x}} + \mu\bar{\mathbf{y}} + \nu\bar{\mathbf{z}}) = \lambda, \quad \mathscr{G}\mathbf{y}\,(\lambda\bar{\mathbf{x}} + \mu\bar{\mathbf{y}} + \nu\bar{\mathbf{z}}) = \mu, \quad \mathscr{G}\mathbf{z}\,(\lambda\bar{\mathbf{x}} + \mu\bar{\mathbf{y}} + \nu\bar{\mathbf{z}}) = \nu,$$

and therefore the three equations ·14 are equivalent simply to

·64
$$\mathbf{r} = \lambda_{\mathbf{r}}\bar{\mathbf{x}} + \mu_{\mathbf{r}}\bar{\mathbf{y}} + \nu_{\mathbf{r}}\bar{\mathbf{z}}:$$

·65 *The vectors* $\bar{\mathbf{x}}$, $\bar{\mathbf{y}}$, $\bar{\mathbf{z}}$ *compose a frame, and the coefficients of any vector in this frame are its projected products in the frame* **xyz**.

The frame $\bar{\mathbf{x}}\bar{\mathbf{y}}\bar{\mathbf{z}}$ is called the *polar* of the frame **xyz**, and the projected products $\lambda_{\mathbf{r}}$, $\mu_{\mathbf{r}}$, $\nu_{\mathbf{r}}$ are called the *polar coefficients* of **r** in **xyz**. The relation between the two sets of vectors **x**, **y**, **z** and $\bar{\mathbf{x}}$, $\bar{\mathbf{y}}$, $\bar{\mathbf{z}}$ defined by ·62 is symmetrical, and ·45 shews that the product of the spatial products of the two sets is unity, confirming that if one set forms a frame, so also does the other. The relations between the fundamental magnitudes of a frame and the fundamental magnitudes of its polar are implied by the symmetry of the relation between the two frames; the fundamentals of the polar are the six numbers such that for every vector

$$\lambda_{\mathbf{r}} = S^1\chi_{\mathbf{r}}, \quad \mu_{\mathbf{r}} = S^2\chi_{\mathbf{r}}, \quad \nu_{\mathbf{r}} = S^3\chi_{\mathbf{r}}$$

is equivalent to $\xi_{\mathbf{r}} = \bar{S}^1 v_{\mathbf{r}}, \quad \eta_{\mathbf{r}} = \bar{S}^2 v_{\mathbf{r}}, \quad \zeta_{\mathbf{r}} = \bar{S}^3 v_{\mathbf{r}}.$

To set out the consequences of this equivalence would be formally to reproduce the algebra of 342·4, which nowhere depends on any hypothesis as to whether the numbers employed are real or complex.

In virtue of ·65, we can replace ·16 by the theorem that

·67 *If* **xyz** *and* $\bar{\mathbf{x}}\bar{\mathbf{y}}\bar{\mathbf{z}}$ *are frames polar to each other, then for any two vectors* **r**, **s**,

$$\mathscr{G}\,\mathbf{rs} = \mathscr{G}\,\mathbf{xr}\,\mathscr{G}\,\bar{\mathbf{x}}\mathbf{s} + \mathscr{G}\,\mathbf{yr}\,\mathscr{G}\,\bar{\mathbf{y}}\mathbf{s} + \mathscr{G}\,\mathbf{zr}\,\mathscr{G}\,\bar{\mathbf{z}}\mathbf{s}.$$

413. Veclines and vecplanes; perpendicularity.

·1. Two vectors of which one is a multiple of the other are said to be
·11 °*parallel* or *collinear*. The zero vector is collinear with every vector, but if **r**, **s** are proper vectors, a proper vector can be collinear with both **r** and **s** only if **r** and **s** are themselves collinear, in which case every vector collinear with one

* The meaning of 1, like the meaning of 0, depends on the numbers which are used, but the property utilised here is common to all numerical meanings of the symbol.

of the two is collinear with the other. The class composed of all the vectors
collinear with a proper vector $\mathbf{r}$ is called the vector line or °*vecline* containing ·12
$\mathbf{r}$. °The zero vector belongs to every vecline, but no two veclines have any ·13
proper vector in common.

If $\mathbf{r}$ and $\mathbf{s}$ are collinear, the spatial product of these two and *any* third vector is zero; on the other hand if $\mathbf{r}$ and $\mathbf{s}$ are not collinear, it follows from 2·37 that it is possible to find a third vector such that the spatial product of the
three is not zero: °two vectors can serve as two of the axes of a vector frame ·15
if and only if they are not collinear.

·2. Two vectors whose projected product is zero are said to be °*perpendicular**. ·21
If two vectors are perpendicular, any multiple of the one is perpendicular to any multiple of the other; if either of the vectors is not zero, we may say that it is the vecline containing this vector that is perpendicular to the other vector; if neither vector is zero, the veclines containing them are perpendicular
veclines. °*The zero vector is perpendicular to every vector and to every vecline,* ·24
and since the simultaneous vanishing of $\lambda_\mathbf{r}$, $\mu_\mathbf{r}$, $\nu_\mathbf{r}$ *identifies* $\mathbf{r}$ with the zero vector, this property belongs to the zero vector alone.

·3. Let $\mathbf{r}$, $\mathbf{s}$ be two vectors that are not collinear and let $\mathbf{t}$ be a third vector associated with them to form a vector frame. Then the vector $\bar{\mathbf{t}}$ determined by the equations

$$\mathscr{S}\,\mathbf{r}\bar{\mathbf{t}} = 0, \quad \mathscr{S}\,\mathbf{s}\bar{\mathbf{t}} = 0, \quad \mathscr{S}\,\mathbf{t}\bar{\mathbf{t}} = 1 \qquad \cdot 31$$

is by definition perpendicular to both $\mathbf{r}$ and $\mathbf{s}$ and is not zero because it is not perpendicular to $\mathbf{t}$; moreover, any multiple of $\bar{\mathbf{t}}$ is perpendicular to both $\mathbf{r}$ and $\mathbf{s}$, and any vector perpendicular to both $\mathbf{r}$ and $\mathbf{s}$ is a multiple of $\bar{\mathbf{t}}$:

If two vectors are not collinear, there is one and only one vecline which is ·32
perpendicular to them both,

and every vector perpendicular to them both is contained in this vecline.

·4. By the vector plane or °*vecplane* determined by two vectors $\mathbf{x}$, $\mathbf{y}$ that ·41
are not collinear, we mean the class to which a vector belongs if and only if it is expressible in the form $\xi\mathbf{x} + \eta\mathbf{y}$. The vectors in the vecplane determined by two vectors $\mathbf{x}$, $\mathbf{y}$ that are not collinear have two distinguishing properties which are easily found by associating with $\mathbf{x}$ and $\mathbf{y}$ a third vector $\mathbf{z}$ to form a frame. The vector $\mathbf{r}$ then belongs to the vecplane determined by $\mathbf{x}$ and $\mathbf{y}$ if and only if for some choice of $\mathbf{z}$ the coefficient $\zeta_\mathbf{r}$ is zero; but for any vector $\mathbf{r}$,

$$\mathscr{S}\bar{\mathbf{z}}\mathbf{r} = \zeta_\mathbf{r}\,\mathscr{S}\bar{\mathbf{z}}\mathbf{z} = \zeta_\mathbf{r}, \qquad \cdot 42$$

where $\bar{\mathbf{z}}$ is the polar vector described in 2·62, and as in 2·53

$$\mathscr{J}\,\mathbf{xyr} = \zeta_\mathbf{r}\,\mathscr{J}\,\mathbf{xyz} = J\zeta_\mathbf{r}, \qquad \cdot 43$$

and therefore the vanishing of $\zeta_\mathbf{r}$ is equivalent both to the vanishing of $\mathscr{J}\,\mathbf{xyr}$, a condition in which $\mathbf{z}$ does not even seem to be involved, and to the vanishing

* Note that the phrase 'at right angles' is to be avoided for the present.

of $\mathscr{S}\bar{\mathbf{z}}\mathbf{r}$. Since $\mathscr{S}\bar{\mathbf{z}}\mathbf{r}$ is zero if and only if the vecline containing $\bar{\mathbf{z}}$, that is, the vecline perpendicular to both **x** and **y**, is perpendicular to **r**,

·44 *The vectors that belong to a particular vecplane are those which are perpendicular to some definite vecline.*

If **r** and **s** are any two vectors in the vecplane determined by **x** and **y**, the vecline perpendicular to **x** and **y** is perpendicular also to **r** and **s**, and therefore if **r** and **s** are not themselves collinear this is the *only* vecline perpendicular to them both, and the vecplane determined by **r** and **s** is identical with the vecplane determined by **x** and **y**. Hence if two vectors are not collinear, the vecplane which they determine is the only vecplane which includes them both, or in other words,

·45 *If two veclines are distinct, there is one and only one vecplane which contains them both.*

The correlative of this result is easily proved. If two vecplanes are distinct, the veclines perpendicular to them are distinct, and the vectors common to the two vecplanes are the vectors perpendicular to the two perpendiculars; hence from ·32

·46 *If two vecplanes are distinct, the vectors common to them compose a single definite vecline.*

·5. Since every vector perpendicular to all the vectors composing a vecplane is in a definite vecline, it is impossible for two vecplanes to be so related that every vector in one is perpendicular to every vector in the other, and the word perpendicular is available to describe some other relation between vecplanes.

·51 ° Two vecplanes are said to be perpendicular to each other if the veclines perpendicular to them are perpendicular veclines. This definition shews the relation to be symmetrical, but there is a condition, unsymmetrical at first sight, which it is useful to know; if **r** and **s** are proper vectors, **r** is in the vecplane perpendicular to **s** if and only if **r** is perpendicular to **s**, that is, if and only if the vecplanes perpendicular to **r** and **s** are perpendicular vecplanes:

·52 *Perpendicular vecplanes are vecplanes one of which contains the vecline perpendicular to the other.*

Thus all the vecplanes which are perpendicular to a given vecplane have one vecline in common, namely, the vecline perpendicular to that vecplane, just as the veclines perpendicular to a given vecline are all in a single vecplane, namely, the vecplane perpendicular to that vecline.

·6. Vectors or veclines to any number are naturally described as coplanar if there is a single vecplane which contains them all:

·62 *A number of vectors are coplanar if and only if there is a vecline to which they are all perpendicular.*

For **r** to be coplanar with **x** and **y** if **x** and **y** are not collinear, $\mathscr{I}\,\mathbf{xyr}$ must be zero; if **x** and **y** *are* collinear, $\mathscr{I}\,\mathbf{xyr}$ is zero whatever **r** may be, but in this case any third vector *is* coplanar with $\mathbf{x}$ and $\mathbf{y}$; thus in the special case of three vectors there is a simple criterion of coplanarity:

Three vectors are coplanar if and only if their spatial products are zero; ·63

if the spatial product of three vectors taken in one order is zero, their spatial product in any other order is of course zero.

We may use ·63 to replace 2·43:

Three vectors can form a frame if and only if they are not coplanar. ·64

To shew that we are gaining real strength and not simply acquiring a useless vocabulary, let us turn to the expansion

$$\mathbf{r}\,\mathcal{T}\,\mathbf{abc} = \mathbf{a}\,\mathcal{T}\,\mathbf{rbc} + \mathbf{b}\,\mathcal{T}\,\mathbf{arc} + \mathbf{c}\,\mathcal{T}\,\mathbf{abr}, \qquad \cdot 65$$

proved in 2·54 on the hypothesis that $\mathbf{a}$, $\mathbf{b}$, $\mathbf{c}$ form a frame. If $\mathbf{a}$, $\mathbf{b}$, $\mathbf{c}$, $\mathbf{r}$ are any four vectors, either they are all coplanar, in which case the four spatial products in ·65 all vanish and ·65 remains formally true, or three vectors can be selected from them in at least one way so as not to be coplanar and these three can form a frame; if $\mathbf{rbc}$ is a frame to which $\mathbf{a}$ is referred, then

$$\mathbf{a}\,\mathcal{T}\,\mathbf{rbc} = \mathbf{r}\,\mathcal{T}\,\mathbf{abc} + \mathbf{b}\,\mathcal{T}\,\mathbf{rac} + \mathbf{c}\,\mathcal{T}\,\mathbf{rba},$$

which is simply a rearrangement of ·65, and a similar reproduction of ·65 occurs if $\mathbf{rac}$ or $\mathbf{rab}$ is the frame. Thus ·65 is true whether or not $\mathbf{a}$, $\mathbf{b}$, $\mathbf{c}$ form a frame:

For any four vectors $\mathbf{r}$, $\mathbf{a}$, $\mathbf{b}$, $\mathbf{c}$, ·66

$$\mathbf{r}\,\mathcal{T}\,\mathbf{abc} = \mathbf{a}\,\mathcal{T}\,\mathbf{rbc} + \mathbf{b}\,\mathcal{T}\,\mathbf{arc} + \mathbf{c}\,\mathcal{T}\,\mathbf{abr}.$$

An immediate corollary is that

If $\mathbf{a}$, $\mathbf{b}$, $\mathbf{c}$ *are coplanar vectors and* $\mathbf{r}$ *is any vector whatever, then* ·67

$$\mathbf{a}\,\mathcal{T}\,\mathbf{rbc} + \mathbf{b}\,\mathcal{T}\,\mathbf{arc} + \mathbf{c}\,\mathcal{T}\,\mathbf{abr} = 0.$$

414. Vector products.

·1. Among the vectors perpendicular to each of two vectors, there is one that is of special importance. Let $\mathbf{x}$, $\mathbf{y}$ be two vectors that are not parallel, and $\mathbf{z}$ a vector taken with them to form a frame. Also let $\mathbf{k}$ be perpendicular to both $\mathbf{x}$ and $\mathbf{y}$, and let $\mathbf{r}$ be an arbitrary vector. Then

$$\mathcal{T}\,\mathbf{xyr} = \zeta_{\mathbf{r}}\,\mathcal{T}\,\mathbf{xyz}, \quad \mathcal{G}\,\mathbf{kr} = \zeta_{\mathbf{r}}\,\mathcal{G}\,\mathbf{kz}. \qquad \cdot 11$$

It follows that if $$\mathcal{G}\,\mathbf{kz} = \mathcal{T}\,\mathbf{xyz}, \qquad \cdot 12$$

then also $$\mathcal{G}\,\mathbf{kr} = \mathcal{T}\,\mathbf{xyr}; \qquad \cdot 13$$

thus ·12, when combined with the conditions of perpendicularity

$$\mathcal{G}\,\mathbf{kx} = 0, \quad \mathcal{G}\,\mathbf{ky} = 0, \qquad \cdot 14$$

does not really involve the vector $\mathbf{z}$. Moreover, ·12 and ·14 together *determine* $\mathbf{k}$, for they give explicitly the three functions $\lambda_{\mathbf{k}}$, $\mu_{\mathbf{k}}$, $\nu_{\mathbf{k}}$ in a frame obtained by associating a third vector $\mathbf{z}$ with $\mathbf{x}$ and $\mathbf{y}$. The vector $\mathbf{k}$, defined by ·12

·15 and ·14, is called the ° *vector product* of **x** and **y**, and denoted by $\mathscr{V}$ **xy**. It is to be observed that since $\mathscr{I}$ **xyx**, $\mathscr{I}$ **xy**^{2} both vanish necessarily, ·12 includes ·14, and ·12 alone may be regarded as defining **k**:

·16 *The vector product* $\mathscr{V}$ **st** *is the one vector* **q** *which is such that for every vector* **r**,

$$\mathscr{G}\ \mathbf{rq} = \mathscr{I}\ \mathbf{rst}.$$

This definition succeeds, where the original investigation fails, with collinear vectors, for if **s** and **t** are collinear, then $\mathscr{I}$ **rst** is necessarily zero, and therefore **q** is not indeterminate but must be the zero vector.

If **a**, **b**, **c** are any three vectors,

$$\mathscr{G}\,(\mathscr{V}\mathbf{ab})\,\mathbf{r} = \mathscr{I}\ \mathbf{abr}, \quad \mathscr{G}\,(\mathscr{V}\mathbf{ac})\,\mathbf{r} = \mathscr{I}\ \mathbf{acr},$$

and therefore $$\mathscr{G}\,(\mathscr{V}\ \mathbf{ab} + \mathscr{V}\ \mathbf{ac})\,\mathbf{r} = \mathscr{I}\ \mathbf{a}\,(\mathbf{b}+\mathbf{c})\,\mathbf{r};$$

hence, because **r** is arbitrary,

·17 $$\mathscr{V}\ \mathbf{a}\,(\mathbf{b}+\mathbf{c}) = \mathscr{V}\ \mathbf{ab} + \mathscr{V}\ \mathbf{ac}.$$

And because $$\mathscr{I}\ \mathbf{bar} = -\ \mathscr{I}\ \mathbf{abr}$$

for every vector **r**, therefore

·18 $$\mathscr{V}\ \mathbf{ba} = -\ \mathscr{V}\ \mathbf{ab}.$$

·2. From 3·66 we see that

·21 *For any five vectors* **l**, **m**, **r**, **s**, **t**,

$$\mathscr{G}\ \mathbf{lm}\ \mathscr{I}\ \mathbf{rst} = \mathscr{G}\ \mathbf{lr}\ \mathscr{I}\ \mathbf{mst} + \mathscr{G}\ \mathbf{ls}\ \mathscr{I}\ \mathbf{mtr} + \mathscr{G}\ \mathbf{lt}\ \mathscr{I}\ \mathbf{mrs},$$

and substituting from ·16 we have the formula

·22 $$\mathscr{G}\ \mathbf{lm}\ \mathscr{I}\ \mathbf{rst} = \mathscr{G}\ \mathbf{lr}\ \mathscr{G}\ \mathbf{m}\,(\mathscr{V}\mathbf{st}) + \mathscr{G}\ \mathbf{ls}\ \mathscr{G}\ \mathbf{m}\,(\mathscr{V}\mathbf{tr}) + \mathscr{G}\ \mathbf{lt}\ \mathscr{G}\ \mathbf{m}\,(\mathscr{V}\mathbf{rs}),$$

which can be written

·23 $$\mathscr{G}\ \mathbf{m}\,(\mathbf{l}\ \mathscr{I}\ \mathbf{rst}) = \mathscr{G}\ \mathbf{m}\,\{\mathscr{V}\mathbf{st}\ \mathscr{G}\ \mathbf{lr} + \mathscr{V}\mathbf{tr}\ \mathscr{G}\ \mathbf{ls} + \mathscr{V}\mathbf{rs}\ \mathscr{G}\ \mathbf{lt}\},$$

since $\mathscr{I}$ **rst**, $\mathscr{G}$ **lr**, $\mathscr{G}$ **ls**, $\mathscr{G}$ **lt** are mere numbers. But ·23 can be true *whatever* vector **m** may be only if

·24 *For any four vectors* **k**, **r**, **s**, **t**,

$$\mathbf{k}\ \mathscr{I}\ \mathbf{rst} = \mathscr{V}\mathbf{st}\ \mathscr{G}\ \mathbf{kr} + \mathscr{V}\ \mathbf{tr}\ \mathscr{G}\ \mathbf{ks} + \mathscr{V}\ \mathbf{rs}\ \mathscr{G}\ \mathbf{kt}.$$

The last theorem shews that

·25 *If the three vectors* **x**, **y**, **z** *form a frame, so also do the three vector products* $\mathscr{V}$ **yz**, $\mathscr{V}$ **zx**, $\mathscr{V}$ **xy**,

and shews that the coefficients of **r** in this frame are $J^{-1}\lambda_{\mathbf{r}}$, $J^{-1}\mu_{\mathbf{r}}$, $J^{-1}\nu_{\mathbf{r}}$. These results are in agreement with ·12 and ·14, which taken together express that in the frame **xyz** the vector product $\mathscr{V}$ **xy** has the polar coefficients 0, 0, J, that is to say, that this vector product is $J\bar{\mathbf{z}}$:

·26 *If* $\bar{\mathbf{x}}\bar{\mathbf{y}}\bar{\mathbf{z}}$ *is the frame polar to* **xyz**, *then*

$$\mathscr{V}\ \mathbf{yz} = J\bar{\mathbf{x}}, \quad \mathscr{V}\ \mathbf{zx} = J\bar{\mathbf{y}}, \quad \mathscr{V}\ \mathbf{xy} = J\bar{\mathbf{z}}.$$

Thus there is no radical difference between ·22 and 2·67.

·3. An elegant use of ·16 is to express the vector product $\mathcal{V}\mathbf{st}$ with reference to a frame **xyz**. In terms of the coefficients of **r**, 2·16 and 2·37 give

$$\mathcal{G}\,\mathbf{qr} = \nu_{\mathbf{q}}\chi_{\mathbf{r}}, \quad \mathcal{J}\,\mathbf{rst} = J\,[[\chi_{\mathbf{p}}]], \tag{·31}$$

and therefore for ·16 to be an *identity* as far as **r** is concerned,

$$(\lambda_{\mathbf{q}}, \mu_{\mathbf{q}}, \nu_{\mathbf{q}}) = J \left\| \begin{matrix} \xi_{\mathbf{s}} & \eta_{\mathbf{s}} & \zeta_{\mathbf{s}} \\ \xi_{\mathbf{t}} & \eta_{\mathbf{t}} & \zeta_{\mathbf{t}} \end{matrix} \right\|; \tag{·32}$$

similarly from 2·16 and 2·46,

$$\mathcal{G}\,\mathbf{qr} = \chi_{\mathbf{q}}\upsilon_{\mathbf{r}}, \quad \mathcal{J}\,\mathbf{rst} = J^{-1}\,[[\upsilon_{\mathbf{p}}]], \tag{·33}$$

and the coefficients of the vector product are given by

$$(\xi_{\mathbf{q}}, \eta_{\mathbf{q}}, \zeta_{\mathbf{q}}) = J^{-1} \left\| \begin{matrix} \lambda_{\mathbf{s}} & \mu_{\mathbf{s}} & \nu_{\mathbf{s}} \\ \lambda_{\mathbf{t}} & \mu_{\mathbf{t}} & \nu_{\mathbf{t}} \end{matrix} \right\|. \tag{·34}$$

·4. An immediate application of ·34 is to the evaluation of $\mathcal{V}\mathbf{r}(\mathcal{V}\mathbf{st})$, a vector which being perpendicular to $\mathcal{V}\mathbf{st}$ is coplanar with **s** and **t**. In a frame **xyz**, the polar coefficients of **x** are the projected products $\mathcal{G}\,\mathbf{x}^2$, $\mathcal{G}\,\mathbf{xy}$, $\mathcal{G}\,\mathbf{xz}$, and the polar coefficients of $\mathcal{V}\mathbf{yz}$ are $\mathcal{J}\,\mathbf{xyz}$, 0, 0. Hence $\mathcal{V}\mathbf{x}(\mathcal{V}\mathbf{yz})$ has the coefficients

$$J^{-1} \left\| \begin{matrix} \mathcal{G}\,\mathbf{x}^2 & \mathcal{G}\,\mathbf{xy} & \mathcal{G}\,\mathbf{xz} \\ J & 0 & 0 \end{matrix} \right\|,$$

that is

$$\left\| \begin{matrix} \mathcal{G}\,\mathbf{x}^2 & \mathcal{G}\,\mathbf{xy} & \mathcal{G}\,\mathbf{xz} \\ 1 & 0 & 0 \end{matrix} \right\|,$$

and therefore if **r**, **s**, **t** are not coplanar,

$$\mathcal{V}\mathbf{r}(\mathcal{V}\mathbf{st}) = \mathbf{s}\,\mathcal{G}\,\mathbf{rt} - \mathbf{t}\,\mathcal{G}\,\mathbf{rs}. \tag{·41}$$

If **s** is collinear with **t**, the vectors $\mathcal{V}\mathbf{r}(\mathcal{V}\mathbf{st})$ and $\mathbf{s}\,\mathcal{G}\,\mathbf{rt} - \mathbf{t}\,\mathcal{G}\,\mathbf{rs}$ are both zero, and if **s** is not collinear with **t**, then **r**, even if coplanar with **s** and **t**, is expressible as the sum of two vectors **l**, **m** neither of which is coplanar with **s** and **t**, and a double application of ·41, justified by ·17, ·18 and 2·18, gives

$$\begin{aligned} \mathcal{V}\mathbf{r}(\mathcal{V}\mathbf{st}) &= \mathcal{V}\mathbf{l}(\mathcal{V}\mathbf{st}) + \mathcal{V}\mathbf{m}(\mathcal{V}\mathbf{st}) \\ &= \mathbf{s}\,(\mathcal{G}\,\mathbf{lt} + \mathcal{G}\,\mathbf{mt}) - \mathbf{t}\,(\mathcal{G}\,\mathbf{ls} + \mathcal{G}\,\mathbf{ms}) \\ &= \mathbf{s}\,\mathcal{G}\,\mathbf{rt} - \mathbf{t}\,\mathcal{G}\,\mathbf{rs}. \end{aligned}$$

Hence there are no cases of exception, and

For any three vectors **r**, **s**, **t**, ·42

$$\mathcal{V}\mathbf{r}(\mathcal{V}\mathbf{st}) = \mathbf{s}\,\mathcal{G}\,\mathbf{rt} - \mathbf{t}\,\mathcal{G}\,\mathbf{rs}.$$

Intimately related to ·42 is a valuable expression for the projected product of two vector products. If **q**, **r**, **s**, **t** are any four vectors, then by a double application of ·16 $\mathcal{G}(\mathcal{V}\mathbf{qr})(\mathcal{V}\mathbf{st}) = \mathcal{J}\,\mathbf{qr}(\mathcal{V}\mathbf{st}) = \mathcal{G}\,\mathbf{q}\,\{\mathcal{V}\mathbf{r}(\mathcal{V}\mathbf{st})\}$,

and therefore from ·42 it follows that

For any four vectors **q**, **r**, **s**, **t**, ·43

$$\mathcal{G}(\mathcal{V}\mathbf{qr})(\mathcal{V}\mathbf{st}) = \left| \begin{matrix} \mathcal{G}\,\mathbf{qs} & \mathcal{G}\,\mathbf{qt} \\ \mathcal{G}\,\mathbf{rs} & \mathcal{G}\,\mathbf{rt} \end{matrix} \right|.$$

This result includes all the relations between the fundamentals of a frame and those of its polar, but it is recorded not for this reason only but because it is of continual service. If the use of ·42 enables us to avoid treating any particular cases of ·43 as exceptional, it is only by going behind ·42 that we can realise that the determinantal form into which the result is thrown is not accidental. One explanation is derived from 2·45, which gives

·44 $$\mathscr{I}\mathbf{rst}\,\mathscr{I}\mathbf{qr}\,(\mathscr{V}\mathbf{st}) = \begin{vmatrix} \mathscr{G}\mathbf{qr} & \mathscr{G}\mathbf{qs} & \mathscr{G}\mathbf{qt} \\ \mathscr{G}\mathbf{r}^2 & \mathscr{G}\mathbf{rs} & \mathscr{G}\mathbf{rt} \\ \mathscr{I}\mathbf{rst} & 0 & 0 \end{vmatrix},$$

implying ·43 unless $\mathscr{I}\mathbf{rst}$ is zero. Or if we go back only to the expression in the last paragraph for the coefficients of $\mathscr{V}\mathbf{x}\,(\mathscr{V}\mathbf{yz})$ in the frame **xyz**, we see that since the vector **q** has in this frame the polar coefficients $\mathscr{G}\mathbf{xq}$, $\mathscr{G}\mathbf{yq}$, $\mathscr{G}\mathbf{zq}$, the projected product $\mathscr{G}\mathbf{q}\,\{\mathscr{V}\mathbf{x}\,(\mathscr{V}\mathbf{yz})\}$ has the value

$$\begin{vmatrix} \mathscr{G}\mathbf{qx} & \mathscr{G}\mathbf{qy} & \mathscr{G}\mathbf{qz} \\ \mathscr{G}\mathbf{x}^2 & \mathscr{G}\mathbf{xy} & \mathscr{G}\mathbf{xz} \\ 1 & 0 & 0 \end{vmatrix},$$

and this again establishes ·43 except for the case in which **r**, **s**, **t** are coplanar. Yet another proof is furnished by the algebraical identity

$$\begin{vmatrix} S\chi_{\mathbf{q}}\chi_{\mathbf{s}} & S\chi_{\mathbf{q}}\chi_{\mathbf{t}} \\ S\chi_{\mathbf{r}}\chi_{\mathbf{s}} & S\chi_{\mathbf{r}}\chi_{\mathbf{t}} \end{vmatrix} = - \begin{vmatrix} L & R & Q & \eta_{\mathbf{q}}\zeta_{\mathbf{r}} - \zeta_{\mathbf{q}}\eta_{\mathbf{r}} \\ R & M & P & \zeta_{\mathbf{q}}\xi_{\mathbf{r}} - \xi_{\mathbf{q}}\zeta_{\mathbf{r}} \\ Q & P & N & \xi_{\mathbf{q}}\eta_{\mathbf{r}} - \eta_{\mathbf{q}}\xi_{\mathbf{r}} \\ \eta_{\mathbf{s}}\zeta_{\mathbf{t}} - \zeta_{\mathbf{s}}\eta_{\mathbf{t}} & \zeta_{\mathbf{s}}\xi_{\mathbf{t}} - \xi_{\mathbf{s}}\zeta_{\mathbf{t}} & \xi_{\mathbf{s}}\eta_{\mathbf{t}} - \eta_{\mathbf{s}}\xi_{\mathbf{t}} & 0 \end{vmatrix}$$

which differs only in notation from 332·87.

A particular case of ·43 is

·45 $$\mathscr{G}\,(\mathscr{V}\mathbf{st})^2 = \mathscr{G}\mathbf{s}^2\,\mathscr{G}\mathbf{t}^2 - (\mathscr{G}\mathbf{st})^2,$$

an identity of fundamental importance.

415. Nul vectors; isotropic veclines and vecplanes.

·11 **·1.** A vector whose projected square is zero is said to be °*nul* or *isotropic**. In ordinary space and in the algebraic space which exactly corresponds to ordinary space the only nul vector is the zero vector. But for **r** to be nul all that is necessary is that the three coefficients of **r** in a frame **xyz** should satisfy

·12 the one equation $$S\chi^2 = 0,$$

and there is therefore in complex space a quadruple† infinity of nul vectors. It is of complex space that we are understood to speak when nul vectors are used or discussed.

* This word was introduced into geometry by Laguerre, who explained his choice carefully (*Nouv. Ann. des Math.*, ser. 2, vol. IX, p. 165, 1870; *Oeuvres*, vol. II, p. 89).

† ·12 is equivalent to two relations between six real numbers.

It would of course be possible nominally to exclude nul vectors or nul vectors other than the zero vector by explicit hypothesis, simply by including among the essential characteristics of a proper vector that the projected square is *not* zero. But (i) nul vectors form the basis of many of the applications of complex geometry to ordinary space; (ii) if their existence was a disease, their exclusion would be no remedy, since it would result in some frames having no polars and some pairs of vectors having no vector product, and would falsify such theorems as 3·46 and 3·62: two vecplanes might have no proper vectors in common, and there would be vecplanes with no veclines perpendicular to them; (iii) it would remain true that in complex space *something* corresponds to a set of coefficients satisfying ·12 just as a proper vector corresponds to a set of coefficients not satisfying ·12; this new concept would demand study, and the change would reduce to a mere change of vocabulary, 3·46 for example taking the form that two distinct vecplanes have in common either a vecline or a quasivecline but not both.

·2. Since every multiple of a nul vector is nul, the nul vectors in complex geometry compose definite veclines, themselves described as nul or isotropic. But the nul vectors in the vecplane through two vectors $\mathbf{x}$, $\mathbf{y}$ that are not collinear are the vectors of the form $\xi\mathbf{x} + \eta\mathbf{y}$ where

$$L\xi^2 + 2R\xi\eta + M\eta^2 = 0,$$ ·23

L, R, M having the same meaning as in 2·11, and since the determinant

$$\begin{vmatrix} 0 & 0 & Q \\ 0 & 0 & P \\ Q & P & N \end{vmatrix},$$

to which [[S]] reduces if L, R, M are simultaneously zero, vanishes identically, one at least of the three coefficients L, R, M must be different from zero, and ·23 is necessarily an effective equation, not an identity. Hence ° there are no vecplanes that consist wholly of nul vectors. ·24

·3. Mere comparison of definitions shews that

A nul vector or vecline is one that is perpendicular to itself. ·31

From ·23 it follows that

Two distinct nul veclines or two nul vectors that are not collinear can not be perpendicular, ·33

for if $\mathbf{x}$ and $\mathbf{y}$ are nul, L and M are zero and it is impossible for R, which is $\mathscr{S}\mathbf{xy}$, also to be zero.

To imagine a paradox in ·31 is to mistake completely the relation of complex geometry to ordinary space. Of the assumptions of Euclidean geometry, complex geometry accepts some and rejects others, and therefore of the properties of ordinary space complex space shares some but not all. There are no self-perpendicular lines in real space, but equally there are no nul vectors except the zero vector. Analogy is to be sought by comparing perpendicular veclines in complex space with conjugate diameters of a given conicoid; in general, conjugate diameters are distinct, but asymptotes, if there are any, are self-conjugate.

·4. Because of ·24, no vecplane can be called nul, but a vecplane is said to be °*isotropic* if the vecline to which it is perpendicular is isotropic. From ·31 and this definition, ·41

·42 *An isotropic vecplane is a vecplane that contains the vecline to which it is perpendicular,*

and ·33 enables us to add that

·43 *If a vecplane is isotropic, the vecline to which it is perpendicular is the only nul vecline that it contains.*

From ·31 and 3·51

·44 *An isotropic vecplane is one that is perpendicular to itself.*

The vecplane containing the two vectors **x**, **y** of a frame **xyz** is isotropic if $\mathscr{G}\bar{\mathbf{z}}^2$ is zero, and therefore if

·45 $$LM - R^2 = 0.$$

Since the equation ·23 is a quadratic equation in $\xi : \eta$ with $LM - R^2$ for its discriminant,

·46 *If a vecplane is not isotropic, it contains two and only two distinct nul veclines.*

On the other hand, if α is a vecline and β is a nul vecline in an isotropic vecplane that contains α, then because the vecplane perpendicular to β contains α, therefore the vecplane perpendicular to α contains β: that is, β is one of the nul veclines in the vecplane perpendicular to α; conversely if β is a nul vecline in the vecplane perpendicular to α, the vecplane perpendicular to β is an isotropic vecplane containing α. Since the vecplane perpendicular to α is or is not isotropic according as α is or is not nul,

·47 *If a vecline is nul, the vecplane to which it is perpendicular is the only isotropic vecplane that contains it,*

and

·48 *If a vecline is not nul, there are two and only two distinct isotropic vecplanes in which it is contained.*

·5. For the vecplane determined by two vectors **r**, **s** that are not collinear to be isotropic, the proper vectors perpendicular to both **r** and **s** must be nul; the vector product $\mathscr{V}\mathbf{rs}$ is not the zero vector unless **r** and **s** are collinear; moreover, if **r** and **s** *are* collinear and the vector-field is complex, there *is* one isotropic vecplane if not two containing them both:

·51 *Two vectors in complex space are contained in a vecplane that is isotropic if and only if their vector product is nul.*

From 4·45 it follows that the equation

·52 $$\mathscr{G}(\mathscr{V}\mathbf{rs})^2 = 0$$

·53 is equivalent to $$\mathscr{G}\mathbf{r}^2\,\mathscr{G}\mathbf{s}^2 = (\mathscr{G}\mathbf{rs})^2,$$

a form which will be found essential to the discovery of the most peculiar properties of vectors in isotropic vecplanes; the condition is expressible readily in words:

·54 *Two vectors in complex space are contained in a vecplane that is isotropic if and only if the product of their projected squares is the square of their projected product.*

CHAPTER IV 2

DIRECTIONS AND ANGLES IN ALGEBRAIC VECSPACE

420. Introduction. 421. The amounts of a vector; measured vectors; directions. 2. Congenial directions; the two aspects of an isotropic vecplane. 423. Traversed vector-irs; cyclic directions; prepared vecplanes; angles; right angles and perpendicularity. 4. Areal products; erection in an anisotropic vecplane. 425. Vector frames in a cplane.

420. Introduction.

Vectors in an algebraic vecspace, real or complex, no less than in the space f real geometry, have directions and amounts. The difference is that directions re defined by means of vectors instead of vectors by means of directions, but he mathematical relations and phraseology are unaltered; moreover, it is a imple step from directions to angles.

The problem of defining direction might be solved for a real algebraic vec-pace by *identifying* a direction with a vector whose projected square is unity, r rather, to use terms that we are about to define, with a measured vector of nit amount. In complex space however, not merely would this obvious plan ail completely, since it would leave nul vectors wholly without direction, but he failure is intrinsic in the nature of the method rather than due to any lifficulty that technical ingenuity might hope to remove. To be applicable niversally a solution must proceed from the start along other lines, and it is ne of the triumphs of the Frege-Russell method of definition to furnish a heory satisfactory in every respect.

421. The amounts of a vector; measured vectors; directions.

·1. The square roots of the projected square $\mathscr{G}\mathbf{r}^2$ are called the °*amounts* of ·11
the vector $\mathbf{r}$. In the real algebraic vecspace constructed to correspond to Euclidean space, the zero vector is the only vector of amount zero, and for every other vector $\mathscr{G}\mathbf{r}^2$ is positive and the amounts are distinct real numbers, one positive and the other negative. In complex vecspace, any vector that is nul has zero for its only amount, and a vector that is not nul has, like the proper vectors of ordinary space, two amounts, each of which is the negative of the other.

·2. A vector associated specifically with one of its amounts is called a
°*measured vector*. A vector $\mathbf{r}$ of which r is an amount gives rise to the two ·21
measured vectors $\mathbf{r}_r$, $\mathbf{r}_{-r}$, which are distinct unless $\mathbf{r}$ is nul.

If r is an amount of the vector $\mathbf{r}$, the vector $k\mathbf{r}$ has the amounts kr, $-kr$; naturally it is the measured vector in which $k\mathbf{r}$ is associated with kr that is
·22 said to be the ° *multiple* of $\mathbf{r}_r$ by k. The measured vector in which $k\mathbf{r}$ is associated with $-kr$ is a multiple of $\mathbf{r}_{-r}$, but not of $\mathbf{r}_r$ unless r is zero.

·31 **·3.** Two measured vectors are said to be ° *codirectional* if one of them is a multiple of the other. For $\mathbf{r}_r$, $\mathbf{s}_s$ to be codirectional, there must be numbers h, k not both zero such that

·32 $$k\mathbf{r} = h\mathbf{s}, \quad kr = hs;$$

in general both numbers h, k are different from zero, but if one but not the other of the vectors is the zero vector, one but not the other of the numbers
·33 must be zero. °If $\mathbf{r}_r$, $\mathbf{s}_s$ are codirectional, $\mathbf{r}$, $\mathbf{s}$ are of course parallel. If either r or s is different from zero, the pair of equations ·32 is equivalent simply to

·34 $$s\mathbf{r} = r\mathbf{s},$$

but we can not reduce the condition always to this form, since ·34 is satisfied by *any* two nul vectors, though ·32 makes no exception in favour of nul vectors in requiring the vectors to be parallel. It is important to observe that

·35 *Two measured vectors that are both codirectional with a measured vector other than that derived from the zero vector are codirectional with each other.*

·41 **·4.** The ° *direction* of a proper measured vector $\mathbf{r}_r$ is defined as *the class formed of all the measured vectors codirectional with* $\mathbf{r}_r$. This class includes the zero measured vector whatever $\mathbf{r}_r$ may be, but it follows from ·35—and this is the value of that proposition—that no two distinct directions have any proper measured vector in common. Since a direction is a class of measured vectors, a happy accident of language enables us to speak of a measured vector quite literally as *in* a direction. Thus

·42 *Codirectional measured vectors are measured vectors in the same direction,*

but there is not even an appearance of circularity in our definitions.

·5. If one measured vector in a direction is derived from a proper vector that is nul, every measured vector in that direction is derived from a nul vector, and the direction is a *nul direction.*

·6. If $\mathbf{r}_r$, $\mathbf{s}_s$ are codirectional, then also $\mathbf{r}_{-r}$, $\mathbf{s}_{-s}$ are codirectional. Thus to every direction corresponds a second direction such that the measured vectors in the two directions are derived from the same vectors, and each of these vectors is associated in each direction with the negative of the amount with which it is associated in the other direction. Of two directions related in this
·64 way, one is said to be opposite to, or the reverse of, the other. °A nul direction is its own reverse, but a direction that is not nul is necessarily distinct from its reverse.

·7. By a direction of a vector $\mathbf{r}$ is meant the direction of the measured vector $\mathbf{r}_r$ obtained by associating $\mathbf{r}$ with an amount r of $\mathbf{r}$, and $\mathbf{r}$ is said to

have the amount r in this direction. Thus °a vector that is not nul, like a ·72
proper vector in real space, has two directions, one the reverse of the other,
and its amount in one direction is the negative of its amount in the other
direction. Also °the zero vector in complex as in real space has every direction ·73
and its amount in every direction is zero. But °a proper nul vector gives rise ·74
to only one measured vector and therefore has but a single direction.

Let Π be the direction of a proper measured vector $\mathbf{p}_p$ that is not nul. Then if r is any number, the vector $(r/p)\,\mathbf{p}$ is a vector, and is the only vector, which has Π for a direction and r for its amount in that direction:

A vector with a direction that is not nul is determined by its amount in that ·75
direction.

But there is no corresponding specification of a nul vector.

If $\mathbf{x}$ is a proper vector, a vector $\mathbf{r}$ collinear with $\mathbf{x}$ can be expressed in one way only as $\xi_{\mathbf{r}}\mathbf{x}$, and if $\mathbf{x}$ is given, $\xi_{\mathbf{r}}$ serves as a numerical measure of $\mathbf{r}$, whether or not $\mathbf{x}$ is nul. That is, quantitative comparison of different vectors in a single vecline is always possible, and the basis of comparison is arbitrary. But vectors in different veclines can not be compared effectively if one of the veclines is nul, even if the other vecline also is nul.

422. Congenial directions; the two aspects of an isotropic vecplane.

·1. One property of codirectional measured vectors has to be recorded. If $\mathbf{r}_r$ is the multiple of $\mathbf{s}_s$ by k, then

$$\mathscr{G}\mathbf{rs} = k\,\mathscr{G}\,\mathbf{s}^2 = ks^2 = rs:$$

If two vectors are parallel, their projected product is the product of their ·11
amounts in a common direction.

In real space the converse of this theorem is true: if the projected product of two vectors is the product of an amount of one and an amount of the other, the vectors are parallel vectors measured in the same direction. In complex space however this converse fails, as is apparent from the identity

$$\mathscr{G}\,\mathbf{r}^2\,\mathscr{G}\,\mathbf{s}^2 - (\mathscr{G}\,\mathbf{rs})^2 = \mathscr{G}\,(\mathscr{V}\,\mathbf{rs})^2$$

of 14·45; if $(\mathscr{G}\,\mathbf{rs})^2$ is the product of $\mathscr{G}\,\mathbf{r}^2$ and $\mathscr{G}\,\mathbf{s}^2$, it is possible to choose square roots of $\mathscr{G}\,\mathbf{r}^2$ and $\mathscr{G}\,\mathbf{s}^2$ whose product is $\mathscr{G}\,\mathbf{rs}$, and therefore by 15·51

The projected product of two vectors is the product of an amount of one and ·13
an amount of the other if the vectors are in an isotropic vecplane.

·2. It is worth while to press a little farther the analysis of this case. Let
us describe two measured vectors as °*congenial* if their projected product is the ·21
product of their amounts; $\mathbf{r}_r$, $\mathbf{s}_s$ are congenial if

$$\mathscr{G}\,\mathbf{rs} = rs. \qquad \cdot 22$$

If two measured vectors are congenial, every multiple of the one is congenial with every multiple of the other. The property therefore belongs essentially to the *directions* of the measured vectors, and the directions also are to be described as congenial. Thus ·11 asserts that

·23 *Every direction is congenial with itself,*

and ·13 that

·24 *If two directions are in an isotropic vecplane, either they are congenial or each is congenial with the reverse of the other;*

1·64 and ·24 emphasise that

·25 *The nul direction in an isotropic vecplane is congenial with every direction in the vecplane:*

the projected product of a proper nul vector **r** and another vector is not in general zero, but the isotropic vecplane which contains **r** is formed of precisely those vectors for which this projected product does vanish.

·3. If **r**, **s**, **t** are any three vectors in a given isotropic vecplane, then because the vectors $\mathcal{V}\,\mathbf{rs}$, $\mathcal{V}\,\mathbf{rt}$ are parallel nul vectors, the projected product of these vector products is zero. But by 14·43,

$$\mathcal{S}\,(\mathcal{V}\,\mathbf{rs})\,(\mathcal{V}\,\mathbf{rt}) = \mathcal{S}\,\mathbf{r}^2\,\mathcal{S}\,\mathbf{st} - \mathcal{S}\,\mathbf{rs}\,\mathcal{S}\,\mathbf{rt}.$$

Hence if $\mathbf{r}_r$, $\mathbf{s}_s$, $\mathbf{t}_t$ are measured vectors derived from **r**, **s**, **t**, and if $\mathbf{s}_s$, $\mathbf{t}_t$ are both congenial with $\mathbf{r}_r$, then

$$r^2\,(\mathcal{S}\,\mathbf{st} - st) = 0,$$

and if r is not zero, $\mathcal{S}\,\mathbf{st}$ is the product st:

33 *If two directions in an isotropic vecplane are both congenial with a third direction that is not nul, they are congenial with each other.*

·34 Thus °the directions in an isotropic vecplane compose two classes such that two directions are congenial if and only if they belong to the same class;
·35 these classes will be called the °*aspects* of the isotropic vecplane. The directions in one aspect of an isotropic vecplane are the reverses of the directions in the
·37 other aspect; °the nul direction in the vecplane belongs to both aspects, and is the only direction common to them both.

·4. To assert that

·41 *The projected product of two vectors in an isotropic vecplane is the product of their amounts in congenial directions*

is to assemble the results at which we have arrived in their most concise and convenient form. To make a direct application of this theorem, let $\mathbf{p}_p$ be a measured vector that is not nul, in an isotropic vecplane, and let $\mathbf{r}_r$, $\mathbf{s}_s$, ... be any measured vectors in the same aspect of the vecplane as $\mathbf{p}_p$, so that

·42 $$\mathcal{S}\,\mathbf{pr} = pr, \quad \mathcal{S}\,\mathbf{ps} = ps, \quad \ldots;$$

from these equations, if the number of vectors is finite,

·43 $$\mathcal{S}\,\mathbf{p}\,(\mathbf{r} + \mathbf{s} + \ldots) = p\,(r + s + \ldots),$$

and therefore $r+s+\ldots$ is the amount of $\mathbf{r}+\mathbf{s}+\ldots$ in the direction of $\mathbf{r}+\mathbf{s}+\ldots$ that is congenial with the direction of $\mathbf{p}_p$:

If any finite number of vectors in an isotropic vecplane, and their sum, are all measured in congenial directions, the amount of the sum is the sum of the amounts. ·44

It will be found that the two aspects of an isotropic vecplane are analogous not to the two cyclic directions by which a plane in ordinary space can be prepared but to the two directions of a line.

·5. It follows from 13·44 and 13·46 that a vecplane which does not consist wholly of vectors perpendicular to a given proper vector $\mathbf{r}$ contains one and only one vecline perpendicular to $\mathbf{r}$. Hence

In general, the vectors in a given vecplane that are perpendicular to a given proper vector in the vecplane compose a definite vecline. Exception occurs only when the vecplane is isotropic and the vector is in the nul vecline which is both in the vecplane and perpendicular to it. ·52

If $\mathbf{r}$ is a vector in an isotropic vecplane, the nul vecline in the vecplane *is* perpendicular to $\mathbf{r}$, and therefore ·52 implies that if $\mathbf{r}$ is not itself nul, the only vectors in the vecplane that are perpendicular to $\mathbf{r}$ are those in the nul vecline:

In an isotropic vecplane, two vectors are perpendicular if and only if one of them is in the nul vecline. ·53

This theorem accounts for some peculiarities in the analysis connected with a vector frame in an isotropic vecplane, to which we refer in the last section of this chapter.

423. Traversed vector-pairs; cyclic directions; prepared vecplanes; angles; right angles and perpendicularity.

·1. The introduction of angles into an algebraic vecspace presents no difficulty. Angles are defined in the first place as related to measured* vectors, but it is immediately evident that directions alone are really relevant.

The angles between the measured vectors $\mathbf{r}_r$, $\mathbf{s}_s$ are the values of $\epsilon_{\mathrm{P}\Sigma}$ that satisfy the equation

$$rs\cos\epsilon_{\mathrm{P}\Sigma}=\mathscr{G}\mathbf{rs}\,; \qquad \cdot 11$$

it is perhaps superfluous to remark that these angles are simply numbers, real or complex according as the field under consideration is real or complex. Since identically

$$\mathscr{G}\mathbf{r}^2\,\mathscr{G}\mathbf{s}^2-(\mathscr{G}\mathbf{rs})^2=\mathscr{G}(\mathscr{V}\mathbf{rs})^2,$$

·11 and 1·11 imply $\qquad r^2s^2\sin^2\epsilon_{\mathrm{P}\Sigma}=\mathscr{G}(\mathscr{V}\mathbf{rs})^2,$ ·12

* The dependence of directions and angles in algebraic space on measured vectors was indicated in a paper read to the Mathematical Association in 1920 (see *Math. Gazette*, vol. x, p. 26).

and therefore

·13 *If* $\epsilon_{P\Sigma}$ *is an angle between* $\mathbf{r}_r$ *and* $\mathbf{s}_s$, *then* $rs \sin \epsilon_{P\Sigma}$ *is an amount of* $\mathcal{V}\,\mathbf{rs}$.

With the aid of this proposition it is easy* to render almost† all the language of elementary geometry concerning angles significant when used of algebraic space.

·2. The ordered pair of measured vectors $(\mathbf{r}_r, \mathbf{s}_s)$ associated with an angle
·21 $\epsilon_{P\Sigma}$ satisfying ·11, I propose to call‡ a °*traversed vector-pair*. A cyclic direction in algebraic geometry is *a class of traversed vector-pairs* with the property that if $\epsilon_{P\Sigma}$ is the angle associated with $(\mathbf{r}_r, \mathbf{s}_s)$ to form a member of the class then $rs \sin \epsilon_{P\Sigma}$ as well as $rs \cos \epsilon_{P\Sigma}$ is determinate. From ·13 it appears that to distinguish between different values of $rs \sin \epsilon_{P\Sigma}$ consistent with ·11 is to distinguish between different amounts of the vector product $\mathcal{V}\,\mathbf{rs}$. If $\mathcal{V}\,\mathbf{rs}$ really has more than one amount, that is, if $\mathcal{V}\,\mathbf{rs}$ is not nul, its two amounts can be separated only if its two directions are known; moreover, $\mathcal{V}\,\mathbf{rs}$ is always perpendicular to $\mathbf{r}$ and $\mathbf{s}$, and therefore for $\mathcal{V}\,\mathbf{rs}$ to be in a given vecline and not to be nul, $\mathbf{r}$ and $\mathbf{s}$ must be in the vecplane perpendicular to that vecline. This is why in algebraic geometry no less than in the space suggested by
·22 experience °it is with *coplanar* directions that cyclic direction is primarily associated. It proves in fact simplest to make coplanarity an essential condition, not a rule to which exceptions can occur, and so we say that the traversed vector-pair in which $\epsilon_{P\Sigma}$ is associated with $(\mathbf{r}_r, \mathbf{s}_s)$ and the traversed
·23 vector-pair in which ϵ_{MN} is associated with $(\mathbf{m}_m, \mathbf{n}_n)$ are °*cyclically codirectional* if and only if the four vectors $\mathbf{r}$, $\mathbf{s}$, $\mathbf{m}$, $\mathbf{n}$ are coplanar and the vector $\mathcal{V}\,\mathbf{rs}$ measured by the amount $rs \sin \epsilon_{P\Sigma}$ is codirectional with the vector $\mathcal{V}\,\mathbf{mn}$
·24 measured by the amount $mn \sin \epsilon_{MN}$. A °*cyclic direction* is then definable as a class of cyclically codirectional traversed vector-pairs such that no traversed vector-pair excluded from the class is cyclically codirectional with every member of the class. With this definition, the vectors from which the different pairs in a cyclic direction are constructed are simply the vectors in a

* For the sake of brevity I have followed the method of the text rather than a line of argument in many respects preferable. If P, Σ, T are coplanar directions and $\epsilon_{P\Sigma}$, $\epsilon_{\Sigma T}$ are angles between P and Σ and between Σ and T, then except in special cases, one but only one of the angles $\epsilon_{P\Sigma} + \epsilon_{\Sigma T}$, $\epsilon_{P\Sigma} - \epsilon_{\Sigma T}$ is an angle between P and T; this consideration may be used to determine without reference to a third dimension which of the angles $\epsilon_{\Sigma T}$, $-\epsilon_{\Sigma T}$ is measured in the same cyclic direction as $\epsilon_{P\Sigma}$. Yet another order is adopted in section 5·3 of my *Fourth Dimension*.

† The exception is that in complex space an angle can not be described as from one direction to another round a third unless the third is perpendicular to each of the others; the complex number $-z$ is the negative of z, but there is no fundamental relation between complex numbers that corresponds to the possession of the same sign by real numbers.

‡ The phrase is suggested by a term in gunnery; my attempts to express the substance of the paragraphs that follow without the adoption of some equivalent abbreviation were verbose.

single vecplane, and the vector products are all measured in a definite direction perpendicular to this vecplane; the vecplane in association with the cyclic direction is said to be °*prepared*, and the perpendicular direction is ·25
called the direction °*normal* to the prepared vecplane or to the cyclic direction; ·26
angles are said to be traversed or measured *in* the cyclic direction or *round* the normal direction.

There are as many cyclic directions that can be given to a vecplane as there are directions perpendicular to the vecplane; that is to say, in a vecplane that is not isotropic angles may be traversed in two different directions, but in an isotropic vecplane only one cyclic direction is possible. If two cyclic directions involve the same pairs of measured vectors but the vector products are measured in opposite directions, each cyclic direction is called the reverse
of the other. °If one cyclic direction can be associated with a given vecplane, ·28
the only other cyclic direction that this vecplane can have is the reverse
direction. °The cyclic direction of a prepared isotropic vecplane is its own ·29
reverse.

·3. It will help us to observe, without distinguishing definitions from deductions, how exactly the assertions of elementary geometry have become
significant and to what an extent they remain true. °If $\mathbf{r}_r$, $\mathbf{s}_s$ are measured ·31
vectors in a prepared vecplane, the angles from $\mathbf{r}_r$ to $\mathbf{s}_s$ in this prepared vecplane are the values of $\epsilon_{P\Sigma}$ such that $rs\cos\epsilon_{P\Sigma}$ is the projected product $\mathscr{S}\,\mathbf{rs}$ and $rs\sin\epsilon_{P\Sigma}$ is the amount of the vector product $\mathscr{V}\mathbf{rs}$ in the direction normal to the prepared vecplane. If the projected product of $\mathbf{r}$ and $\mathbf{s}$ is $rs\cos\epsilon_{P\Sigma}$, the projected product of $h\mathbf{r}$ and $k\mathbf{s}$ is $hr\,ks\cos\epsilon_{P\Sigma}$, and if the vector product of $\mathbf{r}$ and $\mathbf{s}$ has the amount $rs\sin\epsilon_{P\Sigma}$ in a given direction, the vector product of $h\mathbf{r}$ and $k\mathbf{s}$ has the amount $hr\,ks\sin\epsilon_{P\Sigma}$ in the same direction; hence
°the angles defined by the pair of equations ·32

$$rs\cos\epsilon_{P\Sigma} = \mathscr{S}\,\mathbf{rs}, \quad rs\sin\epsilon_{P\Sigma} = p,$$ ·33

where p is the amount of $\mathscr{V}\mathbf{rs}$ in a given direction, depend on the *directions* of $\mathbf{r}_r$ and $\mathbf{s}_s$, and not at all on the individual measured vectors themselves.

The angles from a direction Σ to a direction P in one cyclic direction are the negatives of the angles from P to Σ in the same cyclic direction, and so also are the angles from P to Σ in the reverse direction. In a given prepared vecplane, an angle that differs by an even multiple of π from an angle from P to Σ is itself an angle from P to Σ. An angle that differs by an odd multiple of π from an angle from P to Σ is an angle from P′ to Σ and is also an angle from P to Σ', where P′, Σ' are the directions opposite to P, Σ; the angles from P′ to Σ' are the angles from P to Σ.

·4. For the pair of equations ·33 can be substituted an equivalent pair sometimes more useful. Let $\mathbf{k}_k$ be any measured vector in the direction in which the vector product $\mathscr{V}\mathbf{rs}$ is to be measured. Then

$$kp = \mathscr{S}\,\mathbf{k}\,(\mathscr{V}\,\mathbf{rs}) = \mathscr{T}\,\mathbf{krs},$$ ·41

and therefore if k is not zero the equation

$$rs \sin \epsilon_{\mathrm{P}\Sigma} = p$$

·42 can be replaced by $$krs \sin \epsilon_{\mathrm{P}\Sigma} = \mathscr{J}\,\mathbf{krs}.$$

If the vecplane in which the angles are traversed is not isotropic, k is different from zero if $\mathbf{k}$ is not the zero vector. If the vecplane is isotropic, k can not be different from zero, and ·42 reduces to an identity, but this is precisely the case in which $r^2 s^2 \sin^2 \epsilon_{\mathrm{P}\Sigma}$ is necessarily zero and no information is added by the adjunction of

$$rs \sin \epsilon_{\mathrm{P}\Sigma} = p$$

to the original equation $$rs \cos \epsilon_{\mathrm{P}\Sigma} = \mathscr{G}\,\mathbf{rs}.$$

Thus there is no exception to the rule that

·43 *If* $\mathbf{k}_k$ *is any proper measured vector in a direction* K, *and* $\mathbf{r}_r$, $\mathbf{s}_s$ *are measured vectors in the prepared vecplane to which* K *is the normal direction, the angles from* $\mathbf{r}_r$ *to* $\mathbf{s}_s$ *in this vecplane are the values of* $\epsilon_{\mathrm{P}\Sigma}$ *satisfying the pair of equations*

$$rs \cos \epsilon_{\mathrm{P}\Sigma} = \mathscr{G}\,\mathbf{rs}, \quad krs \sin \epsilon_{\mathrm{P}\Sigma} = \mathscr{J}\,\mathbf{krs}.$$

·51 **·5.** °In general the angles from one direction to another in a prepared vecplane form a single congruence, for unless r or s is zero, both the cosine and the sine of these angles are determinate. If r or s is zero because the corresponding vector is the zero vector, the equations to be satisfied by an angle from $\mathbf{r}_r$ to $\mathbf{s}_s$ reduce to identities and every angle is possible, as is only natural since the zero vector has every direction. But to consider the angles between directions of which one is nul, is to suppose r or s to be zero while $\mathbf{r}$ or $\mathbf{s}$ is nul but not zero. Then either the projected product is zero and the vector product is nul, as happens if the isotropic vecplane containing the direction assumed to be nul contains the other direction also, or the projected product and the amounts of the vector product are simultaneously different from zero, the two directions determining then a vecplane that is not isotropic. The first case does not differ in effect from that in which one vector is zero: every angle is possible; the second case admits no finite angles, but for many purposes any infinite complex number of which the imaginary part is not zero may be regarded as satisfying the necessary conditions. These results may be expressed briefly if a little vaguely in the assertion that

·54 *If* P, Σ *are two directions of which the first is nul, the angles from* P *to* Σ *and the angles from* Σ *to* P *are wholly indeterminate if* Σ *is in the isotropic vecplane that contains* P, *but if* Σ *is not in this vecplane the only angles possible are infinite.*

Here the character of Σ is not described, but since there is only one nul direction in an isotropic vecplane,

·55 *A nul direction makes every angle with itself, but the only angles possible between two distinct nul directions are infinite angles.*

·6. The vanishing of $\mathcal{S}(\mathcal{V}\mathbf{rs})^2$, unlike the vanishing of $\mathcal{S}\mathbf{r}^2$ or $\mathcal{S}\mathbf{s}^2$, introduces peculiarities rather than difficulties. If $\mathbf{r}$ and $\mathbf{s}$ are not nul but $\mathcal{V}\mathbf{rs}$ is nul, then whether $\mathcal{V}\mathbf{rs}$ is the zero vector or a proper nul vector, the angles between $\mathbf{r}_r$ and $\mathbf{s}_s$ are multiples of π, the even multiples or the odd multiples according as $\mathcal{S}\,\mathbf{rs}$ is rs or $-rs$. It is if $\mathbf{r}$ and $\mathbf{s}$ are parallel that $\mathcal{V}\,\mathbf{rs}$ is the zero vector, and in this case our definitions have the desirable consequence that

The angles between two parallel measured vectors that are not nul, in any prepared vecplane that contains the vecline in which they lie, are the even or the odd multiples of π according as they are measured in the same direction or in opposite directions. ·61

For $\mathcal{V}\mathbf{rs}$ to be nul but not zero, $\mathbf{r}$ and $\mathbf{s}$ must belong to the isotropic vecplane perpendicular to $\mathcal{V}\,\mathbf{rs}$, and

In an isotropic vecplane, the angles between two directions that are not nul are the even or the odd multiples of π according as the directions are congenial or uncongenial. ·62

It need hardly be added that if $\sin \epsilon_{\mathrm{P}\Sigma}$ is zero then $\mathcal{V}\mathbf{rs}$ is nul, and that therefore °the directions which make an angle zero with a given direction P are the directions congenial with P in isotropic vecplanes containing P; that in complex space two directions may be distinct when an angle between them is zero is as natural as that in this space the amount of a vector can be zero when the vector itself is not the zero vector. ·63

·7. It is not necessary to prove analytically that if P, Σ, T are directions in a prepared vecplane and if nul directions are in no way involved, then the sum of an angle $\epsilon_{\mathrm{P}\Sigma}$ and an angle $\epsilon_{\Sigma\mathrm{T}}$ is an angle ϵ_{PT}; the reproduction of the formal relations subsisting in real space between angles and vectors is sufficient evidence. A direct proof is however surprisingly simple.

Let $\mathbf{r}_r$, $\mathbf{s}_s$, $\mathbf{t}_t$ be proper measured vectors in the directions P, Σ, T, and let $\mathbf{k}_k$ be a proper measured vector in the normal direction K round which the angles are to be traversed; also let p, q be the amounts of $\mathcal{V}\mathbf{rs}$, $\mathcal{V}\mathbf{st}$ in the direction K. Then

$$rs \cos \epsilon_{\mathrm{P}\Sigma} = \mathcal{S}\mathbf{rs}, \qquad st \cos \epsilon_{\Sigma\mathrm{T}} = \mathcal{S}\,\mathbf{st}, \tag{·71}$$

$$rs \sin \epsilon_{\mathrm{P}\Sigma} = p, \qquad st \sin \epsilon_{\Sigma\mathrm{T}} = q, \tag{·72}$$

$$krs \sin \epsilon_{\mathrm{P}\Sigma} = \mathcal{J}\,\mathbf{krs}, \quad kst \sin \epsilon_{\Sigma\mathrm{T}} = \mathcal{J}\,\mathbf{kst}, \tag{·73}$$

and therefore

$$rs^2t \cos(\epsilon_{\mathrm{P}\Sigma} + \epsilon_{\Sigma\mathrm{T}}) = \mathcal{S}\,\mathbf{rs}\,\mathcal{S}\,\mathbf{st} - pq, \tag{·74}$$

$$krs^2t \sin(\epsilon_{\mathrm{P}\Sigma} + \epsilon_{\Sigma\mathrm{T}}) = \mathcal{S}\,\mathbf{rs}\,\mathcal{J}\,\mathbf{kst} + \mathcal{S}\mathbf{st}\,\mathcal{J}\,\mathbf{krs}. \tag{·75}$$

But since p, q are the amounts of $\mathcal{V}\mathbf{rs}$, $\mathcal{V}\mathbf{st}$ in a common direction,

$$\begin{aligned} pq &= \mathcal{S}\,(\mathcal{V}\mathbf{rs})\,(\mathcal{V}\mathbf{st}) \\ &= \mathcal{S}\,\mathbf{rs}\,\mathcal{S}\,\mathbf{st} - \mathcal{S}\,\mathbf{rt}\,\mathcal{S}\mathbf{s}^2 \\ &= \mathcal{S}\mathbf{rs}\,\mathcal{S}\,\mathbf{st} - s^2\,\mathcal{S}\mathbf{rt}, \end{aligned}$$

and since $\mathbf{r}$, $\mathbf{s}$, $\mathbf{t}$ are coplanar, the universal relation

$$\mathbf{s}\,\mathcal{J}\,\mathbf{krt} = \mathbf{k}\,\mathcal{J}\,\mathbf{srt} + \mathbf{r}\,\mathcal{J}\,\mathbf{kst} + \mathbf{t}\,\mathcal{J}\,\mathbf{krs}$$

implies $$\mathbf{r}\,\mathcal{J}\,\mathbf{kst} + \mathbf{t}\,\mathcal{J}\,\mathbf{krs} = \mathbf{s}\,\mathcal{J}\,\mathbf{krt},$$

and therefore, the spatial products being simply numbers,

$$\mathcal{G}\,\mathbf{rs}\,\mathcal{J}\,\mathbf{kst} + \mathcal{G}\,\mathbf{st}\,\mathcal{J}\,\mathbf{krs} = \mathcal{G}\,\mathbf{s}^2\,\mathcal{J}\,\mathbf{krt}$$
$$= s^2\,\mathcal{J}\,\mathbf{krt}.$$

Hence ·74, ·75 are equivalent to

·76 $$s^2 rt \cos(\epsilon_{\mathrm{P}\Sigma} + \epsilon_{\Sigma\mathrm{T}}) = s^2\,\mathcal{G}\,\mathbf{rt},$$

·77 $$s^2 krt \sin(\epsilon_{\mathrm{P}\Sigma} + \epsilon_{\Sigma\mathrm{T}}) = s^2\,\mathcal{J}\,\mathbf{krt},$$

and if s is not zero, this is the pair of equations defining the angles from P to T; thus we have a result in which are already included all but one of the cases that would have required special examination if the deduction had been made from elementary geometry:

·78 *If* P, Σ, T *are three directions in a prepared vecplane, then provided only that* Σ *is not nul, the sum of an angle from* P *to* Σ *and an angle from* Σ *to* T *is an angle from* P *to* T.

The exception is inevitable, for if Σ is nul, $\epsilon_{\mathrm{P}\Sigma}$ and $\epsilon_{\Sigma\mathrm{T}}$ are arbitrary or infinite, and their sum is subject to no conditions whatever. If neither Σ nor T is nul, then the sum of an angle ϵ_{PT} and an angle $\epsilon_{\mathrm{T}\Sigma}$ is an angle $\epsilon_{\mathrm{P}\Sigma}$, and therefore any angle ϵ_{PT} can be expressed as the difference between an angle $\epsilon_{\mathrm{P}\Sigma}$ and an angle $\epsilon_{\mathrm{T}\Sigma}$, that is, as the sum of an angle $\epsilon_{\mathrm{P}\Sigma}$ and an angle $\epsilon_{\Sigma\mathrm{T}}$; even if the direction T is nul, this result is true in the sense that ϵ_{PT} and $\epsilon_{\mathrm{P}\Sigma} + \epsilon_{\Sigma\mathrm{T}}$ are together arbitrary or together infinite, and therefore ·78 can be replaced by the assertion of an equivalence:

·79 *If* P, Σ, T *are three directions in a prepared vecplane, then provided only that* Σ *is not nul, the angles from* P *to* T *are the angles obtained by adding an angle from* Σ *to* T *to an angle from* P *to* Σ.

There is no failure of ·79 if the vecplane is isotropic, but the result is then a trivial deduction from ·62.

·8. From ·11 and the definition in 13·21, it follows that

·81 *If two directions are at right angles they are perpendicular.*

If we allow that conversely

·82 *If two directions are perpendicular they are at right angles,*

we must be careful not to confuse this assertion with the assertion that "if ϵ is an angle between two directions P, Σ that are perpendicular then ϵ is an odd multiple of $\frac{1}{2}\pi$", which ·54 and ·55 shew to be false in complex vecspace. It is quite true that a nul direction is a direction that is at right angles to itself, but we must not forget three significant facts: the right angle which a complex direction makes with a perpendicular direction is not the *real* number

$\frac{1}{2}\pi$ at all, but is the *complex* number $\frac{1}{2}\pi + 0i$, that is, the pair of numbers $(\frac{1}{2}\pi, 0)$; a nul direction does not succeed in being at right angles to itself *at the expense of* the more commonplace habit of being in the same direction as itself; the complex right angle does not occupy a position in the least privileged among the angles which a nul direction makes with itself, these angles composing simply the entire aggregate of complex numbers.

424. Areal products; erection in an anisotropic vecplane.

·1. Having used vector products for defining cyclic direction, we need not scruple to use them in other definitions associated with a prepared vecplane.

For example, if $\mathbf{r}$, $\mathbf{s}$ are two vectors in a prepared vecplane, the amount of $\mathscr{V}\,\mathbf{rs}$ in the normal direction is the °*areal product* $\mathscr{A}\,\mathbf{rs}$. The identities ·11

$$(\mathscr{A}\,\mathbf{rs})^2 = \mathscr{G}\mathbf{r}^2\,\mathscr{G}\mathbf{s}^2 - (\mathscr{G}\mathbf{rs})^2, \qquad \cdot 12$$

$$\mathscr{A}\,\mathbf{qr}\,\mathscr{A}\,\mathbf{st} = \mathscr{G}\mathbf{qs}\,\mathscr{G}\mathbf{rt} - \mathscr{G}\mathbf{qt}\,\mathscr{G}\,\mathbf{rs} \qquad \cdot 13$$

come from the application of 2·11 to 14·45 and 14·43, and

In an isotropic vecplane, every areal product is zero. ·14

·2. If $\mathbf{r}$ is any vector in an anisotropic vecplane in which $\mathbf{x}$, $\mathbf{y}$ are vectors of reference, the areal products $\mathscr{A}\,\mathbf{rx}$, $\mathscr{A}\,\mathbf{ry}$ are definite numbers, and there is one and only one vector $\mathbf{t}$ which is such that

$$\mathscr{G}\,\mathbf{tx} = \mathscr{A}\,\mathbf{rx}, \quad \mathscr{G}\,\mathbf{ty} = \mathscr{A}\,\mathbf{ry}. \qquad \cdot 21$$

Moreover, these equations imply for any values of the numbers ξ, η

$$\mathscr{G}\mathbf{t}\,(\xi\mathbf{x} + \eta\mathbf{y}) = \mathscr{A}\,\mathbf{r}\,(\xi\mathbf{x} + \eta\mathbf{y}),$$

and therefore in an anisotropic vecplane there is one definite vector $\mathbf{t}$ related to a given vector $\mathbf{r}$ in such a manner that for every vector $\mathbf{s}$ in the plane the numbers $\mathscr{G}\mathbf{ts}$, $\mathscr{A}\,\mathbf{rs}$ are equal; this vector is said to be obtained by °*erecting* ·23
$\mathbf{r}$, and is denoted by $\mathscr{E}\,\mathbf{r}$. For every pair of vectors,

$$\mathscr{G}\,(\mathscr{E}\,\mathbf{r})\,\mathbf{s} = \mathscr{A}\,\mathbf{rs}, \qquad \cdot 24$$

whence from ·12

$$\{\mathscr{G}\,(\mathscr{E}\,\mathbf{r})\,\mathbf{s}\}^2 = \mathscr{G}\mathbf{r}^2\,\mathscr{G}\mathbf{s}^2 - (\mathscr{G}\mathbf{rs})^2. \qquad \cdot 25$$

·3. Since $\mathscr{V}\,\mathbf{r}^2$ is the zero vector, $\mathscr{A}\,\mathbf{r}^2$ is necessarily zero, and ·24 gives as a special case

$$\mathscr{G}\,(\mathscr{E}\,\mathbf{r})\,\mathbf{r} = 0: \qquad \cdot 31$$

$\mathscr{E}\,\mathbf{r}$ is perpendicular to $\mathbf{r}$. This implies that °$\mathscr{E}\,\mathbf{r}$ is nul if and only if $\mathbf{r}$ is nul. ·32

If in the identity

$$\mathscr{A}\,\mathbf{rs}\,\mathscr{A}\,\mathbf{rt} = \mathscr{G}\mathbf{r}^2\,\mathscr{G}\,\mathbf{st} - \mathscr{G}\,\mathbf{rs}\,\mathscr{G}\mathbf{rt},$$

which is a particular case of ·13, we substitute $\mathscr{E}\,\mathbf{r}$ for $\mathbf{s}$ and use ·24 and ·31, we have for all values of $\mathbf{r}$ and $\mathbf{t}$

$$\mathscr{A}\,\mathbf{r}\,(\mathscr{E}\,\mathbf{r})\,\mathscr{A}\,\mathbf{rt} = \mathscr{G}\,\mathbf{r}^2\,\mathscr{A}\,\mathbf{rt}; \qquad \cdot 34$$

unless $\mathbf{r}$ is the zero vector, $\mathscr{A}\mathbf{rt}$ is not necessarily zero, and ·34 implies

·35 $$\mathscr{A}\mathbf{r}(\mathscr{E}\mathbf{r}) = \mathscr{G}\mathbf{r}^2,$$

while if $\mathbf{r}$ is the zero vector both sides of ·35 vanish. Hence

·36 *For any vector* $\mathbf{r}$, $\quad \mathscr{A}\mathbf{r}(\mathscr{E}\mathbf{r}) = \mathscr{G}\mathbf{r}^2.$

Writing $\mathscr{E}\mathbf{r}$ for $\mathbf{s}$ in ·24 we have

·37 $$\mathscr{A}\mathbf{r}(\mathscr{E}\mathbf{r}) = \mathscr{G}(\mathscr{E}\mathbf{r})^2,$$

·38 and this with ·36 implies $\quad \mathscr{G}(\mathscr{E}\mathbf{r})^2 = \mathscr{G}\mathbf{r}^2,$

which we can combine with ·31 in a descriptive proposition:

·39 *The vector obtained by erecting* $\mathbf{r}$ *is a vector perpendicular to* $\mathbf{r}$ *with the same amounts as* $\mathbf{r}$.

But there is nothing in ·39 to distinguish $\mathscr{E}\mathbf{r}$ from its reverse or to enable us to discover $\mathscr{E}\mathbf{r}$ when $\mathbf{r}$ is nul.

·4. If in ·13 we write $\mathscr{E}\mathbf{r}$ for $\mathbf{t}$ we have

·41 $$\mathscr{A}\mathbf{rq}\,\mathscr{A}(\mathscr{E}\mathbf{r})\,\mathbf{s} = -\,\mathscr{G}(\mathscr{E}\mathbf{r})\,\mathbf{q}\,\mathscr{G}\,\mathbf{rs},$$

·42 whence for all values of $\mathbf{s}$ $\quad \mathscr{A}(\mathscr{E}\mathbf{r})\,\mathbf{s} = -\,\mathscr{G}\mathbf{rs},$

·43 that is, $\quad \mathscr{G}\{\mathscr{E}(\mathscr{E}\mathbf{r})\}\,\mathbf{s} = -\,\mathscr{G}\mathbf{rs};$

·44 hence $\quad \mathscr{E}(\mathscr{E}\mathbf{r}) = -\,\mathbf{r}.$

·5. The effect of erecting a nul vector is remarkable. If $\mathbf{r}$ is nul, $\mathscr{E}\mathbf{r}$ is a multiple of $\mathbf{r}$, and in virtue of ·25

·51 $$\{\mathscr{G}(\mathscr{E}\mathbf{r})\,\mathbf{q}\}^2 = -\,(\mathscr{G}\mathbf{rq})^2$$

·52 for any vector $\mathbf{q}$; thus °*the ratio of* $\mathscr{E}\mathbf{r}$ *to* $\mathbf{r}$ *is a square root of* -1. Moreover, ·24 gives for any two vectors

·53 $$\mathscr{G}(\mathscr{E}\mathbf{r})\,\mathbf{s} = -\,\mathscr{G}\mathbf{r}(\mathscr{E}\mathbf{s});$$

if $\mathbf{r}$ and $\mathbf{s}$ are *collinear* nul vectors, $\mathscr{E}\mathbf{r}$, $\mathscr{E}\mathbf{s}$ are collinear with them and both sides of ·53 vanish, but if $\mathbf{r}$ and $\mathbf{s}$ are nul vectors that are not collinear and if

·54 $$\mathscr{E}\mathbf{r} = j\mathbf{r}, \quad \mathscr{E}\mathbf{s} = k\mathbf{s},$$

·55 ·53 implies $\quad j = -\,k:$

·56 *In any prepared anisotropic vecplane, each of the square roots of* -1 *is associated with one of the nul veclines as the ratio of* $\mathscr{E}\mathbf{r}$ *to* $\mathbf{r}$ *when* $\mathbf{r}$ *is in that vecline.*

·57 ° To know which square root belongs to a particular nul vecline is to know the cyclic direction of the vecplane.

·6. In an isotropic vecplane, erection is not a feasible operation. For ·24 to be true for every value of $\mathbf{s}$, the vector $\mathscr{E}\mathbf{r}$ would have to be in the vecline perpendicular to the vecplane, that is to say, in the nul vecline of the vecplane, whatever the value of $\mathbf{r}$, and therefore $\mathscr{E}\mathbf{r}$ could not have the same amounts as $\mathbf{r}$ unless $\mathbf{r}$ itself was nul. The cause of the failure is in ·14, which shews that for an isotropic vecplane the pair of equations ·21 is satisfied if and only if $\mathbf{t}$ is in the nul vecline.

·7. We may use the erected vector $\mathscr{E}\mathbf{r}$ to shew that constructions which we are accustomed to make in ordinary geometry can usually be postulated in algebraic space. Let $\mathbf{r}$ be any proper anisotropic measured vector in a prepared anisotropic vecplane, and let ϵ be any angle, that is to say, any number, real or complex according as the algebraic space with which we are concerned is real or complex. Let s be any number other than zero, and let $\mathbf{s}$ denote the vector $(s/r)\{\mathbf{r}\cos\epsilon + \mathscr{E}\mathbf{r}\sin\epsilon\}$. By ·31, ·38, ·36,

$$\mathscr{S}\,\mathbf{s}^2 = s^2, \quad \mathscr{S}\,\mathbf{rs} = rs\cos\epsilon, \quad \mathscr{A}\,\mathbf{rs} = rs\sin\epsilon; \qquad \cdot 71$$

hence s is an amount of $\mathbf{s}$, and the direction of $\mathbf{s}_s$ makes an angle ϵ with the direction of $\mathbf{r}_r$. Thus

In any prepared anisotropic vecplane there is a direction making any given angle with any given anisotropic direction; ·72

by 3·51, there is not more than one such direction. Construction and result alike fail if the direction is nul or the vecplane isotropic.

425. Vector frames in a vecplane.

·1. It follows from 13·45 that any two vectors in a given vecplane can serve as vectors of reference for that vecplane if they are not collinear. If two vectors $\mathbf{r}$, $\mathbf{s}$ are given in terms of two vectors $\mathbf{x}$, $\mathbf{y}$ by

$$\mathbf{r} = \chi_{\mathbf{r}}\mathbf{f}, \quad \mathbf{s} = \chi_{\mathbf{s}}\mathbf{f}, \qquad \cdot 11$$

where for work in two dimensions we write,

$$\chi = (\xi, \eta), \quad \mathbf{f} = (\mathbf{x}, \mathbf{y}), \qquad \cdot 12$$

then their projected product is given by

$$\mathscr{S}\,\mathbf{rs} = \mathscr{S}\,(\xi_{\mathbf{r}}\mathbf{x} + \eta_{\mathbf{r}}\mathbf{y})(\xi_{\mathbf{s}}\mathbf{x} + \eta_{\mathbf{s}}\mathbf{y}),$$

that is, by $\quad \mathscr{S}\,\mathbf{rs} = E\xi_{\mathbf{r}}\xi_{\mathbf{s}} + F(\xi_{\mathbf{r}}\eta_{\mathbf{s}} + \eta_{\mathbf{r}}\xi_{\mathbf{s}}) + G\eta_{\mathbf{r}}\eta_{\mathbf{s}} = S\chi_{\mathbf{r}}\chi_{\mathbf{s}},$ ·13

where $\quad S^{11} = E = \mathscr{S}\,\mathbf{x}^2, \; S^{12} = S^{21} = F = \mathscr{S}\,\mathbf{xy}, \; S^{22} = G = \mathscr{S}\,\mathbf{y}^2.$ ·14

For the projected products $\mathscr{S}\,\mathbf{xr}$, $\mathscr{S}\,\mathbf{yr}$, denoted by $\lambda_{\mathbf{r}}$, $\mu_{\mathbf{r}}$, we have as in ordinary space

$$\lambda_{\mathbf{r}} = E\xi_{\mathbf{r}} + F\eta_{\mathbf{r}}, \quad \mu_{\mathbf{r}} = F\xi_{\mathbf{r}} + G\eta_{\mathbf{r}}, \qquad \cdot 15$$

or concisely $\quad \lambda_{\mathbf{r}} = S^1\chi_{\mathbf{r}}, \; \mu_{\mathbf{r}} = S^2\chi_{\mathbf{r}}.$ ·16

·2. From 14·17, the vector product of two vectors in the vecplane that includes $\mathbf{x}$ and $\mathbf{y}$ is given by

$$\mathscr{V}\,\mathbf{rs} = (\xi_{\mathbf{r}}\eta_{\mathbf{s}} - \eta_{\mathbf{r}}\xi_{\mathbf{s}})\,\mathscr{V}\,\mathbf{xy}. \qquad \cdot 21$$

When the vecplane is prepared, a direction is given in which vector products are to be measured, and if C is used for the amount of $\mathcal{V}\,\mathbf{xy}$ in this direction, that is, for the areal product $\mathcal{A}\,\mathbf{xy}$, then ·21 implies

·23 $$\mathcal{A}\,\mathbf{rs} = C\,(\xi_{\mathbf{r}}\eta_{\mathbf{s}} - \eta_{\mathbf{r}}\xi_{\mathbf{s}}).$$

Since the vectors $\mathbf{x}$, $\mathbf{y}$ are not collinear, $\mathcal{V}\,\mathbf{xy}$ is not the zero vector, and C is zero if and only if $\mathcal{V}\,\mathbf{xy}$ is in a nul vecline:

·24 *The areal magnitude of a vector frame in a vecplane is zero if and only if the vecplane is isotropic.*

·25 From 4·12, $$C^2 = EG - F^2,$$ whether or not the vecplane is isotropic, and therefore

·26 *If the fundamental magnitudes of a frame in a vecplane are E, F, G, the vecplane is isotropic if and only if $EG - F^2$ is zero;*

this proposition differs from 15·54 only because the vectors of reference can not be collinear.

If the vecplane is not isotropic, ·23 is equivalent to ·21; in the exceptional case, ·23 reduces to 4·14, but ·21 retains its full significance; the vector product is not the zero vector unless $\mathbf{r}$ and $\mathbf{s}$ are collinear.

·3. If the vecplane is not isotropic, there are vectors $\mathcal{E}\,\mathbf{x}$, $\mathcal{E}\,\mathbf{y}$, and we have from 4·24 and 4·31,

$$\mathcal{G}\,\mathbf{x}\,(\mathcal{E}\,\mathbf{y}) = -C,\quad \mathcal{G}\,\mathbf{y}\,(\mathcal{E}\,\mathbf{y}) = 0,$$
$$\mathcal{G}\,\mathbf{x}\,(\mathcal{E}\,\mathbf{x}) = 0,\quad \mathcal{G}\,\mathbf{y}\,(\mathcal{E}\,\mathbf{x}) = C.$$

Hence if $\bar{\mathbf{x}}$, $\bar{\mathbf{y}}$ denote $-C^{-1}\mathcal{E}\,\mathbf{y}$, $C^{-1}\mathcal{E}\,\mathbf{x}$, we have

·31 $$\left[\begin{array}{l}\mathcal{G}\,\mathbf{x}\bar{\mathbf{x}} = 1,\quad \mathcal{G}\,\mathbf{y}\bar{\mathbf{x}} = 0,\\ \mathcal{G}\,\mathbf{x}\bar{\mathbf{y}} = 0,\quad \mathcal{G}\,\mathbf{y}\bar{\mathbf{y}} = 1,\end{array}\right.$$

and therefore from 4·13, $$\mathcal{A}\,\mathbf{xy}\,\mathcal{A}\,\bar{\mathbf{x}}\bar{\mathbf{y}} = 1,$$

·32 that is, $$\mathcal{A}\,\bar{\mathbf{x}}\bar{\mathbf{y}} = C^{-1}.$$

·33 Since ·32 implies that $\mathcal{A}\,\bar{\mathbf{x}}\bar{\mathbf{y}}$ is not zero, the vectors $\bar{\mathbf{x}}$, $\bar{\mathbf{y}}$ form a frame, the *polar* of $\mathbf{xy}$.

If $\mathbf{r}$ is any vector, ·31 implies

$$\mathcal{G}\,\mathbf{x}\,(\lambda_{\mathbf{r}}\bar{\mathbf{x}} + \mu_{\mathbf{r}}\bar{\mathbf{y}}) = \lambda_{\mathbf{r}},\quad \mathcal{G}\,\mathbf{y}\,(\lambda_{\mathbf{r}}\bar{\mathbf{x}} + \mu_{\mathbf{r}}\bar{\mathbf{y}}) = \mu_{\mathbf{r}},$$

·34 that is, $$\mathcal{G}\,\mathbf{x}\,(\lambda_{\mathbf{r}}\bar{\mathbf{x}} + \mu_{\mathbf{r}}\bar{\mathbf{y}}) = \mathcal{G}\,\mathbf{xr},\quad \mathcal{G}\,\mathbf{y}\,(\lambda_{\mathbf{r}}\bar{\mathbf{x}} + \mu_{\mathbf{r}}\bar{\mathbf{y}}) = \mathcal{G}\,\mathbf{yr}.$$

Hence the vector $\lambda_{\mathbf{r}}\bar{\mathbf{x}} + \mu_{\mathbf{r}}\bar{\mathbf{y}}$ has the same projected products in the frame $\mathbf{xy}$ as the vector $\mathbf{r}$. But by ·26, $EG - F^2$ is not zero, and therefore the pair of equations ·15 determines $\xi_{\mathbf{r}}$, $\eta_{\mathbf{r}}$ uniquely in terms of $\lambda_{\mathbf{r}}$, $\mu_{\mathbf{r}}$. It follows that $\lambda_{\mathbf{r}}\bar{\mathbf{x}} + \mu_{\mathbf{r}}\bar{\mathbf{y}}$ has the same *coefficients* in $\mathbf{xy}$ as $\mathbf{r}$, and this implies that the vectors are the same:

·35 $$\mathbf{r} = \lambda_{\mathbf{r}}\bar{\mathbf{x}} + \mu_{\mathbf{r}}\bar{\mathbf{y}}.$$

In other words, $\lambda_{\mathbf{r}}$, $\mu_{\mathbf{r}}$ are the coefficients of $\mathbf{r}$ in the polar frame $\bar{\mathbf{x}}\bar{\mathbf{y}}$.

The definition of the polar magnitudes and their relation to E, F, G follow as for ordinary space in 344.

·4. In an isotropic vecplane, the projected products $\lambda_{\mathbf{r}}$, $\mu_{\mathbf{r}}$ of a vector $\mathbf{r}$ can be defined as usual, and they are related to the coefficients $\xi_{\mathbf{r}}$, $\eta_{\mathbf{r}}$ by the pair of formulae ·15, but it follows from ·26 that this pair of formulae can not be reversed to give $\xi_{\mathbf{r}}$, $\eta_{\mathbf{r}}$ in terms of $\lambda_{\mathbf{r}}$, $\mu_{\mathbf{r}}$, and that the projected products can not be independent.

We understand these peculiarities if, bearing 2·53 in mind, we try to form a frame polar to $\mathbf{xy}$. If neither $\mathbf{x}$ nor $\mathbf{y}$ is nul, *any* two vectors of which one is perpendicular to $\mathbf{y}$ and the other to $\mathbf{x}$ are both nul and are therefore collinear and unable to form a frame. If $\mathbf{x}$ is nul, it is possible to find vectors $\bar{\mathbf{x}}$, $\bar{\mathbf{y}}$ perpendicular to $\mathbf{y}$, $\mathbf{x}$ and not themselves collinear, but since $\mathbf{x}$ is in this case perpendicular to *every* vector in the vecplane, it is certainly impossible to satisfy the further condition

$$\mathscr{G}\mathbf{x}\bar{\mathbf{x}} = 1$$

used to complete the definition of $\bar{\mathbf{x}}$:

In an isotropic vecplane, the definition of the polar of a frame fails completely. ·41

Since the frame in which we are accustomed to find $\lambda_{\mathbf{r}}$, $\mu_{\mathbf{r}}$ serving as coefficients no longer exists, it is not surprising that in fact the two projected products do not suffice to determine the vector.

Formulae are all simpler if the isotropic vecplane is given a definite aspect. In this aspect, let the vectors of reference $\mathbf{x}$, $\mathbf{y}$ have amounts U, V; then by 2·41

$$E = U^2, \quad F = UV, \quad G = V^2, \qquad \cdot 42$$

and the condition in ·26 is reduced to an identity.

If the vector $\mathbf{r}$ has amount r in the same aspect,

$$\lambda_{\mathbf{r}} = Ur, \quad \mu_{\mathbf{r}} = Vr, \qquad \cdot 43$$

and since these projected products depend on the amount alone, not on the direction of $\mathbf{r}$, naturally it is impossible by means of them to infer the direction.

Since $\mathbf{r}$ is the sum of vectors $\xi_{\mathbf{r}}\mathbf{x}$, $\eta_{\mathbf{r}}\mathbf{y}$ which have amounts $U\xi_{\mathbf{r}}$, $V\eta_{\mathbf{r}}$, it follows from 2·44 that because the plane is isotropic with a definite aspect

$$r = U\xi_{\mathbf{r}} + V\eta_{\mathbf{r}}. \qquad \cdot 44$$

This formula combines with ·43 to give ·15, but we might have reversed the argument and made no appeal to 2·44, for ·15, ·42, ·43 give

$$Ur = U(U\xi_{\mathbf{r}} + V\eta_{\mathbf{r}}), \quad Vr = V(U\xi_{\mathbf{r}} + V\eta_{\mathbf{r}}), \qquad \cdot 45$$

and since $\mathbf{x}$, $\mathbf{y}$ are not collinear they are not both nul, and one of the two numbers U, V is certainly different from zero. With this line of reasoning, 2·44 is an obvious *deduction* from ·44.

We have for any two vectors $\mathbf{r}$, $\mathbf{s}$, from ·13 and ·42,

$$\mathscr{G}\mathbf{rs} = (U\xi_{\mathbf{r}} + V\eta_{\mathbf{r}})(U\xi_{\mathbf{s}} + V\eta_{\mathbf{s}}), \qquad \cdot 46$$

but this is only the relation 2·41 which results from confining the measurements to one aspect of the vecplane.

·**5.** If U, V are amounts of the vectors of reference $\mathbf{x}$, $\mathbf{y}$ in any vecplane, then

·51 $$E = U^2, \quad G = V^2.$$

If neither U nor V is zero, the equations

·52 $$UV \cos \omega = F, \quad UV \sin \omega = C,$$

which are compatible in virtue of ·25, determine a congruence of angles, and one member of this congruence can be selected to be *the* angle of the frame formed of the measured vectors $\mathbf{x}_U$, $\mathbf{y}_V$.

If U or V is zero, there is no longer an angle that can serve a useful purpose, but the validity of formulae that involve F and C is not brought into question; the magnitudes E, F, G, C *are* fundamental, and the failure of a derived magnitude such as the angle does not react on theorems in which this derived magnitude is not introduced.

In an anisotropic vecplane, U and V may both be zero, for proper vectors may be taken one from each of the nul veclines to form the frame. Then F, C are definite finite numbers subject to the relation

·55 $$F^2 + C^2 = 0,$$

and the projected product of two vectors is given by the simple formula

·57 $$\mathcal{G}\,\mathbf{rs} = F(\xi_{\mathbf{r}}\eta_{\mathbf{s}} + \eta_{\mathbf{r}}\xi_{\mathbf{s}}).$$

For the polar coefficients of $\mathbf{r}$, we have

·58 $$\lambda_{\mathbf{r}} = F\eta_{\mathbf{r}}, \quad \mu_{\mathbf{r}} = F\xi_{\mathbf{r}};$$

by reversing this pair of formulae, we see that the polar magnitudes are 0, F^{-1}, 0, and that the polar frame is formed of the vectors $F^{-1}\mathbf{y}$, $F^{-1}\mathbf{x}$.

CHAPTER IV 3

ALGEBRAIC SPACE

431. Lines and planes. 432. Parallelism; intersections of lines and planes. 433. Equations of lines and planes. 434. Simultaneous vectorial equations. 435. Measurement in algebraic space. 436. The distribution of isotropic lines and planes; measurement and trigonometry in an isotropic plane.

431. LINES AND PLANES.

·1. The elegance revealed in such theorems as 13·45 and 13·46 must not beguile us into forgetting that veclines and vecplanes are analogous to lines and planes all concurrent in a single point, and that for us the study of vecspace is not an end in itself* but a means to the study of a space resembling the space of elementary geometry. We have to define lines and planes.

If O, P are any two points of space, there is by hypothesis associated with the step from O to P, that is, with the ordered pair of points (O, P), a definite vector, to be called the vector of the step.

° The aggregate of the positions of P for which the vector OP belongs to a ·12
given vecline or vecplane is called the line or plane through O with this vecline or vecplane. If P is on the line or plane through O with vecline or
vecplane α and Q is on the line or plane through P with the same vecline or
vecplane, then OQ, being the sum of OP and PQ, also belongs to α, and
therefore Q is on the line or plane through O with this vecline or vecplane;
that is to say, ° *if P is on the line or plane through O with vecline or vecplane α,* ·13
then the line or plane through P with vecline or vecplane α is contained in the
line or plane through O with vecline or vecplane α. Also because PO belongs
to the same vecline and to the same vecplanes as OP, it follows that ° if P is ·14
on the line or plane through O with a given vecline or vecplane, then O is on
the line or plane through P with the same vecline or vecplane. Combining
this result with the last we can assert that

If P is any point on the line or plane through a point O with a given vecline ·15
or vecplane α, the line or plane through P with the vecline or vecplane α is
identical with the line or plane through O with the same vecline or vecplane.

Thus ° a line or plane, though defined in the first instance with reference to a ·16
particular point, which is a point on it because the zero vector is the vector of

* The student of non-euclidean geometry will find, and will lose his sense of unreality in the subject on finding, that the vector-field of ordinary space *is* an 'elliptic plane'; *as such* it repays careful attention. Compare Sommerville, *Elements of Non-Euclidean Geometry*, p. 90, 1914.

the zero step and is included in every vecline and in every vecplane, bears in fact no relation to any one of its points that it does not bear to any other.

Every line has a definite vecline, every plane a definite vecplane, and the description nul or isotropic is transferred to the line or plane if it belongs to the vecline or vecplane.

·2. If P, Q are any two distinct points, a line through P includes Q if and only if its vecline includes the vector PQ; since this vector is not the zero vector, there is one and only one vecline to which it belongs. Hence

·21 *Through two points that are distinct there passes one and only one line.*

And since any vecplane that includes the vector PQ includes every multiple of this vector,

·22 *Every plane that includes two distinct points of a line contains the whole line.*

·3. If P, Q, R are three points that are not collinear, the vectors PQ, PR are not collinear, and there is therefore one and only one vecplane which includes them both; a plane through P passes through Q and R if and only if it has this vecplane:

·31 *Through three points that are not collinear there passes one and only one plane.*

Hence further:

·32 *If a given point is not on a given line, there is one and only one plane that includes the point and contains the line;*

·33 *If two distinct lines have one point in common there is one and only one plane that contains them both.*

The correlative of this last theorem is proved with equal ease. If two distinct planes have one point O in common, the point P also is common to the two planes if and only if the vector OP is common to the corresponding vecplanes; if these vecplanes were not distinct the two planes through O would coincide; hence the vectors common to the vecplanes compose a definite vecline, and

·34 *If two distinct planes have a single point in common, the points common to them compose a definite line.*

432. Parallelism; intersections of lines and planes.

·1. Two lines with the same vecline or two planes with the same vecplane are said to be parallel, and a line is said to be parallel to a plane if the vecline of the one is contained in the vecplane of the other.

·13 It follows from the definitions of lines and planes that ° parallel lines or parallel planes that have a single point in common coincide completely, and

·14 that ° if a line and a plane that are parallel have one point in common the line is contained in the plane.

·2. Let p, q be two parallel lines, and let P be a point on p and Q a point on q. Then a vecplane that contains the vecline of p and includes the vector PQ also contains the vecline of q; the plane through P with this vecplane contains p and includes Q, and because it includes Q it coincides with the parallel plane through Q, which contains q; hence if two lines are parallel, there is a plane that contains them both, and 1·34 shews that there is not more than one such plane if the lines are distinct:

If two distinct lines are parallel, there is one and only one plane that contains them both. ·21

The converse of the combination of ·21 with 1·33 must be proved. Let p, q be lines in a given plane, let P be a point on p and Q a point on q, and let $\mathbf{p}$ be a proper vector in the vecline of p and $\mathbf{q}$ a proper vector in the vecline of q. Then if p, q are not parallel, $\mathbf{p}$, $\mathbf{q}$ are not collinear, and the vector PQ, being in the vecplane which includes $\mathbf{p}$ and $\mathbf{q}$, can be expressed in the form $\eta\mathbf{p} - \zeta\mathbf{q}$, where η, ζ are numbers. Let R be the point such that the vector QR is $\zeta\mathbf{q}$; then

$$PR = PQ + QR = (\eta\mathbf{p} - \zeta\mathbf{q}) + \zeta\mathbf{q} = \eta\mathbf{p}.$$

Because PR is a multiple of $\mathbf{p}$, the point R is on p, and because QR is a multiple of $\mathbf{q}$, this same point is on q. Hence

If two lines in one plane are not parallel, they have one and only one point in common. ·22

If a line is not parallel to a plane, it is not parallel to any line in that plane. Let p be a line that is not parallel to a given plane, and let Q be any point in the plane. A plane through Q containing p necessarily cuts the given plane, which also includes Q, in a line, and this line, since it is not parallel to p and lies in a plane that contains p, has one point in common with p; this point belongs to both p and the given plane, and no other point can belong to them both since p is not in the plane.

If a line and a plane are not parallel, they have one and only one point in common. ·23

If two vecplanes are distinct, each contains veclines which are not contained in the other. Hence if two planes are not parallel, each contains lines that are not parallel to the other, whence from ·23 and 1·34

Two planes that are not parallel necessarily intersect in a line. ·24

° Parallel planes either coincide or have no points in common. ·25

433. Equations of lines and planes.

·1. The vectorial equations describing the relations of lines and planes to a fixed point, and the algebraic equations of lines and planes referred to an attached vector frame, have the same forms in algebraic space, real or complex, as in ordinary space, and for reasons expressible in the same words.

·2. Thus the reasoning leading to 334·23 and 334·28 may be repeated, to
·21 the conclusions that °every plane has an equation of the form

·22 $$\mathscr{S}\,\mathbf{rk} = K,$$

·23 and that °every equation of this form, if $\mathbf{k}$ is not the zero vector, is the equation of a definite plane. It is to be emphasised that the argument does not suppose $\mathbf{k}$ to be a *unit* vector or a multiple of a unit vector, and is applicable if $\mathbf{k}$ is nul.

Attaching a vector frame $\mathbf{xyz}$ to the point to which ·22 refers the plane, we have the equation in the equivalent forms

·24 $$\chi_{\mathbf{k}}\upsilon = K, \quad \upsilon_{\mathbf{k}}\chi = K.$$

Since the three numbers $\xi_{\mathbf{k}}$, $\eta_{\mathbf{k}}$, $\zeta_{\mathbf{k}}$ are not all zero, one of the three sets of numbers $(K/\xi_{\mathbf{k}}, 0, 0)$, $(0, K/\eta_{\mathbf{k}}, 0)$, $(0, 0, K/\zeta_{\mathbf{k}})$ certainly survives; if $\xi_{\mathbf{k}}$ is not zero, the point whose projections are $K/\xi_{\mathbf{k}}, 0, 0$ is the point in which the plane ·24 is met by the line through O perpendicular to the plane whose vecplane contains $\mathbf{y}$ and $\mathbf{z}$. Similarly if $\lambda_{\mathbf{k}}$ is not zero, the point whose coordinates are $K/\lambda_{\mathbf{k}}, 0, 0$ is the point in which the same plane cuts the line through O whose vecline contains $\mathbf{x}$; certainly one of the three numbers $\lambda_{\mathbf{k}}$, $\mu_{\mathbf{k}}$, $\nu_{\mathbf{k}}$ is different from zero, and therefore one point on the plane can be indicated by its coordinates in the attached vector frame. In real space there is always a vector $(K/\mathscr{S}\,\mathbf{k}^2)\,\mathbf{k}$ which leads from the origin to one point on the plane given by ·22; in complex space, this particular construction fails if $\mathscr{S}\,\mathbf{k}^2$ is zero, but the plane is none the less determinate.

·3. The line through a point S with vecline determined as including a proper vector $\mathbf{k}$ is the locus of a point R which is such that the vector of SR is a multiple of $\mathbf{k}$. If then the vectors of the steps to S, R from an origin O are $\mathbf{s}$, $\mathbf{r}$, the point R is on the line if and only if $\mathbf{r}-\mathbf{s}$ is collinear with $\mathbf{k}$, that is, if and only if the vector product $\mathscr{V}(\mathbf{r}-\mathbf{s})\,\mathbf{k}$ is the zero vector, or if and
·31 only if $$\mathscr{V}\,\mathbf{rk} = \mathbf{K},$$

·32 where $$\mathbf{K} = \mathscr{V}\,\mathbf{sk}.$$

·33 Thus °every line has a vectorial equation of the form ·31, which involves
·34 the condition $$\mathscr{S}\,\mathbf{Kk} = 0.$$

The only difficulty in proving the converse is in shewing that the equation ·31 can not be altogether insoluble if ·34 is satisfied and $\mathbf{k}$ is a proper vector, for the argument used above proves that if there is one point satisfying ·31 the complete locus is a line. A simple plan is to use an attached vector frame. Then ·31, ·34 are equivalent to

·35 $$J^{-1}(\zeta_{\mathbf{k}}\eta - \eta_{\mathbf{k}}\zeta) = \lambda_{\mathbf{K}}, \quad J^{-1}(\xi_{\mathbf{k}}\zeta - \zeta_{\mathbf{k}}\xi) = \mu_{\mathbf{K}}, \quad J^{-1}(\eta_{\mathbf{k}}\xi - \xi_{\mathbf{k}}\eta) = \nu_{\mathbf{K}}$$

·36 with the condition $$\xi_{\mathbf{k}}\lambda_{\mathbf{K}} + \eta_{\mathbf{k}}\mu_{\mathbf{K}} + \zeta_{\mathbf{k}}\nu_{\mathbf{K}} = 0,$$

and also to

·37 $$J(\nu_{\mathbf{k}}\mu - \mu_{\mathbf{k}}\nu) = \xi_{\mathbf{K}}, \quad J(\lambda_{\mathbf{k}}\nu - \nu_{\mathbf{k}}\lambda) = \eta_{\mathbf{K}}, \quad J(\mu_{\mathbf{k}}\lambda - \lambda_{\mathbf{k}}\mu) = \zeta_{\mathbf{K}}$$

·38 with the condition $$\lambda_{\mathbf{k}}\xi_{\mathbf{K}} + \mu_{\mathbf{k}}\eta_{\mathbf{K}} + \nu_{\mathbf{k}}\zeta_{\mathbf{K}} = 0.$$

If $\xi_{\mathbf{k}}$ is not zero, $(0, -J\nu_{\mathbf{K}}/\xi_{\mathbf{k}}, J\mu_{\mathbf{K}}/\xi_{\mathbf{k}})$ is a set of numbers indicating a point on the locus, and since not more than two of the three numbers $\xi_{\mathbf{k}}, \eta_{\mathbf{k}}, \zeta_{\mathbf{k}}$ can be zero, one point certainly is discoverable.

An equation of the form ·39

$$\mathscr{V}\,\mathbf{rk} = \mathbf{K}$$

represents a definite line if only **k** *is a proper vector and*

$$\mathscr{G}\,\mathbf{Kk} = 0.$$

With the line as with the plane one construction possible in real space may fail in complex space: ·34 and 14·42 imply

$$\mathscr{V}(\mathscr{V}\,\mathbf{kK})\,\mathbf{k} = \mathbf{K}\,\mathscr{G}\,\mathbf{k}^2,$$

shewing that if **k** is not nul the vector $\mathscr{V}\,\mathbf{kK}/\mathscr{G}\,\mathbf{k}^2$ determines a point on the line, but the exceptional case must not be overlooked. The fact is that in constructions in real space we use the theorem that *if two proper vectors are perpendicular they are not parallel*, and for complex space the theorem is not true.

·4. In considering what is implied by the equation

$$\mathscr{G}\,\mathbf{rk} = K \qquad \cdot 41$$

in the geometry of a *plane*, we have to be on our guard. If there is one vector **s** which satisfies the equation, the equation is equivalent to

$$\mathscr{G}(\mathbf{r}-\mathbf{s})\,\mathbf{k} = 0 \qquad \cdot 42$$

and expresses that $\mathbf{r}-\mathbf{s}$ is perpendicular to **k**. If two vectors $\mathbf{r}-\mathbf{s}$, $\mathbf{p}-\mathbf{s}$ are both perpendicular to **k**, either they are collinear or **k** is perpendicular to the vecplane that they determine; if by hypothesis **k** *belongs* to the vecplane determined by $\mathbf{r}-\mathbf{s}$, $\mathbf{p}-\mathbf{s}$, the latter case can not arise *unless the vecplane is isotropic*, but in an isotropic vecplane, ·42 asserts only that one of the two vectors $\mathbf{r}-\mathbf{s}$, **k** is nul, and therefore if **k** is itself nul ·42 involves no restriction on $\mathbf{r}-\mathbf{s}$. Again, in an anisotropic vecplane containing **k**, a second vector can be associated with **k** to form a frame, and any vector **r** which has K for its first polar coefficient in this frame satisfies ·41. But in an isotropic vecplane, not only is this process at fault, but the actual existence of the vector is conditional: if **k** is not nul but has an amount k in one aspect of the vecplane, any vector whose amount in the same aspect is K/k satisfies ·41, and there is a vector of this amount in every anisotropic direction in the vecplane; but if **k** is nul, $\mathscr{G}\,\mathbf{rk}$ is zero for every vector in the vecplane and ·41 is ineffective or insoluble according as K is or is not zero.

Thus °·41 represents a definite line perpendicular to **k** if the plane is anisotropic and **k** is not zero, or if the plane is isotropic and **k** is not nul. The observation that in the latter case the line represented necessarily is nul, shews that the converse question, as to what lines are representable in the form ·41, ·43

·44 must not be ignored. °If **k** is a proper vector perpendicular to a given line, and if **r**, **s** are vectors defining points of the line, then

$$\mathscr{G}(\mathbf{r}-\mathbf{s})\mathbf{k}=0$$

and therefore $$\mathscr{G}\,\mathbf{rk}=\mathscr{G}\,\mathbf{sk},$$

·45 an equation of the form ·41; °the vecline to which **k** belongs is determinate unless the plane is isotropic and the given line is nul.

It is to be noticed that the exception is not the same in ·43 as in ·45: in the latter case it is the line concerned that must not be nul, but in the former it is the perpendicular vecline. In an isotropic plane, the lines that *can* be represented in the form ·41 are the nul lines, but the representation is arbitrary in the extreme: *any* anisotropic vector in the plane can be used in the specification of *any* nul line; for a line that is not nul, ·44 remains true, but fails to distinguish the points that belong to the line from those that do not: **k** must be nul, and $\mathscr{G}\,\mathbf{rk}$ is zero for *every* point in the plane, whatever the origin.

In an anisotropic plane, the equation

·46 $$\mathscr{A}\,\mathbf{rk}=A$$

is equivalent to $$\mathscr{G}\,\mathbf{r}(\mathscr{E}\mathbf{k})=-A;$$

·47 °hence ·46 is an alternative form of equation to any line in such a plane, and is effective if $\mathscr{E}\mathbf{k}$ is not the zero vector, that is, if **k** is not the zero vector. Whereas ·41 represents a line perpendicular to **k**, the line given by ·46 is parallel to **k**, as is directly evident since if **s** is any one vector satisfying ·46 the equation is equivalent to

$$\mathscr{A}(\mathbf{r}-\mathbf{s})\mathbf{k}=0.$$

In an isotropic plane, this method of representing a line necessarily fails completely, since the areal product is then always zero.

We must not conclude that there is no representation of a line in a plane that is always valid. If the plane is referred to an attached vector frame, the step from the point Q to the point of coordinates ξ, η has the vector whose coefficients are $\xi-\xi_Q$, $\eta-\eta_Q$, and this vector belongs to the vecline which includes a given proper vector **d** if and only if

·48 $$\eta_{\mathbf{d}}(\xi-\xi_Q)-\xi_{\mathbf{d}}(\eta-\eta_Q)=0;$$

this equation is necessarily significant, since $\xi_{\mathbf{d}}$ and $\eta_{\mathbf{d}}$ are not both zero, and conversely, if two numbers $\xi_{\mathbf{d}}$, $\eta_{\mathbf{d}}$ are not both zero, there is a proper vector **d** of which they are the coefficients, and ·48 expresses that (ξ, η) is in the line through Q whose vecline includes **d**. Thus the assertion that

·49 *In a plane, a line is the locus of a point whose coordinates satisfy a linear equation,*

is true without any reservation as to isotropic planes or lines.

434. Simultaneous vectorial equations.

·1. Theorems regarding intersections of lines and planes can always be interpreted as theorems concerning simultaneous vectorial equations.

·2. If **a** is a proper vector, the equation

$$\mathcal{S}\,\mathbf{ra} = A$$ ·21

represents in a prepared anisotropic plane a definite line, and so also does the equation

$$\mathcal{A}\,\mathbf{ra} = P;$$ ·22

the first line is perpendicular to **a** and the second is parallel to **a**. Hence the two lines have one and only one point in common unless **a** is self-perpendicular, that is, unless **a** is nul.

If **a** *is an anisotropic vector in a given anisotropic vecplane, the vecplane contains one and only one vector* **r** *which satisfies simultaneously the two equations* ·23

$$\mathcal{S}\,\mathbf{ra} = A, \quad \mathcal{A}\,\mathbf{ra} = P,$$

A, P being given numbers.

If **a** is nul, $$(\mathcal{A}\,\mathbf{ra})^2 + (\mathcal{S}\,\mathbf{ra})^2 = 0$$ ·24

identically, by 24·12, and the two equations ·21, ·22 are incompatible unless

$$P^2 + A^2 = 0.$$ ·25

·3. In space, the two planes

$$\mathcal{S}\,\mathbf{ra} = A, \quad \mathcal{S}\,\mathbf{rb} = B$$ ·31

are not parallel unless the vectors **a**, **b** are collinear, and if they are not parallel they intersect in a line whose vecline contains $\mathcal{V}\,\mathbf{ab}$.

If **a**, **b** *are any two vectors that are not collinear, the equations* ·32

$$\mathcal{S}\,\mathbf{ra} = A, \quad \mathcal{S}\,\mathbf{rb} = B$$

can be satisfied simultaneously, and if **d** *is a particular vector satisfying these equations, every solution is of the form* $\mathbf{d} + p\,\mathcal{V}\,\mathbf{ab}$, *where p is a number varying from solution to solution.*

·4. The plane $$\mathcal{S}\,\mathbf{ra} = A$$ ·41

is perpendicular to **a**, and the line

$$\mathcal{V}\,\mathbf{rc} = \mathbf{C}$$ ·42

is parallel to **c**; hence the two are not parallel unless **a** and **c** are perpendicular.

Unless $\mathcal{S}\,\mathbf{ac}$ *is zero, the two equations* ·43

$$\mathcal{S}\,\mathbf{ra} = A, \quad \mathcal{V}\,\mathbf{rc} = \mathbf{C}$$

are satisfied by one and only one vector **r**, *provided only that* $\mathcal{S}\,\mathbf{Cc}$ *is zero.*

An explicit formula comes from 14·42; since identically

$$\mathcal{V}\,\mathbf{a}\,(\mathcal{V}\,\mathbf{rc}) = \mathbf{r}\,\mathcal{S}\,\mathbf{ac} - \mathbf{c}\,\mathcal{S}\,\mathbf{ra},$$ ·44

the equations to be satisfied together imply

$$\mathbf{r}\,\mathcal{S}\,\mathbf{ac} = A\mathbf{c} + \mathcal{V}\,\mathbf{aC}.$$ ·45

If we wish to use vectorial algebra alone to prove ·43, we have only to remark that ·45 implies

·46 $$\mathscr{S}\,\mathbf{ra}\,\mathscr{S}\,\mathbf{ac} = A\,\mathscr{S}\,\mathbf{ac}$$

·47 and $$\mathscr{V}\,\mathbf{rc}\,\mathscr{S}\,\mathbf{ac} = \mathbf{C}\,\mathscr{S}\,\mathbf{ac} - \mathbf{a}\,\mathscr{S}\,\mathbf{Cc},$$

and therefore implies ·41 and ·42 if **c** is perpendicular to **C** but not to **a**.

435. Measurement in algebraic space.

·1. The language concerning directions and angles is transferred bodily to lines and planes from their veclines and vecplanes. And as we have said already, a line with a nul vecline is called a nul line or an isotropic line, and a plane whose vecplane is isotropic is itself said to be isotropic.

·2. The amounts of the vector of the step from P to Q are called the lengths of the step, or the distances from P to Q. If two points are distinct, then if the line through them is nul, zero is the only distance from one to the other, but if the line through them is not nul, there are two distances from one to the other, each distance being the negative of the other.

A step associated with one of its lengths is a measured step, and has, unless it is the zero step, a definite direction. Parallel steps, that is to say, steps whose vectors are collinear, have the same directions. To describe steps which have a common direction and the same length in that direction as congruent is equivalent simply to the definition that

·24 *Congruent steps are steps with the same vector.*

A line associated with one of its directions is a ray, and a step in a ray has in the direction of that ray a length which is completely determinate. Equally definite is measurement in a chosen aspect of an isotropic plane.

A nul line has only one direction, and if P, Q are two points of a nul line, there is only one distance from P to Q, namely, zero; this is not to say that P and Q may not be distinct, or that the vector of QP is not distinguishable from the vector of PQ. If PQ, RS are proper steps in *parallel* nul lines, the vector of PQ can be described as a definite multiple of the vector of RS, although the relation can not be expressed significantly as a relation between lengths; but we can make no quantitative comparison of nul steps that are in different directions.

A Cartesian frame in algebraic space, as in real space, is formed of three rays concurrent in an origin, but it is the essence of Cartesian geometry that the positions of points on the axes are *determined* by distances measured from the origin. The axes of a Cartesian frame must therefore be *anisotropic*. It is not essential to suppose the planes also anisotropic, but if a plane is isotropic, the polar frame is no longer available and all formulae dependent on the polar or involving the biplanar angles of the frame become liable to suspicion. Cartesian formulae can be employed freely only on the understanding that the axes and planes of the frame are all anisotropic; this is sufficient reason for regarding the attached vector frame as the ultimate standard.

The angles of a Cartesian frame belong to six congruences which are definite when the axes and the planes of the frame are given. To correspond at all closely to the system of conventions that is usually adopted for choosing the angles from the congruences in ordinary space, a system of conventions for complex space must be highly artificial, and if we had introduced any particular system of conventions explicitly in our earlier work, we should have been forced now into a digression to consider whether the conventions had in fact influenced the formulae. But by insisting for ordinary space that if only it belongs to the right congruence one angle is as good as another, we have avoided all need to recognise one distinction between real space and complex space that might otherwise have seemed relevant here and elsewhere.

·3. Naturally we attempt to define distances in which lines or planes are involved exactly as in real space, but there are cases that we can not afford to ignore in which the familiar definitions break down. For example, the definition on the plan suggested in 123·1 of the distance from a point P to a plane q in a given direction fails if the direction is parallel to the plane, for then if P is not in q there is *no* second point to which to measure, while if P is in q the second point is arbitrary on a particular line and therefore the distance also is arbitrary unless* the direction is nul. In real space to insist on a definition of a distance from a plane in a direction parallel to the plane is perhaps unnecessary, but in complex space a direction perpendicular to a plane may be parallel also, and to be in doubt as to the meaning of the *normal* distance from a point to a prepared plane would be an intolerable handicap. The difficulty is typical, and so also are the methods by which it is overcome.

There are three of these methods, of which two are not fundamentally distinct. The first, somewhat tentative, aims at discovering an *intrinsic* general formula in which the distance plays a part, and defines the distance when necessary as the number that gives the intrinsic formula freedom from exceptional cases. The second refers the whole problem to a frame of reference having no intrinsic relation to the point and plane concerned, discovers a *formula* for the distance in the general case, and *defines* the distance by the formula in every case of doubt. The third method constructs a space in which the difficulty no longer arises; this is a space with points at infinity where parallel lines do meet, and when we have seen how this space is formed we shall find that the results of the less systematic methods are confirmed.

Let P be a given point and q a given plane, and let n_{N} be a proper vector $\mathbf{n}$ perpendicular to the plane. Then if Q is a point of the plane, the value of the projected product of $\mathbf{n}$ and PQ is a number K which is independent of the position of Q in the plane, and is therefore equal, if the ray through P with direction N does cut the plane in a unique point M, to the product of n by the distance of M from P along the ray, since PM and $\mathbf{n}$ are collinear vectors.

* In fact the distance proves to be arbitrary even in this case, for although every 'accessible' point is at distance zero from P, the distance of the 'point at infinity' is found to be neither definitely zero, although the direction is nul, nor definitely infinite, although the point is 'at infinity', but essentially indeterminate. This subject is considered in 534 below.

That is, if a normal distance d from P to q in the direction N perpendicular to q is definable in the elementary manner, then

·32 $$K = dn,$$

and since K and n are definite numbers in any case, and to replace $\mathbf{n}$ by any other proper vector normal to q is to multiply K and n by the same number, we agree that in every case a distance from P to q is to be any number not inconsistent with ·32. Since n is zero if and only if q is isotropic, and K is zero if and only if P is in q,

·33 *The normal distance from a point to an isotropic plane is indeterminate or infinite according as the point is or is not in the plane.*

If we prefer to attack the problem analytically, we start from the consideration that if an *anisotropic* plane q has its equation given in the form

·34 $$v_{\mathrm{E}}\chi + e = 0$$

where E is a direction normal to the plane, the distance d of a point P from q is given by
$$d = v_{\mathrm{E}}\chi_P + e.$$

·35 To reduce the equation $$v_{\mathbf{K}}\chi + K = 0$$

to the form ·34, it is necessary to divide by a number k such that

·36 $$k^2 = \bar{S} v_{\mathbf{K}}^2,$$

and therefore the distance is given by combining ·36 with

·37 $$d = (v_{\mathbf{K}}\chi + K)/k;$$

the ambiguity in the distance corresponds to the fact that there are two prepared planes related to the one unprepared plane given by ·35. The *process* fails if the plane is isotropic, for then k is zero; if we take the distance d to be defined by the *formula* ·37, the distance is to be indeterminate or infinite according as the numerator is or is not zero, and this agrees with ·33.

·4. To be guided to a definition of distance from a point P to a plane q in a given direction Σ that shall be significant whether or not Σ is in q or q is isotropic, we consider that in ordinary space if Σ is not in q and if d is the distance from P to q in a normal direction N and ϵ is an angle between N and Σ, then the distance is $d \sec \epsilon$, or in other words is the number r which satisfies the equation

·41 $$r \cos \epsilon = d.$$

To remove the cosine, let $\mathbf{n}_n$, $\mathbf{s}_s$ be any proper measured vectors with the directions N, Σ; then ·41 becomes

·42 $$r \mathscr{G} \mathbf{ns} = dns,$$

and from this equality we can remove d by means of ·32, obtaining*

·43 $$r \mathscr{G} \mathbf{ns} = sK,$$

* Generally speaking, this is nothing more than the equation $r \mathscr{G} \mathbf{ns} = s \mathscr{G} \mathbf{nr}$, which expresses an obvious relation between any two codirectional measured vectors $\mathbf{r}_r$, $\mathbf{s}_s$. The discussion shews why this simple consideration is effective.

where K has the same meaning as in the last paragraph. No difficulties attach in any case to the terms $\mathscr{G}\mathbf{ns}$, s, K, and therefore a distance is defined as a value of r which satisfies ·43.

The distance from a point to a plane in a direction parallel to the plane is indeterminate if the point is in the plane or if the direction is nul, but is otherwise infinite. ·44

If it is surprising to find that the distance is not definitely zero but is arbitrary if the direction is nul, it is even more interesting to compare this result with ·33 and to discover that normal distance can not be identified always with distance in a normal direction.

To discuss this problem by means of an attached vector frame is to define the distance r as a number such that the point $\xi_P + r\xi_\Sigma$, $\eta_P + r\eta_\Sigma$, $\zeta_P + r\zeta_\Sigma$ lies in the plane

$$\upsilon_{\mathbf{K}}\chi + K = 0; \qquad \cdot 45$$

thus

$$r = -(\upsilon_{\mathbf{K}}\chi_P + K)/\upsilon_{\mathbf{K}}\chi_\Sigma. \qquad \cdot 46$$

If Σ is given as the direction of a measured vector $\mathbf{s}_s$ that is not nul, ξ_Σ, η_Σ, ζ_Σ must be replaced by $\xi_{\mathbf{s}}/s$, $\eta_{\mathbf{s}}/s$, $\zeta_{\mathbf{s}}/s$, and ·46 becomes

$$r = -s(\upsilon_{\mathbf{K}}\chi_P + K)/\upsilon_{\mathbf{K}}\chi_{\mathbf{s}}, \qquad \cdot 47$$

which is the formula assumed to be general.

·5. Distances between points and lines in a directed plane that is not isotropic are exactly like distances between points and planes in space, nul lines taking the place of isotropic planes. In particular,

In an anisotropic plane, the normal distance from a point to a nul line is indeterminate or infinite according as the line does or does not contain the point. ·51

The peculiarities of isotropic planes are the subject of our next section.

436. The distribution of isotropic lines and planes; measurement and trigonometry in an isotropic plane.

·1. Some conclusions as to the distribution of nul lines and isotropic planes in space are to be drawn from the theorems of 15·4.

°Through a line that is not nul there pass two distinct isotropic planes. ·11
°Through a nul line there passes only one isotropic plane. If P, Q are distinct ·12
points on a line that is not nul, the planes through P, Q perpendicular to the line are distinct parallel planes, for they both have for vecplane the vecplane perpendicular to the vector PQ and this vecplane does not include PQ. But if P, Q are distinct points on a nul line, the vecplane perpendicular to PQ includes PQ, and therefore the plane through P perpendicular to the line includes Q, that is, contains the whole line. To put the same matter differently, the planes perpendicular to a given line are in every case parallel planes; if the line is not nul, these planes are not parallel to the line, and each of them

cuts the line in one and only one point, but if the line is nul, the planes perpendicular to the line are also parallel to the line, and therefore one of them contains the line and none of the others cut the line.

·2. A nul line in a given plane must have for vecline a nul vecline in the
·21 corresponding vecplane. Hence ° in a plane that is not isotropic there are two distinct families of nul lines; each family consists of parallel lines, and through
·22 every point there pass two nul lines, one member of each family. ° In an isotropic plane the nul lines are all parallel, and every point is on one and only one nul line.

·3. In an isotropic plane the elementary definitions of distance to a line do not necessarily fail. On the contrary, if q is any line that is not nul, there is one and only one line through a point P perpendicular to q, namely, the nul line through P, and this line not being parallel to q cuts q in a single point: there is no *difficulty*, but since the distance along the nul line is zero, there is the *peculiarity* that

·31 *In an isotropic plane the normal distance from any point to any ray that is not nul is zero.*

But if q is nul, every direction, including the direction of q itself, is normal to q; the anisotropic lines through any point P of the plane are normal to q and intersect q, and the distances from P to q along these lines are not zero unless P is in q. On the other hand, it follows from ·31 that the points at normal distance zero from a line that is not nul are the points composing the two isotropic planes through the line, and we are tempted to agree that the points at normal distance zero from a nul line are the points forming the one isotropic plane that contains that line, a conclusion that can be drawn only if zero is at least one value of the normal distance from any point to any nul line in an isotropic plane. The convention to which we are driven is that

·32 *In an isotropic plane the normal distance from any point to any nul line is indeterminate.*

To confirm this decision let us appeal to general formulae. In the plane with fundamental magnitudes E, F, G, the normal distance d of the point ξ_P, η_P from the *line*

·33 $$\lambda_{\mathbf{K}}\xi + \mu_{\mathbf{K}}\eta + K = 0$$

·34 is given by $$d = (\lambda_{\mathbf{K}}\xi_P + \mu_{\mathbf{K}}\eta_P + K)/k,$$

·35 where $$k^2 = (G\lambda_{\mathbf{K}}^2 - 2F\lambda_{\mathbf{K}}\mu_{\mathbf{K}} + E\mu_{\mathbf{K}}^2)/(EG - F^2).$$

If the plane is isotropic, $\lambda_{\mathbf{K}}$, $\mu_{\mathbf{K}}$ can not be interpreted as polar coefficients, but ·33 is still the general form of equation for a line, and this line is nul if and only if

·36 $$G\lambda_{\mathbf{K}}^2 - 2F\lambda_{\mathbf{K}}\mu_{\mathbf{K}} + E\mu_{\mathbf{K}}^2 = 0.$$

·37 Since $$EG - F^2 = 0,$$

the value of d given by ·34 and ·35 is necessarily zero unless the line is nul, but if the line is nul, k and d are together indeterminate.

·**4**. The line through ξ_P, η_P in a direction Σ is traced by giving to r different values in $\xi_P + r\xi_\Sigma$, $\eta_P + r\eta_\Sigma$, where ξ_Σ, η_Σ, being the coefficients of a *direction*, satisfy

$$E\xi_\Sigma^2 + 2F\xi_\Sigma\eta_\Sigma + G\eta_\Sigma^2 = 1,$$

and r is the actual distance of the variable point from P. Substituting $\xi_{\mathbf{s}}/s$, $\eta_{\mathbf{s}}/s$ for ξ_Σ, η_Σ we see that in general the distance from the point P to the line given by ·33 in the direction of the measured vector $\mathbf{s}_s$ is the value of r given by

$$(\lambda_{\mathbf{K}}\xi_P + \mu_{\mathbf{K}}\eta_P + K) + (r/s)(\lambda_{\mathbf{K}}\xi_{\mathbf{s}} + \mu_{\mathbf{K}}\eta_{\mathbf{s}}) = 0, \qquad \cdot 42$$

that is, by

$$r = -s(\lambda_{\mathbf{K}}\xi_P + \mu_{\mathbf{K}}\eta_P + K)/(\lambda_{\mathbf{K}}\xi_{\mathbf{s}} + \mu_{\mathbf{K}}\eta_{\mathbf{s}}); \qquad \cdot 43$$

the amount s must satisfy the condition

$$s^2 = E\xi_{\mathbf{s}}^2 + 2F\xi_{\mathbf{s}}\eta_{\mathbf{s}} + G\eta_{\mathbf{s}}^2. \qquad \cdot 44$$

If we use the formula ·43 for a definition and note that the denominator $\lambda_{\mathbf{K}}\xi_{\mathbf{s}} + \mu_{\mathbf{K}}\eta_{\mathbf{s}}$ is zero if and only if the direction is parallel to the line, we find that

In any plane the distance from a point to a line in a direction parallel to the line is indeterminate if the line contains the point or is nul, but otherwise is infinite. ·45

If the direction is not parallel to the line, there is nothing to be learnt from ·43 that is not otherwise evident.

·**5**. Applied verbally to an isotropic plane, the familiar theorems on which ordinary geometry is built are for the most part not false but either tautologous or reducible to simpler terms. The kind of change that takes place is most obvious when the measurement of angles is involved, for as we have seen every determinate angle in an isotropic plane is a multiple of π.

Thus, of the relation

$$b \sin C = c \sin B \qquad \cdot 51$$

between sides and angles of a triangle nothing useful survives, though we may add that unless the side BC is situated in a nul line, zero, which is the value of $b \sin C$ and $c \sin B$, is also the normal distance of A from BC.

The form assumed by

$$a = b \cos C + c \cos B, \qquad \cdot 52$$

the other fundamental formula of plane trigonometry, is made intelligible by **22**·44. If P, Q, R are any three points, then if PQ, QR, and PR are all measured in congenial directions, the length of PR is the sum of the lengths of PQ and QR; thus to reduce ·52 to the form*

$$a = b + c \qquad \cdot 53$$

* Darboux (*Principes*, p. 180) has this theorem in the form $\pm d_{12} \pm d_{23} \pm d_{31} = 0$, but has no plan for disposing of the ambiguities of sign, unless indeed the whole theory of 'aspect' is held to be implicit in the phrase "*exactement comme si les points étaient en ligne droite*", to which he gives the emphasis of italics.

is to suppose CA, AB, and CB (not BC) measured in the same aspect of the plane. It is better to give the theorem a more symmetrical shape and an obvious extension, asserting that

·54 *In an isotropic plane with a definite aspect the perimeter of every closed polygon is zero.*

An important corollary to ·53 comes from the simple observation that a is equal to b if c is zero, that is, if the step of which c is a length is in a nul line:

·55 *In an isotropic plane with a definite aspect, the distance from a point P to a point Q of a nul line q is independent of the position of Q in q.*

·56 In other words, °although the *normal* distance from a point to a nul line in an isotropic plane is indeterminate, there is a definite *oblique* distance in each aspect of the plane. And two nul lines in such a plane stand in a relation to which there is nothing in ordinary geometry to correspond:

·57 *In an isotropic plane with a definite aspect, the distance from a point of one nul line to a point of another depends only on the two lines, not on the positions of the points on the lines.*

CHAPTER IV 4

THE UNIQUENESS OF COMPLEX SPACE

441. General considerations.

·1. When we set up a framework, Cartesian or other, in ordinary space, we have not to consider the possibility that the space owes any properties to the framework, for the space is supposed given in advance. But with algebraic space the constants associated with some one framework have to be assumed, and it is reasonable to ask whether the choice of constants can have any radical effect on the space constructed. In this chapter we are concerned only with complex space, and it must be remembered that the existence of spatial products different from zero is being assumed; in what may be called *isotropic* space there is a type of plane that we do not have to consider.

·2. We must deal first with the vecplane. If for any one pair of vectors of reference $EG - F^2$ is zero, the vecplane is isotropic and $EG - F^2$ is zero for *every* frame. If for any one frame $EG - F^2$ is different from zero, then the vecplane is anisotropic and $EG - F^2$ is different from zero for *every* frame.
°The distinction between the two kinds of vecplane is a fundamental dis- ·23
tinction; what we prove is that there is no other.

When we turn to vecspace we come to a conclusion that is really similar, and appears different only because isotropic vecspace has been explicitly excluded. The reader who takes the trouble to develop the theory will have no difficulty in finding whether or not two isotropic vecspaces necessarily have the same geometry.

·3. It goes without saying that if two vecplanes or vecspaces have the same geometry, two planes or spaces constructed by means of them have the same geometry.

442. The similarity of all isotropic planes.

·1. As described in 25·4, the analytical geometry of an isotropic vecplane with a definite aspect depends wholly on two numbers U, V subject only to the restriction that they are not both zero. It follows that, if in a given isotropic vecplane α can be found a frame **xy** with reference to which the fundamental numbers U, V have the particular values from which an isotropic vecplane β has been constructed, the geometry of α must be the same, qualitatively and quantitatively, as the geometry of β.

Suppose then that α is an isotropic vecplane and that U, V are given numbers, not both zero. In α, let $\mathbf{k}$ be a proper nul vector, and let $\mathbf{d}$, $\mathbf{e}$ be two proper vectors, of amounts d, e, that are neither collinear nor nul*. Then let $\mathbf{x}$ denote $\mathbf{k}$ if U is zero, $(U/d)\,\mathbf{d}$ if U is not zero, and let $\mathbf{y}$ denote $\mathbf{k}$ if V is zero, $(V/e)\,\mathbf{e}$ if V is not zero. With this construction, $\mathbf{x}$ and $\mathbf{y}$ are not collinear; and $\mathbf{x}$ has the amount U and $\mathbf{y}$ the amount V:

·12 *Given any two numbers U, V not both zero, we can find in any isotropic vecplane with given aspect a frame in which these are the fundamental numbers.*

It follows that

·13 *All isotropic vecplanes have the same geometry,*

and also that

·14 *All isotropic planes have the same geometry.*

443. THE SIMILARITY OF ALL ANISOTROPIC PLANES.

·1. A prepared anisotropic vecplane, referred to a frame $\mathbf{xy}$, depends on the four numbers E, F, G, C such that

·11 $$\mathscr{G}\,\mathbf{x}^2 = E, \quad \mathscr{G}\,\mathbf{xy} = F, \quad \mathscr{G}\,\mathbf{y}^2 = G,$$

·12 $$\mathscr{A}\,\mathbf{xy} = C,$$

and these numbers are necessarily subject to the relations

·13 $$C^2 = EG - F^2,$$

·14 $$C \neq 0.$$

We proceed to shew that conversely, given any four numbers satisfying ·13 and ·14, in any complex anisotropic vecplane we can find a pair of vectors $\mathbf{x}$, $\mathbf{y}$ satisfying ·11 and ·12. It is convenient to separate the case in which E and G are both zero.

·2. If E and G are both zero, vectors $\mathbf{x}, \mathbf{y}$ to satisfy ·11 must both be nul, and since they are not to be collinear one of them must belong to each of the two nul veclines. Let $\mathbf{d}$, $\mathbf{e}$ be any proper vectors one in each nul vecline; by 15·33, $\mathscr{G}\,\mathbf{de}$ is not zero; hence there is a vector $(F/\mathscr{G}\,\mathbf{de})\,\mathbf{e}$. If this vector is $\mathbf{g}$,

·21 $$\mathscr{G}\,\mathbf{dg} = F,$$

·22 and since by 24·12 $$(\mathscr{A}\,\mathbf{dg})^2 = -(\mathscr{G}\,\mathbf{dg})^2,$$

we have from ·21 and ·13, which reduces to

$$C^2 = -F^2,$$

·24 the relation $$(\mathscr{A}\,\mathbf{dg})^2 = C^2.$$

* If $\mathbf{d}$ is not nul, $\mathbf{d}+\mathbf{k}$ is neither nul nor collinear with $\mathbf{d}$.

If $\mathscr{A}\,\mathbf{dg}$ is C, ·11 and ·12 are satisfied if $\mathbf{x}$ denotes $\mathbf{d}$ and $\mathbf{y}$ denotes $\mathbf{g}$; if $\mathscr{A}\,\mathbf{dg}$ is $-C$, then $\mathscr{A}\,\mathbf{gd}$ is C and ·11 and ·12 are satisfied if $\mathbf{x}$ is taken as $\mathbf{g}$ and $\mathbf{y}$ as $\mathbf{d}$.

·3. If E is not zero, then by 21·75 we can find in any direction that is not nul a vector $\mathbf{x}$ such that

$$\mathscr{G}\,\mathbf{x}^2 = E, \qquad \cdot 31$$

and by 34·23 we can find then one and only one vector $\mathbf{y}$ satisfying simultaneously the two equations

$$\mathscr{G}\,\mathbf{xy} = F, \quad \mathscr{A}\,\mathbf{xy} = C. \qquad \cdot 32$$

Comparing the identity

$$(\mathscr{A}\,\mathbf{xy})^2 = \mathscr{G}\,\mathbf{x}^2\,\mathscr{G}\,\mathbf{y}^2 - (\mathscr{G}\,\mathbf{xy})^2$$

with ·13, we have
$$E\mathscr{G}\,\mathbf{y}^2 = EG,$$

and since E is not zero this implies

$$\mathscr{G}\,\mathbf{y}^2 = G. \qquad \cdot 33$$

Thus $\mathbf{x}$ and $\mathbf{y}$ together satisfy ·11 and ·12, and since C by hypothesis is not zero, ·12 implies that $\mathbf{x}$ and $\mathbf{y}$ compose a vector frame in the vecplane.

This argument does not require G to be different from zero, and is applicable, *mutatis mutandis*, if E is zero but G is not zero. To construct a direct argument for this last case, starting with $\mathbf{x}$ as a multiple of a definite nul vector, is a good exercise; the steps are similar to those of 4·3 below.

·4. Combining the conclusions of ·2 and ·3 we find that

Given any four numbers E, F, G, C subject to the conditions ·41

$$EG - F^2 = C^2, \quad C \neq 0,$$

we can find in any prepared anisotropic vecplane a frame in which E, F, G are the fundamental magnitudes and C is the areal constant,

from which we infer that

All prepared anisotropic vecplanes have the same geometry, ·42

and that

All prepared anisotropic planes have the same geometry. ·43

444. THE PROOF THAT COMPLEX SPACE IS UNIQUE.

·1. In the three-dimensional problem, we suppose given seven numbers L, M, N, P, Q, R, J subject to the relations

$$J^2 = \begin{vmatrix} L & R & Q \\ R & M & P \\ Q & P & N \end{vmatrix}, \qquad \cdot 11$$

$$J \neq 0, \qquad \cdot 12$$

and we have to discover whether in a given vecspace can be found a frame $\mathbf{xyz}$ in which these numbers play the parts indicated by the notation.

·2. Suppose first that $LM - R^2$ is not zero. Then if two vectors **x**, **y** are such that

·21 $$\mathscr{G}\,\mathbf{x}^2 = L, \quad \mathscr{G}\,\mathbf{xy} = R, \quad \mathscr{G}\,\mathbf{y}^2 = M,$$

they are not collinear and the vecplane containing them can not be isotropic. We begin therefore by taking *any* anisotropic vecplane in the given vecspace. In this vecplane, by 3·41, we can find two vectors **x**, **y** satisfying ·21, and since the vecplane is not isotropic and these vectors are not collinear, the vector product $\mathscr{V}\,\mathbf{xy}$ is not coplanar with **x** and **y**, and a third vector **z** is determinable from the three projected products $\mathscr{G}\,\mathbf{xz}$, $\mathscr{G}\,\mathbf{yz}$, $\mathscr{G}\,(\mathscr{V}\,\mathbf{xy})\,\mathbf{z}$; that is, when **x** and **y** have been chosen there is one and only one vector **z** which satisfies the conditions

·22 $$\mathscr{G}\,\mathbf{xz} = Q, \quad \mathscr{G}\,\mathbf{yz} = P, \quad \mathscr{J}\,\mathbf{xyz} = J.$$

Moreover, 12·47, ·11, ·21, ·22 imply

$$\begin{vmatrix} L & R & Q \\ R & M & P \\ Q & P & \mathscr{G}\,\mathbf{z}^2 \end{vmatrix} = \begin{vmatrix} L & R & Q \\ R & M & P \\ Q & P & N \end{vmatrix},$$

and therefore, since $LM - R^2$ is not zero, imply

·23 $$\mathscr{G}\,\mathbf{z}^2 = N.$$

Taken together, ·21, ·22, ·23 shew that the frame **xyz** has the required relation to the seven numbers.

It is easy to write down the actual expression for **z**. In the frame **xyz**, the vector product $\mathscr{V}\,\mathbf{xy}$ has the polar coefficients 0, 0, J; hence

·24 $$\mathscr{V}\,\mathbf{xy} = J\,(\bar{Q}\mathbf{x} + \bar{P}\mathbf{y} + \bar{N}\mathbf{z}),$$

and therefore

·25 $$(LM - R^2)\,\mathbf{z} = (MQ - RP)\,\mathbf{x} + (LP - QR)\,\mathbf{y} + J\,\mathscr{V}\,\mathbf{xy},$$

and this identity is effective to give **z** unless $LM - R^2$ is zero.

·3. The case in which $LM - R^2$ is zero is equally easy to circumvent and to solve.

If the three numbers L, $LM - R^2$, $LN - Q^2$ were all zero, then the three numbers L, R, Q would all be zero, and therefore J would vanish. That is, if a set of magnitudes polar to the given set is calculated from the formulae of 342·4, one of the three numbers

$$\bar{M}\bar{N} - \bar{P}^2, \quad LM - R^2, \quad LN - Q^2$$

is different from zero. Hence a case in which the process of the last paragraph is *not* effective to describe a frame with the given fundamentals either with its third or with its second vecplane arbitrary, is necessarily a case in which this process *is* effective for the construction of a frame from the *polar* magnitudes with its first vecplane arbitrary, and the polar of any frame so formed is a frame with the given numbers in their required parts.

To deal directly with this case, let U, V be two numbers such that

$$L = U^2, \quad R = UV, \quad M = V^2; \qquad \cdot 31$$

here are such numbers, since by hypothesis

$$LM - R^2 = 0, \qquad \cdot 32$$

and these numbers are not both zero, for the determinant

$$\begin{vmatrix} 0 & 0 & Q \\ 0 & 0 & P \\ Q & P & N \end{vmatrix},$$

to which J^2 would reduce if U and V were both zero, vanishes identically.

In any isotropic vecplane can be found two vectors **l**, **m** satisfying

$$\mathscr{G}\mathbf{l}^2 = U^2, \quad \mathscr{G}\mathbf{lm} = UV, \quad \mathscr{G}\mathbf{m}^2 = V^2, \qquad \cdot 331$$

and not collinear. In space the planes

$$\mathscr{G}\mathbf{lr} = Q, \quad \mathscr{G}\mathbf{mr} = P, \qquad \cdot 334$$

not being parallel, intersect in a line whose vecline is perpendicular to the vecplane containing **l** and **m**, and since this vecplane is isotropic, the line determined by ·334 is parallel to the plane which contains the origin and has **l** and **m** in its vecplane. It follows that ° the spatial product $\mathscr{J}\mathbf{lmr}$ has the same value for every vector **r** satisfying ·334. Moreover, it follows from 12·47 that the value of $(\mathscr{J}\mathbf{lmr})^2$ is given by ·335

$$(\mathscr{J}\mathbf{lmr})^2 = \begin{vmatrix} U^2 & UV & Q \\ UV & V^2 & P \\ Q & P & \mathscr{G}\mathbf{r}^2 \end{vmatrix} = \begin{vmatrix} U^2 & UV & Q \\ UV & V^2 & P \\ Q & P & N \end{vmatrix}$$

since the value of the determinant is actually independent of the value of the element occupying the position of N; hence ° if **r** satisfies ·334, ·337

$$(\mathscr{J}\mathbf{lmr})^2 = J^2,$$

whatever the value of $\mathscr{G}\mathbf{r}^2$.

Let us now take $\quad \mathbf{x} = \mathbf{l}, \quad \mathbf{y} = \mathbf{m}, \quad \mathbf{q} = \mathbf{r},$

if $\mathscr{J}\mathbf{lmr}$ is J, but $\quad \mathbf{x} = -\mathbf{l}, \quad \mathbf{y} = -\mathbf{m}, \quad \mathbf{q} = -\mathbf{r},$

if $\mathscr{J}\mathbf{lmr}$ is $-J$. In either case

$$\mathscr{G}\mathbf{x}^2 = L, \quad \mathscr{G}\mathbf{xy} = R, \quad \mathscr{G}\mathbf{y}^2 = M, \qquad \cdot 34$$

and in either case we deduce that there are values of **q** satisfying

$$\mathscr{G}\mathbf{xq} = Q, \quad \mathscr{G}\mathbf{yq} = P \qquad \cdot 351$$

and that these equations *imply*

$$\mathscr{J}\mathbf{xyq} = J. \qquad \cdot 352$$

If **d** is a *particular* solution of ·351, the general solution was seen in 34·32 to be $\mathbf{d} + p\mathscr{V}\mathbf{xy}$, where p is a variable number, and since $\mathscr{V}\mathbf{xy}$ is nul and **d** satisfies ·352,

$$\mathscr{G}(\mathbf{d} + p\mathscr{V}\mathbf{xy})^2 = \mathscr{G}\mathbf{d}^2 + 2Jp. \qquad \cdot 353$$

Since J is not zero, there is one and only one value of p such that

$$\mathcal{G}\mathbf{d}^2 + 2Jp = N,$$

where N is a given number; thus if

·37 $$\mathbf{z} = \mathbf{d} + \{(N - \mathcal{G}\,\mathbf{d}^2)/2J\}\,\mathcal{V}\,\mathbf{xy},$$

$\mathbf{z}$ satisfies not only

·38 $$\mathcal{G}\mathbf{xz} = Q, \quad \mathcal{G}\mathbf{yz} = P, \quad \mathcal{J}\,\mathbf{xyz} = J,$$

·39 but also $$\mathcal{G}\,\mathbf{z}^2 = N,$$

and ·34, ·38, ·39 are formally the same as ·21, ·22, ·23.

·4. To sum up the conclusions of ·2 and ·3,

·41 *Given any seven complex numbers L, M, N, P, Q, R, J subject to the conditions*

$$J^2 = \begin{vmatrix} L & R & Q \\ R & M & P \\ Q & P & N \end{vmatrix}, \quad J \neq 0,$$

we can find in the complex vecspace constructed from any frame whatever a frame which has L, M, N, P, Q, R for its fundamental magnitudes and J for its spatial constant.

Hence

·42 *All complex vecspaces have the same geometry,*

and

·43 *All complex spaces have the same geometry;*

in fact, if more dimensions than three* are not in contemplation, we may assert that

·44 *There is only one complex space.*

·5. Let us hasten to add that there is nothing surprising in ·41. As a matter of pure algebra, there are six conditions to be satisfied and as many as nine independent variables, namely, the coefficients of the three vectors $\mathbf{x}, \mathbf{y}, \mathbf{z}$ in some one frame of reference. The details of an algebraic proof cease to be tiresome if the necessity of paying attention to the peculiarities of nul veclines and isotropic vecplanes is realised from the first, but there are no advantages, theoretical or practical, in treating the matter as merely one of solving a set of equations of no intrinsic elegance.

* There is a sense in which complex space has *six* dimensions; six *real* numbers are necessary to specify three complex numbers, and the complex *line* corresponds point for point to the real *plane*. To express the arbitrary complex number z in the form

$$(ja + kb)/(j + k),$$

where a, b are given distinct complex numbers and $j : k$ is a variable *complex* ratio, is to relate the value of z to the value of $(z - a)/(z - b)$, a familiar problem in the geometry of the Argand plane.

445. Complex geometry and real space.

·1. The theorems of this chapter explain the part which complex geometry plays in the study of real space. Suppose that a real plane is referred to a frame with fundamental magnitudes E_r, F_r, G_r, C_r, subject necessarily to the conditions

$$C_r^2 = E_r G_r - F_r^2 \neq 0.$$

The complex numbers E, F, G, C which have their imaginary parts zero and have E_r, F_r, G_r, C_r for their real parts satisfy 3·13 and 3·14, and can therefore be used for the construction of an anisotropic complex plane. Let the points in this complex plane whose coordinates have their imaginary parts zero be
called the ° *real points* of the complex plane, and let the real point whose co- ·11
ordinates have the real parts ξ_r, η_r be said to correspond to that point in the
real plane which has the coordinates ξ_r, η_r. Then ° the distances between two ·12
real points of the complex plane are numbers whose imaginary parts are zero and whose real parts are the distances between the corresponding points of
the real plane. It follows that ° if one set of relations among distances between ·13
real points in the complex plane implies another set of relations among distances also between these real points, then the set of relations among distances between points in the real plane which corresponds to the first set of relations *implies* the set of relations among distances between the same points which corresponds to the second set of relations. It does not matter in the least *how* the implication in the complex plane has been established; if none but real points of that plane have been involved in the demonstration, the *proof* can be applied word for word in the real plane, but even if points that are not among the real points have been utilised, the *result* can be transferred back to the real plane.

Real space may be correlated in the same way point for point with a *real part* of complex space; the assumption that the space is not isotropic need not be made explicitly, since it is assumed throughout our work, and our conclusions can be summarised in the statement that

If a theorem concerning an anisotropic complex plane or concerning complex ·15
space can be expressed in such a way as to be significant when asserted of a real plane or of real space, then the theorem is true when so asserted, provided that the conclusion does not assume or assert the existence of any points whose existence is not assumed in the hypothesis.

Needless to say, there are some existence-theorems whose enunciations in the geometries of real and complex space *are* verbally identical; all that the restriction in ·15 implies is that such theorems are not necessarily established for real space when they are proved for complex space.

It is ·15, together with 3·43 and 4·43, that explains why the uncritical use of complex coordinates as a technical device has not led to errors in ordinary geometry, in spite of the indefensible absurdities* of any attempt to introduce complex points into real space merely by letting Cartesian coordinates be complex. "To use geometrical language", writes Russell†, "...is only a convenient help to the imagination", and this is true whether the vocabulary is large or small. Reference should be made to the discussion of the relation of complex geometry to real space in Baker's *Principles of Geometry*‡.

·2. In practice, a converse of ·15 is freely used; theorems proved in elementary geometry are asserted of complex space. To be transferable in this way a theorem must of course retain significance; for example, it must not involve inequalities§, since one complex number can not be described as greater than another, and it must not refer to one of three collinear points as *between* the others, since there is no corresponding relation between three arbitrary complex numbers. A theorem that asserts concurrence of lines is likely to be true in complex space even if nul lines become involved, but if metrical relations occur, a reservation excluding nul lines and isotropic planes may be essential.

The ground for the translation of a theorem from ordinary geometry to the geometry of complex space is that the theorem, however it happens to have been proved, could in fact have been demonstrated analytically, and the analysis, if it used no properties of real numbers that complex numbers do not share, would have proved the result for complex space. As De Morgan says in another connection||, "The perfect confidence which a mathematician puts in these proofs does not arise, as he knows, from their proving that their conclusions are true, but from their proving that they can (otherwise) be proved to be true."

There is little difficulty in deciding of any specific proposition whether or not it can be translated, and for a general theorem we content ourselves with an enunciation somewhat narrow:

·21 *If a theorem concerning real space can be expressed in such a way as to be significant when asserted of complex space, then it is true when so asserted, provided that it does not deny the existence of particular points or the possibility of particular constructions, and provided also that if it is metrical in character none of the lines or planes to which explicit reference is made are isotropic.*

·3. As a result of ·15 and ·21, the mathematician acquires a habit, confusing and illogical at first sight though indeed not merely defensible but inevitable, of carrying on his investigations without premising whether it is with real space or with complex space that they are concerned, and of deducing theorems in ordinary geometry from constructions that may be invalid in real space without giving a hint that he is conscious of a glaring anomaly.

* Compare Russell, *Foundations of Geometry*, pp. 42–46, 1897. † *Loc. cit.*, p. 45.

‡ Vol. I., pp. 142 *et seq.*, 1922. § See in particular the foot-note on p. 299 below.

|| *Trigonometry and Double Algebra*, p. 106, 1849. The reference is to the proofs of propositions in Euclid's second book by methods applicable only to lines commensurable with one another.

BOOK V

IDEAL SPACE

CHAPTER V [1]

IDEAL SPACE IN GEOMETRY

511. Ideal points; accessible ideal points and ideal points at infinity. 512. Cohesion of actual planes with ideal points; ideal lines; cohesion of actual planes with ideal lines. 513. Ideal planes. 514. Intersections of ideal lines and ideal planes.

511. Ideal points; accessible ideal points and ideal points at infinity.

·1. In the conventional language introduced by Kepler and Desargues, there are two cases in which a number of lines are said to be concurrent; if the lines all pass through one point, they are concurrent there, and if they are all parallel, they are said to be concurrent at infinity.

In the treatment which we owe to the genius of von Staudt, the fundamental element is not a point but a class of concurrent lines, the lines being concurrent in the wider sense which allows parallelism as a particular case, and the class being as extensive as possible, that is to say, containing *all* the lines through some one point or *all* the lines with some one vecline. Such a class is called a *sheaf* of lines or an °*ideal point.* ·11

A mere extension of vocabulary does not alter the facts of elementary geometry, and sheaves or ideal points are of two kinds. A sheaf consisting of all the lines through an actual point is said to have that point for °*vertex* or ·12 to be associated with that point. A sheaf composed of parallel lines has no actual point in any special relation to it, and is called an ideal point °*at* ·13 *infinity.* No pretence is made that there are any actual points at infinity; an ideal point at infinity is a class of lines which individually are commonplace straight lines, real or complex according as the space under consideration is itself real or complex. Infinity, in fact, becomes a class of sheaves of lines: if a sheaf belongs to this class, the sheaf is said to be at infinity. If we find it convenient to describe a sheaf or an ideal point that is not at infinity as °*accessible,* this term must not be taken to imply that such a sheaf is logically ·14 on any more secure footing than the sheaves at infinity.

·2. If P is any actual point and A is any ideal point other than the sheaf formed of the lines through P, there is one and only one line through P belonging to A; if A has a vertex, this is the line joining P to that vertex, and if A has no vertex, it is the line through P with the vecline then characteristic of the members of A.

We can express this result by saying that there is one and only one line common to the ideal point A and the ideal point composed of lines through P:

·23 *Unless two distinct ideal points are both at infinity, there is one and only one line which belongs to them both.*

·24 °If the ideal points are both accessible, the common line is simply the line through the vertices.

·31 **·3.** A line p belongs to an infinity of ideal points; °it belongs to every
·32 ideal point which has an actual vertex on p; °it belongs also to one and only one ideal point at infinity, namely, the sheaf formed of those lines which are parallel to p.

Here, and nowhere more mystical, is the meaning of the assertion that every line has one and only one point at infinity associated with it. The student is wholly in the right who refuses to be hypnotised into thinking he believes that there are actual points at infinity to be reached by journeys of infinite length along actual lines, and that the point reached by such a journey in one direction along a line p or along any line parallel to p is the same as the point reached by a similar journey in the opposite direction along any of these lines but different from any point reached by a journey along a line not parallel to p; all statements of this kind are nonsense, not the less because they have proved precious. Infinity is no part of actual space. The points at infinity are ideal points, and it is true, if obvious, that every actual line bears to just one ideal point at infinity the relation of membership which it bears to those accessible ideal points whose vertices it contains.

512. Cohesion of actual planes with ideal points; ideal lines; cohesion of actual planes with ideal lines.

·1. Naturally an ideal line is to be a class of ideal points, and we anticipate that the ideal line associated with an actual line p is to be the class consisting of those ideal points to which p belongs. This however will not provide us with a sufficiently general definition of an ideal line, for just as there are ideal points without vertices, so there are ideal lines to which no actual lines correspond. To encounter the difficulty from another direction, if we set out to find a definition of the ideal line containing two given distinct ideal points Q, R, we can usually find one actual line p which belongs to both these sheaves, and every sheaf that contains p may be regarded as collinear with Q and R; this process succeeds if the ideal points are both accessible, when p is the line through their vertices, or if one of the ideal points is accessible and the other is at infinity, when p is the line through the vertex of the one parallel to the members of the other, but the method fails if both of the ideal points are sheaves of parallel lines, for there is then no actual line common to the two sheaves. Geometry and algebra suggest different definitions of the ideal line, but the two definitions are found to be equivalent.

·2. The relation of a plane to an actual point P when the plane contains P can be expressed directly in terms of the plane and the sheaf with P for vertex: there are lines of the sheaf lying in the plane. If we say that a plane
°*coheres* with a sheaf or an ideal point, whether or not the sheaf is at infinity, ·21
when there are lines of the sheaf lying in the plane, then we can distinguish two cases:

If a plane coheres with an ideal point, then if the ideal point is accessible its ·22
vertex is in the plane, but if the ideal point is at infinity the lines which compose it are parallel to the plane.

It is important to observe that

If a plane includes an actual point P and coheres with an ideal point A, then ·23
unless A is accessible and has P for its vertex, the plane contains the one line which belongs to A and includes P.

·3. In elementary geometry, the line through two distinct points P, Q is the aggregate of points common to all the planes that include both P and Q. Prompted by this consideration, let us examine the planes cohesive with two given distinct ideal points A, B and discover whether there are any ideal points other than A, B with which these planes all cohere.

It follows from ·23 that if B is an ideal point with an actual vertex Q and A is any ideal point distinct from B, every plane that coheres with both A and B contains the line through Q belonging to A. Conversely, since this line belongs to both ideal points, every plane which contains it does cohere with them both. That is,

Unless two distinct ideal points are both at infinity, the planes that cohere ·31
with them both are the planes through the one line common to them.

Hence

If two distinct ideal points A, B have a line p in common, the ideal points ·32
that cohere with all the planes that cohere with both A and B are the ideal points to which p belongs.

If two ideal points A, B are both at infinity, they have no common member if they are distinct, but there are still planes which cohere with them both. In fact if O is any point of space, there are definite lines p, q through O belonging the one to A and the other to B, and the plane that contains p and q coheres with A and B and by ·23 is the only plane through O that does cohere with them both. Since the directions of p and q do not depend on the position of O, any two planes that cohere with both A and B are parallel, while conversely if P is one plane that coheres with A and B, any plane parallel to P also coheres with A and B.

If two distinct ideal points are both at infinity, the planes that cohere with ·33
them both are the parallel planes whose common vecplane contains their two veclines.

Hence

·34 *If two distinct ideal points A, B are both at infinity, the ideal points that cohere with all the planes that cohere with both A and B are the ideal points at infinity with veclines in the vecplane containing the veclines of A and B.*

Considering ·32 without reference to the line p itself, or ·34 without mention of the vecplane, we have in each case a family of planes and a family of ideal points; each plane is cohesive with each ideal point, and any two of the ideal points or any two of the planes determine the whole configuration, for they suffice to give the line or the vecplane. If any two of the ideal points are at infinity, all the ideal points are at infinity, by 1·32; if any two of the planes are parallel, all the planes are parallel.

·35 We can now see the results of defining an ideal line as °a class of ideal points each of which is cohesive with two planes, and therefore with *all* planes, that cohere with any two of them. There are two kinds of ideal line.

·36 °An ideal line may consist of all the ideal points to which a particular actual line, called its axis, belongs. In this case, the ideal line, by 1·32, includes one and only one ideal point at infinity. A plane that coheres with more than one of the ideal points is a plane that contains the axis and is therefore a plane that coheres with every one of the ideal points; such a plane may be said to cohere with the ideal line itself. If a plane that does not contain the axis is parallel to the axis it coheres with the ideal point at infinity to which the axis belongs; if a plane is not parallel to the axis it cuts the axis in a definite point and coheres with the accessible ideal point which has that point
·37 for vertex: in any case, °if a plane does not cohere with every ideal point belonging to the ideal line, there is one and only one of these ideal points with which it does cohere.

·38 °An ideal line of the second type consists of all the ideal points at infinity whose veclines lie in a particular vecplane. Since all the ideal points that compose it are at infinity, such an ideal line is itself said to be at infinity, and by contrast an ideal line with an axis is described as accessible. A plane that coheres with more than one of the ideal points is a plane with the vecplane characteristic of the ideal line and is therefore a plane that coheres with every one of the ideal points; again the plane is said to cohere with the ideal line. The vecplane of the ideal line and the vecplane of any plane that does not cohere with the ideal line have one vecline in common, and the ideal point at infinity which has this vecline is an ideal point that belongs to the ideal line and
·39 coheres with the actual plane: °if a plane does not cohere with every ideal point belonging to the ideal line, there is one and only one of these ideal points with which it does cohere.

·4. The verbal identity of ·37 and ·39 is valuable; we can assert simply that

·41 *A plane that does not cohere with an ideal line coheres with one and only one ideal point on that line.*

The discussion leading to the definition of an ideal line implies that

Given any two distinct planes, there is one and only one ideal line with which they both cohere; ·42

it follows from ·41 and ·42 that

If three planes do not all cohere with a single ideal line, there is one and only one ideal point with which they all do cohere. ·43

Given an actual point O and a line that does not include O, there is one and only one plane that includes O and contains the line; given an actual point and any vecplane, there is one and only one plane that includes O and has the vecplane:

Given any actual point and any ideal line other than an accessible ideal line whose axis passes through the point, there is one and only one plane which includes the actual point and coheres with the ideal line. ·44

Hence comes a correlative of ·43:

If three ideal points are not all at infinity, then if there is no ideal line to which they all belong there is one and only one plane that coheres with them all. ·45

·5. The ideal lines that cohere with a particular plane P are to be found by associating with P a variable plane Q distinct from P. If Q is not parallel to P, the two planes cut in an actual line and determine the accessible ideal line of which that line is the axis. If Q is parallel to P, the two planes determine the ideal line at infinity characterised by the vecplane of P. °Thus P ·51
coheres with a single ideal line at infinity, and with an infinity of accessible ideal lines, namely, the accessible ideal lines whose axes are actual lines in P.
°All the inaccessible ideal points that cohere with P are on the one inaccessible ·52
ideal line that coheres with P; in fact, the ideal line is the aggregate of these ideal points.

Let a, b be any two distinct ideal lines that cohere with P; let Q be a second plane that coheres with a and R a second plane that coheres with b. The three planes P, Q, R do not all cohere with any one ideal line, and therefore by ·43 there is one and only one ideal point with which they all cohere, and this point belongs to a because P and Q cohere with it and to b because P and R cohere with it.

Two ideal lines that both cohere with one plane have an ideal point in common. ·53

If two distinct ideal lines a, b have an ideal point C in common, and if A, B are ideal points distinct from C on a, b, then unless a, b are both at infinity, one at least of the three ideal points A, B, C is necessarily accessible, and therefore by ·45 there is a plane that coheres with the three ideal points; this plane coheres with a, since it coheres with both A and C, and with b, since it coheres with both B and C:

If two distinct ideal lines have an ideal point in common and are not both at infinity, there is a plane that coheres with them both. ·54

Since two ideal lines that cohere with one plane can not both be at infinity, the case excluded from ·54 is excluded also from ·53, and this case must be examined. The vecplanes characteristic of two ideal lines at infinity necessarily have one vecline in common, and the ideal point at infinity with this vecline is an ideal point common to the two ideal lines:

·55 *Any two ideal lines that are both at infinity have an ideal point in common.*

The three results ·53, ·54, ·55 can be combined in a single enunciation:

·56 *Two ideal lines have an ideal point in common if they are both at infinity or if there is a plane which coheres with them both, but not otherwise.*

513. Ideal planes.

·1. If the language of elementary geometry is to be available, an ideal plane must be a class of ideal points determined by three of its members which are not collinear, and such that the ideal line joining any two members of the class is part of the class. Thus to construct from first principles the ideal plane determined by three ideal points A, B, C, we should add to A, B, C first all the ideal points on the ideal lines BC, CA, AB, then all the ideal points on ideal lines joining ideal points on one of these ideal lines to ideal points on another, then all the ideal points on ideal lines joining two ideal points of the last kind, and so on, continuing the process till no new ideal points were introduced; it is obvious that if F, G, H are any three non-collinear ideal points reached by this process, the ideal plane determined by F, G, H is contained in the ideal plane determined by A, B, C, but to prove that the two ideal planes are identical it would be necessary to shew that A, B, C can be reached from F, G, H by a similar process. Actually we avoid work that might prove tedious by appealing to 2·56.

·2. If A, B, C are three ideal points that are not collinear and not all at infinity, a fourth ideal point D is on an ideal line joining A to an ideal point on BC if AD and BC have an ideal point in common, that is, from 2·56, if there is an actual plane P that coheres with the four points A, B, C, D; the plane P is determined by the three given ideal points, and every ideal point that coheres with P is in the ideal plane determined by A, B, C. Since also every ideal point on every ideal line joining two distinct ideal points that cohere with P, itself coheres with P, the process described in the last paragraph can not lead us from ideal points that cohere with P to ideal points that do not cohere with P. Finally, if F, G, H are any three ideal points reached by this process and not collinear, P is the *only* plane that coheres with all three of them, and therefore the ideal plane determined by F, G, H is identical with the ideal plane determined by A, B, C.

If A, B, C are three ideal points at infinity and not collinear, it follows from 2·34 that *every* point to which the process of ·1 leads is at infinity, and from 2·55 that this process leads to every point at infinity.

Thus ideal planes, like ideal lines and ideal points, are of two kinds. °An accessible ideal plane consists of all the ideal points with which some actual plane coheres. °The aggregate of ideal points at infinity also is an ideal plane, naturally called the ideal plane at infinity. ·23 ·24

514. Intersections of ideal lines and ideal planes.

·1. Of two distinct ideal planes, one must be accessible. The ideal points common to an accessible ideal plane and the ideal plane at infinity are the inaccessible ideal points in the accessible ideal plane, and from 2·38 it follows that these compose a definite ideal line. If two ideal planes are both accessible, the ideal points common to the ideal planes are the ideal points with which the corresponding actual planes both cohere, and these are seen by 2·42 to form a definite ideal line.

Any two distinct ideal planes intersect in an ideal line. ·11

This is one example of the simplification introduced into geometrical language by the completing of space; a second, equally useful, is furnished by 2·56, which becomes

Two ideal lines are concurrent if and only if they are coplanar. ·12

From ·11 it follows that if A, B, C are three distinct ideal planes, A, B cut C in ideal lines a, b; unless these ideal lines coincide, ·12 shews that there is one and only one ideal point common to them:

Any three ideal planes have an ideal point in common. ·13

If any number of ideal planes have in common two distinct ideal points, they have the whole ideal line through these two ideal points; if there are three common ideal points that are not collinear, the ideal planes necessarily coincide.

·2. Given an ideal line a we can always find two ideal planes intersecting in a: all that is necessary is to take any ideal point B not in a and a second ideal point C not in the ideal plane that contains a and includes B; the ideal plane that contains a and includes C then cuts the ideal plane that contains a and includes B in the ideal line a itself. It follows from this and ·13 that

Any ideal line that is not contained in a given ideal plane cuts the ideal plane in one and only one ideal point. ·21

It is the entire absence of exceptional cases from propositions such as those of this section that is alike the aim and the justification of the construction of ideal space.

CHAPTER V 2

IDEAL SPACE IN ANALYSIS

521. The specification of an ideal point. 522. Ideal lines and ideal planes in analysis. 523. Conditions for collinearity and coplanarity of ideal points. 524. Tetrahedral coordinates as coefficients in the specification of an ideal point. 525. The loading of ideal points; addition of loads; mean centres. 526. Uses of loaded ideal points; tetrahedral coordinates as multipliers in a loaded tetrahedron. 527. The effect of a change in the tetrahedron of reference; homogeneous linear equations.

521. THE SPECIFICATION OF AN IDEAL POINT.

·1. The introduction of elements at infinity into analytical work follows with surprising fidelity the steps of their introduction into pure geometry.

The position of a point R may be determined from a point Q by means of two vectors, the vector $\mathbf{q}'$ of the step from Q to a fixed point O, and the vector $\mathbf{r}$ of the step from O to R. The step QR is the step which represents the vector $\mathbf{r}+\mathbf{q}'$ with reference to the point Q. If Q is distinct from R, the steps from Q with vectors of the form $k\mathbf{r}+k\mathbf{q}'$ lie all in the line QR, and for different values of k trace out the whole line. Hence given a vector $\mathbf{r}$ and a number t different from zero, the steps which represent from Q the vectors of the form $k(\mathbf{r}+t\mathbf{q}')$, that is, $kt\{(\mathbf{r}/t)+\mathbf{q}'\}$, trace out the line joining Q to the point whose vector from O is $\mathbf{r}/t$, provided only that Q is distinct from this last point. If t is zero but $\mathbf{r}$ is not the zero vector, the vectors of the form $k(\mathbf{r}+t\mathbf{q}')$ *still determine a definite line,* though this is no longer the line through Q and a definite point but is the line through Q *with given directions,* those of the vector $\mathbf{r}$. In either case the line is determined not by $\mathbf{r}$ alone or by t alone, and the same line is given by $k\mathbf{r}$ and kt as by $\mathbf{r}$ and t, provided only that $\mathbf{r}+t\mathbf{q}'$ is not zero. Suppose now that $\mathbf{r}$ and t are given but Q is allowed to vary. To each position of Q, with possibly a single exception, corresponds one and only one line; if t is not zero, the various lines are concurrent in a definite vertex, the point whose vector from O is $\mathbf{r}/t$; if t is zero, the lines are all parallel. In other words,

·13 *The lines determined in this way from a vector* $\mathbf{r}$ *and a number t which are not both zero compose an ideal point.*

Moreover, the same ideal point is determined by $h\mathbf{r}$ and ht as by $\mathbf{r}$ and t, if h has any value other than zero: the specification of an ideal point from an
·14 origin by means of a vector and a number is ° *homogeneous.* The ideal point determined by $\mathbf{r}$ and t will be described simply as the ideal point $(\mathbf{r}, t)$.

·2. The definition of the ideal point $(\mathbf{r}, t)$ is equivalent to the theorem that

If $\mathbf{q}$ *is the vector from the origin* O *to a point* Q, *a line through* Q *belongs to* ·21
the ideal point $(\mathbf{r}, t)$ *if and only if its vecline includes the vector* $\mathbf{r} - t\mathbf{q}$.

If $\mathbf{r} - t\mathbf{q}$ is the zero vector, every vecline includes $\mathbf{r} - t\mathbf{q}$, and the ideal point is accessible and has Q for vertex. In every other case, there is one and only one line through Q that belongs to $(\mathbf{r}, t)$.

·3. The specification of a particular ideal point A by means of a vector $\mathbf{r}$ and a number t depends of course on the origin O. The effect of a change of origin is easily deduced from ·21. If the origin is moved to a point S such that the vector of OS is $\mathbf{s}$, and if $\mathbf{t}$ is the vector of SQ, we have $\mathbf{q} = \mathbf{s} + \mathbf{t}$, and therefore a line through Q belongs to the ideal point A if and only if its vecline includes $\mathbf{r} - t(\mathbf{s} + \mathbf{t})$, that is, includes $(\mathbf{r} - t\mathbf{s}) - t\mathbf{t}$, whence

The ideal point which is $(\mathbf{r}, t)$ *when referred to an origin* O, *is* $(\mathbf{r} - t\mathbf{s}, t)$ *when* ·32
referred to the point S *which is such that the vector of* OS *is* $\mathbf{s}$.

If we have reason to describe the new origin not directly but as the vertex of an accessible ideal point which with reference to O is $(\mathbf{l}, l)$, the new specification $\{\mathbf{r} - t(\mathbf{l}/l), t\}$ is conveniently taken in ° the form $(l\mathbf{r} - t\mathbf{l}, lt)$. But it is ·33
to be observed that ° there is no possibility of using an inaccessible origin in ·34
this way: if l is zero, $(l\mathbf{r} - t\mathbf{l}, lt)$ reduces to $(-t\mathbf{l}, 0)$ and fails to distinguish one accessible ideal point from another. The utilisation of inaccessible ideal points as points of reference is effected along quite different lines.

·4. To describe the ideal point $(\mathbf{r}, t)$ by means of a Cartesian frame $OXYZ$ or an attached vector frame $O\mathbf{xyz}$, what is wanted in addition to the number t is a set of numbers to specify the vector $\mathbf{r}$ by means of the chosen frame. Taking components or coefficients, we have the ideal point indicated in the one case by the set of four numbers x, y, z, t and in the other case by the set of four numbers ξ, η, ζ, τ, where τ is substituted for t for the sake of uniformity in appearance. In each case, one at least of the four numbers is necessarily different from zero, and the ideal point depends only on the ratios $x : y : z : t$ or $\xi : \eta : \zeta : \tau$, being unaltered if the four numbers are multiplied
simultaneously by any number other than zero: in fact, °the specification ·42
remains homogeneous when it is effected by means of four numbers instead of by means of a vector and a number. But it is impossible to replace the homogeneous specification with four numbers by any specification with three numbers only, without loss of efficiency, for although the four numbers can not all be zero together, there is no one of them that is not zero individually for some definite class of ideal points: t and τ are zero for the points at infinity.

Any accessible point A has one and only one specification in which τ_A is 1, and the values of ξ_A, η_A, ζ_A in this specification are the coordinates, in the elementary sense, relative to $O\mathbf{xyz}$, of the actual point which is the vertex of A.

522. Ideal lines and ideal planes in analysis.

·1. In the geometrical theory, an ideal point and an actual plane have been said to cohere if the plane contains a line belonging to the point.

Let the plane be given, with reference to the origin O, by the equation

·11 $$\mathscr{S}\,\mathbf{ar} = A,$$

where $\mathbf{a}$ is a vector perpendicular to the plane and A is a constant for the plane. If $\mathbf{q}$ is the vector from O to a point Q of the plane, the lines* through Q in the ideal point $(\mathbf{l}, l)$ are the lines whose veclines include the vector $\mathbf{l} - l\mathbf{q}$, and there is one of these lines in the plane if and only if

·12 $$\mathscr{S}\,\mathbf{a}(\mathbf{l} - l\mathbf{q}) = 0,$$

that is, since $\mathbf{q}$ satisfies ·11, if and only if

·13 $$\mathscr{S}\,\mathbf{al} = Al,$$

a condition from which $\mathbf{q}$, and with it all reference to the particular point Q, has disappeared.

There is of course nothing surprising in the resemblance of ·13 to ·11. If the ideal point $(\mathbf{l}, l)$ has an actual vertex, this is the point whose vector from O is $\mathbf{l}/l$, and the ideal point coheres with the plane ·11 if the vertex is in the plane, that is, if

$$\mathscr{S}\,\mathbf{a}(\mathbf{l}/l) = A.$$

If on the other hand the ideal point is the sheaf of parallel lines with veclines containing $\mathbf{l}$, the ideal point coheres with the plane if the vector $\mathbf{l}$ is a vector in the corresponding vecplane, that is, if

$$\mathscr{S}\,\mathbf{al} = 0,$$

and this is the form which ·13 assumes if l is zero.

·2. After the manner in which vecplanes are defined, it is natural that when we are given two distinct ideal points $(\mathbf{l}, l)$, $(\mathbf{m}, m)$ we consider the class of ideal points of the form $(i\mathbf{l} + j\mathbf{m},\ il + jm)$ for varying values of i and j. Because the specification of an ideal point is homogeneous, the ideal point $(i\mathbf{l} + j\mathbf{m},\ il + jm)$ depends only on the ratio of i to j, not on the absolute values of these numbers. Moreover, the relation of $(i\mathbf{l} + j\mathbf{m},\ il + jm)$ to $(\mathbf{l}, l)$ and $(\mathbf{m}, m)$ does not depend on the origin of reference, for if $(\mathbf{l}, l)$, $(\mathbf{m}, m)$ are replaced by $(\mathbf{l} - l\mathbf{s}, l)$, $(\mathbf{m} - m\mathbf{s}, m)$, then $(i\mathbf{l} + j\mathbf{m},\ il + jm)$ becomes

$$\{i(\mathbf{l} - l\mathbf{s}) + j(\mathbf{m} - m\mathbf{s}),\ il + jm\},$$

and this, since it can be written

$$\{(i\mathbf{l} + j\mathbf{m}) - (il + jm)\,\mathbf{s},\ il + jm\},$$

represents the same ideal point with respect to the new origin as does $(i\mathbf{l} + j\mathbf{m},\ il + jm)$ with respect to the old.

* Unless the ideal point is the accessible ideal point with vertex Q, there is one and only one line.

It is obvious from ·13 that °for all values of i and j, the ideal point $(i\mathbf{l}+j\mathbf{m},\ il+jm)$ coheres with every plane with which $(\mathbf{l},\ l)$ and $(\mathbf{m},\ m)$ both cohere. ·22

Conversely, if $(\mathbf{l},\ l)$ and $(\mathbf{m},\ m)$ are distinct ideal points cohering with each of the distinct planes $(\mathbf{a},\ A)$, $(\mathbf{b},\ B)$, and if $(\mathbf{n},\ n)$ is a third ideal point which also coheres with each of these planes, then

$$\mathscr{S}\mathbf{al}=Al,\quad \mathscr{S}\mathbf{am}=Am,\quad \mathscr{S}\mathbf{an}=An, \qquad \cdot 231$$

$$\mathscr{S}\mathbf{bl}=Bl,\quad \mathscr{S}\mathbf{bm}=Bm,\quad \mathscr{S}\mathbf{bn}=Bn, \qquad \cdot 232$$

and therefore

$$\mathscr{S}(B\mathbf{a}-A\mathbf{b})\,\mathbf{l}=0,\quad \mathscr{S}(B\mathbf{a}-A\mathbf{b})\,\mathbf{m}=0,\quad \mathscr{S}(B\mathbf{a}-A\mathbf{b})\,\mathbf{n}=0. \qquad \cdot 233$$

Unless A and B are both zero, the vector $B\mathbf{a}-A\mathbf{b}$ is not the zero vector, since the planes are distinct, and therefore ·233 implies that $\mathbf{l}$, $\mathbf{m}$, $\mathbf{n}$ are coplanar, that is, that there are constants f, g, h such that

$$f\mathbf{l}+g\mathbf{m}+h\mathbf{n}=\mathbf{0}; \qquad \cdot 234$$

this being the case, we have from ·231, ·232

$$A\,(fl+gm+hn)=0,\quad B\,(fl+gm+hn)=0,$$

and this requires

$$fl+gm+hn=0. \qquad \cdot 236$$

Since $(\mathbf{l},\ l)$ and $(\mathbf{m},\ m)$ are distinct, h is not zero, for there are no numbers f, g such that simultaneously

$$f\mathbf{l}+g\mathbf{m}=\mathbf{0},\quad fl+gm=0;$$

but if h is not zero, ·234, ·236 become

$$\mathbf{n}=-(f/h)\,\mathbf{l}-(g/h)\,\mathbf{m},\quad n=-(f/h)\,l-(g/h)\,m, \qquad \cdot 237$$

and express that °$(\mathbf{n},\ n)$ is of the form $(i\mathbf{l}+j\mathbf{m},\ il+jm)$. ·24

To deal with the excepted case, we may either move the origin to a point which is not common to the two planes, or observe that if A and B are both zero, $\mathbf{a}$ and $\mathbf{b}$ are not collinear, and ·231, ·232 express that $\mathbf{l}$, $\mathbf{m}$, $\mathbf{n}$ are all multiples of $\mathscr{V}\mathbf{ab}$; writing

$$\mathbf{l}:\mathbf{m}:\mathbf{n}=L:M:N, \qquad \cdot 251$$

then since $mL-lM$ can not be zero, for $m\mathbf{l}-l\mathbf{m}$ is a proper vector, the pair of equations

$$fL+gM+hN=0,\quad fl+gm+hn=0 \qquad \cdot 252$$

can be satisfied by values of f, g, h such that h is not zero.

If $(\mathbf{l},\ l)$, $(\mathbf{m},\ m)$ *are distinct ideal points, and* P, Q *are distinct planes with which they both cohere, the ideal points which cohere with both* P *and* Q *are the ideal points of the form* $(i\mathbf{l}+j\mathbf{m},\ il+jm)$. ·26

That is to say,

If $(\mathbf{l},\ l)$ *and* $(\mathbf{m},\ m)$ *are distinct ideal points, the ideal points of the form* $(i\mathbf{l}+j\mathbf{m},\ il+jm)$ *are the ideal points composing the ideal line through* $(\mathbf{l},\ l)$ *and* $(\mathbf{m},\ m)$. ·27

·31 **·3.** °The expression $(\mathbf{l}+j\mathbf{m},\ l+jm)$ represents by the variation of j all the ideal points of the ideal line joining $(\mathbf{l},\ l)$ to $(\mathbf{m},\ m)$ except the ideal point $(\mathbf{m},\ m)$ itself. Hence if $(\mathbf{l},\ l)$ is not collinear with $(\mathbf{m},\ m)$ and $(\mathbf{n},\ n)$, the expression $(\mathbf{l}+j\mathbf{m}+k\mathbf{n},\ l+jm+kn)$ represents all the ideal points coplanar with these three except those on the ideal line joining $(\mathbf{m},\ m)$ to $(\mathbf{n},\ n)$, and

·32 *If* $(\mathbf{l},\ l)$, $(\mathbf{m},\ m)$, $(\mathbf{n},\ n)$ *are any three ideal points that are not collinear, the ideal points of the form* $(i\mathbf{l}+j\mathbf{m}+k\mathbf{n},\ il+jm+kn)$ *are the ideal points composing the ideal plane through these three ideal points.*

523. Conditions for collinearity and coplanarity of ideal points.

·1. The two ideal points $(\mathbf{l},\ l)$, $(\mathbf{m},\ m)$ coincide if and only if there are numbers i, j' which are not both zero such that

·11
$$j'\mathbf{m}=i\mathbf{l},\quad j'm=il.$$

It is important to observe that in fact *neither* of the numbers i, j' can be zero, for if i is zero but not j', ·11 gives

$$\mathbf{m}=\mathbf{0},\quad m=0$$

and $(\mathbf{m},\ m)$ fails to represent an ideal point at all. Thus we can assert, writing j for $-j'$, both that

·13 *The two ideal points* $(\mathbf{l},\ l)$, $(\mathbf{m},\ m)$ *coincide if and only if there are two numbers* i, j *both different from zero such that*

$$i\mathbf{l}+j\mathbf{m}=\mathbf{0},\quad il+jm=0,$$

and that

·14 *The two ideal points* $(\mathbf{l},\ l)$, $(\mathbf{m},\ m)$ *coincide if and only if there are two numbers* i, j *not both zero such that*

$$i\mathbf{l}+j\mathbf{m}=\mathbf{0},\quad il+jm=0.$$

The difference between the two forms of expression which is trivial in this case acquires significance in the corresponding theorems to which we proceed.

·2. If $(\mathbf{l},\ l)$, $(\mathbf{m},\ m)$ are distinct, a third ideal point $(\mathbf{n},\ n)$ is in the ideal line through them if and only if there are numbers i, j not both zero and a number k' not zero such that

$$k'\mathbf{n}=i\mathbf{l}+j\mathbf{m},\quad k'n=il+jm;$$

remarking that if i is zero, $(\mathbf{n},\ n)$ coincides with $(\mathbf{m},\ m)$, and if j is zero, $(\mathbf{n},\ n)$ coincides with $(\mathbf{l},\ l)$, and replacing $-k'$ by k, we conclude that

·23 *The three ideal points* $(\mathbf{l},\ l)$, $(\mathbf{m},\ m)$, $(\mathbf{n},\ n)$ *are collinear and all distinct if and only if there are three numbers* i, j, k *all different from zero such that*

$$i\mathbf{l}+j\mathbf{m}+k\mathbf{n}=\mathbf{0},\quad il+jm+kn=0.$$

If one of the numbers i, j, k in ·23 is zero but one of them is not zero, the conditions of ·14 reappear; the third number is not zero, and two of the ideal points coincide. If the third ideal point is distinct from these two, there is still one ideal line that includes them all, while in the extreme case in which the three ideal points all coincide, there is an infinity of ideal lines through them.

The three ideal points ($\mathbf{l}$, l), ($\mathbf{m}$, m), ($\mathbf{n}$, n) *are collinear if and only if there are three numbers* i, j, k *not all zero such that* ·24

$$i\mathbf{l}+j\mathbf{m}+k\mathbf{n}=\mathbf{0},\quad il+jm+kn=0.$$

·3. For the ideal point ($\mathbf{p}$, p) to be coplanar with three ideal points ($\mathbf{l}$, l), ($\mathbf{m}$, m), ($\mathbf{n}$, n) that are not collinear, there must be numbers i, j, k not all zero and a number h' different from zero such that

$$h'\mathbf{p}=i\mathbf{l}+j\mathbf{m}+k\mathbf{n},\quad h'p=il+jm+kn.$$

If one of the numbers i, j, k is zero, ($\mathbf{p}$, p) is collinear with two of the three ideal points (l, $\mathbf{l}$), ($\mathbf{m}$, m), ($\mathbf{n}$, n); hence

The four ideal points ($\mathbf{l}$, l), ($\mathbf{m}$, m), ($\mathbf{n}$, n), ($\mathbf{p}$, p) *are coplanar and no three of them are collinear if and only if there are four numbers* i, j, k, h *all different from zero such that* ·33

$$i\mathbf{l}+j\mathbf{m}+k\mathbf{n}+h\mathbf{p}=\mathbf{0},\quad il+jm+kn+hp=0.$$

And corresponding to ·24,

The four ideal points ($\mathbf{l}$, l), ($\mathbf{m}$, m), ($\mathbf{n}$, n), ($\mathbf{p}$, p) *are coplanar if and only if there are four numbers* i, j, k, h *not all zero such that* ·34

$$i\mathbf{l}+j\mathbf{m}+k\mathbf{n}+h\mathbf{p}=\mathbf{0},\quad il+jm+kn+hp=0.$$

524. Tetrahedral coordinates as coefficients in the specification of an ideal point.

·1. If A, B, C, D are any four ideal points that are not coplanar, and G is any ideal point whatever, there is an ideal line that includes D and G, and this ideal line has an ideal point in common with the ideal plane ABC:

If ($\mathbf{l}$, l), ($\mathbf{m}$, m), ($\mathbf{n}$, n), ($\mathbf{p}$, p) *are any four ideal points that are not coplanar, every ideal point can be expressed in the form* ·11

$$(f\mathbf{l}+g\mathbf{m}+h\mathbf{n}+k\mathbf{p},\quad fl+gm+hn+kp).$$

·2. Here is the beginning for completed space of the theory of *tetrahedral coordinates*, which describes a point by its relations to four points of reference, A, B, C, D, themselves subject to no essential condition except that of not being coplanar. It is evident that something must be given in addition to the four ideal points of ·11 themselves if the set of numbers (f, g, h, k) is to characterise a definite ideal point G. For if f, g, h, k are all different from zero and if a, b, c, d are *any* four numbers also all different from zero, then writing

$$\mathbf{l}'=f\mathbf{l}/a,\quad \mathbf{m}'=g\mathbf{m}/b,\quad \mathbf{n}'=h\mathbf{n}/c,\quad \mathbf{p}'=k\mathbf{p}/d,$$
$$l'=fl/a,\quad m'=gm/b,\quad n'=hn/c,\quad p'=kp/d,$$

we have in $(\mathbf{l}', l')$, $(\mathbf{m}', m')$, $(\mathbf{n}', n')$, $(\mathbf{p}', p')$ the *same* ideal points A, B, C, D as $(\mathbf{l}, l)$, $(\mathbf{m}, m)$, $(\mathbf{n}, n)$, $(\mathbf{p}, p)$, and yet since identically

$$a\mathbf{l}' + b\mathbf{m}' + c\mathbf{n}' + d\mathbf{p}' = f\mathbf{l} + g\mathbf{m} + h\mathbf{n} + k\mathbf{p},$$

$$al' + bm' + cn' + dp' = fl + gm + hn + kp,$$

·22 °the ideal point G formed with the four numbers f, g, h, k can equally well be formed from A, B, C, D with the four numbers a, b, c, d chosen almost at
·23 random. By the same argument, °any other ideal point not coplanar with any three of the ideal points A, B, C, D can be associated with the four numbers f, g, h, k first used of G.

This analysis itself shews clearly the point of indetermination and indicates how precision is to be imparted. In passing from f, g, h, k to a, b, c, d as the numbers associated with a particular ideal point, we have to change, not indeed the ideal points A, B, C, D themselves but the vectors and numbers used to specify these ideal points. If $\mathbf{l}, \mathbf{m}, \mathbf{n}, \mathbf{p}$ and l, m, n, p are regarded as *fixed*, as well as the actual point which is used as origin in the specification of the ideal points, and if f, g, h, k are given numbers not all zero, then there is of course one and only one ideal point $(f\mathbf{l} + g\mathbf{m} + h\mathbf{n} + k\mathbf{p}, fl + gm + hn + kp)$. Conversely, for the ideal point $(a\mathbf{l} + b\mathbf{m} + c\mathbf{n} + d\mathbf{p}, al + bm + cn + dp)$ to be the same as the ideal point $(f\mathbf{l} + g\mathbf{m} + h\mathbf{n} + k\mathbf{p}, fl + gm + hn + kp)$, there must be numbers r, s both different from zero such that simultaneously

$$r(a\mathbf{l} + b\mathbf{m} + c\mathbf{n} + d\mathbf{p}) = s(f\mathbf{l} + g\mathbf{m} + h\mathbf{n} + k\mathbf{p}),$$

$$r(al + bm + cn + dp) = s(fl + gm + hn + kp);$$

writing these equations in the form

$$(ra - sf)\mathbf{l} + (rb - sg)\mathbf{m} + (rc - sh)\mathbf{n} + (rd - sk)\mathbf{p} = \mathbf{0},$$

$$(ra - sf)l + (rb - sg)m + (rc - sh)n + (rd - sk)p = 0,$$

we see from 3·34 that they imply either that the four ideal points A, B, C, D are coplanar, which is assumed not to be the case, or that the coefficients $ra - sf$, $rb - sg$, $rc - sh$, $rd - sk$ are all zero, and since neither r nor s is zero, the implication is simply

·26 $$a : b : c : d = f : g : h : k.$$

·27 *Given an actual point as origin of reference, and* definite *specifications* $(\mathbf{l}, l)$, $(\mathbf{m}, m)$, $(\mathbf{n}, n)$, $(\mathbf{p}, p)$ *of four ideal points that are not coplanar, any ideal point can be expressed in the form*

$$(f\mathbf{l} + g\mathbf{m} + h\mathbf{n} + k\mathbf{p}, fl + gm + hn + kp);$$

the four numbers f, g, h, k are not all zero, and the ideal point is determined not by the actual values of these numbers but by the ratios $f : g : h : k$; moreover, to each ideal point corresponds only one set of ratios.

·3. If with the change of origin from O to a point S such that the vector of OS is $\mathbf{s}$ the specifications of the four ideal points $(\mathbf{l}, l)$, $(\mathbf{m}, m)$, $(\mathbf{n}, n)$, $(\mathbf{p}, p)$

ake the simplest modification possible, namely, to $(\mathbf{l} - l\mathbf{s}, l)$, $(\mathbf{m} - m\mathbf{s}, m)$, $\mathbf{n} - n\mathbf{s}, n)$, $(\mathbf{p} - p\mathbf{s}, p)$, then since the pair of equations

$$\mathbf{r} = f\mathbf{l} + g\mathbf{m} + h\mathbf{n} + k\mathbf{p}, \quad t = fl + gm + hn + kp$$ ·31

s equivalent to

$$\mathbf{r} - t\mathbf{s} = f(\mathbf{l} - l\mathbf{s}) + g(\mathbf{m} - m\mathbf{s}) + h(\mathbf{n} - n\mathbf{s}) + k(\mathbf{p} - p\mathbf{s}), \quad t = fl + gm + hn + kp,$$ ·32

the set of ratios $f : g : h : k$ associated with any ideal point G is unaltered, for ·33
$(\mathbf{r} - t\mathbf{s}, t)$ describes G itself with reference to S.

We are prompted therefore to express the relation of the set of ratios $f:g:h:k$ to the ideal point G in a manner independent of any particular actual point used as origin of reference. Two ways in which this elimination of the origin can be effected are described in the following paragraph and in 526 below.

·4. Perhaps the simplest plan is to appeal to the argument of ·2, which
shews that °whatever the origin O we can adapt the specifications of the four ·41
ideal points A, B, C, D to secure that one definite ideal point V not coplanar with any three of these ideal points is associated with any definite set of four numbers a, b, c, d that we choose, subject only to the condition of being all different from zero; in particular, we can assign to a particular ideal point the set of numbers 1, 1, 1, 1. This done, though the specifications of A, B, C, D are not actually *determinate*, the only possible change is a simultaneous multiplication of the four vectors $\mathbf{l}$, $\mathbf{m}$, $\mathbf{n}$, $\mathbf{p}$ and the four numbers l, m, n, p
all by a single number, and this change °leaves unaltered the ratios $f : g : h : k$ ·42
associated with any other ideal point G.

Moreover, it follows from ·33 that if the origin is changed from O to S, the change of specification from $(\mathbf{l}, l)$ to $(\mathbf{l} - l\mathbf{s}, l)$ and so on is sufficient to secure both that V is still associated with $a : b : c : d$ and also that G is still associated with $f : g : h : k$.

If A, B, C, D are any four ideal points that are not coplanar, V a fifth ·44
ideal point not coplanar with any three of them, and a, b, c, d four numbers no one of which is zero, then whatever actual point is adopted for origin of reference there are specifications $(\mathbf{l}, l)$, $(\mathbf{m}, m)$, $(\mathbf{n}, n)$, $(\mathbf{p}, p)$ of A, B, C, D that give to V a specification $(a\mathbf{l} + b\mathbf{m} + c\mathbf{n} + d\mathbf{p},\ al + bm + cn + dp)$, and associated with any ideal point G there is a definite set of ratios $f : g : h : k$ such that all specifications of A, B, C, D that give V this specification allow G to have the specification $(f\mathbf{l} + g\mathbf{m} + h\mathbf{n} + k\mathbf{p},\ \ fl + gm + hn + kp)$.

Any set of four numbers f, g, h, k whose ratios are associated with G in this
manner is called a set of °*homogeneous*, *quadriplanar*, or *tetrahedral** coordinates ·45
of G, determined from the tetrahedron $ABCD$ by assigning to V the chosen coordinates a, b, c, d. If a, b, c, d are taken all to be unity, the system of
coordinates is said to have V for °*unit point.* ·46

* To some early writers, the quadriplanar coordinates of G were distances of G from the faces of the tetrahedron, and the tetrahedral coordinates were ratios of the volumes $GBCD$, $AGCD$, $ABGD$, $ABCG$ to the volume $ABCD$.

525. The loading of ideal points; addition of loads; mean centres.

·1. The alternative method of dealing with the ideal tetrahedron is more elaborate, but the notion involved, which is that of a loaded ideal point, is intrinsically valuable.

·11 The ideal point G is said to be °*properly loaded* if its specification with reference to every actual point is determinate in such a way that if O, S are any two actual points such that the vector OS is $\mathbf{s}$, and if the specification with reference to O is $(\mathbf{r}, t)$, then the specification with reference to S is $(\mathbf{r} - t\mathbf{s}, t)$. If T is a third actual origin and the vector OT is $\mathbf{t}$, the specification with respect to T derived from that with respect to S takes the form $(\mathbf{r} - t\mathbf{s} - t(\mathbf{t} - \mathbf{s}), t)$, and this is identical with $(\mathbf{r} - t\mathbf{t}, t)$, the specification with
·12 respect to T derived directly from that with respect to O: °the definition is therefore consistent.

·13 *A properly loaded ideal point can be determined by its specification with respect to any actual origin,*

·14 while conversely, °an actual point of reference, a vector, and a number, together specify one definite properly loaded ideal point, provided only that the vector
·15 is not the zero vector if the number is itself zero. In any case °the number is independent of the origin of reference.

·2. To define *the load* of a properly loaded ideal point we must have
·21 recourse to the Frege-Russell method and identify the load with °*the class of specifications.* This class is determined by any one of its members, and if we use $(\mathbf{r}^Q, t)$ to denote the association of the vector $\mathbf{r}$ and the number t with the point Q, we may speak of the load $(\mathbf{r}^Q, t)$ briefly when we mean the load of which $(\mathbf{r}^Q, t)$ is one member. In two members of the same load the numbers are necessarily the same, and further, if $(\mathbf{r}^Q, t)$, $(\mathbf{r}^S, t)$ belong to the same load and $\mathbf{s}$ is the vector QS,

·22 $$\mathbf{r}^S = \mathbf{r}^Q - t\mathbf{s}.$$

If we regard the identity ·22 as the fundamental property of a load, we can make an extension apparently trivial but in fact of considerable value. In the specification of an ideal point with reference to an origin by a number and a vector, either the vector must be proper or the number must not be
·23 zero, but °the zero vector and the number zero together *can* be taken in association with an actual point as an element of a load. It follows from ·22 that if these are the vector and number associated with any one origin, they
·24 are also the vector and number associated with any other origin; thus °there is only one load which has an element of this kind, and in this load, which is naturally called the zero load, *every* element consists of the zero vector and the number zero associated with some point.

·3. We can now give a definition of a loaded ideal point that allows the
load to be zero. Let us say that a load is ° *suitable* for an ideal point if on ·31
referring them to a common origin and taking a definite specification for the
ideal point we find that there is a number k such that the vector and number
specifying the load are the products by k of the vector and number specifying
the ideal point, and let us define a loaded ideal point as ° *an ideal point* ·32
associated with a suitable load. Whether or not a load is suitable for an ideal
point does not depend on the origin by means of which the load and the
point are compared.

The definition of a loaded ideal point is designed to be the same in form whether the ideal point is accessible or not, and for this reason it is the more interesting to discover that the definition leads in each case to precisely the concept that would be selected naturally for consideration on its own account.

° If the ideal point to be loaded is accessible, it is completely determined ·33
by its vertex and the number t. Referred to the vertex as origin the ideal
point is simply $(\mathbf{0}, t)$, and referred to any other point S it is $(t\mathbf{r}, t)$ where $\mathbf{r}$ is
the vector of the step from S to the vertex. The idea is the natural adaptation
of the idea of a loaded point in elementary work.

On the other hand, if the ideal point is at infinity, the number t is
necessarily zero and there is neither number nor vertex to distinguish one
point from another. But in this case, because t is zero, the vector $\mathbf{r}$ is independent of the origin of reference. ° *A properly loaded ideal point at infinity* ·34
is simply an inaccessible ideal point specified by a definite proper vector without reference to any particular origin at all.

° The zero load is suitable for every ideal point. An ideal point associated ·35
with the zero load is said to be ° *annihilated*, and an ideal point associated with ·36
any other load is described as properly loaded.

° If a load is proper, there is one and only one ideal point for which it is ·37
suitable; this ideal point is called the ° *point of application* of the load. Our ·38
definitions do not enable us to give the same load to different ideal points,
but the drawback proves to be surprisingly slight.

·4. It is perhaps worth while to emphasise the reasons against the simple plan of identifying the load of a loaded ideal point with the number which occurs in its specification with respect to any origin, for this number is independent of the origin. The method, in addition to its simplicity, would have the advantage of enabling us to ascribe loads almost arbitrarily.

One objection, of which it is not easy to gauge the importance, is in the difficulty of giving a logical meaning on this basis to the ascription of the zero load to a given ideal point.

The second obstacle, complementary to this, is that it becomes impossible to imagine any proper load that can be given to an ideal point at infinity, and this is a more serious matter than is at first apparent: the whole object of the completing of space is the avoidance of exceptional cases, and the more operations we find ourselves unable to perform with ideal points at infinity, the less justification have we for introducing ideal points at all; we might as well treat parallelism itself as the exceptional phenomenon as go to the trouble of inventing infinity only to find ourselves still hampered by its peculiarities.

To admit the necessity of some conception mathematically equivalent to that defined above as the load is not to deny that a simpler notion may have its part to play. We will describe the number which occurs in every speci-
·41 fication of a load as the ° *mass* of the load. Then the special features of the loading of inaccessible ideal points are that

·42 *The ideal point to which a proper load can be given is or is not inaccessible according as the mass of the load is or is not zero.*

·43 ° The zero load is the only load of zero mass that can be given to an accessible ideal point.

·5. The definition of the sum of a finite number of loads is both simple and natural. The individual loads, if proper, imply their points of application, and
·51 ° the process of *adding* a set of loads can be regarded as one of *concentrating* a set of loaded ideal points. Let $A_1, A_2, \ldots A_n$ be ideal points specified with respect to two points Q and S by $(\mathbf{r}_1^Q, t_1), (\mathbf{r}_2^Q, t_2), \ldots (\mathbf{r}_n^Q, t_n)$ and $(\mathbf{r}_1^S, t_1), (\mathbf{r}_2^S, t_2), \ldots (\mathbf{r}_n^S, t_n)$, so that if $\mathbf{s}$ is the vector of QS

·52 $$\mathbf{r}_1^S = \mathbf{r}_1^Q - t_1\mathbf{s}, \quad \mathbf{r}_2^S = \mathbf{r}_2^Q - t_2\mathbf{s}, \ldots \mathbf{r}_n^S = \mathbf{r}_n^Q - t_n\mathbf{s},$$

and let loads suitable for these ideal points be specified by

$$(l_1\mathbf{r}_1^Q, l_1t_1), (l_2\mathbf{r}_2^Q, l_2t_2), \ldots (l_n\mathbf{r}_n^Q, l_nt_n)$$

with respect to Q, and therefore by

$$(l_1\mathbf{r}_1^S, l_1t_1), (l_2\mathbf{r}_2^S, l_2t_2), \ldots (l_n\mathbf{r}_n^S, l_nt_n)$$

with respect to S. Then since ·52 implies

·53 $$(l_1\mathbf{r}_1^S + l_2\mathbf{r}_2^S + \ldots + l_n\mathbf{r}_n^S) = (l_1\mathbf{r}_1^Q + l_2\mathbf{r}_2^Q + \ldots + l_n\mathbf{r}_n^Q) - (l_1t_1 + l_2t_2 + \ldots + l_nt_n)\,\mathbf{s},$$

·54 ° the load whose specification with respect to Q is

$$(l_1\mathbf{r}_1^Q + l_2\mathbf{r}_2^Q + \ldots + l_n\mathbf{r}_n^Q, l_1t_1 + l_2t_2 + \ldots + l_nt_n)$$

is the same as the load whose specification with respect to S is

$$(l_1\mathbf{r}_1^S + l_2\mathbf{r}_2^S + \ldots + l_n\mathbf{r}_n^S, l_1t_1 + l_2t_2 + \ldots + l_nt_n).$$

In other words, this load bears to the given set of loaded ideal points a relation that is independent of any particular origin of reference. If the applied loads are all proper, they determine their points of application, and the resulting load depends only on the loads given. But if some of these loads are not proper, that is, if some of the numbers $l_1, l_2, \ldots l_n$ are zero, these zero loads produce no effect on the final load, whatever their points of application, and therefore in this case also the result is determined by loads alone. The
·55 load found in this way is called the ° *sum* of the loads on which it depends, and if the sum is attached to any ideal point for which it is suitable, the set of loaded ideal points is said to be *concentrated* at that ideal point, which is
·56 called a ° *mean centre.*

If the sum is the zero load, the set of ideal points is said to be ° annihilated by the loading, and in this case any ideal point may be regarded as a mean centre of the loaded set. ° If the set is not annihilated, the mean centre is definite as well as the resultant load. ·57 ·58

° The mass of the sum of a number of loads is the sum of their masses. If this sum is not zero, the mean centre is accessible and the resultant load is determined by the mean centre and the resultant mass. If the resultant mass *is* zero, either the set of loaded ideal points is annihilated by the loading, or the mean centre is at infinity; a knowledge of the mass alone does not enable us to distinguish between these two cases, or in the case of an inaccessible mean centre to discover the resultant load, but the resultant load itself is precise in every event. ·59

·6. The product of the load of which a specification is $(\mathbf{p}^Q, p)$ by a number k is the load of which a specification is $((k\mathbf{p})^Q, kp)$; this is ° a load independent of the origin Q, and suitable for any ideal point for which the original load is suitable. ° Applied to the loads which are all suitable for one and the same ideal point, multiplication and addition stand in their ordinary relation. ·61 ·62

Without defining the ratio of two loads, we can allow the expression that ° the members $L_1, L_2, \ldots$ of one set of loads are proportional to the members $M_1, M_2, \ldots$ of another set if there are numbers r, s not both zero such that the sets $sL_1, sL_2, \ldots$ and $rM_1, rM_2, \ldots$ are identical, and we can express the relation in symbols by writing ·63

$$L_1 : L_2 : \ldots = M_1 : M_2 : \ldots, \qquad \cdot 64$$

and in words by saying that ° the ratios in the two sets are the same. ·65

·7. Applications require the simple theorem that

If each of a set of loads is multiplied by the same number, the sum of the set is multiplied by this number, ·71

utilised often by means of the corollary that

If the loads attached to a number of ideal points are all multiplied by the same number, any ideal point which is a mean centre under the original loading remains a mean centre, ·72

which by ·35 and ·37 includes the theorem that ° if the set is annihilated by the original loading it is annihilated by the subsequent loading. ·73

Since addition is associative both for vectors and for numbers, it is associative also for loads. In other words, we can repeat for loaded ideal points the enunciation of 216·53 above:

In concentrating any finite set of loaded ideal points, we may replace any group contained in the set by the loaded ideal point obtained by concentrating that group. ·74

526. Uses of loaded ideal points; tetrahedral coordinates as multipliers in a loaded tetrahedron.

·1. We can now modify many of the propositions of 2, 3 and 4 to forms independent of any origin of reference.

·11 *Two ideal points are distinct if and only if the only loading that annihilates the pair is that in which the individual loads are zero.*

·12 *The ideal line through two distinct ideal points is the locus of the mean centre for a variable loading in which the individual loads are not both zero.*

·13 *Three ideal points are collinear and all distinct if and only if they form a set that can be annihilated by some loading in which the individual loads are all proper.*

·14 *Three ideal points are collinear if and only if they form a set that can be annihilated by some loading in which the individual loads are not all zero.*

·15 *The ideal plane through three ideal points that are not collinear is the locus of the mean centre for a variable loading in which the individual loads are not all zero.*

·16 *Four ideal points are coplanar but not collinear if and only if they form a set that can be annihilated by some loading in which the individual loads are all proper.*

·17 *Four ideal points are coplanar if and only if they form a set that can be annihilated by some loading in which the individual loads are not all zero.*

·21 **·2.** *Every set of five ideal points can be annihilated by some loading in which the individual loads are not all zero.*

·22 *If A, B, C, D are any four ideal points that are not coplanar and G is any ideal point whatever, there are loads that are not all zero which when attached to A, B, C, D bring the mean centre to G.*

·23 *If A, B, C, D are any four ideal points that are not coplanar to which definite proper loads are attached, then if G is any ideal point whatever, there are four numbers f, g, h, k that are not all zero such that if the loads attached to A, B, C, D are multiplied by f, g, h, k the mean centre of the resultant set of loaded points is G.*

·24 *If a, b, c, d and f, g, h, k are two sets of multipliers that bring the mean centre of a given loaded ideal tetrahedron to the same point, then*

$$a:b:c:d=f:g:h:k.$$

·25 *If the frame of reference is an ideal tetrahedron with given proper loads, every set of four numbers not all zero determines one ideal point, and two sets determine the same point only if the ratios of corresponding members are the same.*

If V is any ideal point that is not coplanar with any three of the four vertices ·26
an ideal tetrahedron and if a, b, c, d are any four numbers all different from
ro, the ideal tetrahedron can be properly loaded so that a, b, c, d are coordi-
tes of V; the ratios of the loads are determinate, and so also are the ratios
the coordinates of every other ideal point.

·3. It is to be observed that tetrahedral coordinates are homogeneous in
far deeper sense than the coordinates (x, y, z, t) or (ξ, η, ζ, τ) of 1·4, for the
rts they play are all of the same kind; they are, so to speak, homogeneous
turally as well as mathematically.

Nevertheless it is important to notice that in the theory of tetrahedral
ordinates as it has been developed here, °the Cartesian frame and the ·33
tached vector frame become, as far as analysis is concerned, *not* limiting
ses but *particular* cases of the general tetrahedral frame. To regard

$$\mathbf{r} = \xi\mathbf{x} + \eta\mathbf{y} + \zeta\mathbf{z}, \quad t = \tau$$

s the form assumed by

$$\mathbf{r} = \xi\mathbf{l} + \eta\mathbf{m} + \zeta\mathbf{n} + \tau\mathbf{p}, \quad t = \xi l + \eta m + \zeta n + \tau p$$

hen

$$\mathbf{l} = \mathbf{x}, \quad \mathbf{m} = \mathbf{y}, \quad \mathbf{n} = \mathbf{z}, \quad \mathbf{p} = 0,$$

$$l = 0, \quad m = 0, \quad n = 0, \quad p = 1,$$

to replace the attached vector frame $O\mathbf{xyz}$ by the loaded ideal tetrahedron
1, B, C, D in which A, B, C are the loaded ideal points at infinity with vectors
, $\mathbf{y}$, $\mathbf{z}$, and D is the accessible ideal point with vertex O and load unity. The
oncepts are different, but the analysis is unchanged.

And here we must recognise that in spite of all appearance to the contrary
n elementary work, °projections and polar coefficients can not be raised to ·35
he same rank as coordinates and components. We might have anticipated
his conclusion when we found that in isotropic planes coordinates and components only are available; the evidence of the last paragraph may be taken
as final.

It is of course easy to construct a system of tetrahedral coordinates in *un-*
completed space, on the basis of the theory of loaded points or by methods
even more elementary. But there are reasons for regarding this development
as actually undesirable. The chief advantage of tetrahedral coordinates is in
their homogeneity, but homogeneity itself loses its charm if exclusion has to
be made of sets of values which algebraically have no essential peculiarities:
simultaneous zero values we must expect to find meaningless, since they
correspond to no definite ratios at all, but with tetrahedral coordinates in
uncompleted space there are proper sets of values which have to be rejected
not because they lead to algebraical difficulties but only because there is no
interpretation for them.

527. The effect of a change in the tetrahedron of reference; homogeneous linear equations.

·1. The character of the formulae for transforming from one set of tetrahedral coordinates to another can be deduced from 5·74. If the tetrahedron of reference is composed of four loads L_1, L_2, L_3, L_4, the ideal point whose coordinates are a, b, c, d is the point of application of the load $aL_1 + bL_2 + cL_3 + dL_4$. If the four loads are themselves described by means of a loaded tetrahedron $QRST$ by

·11 $$L_1 = p_1 P,\ L_2 = p_2 P,\ L_3 = p_3 P,\ L_4 = p_4 P,$$

where $$p = (q, r, s, t),\ P = (Q, R, S, T),$$

·12 then by 5·74 $$aL_1 + bL_2 + cL_3 + dL_4 = qQ + rR + sS + tT,$$

where q, r, s, t have values that we can express briefly in the form

·13 $$q = q_* f,\ r = r_* f,\ s = s_* f,\ t = t_* f$$

by writing f for (a, b, c, d) and using u_* as an umbra of (u_1, u_2, u_3, u_4) for any symbol u. That is to say,

·14 *Coordinates q, r, s, t with reference to the loaded tetrahedron $QRST$ are connected with coordinates a, b, c, d in the loaded tetrahedron $L_1L_2L_3L_4$ by the set of formulae* ·13.

Moreover, since the points of application of Q, R, S, T are not coplanar, 6·17 implies that q, r, s, t are not simultaneously zero, unless a, b, c, d are all zero; hence *the determinant* $[[p_*]]$ *is not zero.* Thus

·15 *To pass from one loaded tetrahedron of reference to another is to submit the coordinates to a homogeneous linear substitution that is not degenerate.*

·2. On the other hand, suppose that we have an undegenerate homogeneous linear substitution

·21 $$q = q_* f,\ r = r_* f,\ s = s_* f,\ t = t_* f,$$

with given coefficients q_1, q_2, and so on, connecting the set of variables a, b, c, d with the set q, r, s, t. This substitution is reversible *algebraically* to the form

·22 $$a = a_* p,\ b = b_* p,\ c = c_* p,\ d = d_* p,$$

and the four loads Q, R, S, T *defined* by

·23 $$Q = f_1 L_*,\ R = f_2 L_*,\ S = f_3 L_*,\ T = f_4 L_*,$$

·24 are such that $$L_1 = p_1 P,\ L_2 = p_2 P,\ L_3 = p_3 P,\ L_4 = p_4 P,$$

and that their points of application are not coplanar. The converse of ·15 is therefore true:

·25 *Any undegenerate homogeneous linear substitution can be effected on tetrahedral coordinates by an appropriate change in the tetrahedron of reference.*

·3 It follows from 2·13 and 13·23 that with reference to a tetrahedron that gives rise to the same formulae as an attached vector frame, an accessible ideal plane is characterised by an equation

$$\lambda_{\mathbf{a}}\xi + \mu_{\mathbf{a}}\eta + \nu_{\mathbf{a}}\zeta = A\tau, \qquad \cdot 31$$

where $\lambda_{\mathbf{a}}$, $\mu_{\mathbf{a}}$, $\nu_{\mathbf{a}}$ are the polar coefficients of the vector **a** in the attached frame and are not simultaneously zero, and conversely any such equation characterises a definite accessible plane. Also the ideal plane at infinity is the aggregate of ideal points satisfying

$$\tau = 0, \qquad \cdot 32$$

which is the form of ·31 in the one excepted case. That is, referred to this tetrahedron every ideal plane has an equation of the form of ·31, and every equation of this form determines one ideal plane. Since a homogeneous linear transformation of the variables changes ·31 into another equation of the same kind, ·15 implies that

Whatever the tetrahedron of reference, every homogeneous linear equation between the coordinates represents a definite ideal plane, and every ideal plane has an equation of this form. ·33

We have used ·15 to avoid a direct examination of this question, but the result can be obtained in many ways; for example, it is a corollary of 4·34.

If two homogeneous linear equations are independent, that is, if one of them is not a mere multiple of the other, then taken together they represent the ideal line which is the common part of the ideal planes represented by the individual equations. But this specification of an ideal line, like the corresponding representation of an actual line, is far from unique, since the equations of any two ideal planes through the line may be used. The canonical representation is not by means of a pair of independent equations, but by means of four interrelated equations obtained by eliminating the variables in turn from a pair of equations; these are equations of the four planes each of which passes through the line and includes one vertex of the tetrahedron of reference. If the line itself passes through a vertex, the corresponding equation disappears, and if the line is coplanar with two of the vertices, two of the equations coincide, but even in the most unfavourable cases two distinct equations survive.

With Cartesian axes or an attached vector frame, the canonical set of equations of a line is the scalar equivalent of one vector equation of the form $\mathcal{V}\,\mathbf{rk} = \mathbf{K}$, and has only three members, but the equation $\mathcal{S}\,\mathbf{rK} = 0$, which corresponds to the fourth equation for tetrahedral coordinates, is often very useful.

In a plane, trilinear coordinates play the part of tetrahedral coordinates in space. Formal investigation is superfluous, and we leave the reader to prove that

In a plane, ideal lines correspond to equations that are homogeneous and linear in trilinear coordinates. ·38

CHAPTER V 3

IDEAL VECTORS

530. Introduction. 531. Ideal vectors and their specifications; infinite ideal vectors; the vecline of an ideal vector. 532. Directions and angles in ideal vecspace; the amounts of an ideal vector; ideal veclines and vecplanes; projected products, spatial products, and vector products, of ideal vectors. 533. Ideal steps; addition of ideal vectors. 534. Measurement in ideal space; focal points.

530. Introduction.

Only to a modified extent are the reasons that lead to the invention of points at infinity operative to prompt a change in the definition of a vector. In the elementary theory of veclines and vecplanes there are no cases of exception to complicate the theorems that deal with intersection; that is to say, the initial impulse to the construction of infinite vectors is lacking completely if the mutual relations of vectors form the only topic of study. Moreover, since the difficulties in the use of numbers actually infinite are not logical but technical, it would seem likely that if the need for infinite vectors should arise it could be met by the simple device of allowing infinite numbers to be associated with directions.

The desirability of infinite vectors is apparent as soon as an attempt is made to extend from actual space to ideal space the relation of vectors to points. Every step from an actual point O with a finite vector $\mathbf{r}$ is a step to another actual point R; we can associate the vector $\mathbf{r}$ with the ideal step from the accessible ideal point whose vertex is O to the accessible ideal point whose vertex is R, but on this plan there can be no finite vector to ascribe to the step from the same ideal point to one that is inaccessible, since we can account for every finite vector without bringing in the inaccessible ideal points. We anticipate that the vector to be associated with the step from an accessible to an inaccessible ideal point is in some sense infinite, but that since there is only one ideal point at infinity on an accessible ideal line there must be only one infinite vector in a given vecline.

The last conclusion makes it difficult to deal with infinite vectors on the basis of directions and amounts. In the realm of the real variable, $+\infty$ is logically distinguishable from $-\infty$, and in the complex domain it is only for some purposes that different infinite numbers are confused. With nul directions in complex space the difficulty is intensified; since every finite vector in a nul direction is of amount zero, any vector obtained by associating a number other than zero with a nul direction would seem to be an infinite multiple of any finite vector in this direction.

531. Ideal vectors and their specifications; infinite ideal vectors; the vecline of an ideal vector.

·1. The solution is along the lines now familiar. A vector associated with
a finite number is called a °*specification of an ideal vector*, and two specifications ·11
(**r**, R), (**s**, S) are said to be °*congruent* if there are numbers h, k not both zero ·12
such that

$$h\mathbf{s} = k\mathbf{r}, \quad hS = kR. \qquad \cdot 13$$

The specification in which the vector and the number are both zero is
called the °*ineffective* specification; this is congruent with every specification. ·14
Two specifications that are both congruent with the same effective specification are congruent with each other, and therefore we can define an °*ideal vector* ·15
as a complete class of congruent specifications—complete in the sense that it includes every specification congruent with its effective members. If (**r**, R) is one effective specification of an ideal vector, the other specifications of the same ideal vector are the various specifications of the form (k**r**, kR) for values
of k other than unity. °Every ideal vector has the ineffective specification, but ·16
two ideal vectors which have an effective specification in common coincide completely. Naturally we speak of the ideal vector (**r**, R) when we mean the ideal vector of which (**r**, R) is one effective specification.

·2. The primary meaning of multiplication of an ideal vector by a number is that the product of (**r**, R) by p is (p**r**, R). It follows that if q is not zero the product of the same ideal vector by p/q is (p**r**$/q$, R), which is (p**r**, qR), and
we therefore say that °(p**r**, qR) is the product of (**r**, R) by p/q whether or not ·21
q is zero. This natural convention has an immediate bearing on our vocabulary. As a rule, the vector and the number used to specify a definite ideal vector vary together. Exception occurs if either the vector or the number is zero, and since (p**r**, qR) has zero vector if p/q is zero and zero number if p/q is infinite, we
are led to call the ideal vector (**s**, S) a °*zero ideal vector* if **s** is the zero vector ·22
and S is not zero and an °*infinite ideal vector* if S is zero and **s** is not zero. ·23

If **r** and **s** are both zero, ·13 can be satisfied whatever the values of R and S; hence

There is only one zero ideal vector. ·24

And since h**s** is zero if **s** is zero,

Every specification of the zero ideal vector involves the zero vector. ·25

Conversely

Every effective specification of a proper ideal vector involves a proper vector. ·26

Similarly

Every specification of an infinite ideal vector involves the number zero; ·27

Every effective specification of a finite ideal vector involves a number that is not ·28
zero.

But $(\mathbf{r}, 0)$, $(\mathbf{s}, 0)$ are congruent only if one of the vectors $\mathbf{r}$, $\mathbf{s}$ is a multiple of the other, and therefore

·29 *There is one and only one infinite ideal vector associated with any vecline.*

·3. To have a particular vecline related intimately to it is not a peculiarity of *infinite* ideal vectors. On the contrary, the vectors involved in the effective specifications of any proper ideal vector are collinear proper vectors. Moreover, any vector collinear with the proper vector $\mathbf{r}$ is expressible uniquely as $k\mathbf{r}$, and therefore there is one and only one specification of $(\mathbf{r}, R)$ corresponding to each vector collinear with $\mathbf{r}$. That is to say,

·31 *The vectors involved in the specifications of a particular proper ideal vector are the vectors composing a definite vecline, and each of these vectors occurs in only one of the specifications.*

·4. Since $(p\mathbf{r}, qR)$ is the zero ideal vector if $p\mathbf{r}$ is zero and qR is not zero,

·41 *Every finite multiple of the zero ideal vector is zero;*

·42 *The product of any finite ideal vector by zero is the zero ideal vector.*

And since if qR is zero and $p\mathbf{r}$ is not zero, $(p\mathbf{r}, qR)$ specifies the same ideal vector as $(\mathbf{r}, 0)$,

·43 *Every proper multiple of an infinite ideal vector coincides with that infinite ideal vector;*

·44 *The infinite multiple of any proper ideal vector is the infinite ideal vector with the same vecline.*

But if $\mathbf{r}$ is not the zero vector and R, p, q are all different from zero, $(p\mathbf{r}, qR)$ coincides with $(\mathbf{r}, R)$, that is, with $(p\mathbf{r}, pR)$, only if p is equal to q:

·45 *A proper finite ideal vector is changed if it is multiplied by any number other than unity.*

·46 °The effect of multiplying the zero ideal vector by infinity or an infinite ideal vector by zero is wholly indeterminate. The first result is natural. It might be supposed that in the second case the product should be associated with the same vecline as the infinite ideal vector; it would be easy to modify the definitions to secure this limitation, but it is doubtful whether this is worth while, for examples can readily be constructed in which two sequences of actual vectors $(r_1)_{\Sigma_1}, (r_2)_{\Sigma_2}, \ldots$ and $(r_1)_{T_1}, (r_2)_{T_2}, \ldots$ are such that the common sequence of amounts $r_1, r_2, \ldots$ tends to infinity, and the sequences of directions $\Sigma_1, \Sigma_2, \ldots$ and $T_1, T_2, \ldots$ tend to limits Σ and T of which each is the reverse of the other, while $(r_1)_{\Sigma_1} + (r_1)_{T_1}, (r_2)_{\Sigma_2} + (r_2)_{T_2}, \ldots$ tends to a limit $\mathbf{r}$ whose directions are *not* Σ and T.

·51 **·5.** °By the *reverse* of $(\mathbf{r}, R)$ is meant $(-\mathbf{r}, R)$ or $(\mathbf{r}, -R)$; it follows from ·41 that

·52 *The zero ideal vector is its own reverse,*

and from ·43 that

An infinite ideal vector is its own reverse, ·53

while ·45 implies the converse that

No proper finite ideal vector is its own reverse. ·54

532. Directions and angles in ideal vecspace; the amounts of an ideal vector; ideal veclines and vecplanes; projected products, spatial products, and vector products, of ideal vectors.

·**1.** Definitions framed in a manner dependent on 1·31 would be inapplicable to the zero ideal vector: for example, we can not define a nul ideal vector as one whose vecline is nul. But 1·31 is invaluable as shewing the precise implication of definitions in the case of proper ideal vectors. We say that °an ideal ·11 vector is nul if the actual vector involved in any of its effective specifications is nul, and then we appeal to 1·31 to deduce that

A proper ideal vector is nul if and only if its vecline is nul, ·12

but our definition has implied also that

The zero ideal vector is nul. ·13

·**2.** By a direction of an ideal vector is meant °a direction of the actual ·21 vector involved in one of its effective specifications. It follows from 1·25 that

The zero ideal vector has every direction, ·22

and from 1·31 that

A proper ideal vector has the directions of its vecline, ·23

whence

A proper ideal vector has one direction or two directions according as it is or is not nul. ·24

Similarly °two ideal vectors are perpendicular if actual vectors involved in ·25 effective specifications of them are perpendicular, and therefore:

The zero ideal vector is perpendicular to every ideal vector; ·26

Proper ideal vectors are perpendicular if and only if their veclines are perpendicular; ·27

Nul ideal vectors are self-perpendicular. ·28

And °the angles between two ideal vectors are the angles between their ·29 directions.

·**3.** If the vector **r** involved in the effective specification (**r**, R) of an ideal vector is of amount r in a direction P, then d is said to be an amount of the ideal vector in the same direction if

$$Rd = r:$$ ·31

·32 *The zero ideal vector is of amount zero in every direction;*

·33 *A proper finite ideal vector that is not nul has equal and opposite amounts in its two directions;*

·34 *A proper finite nul ideal vector has amount zero;*

·35 *An infinite ideal vector that is not nul has an infinite amount in each of its directions;*

·36 *An infinite nul ideal vector is wholly indeterminate in amount.*

The precise significance of ·35 depends on the conventions regarding infinity in the number-system that is being used. It is particularly important to notice that in consequence of ·36 an ideal vector of finite amount is not necessarily a finite ideal vector if the space is complex.

·4. To say that two ideal vectors are collinear if one of them is a multiple of the other, and so to define an ideal vecline without further reference to actual vectors, leads to difficulties where infinite ideal vectors are concerned.
·41 It is better to °define collinear ideal vectors as ideal vectors whose effective specifications involve collinear actual vectors. Then the zero ideal vector is included in every ideal vecline, but a proper ideal vector, finite or infinite, belongs to one and only one ideal vecline.

The ideal vecline that includes the ideal vector $(\mathbf{r}, R)$ is composed of the zero ideal vector together with the ideal vectors of the form $(\mathbf{r}, T)$ for all
·44 possible values of T, or in other words is composed of °all ideal vectors of the form $(p\mathbf{r}, T)$.

·45 *Every ideal vecline includes one and only one infinite ideal vector.*

·5. This method of dealing with the ideal vecline has the advantage that we can apply it to the ideal vecplane before discussing the addition of ideal
·51 vectors. Ideal vectors are °*coplanar* if their effective specifications involve coplanar actual vectors, and an ideal vecplane is a complete class of coplanar ideal vectors. The zero ideal vector is included in every ideal vecplane. Two
·54 proper ideal vectors that are not collinear determine an ideal vecplane. °The ideal vecplane that includes $(\mathbf{r}, R)$ and $(\mathbf{s}, S)$, where $\mathbf{r}$ and $\mathbf{s}$ are not collinear, is composed of all ideal vectors of the form $(p\mathbf{r} + q\mathbf{s}, T)$.

·55 *If two ideal veclines are distinct, there is one and only one ideal vecplane that contains them both.*

·56 *If two ideal vecplanes are distinct, there is one and only one ideal vecline contained in them both.*

·57 It is to be observed that °the infinite ideal vectors in an ideal vecplane do not compose an ideal vecline.

·6. Projected products and spatial products are defined by means of the
·61 same device as amounts. °The projected product of $(\mathbf{r}, R)$ and $(\mathbf{s}, S)$ is $\mathscr{G}\,\mathbf{rs}/RS$
·62, ·63 and °the spatial product of these two and $(\mathbf{t}, T)$ is $\mathscr{J}\,\mathbf{rst}/RST$. °The projected

product of two ideal vectors is indeterminate if the ideal vectors are perpendicular and one of them is infinite, and it is infinite if they are not perpendicular and one of them is infinite; in other cases the projected product has a definite finite value, which is zero if the ideal vectors are perpendicular and both of
them finite. Similarly °the spatial product is infinite if the factors are not ·64
coplanar and one of them is infinite, indeterminate if they are coplanar and one of them is infinite, and otherwise finite and definite. It is true, as with actual vectors, that two vectors are perpendicular if and only if they have projected product zero and that three are coplanar if and only if they have spatial product zero, but we must be careful not to assume, by ignoring the indeterminate cases, that two ideal vectors are not perpendicular if they have a projected product different from zero or that three are not coplanar if they are known to have a proper spatial product.

·7. The vector product of two ideal vectors is actually simpler to express
than their projected product: °the vector product of $(\mathbf{r}, R)$ and $(\mathbf{s}, S)$ is ·71
$(\mathcal{V}\,\mathbf{rs}, RS)$. °The vector product is indeterminate if the factors are collinear ·72
and one of them is infinite; otherwise $(\mathcal{V}\,\mathbf{rs}, RS)$ is an effective specification. The vector product is a definite infinite ideal vector if either of the factors is infinite provided that the factors are not collinear; it is zero if the factors are finite and collinear.

The fundamental identity

$$\mathcal{S}\,\{\mathcal{V}\,(\mathbf{r}, R)\,(\mathbf{s}, S)\}\,(\mathbf{t}, T) = \mathcal{S}\,(\mathbf{r}, R)\,(\mathbf{s}, S)\,(\mathbf{t}, T)$$ ·77

is completely true, that is, true in the sense that any value possible for either of the products is possible also for the other product.

533. Ideal steps; addition of ideal vectors.

·1. The primary relation of ideal vectors to ideal points needs no emphasis,
for the reader will have realised that ideal vectors were virtually used again
and again in the last chapter. °The specifications of an ideal point by reference ·11
to an actual origin are in fact the effective specifications of a definite ideal vector.

·2. If A, B are ideal points, the ideal step AB is simply the pair of ideal points taken definitely in the order indicated; the ideal step BA is the reverse of the ideal step AB. If A is accessible and has vertex P, there is an ideal vector which determines B with reference to P; this ideal vector is the ideal vector of the ideal step AB. If A and the ideal vector AB are known, then B is determinate; B is accessible or inaccessible according as the ideal vector is finite or infinite.

If A, B are both accessible, the ideal step AB itself is said to be accessible. If in this case $(\mathbf{r}, t)$ specifies the ideal vector of AB, and if P, Q are the vertices of A, B, then $\mathbf{r}/t$ is the vector of the actual step PQ, and therefore $-\mathbf{r}/t$ is

·25 the vector of the actual step QP and $(\mathbf{r}, -t)$ is the ideal vector of BA : °if an ideal step is accessible, the ideal vector of its reverse is the reverse of its ideal vector.

If the ideal points A, B, C are all accessible and if A is distinct from B, the ideal vector CA is distinct from the ideal vector CB, and therefore by ·25
·26 the ideal vector AC is distinct from the ideal vector BC: °ideal steps with the same finite ideal vector and different accessible initial points must have different accessible end points.

For ideal steps with infinite ideal vectors the case is altered. It follows from 21·32 that

·27 *All ideal steps with the same inaccessible end point and an accessible starting point have the same ideal vector.*

Since an ideal point at infinity can not be used as an origin for the specification of other ideal points, the ideal vector of an ideal step which has its starting point at infinity must be defined indirectly, if at all. The natural plan is to extend ·25 dogmatically to infinite steps with one accessible extremity;
·28 it follows from 1·53 that this amounts to saying that °if A is an ideal point at infinity, all ideal steps to A from accessible ideal points and all ideal steps from A to accessible ideal points have the same infinite ideal vector.

No plan presents itself for ascribing a definite ideal vector to an ideal step that is wholly at infinity. The question is bound up with the defining of the sum of two ideal vectors, and we shall return to it shortly.

·3. The addition of ideal vectors is of course to be defined in such a way that if AB, BC are ideal steps with ideal vectors $\mathbf{R}$, $\mathbf{S}$, then $\mathbf{R}+\mathbf{S}$ is the ideal vector of AC. Now if the ideal vectors AB, BC are $(\mathbf{r}, R)$, $(\mathbf{s}, S)$ and if AB is finite, the ideal vector BA is $(-\mathbf{r}, R)$ and 21·33 asserts that the ideal vector AC is $(S\mathbf{r}+R\mathbf{s}, RS)$. Thus the fundamental formula would seem to be

·31 $$(\mathbf{r}, R)+(\mathbf{s}, S)=(S\mathbf{r}+R\mathbf{s}, RS),$$

which comes more simply if fractions are removed from

·32 $$(\mathbf{r}/R, 1)+(\mathbf{s}/S, 1)=(\mathbf{r}/R+\mathbf{s}/S, 1);$$

·33 ·31 implies $$\mathbf{R}+\mathbf{S}=\mathbf{S}+\mathbf{R}.$$

If the ideal vectors $\mathbf{R}$, $\mathbf{S}$ are both finite, ·31 is perfectly satisfactory. Moreover, writing

·34 $$\mathbf{T}=(\mathbf{t}, T)=(S\mathbf{r}+R\mathbf{s}, RS),$$

we have $$\mathbf{T}-\mathbf{S}=(S\mathbf{t}-T\mathbf{s}, ST)=(S^2\mathbf{r}, S^2R)=(\mathbf{r}, R),$$

since S is not zero; thus for finite ideal vectors the definition implies that

·35 $$\mathbf{R}+\mathbf{S}=\mathbf{T}$$

·36 is equivalent to $$\mathbf{T}-\mathbf{S}=\mathbf{R}$$

·37 and similarly to $$\mathbf{T}-\mathbf{R}=\mathbf{S}.$$

·**4**. If $\mathbf{S}$ is infinite but $\mathbf{R}$ finite, ·32 fails as a basis for ·31, but 21·33 remains applicable and ·31 becomes

$$(\mathbf{r}, R) + (\mathbf{s}, 0) = (R\mathbf{s}, 0), \qquad \cdot 41$$

that is, $$\mathbf{R} + \mathbf{S} = \mathbf{S}, \qquad \cdot 42$$

which is consistent with ·27. It is true that ·42 is equivalent to

$$\mathbf{S} - \mathbf{R} = \mathbf{S}, \qquad \cdot 43$$

the form assumed in this case by ·37, but $(R\mathbf{s}, 0) - (\mathbf{s}, 0)$ naturally takes the indeterminate form $(\mathbf{0}, 0)$.

If $\mathbf{R}$ is infinite, the original basis of addition is unsound. The assumption that ·33 is to remain true, or the use of ·31 as a definition, gives

$$\mathbf{R} + \mathbf{S} = \mathbf{S} \qquad \cdot 44$$

if $\mathbf{S}$ is finite. We can interpret this to imply that

Any finite ideal step which begins at infinity ends where it begins. ·45

·**5**. There are no considerations which suggest a determinate sum for two infinite ideal vectors. A direct application of ·31 would give the sum as wholly indeterminate, but a slight restriction is imposed if we insist on regarding ·36 and ·37 as equivalent to ·35. For if $\mathbf{T}$ is finite, ·36 and 1·53 imply that $\mathbf{R}$ and $\mathbf{S}$ are identical. We can therefore say that °*the sum of two infinite ideal vectors* ·51
can not be finite if the ideal vectors are different, but °*if two infinite ideal vectors* ·52
are different, any infinite ideal vector may be regarded as a sum of them. That °*by adding an infinite ideal vector to itself any ideal vector whatever, finite or* ·53
infinite, can be obtained, is in keeping with 1·53 and 1·46, for 1·53 compels us to admit that if $\mathbf{R}$ is infinite then

$$\mathbf{R} + \mathbf{R} = \mathbf{R} - \mathbf{R}. \qquad \cdot 54$$

Since in virtue of 1·53 we can not distinguish between $\mathbf{R} - \mathbf{S}$ and $\mathbf{R} + \mathbf{S}$ if $\mathbf{S}$ is infinite, we can deduce from ·51, ·52, and ·53 the conventions to be made as to the ideal vector of a step that is wholly at infinity, if the vector BC is to be in every case the difference between the vectors AB, AC:

If A is an ideal point at infinity, any ideal vector whatever, finite or infinite, ·55
may be regarded as a vector of the ideal step AA;

If A, B are distinct ideal points at infinity, any infinite ideal vector may be ·56
regarded as a vector of the ideal step AB, but no finite ideal vector can be so regarded.

By ·52 and 2·63 we are reassured as to the necessity of dealing first with finite vectors and introducing later the modification that allows vectors to be infinite. For it follows from ·52 that an infinite ideal vector can not be resolved into components from which it can be reconstructed, and from 2·63 that a projected product may be indeterminate when infinite vectors are concerned. That is to say, the two features adopted as characteristic of a vector field are both lacking in ideal vecspace, and it is futile to hope for a method that should depend at the start only on properties common to finite and infinite vectors.

·6. The problem of describing an ideal vector by means of a frame is virtually that considered in 21·4, of describing an ideal point by means of an attached frame. A specification of the ideal vector must be given, and the vector involved in this specification may be described in any way convenient. We may suppose the frame to be composed not of actual vectors but of ideal vectors, but in that case it is essential because of ·52 that these vectors of reference should be finite. Any *finite* ideal vector can be expressed by means of coefficients in a frame itself formed of finite ideal vectors, the analysis being the same as for actual vectors, and the ideal vector $(\mathbf{r}, R)$ is known if the finite ideal vector $(\mathbf{r}, 1)$ and the number R are both given: the coefficients of $(\mathbf{r}, 1)$ in the frame $(\mathbf{a}, A)$, $(\mathbf{b}, B)$, $(\mathbf{c}, C)$ are the same as the coefficients of $\mathbf{r}$ in the frame $\mathbf{a}/A$, $\mathbf{b}/B$, $\mathbf{c}/C$, and these three and R are homogeneous coordinates of $(\mathbf{r}, R)$ in the ideal frame.

·7. The relation of lines and planes to veclines and vecplanes is the same in ideal space as in actual space *provided only that the lines and planes are accessible.* For if O is an accessible ideal point and $(\mathbf{m}, M)$ specifies the vector of a proper step OB, then since $(\mathbf{0}, 1)$ is a specification of OO it follows from 22·27 that the ideal line which contains the two ideal points O, B is the locus of an ideal point P such that the ideal vector OP is of the form $(j\mathbf{m}, i+jM)$, and this is a typical ideal vector collinear with $(\mathbf{m}, M)$. Similarly if $(\mathbf{m}, M)$, $(\mathbf{n}, N)$ are the ideal vectors of proper ideal steps OB, OC that are not collinear, an ideal vector coplanar with these is an ideal vector with a specification of the form $(j\mathbf{m}+k\mathbf{n}, i+jM+kN)$, and by 22·32 this is the ideal vector of a step from O to an ideal point in the ideal plane OBC.

·72 *An ideal line or plane through an accessible ideal point O is the locus of an ideal point P such that the ideal vector of the ideal step OP belongs to a definite ideal vecline or vecplane.*

It is easy to prove that the ideal vecline or vecplane mentioned in this proposition depends only on the ideal line or plane itself, not on the ideal point O.

There is no analogue of ·72 if the ideal point O is at infinity, nor is it possible to associate any definite ideal vecline with an inaccessible ideal line or any definite ideal vecplane with the ideal plane at infinity. This is why work on ideal space is naturally developed in a different order from work on algebraic space. But it is sometimes convenient to regard every ideal vecline as belonging to every inaccessible ideal line and every ideal vecplane as belonging to the plane at infinity. We can then say that any two ideal lines of which one is at infinity are necessarily parallel, and this is consistent both with saying that two ideal lines are parallel if and only if they have an ideal point at infinity in common, and with saying that two ideal lines are parallel if and only if they possess the same ideal vecline. It will be noticed that with the convention just accepted, every line at infinity is both isotropic and anisotropic, and so also is the plane at infinity.

534. MEASUREMENT IN IDEAL SPACE; FOCAL POINTS.

·1. From the ideal vector come the definitions of directions, angles, and lengths in ideal space. If **R** is a vector of the ideal step AB, a direction of **R** is a direction of the step, or a direction of B from A, and an amount of **R** in that direction is a corresponding *length* of the step or *distance* of B from A.

°If A and B are both accessible, the directions and lengths of the ideal step ·13
AB are the same as the directions and lengths of the actual step from the vertex of A to the vertex of B. For this reason, theorems and formulae concerning actual space are necessarily true of the accessible part of ideal space, while conversely results proved of ideal space can always be asserted of actual space if they refer only to ideal points that are accessible. This statement contemplates actual space only as contrasted with ideal space, and therefore as either real or complex; if the actual space is complex, reference may be made to 445·15 and 445·21, and the implication is simply that, subject to certain reservations, a proposition *significant* both of ideal complex space and of actual real space is *true* of either space if it is true of the other.

°The step from one accessible ideal point to another has all directions and ·14
length zero in every direction if the two points coincide. If they are distinct and the step is nul, it has one direction only and its length is again zero. If the points are distinct and the step is not nul, there are two distinct directions, one the reverse of the other, and two distinct lengths, one the negative of the other.

°A step between an accessible ideal point and an ideal point at infinity is ·15
infinite. It has one direction and every length if it is nul, and it has two directions and an infinite length if it is not nul.

°The step from one ideal point at infinity to another has every direction ·16
and every length in each direction if the two points coincide. If the points are distinct, the step must be infinite but it has every direction; in directions that are not nul its length is infinite, but in each nul direction it has every length*.

·2. The conclusions of 435·44 and 436·45 as to the distance from a point to a line or plane in a direction parallel to this line or plane are in entire agreement with the present results.

If P is an accessible ideal point, there is one and only one ideal line p through P with a given direction Δ. An ideal line or plane to which this

* Darboux (*Principes*, p. 141) seems to me mistaken in ascribing only the zero length to the nul directions and looking in other directions for the finite proper lengths. If one of two points moving to infinity at a constant distance apart along a given curve tends to a definite point at infinity, the other tends to *the same point*; in Darboux's own example, a parabola has notoriously only one point at infinity to which the points could tend! By supposing the two points to move away along different arms of the parabola, we have an excellent view of a point at infinity at an infinite distance from itself.

ideal line is parallel either contains p or cuts p definitely at infinity. There is an ideal point Q at distance d from P in the direction Δ whatever the value of d, and in the first case Q is necessarily in the ideal line or plane to which p is parallel; thus the distance from P to this ideal line or plane is indeterminate, and this conclusion is not affected by the fact that if the direction is nul Q is at infinity unless d is zero. In the second case the ideal point in which p is cut is at a distance from P which is indeterminate or infinite according as the direction is or is not nul.

·3. To say that if two ideal lines are parallel and one of them is nul, then the other is nul also, is to assert that if K is the point at infinity on one nul ideal line, then every accessible ideal line through K is nul, and the step to K from any accessible ideal point is a nul step. It appears from ·15 that such an ideal point at infinity as is involved here has special properties in respect of distance, and it is in fact impossible to overrate the importance of ideal points of this kind in metrical geometry. For reasons into which we can not
·31 enter*, an ideal point at infinity on a nul ideal line is called a °*focal point*; then

·32 *A nul ideal line is an ideal line which contains a focal point;*

·33 *Parallel nul ideal lines are ideal lines which contain the same focal point;*

·34 *The distances between two ideal points are wholly indeterminate if one of the ideal points is a focal point.*

·4. From 415·43, 415·46 it follows that

·41 *An accessible ideal plane contains one focal point or two focal points according as it is or is not isotropic.*

We have seen in 424·56 that in a prepared anisotropic vecplane we can distinguish between the two nul veclines by means of the identity

·42 $$(\mathscr{A}\,\mathbf{rs})^2 = -(\mathscr{G}\,\mathbf{rs})^2.$$

* The uncritical reader will find comfort, and the critical, food for thought, in a crude explanation. With rectangular coordinates, the origin is a focus of a given conic if and only if the equation of the conic has the form

$$x^2+y^2=(ax+by+c)^2.$$

The point (h, k) is on a tangent from the origin to the conic if and only if the two values of r for which (hr, kr) is on the conic are equal, that is, if and only if the equation

$$(ahr+bkr+c)^2=h^2r^2+k^2r^2,$$

regarded as an equation in r, has equal roots; the condition is

$$c^2\{(ah+bk)^2-(h^2+k^2)\}=c^2(ah+bk)^2,$$

that is, unless c is zero, $$h^2+k^2=0,$$

which expresses that the distance of (h, k) from the origin is zero, or in other words that (h, k) is on a nul line through the origin. *The point O is a focus of a given conic if and only if the tangents to the conic from O are the lines joining O to the focal points in the plane of the conic.*

If i denotes the complex number (0, 1), we may say that if **r** and **s** are proper vectors in different nul veclines, so that $\mathscr{G}$ **rs** and $\mathscr{A}$ **rs** are different from zero, then if

$$\mathscr{A}\,\mathbf{rs} = i\,\mathscr{G}\,\mathbf{rs}$$ ·43

it is the vecline that contains **r** that is to be called the first nul vecline in the prepared vecplane, and the vecline containing **s** that is to be called the second. This convention extends naturally to the focal points in any anisotropic prepared ideal plane. The two focal points in such a plane are denoted by* I and J, and in the absence of indication to the contrary it is to be assumed† that I is the first and J the second.

A characteristic property of an isotropic ideal plane may be expressed in the form that

In an isotropic ideal plane the two focal points coincide. ·46

The association with the two square roots of -1 fails because nothing significant survives of ·43: $\mathscr{A}$ **rs** is zero if **r**, **s** are *any* two vectors in the vecplane, and $\mathscr{G}$ **rs** is zero if *either* of the two is nul. We shall use K to denote the one focal point in an isotropic ideal plane.

* Or often by ω and ω' or by Ω and Ω'.

† The convention suggested by Laguerre and usually adopted is the reverse of this, and an inversion of order disfigures Laguerre's angle-formula in consequence. If we have to change from rectangular axes OX, OY in a plane to axes which are such that OX bisects the angle between them, it seems natural to take the direction in the fourth quadrant as that of the new x-axis, and that in the first quadrant to describe the new y-axis: in other words, if the new axes are $y = \pm x \tan a$, to suppose the angle from the new x-axis to the new y-axis to be $2a$, not $-2a$. By analogy, we should take $y = -ix$ to contain I and $y = ix$ to contain J; if **r** is the vector $(1, -i)$ and **s** the vector $(1, i)$, then $\mathscr{A}$ **rs** is $2i$ and $\mathscr{G}$ **rs** is 2.

Scott (*Modern Analytical Geometry*, p. 253, 1894) avoids inelegance in the angle-formula by using $\overline{pq}$ for an angle *to* a ray p *from* a ray q.

CHAPTER V 4

INTERSECTION AND ALTERSECTION OF LINES WITH PLANE CURVES AND WITH SURFACES

540. Introduction. 541. Plane curves and surfaces; composite loci; the order of a plane curve or a surface. 542. The order of a point on a plane curve or a surface. 543. The order of intersection of a line with a plane curve or a surface; tangents; segments of a line. 544. Altersection and altercontact. 545. The relation between orders of altersection with a surface and orders of altersection with plane sections of the surface. 546. Asymptotes. 547. Definitions of conics and conicoids; degenerate conics; parabolas; the existence of a conic through five coplanar points.

540. Introduction.

Except on questions of existence, it is only if isotropic lines or planes or inaccessible points become involved that a proposition may differ in enunciation according as it is asserted of actual real space or of ideal complex space.

For example, if BA, CA are steps of equal finite length with vectors $\mathbf{r}$, $\mathbf{s}$, then since the equality

$$\mathcal{G}\,\mathbf{r}^2 = \mathcal{G}\,\mathbf{s}^2$$

is equivalent to

$$\mathcal{G}\,\mathbf{r}\,(\mathbf{r}-\mathbf{s}) = \mathcal{G}\,\mathbf{s}\,(\mathbf{s}-\mathbf{r}),$$

the angles between BA and BC are the same definite angles as those between CA and CB unless one of the sides is nul, and even in the exceptional case the angles at B and at C are equally indeterminate. We may go even further; the identity $\mathcal{A}\,(\mathbf{r}-\mathbf{s})^2 = 0$ can be written as

$$\mathcal{A}\,\mathbf{r}\,(\mathbf{r}-\mathbf{s}) = -\mathcal{A}\,\mathbf{s}\,(\mathbf{s}-\mathbf{r}),$$

and this combined with

$$\mathcal{G}\,\mathbf{r}\,(\mathbf{r}-\mathbf{s}) = \quad \mathcal{G}\,\mathbf{s}\,(\mathbf{s}-\mathbf{r})$$

enables us to compare angles between definite directions: if b is a length common to AB and AC, the angles from the direction in which BA has the length b to one direction along BC are the negatives of the angles from the direction in which CA has the length b to the opposite direction along BC.

To illustrate the kind of care that is necessary, we will consider in the next two chapters the nature of circles and spheres in ideal complex space. The subject is intrinsically important, and the student who appreciates the modifications of elementary theorems concerning circles and spheres is in little danger of overlooking exceptional cases in more advanced work.

In order that the discussion of circles and spheres may be as free from interruption as possible, an explanation of certain terms used in connection with curves and surfaces occupies the present chapter; the actual requirements could have been met by a treatment less general than is given here, but it is necessary to shew that as far as conics and conicoids are concerned the idea of a tangent need not presuppose that of a limit, and the generality consists in postponing restriction on the degree of certain polynomials as long as the restriction is irrelevant.

541. Plane curves and surfaces; composite loci; the order of a plane curve or a surface.

·1. Throughout this chapter we shall use homogeneous coordinates, which we shall denote by α, β, γ or by $\alpha, \beta, \gamma, \delta$ according as points in a plane or in space are under consideration; also we shall write ϵ for (α, β, γ) or $(\alpha, \beta, \gamma, \delta)$, and $\Phi\epsilon^n$ will denote a homogeneous polynomial of degree n in the coordinates. The aggregate of points whose coordinates satisfy the equation

$$\Phi\epsilon^n = 0$$ ·13

is called simply the *locus* Φ, and is described as a plane curve or a surface according as the number of variable coordinates is three or four. We make no attempt to define functions or curves or surfaces in general.

In general a polynomial in more than two variables can not be resolved into polynomial factors of lower degree, but it is better for us to classify than to stipulate. If identically $\Phi\epsilon^n$ is the product of polynomials

$$\Phi_1\epsilon^{n_1},\ \Phi_2\epsilon^{n_2},\ \ldots\ \Phi_m\epsilon^{n_m},$$

where $n_1 + n_2 + \ldots + n_m$ must equal n, then $\Phi\epsilon^n$ is said to be *reducible*; a point belongs to the locus Φ if and only if it belongs to one or other of the loci $\Phi_1, \Phi_2, \ldots \Phi_m$, and Φ is said to be *degenerate* or to be a *composite* locus of which $\Phi_1, \Phi_2, \ldots \Phi_m$ are *constituents*. Since a transformation of coordinates which changes

$$\Phi_1\epsilon^{n_1},\ \Phi_2\epsilon^{n_2},\ \ldots\ \Phi_m\epsilon^{n_m}$$

into

$$\Phi_1^*\dot\epsilon^{n_1},\ \Phi_2^*\dot\epsilon^{n_2},\ \ldots\ \Phi_m^*\dot\epsilon^{n_m}$$

necessarily changes the product of the original polynomials into the product of the transformed polynomials, the question whether one locus forms part of another does not depend for its answer on the coordinates employed.

·2. The formulae of transformation in 27 have their counterparts in plane geometry, and from these formulae it is evident that a homogeneous polynomial of any degree in the coordinates with one triangle or tetrahedron of reference transforms into a homogeneous polynomial of the same degree with reference to any other triangle or tetrahedron. Thus if a curve referred to one triangle, or a surface referred to one tetrahedron, has an equation $\Phi\epsilon^n = 0$, the *degree* of $\Phi\epsilon^n$ does not depend on the particular triangle or tetrahedron but is a number associated intrinsically with the curve or surface; it is called the °*order* or the *degree* of the curve or surface. From 27·38 and 27·33, ·21

A curve of the first order is a straight line, a surface of the first order is a plane. ·22

·3. The significance of the order of a curve or surface is exhibited by a method due to Joachimsthal. If $(\alpha_P, \beta_P, \gamma_P), (\alpha_Q, \beta_Q, \gamma_Q)$ or $(\alpha_P, \beta_P, \gamma_P, \delta_P), (\alpha_Q, \beta_Q, \gamma_Q, \delta_Q)$ are *definite* sets of coordinates of two points P, Q, or in other words specify definite loads attached to these points, then provided only that the points P, Q are distinct,

$$(h\alpha_P + k\alpha_Q,\ h\beta_P + k\beta_Q,\ h\gamma_P + k\gamma_Q)$$

or $$(h\alpha_P + k\alpha_Q,\ h\beta_P + k\beta_Q,\ h\gamma_P + k\gamma_Q,\ h\delta_P + k\delta_Q)$$

is a set of homogeneous coordinates of a point on the line PQ; the particular point, which we may call the point $hP + kQ$, depends on the ratio $h : k$, not on the absolute values of h and k, and to each value of this ratio corresponds one and only one point on the line.

The condition that the point $hP + kQ$ should be on the locus Φ is

·31 $$\Phi\,(h\epsilon_P + k\epsilon_Q)^n = 0,$$

and the expression here equated to zero is homogeneous and of degree n in h and k, with coefficients dependent on the coefficients in the equation of the curve and on the coordinates of P and Q.

There are two possibilites: ·31 is either an identity or an equation of the
·32 nth degree. Hence °*if a line has more than n points in common with a curve or surface of the nth degree, every point of the line belongs to that curve or surface.* If ·31 is not an identity, it is equivalent to an equation

·33 $$(hk_1 - kh_1)^{n_1}(hk_2 - kh_2)^{n_2} \ldots (hk_m - kh_m)^{n_m} = 0$$

·34 where $$n_1 + n_2 + \ldots + n_m = n,$$

and just as the equation

$$(z - z_1)^{n_1}(z - z_2)^{n_2} \ldots (z - z_m)^{n_m} = 0$$

is said to have not m roots but n, namely, n_1 all equal to z_1, n_2 all equal to z_2, and so on, so the line PQ is said to intersect the curve or surface in n points, the points of intersection being $h_1P + k_1Q$ counted n_1 times, $h_2P + k_2Q$ counted n_2 times, and so on. This language is of course conventional, and it proves to be invaluable. To absorb ·32 in the more complete statement that

·35 *If a line does not form part of an algebraic curve or surface, the number of points common to the line and the curve or surface is equal to the order of the curve or surface but the points of intersection are not necessarily all distinct,*

is merely to assert the possibility of laying down conventions having the desired result.

It should be added that on the one hand nothing that has been said assumes the line PQ or either of the points P, Q to be accessible, and that on the other hand in saying that to *every* ratio $h : k$ there is some one point of PQ to correspond we *are* assuming that space is ideal; in a space without points at infinity, one factor of ·33 may be insusceptible of interpretation, and since the power to which that factor is raised may have any value not greater than n, the convention as to multiplicity of accessible points of intersection fails altogether to provide a passage from ·32 to ·35.

·4. If ·13 is the equation of a surface and P, Q, R are three points that are not collinear, the condition for the point $iP+jQ+kR$, a typical point in the plane PQR, to be in this surface is

$$\Phi(i\epsilon_P+j\epsilon_Q+k\epsilon_R)^n=0,$$ ·41

and this is either an identity or an equation homogeneous and of degree n in the set of variables i, j, k. Since i, j, k are themselves homogeneous coordinates referring a variable point of the plane PQR to the triangle PQR,

If a plane does not form part of a given algebraic surface, the points common to the two compose a curve of the same order as the surface; ·42

this is a corollary of ·35, but not of ·32. If the surface has no plane constituents, and in particular if it is not composite, there is no restriction on the plane.

·5. The coefficient of $h^{n-r}k^r$ in $\Phi(h\epsilon_P+k\epsilon_Q)^n$ is both a homogeneous polynomial of degree $n-r$ in the coordinates of P and a homogeneous polynomial of degree r in the coordinates of Q: it may be regarded as a polynomial in one set of coordinates with coefficients that are themselves polynomials in the other set. If Q coincides with P, the function $\Phi(h\epsilon_P+k\epsilon_Q)^n$ becomes $(h+k)^n\Phi\epsilon_P{}^n$, and the coefficient of $h^{n-r}k^r$ reduces to the product of $\Phi\epsilon_P{}^n$ by the binomial coefficient $\binom{n}{r}$. There is therefore no confusion, and there are many advantages, in denoting the coefficient in general, divided by this same binomial coefficient, by $\Phi\epsilon_P{}^{n-r}\epsilon_Q{}^r$, that is, in writing

$$\Phi(h\epsilon_P+k\epsilon_Q)^n$$ ·51
$$=h^n\Phi\epsilon_P{}^n+\binom{n}{1}h^{n-1}k\,\Phi\epsilon_P{}^{n-1}\epsilon_Q+\binom{n}{2}h^{n-2}k^2\,\Phi\epsilon_P{}^{n-2}\epsilon_Q{}^2+\dots+k^n\Phi\epsilon_Q{}^n;$$

this formula *defines* the meaning of $\Phi\epsilon_P{}^{n-r}\epsilon_Q{}^r$. The more general formula

$$\Phi(k_1\epsilon_1+k_2\epsilon_2+\dots+k_n\epsilon_n)^n=\Sigma\frac{n!}{p!q!r!\dots}k_1{}^pk_2{}^qk_3{}^r\dots\Phi\epsilon_1{}^p\epsilon_2{}^q\epsilon_3{}^r\dots,$$ ·52

the summation being for all positive integral values of $p, q, r, \dots$ such that

$$p+q+r+\dots=n,$$

defines the multinomial $\Phi\epsilon_1{}^p\epsilon_2{}^q\epsilon_3{}^r\dots$, or alternatively if the *multilinear* function $\Phi\epsilon_1\epsilon_2\dots\epsilon_n$ is defined as the quotient by $n!$ of the coefficient of $k_1k_2\dots k_n$ in $\Phi(k_1\epsilon_1+k_2\epsilon_2+\dots+k_n\epsilon_n)^n$, the multinomial $\Phi\epsilon_1{}^p\epsilon_2{}^q\epsilon_3{}^r\dots$ is definable as the function derived from $\Phi\epsilon_1\epsilon_2\dots\epsilon_n$ by repetition of terms.

If a change of coordinates replaces the multilinear function $\Phi\epsilon_1\epsilon_2\dots\epsilon_n$ by $\Phi^*\dot\epsilon_1\dot\epsilon_2\dots\dot\epsilon_n$, the *same* change replaces $\Phi\epsilon_1{}^p\epsilon_2{}^q\epsilon_3{}^r\dots$ by $\Phi^*\dot\epsilon_1{}^p\dot\epsilon_2{}^q\dot\epsilon_3{}^r\dots$ for all values of $p, q, r, \dots$, and in particular replaces $\Phi\epsilon^n$ by $\Phi^*\dot\epsilon^n$. Thus °if a relation between ·56
the points P, Q, R, ... and the locus Φ is expressed with reference to one triangle or tetrahedron by an equation of the form $\Phi\epsilon_P{}^p\epsilon_Q{}^q\epsilon_R{}^r\dots=0$, it is the *same* relation that is expressed with reference to another triangle or tetrahedron by the equation $\Phi^*\dot\epsilon_P{}^p\dot\epsilon_Q{}^q\dot\epsilon_R{}^r\dots=0$, where the function $\Phi^*\dot\epsilon_P{}^p\dot\epsilon_Q{}^q\dot\epsilon_R{}^r\dots$ is formed from the function $\Phi^*\dot\epsilon^n$ into which $\Phi\epsilon^n$ changes by the same rules as $\Phi\epsilon_P{}^p\epsilon_Q{}^q\epsilon_R{}^r\dots$ from $\Phi\epsilon^n$.

542. The order of a point on a plane curve or a surface.

·1. Suppose the point P to be on the locus Φ. Then the equation 1·31 lacks the term in h^n, whatever the position of Q. It is possible, though exceptional, for the equation without reducing to an identity to lack also any number smaller than n of successive terms following this first term: for example, in space, if P is the point for which δ is unity and the other coordinates are zero, $\Phi(h\epsilon_P + k\epsilon_Q)^n$ becomes $\Phi(k\alpha_Q, k\beta_Q, k\gamma_Q, h+k\delta_Q)^n$, and if further $\Phi\epsilon^n$ does not contain δ, no change is made by the substitution of $k\delta_Q$ for $h+k\delta_Q$ in this expression, a substitution that reduces $\Phi(h\epsilon_P + k\epsilon_Q)^n$ in this case to the term $k^n\,\Phi\epsilon_Q{}^n$ without imposing any condition on Q.

In other words, it is *possible* for a point P on a curve or surface to be such that on *every* line through P that does not lie wholly in the curve or surface, P is a multiple point of intersection. If P is a point such that every line through P that does not form part of a given curve or surface cuts this curve or surface m times at P but that on some lines through P the multiplicity is not
·12 greater than m, then P is called a ° *point of order* m on the curve or surface. Algebraically, the condition is that in the function $\Phi\epsilon_P{}^{n-r}\,\epsilon_Q{}^r$, regarded as a polynomial in the coordinates of Q, every coefficient vanishes if r is less than m, but at least one coefficient is not zero when r has the value m. If every term in the polynomial $\Phi\epsilon_P{}^{n-s}\,\epsilon^s$ vanishes, so does every term in the symmetrical multilinear function $\Phi\epsilon_P{}^{n-s}\,\epsilon_1\epsilon_2\ldots\epsilon_s$, and therefore so does every term in the
·13 polynomial $\Phi\epsilon_P{}^{n-r}\,\epsilon^r$ if r has any value less than s. Hence ° the order of P on Φ is definable as *the number m which is such that $\Phi\epsilon_P{}^{n-m+1}\,\epsilon^{m-1}$ vanishes identically but $\Phi\epsilon_P{}^{n-m}\,\epsilon^m$ does not*, explicit reference to polynomials of degree lower than $m-1$ being superfluous. The equation

·14 $$\Phi\epsilon_P{}^{n-m}\,\epsilon^m = 0$$

is an effective equation, not an identity, and the line PQ cuts Φ at P exactly m times provided that Q is *not* on the locus corresponding to this equation.

·15 According to the definition just given, ° a point that does not belong to the curve or surface at all can be regarded as a point of order zero. The vanishing of $\Phi\epsilon_P{}^n$ does not as a rule imply the vanishing of the coefficients of the coordinates of Q in $\Phi\epsilon_P{}^{n-1}\,\epsilon_Q$, and therefore in general the order of a point taken at random on a curve or surface is unity. A point of order unity is called a
·16, ·17 ° *simple** point, a point of higher order a ° *multiple point.*

·2. The order of a point on a curve or surface is not wholly independent of the form of the equation of the curve or surface. The points that satisfy the
·21 equation

$$\{\Phi\epsilon^n\}^p = 0,$$

where p is an integer greater than unity, are the same as the points that satisfy

·22 $$\Phi\epsilon^n = 0,$$

* A distinction can be made between *simple* points and *ordinary* points, points that are simple when the locus is given by ·22 being distinguished as ordinary when it is given by ·21.

but if ·22 leads to 1·33, then ·21 leads to

$$(hk_1 - kh_1)^{pn_1}(hk_2 - kh_2)^{pn_2} \dots (hk_m - kh_m)^{pn_m} = 0: \quad \cdot 23$$

a line that cuts ·22 in m points coincident at P cuts ·21 in pm points coincident at the same place, and ° the order of any point with respect to ·21 is p times ·24
the order of the same point with respect to ·22. It is for this reason that ·21 is said to represent not the same locus as ·22 but this locus taken p times. No point of ·21 is a simple point, for points that are simple on ·22 are points of order p on ·21.

·3. If the several loci

$$\Phi_1 \epsilon^{n_1} = 0, \quad \Phi_2 \epsilon^{n_2} = 0, \dots, \quad \cdot 31$$

finite in number, are regarded as forming a single composite locus

$$\Phi \epsilon^n = 0, \quad \cdot 32$$

where $$n = n_1 + n_2 + \dots, \quad \Phi \epsilon^n = \Phi_1 \epsilon^{n_1} . \Phi_2 \epsilon^{n_2} . \dots, \quad \cdot 33$$

a line lies wholly in Φ if and only if it lies wholly in one of the constituents $\Phi_1, \Phi_2, \dots$, and if P is any point on a line Λ that does not lie wholly in Φ, ° *the* ·34
order of P as an intersection of Λ with Φ is the sum of the orders of P as an intersection of Λ with the constituents of Φ, for the binomial 1·33 whose roots determine the intersections of Λ with Φ is the product of the corresponding binomials for $\Phi_1, \Phi_2, \dots$; the order of intersection for a constituent which does not contain P is of course zero.

It follows from ·34 that the order of a point P on a composite locus is *not less than* the sum of the orders of P on the constituents. Moreover, we have seen that the lines through a point P of order m for which the order of intersection at P is exactly m are the lines joining P to points which do *not* satisfy a certain equation. Given any finite number of equations, it is always possible to find a set of values of the variables which does *not* satisfy *any* of the equations. Hence

The order of a point on a composite locus is the sum of the orders of that ·36
point on the constituent loci.

We have had a particular case of this theorem in ·24.

543. The order of intersection of a line with a plane curve or a surface; tangents; segments of a line.

·1. If P is a point of order m on Φ, every line through P either forms part of Φ or has at P an intersection of order at least as great as m, and distinction is drawn between those lines on which the order is exactly m and other lines through P; the exceptional lines are said to *touch* the curve or surface at P:
in other words a ° *tangent* to a curve or surface at a point P is a line through ·11
P which either forms part of the curve or surface or has at P an intersection of an order higher than is implied by the mere fact of passing through P.

To see that in complex space tangents, in this sense of the word, exist if m is not zero, we have only to consider the relation

·12 $$\Phi \epsilon_P^{\,n-m} \epsilon_Q^{\,m} = 0.$$

This relation can not be satisfied for *all* positions of Q, for if it were, P would be a point of order greater than m; since the variables are complex, there are *some* values of the coordinates of Q that satisfy the relation. That is to say,

·13 $$\Phi \epsilon_P^{\,n-m} \epsilon^m = 0$$

is a significant equation, and the line joining P to a point Q distinct from P is a tangent to Φ at P if and only if Q is on the curve or surface represented by this equation; the condition is satisfied if the line forms part of the curve or surface, and this is one reason for regarding such a line as itself a tangent. Moreover, if the condition is satisfied by a point Q, it is satisfied by every point of the line PQ. Hence

·14 *If P is a point of order m on the curve or surface*

$$\Phi \epsilon^n = 0,$$

the equation $$\Phi \epsilon_P^{\,n-m} \epsilon^m = 0$$

is the equation of the aggregate of tangents to the curve or surface at P.

·2. If P is a simple point of a *curve*, m is unity, and the equation

·21 $$\Phi \epsilon_P^{\,n-1} \epsilon = 0$$

is the equation of a single line, *the* tangent at P; every line through P except the tangent cuts the curve once at P; the tangent can not cut the curve only once, but there is nothing to prevent the tangent from cutting the curve *more than* twice at P, or from forming part of the curve.

If P is a simple point of the curve

·22 $$\Phi \epsilon^n = 0$$

and if PT is the tangent at P, any line through P other than PT cuts

·23 $$\{\Phi \epsilon^n\}^p = 0$$

p times at P but PT cuts this curve *at least* $2p$ times or forms part of the curve. Thus the only line which *touches* ·23 at P is the line which touches ·22 at P, but a property that depended on a line *having multiple intersection* at P would belong for ·23 to *every* line through P and for ·22 to the tangent alone.

If it is with a curve that we are dealing, and if the order of P is m, the equation ·13, since it represents nothing but lines through P, represents not more than m of these lines:

·25 *At a multiple point of order m, a plane curve has m tangents but these are not necessarily all distinct.*

It is to be noticed that the equation ·13 derived from the equation of a plane curve does not *as a rule* represent a group of lines; it is from the assumption that P is of order m that we have deduced that the locus has this character.

·3. If P is a simple point on a surface, ·13 becomes the equation of a plane:

At a simple point of an algebraic surface, the tangents compose a plane, the tangent plane at that point. ·31

But there is no reason to suppose that in general, because it represents nothing but lines through P, ·13 factorises and represents a number of planes: all that can be done is to define a cone with vertex P as a surface composed of lines through P, and to assert that

At a point of order m on a surface, the tangent lines compose a cone of order m; ·32

in general this cone is not composite, but exceptions are possible.

If the tangent plane at a simple point P of a surface is not a constituent of the surface, any line through P in the tangent plane has the same order of intersection at P with the curve in which this plane cuts the surface as it has with the surface itself; comparing the definition of a tangent to a surface with that of a multiple point on a curve, we infer that

If the tangent plane at a simple point of a surface does not form part of the surface, the section of the surface by this plane has the point of contact for a multiple point. ·33

·4. There is intrinsically no difference between supposing a point A to belong to a given curve or surface and supposing a number of points coincident in A to belong to that curve or surface. But if we associate with A a definite line through A, it becomes possible for us to discriminate, naturally if conventionally, between a curve or surface that has one point in common with the line at A and one that has several coincident* points in common with the line there.

For many reasons, *double* intersection figures not merely as the simplest type of multiple intersection but with an importance that is fundamental, and it is the vocabulary by means of which we include double intersection at one point and simple intersections at two distinct points in one description that must now be explained.

Two points together with a line containing them are said to constitute a °*linear segment* or a *segment of a line*; the points are called the *ends* of the segment, and the line is called its *axis*. Unless the points A, B coincide, there is only one line which contains them both, and therefore there is only one linear segment to which they belong; this is called the segment AB. If the points coincide, the propositions which we have in view require us to consider them as coincident in a *definite* line, and it is for this reason that the idea of the segment is necessary. Any theorem concerning a *proper* linear segment, that is, a linear segment with distinct points A, B, can be expressed as a theorem regarding the pair of points, and differs from a theorem regarding the step AB only in imposing no order on the two points: °the segment BA is the same as the segment AB. But if B coincides with A, the identity of the segment depends on the line through A in which the two coincident ·41 ·42

* But not, on any tenable interpretation, *consecutive*.

points are conceived to be situated; if for brevity we speak of *the* segment AB even in this case, it must be understood that the axis of the segment is assigned in some way.

In accepting the meaning now suggested for the word segment, we have to realise that in complex space there is no sense in which a point can be described as *between* two given points of a line on which it lies, and that therefore the word is not required with its familiar intension. The use of the word *end* in connection with complex segments is purely conventional; a segment does not terminate at its ends. Just as we speak of a segment of a line, so we may define a segment of any curve by associating the curve with two of its points; for the present we are concerned only with segments of lines, and the word segment unqualified is to be held to refer to a linear segment.

There is no need to indulge in formal explanations of such phrases as 'a length of a segment', 'perpendicular segments', 'the angles between two
·43 segments', which bear their obvious meanings. °A segment is called finite if it has no infinite length, that is, if both its ends are accessible. A segment AB that is not wholly inaccessible has a *midpoint*, which is a point C such that the steps AC, CB are congruent; this midpoint is accessible if and only if both ends of the segment are accessible, that is, if and only if the segment is finite. To a segment of a line at infinity no definite midpoint can be assigned; every point of the line can serve as a midpoint of any segment of the line. But it is to be remarked that the definition of the midpoint depends on the identity of two *vectors*, not on the equality of two *lengths*, and that therefore the midpoint of a segment not wholly at infinity is no more uncertain if the axis is nul than if the axis is not nul.

·45 °A proper segment AB is said to be inscribed in a curve or surface if the points A, B both belong to the curve or surface, and the curve or surface
·46 is said to be a curve or surface *through* the segment. °When the segment degenerates into two coincident points A, A in an axis l, it is only if a locus has double intersection with l at A that the segment is said to be inscribed
·47 in the locus. °If A is a simple point, to say that a zero segment AA with a given axis is inscribed in the locus is equivalent to asserting that the axis is a tangent at A.

544. Altersection and altercontact.

·1. The definition of the order of intersection of a line with a locus fails altogether if the line forms part of the locus. By regarding the order as infinite we can reach some measure of uniformity, but this convention puts all the points of the line on the same level, whereas it is evident, for example, that in a composite locus formed of a line and a conic the points of intersection of the line and the conic have *some* peculiarity in relation to the locus as a whole and that this peculiarity is modified if the line touches the conic.

A plane locus which includes the whole of a line is necessarily composite;

definitions are obvious when the locus is decomposed, and have to be changed into a form that is applicable not only to a curve for which the decomposition has not actually been effected but also to a surface.

Let the equation 1·13 represent a plane locus that includes the whole of the line whose equation is the linear equation

$$\Lambda\epsilon = 0. \qquad \cdot 11$$

Then $\Lambda\epsilon$ is a factor, but not necessarily a simple factor, of $\Phi\epsilon^n$. Let

$$\Phi\epsilon^n \equiv (\Lambda\epsilon)^l\, \Psi\epsilon^{n-l}, \qquad \cdot 12$$

where $\Psi\epsilon^{n-l}$ does not contain $\Lambda\epsilon$ as a factor; l is the °*order* of the line Λ as a constituent of the locus. The line Λ does not form part of the locus ·13

$$\Psi\epsilon^{n-l} = 0 \qquad \cdot 14$$

and therefore cuts this locus in $n-l$ points, not necessarily distinct; these points are the °*altersections* of Λ with the original locus Φ, and °the order of intersection with Ψ is the order of altersection with Φ. With the natural convention that a line which does not form part of a plane locus is a constituent of order zero, we can assert that ·15, ·16

The sum of the order of a line as a constituent of a plane locus and the orders of its altersections with that locus is the order of the locus itself. ·17

2. It follows from 2·36 that the order on Φ of a point on Λ is equal to or greater than l according as its order on Ψ is or is not zero, that is, according as it does or does not belong to Ψ. Hence

The order of a line Λ as a constituent of a plane locus Φ is the least value which the order of a point P can have on Φ if P belongs to Λ. ·21

This theorem suggests a definition: by °the order of a line *in* a locus, plane or spatial, composite or undegenerate, is meant the least value which the order of a variable point of the line can have on the locus. With this definition ·21 becomes ·22

The order of a line as a constituent of a plane locus is its order in that locus. ·23

If now we define the °altersections of a line Λ with a locus Φ as the points of Λ whose order on Φ is greater than the order of Λ in Φ, we have a definition not inconsistent with ·15 and significant when the locus is a surface in space. ·24

°If there are any points of Λ which do not belong to Φ, the order of these points on Φ, and therefore of Λ in Φ, is zero, and the altersections become the points of Λ whose order on Φ is not zero, that is, become the intersections in the elementary sense. ·25

·3. To say that the order of intersection of a line with a locus at a point P may be greater than the order of P on the locus is only to assert that the line may touch the locus at P. In the case of the composite plane locus, if h is the order of altersection of Λ with Φ at P and m is the order of P on Φ, then $m-l$ is the order of P on Ψ, and this is less than or equal to h according as Λ is or is not a tangent to Ψ at P.

·31 °If the multiplicity of Λ as a tangent to Φ at P is l, then h is determinable as $m-l$, but in general h does not depend on l and m alone.

If P is on Λ, the linear function $\Lambda(i\epsilon_P + j\epsilon_Q)$ reduces to $j\Lambda\epsilon_Q$, and therefore with the notation of ·12

·32 $$\Phi(i\epsilon_P + j\epsilon_Q)^n = j^l (\Lambda\epsilon_Q)^l \, \Psi(i\epsilon_P + j\epsilon_Q)^{n-l},$$

whence for all values of r from l to n

·33 $$\binom{n}{r} \Phi \epsilon_P{}^{n-r} \epsilon_Q{}^r = \binom{n-l}{r-l} (\Lambda\epsilon_Q)^l \, \Psi \epsilon_P{}^{n-r} \epsilon_Q{}^{r-l}.$$

If the order of intersection of Λ with Ψ at P is h, the coefficients of the highest h powers of i in $\Psi(i\epsilon_P + j\epsilon_Q)^{n-l}$ vanish if Q is on Λ, but there are positions of Q on Λ for which the coefficient of i^{n-l-h} does not vanish; in other words, the polynomial $\Psi\epsilon_P{}^{n-r}\epsilon^{r-l}$ vanishes identically or contains $\Lambda\epsilon$ for a factor if r has any value from l to $l+h-1$ but not if r has the value
·34 $l+h$, and therefore °*the polynomial* $\Phi\epsilon_P{}^{n-r}\epsilon^r$ *vanishes identically or contains* $\Lambda\epsilon$ *for a factor to a power greater than* l *if* r *is less than* $l+h$ *but contains* $\Lambda\epsilon$ *only to the power* l *if* r *is equal to* $l+h$. Retranslating the occurrence of $\Lambda\epsilon$ as a factor of a polynomial into geometrical terms we have the following enunciation, which is consistent with ·16 for a curve and *defines* the order of altersection for a surface:

·35 *Let* Φ *be a locus of order* n, *let* Λ *be a line whose order in* Φ *is* l, *and let* P *be a point of altersection of order* h *on* Λ. *Then the equation*

$$\Phi\epsilon_P{}^{n-r}\epsilon^r = 0$$

reduces to an identity for all values of r *from* 0 *to* $l-1$, *either reduces to an identity or represents a locus in which* Λ *is of order greater than* l *for all values of* r *from* l *to* $l+h-1$, *represents a locus in which* Λ *is of order exactly* l *when* r *has the value* $l+h$, *and either reduces to an identity or represents a locus in which* Λ *is of order not less than* l *for all values of* r *from* $l+h+1$ *to* n.

Recalling that the order m of P on Φ is definable by the property that $\Phi\epsilon_P{}^{n-r}\epsilon^r$ vanishes identically for all values of r from 0 to $m-1$ and not when r has the value m, we see that m is not less than l and not greater than $l+h$. In the tangent locus

$$\Phi\epsilon_P{}^{n-m}\epsilon^m = 0,$$

Λ is of order not less than l and not greater than m, and we have only to
·38 compare the definitions of m and h to find that °if the order of Λ in the tangent locus is exactly l, then $l+h$ and m are identical, thus extending to the general locus, curve or surface, a property asserted in ·31 of the decomposed plane curve; to find h in general we have to find a locus in which

the order of Λ *is* l, and that is why the order of Λ in the tangent locus is irrelevant except in the case when it has this particular value.

·4. The number associated most simply with the contact of a line Λ with a locus Φ at a point P is the excess of the order of intersection at P over the order of P on Φ. To say that Λ is a tangent is simply to assert that this
excess is not zero, and the excess is called the °*order of contact.* If Λ forms ·41
part of Φ, the order of contact is infinite, and its place is taken by the °*order* 42
of altercontact, defined as the number by which $l+h$, the sum of the order of Λ in Φ and the order of altersection at P, exceeds m, the order of P; this number is zero if and only if the order of Λ in the tangent locus at P is the same as its order in Φ itself.

The orders of contact and altercontact make no allowance for a possible multiplicity of the tangent as a constituent in the tangent locus, and in some problems a number occurs that differs for this reason from the order of altercontact.

In the simple case of a plane curve, a line that cuts the curve at a point P of order m and is not itself a tangent has an intersection of order m; whether
a line touches the curve or not at P, we may say that °a tangent distinct from ·43
Λ and of multiplicity f accounts for f of the intersections or altersections of
Λ at P, and the °*index* of contact or altercontact of Λ at P is the number of ·44
intersections or altersections for which tangents distinct from Λ do not account. Since the total number of tangents at P is m, the order of P, the number distinct from Λ is $m-g$ where g is the multiplicity of Λ as a factor of the tangent locus

$$\Phi \epsilon_P^{n-m} \epsilon^m = 0,$$

and by replacing multiplicity in the tangent locus by *order* in this locus we
can frame a definition applicable equally to plane curves and to surfaces: °if ·45
the order of altersection of Λ with Φ at P is h and if the orders of P on Φ and of Λ in the tangent locus at P are m and g, the index of altercontact is
the number $g+h-m$; °the index of contact is the same as the index of alter- ·46
contact if Λ does not form part of Φ but is infinite if Λ is in Φ.

The index of contact exceeds the order of contact by the multiplicity of the tangent; the difference between the index of altercontact and the order of altercontact is the same as the difference between the order of the tangent in the original locus and the order of the tangent in the tangent locus.

Since g is not less than l, the order of Λ in Φ, and m is not greater than $l+h$, the index defined is not negative. For the index to be zero, m must be as large as possible and g as small, that is, Λ must not be a tangent at all. If Λ is a tangent, g is not less than $l+1$, and m is not equal to $l+h$ and therefore is not greater than $l+h-1$: the index is not less than 2.

If the index of altercontact of a line Λ at a point of altersection P with a *plane* locus is k, then the number of tangents at P distinct from Λ is $h-k$; it follows from ·17 that

·49 *If the order of a line Λ in a plane locus Φ of order n is l, the number of tangents distinct from Λ whose points of contact are points of Λ is less than $n-l$ by the sum of the indices of altercontact of Λ at its points of altersection with Φ.*

545. The relation between orders of altersection with a surface and orders of altersection with plane sections of the surface.

·11 **·1.** It follows from 2·13 that if P, Q are any two distinct points, °the point $iP+jQ$ is of order m on the locus Φ if $\Phi\,(i\epsilon_P+j\epsilon_Q)^{n-m+1}\,\epsilon^{m-1}$ vanishes identi-
·12 cally but $\Phi\,(i\epsilon_P+j\epsilon_Q)^{n-m}\,\epsilon^m$ does not. Hence °the order of the line PQ is the number l which is such that $\Phi\,(i\epsilon_P+j\epsilon_Q)^{n-r}\,\epsilon^r$ is identically zero for all values of $i:j$ if r is equal to $l-1$ but not for *all* values of $i:j$ if r is equal to l, and
·13 °the altersections of PQ with Φ are the points that correspond to values of $i:j$ for which every coefficient in the polynomial $\Phi\,(i\epsilon_P+j\epsilon_Q)^{n-l}\,\epsilon^l$ does vanish.
·14 °If for a *particular* value of s we know that $\Phi(i\epsilon_P+j\epsilon_Q)^{n-s}\,\epsilon^s$ vanishes identically for all values of i and j, we can assert that the order of PQ in Φ is *greater than s*. In the function $\Phi\,(i\epsilon_P+j\epsilon_Q)^{n-l}\,\epsilon_R{}^l$ regarded as a polynomial in the coordinates of R, each coefficient that does not vanish identically is a homogeneous binomial in i and j of degree $n-l$, with coefficients depending on the relation of P and Q to the locus Φ. We have therefore a number of equations, not more than $\frac{1}{2}(l+1)(l+2)$ if Φ is a curve and not more than $\frac{1}{6}(l+1)(l+2)(l+3)$ if Φ is a surface, each of degree $n-l$ in $i:j$, such that the ratios corresponding to the altersections of PQ with Φ are the common roots of these equations.

If j is a factor of degree h in every one of these equations, it is a factor of this degree in the function $\Phi\,(i\epsilon_P+j\epsilon_Q)^{n-l}\,\epsilon^l$ from which the equations are derived; that is to say, the function $\Phi\epsilon_P{}^{n-l-s}\,\epsilon_Q{}^s\,\epsilon^l$ vanishes identically for every value of s from 0 to $h-1$, and so also does the function $\Phi\epsilon_P{}^{n-l-s}\,(i\epsilon_P+j\epsilon_Q)^s\,\epsilon^l$ for every one of these values of s and for arbitrary values of i and j. Conversely if the function $\Phi\epsilon_P{}^{n-l-s}\,(i\epsilon_P+j\epsilon_Q)^s\,\epsilon^l$ vanishes identically for arbitrary values of i and j and for every value of s from 0 to $h-1$, the function $\Phi\epsilon_P{}^{n-l-s}\,\epsilon_Q{}^s\,\epsilon^l$ vanishes identically and j^h is a factor of $\Phi\,(i\epsilon_P+j\epsilon_Q)^{n-l}\,\epsilon^l$. By referring the points of the line PQ not to the points P, Q but to one of these
·16 points and the point $fP+gQ$ we deduce that °the function $\Phi\,(i\epsilon_P+j\epsilon_Q)^{n-l}\,\epsilon_R{}^l$ has a factor $(ig-jf)^h$ independent of the coördinates of R if and only if $\Phi\,(f\epsilon_P+g\epsilon_Q)^{n-l-s}\,(i\epsilon_P+j\epsilon_Q)^s\,\epsilon^l$ vanishes identically for arbitrary values of i and j for every value of s from 0 to $h-1$, that is, by ·14, if and only if the order of PQ in the locus $\Phi\,(f\epsilon_P+g\epsilon_Q)^{n-l-s}\,\epsilon^{l+s}$ is greater than l for every value of s from 0 to $h-1$, that is, by 4·35, if and only if the order of altersection of PQ with Φ at $fP+gQ$ is greater than $h-1$:

·17 *The degree in which $ig-jf$ occurs as a factor of every coefficient in the function $\Phi\,(i\epsilon_P+j\epsilon_Q)^{n-l}\,\epsilon^l$ is the order of altersection of the line PQ with the locus Φ at the point $fP+gQ$.*

That is to say, °if the line PQ is of order l in Φ and its altersections with Φ are i_1P+j_1Q, i_2P+j_2Q, ... i_mP+j_mQ, of orders h_1, h_2, ... h_m, the function $\Phi(i\epsilon_P+j\epsilon_Q)^{n-l}\epsilon^l$ is the product of the binomial ·18

$$(ij_1-ji_1)^{h_1}(ij_2-ji_2)^{h_2}\ldots(ij_m-ji_m)^{h_m}$$

by a function of degree l whose coefficients are of degree $n-l-\Sigma h$ in i and j and do not vanish simultaneously for any values of i and j.

·2. It is an immediate deduction from ·18 that

The sum of the orders of altersection of a line with a locus of order n in which its own order is l is not greater than $n-l$. ·21

We saw in 1·35 that if the altersections are intersections, that is if l is zero, the sum is n, and in 4·17 that in the case of a plane curve the sum is actually equal to $n-l$ whatever the value of l; by considering the sections of a surface by planes through a line it is easy not only to see that °*for a surface the maximum $n-l$ is not necessarily attained unless l is zero* but to account for the deficiency. ·22

Let Π be the section of a surface Φ by a plane which does not form part of Φ, and let P be a point of this plane. Then if the order of P on Φ is m, there are lines through P which cut Φ only m times at P, and in general some of these lines are in the plane of the section; if there are such lines, the order of P on Π is not greater than m, and since this order is manifestly not less than m, °*the order of P on Π is equal to the order of P on Φ unless the plane of section forms part of the tangent locus to Φ at P.* ·23

Since the order of the tangent locus is m, this locus can not include more than m distinct planes, and therefore °if P is a *given* point, the order of P on a section by a plane through P is the same as the order of P on Φ except possibly for m special planes. ·24

If Λ is a line of order l in Φ, there are points on Λ whose order on Φ is l; indeed, the altersections are not more than $n-l$ in number, since the sum of their orders of altersection is not greater than $n-l$. It follows from ·24 that °there are not more than l planes through Λ which yield sections of Φ in which Λ is not of order l. Since the order of altersection of Λ with a locus Φ at a given point can be discovered by inspection of the orders of Λ in a finite number of loci derived from Φ, °there is at most a finite number of planes through Λ which cut Φ in sections which do not have at the altersections of Λ with Φ altersections of the same order as those of Λ with Φ itself. If Π is a section with which Λ has the altersections which it has with Φ, and in which Λ is of order l, and if the sum of the orders of altersection of Λ with Φ is not $n-l$ but $n-l-k$, 4·17 implies that °there are altersections of Λ with Π which are not altersections of Λ with Φ and that °the sum of the orders of these additional altersections is k, a number independent of any particular plane through Λ. ·25 ·26 ·27 ·28

·3. The entry of the additional altersections is explained by ·23. A point Λ has an order on Π greater than l if its order on Φ is greater than l, or if it has a higher order on Π than on Φ. In the first case the point is an altersection of Λ with Φ; in the second case, which does not exclude the first, the plane of section is part of the tangent locus to Φ at the point. If P is a point of Λ which is not an altersection with Φ and if the plane of Π is part of the tangent locus at P, every line through P in this plane has an intersection with Π at P of order greater than l; hence Λ altersects Π at P unless Λ has an order greater than l in Π, while for Λ to have an order greater than l in Π, the plane of section must touch Φ at every point of Λ except possibly at the altersections of Λ with Φ.

The reader familiar with ruled surfaces should consider the case of a developable of which Λ is a generator, and distinguish between the general case of a developable with an edge, touched by Λ at a midpoint C, and the case of a cone with a vertex V. As a rule in the general case every point of Λ except C is of the first order on the surface and C is of the second order; with the definitions we are using, the plane which touches the surface elsewhere on Λ touches it also at C, for lines through C in this plane have triple intersection there with the surface. The tangent locus at the vertex V of a cone is identical with the cone itself and does not as a rule include the plane which touches the cone at other points of the generator Λ.

546. Asymptotes.

·**1**. No distinction has yet been made in this chapter between accessible and inaccessible points, but it is on the disposition of their inaccessible points that the classification of conics and conicoids depends.

A point at infinity is characterised by a definite vecline, and the veclines corresponding to the points at infinity on a given curve or surface are called
·11 the °*asymptotic* veclines of that curve or surface; their directions are the asymptotic directions.

The inaccessible points of a plane curve are the points which the curve has in common with the line at infinity in its plane. If the line at infinity is a constituent of the curve, every direction in the plane is asymptotic, but if the line at infinity is not a constituent, the number of asymptotic veclines is not greater than the order of the curve and is actually equal to this order if the intersections of the line at infinity with the curve are all simple.

·12 A tangent at an inaccessible point of a curve is called an °*asymptote* of the curve. The tangent may be the line at infinity itself, but it is of course the exception for the line at infinity to be a tangent, just as it is the exception for an accessible line taken at random to be a tangent. If the intersections of the curve by the line at infinity are all simple, the number of them is equal to the order of the curve, and the asymptotes are all accessible; also no two of the asymptotes are parallel, for a point at infinity common to two distinct asymptotes would be a multiple point of the curve and would give a multiple intersection with the line at infinity, contrary to hypothesis:

·13 *If as is generally the case the intersections of a plane curve of order n by the line at infinity in its plane are all simple, then the asymptotes of the curve are n distinct accessible lines no two of which are parallel.*

If the intersection of the line at infinity with a curve at a point P is of multiple order h, two possibilities, different in their effects but not mutually exclusive, have to be considered. If the order of the point P *on the curve* is m, then °if h is equal to m, the line at infinity is not a tangent at P, and there ·14
are m tangents, not necessarily distinct, which, because they are accessible lines through P, are parallel lines. But °if h is greater than m, the line at ·15
infinity is a tangent at P, and accounts for a number g of the asymptotes through P, but this number is the multiplicity of the line as a factor of the tangent locus at P, and is not a function of m and h; the number of *accessible* asymptotes through P is $m-g$, and in general no two of them coincide.

Should the line at infinity be a constituent of order l in the curve, it is an l-fold asymptote on that account, and the points to be examined are its points of altersection with the curve. If the altersections are simple, there are $n-l$ distinct accessible asymptotes of which no two are parallel, and if the altersections are multiple but do not number among them any points of altercontact there are still $n-l$ accessible asymptotes of which some perhaps coincide and some are certainly parallel. If there are points of altercontact, the number of accessible asymptotes can not be predicted; the problem of counting the accessible asymptotes exactly is a particular case of the problem solved in 4·49.

·2. If the triangle of reference has two of its vertices at infinity, or if the plane is referred to a vector frame attached to an accessible origin,—which comes to the same thing—the coordinates are naturally denoted, as explained for three dimensions in 21·4 and 26·3, by ξ, η, τ, and the asymptotic directions of the curve

$$\Phi\,(\xi,\ \eta,\ \tau)^n = 0$$ ·21

are given immediately by the equation

$$\Phi\,(\xi,\ \eta,\ 0)^n = 0,$$ ·22

which interpreted as an equation between the coordinates of a point is the equation of the lines through the origin with asymptotic directions. If $\Phi\epsilon^n$ has τ for a factor, to power l, then the line at infinity is of order l in the curve, and if the quotient of $\Phi\epsilon^n$ by τ^l is $\Psi\epsilon^{n-l}$, the points of altersection of the line at infinity are determined by the equation

$$\Psi\,(\xi,\ \eta,\ 0)^{n-l} = 0.$$ ·23

·3. Two curves are said to be asymptotic °*along* a given accessible line if ·31
they have in common the point at infinity on the line and if also the line is a tangent to both of them there, in short, if the line is an asymptote of them both. If two curves have a common point P at infinity and if the line at infinity is not a tangent to either of them at P, the curves are described as asymptotic °*at P* if they have there the same asymptotes each with the same ·32
multiplicity for the two curves. We call two curves neither of which has the line at infinity for a tangent °asymptotic to each other if their asymptotes, ·33
each with its appropriate order, are the same.

·35 °If the plane at infinity is not part of the tangent locus at any point of either of two surfaces, the surfaces are said to be asymptotic to each other if they have the same points at infinity and if also at each of these points they have the same tangent locus: the surfaces touch each other along their common intersection with the plane at infinity.

No mention has been made of the property most intimately associated with the word asymptotic, namely, the property of indefinitely near approach of a variable point on a curve to a variable point on a line, or more generally of indefinitely near approach of a variable point on one curve or surface to a variable point on another. This is because all questions involving limits are being deliberately avoided. But it must not be forgotten that questions of this kind concerning asymptotes have their exact counterparts in questions of orders of approximation relating to accessible tangents; there is no logical ground for dealing with the former type of question and not with the latter*, and what we have omitted to consider is not *the* point from which problems of asymptotes *should* be approached but *a* point from which geometrical problems of many kinds *may* be approached.

With regard to asymptotic surfaces, little can be said without mention of *developables*, and the definition in ·35 is designed solely to meet our requirements with regard to spheres.

547. Definitions of conics and conicoids; degenerate conics; parabolas; the existence of a conic through five coplanar points.

·1. Second only to lines and planes in importance are curves and surfaces
·11 of the second order. Plane curves of the second order are called °*conics*, surfaces
·12 of the second order °*conicoids*. It is not to be imagined that in interest to the mathematician these curves and surfaces are merely somewhere between loci of the first order and loci of the third order, for in fact the place of conics and conicoids in the art is fundamental. A mathematician who is not investigating curves and surfaces of the third order or of some definite higher order on their own account, is little likely to require ever to be acquainted with even their simplest properties, but conics and conicoids, of special forms if not in complete generality, recur in every branch of mathematics.

It is only with certain special kinds of conics and conicoids that we shall deal explicitly, and the present section merely contains those properties of conics and conicoids in general that follow directly from the principles of the earlier sections of this chapter and are required in the chapters that conclude our work.

·2. Applied to the case when n is two, 1·32 asserts that

·21 *If a line has more than two points in common with a conic, then the conic is degenerate and has the line for a constituent,*

and that

·22 *If a line has more than two points in common with a conicoid, then every point of the line belongs to the conicoid.*

* With regard to such questions see Fowler's tract, *Elementary Differential Geometry of Plane Curves* (1920), which deals only with the real plane and makes no reference to points at infinity, but does not restrict the curves to be algebraic.

The points in these propositions need not be distinct:

If a line has double intersection with a conic at one point, the two have no other point in common unless the conic is degenerate and has the line for a constituent; ·23

If a line has intersection of higher order than the second with a conic, the conic is degenerate and has the line for a constituent. ·24

From 3·25 it follows that if a conic has a double point C, there are two lines through C which have intersections of order higher than two; hence from ·24

A conic is degenerate if and only if it has a double point. ·25

Similarly

If a line has intersection of higher order than the second with a conicoid, the line lies wholly in the conicoid; ·26

A conicoid that has a double point is identical with its tangent cone at that point. ·27

From 1·42,

Any plane section of an undegenerate conicoid is a conic, ·28

and therefore from ·25 and 3·33,

The tangent plane at any simple point of an undegenerate conicoid cuts the surface in two lines both of which pass through the point of contact. ·29

·3. Conics are classified by their inaccessible points. A °*parabola* is a conic which has *double* intersection with the line at infinity at some point. A conic that is not a parabola has simple intersection with the line at infinity at each of two distinct points. Hence as a special case of 6·13*, ·31

An aparabolic conic has two distinct accessible asymptotes, and these are not parallel. ·32

Also by ·25, the point which the line at infinity has in common with a parabola is a simple point on the parabola if the parabola is not degenerate:

An undegenerate parabola has the line at infinity for its only asymptote. ·33

A constituent of a degenerate conic is a tangent to the conic at every one of its own points, and therefore

If a conic is degenerate, its asymptotes are the two constituents themselves. ·34

If the constituents are accessible and not parallel, the points in which they cut the line at infinity are distinct. If one of the constituents is the line at infinity and the other is accessible, the conic satisfies the definition of a parabola, which does not require the point of intersection to be unique, and it remains true that the line at infinity is an asymptote, but this line is no

* Thus in complex geometry the names 'ellipse' and 'hyperbola' are misleading and out of place. For a given conic, the square of the eccentricity is a definite complex number; to say that this number is not equal to the complex number 1 is intelligible, but to say that it is greater than 1 or that it is less than 1 is nonsense.

longer the *only* asymptote, unless indeed the conic is merely this one line duplicated. If the constituents are accessible and parallel, having a common point P at infinity, the line at infinity has double intersection with the conic at P, and therefore the conic is a parabola, but the line at infinity is *not* one of the tangents at P, that is, is not an asymptote.

·4. It might be questioned whether the definition of a parabola is not undesirably wide, whether in fact the line at infinity should not be required to be a tangent rather than to have double intersection. The answer is made most convincingly by means of the general equation of a conic referred to a triangle with two vertices at infinity. This equation is

·41 $$a\xi^2 + 2h\xi\eta + b\eta^2 + 2g\xi\tau + 2f\eta\tau + c\tau^2 = 0,$$

and the points at infinity correspond to the equation

·42 $$a\xi^2 + 2h\xi\eta + b\eta^2 = 0.$$

If this last equation is significant, it indicates two and only two points at infinity, and the condition for these points to coincide is

·43 $$ab - h^2 = 0.$$

If the coefficients in ·42 are all zero, ·41 reduces to

·44 $$(2g\xi + 2f\eta + c\tau)\,\tau = 0,$$

the equation of a degenerate conic of which the line at infinity is one constituent, but ·43 does remain true. Thus according to the definition we are using, ·43 is the *necessary and sufficient* condition for ·41 to represent a parabola.

If ·43 is satisfied but a, h, b are not all zero, there are numbers p, q such that identically

·45 $$a\xi^2 + 2h\xi\eta + b\eta^2 \equiv (p\xi + q\eta)^2,$$

and ·41 represents parallel straight lines if and only if $g\xi + f\eta$ is a multiple of $p\xi + q\eta$, that is, if and only if

$$fp - gq = 0,$$

a condition which is equivalent in virtue of ·45 to

·46 $$af^2 - 2hfg + bg^2 = 0.$$

To couple the positive condition ·43 in an analytical investigation either with the negative condition that a, h, b are not all to vanish or with the negative condition that $af^2 - 2hfg + bg^2$ is not to vanish—a condition that introduces the ratio of f to g which is not otherwise involved in the discrimination—could lead to nothing but confusion, and therefore we are content with the definition that leads to a simple result:

·47 *If the triangle of reference in a plane is equivalent to a vector frame attached to an accessible origin, the necessary and sufficient condition for the conic*

$$a\xi^2 + 2h\xi\eta + b\eta^2 + 2g\xi\tau + 2f\eta\tau + c\tau^2 = 0$$

to be a parabola is $$ab - h^2 = 0.$$

·5. In the general equation of a conic, as given in ·41, there are six coefficients, and *whatever* the values of these coefficients, unless indeed they are all zero, it is a conic that the equation represents. To multiply the equation throughout by a constant other than zero does not affect the locus represented; in other words, the locus depends on the *five* independent ratios of the coefficients, not on the actual values of the coefficients individually.

In general, there is one and only one conic which contains five given points in ·51
a plane.

In fact the conditions that five points P, Q, R, S, T should lie on the conic, that is, that the coordinates of these five points should satisfy the equation ·41, are five equations linear and homogeneous in the coefficients a, h, b, g, f, c, and unless there is some special relation between the five given points these equations *determine* the mutual *ratios* of the coefficients and therefore give the equation of a *unique* conic through the points. Instead of solving the five equations and making a substitution, we have only to eliminate the six coefficients between the general equation itself and the five equations expressing that the points lie on the conic to have the actual equation of the conic in the determinantal form

$$\begin{vmatrix} \xi^2 & \xi\eta & \eta^2 & \xi\tau & \eta\tau & \tau^2 \\ \xi_P^2 & \xi_P\eta_P & \eta_P^2 & \xi_P\tau_P & \eta_P\tau_P & \tau_P^2 \\ \xi_Q^2 & \xi_Q\eta_Q & \eta_Q^2 & \xi_Q\tau_Q & \eta_Q\tau_Q & \tau_Q^2 \\ \xi_R^2 & \xi_R\eta_R & \eta_R^2 & \xi_R\tau_R & \eta_R\tau_R & \tau_R^2 \\ \xi_S^2 & \xi_S\eta_S & \eta_S^2 & \xi_S\tau_S & \eta_S\tau_S & \tau_S^2 \\ \xi_T^2 & \xi_T\eta_T & \eta_T^2 & \xi_T\tau_T & \eta_T\tau_T & \tau_T^2 \end{vmatrix} = 0. \qquad \cdot 52$$

It is not necessary for us to examine the cases in which this equation is evanescent, or even to prove formally that the equation is usually significant, for the use we have to make of ·51 is purely tentative. But we note that there is no distinction of rôle in ·52 between the coordinate τ and the coordinates ξ and η; no distinction has to be drawn between accessible and inaccessible points in the discussion of the existence and uniqueness of a conic through five of them.

CHAPTER V 5

CIRCLES IN IDEAL COMPLEX SPACE

551. Ordinary circles; nul circles and degenerate circles. 552. The perpendicular bisector of a segment; the centres and radii of ordinary circles. 553. The general definition of a circle; infinite circles; undegenerate parabolic circles in an isotropic plane; centres and radii in general. 554. The properties of the constant rectangle and the constant angle. 555. Circles about a pair of points; associated linear segments; measures of separation; coaxal systems of circles in general; associated coaxal systems. 556. Exceptional forms of coaxal systems.

551. Ordinary circles; nul circles and degenerate circles.

·1. Naturally we wish the locus of a point in a plane at a constant distance from a fixed point of the plane to have the name of circle, at any rate if the fixed point is accessible and the distance is finite. To avoid exceptional cases it is necessary in due course to allow the distance to be infinite or the fixed point to be at infinity, but the locus may not then be *definable* by means of the point and the distance, and to understand the extensions to be made we must first discover properties that are characteristic of the locus when the
·11 difficult cases are expressly excluded. We define then an °*ordinary* circle* as the locus of a point in a plane at a constant finite distance from a given accessible point of the plane. The distance is called a radius of the circle, and the fixed point a centre; we must not prejudge such questions as whether a circle in a complex plane can have more than one centre.

The ideal vector of which $(\mathbf{r}, R)$ is an effective specification is the vector of a step from Q to the ordinary circle with centre Q and radius q if and only if

·12 $$\mathscr{G}\mathbf{r}^2 = q^2R^2,$$

it being assumed that $\mathbf{r}$ belongs to the necessary vecplane.

The condition for $(h\mathbf{r}, kR)$ to lead from Q to the circle is

$$h^2\mathscr{G}\mathbf{r}^2 = k^2q^2R^2.$$

Supposing R not to be zero, we can distinguish four possibilities. If neither $\mathscr{G}\mathbf{r}^2$ nor q is zero, the equation is satisfied by two distinct values of h/k, both finite, one the negative of the other. If $\mathscr{G}\mathbf{r}^2$ is zero, but not q, the equation requires k to be zero. If q is zero, but not $\mathscr{G}\mathbf{r}^2$, the equation requires h to be zero. If both q and $\mathscr{G}\mathbf{r}^2$ are zero no condition is imposed on h and k. Thus:

* In one respect the adjective is misleading: we shall find that in an isotropic plane it is the exception for a 'circle' to be in this sense 'ordinary'. If we are to use 'actual' still as the opposite of 'ideal,' we must describe the circles of elementary geometry as *actual real* circles.

If an ordinary circle has centre Q and radius different from zero, an anisotropic line through Q lying in its plane cuts the circle in two distinct accessible points, and an isotropic line through Q cuts it at infinity only; ·13

If an ordinary circle has centre Q and radius zero, an anisotropic line through Q in its plane cuts it nowhere except at Q, but every point of an isotropic line through Q belongs to the circle. ·14

A circle is said to be *degenerate* if there is a line whose points all belong to the circle, and ·14 implies that °*every circle of radius zero is degenerate.* ·15

·2. The last proposition is evident on a direct examination of the conditions involved. An ordinary circle of radius zero is called* a °nul circle. In real ·21
space, such a circle consists of a single point, its centre, but in complex space, with which alone we are now concerned, °the nul circle with centre Q is formed ·22
of the same points as the nul lines through Q; a line through Q either coincides with one of these lines or cuts it nowhere except at Q. As we proved in 436·2, if the plane is anisotropic there are two nul lines through each point, but if the plane is isotropic there is only one. That a circle should in any circumstances degenerate into a pair† of lines is enough to warn us against taking for granted that all the properties of actual real circles have their counterparts in ideal complex space.

·3. In an isotropic plane it is not only nul circles that are degenerate. We have seen in 436·5 that in an isotropic plane the points whose distances from a point Q in one aspect of the plane have a given value q compose a definite nul line; those whose distances from Q in the other aspect have the value q compose another nul line, distinct from the first unless q is zero, and the circle with centre Q and radius q is formed of the points of these two lines:

In an isotropic plane, an ordinary circle with radius different from zero has the form of two distinct nul lines. ·31

Whether it is from a nul circle in an anisotropic plane or from a circle with proper radius in an isotropic plane that we regard a nul circle in an isotropic plane as degenerating, we have to think of the line as °*double* to find a con- ·32
ventional interpretation of general theorems applicable to this extreme case.

It is evident that °in an isotropic plane every ordinary circle has an infinity ·33
of centres: if Q is one centre, every point on the nul line through Q is a centre also.

·4. The most striking difference descriptively between the circles of ideal complex space and the circles known to the Greeks was discovered by Poncelet‡.

* It will be proved that a circle can not be of zero radius with respect to one centre and of radius different from zero with respect to some other centre.

† To speak of the circle as a pair of lines is a convenient illogicality, too glaring to be harmful: the circle *is* a class of points, not of lines.

‡ *Propriétés Projectives des Figures*, p. 49, 1822.

Whatever the value of q, the fundamental equation ·12 is satisfied if R is zero if and only if **r** is nul: whatever its radius, an ordinary circle with centre Q contains no inaccessible points except those on the nul lines through Q, which we have already noticed to belong to the circle. In other words

·41 *Every ordinary circle contains the focal points of its plane, and no ordinary circle contains any points at infinity except these.*

On account of their relation to circles, the focal points in a plane are often
·42 called the *circular points* of the plane, or more fully the °*circular points at infinity* in the plane.

552. The perpendicular bisector of a segment; the centres and radii of ordinary circles.

·1. Let us consider the locus in space of an accessible point equidistant from two given accessible points A, B. If N is the midpoint of AB, the equation

$$\mathscr{G}(QN+NA)^2 = \mathscr{G}(QN+NB)^2$$

is equivalent, if all the vectors involved are finite, to

$$\mathscr{G}NA^2 - \mathscr{G}NB^2 = 2\mathscr{G}QN.AB,$$

and therefore to $\mathscr{G}QN.AB = 0$:

·11 °the step QN must be perpendicular to the step AB. Expressed in this form the result is not actually false if A and B coincide, but if we suppose these points distinct we can envisage a definite locus. The midpoint N is a definite point, since A and B are assumed to be accessible, and if A and B are distinct, the vector AB belongs to only one vecline and ·11 asserts that QN belongs to the vecplane to which this vecline is perpendicular:

·12 *If two accessible points A, B are distinct, the perpendicular bisector of AB is a definite plane, and the accessible points of this plane are the accessible points equidistant from A and B.*

·2. We can now discover the positions in a given plane possible for a centre of a circle through two distinct accessible points A, B of the plane. The perpendicular bisector of AB has certainly one point in common with the given plane, namely, the midpoint of AB; it therefore either coincides with the given plane or cuts the given plane in a definite line. Coincidence requires that a plane perpendicular to AB should contain AB, that is, that AB should be nul, and requires further that the plane under consideration should itself be the isotropic plane containing AB.

·21 *In general, the accessible points in a given plane equidistant from two distinct accessible points A, B of the plane are the accessible points of a definite line, and this is the only line in the plane to bisect AB perpendicularly; exception occurs only when the plane is isotropic and the line AB is nul, in which case* *every point of the plane is equidistant from A and B and every line in the plane is perpendicular to AB.*

°If AB is nul but the plane is not isotropic, the peculiarity is that the perpendicular bisector coincides with AB. ·22 °If the plane is isotropic but AB is not nul, the perpendicular bisector is the nul line through the midpoint of AB. ·23 From the present point of view, the fact that if two accessible points in an isotropic plane are on the same nul line *every* accessible point of the plane is equidistant from them seems quite natural, and yet this is only another way of saying that

In an isotropic plane, every ordinary circle that contains a point P includes the whole of the nul line through P, ·24

and 1·31 is an immediate deduction from this.

For the sake of reference later, we must supplement ·22; if A is an accessible point in a nul line l and if Q is any accessible point of l, the circle with centre Q which contains A must have zero radius, since the length of QA is zero. Thus, °if A, B are distinct accessible points of a nul line in an anisotropic ·25 plane, every ordinary circle through A and B in that plane is a nul circle of which the line AB forms part.

·3. If two accessible points A, B coincide, there is no sense in which any point can fail to be at the same distances from A as from B. Also there is no plane which can be regarded as the perpendicular bisector of the zero *step* AB.

But the midpoint of the step is perfectly definite, and if the coincident points are associated with a definite line through them, there is only one plane through the midpoint perpendicular to this line. In other words, °if it is ·31 ascribed to a *segment* rather than to a step or to a pair of points, the perpendicular bisector does not evade us when the points happen to coincide. Moreover, if the segment lies in a given plane, that is, if the axis of the segment is in that plane, the perpendicular bisector cuts the plane in a definite line unless the axis is nul and the plane isotropic, whether or not the ends of the segment coincide.

Again, although if A and B coincide every point is equidistant from A and B, so that if Q is any accessible point in a plane containing A there is a circle with centre Q which contains both A and B, it is not true that if A and B coincide in a line l there is necessarily a circle with a given centre Q which circumscribes the *segment* obtained by associating A and B with l. If $\mathbf{l}$ is a proper vector in the vecline of l, a point P for which AP has the vector $r\mathbf{l}$ is on the circle with centre Q which passes through A if and only if

$$\mathscr{G}(QA + r\mathbf{l})^2 = \mathscr{G}\, QA^2, \qquad ·32$$

that is, if and only if $$r^2\mathscr{G}\,\mathbf{l}^2 + 2r\mathscr{G}\,\mathbf{l}.QA = 0; \qquad ·33$$

this equation has one zero root, because the circle by hypothesis contains A. The second root satisfies the equation

·34 $$r\mathscr{G}\mathbf{l}^2 + 2\mathscr{G}\mathbf{l}.QA = 0,$$

which can be satisfied with r zero only if $\mathscr{G}\mathbf{l}.QA$ is zero, that is, only if Q is in the plane through A perpendicular to l. If l is not nul, r must then be zero, and l cuts the circle twice at A but does not form part of the circle. If l is nul, r is indeterminate, and l is a constituent of the circle, but it is still necessary for AQ to be perpendicular to l.

What we have just proved may be expressed in the form that

·35 *If a line l has double intersection with a circle at an accessible point A and Q is a centre of the circle, then Q is in a line through A perpendicular to l.*

The point we are concerned to emphasise is that this result and ·21 are included in the single assertion that

·36 *The centres of ordinary circles circumscribed to any finite segment belong to the perpendicular bisector of the segment. If the plane of the circles is given, then unless this plane is isotropic and the axis of the segment is nul, the centres are the accessible points of a definite line, which is the only line in the plane that bisects the segment perpendicularly. In the exceptional case, every ordinary circle through either end of the segment circumscribes the segment, and every line that passes through the midpoint and lies in the plane is a perpendicular bisector of the segment.*

·4. To find the points which a given line has in common with the ordinary circle with centre Q and radius q, let us take a definite point A of the line and a definite vector $\mathbf{p}$ in the corresponding vecline; the point P is in the line if and only if the vector of AP is a multiple of $\mathbf{p}$, and if this vector is $r\mathbf{p}$, one and only one position of P in the line corresponds to each value of r. The point P belongs to the circle if and only if

·41 $$\mathscr{G}(QA + r\mathbf{p})^2 = q^2,$$

that is, if and only if

·42 $$r^2\mathscr{G}\mathbf{p}^2 + 2r\mathscr{G}\mathbf{p}.QA + \mathscr{G}QA^2 - q^2 = 0,$$

and since this equation is quadratic in r,

·43 *If a line has more than two points in common with an ordinary circle, the circle is degenerate and the line is a constituent of it.*

A line which is a constituent of a circle has multiple intersection with the circle at every point. It follows from ·35 that if l is such a line and Q is a centre of the circle, and if A, B are two points of l distinct from each other and from Q, then both QA and QB are perpendicular to l. The lines QA, QB can not be parallel unless they coincide, that is unless Q is in l. For proper steps which are perpendicular to l to be in l, the line l must be nul; on the other hand, for two steps coplanar with l but not parallel to each other both to be perpendicular to l, the plane must be isotropic and still l must be nul.

If an ordinary circle is degenerate, its constituents are nul lines. ·44

°In an isotropic plane, any two nul lines together constitute an ordinary circle, and the circle itself is not nul unless the constituents coincide. But if the plane is not isotropic, any centre Q necessarily belongs to any constituent l, and since l is nul, zero is the only distance between Q and a point of l, and the circle is the nul circle whose centre is Q: 45

If an ordinary circle in an anisotropic plane is degenerate, the constituents are nul lines which are not parallel, the only centre is the point of intersection of the constituents, and zero is the only value of a radius. ·46

It is sometimes convenient to speak of two nul lines in a given plane as °*complementary* if together they form an ordinary circle in the plane. ·47

·5. In an anisotropic plane, if A, B, C are three accessible points that are not collinear, the perpendicular bisectors of AB and BC, not being parallel, intersect in an accessible point Q which is the only point common to them and is therefore the only point equidistant from the three points A, B, C. Combining this result with ·43 and ·46 we can assert that

In an anisotropic plane, no ordinary circle has more than one centre, ·51

a proposition of which 1·33 shews a proof to be by no means superfluous. If Q is the only centre of a given circle and A is an accessible point of the circle, a radius of the circle must be a length of QA, and therefore

In an anisotropic plane, an ordinary circle that is not nul has only two radii, and each of these is the negative of the other. ·52

In the course of proving ·51, we have shewn incidentally that

If three accessible points of an anisotropic plane are not collinear, there is one and only one ordinary circle through them. ·53

This conclusion is supplemented by means of ·43 and ·46 and of 1·41: °if ·54
in an anisotropic plane three points are collinear, then unless the line in
which they lie is nul there is no ordinary circle that contains them; °if three ·55
points in an anisotropic plane are not all accessible, there is an ordinary circle
through these points if and only if each of them which is at infinity is a focal
point of the plane. In the exceptional cases of ·54 and ·55, the circle is not
unique: °if three points are collinear in a nul line, any nul circle with its ·56
centre on this line includes them all; °if A and B are accessible points and C ·57
is a focal point, there is an infinity of ordinary circles through A and B in
the plane ABC, and each of these circles includes C.

·6. In an isotropic plane, an ordinary circle with a radius different from zero consists of two *distinct* nul lines; if then the nul circle with centre O has also centre Q, this circle must be the *nul* circle with centre Q, and therefore O and Q lie in the same nul line:

The centres of a nul circle in an isotropic plane are the points composing the circle itself, and zero is the only radius. ·61

From ·23 it follows that if a, b are distinct nul lines in an isotropic plane, and if A, B are points of a, b, the circle formed of the points of a and b can not have a centre that is not on the nul line p through the midpoint of AB. Every point of p is however a centre of the circle, and if O, Q are two points of p, the two distances of A from Q are the same as the two distances of A from O:

·62 *In an isotropic plane, the centres of any ordinary circle are the accessible points of one definite nul line;*

·63 *In an isotropic plane, an ordinary circle that is not nul has only two radii, and each of these is the negative of the other; either radius may be used in connection with any of the centres of the circle.*

From the degenerate nature of the circle we conclude that

·64 *For there to be an ordinary circle through three given accessible points in an isotropic plane, two of the three points must be in one nul line.*

If one of the points is at infinity, it is necessary and sufficient that this point should be the focal point of the plane; if two of the points are at infinity, no ordinary circle is possible.

In ·64 we have the first direct intimation that the conception of a circle as arising from a centre and a radius is too narrow to be adapted to the isotropic plane. But it is evident that *any* definition of a locus in terms of distances must reduce the locus in an isotropic plane to a set of nul lines; to admit of a genuine extension, a definition must be either analytical or descriptive.

553. The general definition of a circle; infinite circles; undegenerate parabolic circles in an isotropic plane; centres and radii in general.

·1. With the homogeneous coordinates of 21·4 restricted to a plane, one specification of the ideal vector of the step from (ξ_Q, η_Q, τ_Q) to (ξ, η, τ) combines the vector whose coefficients are $\tau_Q\xi - \xi_Q\tau$, $\tau_Q\eta - \eta_Q\tau$ with the number $\tau_Q\tau$, and this specification is effective unless the ideal step is wholly at infinity. Hence in the notation of 425 the equation of the ordinary circle with centre Q and radius q is

·11 $$S(\tau_Q\chi - \chi_Q\tau)^2 = q^2\tau_Q^2\tau^2,$$

and since this is homogeneous and quadratic in the variable coordinates ξ, η, τ,

·12 *An ordinary circle is a conic.*

But of course not every conic is a circle, and we have to find a condition, independent of any particular frame of reference, by which to recognise or to define a circle.

It is 47·51 that suggests the course to be taken. If A, B, C are three accessible points of an anisotropic plane whose focal points are I and J, in general there is only one circle through the three points A, B, C, and there is only one *conic* through the five points A, B, C, I, J, and since the circle itself is a conic containing I and J, the circle appears definable as this particular conic. Given any conic through I and J, we should expect by taking A, B, C arbitrarily upon it to be able as a rule to prove that the conic is a circle. That is, we suspect that a conic is usually a circle if it contains I and J, but since we have not examined the cases of exception to 47·51 we must make a direct examination of conics through I and J. We observe in advance that a conic that degenerates into two lines of which one is the line at infinity contains the focal points; since no ordinary circle has this form, we commence by discussing conics through I and J which do not include the whole of the line at infinity.

For the conic

$$a\xi^2 + 2h\xi\eta + b\eta^2 + 2g\xi\tau + 2f\eta\tau + c\tau^2 = 0$$

to contain the focal points and no other points at infinity, the equation

$$a\xi^2 + 2h\xi\eta + b\eta^2 = 0$$

must be the equation satisfied by a vector if and only if the vector is nul, that is, must be the equation

$$S\chi^2 = 0,$$

and we may take $a\xi^2 + 2h\xi\eta + b\eta^2$ to be $kS\chi^2$, where k is not zero. For any values of ξ_Q, η_Q, τ_Q,

$$S(\tau_Q\chi - \tau\chi_Q)^2 = \tau_Q^2 S\chi^2 - 2\tau_Q\tau S\chi_Q\chi + \tau^2 S\chi_Q^2,$$

and therefore if τ_Q is not zero, the equation

$$kS\chi^2 + 2g\xi\tau + 2f\eta\tau + c\tau^2 = 0 \qquad \cdot 13$$

is equivalent to

$$kS(\tau_Q\chi - \tau\chi_Q)^2 + 2\tau_Q\{(kS^1\chi_Q + g\tau_Q)\xi + (kS^2\chi_Q + f\tau_Q)\eta\}\tau = (kS\chi_Q^2 - c\tau_Q^2)\tau^2. \qquad \cdot 14$$

Since by hypothesis neither k nor $EG - F^2$ is zero, the equations

$$kS^1\chi + g\tau = 0, \quad kS^2\chi + f\tau = 0 \qquad \cdot 15$$

represent two lines that are not parallel, and if Q is the point common to these lines, ·14 is equivalent to

$$kS(\tau_Q\chi - \tau\chi_Q)^2 = (kS\chi_Q^2 - c\tau_Q^2)\tau^2$$

and represents the ordinary circle with Q for centre and $(kS\chi_Q^2 - c\tau_Q^2)/k\tau_Q^2$ for the square of its radii. Hence

In an anisotropic plane, every conic whose only points at infinity are the focal points is an ordinary circle. ·16

This proposition combines with ·12 and 1·41 to give an assertion of equivalence from which explicit reference to distance has disappeared:

In an anisotropic plane, ordinary circles are conics which contain the two focal points and no other points at infinity. ·17

We note in passing that ·12 converts 2·43 into a case of 47·21.

·2. The transformation of ·13 depends only on the *existence* of a solution of ·15 for which τ_Q is not zero, not on the *uniqueness* of this solution. If the plane is isotropic, the lines given by ·15 must be parallel, but they may coincide; since the equations are equivalent, if the plane is isotropic, to

$$kU(U\xi + V\eta) + g\tau = 0, \quad kV(U\xi + V\eta) + f\tau = 0, \qquad \cdot 21$$

the condition for coincidence is

·22 $$Uf - Vg = 0,$$

that is, is the existence of a number j such that

·23 $$g = Uj, \quad f = Vj,$$

and if this condition is satisfied, and Q is *any* point of the nul line

·24 $$k(U\xi + V\eta) + j\tau = 0,$$

the reduction of ·13 can be made as in the previous case. In this special case, since $S\chi^2$ is $(U\xi + V\eta)^2$, ·13 is equivalent to

$$k(U\xi + V\eta)^2 + 2j(U\xi + V\eta)\tau + c\tau^2 = 0,$$

·25 that is, to $$\{k(U\xi + V\eta) + j\tau\}^2 = (j^2 - kc)\tau^2,$$

and represents a pair of nul lines: the peculiar character of an ordinary circle in an isotropic plane is disclosed analytically.

·3. The expression for the square of the radius of the circle represented by ·13 can undergo a useful modification, for since $S\chi^2$ is identically equal to $\xi S^1\chi + \eta S^2\chi$, substitution from ·15 gives

$$kS\chi_Q^2 = -(g\xi_Q + f\eta_Q)\tau_Q:$$

·31 *If Q is a centre of the ordinary circle represented by the equation*

$$k(E\xi^2 + 2F\xi\eta + G\eta^2) + 2g\xi\tau + 2f\eta\tau + c\tau^2 = 0,$$

the square of the radii of this circle is

$$-(g\xi_Q + f\eta_Q + c\tau_Q)/k\tau_Q.$$

Eliminating ξ_Q, η_Q, τ_Q from the three equations

$$kE\xi_Q + kF\eta_Q + g\tau_Q = 0,$$
$$kF\xi_Q + kG\eta_Q + f\tau_Q = 0,$$
$$g\xi_Q + f\eta_Q + (c + kq^2)\tau_Q = 0,$$

we find that

·32 *In an anisotropic plane, the square of the radii of the circle*

$$k(E\xi^2 + 2F\xi\eta + G\eta^2) + 2g\xi\tau + 2f\eta\tau + c\tau^2 = 0$$

is $$-\begin{vmatrix} E & F & g \\ F & G & f \\ g & f & kc \end{vmatrix} \Bigg/ k^2(EG - F^2).$$

Replacing $g\xi_Q + f\eta_Q$ by $j(U\xi_Q + V\eta_Q)$ from ·23 and this last expression by $-j^2\tau_Q/k$ from ·24, we infer also that

·33 *In an isotropic plane, the square of the radii of the circle*

$$k(U\xi + V\eta)^2 + 2j(U\xi + V\eta)\tau + c\tau^2 = 0$$

is $(j^2 - kc)/k^2$;

this result of course follows directly from the form ·25 of the equation.

·4. In favour of extending* the word circle to cover *every* conic in an anisotropic plane that passes through the focal points of the plane there are many

* The extension was made by Poncelet, *loc. cit.* p. 303 above.

arguments, cumulatively adequate, of which two can be advanced now. It is a general principle* that definitions should use positive properties, not negative: with all their peculiarities, isotropic planes are not refused the title of plane, nor do we deny that the zero vector is a nul vector. And by means of the degenerate conic formed of two lines of which one is the line at infinity we can remove the restrictions from 2·53: if three accessible points are collinear, the line containing them and the line at infinity together form a degenerate conic of this kind; and given two accessible points and one point at infinity, the line through the accessible points and the line at infinity again compose a degenerate conic containing the three points and the focal points.

Consistent with the definition of a circle in an anisotropic plane as a conic through the two focal points, two definitions that are not equivalent suggest themselves for a circle in an isotropic plane: a circle must pass through the focal point K, and if it does not include the line at infinity must be characterised either by having the line at infinity for a tangent at K or by having intersection of the second order with this line there. The question is similar to the question whether the name of parabola is to cover a pair of parallel lines, and the arguments valid in the discussion of this other matter are reinforced by the observation that the Euclidean definition of a circle has already led us to regard pairs of nul lines in an isotropic plane as circles. Hence a circle in an isotropic plane is to be defined as a conic which has the focal point as a *multiple* point of intersection with the line at infinity. As in an anisotropic plane, the line at infinity combines with any line to form a circle of a special kind. But a circle which does not include the line at infinity is not usually, in an isotropic plane, an ordinary circle in the sense of 1·11, for it is not as a rule degenerate.

To resume formally, we define a °circle in an anisotropic plane as a conic ·41
containing the two focal points, a °circle in an isotropic plane as a parabola ·42
containing the focal point. By 47·21 and 47·23, °a circle either includes the ·43
whole of the line at infinity or contains no points of this line that are not focal; it is convenient to call a circle of which the line at infinity forms part an °*infinite* circle. ·44

We have seen in ·1 that in an anisotropic plane, for values of k other than zero, the equation

$$kS\chi^2 + 2g\xi\tau + 2f\eta\tau + c\tau^2 = 0 \qquad \cdot 45$$

represents an ordinary circle. In an isotropic plane, the nul vectors are those for which $U\xi + V\eta$ is zero, and the general equation

$$a\xi^2 + 2h\xi\eta + b\eta^2 + 2g\xi\tau + 2f\eta\tau + c\tau^2 = 0$$

* There is no opposition to this principle in our neglect of isotropic space: we do not deny the name of vecspace to a class of vectors constructed with the condition $J=0$ instead of the condition $J\neq 0$, but the subject of our work is anisotropic Euclidean space, not space of three dimensions in general. The study of complex anisotropic space of n dimensions always involves that of isotropic space of $n-1$ dimensions.

represents a circle that does not include the line at infinity only if

$$a\xi^2 + 2h\xi\eta + b\eta^2$$

is a multiple of $(U\xi + V\eta)^2$, that is, of $S\chi^2$. Thus whether the plane is or is not isotropic, ·45 for values of k other than zero is the general equation of a circle that does not include the line at infinity. But when k is zero, ·45 reduces to

·46 $$(2g\xi + 2f\eta + c\tau)\,\tau = 0,$$

and represents a combination of two lines of which one is the line at infinity
·47 and the other, which will be called the °*distinctive constituent* of the circle, is subject to no restriction whatever. That is to say,

·48 *The general equation of a circle in any accessible plane, isotropic or anisotropic, is*

$$k\,(E\xi^2 + 2F\xi\eta + G\eta^2) + 2g\xi\tau + 2f\eta\tau + c\tau^2 = 0,$$

and in this theorem we have the most straightforward reason for extending
·49 the name of circle precisely as we do. °The circle represented by the equation in ·48 is or is not infinite according as k is or is not zero. The distinctive constituent of an infinite circle may itself be the line at infinity; the circle is then this line duplicated.

·5. The theorem ·16 can be expressed in the form that

·51 *In an anisotropic plane, a circle that is not infinite is an ordinary circle,*

and we may appeal to 2·46 in order to add that

·52 *In an anisotropic plane, a circle is degenerate if it is infinite or nul, but not otherwise,*

but it is better to deduce ·52 from the relation of a circle to the focal points: if a conic consisting of two lines contains the two points I, J, either one of the lines is the line IJ, the line at infinity, or one of the lines contains I and not J, the other J and not I; in the former case the circle is infinite, in the latter it is formed of two nul lines that are not parallel and is therefore the nul circle whose centre is the point of intersection of these lines.

In an isotropic plane ·51 has no counterpart. But if a conic consisting of two accessible lines has double intersection with the line at infinity at K, each of the constituent lines passes through K, and is therefore nul:

·53 *In an isotropic plane, a circle is degenerate if it is infinite or ordinary, but not otherwise.*

We can combine ·52 and ·53 in a single enunciation which indicates the common basis of the theorems:

·54 *If a circle is degenerate, either its constituent lines are both nul or one of them is the line at infinity.*

Since a circle is a conic, a line in the plane of a circle either cuts the circle in two distinct points, or has double intersection with the circle at one point, or is a constituent of the circle. If the line is accessible and is not a constituent of the circle, there are four cases to distinguish, for there may be intersection in two distinct accessible points, simple intersection at infinity accompanied by simple intersection at one accessible point, double intersection at an accessible point, or double intersection at infinity.

If a line m that is not nul cuts a circle at an inaccessible point M, the line at infinity cuts the circle at M and therefore is a constituent of the circle: the circle is infinite, and the intersection with m is simple unless the distinctive constituent also contains M; the intersection is double if the distinctive constituent is the line at infinity or is a line parallel to m, and any order whatever may be ascribed to the intersection if m is itself the distinctive constituent.

We have just seen that

If a circle is finite and a line in its plane is not nul, the two must have simple intersection at each of two accessible points or double intersection at a single accessible point. ·55

This conclusion does not depend on the nature of the plane, but in discussing the intersections of a nul line with a circle the nature of the plane has to be taken into account.

In any plane, a nul line cuts any circle at infinity. If the plane is isotropic, the focal point is a double intersection of the line at infinity with any circle; if this same point is a double intersection of any other line with the circle, it is a double point on the circle and the circle is degenerate:

In an isotropic plane, any undegenerate circle cuts any nul line in one and only one accessible point, and the intersection is simple. ·56

If the circle is infinite, the intersection at infinity is simple unless the distinctive constituent is nul. If the circle is ordinary, the intersection at infinity is exactly double unless the circle includes the line.

In an anisotropic plane, the nul line joining the centre of a finite circle that is not nul to a focal point has no accessible points in common with the circle, and therefore has double intersection with the circle at the focal point; if any other line had double intersection there, the point would be a double point of the circle and the circle would be degenerate. Hence

In an anisotropic plane, a nul line through the centre of an ordinary circle has double intersection with the circle at infinity and has no accessible points of intersection unless the circle is nul; a nul line that does not contain the centre has simple intersection at infinity and simple intersection at one accessible point. ·57

Combined with 1·41, ·57 implies that

The asymptotes of an ordinary circle in an anisotropic plane are the nul lines through the centre of the circle, ·58

and ·56 implies that

The only asymptote of an undegenerate circle in an isotropic plane is the line at infinity itself. ·59

If a circle is degenerate, the constituents are themselves the asymptotes.

·6. If A, B, C are three given points, distinct from each other and from the focal point or points, the equation

·61
$$\begin{vmatrix} S\chi^2 & \xi\tau & \eta\tau & \tau^2 \\ S\chi_A^2 & \xi_A\tau_A & \eta_A\tau_A & \tau_A^2 \\ S\chi_B^2 & \xi_B\tau_B & \eta_B\tau_B & \tau_B^2 \\ S\chi_C^2 & \xi_C\tau_C & \eta_C\tau_C & \tau_C^2 \end{vmatrix} = 0$$

if it is not an identity represents a circle through A, B, C. In this equation, the coefficient of $S\chi^2$ is the product of $\tau_A\tau_B\tau_C$ by a determinant that is zero if and only if the points are collinear. Hence whether a plane is isotropic or not, three accessible points that are not collinear determine one and only one circle, and this is not an infinite circle; for an anisotropic plane, we have here a verification of 2·53. If the three points are collinear, any conic to which they belong, and in particular any circle, must include the whole of the line containing them. Hence from 47·21 and ·54, if the points are collinear in an accessible line that is not nul, the circle formed of this line and the line at infinity is the *only* circle through them. If one of the points is at infinity, then by ·43 the circle includes the line at infinity, and therefore if one of the points is at infinity and two are accessible, the circle consists of the line at infinity and the line through the accessible points; in this case also the circle is unique. But if the three points are collinear in a nul line, this line may be combined with any complementary nul line or with the line at infinity, if two of the points are at infinity and one is accessible, the line at infinity may be combined with any line through the accessible point, and if the three points are at infinity, they are on every infinite circle.

The results for an anisotropic plane can be summarised as follows:

·62 *If I, J are the focal points of an anisotropic plane and A, B, C are any three points of the plane distinct from the focal points and from each other, then there is one and only one circle through A, B, C unless four of the five points A, B, C, I, J are collinear; if four of these points are collinear, but not all five of them, the line which contains the four combines with any line through the fifth point to give a circle through A, B, C, and if the five points are collinear, the line through them, which is the line at infinity, may be associated with any line in the plane to give a circle with the required property.*

If three of the points, but not four, are collinear, the circle is formed of the line through these three and the line through the other two, and is nul or infinite according as one of the points I, J is on each line or both of these points
·64 are on one line; that is, °the circle is nul if and only if two of the points A, B, C are collinear with one of the points I, J.

For an isotropic plane the summary is less concise:

·65 *If K is the focal point of an isotropic plane and A, B, C are any three points of the plane distinct from K and from each other, then there is one and only* *one circle through A, B, C unless either the four points A, B, C, K are collinear or two of the points A, B, C are at infinity; in the first case, any circle formed of the line through the points combined with a line through K, that is, with the line at infinity or with a nul line, is a circle through A, B, C; in the second case, if one of the points A, B, C is accessible, a circle through the three points is formed by the line at infinity and any line through the accessible point, while if the three points are all at infinity, the line at infinity can be associated with any line whatever in the plane.*

This is precisely the form taken by ·62 if I and J are both replaced by K and the line IJ remains definitely the line at infinity.

·7. To discover whether centres can be ascribed to circles that are not ordinary, we appeal to equations satisfied by the coordinates of a centre of an ordinary circle; a pair of such equations we have seen in ·1 and ·2 to be

$$kS^1\chi + g\tau = 0, \quad kS^2\chi + f\tau = 0, \qquad \cdot 71$$

and we *define* a centre of the circle

$$kS\chi^2 + 2g\xi\tau + 2f\eta\tau + c\tau^2 = 0, \qquad \cdot 72$$

whatever the plane and whatever the nature of the circle, as a point that satisfies this pair of equations; it appears on investigation that whether a given point is or is not a centre of a given circle does not depend on the frame of reference used.

The case of an ordinary circle in a plane that is not isotropic needs no further examination; there is one centre, and that is the centre in the elementary sense. For an ordinary circle in an isotropic plane the centres are the points of a certain nul line; the accessible points of this line are the centres in the elementary sense, but we have to add to them the point at infinity on the line, that is, the focal point of the plane.

If the plane is isotropic but the circle is not degenerate, neither k nor $Uf - Vg$ is zero, and the equations ·71, taking the form

$$kU(U\xi + V\eta) + g\tau = 0, \quad kV(U\xi + V\eta) + f\tau = 0, \qquad \cdot 73$$

represent *distinct* parallel lines, and °these lines have no common point except the focal point of the plane, which is therefore the only centre. ·74

There remain for consideration the infinite circles in planes of both kinds, and it is in discussing them that we find algebraic support most useful. If a conic degenerates into two distinct lines whose common point is accessible, this common point is alone the centre of the conic, but to insist that the common point is to be the only centre whenever the conic is degenerate would contradict 1·33. Moreover, in relation to the circle formed of the line at infinity and a given accessible line in an anisotropic plane, some of the properties associated with the centre of a circle in elementary geometry attach themselves to the point at infinity whose vecline is perpendicular to the vecline of the accessible part of the circle, for the perpendicular bisectors of all accessible chords of the circle are concurrent in this point. Let us refer to ·71; k being zero, the circle is formed of the line at infinity and the distinctive constituent

$$2g\xi + 2f\eta + c\tau = 0,$$

which is accessible unless both g and f are zero, and the equations to be satisfied by the centre are

·76 $$g\tau = 0, \ f\tau = 0,$$

which require τ to be zero except in the same special case, when the centre is subject to no conditions whatever:

·77 *In any plane, the circle formed of the line at infinity taken twice has every point of the plane for a centre, and every other infinite circle has for its centres the points at infinity and those only.*

·78 °If A is an accessible point and B is a point at infinity that is not a focal point, no ordinary circle contains B, and therefore the circles through A and B are the infinite circles whose distinctive constituents contain A. This result may be absorbed into 2·36. For since B is itself the midpoint of AB, and since the accessible lines through B are parallel to AB and therefore are not perpendicular to AB, the segment AB has the plane at infinity definitely for its perpendicular bisector.

·79 *If one end of a segment in a given plane is accessible and the other end is not a focal point, then unless the plane is isotropic and the axis of the segment is nul, the segment has a definite perpendicular bisector in the plane. Every point of this bisector is a centre of a circle through the segment, and no accessible point of the plane is a centre of any such circle unless it does belong to the bisector.*

It is to be noticed that to include ·78 in ·79, it is necessary to recognise the point at infinity on the perpendicular bisector of a finite segment as a centre of the infinite circle in which the axis of the segment is combined with the line at infinity. Since every point at infinity is a centre of this circle, we can not rest satisfied with ·79, and the question of the centres of circles circumscribing a given segment is one to which we shall return.

·8. A radius of a circle should satisfy two conditions: it should be one distance from a centre to any point of the circle, and its square should be not inconsistent with the formulae of ·3; we have to see whether these conditions can be fulfilled.

The case of an ordinary circle presents no difficulties. If the plane is anisotropic, the centre and the squared radius are those from which the circle was first defined. If the plane is isotropic, the additional centre is the focal point and any value may be assigned to the distance between this point and points of the circle.

If the plane is isotropic and the circle undegenerate, $g\xi + f\eta$ is not a multiple of $U\xi + V\eta$, and therefore $g\xi_Q + f\eta_Q + c\tau_Q$ is not zero if Q is the focal point. Since in this case τ_Q is zero, the formula of ·31 requires the radius to be infinite:

An undegenerate circle in an isotropic plane has the focal point for its only centre and its radius is infinite. ·83

For an infinite circle, whether the plane is anisotropic or not, $k\tau_Q$ is zero and the radius as given by ·31 is indeterminate or infinite according as $g\xi_Q + f\eta_Q + c\tau_Q$ is or is not zero at the centre Q. If the distinctive constituent is accessible, the centres are all at infinity, and the only one of them for which $g\xi + f\eta + c\tau$ is zero is the point at infinity on the accessible constituent itself; denote this point by M. For any centre except M, the formula prohibits a finite radius; for any centre that is not a focal point, the distance from an accessible point can not be finite; an infinite value of the radius satisfies both the prescribed conditions, but no finite value does so unless M is a focal point:

An infinite circle with an accessible constituent p has an infinite radius at every centre; if p is not nul, the circle has no finite radii, but if p is nul, the radius at the focal point on p is arbitrary while the radius at every other centre is infinite. ·84

There remains the case of the circle formed of the duplicated line at infinity. The formula for the square of the radius reduces to $-c\tau_Q/k\tau_Q$ with k zero and c different from zero, and the result must be reckoned as indeterminate for centres at infinity, but infinite at accessible centres; this is in agreement with 34·15 and 34·16.

We can speak of *the* circle with centre Q and radius q unless q is finite and Q is a focal point or q is infinite and Q inaccessible; if Q is accessible and q finite, the circle is the ordinary circle described in this way; if Q is at infinity and not focal and q is finite, or if Q is accessible and q infinite, the phrase denotes the duplicated line at infinity.

·9. In an isotropic plane all undegenerate circles have an infinite radius. But just as it is possible to make metrical comparison of two nul steps provided that they are in parallel lines, so it is possible to make metrical comparison of two undegenerate circles in isotropic planes if only the planes are parallel.

Suppose that a reference frame for a given isotropic plane is constructed from a vector frame in which the first vector is a nul vector $\mathbf{x}$ and the second is a unit vector $\mathbf{y}$, and that homogeneous coordinates are introduced by means of the constant unity. Then since every nul vector in the plane is a multiple of $\mathbf{x}$ and every unit vector differs either from $\mathbf{y}$ or from the reverse of $\mathbf{y}$ by a multiple of $\mathbf{x}$, the most general substitution which preserves the features of the frame leaves τ unchanged and replaces ξ, η by $p\xi + q\eta + r\tau$, $\pm\eta + s\tau$, where p, q, r, s are arbitrary constants. The general equation of a finite circle with these coordinates is

$$\eta^2 + 2g\xi\tau + 2f\eta\tau + c\tau^2 = 0, \qquad \cdot 91$$

and the substitution just indicated replaces g by pg and therefore is without effect on g provided that p is unity, that is, provided that the scale on which the nul vectors are measured is unaltered. If g_1 and g_2 are the coefficients for two different circles, the ratio of g_1 to g_2 depends only on the circles, not on the frame of reference. The value of g measures the circle with reference to a particular scale of nul vectors. Two undegenerate circles which have the same size with reference to one scale have the same size with reference to any
·92 other scale and are said to be °*equal.*

If g is zero, ·91 represents a pair of accessible nul lines, that is, an ordinary circle. If g is not zero, the equation can be put into the form

$$(\eta + f\tau)^2 + 2g\,[\xi + \{(c - f^2)/2g\}\,\tau]\,\tau = 0$$

·93 and reduced to $$\eta^2 + 2g\xi\tau = 0$$

by a change of origin alone. The line $\xi = 0$ has double intersection with ·93 at the origin, but no accessible line parallel to this has double intersection
·94 with the circle. Hence °given any line l in the plane, there is one and only one accessible point of the circle at which the tangent is parallel to l, provided only that l is not nul.

A nul line cuts an undegenerate circle in one and only one accessible point; the equation of the circle takes the form ·93 if the axes of reference are *any* nul line and the tangent at its accessible point of intersection with the circle, and takes the form

$$\eta^2 + 2g\xi\tau + c\tau^2 = 0$$

if the first axis is nul and the second is parallel to the tangent at the point where the first axis cuts the curve.

In elementary algebraic geometry, we reduce the equation of a parabola to the form

$$y^2 = 2lx$$

by taking a diameter and a tangent for axes of reference, and the value of l depends on the point of contact of the tangent, l being the semilatusrectum only if this point is the vertex. If the equation ·91 is reduced by change of axes to the form

$$\eta^2 + 2g\xi\tau = 0,$$

the value of g depends on the nul scale adopted and on the circle, but *not* on the point chosen for origin. But we must remember that at *every* point of ·91 the tangent is perpendicular to the ξ-axis.

In an isotropic plane as in an anisotropic plane, if a parabola that is *not* circular is referred to the diameter and the tangent through one of its points, the coefficient that occurs in the equation varies with the position of the origin if the scales of measurement are not altered.

Taking an arbitrary value of q, we can replace ·91 by

$$\eta^2 + 2g\,(\xi + q\eta)\,\tau + 2\,(f - gq)\,\eta\tau + c\tau^2 = 0$$

and therefore by

$$\{\eta + (f - gq)\,\tau\}^2 + 2g\,(\xi + q\eta)\,\tau + \{c - (f - gq)^2\}\,\tau^2 = 0.$$

Ve can therefore reduce the equations of two finite circles in an isotropic plane *simultaneously* to the forms

$$\eta^2 + 2g_1\xi\tau + c_1\tau^2 = 0, \quad \eta^2 + 2g_2\xi\tau + c_2\tau^2 = 0 \qquad \cdot 95$$

f and only if there is a value of q that satisfies the condition

$$f_1 - g_1 q = f_2 - g_2 q.$$

The circles whose equations are given in ·95 are parallel, that is, have parallel tangents, where they cut the nul line $\eta = 0$, and conversely if two circles are parallel where they cut a given nul line the choice of this line for an axis reduces their equations simultaneously to the forms in ·95. Hence

If two undegenerate circles in an isotropic plane are unequal, there is one and only one nul line that cuts them in points at which they are parallel. ·96

But if g_1 and g_2 are equal, the condition imposes itself on f_1 and f_2:

In general there is no nul line that cuts two given equal circles in an isotropic plane in points where the circles are parallel, but if two such circles are parallel where they are cut by one nul line they are parallel where they are cut by any nul line. ·97

Two undegenerate circles in an isotropic plane which are equal and are parallel where they are cut by a nul line are said to be °*parallel*. The equations of parallel undegenerate circles can be reduced simultaneously to the forms ·98

$$\eta^2 + 2g\xi\tau + c_1\tau^2 = 0, \quad \eta^2 + 2g\xi\tau + c_2\tau^2 = 0,$$

and it is evident therefore that

Distinct parallel undegenerate circles in an isotropic plane have no accessible points in common. ·99

554. The properties of the constant rectangle and the constant angle.

·1. There is no need for us to prove that *in general* if a line through a point O cuts a circle in R and S, the product of the lengths OR, OS measured in a common direction depends only on the position of O in relation to the circle, not on the line to which R and S belong; the classical proofs of this theorem, as of any other, fail if at all only in particular cases. But it is worth while to see in an actual proof which cases have to be set aside for special examination, for these cases are fewer than we might expect.

If P is a point of the ordinary circle with centre Q and radius q and if O is any accessible point of the plane, the condition that P belongs to the circle can be written in the form

$$\mathscr{G}(QO + OP)^2 = q^2,$$

that is,

$$\mathscr{G}\,OP^2 + 2\,\mathscr{G}\,QO.OP + (\mathscr{G}\,QO^2 - q^2) = 0.$$

If $\mathbf{p}$ is a *given* proper vector in the line OP and the vector of OP is $r\mathbf{p}$, the factor r satisfies the equation

·11 $$r^2 \mathscr{G}\mathbf{p}^2 + 2r\mathscr{G}\mathbf{p}.QO + (QO^2 - q^2) = 0.$$

If the line OP is not nul, we may take a unit vector in this line for $\mathbf{p}$, and r is then the length of OP in the direction of this unit vector; ·11 determines two values of r, finite but not necessarily different, and since $\mathscr{G}\mathbf{p}^2$ is unity, the product of the two values is $QO^2 - q^2$. From its relation to the line OP, the number $QO^2 - q^2$ is not affected by any freedom possible in the choice of Q or q, while from its relation to Q and q the number is equally independent of the direction of OP. That is, $QO^2 - q^2$ depends only on the circle itself and
·12 on the position of the point O; this number is called the °*power* of the circle and the point with respect to each other, and ·11 implies that

·13 *If any anisotropic line through an accessible point O cuts an ordinary circle in R and S, the product of the lengths OR, OS, measured in a common direction, is equal to the power of the circle with respect to O.*

Even in this proof nul circles and isotropic planes do not call for special treatment, but an algebraic proof that is equally simple is of wider application. With respect to a frame of the kind already used in this chapter, let the equation of the circle be

·14 $$kS\chi^2 + 2g\xi\tau + 2f\eta\tau + c\tau^2 = 0,$$

and let a finite ideal vector be determined by a vector $\mathbf{p}$ with coefficients $\xi_{\mathbf{p}}$, $\eta_{\mathbf{p}}$ and a number $\tau_{\mathbf{p}}$; the ideal vector of the step from the origin to the point $(r\xi_{\mathbf{p}}, r\eta_{\mathbf{p}}, s\tau_{\mathbf{p}})$ is the product of this ideal vector by r/s, and if p is an amount of $\mathbf{p}$, the distance from the origin to the point $(r\xi_{\mathbf{p}}, r\eta_{\mathbf{p}}, s\tau_{\mathbf{p}})$ in the direction in which $\mathbf{p}$ has the amount p is $rp/s\tau_{\mathbf{p}}$. For the point in question to be on the circle ·14, the ratio $r:s$ must satisfy the equation

·15 $$r^2 kS\chi_{\mathbf{p}}^2 + 2rs(g\xi_{\mathbf{p}} + f\eta_{\mathbf{p}})\tau_{\mathbf{p}} + s^2 c\tau_{\mathbf{p}}^2 = 0,$$

and the product of the two distances corresponding to the two roots of this equation is $cp^2/kS\chi_{\mathbf{p}}^2$. But p^2 is equal to $S\chi_{\mathbf{p}}^2$; if then we define c/k, a number
·16 in which $\mathbf{p}$ is not involved, as the power of the origin, we can assert that °*the product of the two distances is equal to the power unless the direction is nul, and is indeterminate in the exceptional case.* Since c is zero if and only if the
·17 origin is on the circle, and k is zero if and only if the circle is infinite, °the power is indeterminate only in the case of an infinite circle and a point actually upon it, is zero for a point on a circle that is not infinite, is infinite for an infinite circle and a point not on the circle, and in other cases is a definite proper finite number.

This second proof applies equally to ordinary and extraordinary circles, but in referring the plane to a vector frame attached to the point whose power is in question, we have tacitly supposed this point to be accessible. To secure complete generality, we must calculate the power of a point not assumed to be the origin.

·2. The sum of the ideal vector which combines the vector (ξ_P, η_P) with the number τ_P and the ideal vector which combines the vector $(r\xi_{\mathbf{p}}, r\eta_{\mathbf{p}})$ with the number $s\tau_{\mathbf{p}}$ is the ideal vector which combines the vector

$$(r\tau_P\xi_{\mathbf{p}} + s\xi_P\tau_{\mathbf{p}},\ r\tau_P\eta_{\mathbf{p}} + s\eta_P\tau_{\mathbf{p}})$$

with the number $s\tau_P\tau_{\mathbf{p}}$. The step from the origin with this ideal vector leads to a point on the conic

$$a\xi^2 + 2h\xi\eta + b\eta^2 + 2g\xi\tau + 2f\eta\tau + c\tau^2 = 0$$ ·21

if $$r^2\tau_P^2(a\xi_{\mathbf{p}}^2 + 2h\xi_{\mathbf{p}}\eta_{\mathbf{p}} + b\eta_{\mathbf{p}}^2) + 2rs\tau_P\tau_{\mathbf{p}}\{(a\xi_P + h\eta_P + g\tau_P)\xi_{\mathbf{p}} + (h\xi_P + b\eta_P + f\tau_P)\eta_{\mathbf{p}}\} + s^2\tau_{\mathbf{p}}^2(a\xi_P^2 + 2h\xi_P\eta_P + b\eta_P^2 + 2g\xi_P\tau_P + 2f\eta_P\tau_P + c\tau_P^2) = 0.$$ ·22

Hence °the product of the lengths, measured in the direction in which the vector $\mathbf{p}$ is of amount p, of the distances from P to the points in which the line through P with this direction cuts the conic ·21, is ·23

$$p^2(a\xi_P^2 + 2h\xi_P\eta_P + b\eta_P^2 + 2g\xi_P\tau_P + 2f\eta_P\tau_P + c\tau_P^2)/(a\xi_{\mathbf{p}}^2 + 2h\xi_{\mathbf{p}}\eta_{\mathbf{p}} + b\eta_{\mathbf{p}}^2)\tau_P^2.$$

From the value of p^2 it follows that

The power of the point (ξ, η, τ) with respect to the circle ·24

$$kS\chi^2 + 2g\xi\tau + 2f\eta\tau + c\tau^2 = 0$$

is $$(kS\chi^2 + 2g\xi\tau + 2f\eta\tau + c\tau^2)/k\tau^2.$$

As in other cases, the formula provides a definition when the elementary definition fails. For a point at infinity, the denominator is zero and the numerator is or is not zero according as the point is or is not on the circle: °*the power of an inaccessible point with respect to a circle is indeterminate or infinite according as the point is or is not on the circle.* At the cost of repetition, it is useful to set down that °*the power of a point with respect to a circle to which it belongs is zero if the point is accessible and the circle is not infinite but is indeterminate in both the exceptional cases.* ·25 ·26

A comparison of conventions shews that the expression $QO^2 - q^2$ is in no case inconsistent with the value attached to the power, though one of these numbers may be indeterminate when the other has a definite value. For example, if O is at infinity and q is finite, $QO^2 - q^2$ is infinite if Q is accessible and O is not a focal point, that is, if the circle is an ordinary circle and does not contain O, but $QO^2 - q^2$ is indeterminate if Q is at infinity, that is, if Q is focal or the circle is the duplicated line at infinity, or if O is focal. It is particularly important to notice that

The square of the distances between two points is the power of one of them with respect to a nul circle which has the other for centre. ·27

The nul circle is unique unless the point to serve as a centre is a focal point, but in this exceptional case the power and the distance are alike arbitrary.

If P is at infinity, ·22 has no validity in determining distances from P. But if O is at infinity, the product of lengths OR, OS is either infinite or indeterminate, wherever R and S may be, and so also is the power of O with respect to a given circle. We can therefore affirm that

·28 *If O, R, S are collinear, the power of O with respect to any given circle through R and S and the product of the lengths OR, OS measured in a common direction are equal unless one or other of these numbers is wholly indeterminate.*

·29 From ·23 we see that °*the property of the constant rectangle is characteristic of finite circles*, no less in isotropic than in anisotropic planes, for the expression given there for the product is independent of $\mathbf{p}$, for all positions of P, *if and only if* $a\xi_{\mathbf{p}}^2 + 2h\xi_{\mathbf{p}}\eta_{\mathbf{p}} + b\eta_{\mathbf{p}}^2$ is a multiple of p^2, that is, of $E\xi_{\mathbf{p}}^2 + 2F\xi_{\mathbf{p}}\eta_{\mathbf{p}} + G\eta_{\mathbf{p}}^2$, for all values of $\xi_{\mathbf{p}}$ and $\eta_{\mathbf{p}}$.

·3. Closely allied to the property of the constant rectangle is that of the constant angle. If P, Q are points on one line through O and R, S are points on another, and if the rectangles $OP.OQ$, $OR.OS$ are equal, then the triangles OPS, ORQ are inversely similar, and the angles PSO, OQR determine the same congruences:

·31 *If the points P, Q, R, S are concyclic, the angles between QP and QR are the same as the angles between SP and SR unless the angles in one case or the other are wholly indeterminate.*

An examination of different cases shews that the result ·31 is true even when the proof is invalid. For example, if S is at infinity but is not a focal point, and if P and R are accessible and the line joining them is not nul, the circle consists of the line at infinity and the line PR, and the angles between SP and SR are the multiples of π; if Q, assumed neither to be a focal point nor to coincide with P or R, is not at infinity it is collinear with P and R, and in either case the lines QP and QR have the same vecline and the angles between them also are the multiples of π.

It is necessary to remember that the circle of complex space is not in any sense cut into two parts by a pair of its points. The points of a complex line or of a complex circle are as numerous as the values of a complex variable, that is, as numerous as the points of a real sphere, and the removal of one or two of them, or of any finite number, does not destroy the unity of the line or circle.

Nor is there any division of the circle latent in ·31. Different angles determined by a pair of points P, R at a variable point of the circle may have either their difference or their sum a multiple of 2π; to compare one of the *congruences* at Q with one of the *congruences* at S, it is necessary to correlate one direction of QP with one of SP and one direction of QR with one of SR, that is, to correlate one *length* of QP with one of SP and one *length* of QR with one of SR. This is precisely the correlation which, effected in real space by means of signs, has no natural basis in complex space, except in isotropic planes. In an isotropic plane, ·31, like all angular relations, is necessarily trivial*.

But although the circle can not be divided, the distinction between the two circles on which a given pair of points determines the same sets of angles can be made in the same way for the anisotropic as for the real plane. If l, m are two anisotropic lines in a prepared plane, any angle from a direction of l to a direction of m differs from any other angle which is also *from* a direction of l *to* a direction of m by a multiple of π. That is, °an ordered line-pair has an ·32
angular measurement, which is definite to within a multiple of π if neither line is inaccessible or nul. By an °*angle subtended* at a point C by an ordered ·33
pair of points AB is meant† an angular measurement of the line-pair (AC, BC).

Inverse similarity of two triangles OPS, ORQ implies that the angles subtended by OR at Q are the negatives of those subtended by OP at S and are therefore the same as those subtended by PO at S. But if P is in OQ, the angles subtended at Q by PO are by definition the same as those subtended at Q by PR, and similarly if R is in OS the angles subtended at S by PO are the same as those subtended at S by PR. The steps of this argument are reversible, and ·31 can be replaced by the more exact theorem that

Four distinct accessible points P, Q, R, S in an anisotropic plane are con- ·34
cyclic if and only if the pair of points PR subtends the same angles at Q as at S.

Not only segments in general, in the sense of portions of circles, but semicircles, are lacking in complex geometry. We can however say that °two ·35
points P, R are diametrically opposite on a circle if the midpoint of PR is a centre of the circle, and classical proofs shew that in general a right angle is among the angles subtended at a variable point of a circle by a pair of points diametrically opposed. Euclid's proof and the use of straight angles are alike ineffective to discover whether the theorem is true of nul circles, but a vectorial proof applicable to every ordinary circle is easily found. °A pair of ·36
points AB subtends a right angle at a point C if and only if the lines AC, BC are perpendicular, and instead of referring to angles we may say that

In any plane, the locus of a variable point Q which is such that there are ·37
perpendicular lines joining Q to two given accessible points P, R is the ordinary circle on PR as diameter.

If for an isotropic plane we make the natural convention that °the focal ·38
point is diametrically opposite to every point of an undegenerate circle, then since PQ and RQ are necessarily perpendicular if either P or R is the focal point, it is true that

* In contrast with ·13, which we have seen to be a significant property of finite circles, undegenerate as well as degenerate. This observation acquires interest from the fact that it is not unusual in elementary geometry to deduce the property of the constant rectangle from the property, seen to be in one sense narrower in scope, of the constant angle.

† This meaning, to the value of which for elementary geometry Picken has recently called attention, was familiar to Laguerre and is implicit throughout Darboux's *Principes*.

·39 *On any circle that is not infinite, the lines joining one point to two points that are diametrically opposed are perpendicular.*

·4. Interesting cases of ·34 and ·37 are those in which the circle is a nul circle in an anisotropic plane. If PR, QS are complementary nul lines, then unless one of the points P, Q, R, S is either the point of intersection of these lines or a focal point, the lines PQ, QR, PS, SR are not nul, and the general proof of ·34 applies without modification. The complete circle through the four points is formed by the two lines, but since if O is any point of PR any value can be ascribed to an angle subtended at O by PR, the significant deduction from the general theorem is that

·41 *If P, R are distinct accessible points of a nul line l in an anisotropic plane, the line joining two accessible points Q, S neither of which belongs to l is a nul line complementary to l if and only if PR subtends the same angles at Q as at S.*

This result can not be established by Euclid's method of proving ·34. The corresponding case of ·37 is that

·42 *In an anisotropic plane, the points at which an accessible pair of points PR belonging to a nul line l subtends a right angle without subtending an arbitrary angle are the points of the nul line m complementary to l which bisects PR, exception being made of the focal point on m and of the midpoint of PR.*

Theorems involving nul lines always evade pictorial representation, but rarely with more success than here.

555. Circles about a pair of points; associated linear segments; measures of separation; coaxal systems of circles in general; associated coaxal systems.

·1. If A, B are given points and r, s given numbers, the condition

·11 $$s\,.\,AP^2 = r\,.\,BP^2$$

becomes in terms of homogeneous coordinates

$$s\tau_B^2\, S\,(\tau_A\chi - \chi_A\tau)^2 - r\tau_A^2\, S\,(\tau_B\chi - \chi_B\tau)^2 = 0,$$

and the terms independent of τ in this equation are

$$(s - r)\,\tau_A^2\,\tau_B^2\, S\,\chi^2.$$

·12 *In any plane, the locus of a variable point the squares of whose distances from two distinct accessible points are in a given ratio other than unity is a finite circle.*

Readers of Darboux's last work will find this theorem exhibited there* in intimate relation to the property of the constant angle; here we are concerned with only its most elementary aspect.

In an isotropic plane, if R is one point satisfying ·11, every point of the nul line through R also satisfies ·11; hence the circle is not merely finite but ordinary, whatever the nature of the plane.

* *Principes*, p. 151.

In 2·2 we found the accessible points equally distant from A and B to be in general the accessible points on a definite line, the perpendicular bisector of AB. It now appears that °if the equation ·13

$$AP^2 = BP^2$$

is to be regarded as a particular case of ·11, the locus represented is the infinite circle compounded of the line at infinity and the perpendicular bisector. Nor is this at variance with the natural theorem that

The centres of circles through two given points in a given plane is the locus of points from which these two are equidistant: ·14

if the plane is anisotropic, each accessible point of the perpendicular bisector of AB is *the* centre of one and only one of the finite circles through A and B, and every point at infinity is *a* centre of the infinite circle formed of the line AB and the line at infinity; if the plane is isotropic and the line AB is not nul, every point of the nul line bisecting AB is *a* centre of the ordinary circle through A and B, every point at infinity is *a* centre of the infinite circle formed of the line AB and the line at infinity, and the focal point is *the* centre of every undegenerate circle through A and B; if the plane is isotropic and the line AB is nul, every point of the plane is a centre of a circle through A and B, and at the same time every point of the plane is at the same distances from A as from B.

·2. Except when the plane is isotropic and the line AB is nul, the condition ·11 associates a particular circle with each value of the ratio $r:s$. The circles of this kind are said to be described °*about* the pair of points A, B. ·21

Let Q be any accessible point of the plane. Then the condition for the circle about A, B with ratio $r:s$ to contain Q is

$$s \,.\, AQ^2 = r \,.\, BQ^2. \qquad \cdot 22$$

°If either of the lengths AQ, BQ is different from zero, there is one and only ·23
one circle about A, B through Q, but °if both these lengths are zero every ·24
circle about A, B contains Q. To put the argument differently, because ·11 is linear and homogeneous in r and s, any point that is common to *two* circles about A, B belongs to *every* circle about this pair of points; the circle for which r is zero is the nul circle with centre A, and the circle for which s is zero is the nul circle with centre B, and to say that a point is common to these circles is to assert that its distances from A and B are zero.

Suppose first that the plane is not isotropic and the line AB is not nul. Then the points at zero distance from A compose the lines AI, AJ, and the points at zero distance from B compose the lines BI, BJ, and no two of these four lines coincide. The lines AI, BJ are not parallel and therefore cut in a definite accessible point C; similarly AJ, BI cut in a definite accessible point D. Since C is on BJ but A is not, C is distinct from A; similarly C is distinct from B, and D also is distinct from both A and B; further, since C

is on AI and is distinct from A, C is not on AJ and is therefore distinct from D.

·246 From ·24, °every circle about A, B contains C and D. Conversely, if Q is a point distinct from C and D and from the focal points and situated on a given circle through C and D, there is a unique circle through Q about A, B, and since
·247 this circle does contain C and D, it is the given circle: °every circle through C and D is a circle about A, B.

Also because A is the intersection of CI and DJ and B is the intersection
·25 of CJ and DI, °*the relation between the pairs of points A, B and C, D is re-*
·26 *ciprocal*, and ·246 and ·247 imply that °*the circles about one of these pairs are the circles through the other pair.* From 2·36, A and B, being the centres of nul circles through C and D, are on the perpendicular bisector of CD, and the symmetry implies that C and D are on the perpendicular bisector of AB. To
·27 put the matter otherwise, °the figure $ABCD$ is a parallelogram whose sides are all of zero length, and the diagonals AB and CD, like those of any other rhombus, bisect each other at right angles. If O is the common midpoint of
·28 AB and CD, °the sum of the squares on OA and OC is the square on AC, which is zero; hence

·29 $$AB^2 + CD^2 = 0.$$

·3. To connect with a pair of points in a plane the pair related to it as is C, D to A, B is often useful. But if theorems are to be enunciated in the most general manner, allowance must be made for the possibility of degeneration: definitions must be framed with reference to segments rather than to pairs of points. In an anisotropic plane, if B coincides with A in an accessible point O, then C and D, defined as the intersection of AI with BJ and of AJ with BI, coincide in the same point O, and ·29 remains true, but the various collinearities do not connect an axis for C and D with a given axis for A and B; the perpendicularity of the axes has to be secured by definition.

·31 Accordingly, two coplanar segments AB, CD are described as °*associated segments* if their axes are perpendicular while one focal point is collinear both with A and C and with B and D and the other focal point is collinear both with A and D and with B and C; the relation between the segments is symmetrical.

·32 °If the plane is anisotropic and one of two associated segments is finite, proper, and anisotropic, the other segment also is finite, proper, and anisotropic, and the relation between the pairs of points that determine the segments is that between the pairs A, B and C, D in ·2. The perpendicularity of the axes follows, as we have seen, from the four collinearities, and is redundant in the definition. If we call the circles about the pair of points A, B circles about the segment AB, we can replace ·26 by the self-contained assertion that

·33 *In an anisotropic plane, if two associated segments are finite, proper, and anisotropic, the circles about either of them are the circles through the other.*

The restriction that the segments are to be anisotropic is easily removed. It is evident that

In an anisotropic plane, a finite segment in a nul line is its own associate, ·34

whether or not the segment is proper. Also, it follows from 2·25 that if the segment is proper and nul, the circles through the segment are the degenerate circles which have the axis of the segment for a constituent. On the other hand, merely from ·24 it follows that the circles about the ends of the segment also have the axis for a constituent. If Q is any point of the plane that is neither a focal point nor a point of the axis, then whether Q is accessible or not there is one and only one circle which contains Q and has the axis for a constituent, and this is therefore both the circle through Q about the segment and the circle through Q circumscribed to the segment:

In an anisotropic plane, the circles about a finite proper segment in a nul line ·35
are the circles through the same segment.

To combine ·34 with ·35 is to allow the segments in ·33 to be isotropic. The peculiarity is not in any failure of the definitions, but in the fact that if AB and EF are proper finite segments of the same nul line, the circles through and about AB are also the circles through and about EF; in general the associate of a segment AB can be *identified* as the segment inscribed in all the circles about AB, but if AB is in a nul line this property is *not* special to AB itself.

To allow the segments in ·33 to degenerate is a matter only of definition. The ordinary circles through a degenerate segment AA with axis l have been considered in 2·3, and if A is accessible and the plane is anisotropic, the segment with which AA is associated degenerates into the pair of coincident points AA in the axis perpendicular to l. To maintain ·33 is to *define* the circles about the latter segment as the circles through the former. This is
equivalent to saying that °in an anisotropic plane, by an ordinary circle about ·36
a segment AA degenerate at an accessible point of a line l is meant an ordinary circle through A with its centre in l, and by the infinite circle about the same segment is meant the infinite circle whose distinctive constituent is the line through A perpendicular to l. For a point Q on the nul circle with centre A, the fundamental condition ·22 is satisfied whatever the ratio of r to s; for an accessible point on any undegenerate circle about the segment, ·22 is satisfied only if r and s are equal, and a value of $r:s$ does not characterise a circle; for the accessible points of the infinite circle, $r:s$ must be unity unless l is nul but is arbitrary in the exceptional case.

We can now say that

In an anisotropic plane, if two associated segments are finite the circles about ·37
either of them are the circles through the other.

The consideration of infinite segments and of segments in an isotropic plane is postponed.

·4. The proof that the condition

$$s \, . \, AP^2 = r \, . \, BP^2$$

leads to the equation of a circle depends not on the precise formulae for the squares of the distances involved but on the fact that in each of these formulae the terms independent of τ compose a multiple of $S\chi^2$. Let us write Σ for

$$kS\chi^2 + 2g\xi\tau + 2f\eta\tau + c\tau^2,$$

so that the equation $$\Sigma = 0$$

if significant represents a circle, finite unless k is zero, which we may call the circle Σ. Given any finite number of circles Σ_1, Σ_2, ... and a corresponding number of constants p_1, p_2, ..., the terms independent of τ in the function
·41 $p_1\Sigma_1 + p_2\Sigma_2 + \ldots$ take the form $(p_1k_1 + p_2k_2 + \ldots)\, S\chi^2$; hence °the equation

$$p_1\Sigma_1 + p_2\Sigma_2 + \ldots = 0$$

if not satisfied identically is the equation of a circle, finite or infinite. To interpret this result, which we propose to use only in the simplest case, we must connect some number which does not depend on the frame of reference with the value of the *function* Σ for the coordinates of points that do not lie on the circle for which the function vanishes.

In the case of a finite circle there is no difficulty: we have seen in 4·24 that Σ/τ^2 is proportional to the power of the circle with respect to the variable
·42 point (ξ, η, τ), and therefore °$p\Sigma/\tau^2$ is the product of the power, not as a rule by p, but by some number entirely independent of the variable point.

If the circle is infinite, k is zero and the circle is compounded of the line at infinity and the line

$$2g\xi + 2f\eta + c\tau = 0,$$

the distinctive constituent of the circle; in this case Σ/τ^2 reduces, for accessible points, to Λ/τ, where Λ denotes $2g\xi + 2f\eta + c\tau$. If the distinctive constituent is accessible and if $\mathbf{p}$ is any unit vector not parallel to this line, the line through (ξ, η, τ) with vecline containing $\mathbf{p}$ cuts the line in a definite point, and the distance from this point to (ξ, η, τ) is r, given by the equation

$$2g(\xi - r\tau\xi_{\mathbf{p}}) + 2f(\eta - r\tau\eta_{\mathbf{p}}) + c\tau = 0,$$

that is, is $\Lambda/\{2\tau(g\xi_{\mathbf{p}} + f\eta_{\mathbf{p}})\}$. The factor $g\xi_{\mathbf{p}} + f\eta_{\mathbf{p}}$ is independent of the co-
·43 ordinates ξ, η, τ, and therefore in this case °$p\Sigma/\tau^2$ is a multiple of the distance of (ξ, η, τ) from the distinctive constituent of Σ in a prescribed direction. Lastly, if the distinctive constituent is the line at infinity, Σ/τ^2 has the
·44 constant value c, and °$p\Sigma/\tau^2$ is an arbitrary constant.

·45 For the sake of brevity we shall call Σ/τ^2 a °*measure of separation* of the point (ξ, η, τ) from the circle Σ. There is necessarily an arbitrary factor in this measure, since to multiply the *function* Σ by an arbitrary constant does not affect the circle. But unless the circle is the duplicated line at infinity, to say that two accessible points have the same measures is to make a sig-

nificant assertion, implying that if the circle is finite the points have the same power and that if the circle is infinite the line through one of the points parallel to the distinctive constituent of the circle contains the other point.
°For an accessible point a measure is zero only if the point is on the circle, ·47
and in this case every measure is zero. A measure of separation becomes definite if its value is given for any one accessible point that is not on the circle.

·5. We can now study the equation

$$s\Sigma_1 - r\Sigma_2 = 0,$$ ·51

which is not an identity unless Σ_1 and Σ_2 are the same circle. From its form, this equation represents a circle, finite unless $sk_1 - rk_2$ is zero; °the circle is ·52
said to be described about the pair of circles Σ_1, Σ_2; to each value of the ratio $r:s$ corresponds one and only one circle about Σ_1, Σ_2.

A circle about two circles is a circle whose accessible part is the locus of a ·53
point for which definite measures of separation with respect to the two circles have a constant ratio.

It will be noticed that a circle is determined by its accessible points except in one case; the accessible points of a nul line in an isotropic plane are the accessible points both of the nul circle formed by duplicating the line and of the infinite circle formed by combining the line with the line at infinity.

Let Σ_3 and Σ_4 be two different circles described about the circles Σ_1, Σ_2, and suppose that

$$\Sigma_3 = s_3\Sigma_1 - r_3\Sigma_2, \quad \Sigma_4 = s_4\Sigma_1 - r_4\Sigma_2.$$ ·54

Since a linear combination of Σ_3 and Σ_4 is expressible by means of ·54 as a linear combination of Σ_1 and Σ_2, *every circle about* Σ_3, Σ_4 *is a circle about* Σ_1, Σ_2. But since Σ_3, Σ_4 are distinct, $r_3s_4 - s_3r_4$ is not zero and therefore ·54 can be used to express Σ_1 and Σ_2 as linear combinations of Σ_3 and Σ_4. That is to say, Σ_1 and Σ_2 are circles about Σ_3, Σ_4, and therefore *every circle about* Σ_1, Σ_2
is a circle about Σ_3, Σ_4. Hence °the circles about two given circles form a ·55
system in which the original circles retain no distinctive feature; some one pair of circles renders easy the identification of the system, just as some one
pair of points is useful in the specification of a line, but if we define a °*coaxal* ·56
system or a system of coaxal circles indirectly by defining *the* coaxal system containing two given circles as the aggregate of circles described about those two, we must add at once that

Of any three circles of a coaxal system, each is a circle about the other two, ·57
and that

Every circle about any two members of a coaxal system is itself a member of ·58
the system.

We can describe the structure of a coaxal system otherwise by saying that
°*three* circles Σ_1, Σ_2, Σ_3 are coaxal if there are constants f, g, h not all zero ·59

such that $f\Sigma_1 + g\Sigma_2 + h\Sigma_3$ is *identically* zero, and that a family of circles is a coaxal system if three circles chosen arbitrarily from the family are necessarily coaxal but no three distinct circles can be coaxal if two of them belong to the family and one does not.

·6. The condition for the circle ·51 to be infinite is

·61 $$sk_1 - rk_2 = 0,$$

and unless k_1 and k_2 are both zero this condition is satisfied by one and only
·62 one value of the ratio $r:s$: °in a system of coaxal circles there is in general one and only one infinite member; there is always one infinite member, and if there are two infinite members every member is infinite.

The distinctive constituent of an infinite member of a coaxal system is
·63 called a °*radical axis* of the system. Usually there is only one such line, and to speak of *the* radical axis is to assume implicitly that the system is not formed of infinite members. As a rule, the radical axis is accessible, but we shall have to recognise the peculiarities of a system with the line at infinity for its only radical axis.

If Σ_1 and Σ_2 are both finite, k_1 and k_2 are both different from zero, and we can satisfy ·61 by taking $1/k_1$ for s and $1/k_2$ for r; the equation of the infinite circle is then

$$\Sigma_1/k_1 = \Sigma_2/k_2,$$

whence from 4·24

·64 *Any accessible point for which two finite circles are equipotent is on the radical axis of the coaxal system containing these circles,*

and conversely

·65 *All the circles of a coaxal system have the same power for any accessible point on the radical axis of the system.*

From the fundamental property of a circle described about two others,

·66 *If a variable point is confined to one circle of a coaxal system with an accessible radical axis, its power with respect to any other circle of the system is proportional to its distance from the radical axis, the distance being measured in any fixed direction;*

·67 *If a coaxal system has the line at infinity for radical axis, the power of a variable point on one circle of the system with respect to any other circle of the system depends only on the two circles.*

·7. The form of the equation ·51 shews that any point which is common to two circles is on every circle described about those two; hence if two members of a coaxal system have a point in common, that point belongs to every member of the system. For accessible points this result is a corollary of ·59 and ·47, for if there is a homogeneous linear relation between three measures of separation, a point for which two of the measures are zero is a point for which the third also is zero; but the algebraic proof, making no distinction between accessible and inaccessible points, is the more powerful.

If Q is any point, accessible or inaccessible, that is not on both the circles Σ_1, Σ_2, the numbers $\Sigma_1(Q)$, $\Sigma_2(Q)$ are not both zero and

$$\Sigma_2(Q)\,\Sigma_1 - \Sigma_1(Q)\,\Sigma_2 = 0$$

is a significant equation; it is the equation of a member of the coaxal system to which Σ_1 and Σ_2 belong, and it is satisfied by the coordinates of Q. Thus there is one member of the system which contains Q; if there were two such members, Q would belong to every member, and in particular to both Σ_1 and Σ_2, contrary to hypothesis:

Through any point, accessible or inaccessible, that does not belong to every member of a system of coaxal circles, there passes one and only one member of the system. ·71

If P is the radical axis of a system which contains a finite member Σ, the points common to any two circles of the system are the points common to Σ and the infinite circle of which P is the distinctive part, that is, are the focal points of the plane together with the points common to Σ and P. This consideration enables us to describe the features usually possessed by a coaxal system, and to discover which systems are to be regarded as peculiar. It is the exception for a plane to be isotropic or a line nul, or for a line to cut a circle otherwise than in two distinct accessible points only. We suppose therefore in the first place that the plane is not isotropic, that P is not nul, and that Σ and P have in common two accessible points C, D and no other points; it is not necessary for us to suppose C and D to be distinct. Then every member of the coaxal system circumscribes the segment of which C and D are the ends and P is the axis. Conversely, if T is any circle through the segment and Q is any point of T that is distinct from C and D and is not a focal point, T is the *only* circle through Q circumscribing the segment, and therefore T *is* the circle through Q that belongs to the coaxal system: every circle that circumscribes the segment belongs to the system.

In general, the circles forming a coaxal system can be described as the circles through a definite segment; the axis of the segment is the radical axis of the system, and the ends of the segment are the distinctive common points. ·72

If the circles of a system can be described as the circles through a finite segment CD, they can be described also as the circles about the segment AB which is the associate of CD. By ·13 and ·14 the axis of AB is the distinctive constituent of the infinite circle formed of centres of circles through AB, and for this reason the axis of AB is called the °*central axis* of the system. By ·73
the definition of associated segments, the nul circles whose centres are A and B both contain C and D and therefore both belong to the coaxal system; they are the only nul members of the system. A centre of a nul circle belonging to a coaxal system is called a °*limiting point* of the system. ·74

·75 *In general, the circles forming a coaxal system can be described as the circles about a definite segment; the axis of the segment is the central axis of the system, and the ends of the segment are the limiting points.*

If the limiting points A, B are distinct, the nul circles with these points for centres are two distinct members of the system, and the system may be constructed either about the two points, in the sense of ·21, or about the two circles, in the sense of ·52; this concordance has its origin in 4·27.

Since a circle in an anisotropic plane is degenerate only if it is nul or infinite,

·76 *In an anisotropic plane, a coaxal system in general includes only three degenerate circles, namely, the two nul circles whose centres are the limiting points and the infinite circle whose distinctive constituent is the radical axis.*

But

·77 *If a coaxal system in an anisotropic plane has an anisotropic radical axis which has double intersection with the finite members of the system at a point O, the two limiting points coincide at O, and of the three degenerate circles of the system the two that are nul coincide.*

·8. We have seen that

·81 *In general in an anisotropic plane the segment determined by the distinctive common points of a coaxal system in the radical axis is the associate of the segment determined by the limiting points of the system in the central axis.*

The symmetry of the relation between associated segments prompts us to
·82 °*associate* with the coaxal system through CD and about AB the coaxal system through AB and about CD.

·83 *In general, with a coaxal system of circles in an anisotropic plane can be associated a second coaxal system such that the radical axis of each system is the central axis of the other and the limiting points of each system are the distinctive common points of the other.*

Through any point Q which is distinct from the common points and limiting points and from the focal points there passes one circle of each system, and if Q is accessible and is not on either of the lines AB, CD, the circle QCD has for centre an accessible point P on AB and the circle QAB has for centre an accessible point R on CD. Also if O is the common midpoint of AB and CD,

$$PQ^2 = PC^2 = PO^2 + OC^2, \quad RQ^2 = RA^2 = RO^2 + OA^2,$$

since AB and CD are perpendicular; for the same reason

$$PR^2 = PO^2 + RO^2,$$

and therefore by ·28 $\qquad PR^2 = PQ^2 + RQ^2$:

the steps PQ and RQ are perpendicular. To suppose one of the steps PQ, RQ to be zero is to suppose not only that the corresponding circle is nul but that Q is at the centre of this circle, that is, at one of the points A, B, C, D. This being contrary to the assumption already made, it follows that the circles QAB, QCD have definite tangents at Q, and that these tangents contain the steps PQ, RQ and are perpendicular to each other. We may allow Q to be on AB if only it is kept distinct from A and B and from O: if Q is on AB but not at A or B or at infinity, the circle QAB is the infinite circle which includes the line AB, and the tangent to this circle at Q is the line AB itself; if Q is not at O, the circle QCD is a finite circle with its centre at an accessible point P of AB distinct from Q, and the tangent to this circle at Q is perpendicular to PQ, that is, to AB, and therefore perpendicular to the tangent at Q to the circle QAB. Similarly, Q may be on CD if it is not at C, D, or O. Lastly, if Q is at O, the circles QAB, QCD degenerate and have constituents AB, CD, the tangents at Q are the lines AB, CD themselves, and again the tangents are perpendicular. Hence

If two circles belonging one to each of two associated coaxal systems intersect at an accessible point that is not a common point of either system, they intersect at right angles. ·84

Briefly,

Associated coaxal systems of circles are mutually orthogonal. ·85

Neither ·83 nor ·85 requires modification in the case in which the limiting points coincide, provided that the system presents no other peculiarity, that is, provided that the plane and the radical axis are anisotropic and the point in which the distinctive common points coincide is accessible; the formulae used in the proof of ·85 are simplified, but not invalidated.

From ·84 we can derive an excellent example of the services which complex geometry can render to real geometry. From ·29 it is evident that in a real plane there are no pairs of associated segments except segments of zero length in perpendicular lines. But we can express ·84, except for special cases, in the form that

If A, B are distinct accessible points in an anisotropic plane and Q is any accessible point of the plane that is neither on AB nor on the perpendicular bisector of AB, the circle through Q about A and B and the circle through Q which contains A and B are perpendicular at Q.

If the plane is supposed to be real, this proposition remains significant *and therefore is true*; it is a well-known and important theorem, but there is no proof of it in terms of real points alone which compares for simplicity with the deduction of ·84 from the theorem of Pythagoras.

For subsequent use we must render the proof of ·84 independent of reference to the point O. If A, P, C, R are any four points of space, then identically

$$\mathcal{G}\, PC^2 = \mathcal{G}\,(PA + AC)^2 = \mathcal{G}\, PA^2 + \mathcal{G}\, AC^2 + 2\,\mathcal{G}\, PA\,.\,AC,$$

$$\mathcal{G}\, AR^2 = \mathcal{G}\,(AC + CR)^2 = \mathcal{G}\, CR^2 + \mathcal{G}\, AC^2 + 2\,\mathcal{G}\, AC\,.\,CR,$$

$$\mathcal{G}\, PR^2 = \mathcal{G}\,(PA + AC + CR)^2$$
$$= \mathcal{G}\, PA^2 + \mathcal{G}\, CR^2 + \mathcal{G}\, AC^2 + 2\,\mathcal{G}\, PA\,.\,AC + 2\,\mathcal{G}\, AC\,.\,CR + 2\,\mathcal{G}\, PA\,.\,CR;$$

hence

·86 *For any four points A, P, C, R of space*

$$\mathcal{G}\,CP^2 + \mathcal{G}\,AR^2 = \mathcal{G}\,PR^2 + \mathcal{G}\,AC^2 + 2\,\mathcal{G}\,AP.CR,$$

so that in particular

·87 *If A, P, C, R are four points in space, then*

$$CP^2 + AR^2 = PR^2 + AC^2$$

if and only if the steps AP, CR are perpendicular,

and further

·88 *If the steps AP, CR are perpendicular and the step AC is nul, then*

$$CP^2 + AR^2 = PR^2.$$

Pythagoras' theorem is the special case of ·88 in which AC is not merely nul but zero. To deduce ·84 we have only to add as a corollary to ·88 that

·89 *If AP and CR are coplanar and perpendicular and AC is nul, then if a circle through C with centre P and a circle through A with centre R cut in an accessible point Q the tangents to these circles at Q are perpendicular.*

556. Exceptional forms of coaxal systems.

·1. Having discussed the form which a coaxal system of circles normally assumes in an anisotropic plane, we must examine the exceptional forms that are possible, and the nature of coaxal systems in an isotropic plane. If the system contains any finite members, the classification is made to depend on the relation of the system to its radical axis.

The existence of a central axis has been deduced virtually from 3·79. An alternative deduction, from 5·87, is subject to different exceptions and is more useful to us at this stage. Let a coaxal system have an accessible common point C and a unique radical axis, and let one circle of the system have an accessible centre F. Then by 4·12, if G and Q are any two accessible points of the plane, the powers of Q for the circles through C with centres F, G are $FQ^2 - FC^2$, $GQ^2 - GC^2$, and by 5·87 these two powers are equal if and only if CQ and FG are perpendicular. Taking Q in the radical axis, we infer from 5·64 that G is a centre of a circle of the system if and only if FG is perpendicular to the radical axis. If F, G, H are three points that are not collinear, the lines FG, FH can not both be perpendicular to a given line in the plane FGH unless the plane is isotropic and the given line is nul. Hence

·11 *If a coaxal system has a unique radical axis and if there is one accessible common point, then unless the plane of the system is isotropic and the radical axis is nul, the accessible centres of circles of the system are the accessible points of a definite line, and this central axis is perpendicular to the radical axis.*

It follows from 3·55 that for an anisotropic plane the contrast between 5·75
·12 and ·11 is that in the later proposition °the radical axis may be supposed nul;

the central axis, whose existence is proved, is then parallel to the radical axis. Combining ·11 with 3·57, we find that

One exceptional form of coaxal system of circles in an anisotropic plane is composed of the circles with centres on a given accessible nul line and a common point that is accessible and is not on the central axis; the radical axis of the system is the nul line through the common point parallel to the central axis. ·13

°The only finite nul circle of the system is formed of the central axis, which ·14
we will denote by Π, together with the nul line complementary to Π through the common point C. The centre A of this nul circle is the only accessible limiting point. But °the circle formed of the radical axis P and the line at ·15
infinity serves not only in its ordinary capacity as the infinite circle of the system but also as one of the nul circles, and the focal point on the radical axis acts therefore not only as one of the distinctive common points but also as one of the limiting points; this same focal point is also the centre of the system, for it is the point common to the radical axis and the central axis.

To regard the present system as degenerating from the usual form we have only to suppose the common point D to coincide with the focal point J while the line DJ assumes the position of a definite accessible nul line Π and C remains accessible and does not lie in Π. Then A is the intersection of CI and Π, and DI is the line at infinity and cuts CJ nowhere except at J: °the ·16
two point pairs AB, CD are associated if B and D coincide in one focal point and A and C are collinear with the other focal point.

°The system of circles to be associated with the coaxal system having Π for ·17
central axis and C for common point is the system of the same kind with P for central axis and A for common point. As in general, the radical axis and the common points of each system are the central axis and the limiting points of the other. Moreover, 5·89 is valid to shew that the two systems are orthogonal.

·2. The radical axis of a system, if nul, may be an asymptote or a constituent of one member of the system, and therefore of every member; in other words, the centres of the finite circles of the system may belong to the radical axis. From 4·12, *any* point on a nul line through a centre of an ordinary circle of radius q has power $-q^2$ with respect to the circle. Hence °if ·21
two finite circles have centres in a nul line P, *no* point of P is equipotent for the two circles if they are unequal, but *every* point of P is equipotent for them if they are equal; that is, P is the radical axis in the latter case but not in the former. Hence °if in an anisotropic plane the central axis and the ·22
radical axis of a system coincide in a nul line P, the finite circles belonging to the system are all equal; P is a constituent of the circles if they are nul, but not otherwise. Further, if P is a given nul line and Q is any accessible point not on P, and if q is any given number, the circle with centre Q and radius q has one of its asymptotes parallel to P and distinct from P and

therefore cuts P in one and only one accessible point R; the circle with centre R and radius q is the *only* circle with centre on P and q for a radius which passes through Q. From this it follows that

·23 *If the radical axis of a coaxal system in an anisotropic plane is an asymptote but not a constituent of the finite circles of the system, the finite circles are those circles with a given radius different from zero which have their centres in the radical axis.*

·24 °In this system, the distinctive common points and the limiting points all coincide in the focal point on the radical axis. The only degenerate member is formed of the radical axis and the line at infinity.

The system to be associated with a system of this kind must have its own radical axis and central axis coincident in the line P that plays the double part for the original system, and must have no accessible common points or limiting points; that is, the associated system must share the peculiarities of the original system. This condition does not define the associated system, for it leaves the size of the circles undetermined, and we appeal to the property of orthogonality to suggest a definition. If P, R are two accessible points of a nul line, PR^2 is zero, and therefore two accessible steps PQ, RQ are perpen-
·25 dicular if and only if $PQ^2 + RQ^2$ is zero. For this reason we °define two systems of the present type to be associated if they have a common axis and the sum of the squared radii of the finite members of one and the squared
·26 radii of the finite members of the other is zero. With this definition, °associated systems are orthogonal.

If a nul line P is a constituent of a finite circle Σ, it is a constituent of every member of the coaxal system which includes Σ and has P for radical axis; that is to say, every finite circle of the system is a nul circle with its centre on P. Conversely, since through any accessible point Q that is not on P there passes one and only one nul circle with P for a constituent, namely, the circle formed of P itself and the nul line through Q that is not parallel to P, every nul circle with its centre on P belongs to the system.

·27 *The circles obtained by combining a definite nul line* P *with the line at infinity and with the nul lines that are complementary to* P *form a coaxal system of which* P *is at once the radical axis and the central axis.*

·28 °Every point of the axis P is both a common point and a limiting point. Every member of the system is degenerate, but only one member is infinite. The system is its own associate, and is orthogonal to itself, for if Q is any accessible point that is not on the axis P, the tangent at Q to the member of the system through Q is the nul line which combines with P to form the circle, and this tangent is self-perpendicular.

The system of ·27 can be regarded as degenerating from every one of the cases already treated. The circles of this system have in common distinct accessible points, but these points are on a nul line and there are more than two of them. All the circles have multiple intersection with a line at the same accessible point, but the line is nul and the point is not unique. The circles have their centres in one nul line and have a common accessible point, but there is no common point that is not on the line of centres. The circles are equal and have their centres in a nul line, but they have no common radius other than zero. The radical axis is asymptotic to all the circles, but it is also a constituent of them.

Taken together, ·23 and ·27 enable us to remove one of the restrictions from ·11, for they shew that if the radical axis is itself accessible, the common points may be coincident at infinity:

If a coaxal system in an anisotropic plane has an accessible radical axis and does not consist only of infinite circles, then it has an accessible central axis and the two axes are perpendicular. ·29

·3. For an anisotropic plane, the forms possible to a coaxal system of circles with a unique accessible radical axis have all been described. There remain two possibilities to consider.

The form of the system which has the line at infinity for radical axis and includes an ordinary circle Σ is shewn by 5·67: since the points which have a constant power with respect to Σ are the points at a constant distance from the centre of Σ, and since there is only one circle with a given centre which passes through a given point,

A coaxal system of which the line at infinity is the only radical axis is a family of concentric circles. ·31

°The duplicated line at infinity is the only infinite member of the system, the nul lines through the common centre form the only finite nul member. The focal points are the distinctive common points, and the common centre is one limiting point, but it proves useful to regard every point at infinity also as a limiting point of the system, a convention that we may justify by recalling that the duplicated line at infinity has all points at infinity for centres and has zero for a radius about every one of them. ·32

The coaxal system described about two infinite circles Σ, T has no finite members. If the point of intersection of the distinctive constituents of Σ and T is an accessible point C, every circle of the system consists of the line at infinity together with a line through C, and conversely every line through C combines with the line at infinity to form a circle coaxal with Σ and T.

In one form of coaxal system, the various circles are formed by combining the line at infinity with the different lines through a definite accessible point. ·33

°This system has for its distinctive common points the vertex C of the pencil formed by the distinctive constituents and also all the points at infinity in the plane. The only members of the system that can be called nul are the two that involve the nul lines through C, and although each of these circles has every point at infinity for a centre, it is only about a focal point that zero ·34

is a possible radius, and therefore only the focal points are to be regarded as limiting points. The system to be associated with this must have the focal points for its distinctive common points, and the point C and the points at
·35 infinity for its limiting points; hence °the associated system is formed of concentric circles, the common centre being C. And to say that in this case also the two systems are orthogonal is only to repeat that at any point of an ordinary circle the diameter and the tangent are perpendicular.

One difficulty must not be overlooked. There is nothing unnatural in describing the line at infinity, which is the radical axis of a concentric system, as the central axis of the associated system of infinite circles. But the grounds for regarding every radical axis of the latter system as a central axis of the former are more obscure, for the lines through the common centre are not *composed* of centres of finite circles of the system, and it may be urged that the *name* of central axis is misleading. Nevertheless, these lines do acquire properties that in general belong to the central axis alone, since each of them is a diameter of every finite circle of the system and an axis of symmetry of every circle. Since it is not easy to see in what sense the line at infinity can be an axis of symmetry of some circles and not of others, we may be content to define a central axis of a coaxal system as a radical axis of the associated system. With this *definition*, the significant propositions are that in every case a central axis contains a centre of every circle and that *in general* the central axis is unique and is composed of centres of circles belonging to the system.

There remain for consideration the cases in which Σ and T are infinite and their distinctive constituents intersect at infinity. Then any circle about Σ and T is an infinite circle whose distinctive constituent has no accessible point in common either with the distinctive constituent of Σ or with the distinctive constituent of T.

·36 *In one kind of coaxal system, lines all parallel to each other are combined severally with the line at infinity to form the circles.*

Systems of this kind have the duplicated line at infinity for one member, and therefore share some of the characteristics of systems of concentric circles as well as some of those of systems of the type of ·33. The common points of the system compose the line at infinity, and the distinctive constituents, including among them the line at infinity, are all radical axes. Every point at infinity is a limiting point, for the same reason as in ·32; the distinctive constituents may form one of the two families of nul lines in the plane, and then every circle of the system is nul, but as a rule the duplicated line at infinity is the only nul member of the system.

·37 °The associate of a system of this kind is a system of the same kind, chosen to preserve the property of orthogonality, that is, formed with distinctive constituents perpendicular to those of the original system. The two systems

coincide if and only if the distinctive constituents are nul. In any system of
the kind described in ·36, °every line that is perpendicular to the parallel ·38
constituents is a central axis.

·4. A contrast is to be observed between the association of segments and
the association of coaxal systems. If B and D coincide in I, the condition for
AB and CD to be associated does not render one of these segments determinate
when the other is given. Also °the focal segment IJ is itself *an* associate of ·41
any infinite segment, and is actually *the* associate of any infinite segment
whose axis is not nul; for this very reason, there is no segment that can be
called *the* associate of IJ. In fact, we have to admit that

No infinite segment whose axis contains a focal point has a unique associate. ·42

But the assertions with regard to associated coaxal systems in an anisotropic plane are perfectly general:

In an anisotropic plane, every coaxal system, whatever its form, has a definite ·43
associate;

°the common points of each of two associated systems are the limiting points ·44
of the other; °through any ordinary point, that is, any point which is neither ·45
a focal point nor one of these common and limiting points, there passes one
and only one circle of each system; °the two circles through any ordinary ·46
point have definite tangents there, and these tangents are perpendicular.

·5. No attempt to adapt to an isotropic plane an argument dependent on associated segments can be successful. If K is the focal point and AB is a given segment, the lines AK, BK either cut in K alone or coincide. If AB is not nul, the associate of AB is an improper segment KK to which it is natural to ascribe for axis the nul line bisecting AB. If AB is nul, different comparisons provide different suggestions for the associate: it would seem absurd that KK in the axis of AB should not be one associate, or that AB should not be self-associated, or that the zero segment OO in *any* line through the midpoint O of AB should not serve.

But the reasoning in articles 5·4, 5·5, 5·6, and in the beginning of article 5·7
is valid, and it is unnecessary for us to reassert any of the results from 5·41
to 5·72. °In general, a coaxal system consists of the circles through some ·51
definite segment. The axis of this segment is the radical axis of the system,
and the only infinite member of the system is formed of the radical axis and
the line at infinity. The circumstances to be regarded as normal are those in
which the radical axis is not nul. The distinctive common points C, D are
then accessible points, and the system has one degenerate member that is
finite, namely, the ordinary circle formed of the nul lines through C and D;
it is only if C and D coincide that this finite degenerate circle is of zero radius
about any centre except the focal point K.

°Coaxal systems of infinite circles have the same form in an isotropic plane ·52
as in a plane that is not isotropic; the members of such a system consist of

the line at infinity together with the various lines through some definite point, accessible or inaccessible. The systems for which a special investigation is required are those for which the radical axis is unique but nul or inaccessible.

We saw in 3·9 that if vectors of reference are suitably chosen the typical equation of a finite circle Σ in an isotropic plane is

·53 $$\eta^2 + (2g\xi + 2f\eta + c\tau)\,\tau = 0.$$

This circle is degenerate if g is zero, and two circles Σ_1, Σ_2 are equal if g_1 and g_2 are equal. For τ to be a factor of $s\Sigma_1 - r\Sigma_2$ we must have r and s equal: the radical axis of the coaxal system defined by the two circles Σ_1, Σ_2 is

·54 $$2\,(g_1 - g_2)\,\xi + 2\,(f_1 - f_2)\,\eta + (c_1 - c_2)\,\tau = 0.$$

Hence follows a proposition fundamental in the classification of coaxal systems:

·55 *The radical axis of the coaxal system described about two finite circles in an isotropic plane is accessible and anisotropic if and only if the circles are unequal.*

Since a nul line which is not a constituent of a circle can not cut the circle in more than one accessible point, ·55 implies that

·56 *Two equal undegenerate circles in an isotropic plane can not have two accessible points in common.*

It follows from ·55 that each of the systems that we have yet to consider is formed, except for its infinite member, of equal circles. Suppose first that a system includes one finite undegenerate circle Σ and has for radical axis an accessible nul line P. Then, by 3·56, the intersection of P with Σ at K is simple, and there is one accessible common point C. Every finite circle of the system is a circle through C equal to Σ. Conversely, if T is a circle through C equal to Σ and Q is any accessible point of T other than C, the circle through Q belonging to the coaxal system is a circle equal to T, and, by ·56, this circle, since it has the two points C, Q in common with T, is T itself: every circle through C equal to Σ belongs to the system.

·57 *In one form of coaxal system in an isotropic plane, the distinctive common points are the focal point and an accessible point C; the radical axis is the nul line through C, and the circle formed of the radical axis and the line at infinity is the only degenerate member of the system; the undegenerate members of the system form a complete family of equal circles through the common point.*

The nature of a system which contains an undegenerate circle Σ and has the line at infinity for radical axis is now evident by mere exhaustion: the finite circles are the circles parallel to Σ. This conclusion is confirmed by the simplest analysis, for if the equation of Σ is

$$\eta^2 + 2g\xi\tau = 0,$$

the equation $$\eta^2 + 2g\xi\tau + c\tau^2 = 0$$

for variable values of c represents both an arbitrary circle parallel to Σ and an arbitrary finite member of the system described about Σ and the duplicated line at infinity.

In an isotropic plane, a family of parallel undegenerate circles forms together with the duplicated line at infinity a coaxal system which has the line at infinity for radical axis and the focal point for the only common point. ·58

·6. In conclusion we have to suppose a coaxal system in an isotropic plane to include an ordinary circle, that is, a circle formed of a pair of accessible nul lines, and to have a radical axis that is either an accessible nul line or the line at infinity.

Suppose first that the radical axis is accessible and is taken for the first axis of reference. Then the infinite circle formed of this axis and the line at infinity has the equation

$$\eta\tau = 0, \tag*{·61}$$

and if one ordinary circle of the system is

$$\eta^2 + 2f\eta\tau + c\tau^2 = 0, \tag*{·62}$$

any other ordinary circle of the system is

$$\eta^2 + 2(f + k)\eta\tau + c\tau^2 = 0, \tag*{·63}$$

where k is a variable parameter. Since the product of the distances of the constituents of this circle from the radical axis, in either aspect of the plane, is c, a number independent of k,

One form of coaxal system in an isotropic plane consists of pairs of nul lines such that the product of the distances of the lines in each pair from a definite nul line in the plane is constant, the distances being measured in the same aspect of the plane; the fixed nul line is the radical axis of the system. ·64

° A special case occurs when the constant is zero; in this case, which is covered by ·27 as well as by ·64, the radical axis is a constituent of every circle of the system. ·65

If the radical axis is the line at infinity, the infinite member of the system has the equation

$$\tau^2 = 0, \tag*{·66}$$

and the equation of a typical member is

$$\eta^2 + 2f\eta\tau + (c + k)\tau^2 = 0: \tag*{·67}$$

In one form of coaxal system in an isotropic plane, the members are pairs of nul lines such that the nul line midway between them is fixed; the radical axis is the line at infinity. ·68

It must not be overlooked that there is a system in which the line at infinity is combined with the nul lines of the plane; every nul line, including the line at infinity, is a radical axis. But this system is covered by ·52 and is in no respect peculiar to the isotropic plane.

The reader will recognise that ·64 and ·68 can be expressed together in the form that the pairs of lines cut any anisotropic line in pairs of points *in involution*, and that the radical axis is the nul line through the centre of the involution. The nature of involution, and the intersection of coaxal systems in general with a transversal, are not merely outside our scope to discuss, but are projective matters that it would be a mistake to approach from our metrical standpoint.

CHAPTER V 6

SPHERES IN IDEAL COMPLEX SPACE

561. Ordinary spheres; nul spheres; the centre and the radii of an ordinary sphere; infinite spheres. 562. Sections of spheres by planes the focal circle; tangents and tangent planes. 563. Generators.

561. Ordinary spheres; nul spheres; the centre and the radii of an ordinary sphere; infinite spheres.

·11 **·1.** An °*ordinary sphere* is the locus of a point in space at a given finite distance from a definite accessible centre.

The ideal vector $(\mathbf{r}, R)$ is the vector of a step from Q to some point of the ordinary sphere with centre Q and radius q if and only if

·12 $$\mathscr{S}\mathbf{r}^2 = q^2 R^2.$$

·13 °The section of an ordinary sphere by a plane through its centre is an ordinary circle with that centre. If the sphere had two centres P, Q, the section by any plane through the line PQ would be an ordinary circle with more centres than one, and therefore the plane would be isotropic; since no line has the property that *every* plane through it is isotropic,

·14 *An ordinary sphere has only one centre, and the square of its radii is unique.*

·2. Many of the arguments used in the last chapter can be adopted almost word for word. For example, we need only refer to the proof of 51·13 and 51·14 to realise that corresponding propositions are true:

·21 *If an ordinary sphere has centre Q and radius different from zero, an anisotropic line through Q cuts the sphere in two distinct accessible points, and an isotropic line through Q cuts it at infinity only;*

·22 *The points of an ordinary sphere with centre Q and radius zero are the points belonging to the nul lines through Q; an anisotropic line through Q cuts the sphere nowhere except at Q.*

·23 A sphere of zero radius is called a °*nul sphere*; ·22 implies that

·24 *A nul sphere is a cone whose vertex is the centre of the sphere.*

·31 **·3.** From ·21 and ·22, °an ordinary sphere, whatever its centre and radius, contains all the focal points of space, and contains no other points at infinity.

Also, with coordinates (ξ, η, ζ, τ) derived from a vector frame as in 21·4, the equation of the ordinary sphere with centre Q and radius q is

$$S(\tau_Q\chi - \tau\chi_Q)^2 = q^2\tau_Q^2\tau^2, \qquad \cdot 32$$

which is homogeneous and quadratic. Hence

An ordinary sphere is a conicoid that contains all the focal points. ·33

For a conicoid to contain all the focal points and no other points at infinity, the equation of the conicoid must be of the form

$$kS\chi^2 + 2u\xi\tau + 2v\eta\tau + 2w\zeta\tau + d\tau^2 = 0, \qquad \cdot 34$$

with k different from zero, and this, for arbitrary values of $\xi_Q, \eta_Q, \zeta_Q, \tau_Q$, is equivalent, if τ_Q is not zero, to

$$kS(\tau_Q\chi - \tau\chi_Q)^2 + 2\tau_Q\{(kS^1\chi_Q + u\tau_Q)\,\xi + (kS^2\chi_Q + v\tau_Q)\,\eta + (kS^3\chi_Q + w\tau_Q)\,\zeta\}\,\tau \qquad \cdot 35$$
$$= (kS\chi_Q^2 - d\tau_Q^2)\,\tau^2.$$

Since neither k nor the value of the determinant $[[S]]$ is zero, it is possible to satisfy the set of equations

$$kS^1\chi_Q + u\tau_Q = 0, \quad kS^2\chi_Q + v\tau_Q = 0, \quad kS^3\chi_Q + w\tau_Q = 0 \qquad \cdot 36$$

by a set of values $\xi_Q, \eta_Q, \zeta_Q, \tau_Q$ such that τ_Q is not zero and ξ_Q, η_Q, ζ_Q are all finite. If Q is the accessible point whose coordinates satisfy ·36, the equation ·35 is equivalent to ·32 if

$$q^2 = (kS\chi_Q^2 - d\tau_Q^2)/k\tau_Q^2, \qquad \cdot 37$$

and since this value of q^2 is finite

Every conicoid that contains all the focal points and no other points at infinity is an ordinary sphere. ·38

·4. With k different from zero, ·34 is the general equation of an ordinary sphere. Writing $\xi_Q S^1\chi_Q + \eta_Q S^2\chi_Q + \zeta_Q S^3\chi_Q$ for $S\chi_Q^2$ in ·37 and substituting from ·36 we can replace ·37 by

$$q^2 = -(u\xi_Q + v\eta_Q + w\zeta_Q + d\tau_Q)/k\tau_Q, \qquad \cdot 41$$

and if we express this last formula in the form

$$u\xi_Q + v\eta_Q + w\zeta_Q + (d + kq^2)\,\tau_Q = 0 \qquad \cdot 42$$

and eliminate the coordinates of Q between ·36 and ·42 we find that

The square of the radii of the sphere ·43

$$kS\chi^2 + 2u\xi\tau + 2v\eta\tau + 2w\zeta\tau + d\tau^2 = 0$$

is the quotient of

$$\begin{vmatrix} L & R & Q & u \\ R & M & P & v \\ Q & P & N & w \\ u & v & w & kd \end{vmatrix}$$

by $-k^2J^2$, *where* J^2 *denotes the value of*

$$\begin{vmatrix} L & R & Q \\ R & M & P \\ Q & P & N \end{vmatrix}.$$

·5. There are fewer varieties of spheres to be considered than of circles. This is not merely because we are not contemplating isotropic *space*, for in isotropic space there are planes with properties different from those of any planes in anisotropic space, and a discussion of isotropic space while it would involve new kinds of spheres would introduce also new kinds of circles.

·51 The general definition in anisotropic space is that a °sphere is a conicoid that contains all the focal points. It follows that

·52 *The general equation of a sphere, referred to a vector frame attached to an accessible origin, is*

$$kS\chi^2 + 2u\xi\tau + 2v\eta\tau + 2w\zeta\tau + d\tau^2 = 0.$$

If k is not zero, the equation in ·52 has already been shewn to represent an ordinary sphere. If k is zero, the equation reduces to

·53 $$(2u\xi + 2v\eta + 2w\zeta + d\tau)\,\tau = 0$$

and represents the combination of two planes of which one is the plane at infinity and the other is arbitrary; such a combination, regarded as a sphere, is

·54 called an °*infinite sphere.* The infinite sphere whose equation is ·53 has the plane

·55 $$2u\xi + 2v\eta + 2w\zeta + d\tau = 0$$

·56 for its °*distinctive constituent.*

562. Sections of spheres by planes; the focal circle; tangents and tangent planes.

·1. From 1·31 and 47·28, combined with 53·41, 53·42, and 53·43, it follows that

·11 *The points common to an accessible plane and an ordinary sphere compose in all cases a finite circle.*

This result is more general than 1·13, since the plane is not required to contain the centre of the sphere, but it is to be observed that the circle is now described only as finite, not as ordinary.

If the plane is anisotropic, the circle is of course ordinary—there is no finite circle in the plane that is not. We can confirm this conclusion by direct calculation. There is a line through the centre Q of the sphere perpendicular to the plane, and because the plane is anisotropic this line is not parallel to the plane but cuts it in a definite accessible point O. If P is any point of the plane, the steps OP, OQ are perpendicular, and therefore the equation

$$QP^2 = q^2$$

is equivalent, for points in the plane, to

$$OP^2 = q^2 - QO^2.$$

The curve of section of an ordinary sphere of radius q by an anisotropic plane is an ordinary circle whose radii have the square $q^2 - n^2$, *where n is a perpendicular distance of the centre of the sphere from the plane; the centre of the circle is the foot of the perpendicular from the centre of the sphere on the plane.* ·12

·2. It follows from ·12 that the ordinary spheres which contain a given finite circle in an anisotropic plane all have their centres in a definite line perpendicular to the plane. An alternative proof of this proposition dispenses with the condition that the plane is anisotropic and enables us to describe the section of a sphere by any plane. If AB, BC are finite segments inscribed in a finite circle, with axes l, m that are not parallel, it follows from 52·12 that every ordinary sphere through AB has its centre in a definite plane perpendicular to l and that every ordinary sphere through BC has its centre in a definite plane perpendicular to m; since l and m are not parallel, the planes are not parallel but intersect in an accessible line which is perpendicular to l and m, that is, to the plane of the circle, and if Q is any accessible point of this line, the sphere with centre Q which contains the point B contains both the segments and therefore contains the circle through them.

The centres of ordinary spheres through a given finite circle are the accessible points of a definite line perpendicular to the plane of the circle. ·21

The line is called the °*axis* of the circle. ·22

For an anisotropic plane the latter part of ·12 is reproduced. But ·21 implies also that

Every ordinary sphere through an ordinary circle in an isotropic plane has its centre in the line of the plane which contains the centres of the circle itself, ·23

and that

The centres of ordinary spheres through an undegenerate circle in an isotropic plane occupy a nul line parallel to the plane but not included in the plane. ·24

We have only to look at these same propositions from a different point of view to assert that

The finite circle in which an isotropic plane cuts an ordinary sphere is degenerate or undegenerate according as the plane does or does not contain the centre of the sphere. ·25

·3. Suppose that we are given a finite circle, not necessarily ordinary, and a finite segment AB which has one end A in the circle but is not inscribed in the circle. Then the ordinary sphere with centre Q which contains A includes the whole circle if and only if Q is in the axis of the circle, and circumscribes the segment if and only if Q is in the perpendicular bisector of the segment. The axis of the circle is parallel to the perpendicular bisector of the segment if and only if the axis of the segment is parallel to the plane of the circle, that is, since the latter axis and plane have the point A in common, if and only if the axis of the segment is *in* the plane of the circle.

·31 *Given a finite circle and a finite segment with one end in the circle, then unless the axis of the segment is in the plane of the circle there is one and only one ordinary sphere which includes the circle and is circumscribed to the segment.*

Since the infinite sphere through the circle contains the segment if the axis of the segment is in the plane of the circle or if the segment is infinite, but not otherwise, and since the circle must be the *complete* intersection of its plane with any ordinary sphere that includes it, ·31 admits of an extension in which the restriction on the segment is removed. Moreover, a sphere contains an infinite circle if and only if* the sphere is an infinite sphere whose distinctive constituent includes the distinctive constituent of the circle, and since the addition of an accessible point not on the circle or of an accessible line intersecting the distinctive constituent of the circle renders the distinctive constituent of the sphere determinate the restriction on the circle can be removed also.

·32 *Given any circle, and any segment which has one end in the circle but is not inscribed in the circle and has neither end at a focal point, there is one sphere, and unless the circle is infinite and the axis of the segment is at infinity there is only one sphere, which includes the circle and is circumscribed to the segment; the sphere is infinite if the circle or the segment is infinite, or if the axis of the segment is in the plane of the circle, but not otherwise.*

If we separate the case of a proper segment from that of a degenerate segment we have propositions simpler in form than ·31 and ·32:

·33 *Given a circle and a point that is neither a focal point nor a point of the circle, there is one and only one sphere that includes the circle and contains the point; the sphere is infinite if the point is at infinity or is in the plane of the circle, or if the circle is infinite, but not otherwise;*

·34 *Given a circle and an accessible line which has simple intersection with the circle at a point P that is not a focal point, there is one and only one sphere that includes the circle and has double intersection with the line at P; the sphere is infinite if the line is in the plane of the circle or if the circle is infinite, but not otherwise.*

From ·33 can be deduced the fundamental propositions relating to spheres through given points:

·35 *Through any four points a sphere can be passed;*

·36 *An infinite number of spheres can be passed through four given points if the points are concylic, if one of the points is focal, or if two of the points are at infinity; except in these cases, the sphere through the points is unique;*

* The convention that renders this statement true if the circle is a duplicated line at infinity is easy to frame.

Four points are not on any finite sphere if they are coplanar but are not contained in any finite circle, or if one of them is inaccessible but not focal; ·37

If four points are on more than one infinite sphere, every sphere through them is infinite. ·38

·4. °If two ordinary spheres have the same centre, they have no common accessible points, and therefore no common points except the focal points, unless they have the same radii. Hence °the sections of two distinct concentric spheres by any plane, isotropic or anisotropic, are two circles which have no common points except the focal points of their plane. If the plane is anisotropic, the circles are concentric circles, as we have seen already in ·12. But we now see also that ·41 ·42

The parabolic circles in which an isotropic plane cuts a number of concentric spheres are parallel circles. ·43

°The circles in ·43, being parallel, are equal, and their size depends only on the relation of the plane to the centre of the spheres. Let $\mathbf{x}$ be a proper nul vector in the plane, let $\mathbf{y}$ be a unit vector in the plane, and therefore perpendicular to $\mathbf{x}$, and let $\mathbf{z}$ be the vector of a step from the centre Q of a sphere to some point O of the plane. Then if P is any accessible point of the plane, the vector QP can be expressed in the form $\xi\mathbf{x} + \eta\mathbf{y} + \mathbf{z}$, and since $\mathscr{S}\mathbf{x}^2$ and $\mathscr{S}\mathbf{xy}$ are zero and $\mathscr{S}\mathbf{y}^2$ is unity, the condition for P to belong to the sphere with centre Q and radius q is ·44

$$\eta^2 + 2\xi\,\mathscr{S}\,\mathbf{xz} + 2\eta\,\mathscr{S}\,\mathbf{yz} + \mathscr{S}\,\mathbf{z}^2 = q^2; \qquad ·45$$

hence the circle is measured, with respect to the nul vector $\mathbf{x}$, by the projected product $\mathscr{S}\,\mathbf{xz}$, which is of course independent not only of the radius q but of the position of O in the plane.

If $\mathbf{x}$ *is a proper nul vector, the isotropic plane whose equation with respect to a given point Q is* ·46

$$\mathscr{S}\,\mathbf{xr} = A,$$

where A is a constant and $\mathbf{r}$ *is the vector of the step from Q to a variable point of the plane, cuts every ordinary sphere whose centre is Q in a circle whose measure with respect to* $\mathbf{x}$ *is A.*

If A is zero, Q is in the plane and the circle degenerates into the ordinary circle whose radii are the radii of the sphere. That the circles for different spheres are in any case parallel as well as equal is apparent in ·45 from the fact that the coefficient of η as well as the coefficient of ξ is independent of q.

·5. Since every accessible plane cuts any ordinary sphere in a circle, the name of circle is allowed to the aggregate of points common to an ordinary sphere and the plane at infinity; the focal points of space, the points at infinity on nul lines, are said to compose °*the focal circle.* This circle is a ·51
conic, but no definite centre or radii can be ascribed to it. The focal points of any plane are the points in which the plane cuts the focal circle, that is, in

·52 which the line at infinity in the plane cuts the focal circle; °if the line is a tangent to the circle, the focal points of the plane coincide and the plane is isotropic.

No conic in the plane at infinity except the focal circle is given the name of circle, for no other conic contains *all* the focal points that are in that plane;
·53 the focal circle can therefore be called °*the* circle at infinity.

If the focal circle had a constituent line l, any accessible plane through l would be such that every line in it was nul, and the corresponding vecplane would include no anisotropic vectors; we have seen in 415·24 that no such vecplane exists. Hence

·54 *The focal circle is not degenerate.*

·6. For the complete generalisation of ·11 we must examine not only the cases in which the plane is inaccessible but also the cases in which the sphere is infinite. If the sphere is infinite, any plane which is neither the plane at infinity nor the distinctive constituent of the sphere cuts the sphere in two lines of which one is at infinity; that is, the section is an infinite circle whose distinctive constituent is the line in which the plane cuts the distinctive constituent of the sphere. If the plane is parallel to the distinctive constituent of the sphere, the circle is a duplicated line at infinity.

·61 *The points common to a plane and a sphere compose a definite circle unless the sphere is infinite and the plane is one of its constituents; the circle is an ordinary circle if the plane is accessible and the sphere is finite, an infinite circle if the plane is accessible and the sphere is infinite, and the focal circle if the plane is at infinity and the sphere is finite.*

·7. If a line has double intersection with a sphere at a point P, it has double intersection at P with the section of the sphere by any plane that includes the line, and in particular with the section by a plane that includes the line and contains the centre Q. And conversely, if a line has double intersection at P with this one circle it has double intersection at P with the sphere. Hence from 52·35,

·71 *A line through an accessible point P of an ordinary sphere whose centre is Q has double intersection with the sphere at P if and only if it is perpendicular to the step QP.*

Two cases are to be distinguished, for the line is unrestricted or is limited to a definite plane according as the step is or is not a zero step. For the step to be a zero step, the sphere must be a nul sphere, since the radii of the sphere are the lengths of the step, and even for a nul sphere there is no exception unless P is at the centre. It is obvious that a line through the centre of a nul sphere has intersection with the sphere there of order two or of order greater than two according as it is anisotropic or isotropic:

·72 *The centre of a nul sphere is a double point on the sphere, and the tangents there are the nul lines that compose the sphere.*

And from ·71,

Every accessible point of an ordinary sphere that is not nul, and every accessible point of a nul sphere except the centre, is a simple point of the surface; the tangents at a simple accessible point of an ordinary sphere compose the plane through that point perpendicular to the diameter. ·73

It is sometimes useful to have for reference the explicit statement, implied in ·73, that

If an ordinary sphere has a double point, the sphere is nul and the point is its centre. ·74

As for the inaccessible points, they are all simple. For if K is a focal point, then because the focal circle is undegenerate, every line at infinity through K except the tangent to the focal circle has simple intersection with the focal circle at K, and therefore also has simple intersection with any ordinary sphere there. The tangent at K to the focal circle is one line having double intersection with the sphere at K; also the diameter QK has multiple intersection with the sphere at K; hence the tangent plane at K is the isotropic plane through the nul line QK.

We can verify this conclusion without reference to the focal circle. If K is a point at infinity on an ordinary sphere with centre Q, and if P is any accessible point, the line PK is a nul line, and the isotropic plane through PK cuts the sphere in an undegenerate parabolic circle unless this plane contains Q. Hence by 53·56 the line PK has simple intersection at K with this section, and therefore with the sphere, unless the plane contains Q. But if the plane does contain Q, the section is an ordinary circle in the isotropic plane, that is, is a pair of lines through K, and the intersection of PK at K is double even if PK is not itself one of the lines.

The focal points are all simple points on any ordinary sphere; the tangent plane at a focal point is the isotropic plane through the nul line joining that point to the centre of the sphere. ·75

It follows from ·75 that

Ordinary spheres that are concentric are asymptotic to each other, ·76

and therefore that

The nul sphere concentric with a given ordinary sphere is a cone asymptotic to the surface. ·77

563. Generators.

·1. If a nul line has double intersection with an ordinary sphere at an accessible point P, then since the line also has one intersection with the sphere at infinity every point of the line belongs to the sphere. To say that if P is a *double* point of the sphere then every nul line through P lies wholly in the surface is merely to associate 1·22 with 2·74. But if P is any accessible *simple* point of the sphere, the tangent plane at P includes two nul lines, distinct or coincident, through P, and these lines do have double intersection at P.

A different argument, more powerful because it allows P to be at infinity, has been used already in 43·3. If through a point P of a sphere there passes a plane such that *every* line through P in the plane has double intersection with the sphere at P, then the section of the sphere by the plane is a circle such that every line through P in the plane has double intersection with the *circle* at P. The circle is therefore degenerate, and its constituents are lines that lie in the surface. Such lines are necessarily nul and accessible, since they can have no points at infinity that do not belong to the sphere, that is,
·11 that are not focal. Thus °in every plane through the centre of a nul sphere
·12 the nul lines through the centre lie in the surface, and °the tangent plane at any simple point, accessible or inaccessible, of any ordinary sphere cuts the surface in a pair of complementary nul lines.

The lines whose existence we have just proved, which lie wholly in a given
·13 ordinary sphere, are called the °*generators* of the sphere. Because these lines are nul lines, it is unprofitable to study complex space without paying attention to the peculiarities of nul lines and isotropic planes.

·2. In all that concerns generators, nul spheres and spheres that are not nul have little in common. What we have to say of generators on nul spheres can be said at once.

·21 °The generators of a nul sphere are the nul lines through the centre of the
·22 sphere. °Every anisotropic plane through the centre cuts the surface in a pair
·23 of distinct generators. °An isotropic plane through the centre touches the surface at every point of the nul line through the centre which it includes,
·24 except at the centre itself. °Planes which do not contain the centre cut the sphere in undegenerate circles.

·3. If P is an accessible point of an ordinary sphere that is not nul and that has centre Q and radius q, the step QP is not a zero step since q is not zero, and the line QP is not nul since P is not at infinity. There is a definite plane through P perpendicular to QP, this plane is anisotropic, P is itself the foot of the perpendicular from Q on the plane, and q, being a distance from Q to P, is a perpendicular distance from Q to the plane. Hence by 2·12 the section of the sphere by this plane is a circle of radius zero with centre P, that is, has the form of the two nul lines through P in the plane. Conversely, if two nul lines l, m through P both belong to the surface, the section of the surface by the plane which includes both lines has P for centre and therefore, by 2·12, QP is perpendicular to this plane. Thus we have a direct verification of the conclusions already reached:

·31 *Through any accessible point P of an ordinary sphere with centre Q and radii different from zero there pass two and only two generators of the sphere;*

these are the nul lines through P in the plane perpendicular to QP, and they are distinct.

At a focal point, the tangent plane is an isotropic plane through the centre, and because this plane contains the centre the section is an ordinary circle with the same radii as the sphere. If the sphere is not nul, the circle is not nul and the nul lines that form it are distinct.

Through a focal point K there pass two and only two generators of an ordinary sphere with centre Q and radii different from zero; these are nul lines in the isotropic plane through QK, and they are distinct. ·32

To a certain extent ·31 and ·32 can be combined:

Through any point of an ordinary sphere that is not nul, there pass two and only two generators; these are distinct nul lines in the tangent plane at the point. ·33

°In all cases the generators determine both the tangent plane and its point of contact, but the point and the plane suffice to determine the generators only if the point is accessible. ·34

Since a circle that contains all the points of one line is a degenerate circle formed of this line together with a second line, the section of a sphere by any plane through one generator consists of this generator together with a second line; if the two lines have a point P in common, *every* line in the plane which passes through P has double intersection with the sphere at P, and therefore the plane is the tangent plane at P and the two lines are the two generators through P.

Any plane through one generator of an ordinary sphere that is not nul includes a second generator distinct from the first, and is the tangent plane at the point, accessible or inaccessible, in which these two coplanar generators intersect; the two generators together form the complete intersection of the plane with the sphere. ·35

·4. Not only are the two generators through any one point distinct, but it is possible by means of ·35 to divide all the generators of the sphere into two distinct families. Let a be a given generator, and P a point of the sphere that is not on a. The plane through a which contains P includes a second generator p distinct from a. Since the two generators a, p together form the complete intersection of the plane with the sphere, the point P which is common to the plane and the sphere and is not a point of a is necessarily a point of p; that is, p is one of the generators through P. Also p, being coplanar with a, intersects a. But the second generator through P is not identical with p, since the two generators through P are distinct, and is not identical with a, since P belongs to one of the lines and not to the other; hence this second generator has points that do not belong to either a or p, and these points, since they belong to the surface, are not in the plane whose *complete* intersection with the sphere consists of the lines a and p. It follows that the second generator through P does *not* lie in the plane through P and a, and therefore does *not* intersect a.

·41 *If a is any generator of an ordinary sphere that is not nul, and P is any point of the sphere that is not on a, then one of the generators through P intersects a and the other does not.*

Next let a, b be two generators that do not intersect, and let p be a generator distinct from b which intersects b. If P is the point in which p cuts b, then that one of the generators through P which intersects a is not b *and therefore is* p:

·42 *If two generators of an ordinary sphere that is not nul do not intersect, the generators which intersect one of them are the generators which intersect the other.*

Note also that if two distinct generators p, q both intersect a generator a distinct from them both, then p and q can not intersect each other in a point of a, since there can not be three generators through one point, and can not intersect each other in a point that is *not* on a, since of the two generators through any such point one does *not* intersect a. In short,

·43 *If two generators of an ordinary sphere that is not nul both intersect a third generator, they do not intersect each other.*

Suppose now that p, q are two generators each of which intersects a given generator a, but does not coincide with a, and that m, n are two generators each of which either coincides with a or does not intersect a. Then by ·43 p does not intersect q, by ·42 both p and q intersect both m and n, and therefore by ·43 m does not intersect n. That is to say,

·44 *The generators of an ordinary sphere that is not nul fall into two mutually exclusive families such that every member of each family cuts every member of the other but no two members of either family cut each other.*

·45 Briefly, °*generators do or do not intersect according as they belong to different families or to the same family.*

It is an immediate deduction from 47·29 that in complex space all conicoids have generators, and one reason why the treatment of conicoids in general and of spheres in particular is in many respects easier for complex space than for real space is that the existence of these lines renders available both geometrical arguments and analytical devices which in elementary geometry are valid only for hyperboloids. In ·3 the nul character of the generators was assumed, but the whole of ·4 will be recognised to be verbally indistinguishable from a discussion of the generators of an ordinary hyperboloid, and to be verbally applicable to the general conicoid in complex space.

·51 **·5.** If a is any generator of an ordinary sphere that is not nul, °an individual generator of the family that does not contain a may be identified by means of the point in which it intersects a. This point, which we will denote by R, can not be determined by *distances* along a, for a is nul, but it can be determined by the ratios of vectors. For example, if $\mathbf{a}$ is a given proper vector in the vecline of a and A is a given point of a, the vector of the step AR is a definite multiple $r\mathbf{a}$ of $\mathbf{a}$, and the *number* r characterises the point R and the generator distinct from a through R. Or again, if A_1, A_2 are given distinct points of a, the vectors of A_1R and RA_2 are collinear, and two numbers having the ratio of these two vectors can be used as homogeneous coordinates for R.

°There is no reason why a variable generator that intersects a should not be identified directly by means of the *plane* through a in which it lies, instead of by means of its intersection with a. The plane can be determined by means of the point in which it cuts some line not coplanar with a. To suppose this line itself to be a generator b is merely to identify the variable generator by its intersection with b instead of by its intersection with a. Thus the second method includes the first as a special case. It is essentially the more adaptable method, but properties of the sphere are likely to take a far more elegant form if associated with a line related intrinsically to the sphere than if developed by means of an arbitrary line in space. ·52

To say that

Through every point of an ordinary sphere that is not nul passes one and only one member of each family of generators ·53

is merely to call attention to the fact that *every* generator belongs to one of the two families. But any method of identifying the two generators in their respective families is implicitly a method of identifying their point of intersection. Thus the considerations of the last two paragraphs lead to various plans for associating with each point on the sphere a definite pair of numbers to serve as coordinates, in an extended sense of the word, or even a pair of pairs of numbers to serve as homogeneous coordinates. For developments the reader must look elsewhere; should mathematics make no aesthetic appeal to him, he will still find that the ideas, far from remaining abstract, yield immediately in Darboux's skilful hands the practical formulae of spherical trigonometry.

APPENDIX

POINTS AS LIMITS IN COMPLEX SPACE AND IN IDEAL SPACE

APPENDIX

POINTS AS LIMITS IN COMPLEX SPACE AND IN IDEAL SPACE

FOR elementary geometry, the ρ-neighbourhood of a point P is the aggregate of points at distances numerically less than ρ from P, and P is a limit of a set of points Γ if every existent* neighbourhood of P includes some member of Γ other than P.

If we attempt to apply these definitions either to complex space or to ideal space simply by using the modulus of a distance, we meet with difficulties. For complex space, the ρ-neighbourhood of P would include every point on every nul line through P, and if Q is any member of a set Γ, every point except Q on any nul line through Q would satisfy the definition of a limit of Γ. For ideal space, a finite neighbourhood of a point at infinity would not include any accessible points, unless the point was focal, and there would be no analytical interpretation of our instinctive conception of a point at infinity as a limit of a set of accessible points. One natural method of avoiding the difficulty for actual complex space can be modified to apply to ideal space, real or complex.

We require first to associate with any pair of points some number which is zero if *and only if* the points coincide. Given a finitely numerous set of numbers $(p_1, p_2, \dots p_n)$, real or complex, let the greatest among the moduli $|p_1|, |p_2|, \dots |p_n|$ be called the *number dominating* the set and be denoted by $|p|$. And if $(p_1, p_2, \dots p_n)$, $(q_1, q_2, \dots q_n)$ are ordinally similar sets of numbers, let the number dominating the set of differences $(p_1 - q_1, p_2 - q_2, \dots p_n - q_n)$ be called the *gap*† between the sets of numbers and be denoted by $|p - q|$. The number dominating a set is zero if and only if every constituent of the set is zero; the gap between two sets is zero if and only if the sets coincide.

If a finite vector $\mathbf{r}$ is referred to a vector frame $\mathbf{xyz}$, the number that dominates the set of coefficients $(\xi_\mathbf{r}, \eta_\mathbf{r}, \zeta_\mathbf{r})$, a number that we denote by $|\chi_\mathbf{r}|$, is zero only if the vector is zero, not if the vector is nul; we will call $|\chi_\mathbf{r}|$ the number that dominates $\mathbf{r}$ with reference to $\mathbf{xyz}$. If $\mathbf{r}$ is the vector of a step PQ, the number $|\chi_\mathbf{r}|$ may be called the gap between P and Q relatively to $\mathbf{xyz}$.

* In real space, the zero-neighbourhood of P has no members, and in this sense is non-existent.

† For the purposes of this note, Jordan's 'écart', which is the sum

$$|p_1 - q_1| + |p_2 - q_2| + \dots + |p_n - q_n|,$$

could be used instead of the gap as here defined. But it is the gap that lends itself to the extensions, of which every day shews more clearly the importance, in which the number of variables is not restricted to be finite.

It is impossible to express the number that dominates a vector with reference to one frame in terms of the number that dominates the same vector with reference to another frame. But it follows from the ordinary formulae of transformation, given in 355·43 on p. 184 above, that if the greatest among the moduli of the nine elements in a scheme giving the coefficients of the vectors **x**, **y**, **z** in a frame $\mathbf{x}^0\mathbf{y}^0\mathbf{z}^0$ is m, the dominating number $|\chi^0\mathbf{r}|$ is not greater than $3m|\chi\mathbf{r}|$. Similarly if m^0 dominates the reciprocal scheme, $|\chi\mathbf{r}|$ is not greater than $3m^0|\chi^0\mathbf{r}|$. Hence there are definite numbers f, g, dependent only on the two frames, such that for any vector **r**, the number $|\chi^0\mathbf{r}|$ is somewhere in the interval from $f|\chi\mathbf{r}|$ to $g|\chi\mathbf{r}|$.

If a class of finite vectors and a vector frame **xyz** are given, the numbers each of which dominates one or more of the vectors form a definite class, and this class, whether finitely numerous or not, has a lower bound l, which may be either an isolated member of the class, or an attained lower limit, or an unattained lower limit. From the result of the last paragraph, it follows that if f and g have the same values as there, the lower bound l^0 with reference to a frame $\mathbf{x}^0\mathbf{y}^0\mathbf{z}^0$ is necessarily in the interval from fl to gl. Hence l^0 is zero if and only if l is zero:

If a class of vectors is such that the lower bound of the class of numbers dominating its members with respect to one frame of reference is zero, then the lower bound of the class of numbers dominating its members with respect to any other frame is zero also.

In general, a change in the frame of reference may change the character of the lower bound of the class of dominating numbers associated with a given class of vectors, but if the lower bound is zero such a change is impossible. For zero is a member of the class of numbers dominating a class of vectors with reference to a particular frame if and only if the class of vectors has the zero vector for one of its members, and in this exceptional case zero belongs to the class of dominating numbers for any frame of reference. Hence

If the class formed of the numbers that dominate the vectors belonging to a given class with reference to some one vector frame has zero for an unattained lower limit, the class formed of the numbers that dominate the vectors belonging to the same class with reference to any other vector frame also has zero for an unattained lower limit.

Now let C denote a class of vectors of which the zero vector is a member, but not the only member, and let C' denote the class consisting of all the members of C except the zero vector. Whatever the frame of reference, zero is the lower bound of the class of numbers dominating members of C; but zero is a limit as well as a member of this class only if it is the lower bound of the class of numbers dominating members of C', and this is a condition independent of the choice of frame. Thus

If the class of numbers dominating the members of a given class of vectors

with reference to one frame has zero for a limit, the class of numbers dominating the members of the same class of vectors with reference to any other frame also has zero for a limit.

We are now in a position to frame a definition:

The zero vector is a limit of a given set of finite vectors if when the vectors are referred to some one vector frame the numbers which dominate them form a class of which zero is a limit.

The proposition that concludes the preceding paragraph implies that with this definition,

If a given set of finite vectors has the zero vector for a limit, then if the vectors are referred to any vector frame whatever, the numbers which dominate them form a class of which zero is a limit.

We add that a set C of vectors is said to have a vector $\mathbf{s}$ for a limit if the set whose typical member is obtained by subtracting $\mathbf{s}$ from the typical member of C has the zero vector for a limit.

Returning from vectors to points, we say that an actual or accessible point P is a limit of a set Γ of actual or accessible points if the set of vectors each of which is the vector of the step from P to some member of Γ has the zero vector for a limit. Reduced to more elementary terms, this definition is equivalent to the following theorem:

The point P is a limit of the set Γ if given a vector frame of reference and an arbitrary signless number ρ other than zero, independent of the frame, there is some member of Γ distinct from P separated from P relatively to the given frame by a gap that is less than ρ.

In other words, P is a limit of Γ if given an attached frame $O\mathbf{xyz}$ and an arbitrary number ρ that is not zero, there is always some member Q of Γ such that the moduli $|\xi_P - \xi_Q|$, $|\eta_P - \eta_Q|$, $|\zeta_P - \zeta_Q|$ are all less than ρ but are not all zero. This is only the result at which it is natural to aim, but it has been necessary to establish that it is not possible for the result to hold for some frames of reference and not for others.

To be of practical value in analytical geometry, a discussion of limits that is designed to be applicable equally to accessible and to inaccessible points must admit of being put into relation with the theory of homogeneous coordinates. And we recognise at the outset that if coordinates are homogeneous, the simple gap between a set of coordinates of a point P and a set of coordinates of a point Q can not be of fundamental importance, for the coordinates individually, and therefore the gap between two sets of them, can be made arbitrarily small without ceasing to refer to the same two points P, Q, while on the other hand the gap between two different sets of coordinates of one given point with reference to a given tetrahedron is not zero.

Let ϵ denote as in Chapter V 4 an umbra of the coordinates with reference to a definite tetrahedron. Then $|\epsilon_P|$ is the greatest among the numbers $|\alpha_P|$,

$|\beta_P|$, $|\gamma_P|$, $|\delta_P|$, and for a given pair of numbers h, k, $|h\epsilon_P - k\epsilon_Q|$ is the gap between the set of numbers $(h\alpha_P, h\beta_P, h\gamma_P, h\delta_P)$ and the set of numbers $(k\alpha_Q, k\beta_Q, k\gamma_Q, k\delta_Q)$.

Although with assigned values of the coordinates of P and Q the gap $|h\epsilon_P - k\epsilon_Q|$ may be made to assume any value whatever by an appropriate choice of h and k, this gap is not arbitrary to the same extent when k alone is allowed to change. To prove this, let us consider the gap $|\epsilon_P - k\epsilon_Q|$ as a function of k. Since for any two values k', k'' of k we have

$$|\epsilon_P - k'\epsilon_Q| \sim |\epsilon_P - k''\epsilon_Q| \leqslant |k' - k''|\,|\epsilon_Q|,$$

$|\epsilon_P - k\epsilon_Q|$ is a continuous function of k. Hence for variation of k, this gap has a lower limit which is either approached as k tends in some manner to infinity or attained for one or more finite values of k. The first alternative is impossible, since the gap tends to infinity with $|k|$. It follows that the lower bound of the class of numbers of which $|\epsilon_P - k\epsilon_Q|$ is the typical member is a minimum that is attained. In general there is only one critical value of k for which the minimum is reached, but this uniqueness is irrelevant to our purpose and we will not delay to establish it.

The minimum of $|\epsilon_P - k\epsilon_Q|$ may be zero. That is, there may be a number k_c such that simultaneously

$$\alpha_P - k_c\alpha_Q = 0, \quad \beta_P - k_c\beta_Q = 0, \quad \gamma_P - k_c\gamma_Q = 0, \quad \delta_P - k_c\delta_Q = 0.$$

But this set of equations, which implies incidentally that in this case k_c is not zero, expresses that Q is the same point as P. Since zero, if it is a value of $|\epsilon_P - k\epsilon_Q|$, is necessarily the minimum, the converse also is true.

The minimum of $|\epsilon_P - k\epsilon_Q|$, *regarded as a function of* k, *is zero if and only if* Q *coincides with* P.

This result proves that to say for a given specification of P and a given point Q that there are *some* sets of coordinates of Q that are separated from the given set of coordinates of P by gaps less than an assigned number ρ is to make a statement that is significant provided only that Q is distinct from P. Hence further, to say that a set of points Γ is such that some member of Γ distinct from P has some sets of coordinates that are separated from a given set of coordinates of P by gaps less than an assigned number ρ is to describe a relation of P to Γ that is not the less definite because it involves both the tetrahedron of reference and the particular load attached to P.

In other words, if from a given set of coordinates of a point P and a given set of points Γ is formed the class of numbers each of which is the gap between the set of coordinates of P and *some* set of coordinates of *some* member of Γ distinct from P, the lower bound of this class of numbers is not necessarily zero, and if this bound is zero it is an unattained limit. Arguing from formulae of transformation for tetrahedral coordinates, that if the gap between two sets of coordinates relative to one tetrahedron is g then the gap between the corresponding sets relative to another tetrahedron is not greater than $4mg$, where m is a constant depending only on the two tetrahedra, we deduce that if the class of numbers derived from P and Γ by means of one tetrahedron has zero for its lower bound, then the class derived from P and Γ by means of any other tetrahedron also has zero for its lower bound.

There is still a tacit reference to a particular set of coordinates of P. But if $|\epsilon_P - k\epsilon_Q|$ is l, then $|h\epsilon_P - hk\epsilon_Q|$ is $|h|l$; hence if the lower bound of the class of gaps derived from ϵ_P and Γ is g, the lower bound of the class derived from $h\epsilon_P$ and Γ is $|h|g$, and if either bound is zero, so also is the other, since h must not be zero.

A point P is a limit of a set of points Γ if given any one tetrahedron of reference, and any one set of coordinates of P in that tetrahedron, the class of numbers each of which is the gap between the given set of coordinates of P and some set of coordinates relative to the given tetrahedron, of some member of Γ distinct from P, has zero for its lower bound.

In other words, given any number ρ other than zero, it must be possible to find some specification $(\alpha_Q, \beta_Q, \gamma_Q, \delta_Q)$ of some member Q of Γ distinct from P such that $|\epsilon_P - \epsilon_Q|$ is less than ρ. And if this condition is satisfied with any one set of coordinates of P in any one tetrahedron, then it is satisfied also with any set of coordinates in any tetrahedron.

It will be noticed that the condition that Q is to be distinct from P is not avoided in this method of presenting the result, for if P is a member of Γ, zero is for that reason alone a limit of the class of gaps that has been used, and can not be an isolated minimum. For this reason, it is perhaps worth while to associate with P and Q not every gap of the form $|\epsilon_P - k\epsilon_Q|$ but only the least gap of this form. If to emphasise that this minimum is not derived symmetrically from the two points and depends on the actual coordinates in use for P we call the minimum the gap from ϵ_P to Q, the validity of the earlier arguments is restored, with the result that

The point P is a limit of the set Γ if, given one tetrahedron of reference and one set of coordinates of P in that tetrahedron, the class of numbers each of which is the gap from ϵ_P to some member of Γ has zero for a limit.

But in practice it may be tiresome as well as superfluous to find the minimum of $|\epsilon_P - k\epsilon_Q|$.

If the gap from ϵ_P to Q is γ, the gap from $h\epsilon_P$ to Q is $|h|\gamma$. Hence the quotient $\gamma/|\epsilon_P|$ is independent of the load attached to P. Since $|\epsilon_P|$ is itself the value of $|\epsilon_P - k\epsilon_Q|$ when k is zero, $|\epsilon_P|$ can not be less than the minimum of $|\epsilon_P - k\epsilon_Q|$. That is, the quotient $\gamma/|\epsilon_P|$ is a number which can be used to measure, relatively to a given tetrahedron of reference, the gap from P to Q; this number is independent of any load attached to either point, it is zero only if the points coincide, and unity only if the critical value of k is zero, and in every other case the number has a definite value between zero and unity. The number is however not symmetrical as between P and Q, and its value in relation to one tetrahedron is not deducible from its value in relation to another.

As an example of the application of the definition of a limit, consider the set of points of which the typical member Q_n has in a frame O**xyz** the coordinates $(4+3n, 5+n, 6+2n)$, for an integral value of n; this is a set of points uniformly spaced on a line. With homogeneous coordinates, the typical set of coordinates is $(4+3n, 5+n, 6+2n, 1)$, and one loaded point at infinity on the line is $(3, 1, 2, 0)$, which does not belong to the set. The gap from the loaded point at infinity to Q_n is the smallest value possible for the greatest among the numbers

$$|3-(4+3n)k|, \quad |1-(5+n)k|, \quad |2-(6+2n)k|, \quad |-k|.$$

It is not necessary to determine this value, since it is certainly not greater than the greatest among the four numbers that correspond to the particular value $1/n$ of k, which are $4/|n|$, $5/|n|$, $6/|n|$, $1/|n|$. That is, the gap is not greater than $6/|n|$, and therefore the class of gaps has zero for a limit, and the class of points has the point at infinity for a limit. Actually, for any positive value of n the critical value of k is $4n/(4n+9)$ and the gap is $11/(4n+9)$.

If we transform coordinates (ξ, η, ζ) in a vector frame into homogeneous coordinates (ξ, η, ζ, τ), we have for accessible points two definitions of a limit that are not literally identical; if P is a given accessible point and Q a variable point that belongs to a set Γ but is distinct from P, then according to one definition, P is a limit of Γ if zero is a limit of

$$|\xi_P-\xi_Q, \eta_P-\eta_Q, \zeta_P-\zeta_Q|,$$

but according to the other, it is sufficient if zero is a limit of

$$|\xi_P-k\alpha_Q, \eta_P-k\beta_Q, \zeta_P-k\gamma_Q, 1-k\delta_Q|,$$

where k is variable, δ_Q is zero if Q is at infinity, and

$$\alpha_Q:\beta_Q:\gamma_Q:\delta_Q=\xi_Q:\eta_Q:\zeta_Q:1$$

if Q is accessible. In proving that the second condition does imply the first, it is not necessary to assume the multiplicative axiom.

Let the set Γ be divided into two parts Γ_1, Γ_2, of which the second contains all the points of Γ at infinity and also any accessible point for which

$$|\chi| \geqslant 2|\chi_P|+1;$$

we shew first that $|\epsilon_P-k\epsilon_Q| \geqslant \frac{1}{2}$ for every point Q of Γ_2 and for every value of k. If Q is at infinity, then $|1-k\delta_Q|=1$, and therefore $|\epsilon_P-k\epsilon_Q| \geqslant 1$. If Q is not at infinity, and if $|1-k\delta_Q|<\frac{1}{2}$, then $|k\delta_Q|>\frac{1}{2}$, and we have

$$\begin{aligned}|\epsilon_P-k\epsilon_Q| &\geqslant |\xi_P-k\delta_Q\xi_Q, \eta_P-k\delta_Q\eta_Q, \zeta_P-k\delta_Q\zeta_Q| \\ &\geqslant |k\delta_Q\xi_Q, k\delta_Q\eta_Q, k\delta_Q\zeta_Q| \sim |\xi_P, \eta_P, \zeta_P| \\ &\geqslant \tfrac{1}{2}\{2|\chi_P|+1\}-|\chi_P| \geqslant \tfrac{1}{2},\end{aligned}$$

as required. It follows that zero is a limit of $|\epsilon_P-k\epsilon_Q|$ when Q belongs to Γ if and only if it is a limit when Q is confined to Γ_1; that is, we may replace the gap $|\epsilon_P-k\epsilon_Q|$ by the gap

$$|\xi_P-k\xi_Q, \eta_P-k\eta_Q, \zeta_P-k\zeta_Q, 1-k|,$$

with the condition $|\chi_Q| < m$, where m is a definite finite number independent of the position of Q in Γ_1 and not less than unity.

Suppose now that the lower limit of $|\chi_P - \chi_Q|$ when Q is confined to Γ_1 is a number l that is not zero. We have

$$|\chi_P - k\chi_Q| \geqslant |\chi_P - \chi_Q| \sim |1-k||\chi_Q|;$$

if k has any value such that $|1-k| \leqslant \frac{1}{2}l/m$, then if Q is confined to Γ_1,

$$|\chi_P - \chi_Q| \geqslant l, \quad |1-k||\chi_Q| < \tfrac{1}{2}l,$$

and therefore $|\chi_P - k\chi_Q| > \frac{1}{2}l$. That is, if Q belongs to Γ_1, one of the two conditions

$$|\chi_P - k\chi_Q| > \tfrac{1}{2}l, \quad |1-k| > \tfrac{1}{2}l/m$$

must be satisfied whatever the value of k. But the gap

$$|\xi_P - k\xi_Q, \eta_P - k\eta_Q, \zeta_P - k\zeta_Q, 1-k|$$

is itself the greater of the two numbers $|\chi_P - k\chi_Q|$, $|1-k|$, and since $m \geqslant 1$, it follows that the gap is greater than $\frac{1}{2}l/m$, a number independent both of the value of k and of the position of Q. Hence the lower limit of the gaps for different values of k and different positions of Q in Γ_1 is not less than $\frac{1}{2}l/m$, and is not zero since l is not zero.

For accessible points, the definition of a limit in terms of tetrahedral co-ordinates is equivalent to the definition in terms of an attached vector frame.

INDEX OF DEFINITIONS

The references are to pages. As in the text, actual *is opposed to* ideal.

INDEX OF NAMES

The references are to pages.

CAMBRIDGE: PRINTED BY J. B. PEACE, M.A., AT THE UNIVERSITY PRESS

www.ingramcontent.com/pod-product-compliance
Lightning Source LLC
LaVergne TN
LVHW020603110826
845149LV00002B/364

* 9 7 8 1 4 1 8 1 8 3 4 4 8 *